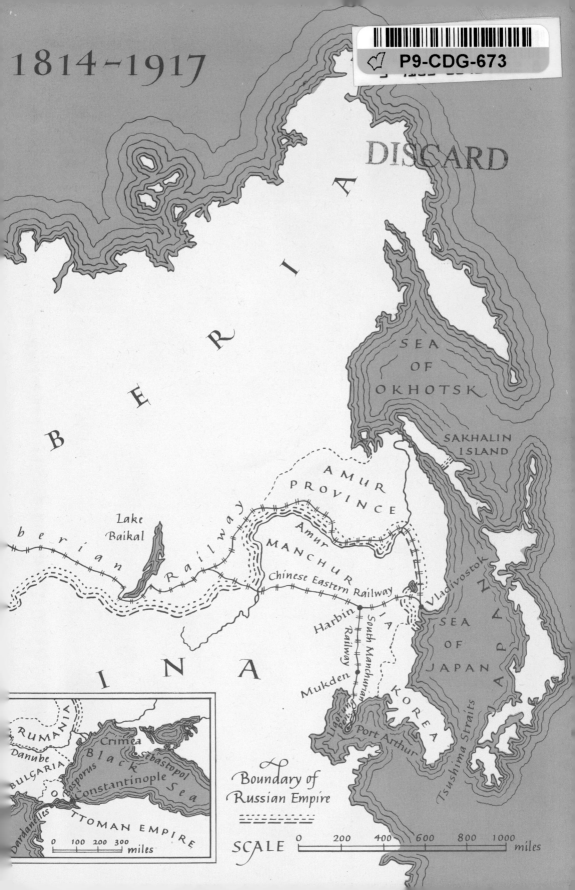

1814~1917

S I B E R I A

SEA
OF
OKHOTSK

SAKHALIN
ISLAND

AMUR
PROVINCE

Lake
Baikal

Amur

berian MANCHUR

Railway

Chinese Eastern Railway

Vladivostok

I A

SEA
OF
JAPAN

Harbin

South Manchurian
Railway

C H I N A

Mukden

Liaotung Peninsula

KOREA

Port Arthur

Tsushima Straits

J A P A N

RUMANIA

Danube

BULGARIA

Crimea

Black

Sebastopol

Bosporus

Constantinople

Sea

Dardanelles

OTTOMAN EMPIRE

0 100 200 300
miles

Boundary of
Russian Empire

SCALE 0   200   400   600   800   1000
miles

Years of the Golden Cockerel

YEARS OF THE
Golden Cockerel
THE LAST ROMANOV TSARS
1814-1917

by

SIDNEY HARCAVE

The Macmillan Company, New York

Collier-Macmillan Limited, London

The Macmillan Company, New York
Collier-Macmillan Canada Ltd., Toronto, Ontario

Printed in the United States of America

CONTENTS

Preface

DURING the final, turbulent hundred years of the Romanov
dynasty, two illustrious and imaginative Russians expressed their
view of tsarism through a satirical allegory that remains today an appropriate commentary on it: Alexander Pushkin, in his poem "The
Tale of the Golden Cockerel," [1] and Nicholas Rimsky-Korsakov, in
his opera *The Golden Cockerel*.[2]

Between them, the two were acquainted with Russian life under
the five tsars of the century. Pushkin knew it under Alexander I and
Nicholas I; Rimsky-Korsakov, under Alexander II, Alexander III,
and Nicholas II. That the composer, in the last quarter of the century, braved the imperial censors with an opera based on the plot
and characterization employed by the poet in the first quarter sug-
gests that the specific object of the satire, Russian autocracy, had remained sufficiently unchanged during the intervening years to be still
a fit target.

History endorses the suggestion. Indeed it is easy, conceding the
license of satire, to read "the last Romanovs" for "Tsar Dadon," the
Everytsar of the allegory. As Pushkin represents him, aging Dadon,
after years of war and labor, realized that he had finally achieved a
station "second in renown to none"; and, "having earned a rest, he
took it." To safeguard the imperial eminence on which he rested,
he relied on the magic of the golden cockerel, a gift from his court
astrologer. Other matters were of small concern to him:

[vii]

> Lawful vouchers? How confusing!
> I don't get these words you're using.
> My caprice and my command
> Always serve to rule my land.

The last Romanov tsars, likewise, sought to safeguard attainments which, by 1814, had made their dynasty in some respects "second in renown to none." According to an increasing number of their disenchanted subjects, they chose to take a "rest" that was wholly unjustifiable in view of Russia's accumulating problems. They also claimed recourse to a supramundane source of guidance, citing divine authority in defense of their autocratic rule: "The tsar's heart is in God's hands." Finally, in their realm as in Dadon's, misplaced action and culpable inaction marked the way to destruction.

Of course, Pushkin and Rimsky-Korsakov undertook to be no more than artistic commentators; certainly they were neither prophets nor political analysts.

It would be convenient if historical judgments could be made as easily as the allegorical, but characters and events in history have a way of resisting facile manipulation. Yet it is demonstrable that each of Russia's last five tsars was nearly enough a Dadon to give the combined years of their rule the "golden cockerel" aura. Though each was significantly individual in many respects, each, like Dadon, cherished a passion he could not reconcile with the demands made upon him; and his inability to do so contributed to the downfall of tsarism.

Explanations of the decline and fall of the Romanov dynasty range from those that fix attention exclusively on personal responsibility—whether of the tsars or of the men who made up the unrelenting opposition—to those of analysts like Trotsky, who dismissed personal influence as "merely individual scratches made by a higher law of development." Evidence and events support neither extreme. It is undeniably tempting to settle the affairs of the past by attributing great results to slight causes or by devising patterns and fitting past events into them—to join the ranks of Schlegel's "prophets who look backward." However, being human, we are on safest ground when we approach judgments by way of what is readily within our human competence, the expressed thoughts and observable personal responses of those most closely associated with the subject of our judgment. Hence this book, a look at some of Russia's compelling problems as they appeared to the tsars and the men and women who influenced them, either through approval or disapproval, during the century when the Romanov dynasty was moving toward its disintegration.

Why the end came in the exact way that it did and at the exact time that it did will remain an unanswered "why?" as long as there are men to study and speculate about what took place. But even a premise should take into account the personal influence exerted by those intimately concerned with the problems of the government and the people of Russia at this time. Particularly it should recognize the five who represented the ruling dynasty during this period not merely as immobile figures on a frieze of Clio's temple but as human beings affected by other human beings. The tsars by no means had complete control of the destiny of Russia, but they had much responsibility and some freedom in the choice of policies. Their freedom was limited, and, as the years passed, it narrowed. Yet the manner in which they exercised it, their motivations, and their intentions were factors in determining the fate of the dynasty and the monarchy.

Why choose 1814 as the year with which to begin the appraisal? At that time, the Russian monarchy was strong at home and abroad, having just emerged from intermittent war with France as the greatest power on the European continent. At that time, too, the institutions upon which the strength of the monarchy depended were beginning to show evidence of strain, and Russia was becoming susceptible to the influence of liberal and revolutionary ideas as well as the pressures of industrial capitalism. At that time, the tsar and many of his nobles were growing especially sensitive to the needs of the country, and it appeared likely that great changes and new beginnings were in store for Russia.

In the next hundred years, five Romanov tsars undertook the task of leading Russia through the developments of an era without precedent in its history. Each was the beneficiary and the prisoner of the country's past, which had produced an autocratic state closely allied with the Russian Orthodox Church and the landed nobility and scarred by centuries of serfdom. Each, sincerely devoted to Mother Russia, wrestled with the problems of his great realm, beginning his reign with the heartfelt wish to promote the welfare of the people, facing crisis after crisis, then retreating from progressive policies and falling back on regressive ones. Each was tested by the necessity to struggle with domestic problems and meet crises while attending to the needs of Russia as a great power. By the time of Nicholas II, to whom most attention is given in this book, the strength of hostile forces and the challenges to stability had become so

great, the incidence of crises so increased, that the administrative practices of preceding tsars—that is, reform followed by reaction—had become highly ineffective as a means of protecting the autocratic
prerogatives.

In February 1917, with Russia's basic problems still unsolved and
her great-power status shaken by involvement in three debilitating
wars, the Romanov dynasty faced a crisis that was unplanned,
localized, initially undramatic, and—almost unbelievably—final. The
years of the "golden cockerel" had run out.

Unless otherwise indicated (by N.S. for New Style), all dates in this
book are given according to the Julian calendar, used in Russia until
1918. In the nineteenth century, this calendar lagged twelve days
behind the Gregorian calendar, with which the West is most familiar;
in the twentieth century, thirteen days.

I acknowledge with sincere thanks the assistance of the archivists
and librarians in this country, England, France, Germany, and
Russia who have made available to me countless sources of information and confirmation in the course of my study of this period of
Russian history.

Quotations from the following are used with the generous permission of Random House: "The Tale of the Golden Cockerel," translated by Babette Deutsch, in *The Poems, Prose, and Plays of Alexander
Pushkin,* edited by Avrahm Yarmolinsky; "The Trouble with Reason," by Alexander Griboedov, in *Anthology of Russian Plays,* Vol.
I, edited and translated by F. D. Reeve.

S. H.

Binghamton, New York

Years of the Golden Cockerel

I

"Second in Renown to None"

ALEXANDER I, 1814-1815

T H E House of Romanov, ruling dynasty of the Russian empire, reached the zenith of its distinction on the last day of March, 1814 (N.S.). There had been nothing comparable in the two centuries of its past, nor would there be a repetition in the one century that history was to allot its future.

The occasion was celebrated not in the splendid halls of St. Petersburg but on the Champs Élysées of Paris, where Alexander I, then beginning his fourteenth year as Emperor and Autocrat of All the Russias,* represented the dynasty in a role that would have been strange indeed for any of his predecessors: the benevolent protector of European civilization.

Beside him, sharing the place of honor, were King Frederick William III of Prussia and Prince Karl Philip von Schwarzenberg, deputy for Emperor Francis I of Austria. But to the thousands of Parisians who applauded the appearance of these three foreigners in their city, Alexander was the focus of attention. Though Prussia and Austria had joined their fighting strength to that of Russia, and England and Sweden had given support, in the coalition that had forced Napoleon from his gains in eastern Europe and freed France

---

* Instead of this formal title, the traditional "tsar" commonly used to designate the ruler of imperial Russia will be used in this book. For the tsar's consort, the formal "empress" will be used (instead of "tsarina") since custom—however inconsistent—favors that title for her.

from the desperate embrace of his waning potency, the grateful French credited these accomplishments in large part to the military and diplomatic guidance of the gallant Russian, hailing him as *le libérateur*.

There were some Frenchmen, of course, who did not share the mood of gratitude and jubilation that had drawn this throng into the heart of Paris. Among them were those restrained by continued loyalty to Napoleon or simply by the popular Western notion that Russia was still a rough bear of a country sprawled on the eastern periphery of the civilized world and that, behind any evidence of its good nature, there lurked an untamed malevolence. They were the ones who, a little more than two years before, had eagerly anticipated the prospect of which Napoleon had boasted: that he would "finish off, once and for all, the Colossus of Northern Barbarism" and thrust the Russians "back into their snow and ice, so that for a quarter of a century at least they will not be able to interfere with civilized Europe." [1] Others, still loyal to the ousted Bourbon autocrats, were sobered by doubts about the kind of political adjustments that Alexander, known by this time as a "reforming tsar," would now favor for France. Some may have been remembering that he had come to power after the murder of his father, the cruel and mildly mad Tsar Paul, with whose death gossip had linked him as a possessor of guilty knowledge, if not an actual accessory.

Adverse sentiment, however, was all but submerged by the realities of the moment. It could not be denied that Alexander had conceived, activated, and led the coalition that had driven Napoleon from offensive strength to defensive weakness and, from there, to his present humiliation—waiting in impotence at Fontainebleau. In recognition of that accomplishment, the disillusioned citizens of the French capital saw nothing unpatriotic in opening their arms to this foreign monarch nor in cheering the magnificent display as rank on rank of foreign infantry, cavalry, and artillery swept up the avenue where they had once thrilled to the military pomp and parade of Napoleon's brave campaigners. And if any recalled the taunt of barbarism as they watched the Russian units, it was only to smile at the palpable absurdity of it. Except for the dashing equipage of the red-coated Cossacks, there was nothing to mark them as different from their Prussian and Austrian counterparts.

Only Alexander himself drew more attention and admiration than his men. As the crowds surged against the cordons shouting *"Vive*

Alexandre!" and aristocratic young ladies, sacrificing modesty to curiosity, mounted the rumps of aides' horses to catch a glimpse of the handsome blond *libérateur,* he sat quietly on his gray mare Eclipse (a gift from Napoleon, ironically enough) and received the homage with dignity and apparent ease. His bearing suggested nobility without pomposity; in the dress uniform of the Imperial Guard—every feature of which, from the high boots of burnished cordovan to the plume on the cocked hat, defined his tall and youthful figure—he inspired acceptance as *le chevalier sans peur et sans reproche.* Those personally acquainted with him knew that his French was as impeccable as his uniform, and his manner—when he chose to make it so—as flawless as his speech. Certainly nothing in his appearance suggested the agony of the achievement by which he had brought the name of Romanov to this high point in Russian history.

At the time of Alexander's accession, in 1801, Russians had felt assured that their country, even though lacking in popularity abroad, was at least in a position of recognized importance in European affairs and, to a lesser degree, in wider international affairs. But by 1812, when Napoleon had been able to lead more than half a million men of his Grand Army into the very heart of Russia and confidently begin to lay plans for the death thrust, many had begun to have misgivings about the endurance of that position. Alexander, however, had refused to interpret the flames of burning Moscow as the battle flags of Armageddon. It had taken courage, under the circumstances, to defy the threat of the invader and to undertake the rekindling of morale in a frightened populace; fortunately for Russia, the tsar had the courage. He vowed that he would not enter into, nor allow, any negotiations with Napoleon as long as one enemy soldier remained on Russian soil.

He might have judged his obligation under that vow fully discharged when Napoleon, who had overreached himself in this Russian campaign almost to the point of self-defeat, had been harried across the frontier. Instead he widened his field. On New Year's Day of 1813, he left Russia to throw his country's military power into the pursuit of Napoleon, thus inspiring a war to liberate the countries that had been annexed or subordinated in the eastward sweep of the Grand Army. His allies in that enterprise had generally, though not always wholeheartedly, proved acquiescent to his advice and compliant to his strategy. Together they had battled Napoleon until this day of triumph, when Paris had been recommended "to the generosity of the allied monarchs" and Napoleon had ostensibly retired from the field.

From the height he now commanded, Alexander could envision a future transcending all that had gone before in Russian history. His country, beginning as a minor principality that could be crossed in a single day by a swift horseman, had grown to a great Eurasian state covering one-ninth of the world's surface. Its westernmost border, in Europe, was halfway around the world from its easternmost, in Russian Alaska. Its European provinces included one-seventh of that continent's entire population. On March 31, 1814, it was able and ready to hand down judgment on the fate of Europe.

Moreover, the day was one of special diplomatic significance for Russia: it brought the prospect of a long-delayed adjustment of relations with France. During the preceding years of Romanov rule, the two countries had been almost continually in contention, it having been the French policy to oppose, wherever and however conveniently possible, both the Romanov and the Hapsburg dynasties. Russia had suffered from that position particularly as she had pursued her own policy in involvements with the Ottoman empire, Poland, and Sweden. The French had usually managed to use their aid and influence to Russia's disadvantage in those areas without becoming directly involved; however, when they had finally taken to the field against Russia in 1733, in an unsuccessful effort to save the Polish throne for Louis XV's father-in-law, King Stanislaw Leszczynski, the fighting had dragged on for ten years. Only once had these traditional opponents fought as allies—against Prussia during the Seven Years' War. And through the nearly two centuries of their relationship, Russia had not been able to challenge France's position as hub of the European system of states. Now it appeared that the coveted position could fall to Russia. There were many who believed that outcome to be imminent, among them Alexander.

For a time his belief was sustained by stirring expressions of gratitude, trust, and admiration from all sides. While still in Paris, where he continued to hear echoes of the triumphal parade, he was honored in the salons as one who, in the words of Madame de Staël, had reached "the summit of human success." And as a house guest of the brilliant French diplomat Talleyrand, exchanging views with statesmen and politicians, he was given a feeling of "closeness to the heart of diplomacy" and an intimation of things to come. He was

warmed by the deference shown him when, against the known wishes
of his allies, he insisted that the French be treated as a liberated, not
a conquered, people. He became so confident of his influence that he
expected Louis XVIII to accept his counsel on the reinstatement of
the Bourbon dynasty—according to constitutional principles. Then,
when he went with King Frederick William directly from France to
England, he was still further cheered to share an enthusiastic reception from both high and low ranks, to receive an honorary degree
from Oxford University, and to take counsel with crown officials on
problems of government.

When he finally turned toward Russia, in June, Alexander seemed
inclined to consider the period of congratulations and ceremonies
at an end and anxious to be about the business of his newly recognized position in European affairs. But others would not have it so.
The spirit expressed in a letter received from one of his former
confidants, Georg-Friedrich Parrot, rector of Dorpat University, was
typical of the countless messages he received en route: "You are now
the most fortunate of sovereigns. The point at which you are now,
in relation to your nation and Europe, is that which Napoleon had
reached when he became Emperor, master of public opinion and of
supreme power. You will use them for the happiness of mankind." [2]

Russian officials, wishing to honor his return with appropriate
splendor, sent a request for his approval of elaborate plans for celebrations in the capital and other Russian cities. He vetoed the plans,
declaring his unwillingness to be honored above other Russians who
had been involved in the war effort. A deputation of representatives
from the Holy Synod, the State Council, and the Senate asked permission for the erection of a monument in St. Petersburg, to be
dedicated to "Alexander the Blessed, Emperor of All the Russias,
magnanimous restorer of the Powers of Europe." Honoring him in
this way would have been wholly in keeping with the three-centuries-
old tradition of tsarism that had elevated Russian rulers to a quasi-
divine status in which, as it was defined by the Church, they were
"viceroys of God on earth." But Alexander declined the proffered
title on the grounds that to accept it would be to set an example
for his subjects "contrary to the sentiments of moderation and the
spirit of humility" which he sought to inspire in them. These sober
expressions were evidences of a subtle metamorphosis that was taking
place in the tsar as he approached the routines of home and throne.

Back in Russia at last, after eighteen months abroad, Alexander was faced with something quite different from that with which he had recently been concerned, and he met it as a different man. Behind the façade of the brilliant knight whose touch was diplomatic magic and whose energy and ability were sufficient for anything he undertook, he was now the unfulfilled ruler of a land whose façade, like his own, was subject to easy misinterpretation.

The official ceremonial duties that traditionally marked the victorious conclusion of an important military undertaking occupied him only briefly: the provision of service medals for all classes that had served in the war effort; in addition, as practical expressions of imperial gratitude, the remission of certain tax arrears throughout the realm, the granting of pardons to noncriminal prisoners, and the repayment of individual loans to the government. After that, no pressing commitment stood between him and the domestic responsibilities that had accrued to him through two hundred years of Romanov rule.

Alexander was returning to a throne he had never wanted. Five years before he had been propelled into power by the murder of his father, in 1801, he had written to his friend Count Victor Kochubei: "I am aware that I was not born for the position I now occupy and even less for the one I am destined to hold, a position that I am determined to give up by one means or another." [3] Twelve years as tsar had only given him a more cheerless view of his imperial station. As he explained to the English general Sir Robert Wilson shortly before leaving for the war: "I am to be pitied, for I have few about me who have any sound education or fixed principles: my grandmother's court vitiated the whole education of the empire, confining it to the acquisition of the French language, French frivolities and vices, particularly gaming. I have little, therefore, on which I can rely firmly; only impulses . . ." [4]

He was faced again with the conditions that had occupied his thoughts before the so-called War of Liberation drew him into the position of absentee tsar. He now recognized all too vividly the paradoxes and intricacies with which he had wrestled, and he found them no less frustrating. He abhorred serfdom; yet he was sovereign of a state in which some thirty-two million of his subjects were peasants bound to the lands of the government, the imperial family, or the nobility. He viewed the numerous noble class of his subjects unsympathetically, regarding its pretensions as excessive and its contributions as inadequate; yet he understood that the stability of the state depended on the nobility. He sincerely believed that all human beings should enjoy inviolable civil and political rights; yet, according to the fundamental laws of the empire, he was the holder of supreme power, "autocratic and unlimited," and his subjects were obliged to obey him not only out of fear but also out of "duty commanded by God Himself." He was the source of law and, as such, stood above the law. He was the source of titles, distinctions, privileges, and honors. He alone could declare war or conclude peace. He was the "supreme leader" of the armed forces. He was the "supreme defender and protector" of the dogmas of the Russian Orthodox Church, over which he exercised administrative authority through the Holy Synod, consisting of prelates appointed by him and supervised by a lay overprocurator appointed by him. The only formal limitations imposed on him were that he be of the Eastern Orthodox faith and that he marry within that faith. It was generally assumed that he was bound by oath to respect the order of succession devised by his father, Tsar Paul, who, intending to eliminate such irregularities as those involved in many past successions, had decreed that, though either male or female members of the imperial family might succeed, precedence be given to the males, the oldest son of the sovereign being first among them. Yet, since the tsar was formally privileged to deprive any member of the imperial family of title—and thereby of the right to succeed—he could, if he believed that circumstances warranted, avoid the limitation of even that important decree. Indeed, the Russian tsar wielded far greater authority than did the most powerful of Western European monarchs, was more nearly immune than they had ever been from hampering restraints, whether imposed by their clergy, nobility, middle class, or bureaucracy. This fact weighed on Alexander's mind particularly when he had just returned from the West, where monarchs were subject to time-honored checks and balances, the dignity of man and the sovereignty of the people were beginning to be proclaimed, and constitutionalism was gaining ground. The only checks he had to respect were those imposed by his country's vastness and the backwardness of his subjects, factors that made effective administration difficult, and by the enduring possibility of assassination, a matter of much more intimate concern to a ruler who embodied supreme power, and was therefore held personally responsible for all grievances, than to those who shared their power.

Alexander faced also the remnants of the reforms he had begun, then abandoned. He could draw satisfaction from them only as evidences of his good intentions. When he had come to the throne, he had tried to submerge his aversion to the affairs of state, had accepted what he called the "burden of rule," and had planned in the manner of an enlightened autocrat—as he considered himself to be—to right some of the wrongs that abounded in the immense and complex Russian empire. He had, in fact, taken up his duties with such a willingness to make changes that the traditionalists in the government were soon protesting his "liberal dreams," while the young and progressive thinkers of the country were taking heart at the prospect of an "emancipated Russia." Predictions as to just how he would proceed had been made by many, relied upon by few. His character did not admit of precise interpretation, and his acts, therefore, of no accurate foreseeing.

In 1814, Alexander was no less an enigma than he had been in years past. He had changed only insofar as some of the elements in the definitely identifiable facets of his personality had been intensified, others subordinated.

As Alexander the Liberal, he was the product of an education ordered by his grandmother Catherine II and directed by the Swiss tutor Frederick La Harpe, through which he had come to accept the tenets of the French Enlightenment: belief in natural rights, man's perfectibility, the idea of progress, and deism. This was the idealistic Alexander who had come to power imbued with lofty notions of reform but quite unacquainted with the realities of the realm he had inherited.

Knowing that his ideas would have the support of neither his imperial relatives nor the experienced members of his government, he had sought it elsewhere. He had gathered around himself a number of sympathetic young men, most of them companions of his youth, whom he knew to be tolerant of ideas challenging tradition and established institutions—in short, liberals (a term not commonly employed in a political sense at the beginning of the nineteenth century, but soon to be applied to any person of this leaning). Prominent and very influential among them were Prince Adam Czartoryski, crusader for the restoration of Poland; Count Paul Stroganov, former member of the Jacobin club *Amis de la Loi* in Paris; and two who were enthusiastic admirers of English constitutional ideas, Count Victor Kochubei and Nicholas Novosiltsev. These four, as a group, were variously known as the Secret Committee, the Committee of Friends, the Committee of Public Welfare, the Jacobin Band—the name depending on the prejudice of the user, for the group had no official designation. To them the tsar had assigned the task of studying the needs of the country and outlining a constitution. Another young friend on whom he leaned particularly was Prince Alexander Golitsyn, who some years previously had forsaken the security of a career in the distinguished Preobrazhensky Guards to lead a life of self-indulgence and establish a reputation as a Voltairean in religion and a conservative in politics. Alexander, characteristically ignoring his friend's unsympathetic political bent in admiration for other aspects of his nature, had prevailed upon him to accept, at the age of thirty, the most powerful religious post in the country, that of Over-Procurator of the Holy Synod of the Russian Orthodox Church. Thus the liberal tsar had provided himself with supporters and willing administrators.

Then there was Alexander the Autocrat. While La Harpe's teachings had turned him toward idealistic convictions, his observation and participation in the military ceremonials at Catherine's court and his experience at his martial-minded father's palace at Gatchina had led him to an early admiration for practices that appeared quite incongruous with those convictions. He had developed an almost maniacal devotion to parades, close-order drills, and all the outward trappings of the military life. That devotion had led him easily to a liking for the commander of his father's private army, the notorious Count Alexis Arakcheev, and later to the enjoyment of the atmosphere on the Arakcheev estate in Gruzino, where the count and his mistress, Nastasya Minkin, maintained a scrupulously disciplined establishment. Alexander's admiration for ordered authority often extended beyond the military plane, expressing itself in arbitrary action that belied his liberalism, or in insistence on his own point of view regardless of the validity of contrary views. Even his most loyal friends deplored this trait in the otherwise tolerant man. Czartoryski's judgment of it was perhaps as generous as any: "In a word, he would willingly have agreed that every man should be free, on the condition that he should voluntarily do only what the Emperor wished." [5]

At times the tsar's arbitrariness outdid that of his autocratic predecessors, particularly in foreign affairs, where he frequently ignored established channels and handled matters either directly—with the justification that "I am my own minister"—or through some irregularly appointed personal representative. Another of his autocratic tendencies was to resort to diplomatic intrigue or duplicity in order to achieve desired ends; for instance, he treated covertly with Talleyrand against Napoleon in 1808 while openly avowing steadfast friendship for the latter. Also basically autocratic were his earnest pursuit of territorial expansion and his devotion to that supreme mark of imperial prestige, a large army.

The one consistent element in Alexander's character was seeming contradiction. The counterpoise of Alexander the Autocrat was a beneficent, mild man of quiet dignity and limitless love of mankind: Alexander the Religious Mystic. This phase of his personality had come into focus during the agony of near-disaster for Russia at the time of the Napoleonic invasion, when Prince Golitsyn suggested that the Bible might prove a source of solace and release from the tensions of daily crises (the prince himself having turned to a study of it rather belatedly, after his appointment to the office of over-procurator). The tsar, until then completely unacquainted with the Bible, adopted it as his daily guide. Thereafter it became the one source he depended upon for infallible direction in both personal and public affairs. Already interested in mysticism, with its emphasis on the individual's sensibility, he chose to seek God through personal experience, not through the intercession of the Church—though he attended services faithfully and prayed often at holy places. Once committed to the pious life, he fell easily into relationships with kindred persons and spent much time with Quakers, Moravian Brethren, and various devout monks. He welcomed particularly the friendship of mystics. In his own government he cherished two "brothers in Christ," Golitsyn and Rodion Koshelev, through whom he had introductions to many mystics of prominence throughout Europe.

The facets of Alexander's personality were not actually as disparate as they appear in cold enumeration. It is true that, because of the warring elements in his makeup, he was a man of many moods. He was capable of enthusiasms so intense that they were likely to burn themselves out and give way to what appeared to be indifference or an irresponsible shift in interest. Moreover, it was easy for him to see harmony where, to practical minds, there was none, and, lacking as he did the capacity for sustained commitment when severe opposition or more impelling interests presented themselves, to walk away from unfinished tasks. Yet there was a core of firmness in him. He was, in fact, a man of patent sincerity and a deep conviction about the rightness of whatever he was doing. Throughout his life, he was faithful to certain friends and to certain ideas regardless of changes that might have been expected to alter his attitude. Neither his extended love affair with Marie Naryshkin, wife of a court official, nor his many celebrated brief infatuations displaced his deep respect and consideration for his wife, Empress Elizabeth, as he proved in the years after he finally put aside the gallant's cape. The fact that he himself turned to Christian mysticism did not lessen his affection for his deist tutor, La Harpe. Even Napoleon stayed in his memory as an able and courageous soldier, and he did what he could to mitigate the humiliation and punishment measured out to him in defeat. Though he shied away from any practical action on what he considered the chief aim of his reign, to effect realistic and liberalizing changes in Russia, he did not abandon his basic conviction that change was needed. His enthusiasm and vigor waned, it is true, and his personal supporters despaired of him and withdrew; yet he remained steadfastly loyal to his ideals.

In one aspect of his life, Alexander was impelled toward the observance of ceremonies and the discharge of duties that were wholly antipathetic to the liberal in him. He had inherited the responsibility for a court that, despite his father's efforts to tone it down, was one of the most grandiose in Europe, and the leadership of a court society of unrivaled brilliance, both of which by their very nature set him apart from the people toward whom his liberalism drew him.

Court society revolved about whatever residence the imperial couple were occupying at a particular time, and that residence was popularly called the court. But in strict and legal terminology, the Russian imperial court was made up of holdings so extensive and of such specialized administration as virtually to constitute a separate state within the empire. It included millions of acres of appanage land, set aside to provide revenue for the imperial family through the labor of over a million appanage peasants; dozens of palaces and parks, the finest of them in St. Petersburg, in nearby Tsarskoe Selo (Tsar's Village), Peterhof, Gatchina, Pavlovsk, and in Moscow and Kiev; theaters for the presentation of imperially supported drama, music, and ballet; museums in which were collected rich displays of art, gems, and treasures of various other kinds from all parts of the world. In addition, there were a number of hunting preserves, where imperial hunting parties had the exclusive use of thousands of acres for sports, including grouse shooting, small-game coursing, and the taking of large game—bear, deer, boar, or wolf. Accessory to the preserves was a variety of so-called service establishments, the most widely known of which were the kennels maintained to supply the huntsmen with the dogs for which Russian breeders were noted, such as the swift borzoi, used especially for wolf hunting, and the large, strong-hearted beasts bred for the stamina and courage required for bear hunting.

The chief administration of these properties and the supervision of all activities involving them were in the hands of court officials answerable to the tsar; their number ran into the hundreds. Alexander took them, on the whole, as he found them. Since the designations as well as the basic duties and order of precedence assigned to their offices had come down almost unchanged from the time of Peter the Great, who chose German models of both function and nomenclature, these officials still followed the old, formal, and often cumbersome, German ways and carried such titles as *Ober-hofmarschall, Ober-jägermeister, Ober-schenk,* and *Ober-stallmeister* (the spelling modified only to the extent made necessary because of the differences between the Latin and Cyrillic alphabets). Below the chief administrators were tens of thousands of individuals, ranging from lower honorary to service ranks, whose tasks were the overseeing, upkeep, or operation of the properties—all of them personal employees of the tsar.

Court obligations requiring Alexander's personal attention included also the interpretation and application of the specific regulations pertaining to members of the imperial family—during his reign, Dowager Empress Marie Fedorovna, Empress Elizabeth, the grand dukes, the grand duchesses—and the setting of mood and pace for upper-class social activities.

He had come to the throne with the apparent intention of observing, in each area, what custom dictated. That task, by the beginning of the nineteenth century, was far from easy, entailing as it did the need to educe congeniality—or, at the least, workability—from what appeared to be a congeries of entirely inharmonious factors. The Russian court was, in fact, one of the most heterogeneous, and on the whole non-Russian, establishments within the empire. In addition to the German organization and titles of its officials, it included much on which the preceding century had set a foreign stamp. The palatial residences had been designed chiefly by Italian, French, and Scottish architects and surrounded by elaborate gardens modeled after those of France (if ordered by Alexander's great-grandaunt Elizabeth) or of England (if ordered by his grandmother Catherine). The regulations governing the imperial succession, which Tsar Paul had handed down, were German-Dutch in origin. The established rules of official etiquette followed quite faithfully those observed by

Austrian royalty. Among members of court society, the intellectual atmosphere, elegancies, and language of polite intercourse were French. And the tradition of imperial ceremonial practices were, in both grandeur and color, unabashedly oriental.

So far as the social life of the court was concerned, Alexander, trained as he had been at the direction of his grandmother, could approach it with easy competence notwithstanding his personal disfavor for some of high society's standards. Catherine, amply meriting Voltaire's description of her as the "Semiramis of the North," had not turned the court life of Russia into Babylonian revel, but she had marked it firmly with her liberal interpretation of *somptuosité* and *joie de vivre*. Determined that her favorite grandson be groomed for the "greatness" she visualized for him when she had him christened Alexander, she had ordered that his training for the imperial estate produce in him, in addition to the manly ruggedness and political awareness that it would demand, a familiarity with its embellishments.

The training was effective up to a point. During the first years of his reign, Alexander not only adhered to a personal regimen of austerity (sleeping on a hard camp bed and taking regular exercise) and attempted to apply the political principles he had been taught, but also restored much of the court display and exuberance that his father had spent five years in reducing. Though he declined to reinstate the court dwarfs and fools whose contribution to conviviality Catherine had enjoyed, he kept such symbols of former ostentation as the court "Arabs," a succession of tall, handsome, well-muscled Negroes, strikingly outfitted in scarlet, blue, and gold, whose presence always heralded the approach of the tsar; and he revived most of the grand formalities. These early responses of his encouraged the noble families to anticipate a return to the halcyon days when they had felt appreciated and secure. Indeed, almost every court function, for a time, recalled those days.

Perhaps, as some said, Alexander began to play the autocrat at court in a manner agreeable to members of upper-class society in order to mollify their expected opposition to his liberalism in government. Whatever his purpose, he accepted the traditional social obligations of the court along with all the others, and he and Empress Elizabeth made a notable beginning in their observation of the social calendar. It was a strict calendar and, considered in the light of the time and energy required by their activities beyond the court, quite a taxing one. There were many calls on a ruler's time. Alexander's presence was expected at military maneuvers. He and the empress might receive royal relatives from Western Europe at any time of the year, and they repaid many visits. In addition, as the reign advanced, he became more and more involved with regular visits to the country's holy places, such as the Trinity-Sergei Monastery outside Moscow, which drew tens of thousands of pilgrims each year, and with his trips abroad in the interest of international affairs. All this, in addition to the details of ruling Russia.

The ordinary social activities of the court could be observed without the participation of the imperial couple; however, when they chose to take part, they were expected to follow an established program. They spent the winter social season, from New Year's Day to the eve of Lent, in the St. Petersburg imperial residence, the Winter Palace, and kept up the conventions of the life for which it was designed. Its original 1,500 elegant rooms had been built half a century earlier to the plans of the architect Bartolomeo Rastrelli, who had accented the magnificence of the baroque interior by floors intricately inlaid with mother-of-pearl and rare, contrasting woods, by paintings on ceilings and walls, fine paneling, and the lavish use of such materials as colored marble, porphyry, malachite, jasper, and lapis lazuli. Catherine II had enlarged it by the addition of equally splendid apartments, pavilions, and galleries in her favored style, neoclassic. There, in the twenty halls specially appointed for the purpose, Alexander and Elizabeth received aristocrats, diplomats, and royalty at state receptions, masquerade balls, and banquets—sometimes as many as 3,000 of them at one function. Every occasion was a display of surpassing luxury: lights reflected from galaxies of precious lusters; bowers of exotic flowers gathered from the imperial hothouses or brought from the south; fine food and imported, out-of-season delicacies, presented on crested services of gold and silver hallmarked by German artisans or porcelain from Dresden and Sèvres; often, hours of dancing to the accompaniment of select musicians, both Russian and foreign.

When the winter season ended, rounded out by attendance at various theatrical performances and functions in the local palaces of other members of the family and the town houses of the upper nobility, custom decreed that the imperial couple leave for one of their residences outside the capital. Usually, at the beginning of the spring season, they went to Tsarskoe Selo, sixteen miles south of St. Petersburg. Their home there was the Great Imperial Palace, another Rastrelli monument to pretentiousness, renowned for its arcaded galleries and agate pavilion walled in jasper. Many members of the imperial family and others of court society moved also, to nearby villas and estates, where they continued their privileged lives, altered only to suit the changed season and environment. Here, no less than in St. Petersburg, the tsar lived, as far as the majority of Russians were concerned, at a sublime height. The chief difference, according to popular observations, was that the imperial surroundings at Tsarskoe Selo were more "foreign" than those in the capital: an "Italian" palace, an "English" park, a "Chinese" village for aides-de-camp, even an "Egyptian" memorial (actually a granite pyramid that had been built over the burial place of Catherine's favorite dogs). In time, Alexander himself unintentionally helped to emphasize the exclusiveness of the people with whom he consorted, here as well as elsewhere: he provided for the establishment of the Tsarskoe Selo Lycée and designated it as an institution for the instruction of sons of nobles—an act that could easily be taken as an indication that some of the choice blessings he had promised were to be limited in their distribution.

With the coming of summer, there was another move—this one to Peterhof, overlooking the Gulf of Finland, where the seasonal heart of the court became another Imperial Palace. Peter the Great had planned and begun here what he intended to be a Russian Versailles, and the central structure he built had been so elaborately expanded during the succeeding reigns that it came to Alexander as one of the most spectacular of his residences. The extravagance of its interior could not outdo that of the Winter Palace; but its exterior and its setting, a panorama of splendor overlaid by splendor, gave it a more imposing appearance. Its richly gilded domes rose above twin cascades rushing from the main courtyard down wide marble terraces; in every direction, there were acres of gardens and parks with formal and fanciful designs worked out in flowers, hand-smoothed walkways, waterfalls, fountains, statuary, and the famous "follies" which Peter had devised to tease the imagination or invite ribaldry (where, for example, a moment's rest on an inviting bench might leave an elegantly dressed lady embarrassed by a sudden skirt-ballooning wind or drenched by a chilly spray, which she had unwittingly triggered by sitting down).

From whatever point observed, the imperial court represented a life and culture alien to that of the majority of Russian people. Consequently, to the extent that Alexander attended to the routine proprieties of his position and respected the tradition providing for his personal involvement in the social life of it, he accented the anomaly of the liberalism he wanted his reign to reflect.

Because the combination of Alexander's inner selves functioned in no discernible order, his reign, like a receding glacier, was to leave a series of ill-assorted and irregular features on the surface of Russian history. The years between 1801 and 1814 had already been definitely marked by his individuality. During that time he had, in fact, so disturbed the tenor of tsarist rule that many, both at home and abroad, had come to believe that basic changes were imminent.

It was as the liberal that Alexander had sought an exchange of views with foreign heads of state and other men of stature in contemporary thinking when he came to power, a young man eager to learn. His correspondence with President Thomas Jefferson and his interest in relations with the United States were typical. Jefferson was sufficiently impressed by him to write a friend: "A more virtuous man [than Tsar Alexander], I believe does not exist, nor one who is more enthusiastically devoted to better the condition of mankind." [6] The general feeling of friendliness that he took pains to preserve between Russia and the United States had helped to moderate the discord growing out of the rivalry for fur trade and territory in Alaska and California. Nearer home, he had found a kindred spirit in Prussia's Frederick William III and had shared his political attitude to the extent of approving the king's toleration of secret patriotic societies, which, to most monarchists, represented dangerous revolutionary elements.

The same liberalism had marked Alexander's interest in all serious thinkers and led him to provide patronage for various learned men, among them some of quite uncongenial views. Two such were the English liberal Jeremy Bentham, whose treatise on civil and penal law he had ordered to be translated and published in Russia, and the Russian conservative Nicholas Karamzin, whom he had appointed court historiographer at a generous salary in order to encourage his writing plans, carried out as the twelve-volume *History of the Russian State*.

Some of the liberal measures he had enacted during his first five years of rule—when there was peace and when enthusiasm and hope ran highest in him—would have proved bases for extensive improvement if they had been supplemented in the years following. The machinery of the central government had been overhauled to the

extent of replacing the hundred-year-old collegiate system by ministries modeled after those of Western Europe, and of redefining the
powers of the Senate to make it more efficient as the highest judicial
and administrative body of the state—though still subject to the supreme authority of the tsar. To carry fundamental state reorganization any further would have entailed reassessing the basic principles
of tsarism, and even Alexander in his most liberal mood had not
proposed to undertake that task.

In the field of education, on the other hand, the beginning promised the possibility of continuing development. A ministry of education had been formed to centralize authority and policy. The number
of institutions of higher learning had been increased from one (Moscow University, founded in 1755) to six by the founding of new
universities in Kazan and Kharkov, the establishment of a pedagogical
institute in St. Petersburg, the reopening of the German-speaking
university at Dorpat, and the raising of the Polish-speaking Jesuit
academy at Vilna to the status of university. At the same time, definite
arrangements for the autonomous operation of these institutions had
been prescribed, the faculties being granted extensive freedom in
their administration. In addition, the framework for a countrywide
system of primary and secondary education had been set up, to function through parish and district schools, gymnasiums (secondary
schools), corps of cadets (for the military education of noble youths),
and ecclesiastical schools.

Of the less comprehensive measures undertaken by Alexander, a
few had been enforced with immediate and worthwhile results: the
granting of amnesty to those thousands whom Tsar Paul had deprived
of freedom, the abrogation of repressive measures against foreign
literature, the alleviation of censorship, the affirmation of the rights
of cities and the privileges of nobles, and the termination of restrictions on travel. Others, such as the abolition of torture as a means of
obtaining evidence and the elimination of secret police activity, had
been virtually annulled through lack of enforcement.

But these early measures, even if all had been enforced, could not
have been expected to have any discernible effect in the areas where
the realities were at greatest variance with Alexander's ideals, where
the great issues of the century and the critical tests of tsarist rule
were developing: serfdom and constitutionalism. Not that he had
neglected these areas; he had not. He had set out enthusiastically to
come to grips with the problems and to plan reforms, but he had

drawn up short of effective action. His timid efforts toward the liberation of the serfs through the establishment of a new peasant class of so-called free farmers had been all but fruitless: fewer than 50,000 male adults, little more than 1 percent of the peasant population, had been affected. And constitutionalism had developed no further than untried plans, which now lay dormant.

That Alexander's reforms were at a standstill when he returned to Russia in 1814 could not be ascribed solely to his having been abroad, absorbed in the War of Liberation, for the past year and a half. His schemes had been drifting into difficulties as early as 1805, when Russia, as a member of the Third Coalition, took up arms against Napoleon for the second time. The two years following had brought the costly defeats at Austerlitz and Friedland and the Treaty of Tilsit, which few Russians could accept as justification for the tsar's opinion that Russian had come out of the war "with a kind of luster." Many, including some of his closest friends and endorsers of his liberal efforts, had believed on the contrary that Tilsit was a diplomatic travesty and its binding of Russia to the Continental System an economic tragedy. When this opposition to his foreign policy had been added to what was becoming open petitioning for a recession of his reforming zeal at home, Alexander had been faced with a kind of crisis he had no adeptness in handling.

Those importuning for a change in his domestic policy had come to include not only members of the conservative nobility, whose oppostion to liberalism was to be expected, but also Dowager Empress Marie Fedorovna and his sister the Grand Duchess Catherine, who had at first indulged his idealism. To avoid conflict with such established and respected people, Alexander had set himself busily to ignoring their arguments. He had directed the government's immediate attention to the problems of the old and continuing wars with Persia and Turkey and a revival of hostilities with Sweden. Also, with courteous inattention to contrary advice, he had managed to revive some interest among liberals and some popular hope by reactivating, in the latter part of 1808, a part of his program of reforms. However, the vigor and dash of earlier efforts had not been retrievable.

Placed almost completely under the direction of Michael Speransky, who had proved his capability in the earlier reform period, the renewed efforts had been concentrated on the planning of constitutional reform aimed at the establishment of the rule of law in Russia without violating the monarchical principle. Speransky had applied himself diligently, but the outlook for his work had been at no time promising. Any change with which his name could be even remotely associated had become suspect among government officials after the spring of 1809, when the tsar, on his advice, had decreed two reforms highly objectionable to them: one specifying that court appointments were not *per se* steps to civil service positions, as they had previously been; the other making a university degree and the passing of a difficult examination requisite for holding civil service office. The immediate effect of such meddling with the status quo was increased opposition to reform in any guise. The growing opposition disturbed Alexander; yet, though he did not try overtly to allay it, he did try to avoid aggravating it unduly.

When Speransky had completed his detailed and ambitious plan for constitutional reform, late in 1809, Alexander had seen fit to put into effect only two parts of it. He had given his approval, in 1810, to the establishment of a state council (to be appointed by the tsar) privileged to consider new laws as well as watch over the legality of administration and to the reorganization of the ministries, the executive departments of the central government. He had thereby allowed some changes while abdicating none of his autocratic prerogatives. At the same time, he had restored somewhat his standing among the liberal thinkers—and perhaps eased his conscience a bit. But he had quietly shelved the remaining, and very important, parts of Speransky's plan without ever having made them public.

Unfortunately, however, he had again stirred the very hornet's nest he wanted to avoid. His acts had prompted the antireform forces to intensify their opposition, which now culminated in the charge that Speransky had been revealing state secrets to the French; finally, in March 1812, Alexander had found it expedient to dismiss him.

For a time, it appeared that the tsar's liberal "sins" had been carried away by the scapegoat Speransky. Shortly thereafter, the superficial alliance with Napoleon broke down, war was reopened, and the various reform projects joined other infrequently recalled memories.

By the time he returned from the War of Liberation, Alexander had become preoccupied with ideas that were to overshadow, and finally eclipse, his concern with domestic reform. He was beginning to see himself as one whose mission was to lend guidance to a confused world, a leader whose obligations had become international in scope. He judged his first duty to be the overseeing of arrangements for peace in Europe, and he intended that, in both the establishment and the preservation of peace, Russia should have a deservedly leading part.

Still, he had some difficulty in disengaging his new character from the old: the quirk in his nature that sometimes drew the left hand to one task and the right to another led him, in 1814, to make a token move toward renewing the central project of his uncompleted reform program. This time, he selected for the undertaking Baron Gustav Rosenkampf, a Baltic German with not the slightest enthusiasm for it, and directed him to "draft a suitable constitution for Russia." The act was not made public, however, and, as others before it, finally came to nothing as the tsar's energies became absorbed by his driving concern with foreign affairs. After all, any doubts he had concerning autocracy, the nobility, and serfdom derived from moral rather than practical considerations; he therefore found it easy to become so involved elsewhere that he was soon giving only desultory attention to his realm's internal affairs. As he said, "One cannot do all things at once."

Alexander gave himself wholeheartedly to his new crusade as he left Russia, within two months after his return as the "hero of the liberation," for the Congress of Vienna. Since he considered his mission in Europe to be a personal one, he had no thought of trusting it to a diplomatic representative. Let Francis I speak through his Metternich; Louis XVIII, his Talleyrand; the English regent, his Castlereagh and Wellington; Frederick William III, his Hardenberg and Humboldt; Alexander would speak for himself. He was glad to have his minister of foreign affairs, Count Karl Nesselrode, at his side when he needed an intelligent, loyal, and competent aide, an agreeable companion, or a reliable messenger; but Nesselrode was to be neither a maker of policy nor a responsible team member in the game of diplomacy. Others in his retinue were likewise only favored subordinates, though they included such trusted friends as Czartoryski and the Greek liberal Giovanni Capo d'Istria, soon to share the foreign ministry post with Nesselrode.

Alexander let it be known at once that he expected Russia to have a decisive voice—along with Austria as a major partner, Prussia as a minor one, and England as an intermittent force—in all decisions concerning the nine European nations now involved in the postwar territorial and political adjustments. He made his policy clear on all issues and, disregarding the positions of others, backed his proposals so stubbornly as to indicate that he would risk war in order to have his own way.

The fact that he was behaving like a willful autocrat did not prevent his insisting on principles and measures representing his liberal inclination. Just as liberalism had prompted his wish that France be governed in a constitutional manner, it now prompted his insistence on the restoration of the kingdom of Poland (though some were quick to infer that his vision of that country's future did not exclude a bit of autocratic self-interest). Deeply ashamed of the dismemberment of Poland, in which Catherine II had played so crucial and inglorious a part, he was dedicated to the ambition, as he confided to Czartoryski, to effect "the reunion of everything that formerly constituted Poland" except White Russia. The scheme met with immediate opposition from the assembled heads of state and diplomats; as a result, Alexander found himself the intended victim of a neat little movement of resistance planned by Talleyrand, Castlereagh, and Metternich.

Just as the Polish question was building to decided unpleasantness, crisis overrode crisis. Napoleon's return from Elba broke into the work of the Congress of Vienna and drew the participants once more into a common undertaking.

During the Hundred Days, beginning on March 20, 1815 (N.S.), while all turned their attention to the renewed conflict with Napoleon (finally, under Wellington, defeating him at Waterloo), Alexander underwent one of his personality changes. Distressed over the general discord in the congress and the opposition he had personally encountered, he seemed to lose spirit and become self-absorbed. As he recalled in later years, "My heart was indeed oppressed." When he and his Russian army were denied an honored part in the final victory over Napoleon, his dedication to international leadership was shaken by frustration. Religious mysticism was now, as it had been before, an inviting sanctuary for him; in it he was able to find a reason to redirect his leadership.

One person who took advantage of his unsettled state was the shrewd mystic Baroness von Krüdener, whom Alexander first met during this intermission of the congress. She urged him to think of himself not as a mere leader but as the man foreordained to prepare the world for the advent of the millennium. Surely, she argued, it was not to be doubted that he met the Lord's specifications as set down in Isaiah's prophecy:

> I stirred up one from the north, and he has come,
>   from the rising of the sun, and he shall call on my name;
> he shall trample on rulers as on mortar,
>   as the potter treads clay.[7]

The idea was both reasonable and appealing to Alexander. It had the merit of coinciding with his belief that he had already begun the shaping of destinies: he had liberated the Germans, he had restored the Bourbons and gained benevolent consideration for France in the First Treaty of Paris, and he intended to bring justice to the Poles.

His belief in his inspired leadership thus reinforced and a new goal identified, Alexander was more eager than ever to resume what he considered his personal responsibility in international diplomacy. Accordingly, after Napoleon was defeated and Louis XVIII once more had returned to Paris "in the baggage of the allies," he took up anew, in the reassembled congress, his fight on behalf of Poland. Though he could not get agreement on the whole of his plan for territorial restoration (by the final arrangement, Austria kept Galicia, Prussia kept Posen, and Cracow was declared free under the protection of Russia, Prussia, and Austria), he was reasonably satisfied when Poland as a national entity was restored. The new kingdom of Poland was bound by a very significant condition: while it would be a self-governing state, it was to be so under the scepter of the Russian tsar. That condition was viewed by the Poles with distaste, and by many others with grudging acquiescence and ill-concealed suspicion. As Alexander interpreted the matter, his position was one of complete generosity, for he planned to allow a liberal Polish constitution as well as to transfer to the restored kingdom at a later time some of the provinces taken by Russia during the partitions; if he had to use the bludgeon of power to defend that position, he felt that the end would justify the means.

When the major problems of the congress had been taken care of, Alexander turned resolutely to what he now considered his sacred mission. He urged the rulers of Europe—and generously included one outsider, the President of the United States—to enter with him into an agreement to respect the "supreme truths dictated by the eternal law of God the Saviour" and to apply the Christian principles of "justice, charity, and peace" in all their dealings with one another and with their subjects—to form the Holy Alliance. All of the European heads of state, with the exception of England's prince regent, the sultan of Turkey, and the Pope, promised adherence to the alliance. On the whole, however, neither they nor their ministers attached to it the profound importance that Alexander did. Observers from the vantage point of England expressed their sentiments with the forthright temerity of nonparticipants: Sydney Smith saw its adherents as "crowned conspirators"; Castlereagh called it "a piece of sublime mysticism and nonsense," which, if actually applied, would turn world affairs back to the "epoch of the Saints." But such disparagement did not cloud the renewed self-confidence of Russia's tsar.

So far, it appeared to Alexander that he was making progress, without significant challenge, toward his aim of consolidating his country's newly acquired position. He confidently expected Russian preeminence to be continued in the West through his leadership in the Holy Alliance and the plans he had for increasing his country's military strength. And in the East, where the rise of the imperial sun was already to be seen in Transcaucasia, Turkestan, across Siberia, and even along the Pacific coast of North America, the prospect was altogether promising.

But here and there in diplomatic circles different views were being expressed. There were some doubts about the practicality of Alexander's leadership as well as uneasiness about Russia's ascendant position among the great powers. The dissidence had so far been mild, but it had been quite apparent—in the strategy that precluded Russian participation and sharing of honors at Waterloo, in the amendments to the Polish settlement, and in the Second Treaty of Paris, which was harsher than the tsar wished—and it was growing.

Austria's minister of foreign affairs, Prince Clemens von Metternich, one of the most vigorous-minded of European diplomats, was pointedly frank in giving his assessment of the situation from a point of view agreeable to most European monarchists. He saw Europe still walking a tightrope over a fiery pit of revolution, the heat maintained by liberal and radical ideas sparked in France, and he felt that the time had come to restore some semblance of security by complete and unequivocal support of the spirit of conservative monarchism. The continent, he was convinced, would never be secure as long as there was any traffic with ideas of popular sovereignty, constitutionalism, and representative government. Moreover, he saw it as the task of the throne and the established church in each country to stop such traffic and to hold fast to the eternal verities of throne and altar. He feared, however—and rightly so—that Tsar Alexander did not share his views. Of still greater importance, he lacked confidence in the tsar's dependability as a leader, regardless of his views at a particular time. Embarrassingly enough, he recognized that his judgment was closely in agreement with that of the recent enemy: Napoleon, reflecting on Alexander's ability to play seemingly contradictory roles, had called him the "Talma of the North" (Talma being an unusually versatile French actor).

After years of dealing with Alexander, Metternich altered only slightly this evaluation—and that, merely in being more explicit:

The Emperor seized an idea, and followed it out quickly. It grew in his mind for about two years, till it came to be regarded by him as a system. In the course of the third year he remained faithful to the system he had adopted and learned to love, listened with real fervour to its promoters, and was inaccessible to any calculation as to its worth or dangerous consequences. In the fourth year the sight of those consequences began to calm down his fervour; the fifth year showed an unseemly mixture of the old and nearly extinct system with the new idea. This new idea was often diametrically opposite to the one he had just left.[8]

Alexander's diplomatic contradictoriness, however, did not obscure for the discerning Metternich what many of his contemporaries failed to see: that his "disposition was noble, and his word was sacred." [9]

II

"Having Earned a Rest, He Took It"

ALEXANDER I, 1815-1816

WHEN Alexander returned from Vienna to St. Petersburg, in December 1815, a renewal of interest in his own people was in order—overdue, in fact. In the three years since he left for the War of Liberation, he had been in Russia for only one period, of less than two months. There was some speculation, of course, about what he would turn to, now that the Eagle was safely pinioned on St. Helena, the Final Act of the Congress of Vienna had been signed, and the Holy Alliance had been formed.

It was not to be expected in autocratic Russia, however, that there would be much discussion of any of these speculations that might touch on politics. That had never been considered a safe topic of conversation, even for the privileged of government and court; since Speransky's shadow no longer darkened their days and since most of those reforming young confidants of the tsar had drifted away from him as his zeal for domestic reform had abated, there was no particular reason to be concerned with politics. Anyway, gossip and frivolous anecdote, both accepted as social currency, were far more interesting.

The findings in that area were, as usual, satisfyingly plentiful:
. . . The tsar, though only thirty-eight, was already graying and looking dispirited. His customary charm and gentleness were known

recently to give way to frequent bursts of anger. . . . It was remarkable that his wife, Elizabeth Alexeevna, whom Catherine had chosen over ten other German princesses as a child bride for Alexander more than two decades ago, could have so patiently endured his neglect while he had openly continued—for eleven years—his adulterous affair with the "Beautiful Pole," Marie Naryshkin. Could it be that the empress judged him generously because she understood his disappointment that she had borne him no heir, only two daughters, who had died in infancy?

. . . The tsar's oldest brother, the brusque and reputedly callous Constantine (it was said that he actually shot live rats from a cannon as a birthday salute to Alexander), was growing into a real fire-breathing martinet as he faced the hatred he had stirred up in the seven months since the tsar gave him command of the Polish army. Heaven help Russia if he should ever become tsar—a definite likelihood since, as long as Alexander and Elizabeth had no son, Constantine was the legal heir to the throne. No doubt he was now rehearsing more specifically for the role his grandmother Catherine had selected for him when she chose his name: the future "Emperor Constantine," ruling from Constantinople the reconstituted Byzantine Empire. Still, he would perhaps be less irascible if the tsar and his mother could bring themselves to allow him the privilege of divorcing his wife, who had gone home to Saxe-Coburg years ago, and make it possible for him to marry again. There was a possibility, it had to be admitted, that no woman would accept him, the poor unfortunate, cursed with his father's forbidding countenance and unruly temper. With his father's touch of madness also? Probably not. Though stubborn, self-indulgent, and sometimes apparently unfeeling, he could be reasonable and kind when he chose, even affectionate.

. . . The two younger grand dukes, Nicholas and Michael—more like sons than brothers to the tsar, of course, he being nineteen years older than Nicholas and twenty years older than Michael—were happily giving promise of being quite different from Alexander in cast of mind. Their private education, based on traditionally proper military training rather than liberal ideas, probably had something to do with it. Indeed, their mother, Dowager Empress Marie Fedorovna, was understood to complain that they gave too much attention to "military trifles."

. . . Back to the subject of Poland: it was authoritatively reported that Prince Czartoryski was still smoldering because the tsar had chosen the obscure General Zaionczek as viceroy of the new Polish

state when the prince—and everyone else, for that matter—had expected that he himself would receive the appointment.

. . . Catherine, the tsar's favorite among the three of his still living
sisters, had apparently decided that three years of widowhood were
enough: she had been observed flirting with Prince Wilhelm of
Württemberg at the time of the Congress of Vienna. After all, no
one expected her to upset gossip's rule that Germany was Russia's
"stud farm," the chief source of husbands for Romanov daughters.
The current generation was, in fact, not only observing the rule
rather consistently but applying it in reverse as well. Four of Alexander's sisters, including Catherine, had married Germans, while
only one had chosen from another royal house, the Dutch; and, since
the tsar himself as well as the Grand Duke Constantine had married
German princesses, there remained only the Grand Duke Nicholas
—already engaged to the lovely daughter of Prussia's King Frederick
William III—and the young Michael to complete the program.
. . . *Eh bien, nous verrons ce que nous verrons.*

Here and there beyond the untroubled coteries of court and upper-
class society, a few were beginning to disregard the traditional taboo
on political discussion, some of them interpreting the permissiveness
of Alexander's rule as encouragement to declare themselves for reform and others interpreting it as a compelling reason to make clear
their distaste for reform. The return of the tsar, ostensibly free now
to give his attention to domestic affairs, quickened both groups, the
one to hope, and the other to fear, that he would resume the course
of reforms with which he had begun his reign.

The champions of change, usually well educated and alert young
men, were proud of their liberal views and eager to defend them
against views which, in the challenging world as they saw it, were
inadequate and dangerously outmoded: the views identified as conservative, reactionary, obscurantist—by whatever name, those representative of complacency and tolerant of inaction.

In contrast to the vigorous young liberals, the so-called conservatives and their fraternal supporters were generally of an older generation, solidly and complacently identified with some aspect or
other of the established order: the Holy Synod of the Russian Orthodox Church, for example, the privileged nobility, some of the
ministries, or the Russian Academy, Russia's inferior counterpart of
the Académie Française. Admiral Alexander Shishkov, who was president of the Academy for twenty-five years after the war, was typical

of those who could, and did, use their positions as redoubts against reform in very important areas. As state secretary during the war years, he had written most of the imperial manifestoes and rescripts issued during that period, but his personal acquaintance with Alexander had in no way altered his disapproval of the liberalism so obviously basic to the tsar's intentions. He lost no time, therefore, in turning the power of his Academy postion not only to the defense of the Russian language against the "corrupting" effect of French words but also to the protection of Russian society from the "corrupting" effects of French ideas—that is, from reform.

Though Alexander had no obligation to share his postwar plans with the liberals, the conservatives, or any of his other subjects, he was obliged by tradition to issue a manifesto announcing the end of war. And this he did—in a rather perfunctory way. Revising and updating the pigeonholed draft of a manifesto Shishkov had prepared a year earlier, on the occasion of Napoleon's first surrender, he issued it on New Year's Day, 1816. It was simply an expression of thanks to God for leading Christian Russia to victory and a call for humility toward Him. Neither dramatic nor revealing, it kindled no hope in liberals, evoked no fears among conservatives. It was not intended as a statement of intention; yet those who shrank from change and had been troubled by the early evidences of the tsar's penchant for reforms, took comfort in the familiarity of its religious phrasing and its archaic language.

In fact, there was no immediately discernible evidence anywhere that the traditional rhythms of Russian life were to be interrupted or changed. Russia seemed to be slipping back into her accustomed ways as if there had been no French Revolution, no Napoleon; as if the trace of light to which some had looked hopefully during the brief reform period had simply guttered out like that of a spent candle. The reforms inaugurated in France since 1789, which had directly or indirectly altered the institutions of most of Western and Central Europe, had occasioned no change in either the social or the political fabric of Russia; indeed, the French ideas of liberty and human rights were practically unknown to all but the small educated class—and rejected by most of them. It was a situation that might have dashed the hopes of the country's nascent liberals had they not been fortified by the resilience of youth and the confidence of upper-class status.

Even in the recovery from the physical ravages of the war, every effort was being made to restore the old rather than to replace it with something different or better. Moscow, three-quarters of which had been burned in 1812, was to be reconstructed but not remodeled. Plans called for a few more gardens and for fireproof, metal roofs (green, to blend pleasingly with the soft tints of the buildings); but in most respects the city was to resume its look of splendid medieval disorder. In the many towns and villages of the provinces of Smolensk, Mogilev, Grodno, Kovno, and Vilna, where devastation had been extensive, postwar emphasis was on restoration, not change.

It is true that in St. Petersburg the neoclassic style currently popular in western Europe was being followed in the construction of the Kazan Cathedral, the Exchange, and the New Admiralty; yet, even there, tradition was not being abandoned. St. Petersburg had always been an anomalous city, whose chief excuse for existence was that it had been designated as the capital; over the years, it had become a mélange of the old and the new. The personal vanity of the ambitious empresses Elizabeth and Catherine II was responsible for the architectural features that provided its "modern" aspect. The buildings now under way were simply to continue what they had started. It remained a place of would-be grandeur arbitrarily set in place above a chill Finnish swamp; a city without public transportation, water supply, sewage system (a network of open canals and branches of the Neva still carried its fetid waste), regular fire department, or sidewalks; a city where the guards drilled their horses in buildings that looked like Greek temples, and the poor lived in quarters that looked like stables. Its population of 385,000 was presently growing at the rate of fewer than a hundred persons a year. In fact, except for the shipyards of the energetic Scottish entrepreneur Charles Baird, where his ships were being fitted with steam engines, there was precious little in or around St. Petersburg to suggest that it had entered the nineteenth century.

As with so much that was Russian, the people themselves, with few exceptions—and those limited chiefly to the nobility—seemed to belong to the pre-Petrine world, untouched by what went on in the more progressive Western world. The majority of them, peasants and those of peasant origin (the so-called dark people), had little hope of change. Others clung to the old days because of indifference or complacency or, like the peasants, because of necessity imposed by unchallenged tradition.

The nineteenth century clergy, despite the Church's successive losses to the state over the years—power, under Peter I; property, under Peter III and Catherine II—was little different from the clergy of centuries earlier. Its members bore practically the same relation to one another and to the people, were organized in much the same way, and discharged their several duties in much the same manner. There were still the sharp class differences between the monastic and the secular branches, the "black clergy" and the "white clergy," which seemed to mark the one as the Almighty's noblemen, the other as His serfs. From the black clergy, those who had taken monastic vows, came the elite. Standing at the right hand of the tsar, who ruled by divine right, they constituted what amounted to the spiritual department of the government. All of them, from the eminent metropolitans down to the abbots of the meanest monasteries, served well in return for the personal gain, influence, and respect that went with their ranks; as shapers and directors of the people's attitude toward the tsar, they were important supports of the whole imperial scheme. The white clergy lived among the laity as the parish priests, did the yeoman work laid out by their superiors, were among the lowliest of the lowly in the social scale and as ill-rewarded in the goods of the profane world. Catherine II had sought to help them by providing schools for their children and by freeing them from corporal punishment at the hands of their superiors, but their lot was still a wretched one. Barely literate, they fulfilled their ritual duties in the parish by dint of memorizing the necessary services or Biblical passages, and they eked out their wholly inadequate allowances by paltry fees from their parishioners and hard work on the small plots allotted them. They were required to marry, and it was expected that their sons would follow them into the priesthood, thus making it primarily a hereditary arm of the Church organization (while it was possible for outsiders to enter the ranks of the white clergy, it was quite unusual). But gradually the number of aspirants had become greater than the number of vacancies, and many were now being forced to seek lay occupations.

The effectiveness of the labor of these ecclesiastical classes was evident everywhere. Religious ritual was part of almost every activity, from the coronation of a tsar to the baptism of a serf's infant. Its cadence was the pulse of everyday life: the never-ending tramp of pilgrims' feet, the gently repeated sign of the cross before familiar icons, the liturgical chants in the great cathedrals, the drone of responses in village services. Peasants in particular embraced their religion wholeheartedly and humbly, trusted its promises, and reverenced the Little Father, the tsar, as God's representative on earth.

They were the better prepared therefore to accept their lot, pay their taxes, and follow the holy icons into battle for the tsar.

Members of the merchant class, the backbone of both domestic and foreign commerce, had prospered and grown in number, but their position in the scheme of Russian life remained the same. Their unrefined business methods had endured almost unaltered since the days of Ivan IV. Each merchant still dominated what amounted to a private economic empire, having his own countinghouse system of banking, owning stalls for his specialties at the great fairs, contracting directly in both buying and selling, and often trading in the products of home industries under his personal management. The merchants clung jealously to the distinction, exclusiveness, and advantages guaranteed by their membership in the old merchant guilds, displayed the snobbishness or the humility appropriate to whatever station they occupied in the rigid economic hierarchy recognized within their class, and shrugged contemptuous shoulders at the burghers, tradesmen whose capital was insufficient to give them merchant status. Although Catherine II had relieved them of the poll tax and the liability to military draft, class stigmas that they had long borne, they still existed in a kind of no man's land between the upper and lower strata of Russians. Regardless of their degree of prosperity, they were excluded from the salons of the upper class and from government officialdom. Their position was a solid one, however, and apparently a satisfying one. The tsar expected no disturbing change in their quarter.

The common lot of the peasant—whether state peasant attached to government-owned lands, appanage peasant attached to lands of the imperial family, or privately owned peasant (serf)—was such that his most likely chance of change was, as his already heavy burdens grew heavier, to sink to a lower and more hopeless level. So little improvement had come into the life of his kind that, in the first quarter of the nineteenth century, he could have merged unobserved into almost any scene from the life of his forebears of three hundred years earlier. Tradition and experience had seared him with a deep brand. Centuries of subservience to the two forces he was helpless to oppose, his immediate masters and the supernatural presences which he recognized all about him, had imposed docility, humility, and superstition upon him. His simple faith in the Almighty and His earthly representative, the tsar, had led to piety out of respect for the one, to bravery and long-suffering obedience out of respect for the other. The average peasant believed that the Little Father possessed the heaven-given right of ownership of everything in Russia, that he sincerely loved his lowly subjects, and that his beneficence was denied them by his unprincipled deputies, the noble-landlords.

If a peasant was one of the majority, whose life was never-ending hard work, his aspect was likely to justify the epithet *chern* ("filth" or "darkness"), by which he was known among his betters: his hair and beard uncut and matted with the sweat and dirt of his toil; his tattered coat hanging from stooped shoulders; his legs swathed in woolen strips; his feet thrust into bast shoes—boots, if he were exceptionally prosperous—and his unwashed body giving acrid testimony of the chief elements in his daily monotonous routine—manure, earth, onions, cabbage. If he were one of the minority fortunate enough to be assigned to special work, his appearance differed accordingly, and his dress reflected his improved station. In case he was endowed with outstanding intelligence, comeliness, or talent, he might find favor with his master and be given instruction or training in such fields as nursing, weaving, wood carving, dancing, music; even painting, writing, or accounting. A notable example of generous treatment during this period was to be found in Ostankino, where serfs provided the entire cast of an opera company maintained in the palace of the noble Sheremetev family.

There were peasants in some capacity or other in every area of Russian life: as farmers providing the substance that supported the economy of the country; as servants in noble households; as laborers in the mines and factories or in the service of the state, driving postal carriages, timbering for the Admiralty in state-owned forests, constructing buildings, bridges, or roads (forced peasant labor built with hand-cut logs the nearly 500 miles of joggle-and-jolt road between St. Petersburg and Moscow); as privates in the guards or line regiments —wherever there was work to be done, lives to be spent. Sixty percent of the inhabitants of the most Westernized of Russian cities, St. Petersburg, were peasant-born, most of them—that is, those not in the military units or in the city households of their masters—on leave from their villages to eke out their income by the heavy labor to be found in the capital.

There was ample reason to believe that, as there had been little change for these thirty-two million Russians in the past, there would be little now or in the foreseeable future. Of those who might have brought it, the upper class and the government, the majority wanted no change that would disrupt the class structure; no one had conceived of any significant change that would not disrupt it.

As for Alexander himself, when he returned to Russia at the end of 1815, his concern with domestic reform and change had been all but eclipsed. He was now at such an elevated level of idealism that what he saw in the distance was clearer to him than what was near at hand. The responsibilities of his personal stewardship, as he now interpreted it, was no longer limited to his Russian subjects but ranged over all of mankind. He was not insensible to the needs for improvement in his own country, although he seemed to have lost the impetus to try to improve it through liberal changes. Most of the fruits of his liberalism had proved bitter, and he did not care to harvest more of the same just then. So far as Russia was concerned, he had become "Tsar Dadon," intent chiefly on its relation (as personified by himself) to other countries. Whatever changes might be needed to support this new interest would be imposed expeditiously by his direct order and would involve no disturbing adjustments in his autocratic rule.

If the tsar's aspiration to be a recognized and respected arbiter among nations were to be realized, his own empire would have to remain secure in its position as first among the great powers. At the time, there seemed to be no reason to doubt that the condition could be met. Yet there were built-in contingencies.

The strength of Russia had developed from, and now rested firmly on, four institutions: autocracy, the nobility, serfdom, the Russian Orthodox Church. Any ruler who let his attention wander from them did so at his peril. Century after century, each of them had done its part as needed to make Russia powerful and bring it to the point of supremacy in European affairs. Autocracy had served by giving cohesion, security, and domestic tranquility to a sprawling and heterogeneous land; the nobility, by providing responsible civil and military service to the state; serfdom, by making available millions of men for military service as well as furnishing the labor necessary to support the nobility and the state; and the Church, by inducing moral support for autocracy as a divinely sanctioned institution and by fostering loyalty to throne and fatherland.

As these institutions had served well in the distant past, so they had served in the war just concluded. Alexander had represented autocracy nobly in the crises by his steadfastness, personal bravery, and diplomatic effectiveness; the nobles had served patriotically in positions of government and military leadership, and some of them had been able to provide emergency funds for the national treasury;

the serfs, with very few exceptions, had been loyal to their masters
and the sovereign, had worked hard and given lives by the tens of
thousands; and the Church, eagerly championing the brave new
David against the bold Goliath from the West, had contributed
significant moral support to what it interpreted basically as a struggle
against the evil designs of antichristian forces.

In 1815, the stability of these institutions was taken for granted by
most of the country's articulate commentators. The tsar had been
pointedly reminded of this serene conservative view through a memorandum from court historiographer Karamzin at the time of the anti-
Speransky agitation in 1811, and there had been no change in this
view. Karamzin's argument was that the "sensible political system"
of a country such as Russia, where "the people labor, the merchants
trade, and the nobility serve," being properly rewarded with "distinction and benefits, respect and comfort," was in no need of change;
that, though admittedly there were some abuses in administration,
they could be corrected by a good autocrat served by "good" governors and "good" priests; and that, finally and without equivocation,
autocracy stood firm, the "Palladium of Russia."

As Alexander's interest shifted from national to international affairs, he could take comfort in such complacency. The conservatives
in his government lost no opportunity to assure him that basically
all continued to be well despite the few who openly persisted in de-
crying certain objectionable conditions, particularly those inherent
in serfdom. Changing times had no effect on their views: twenty years
after the tsar's first tentative and ineffectual gestures toward removing
some of the glaring injustices imposed on the "dark people," he received this assurance in a special report from a highly respected
guards general, Alexander Benckendorff: "Always and everywhere
the *chern* have been and will continue to be the *chern*. . . . Russians
are so accustomed to the existing order, under which they live peacefully and happily and which is so much in accord with the environment and with their nature, that they will not permit themselves
to think of change." [1]

Assurances notwithstanding, the fact was that Russia was slowly,
almost imperceptibly, drifting into a new era. A more sudden and
dramatic confrontation between the realities of the old order and the
challenges of changing conditions might have caused Alexander to assign a higher priority to the consideration of domestic needs. As it
was, he allowed himself to be lulled into ignoring a number of
danger signals.

The most imporant of these appeared in the countryside, where the nobility and the serfs were feeling the first mild tug of currents that would draw them inexorably into a maelstrom unless their predicament were recognized and efforts made to rescue them. It was unfortunate that the conditions underlying the adversity, having developed gradually and lacking the distinct outlines of ponderable problems, could not be easily recognized.

Whereas the great noble estates had once sustained the strong heart of Russia's nearly self-sufficient agricultural society, in recent years most of them had declined into a condition definitely threatening to that function.

The serfs on these lands had to endure enslavement not only to their lords but also—as did many of the peasants tilling state lands—to an antiquated, inefficient, and inflexible agricultural system that was little more than a latter-day counterpart of the medieval manorial system. Most of them were condemned to the open, three-field scheme of planting, the use of primitive implements, and the lack of such essentials as fertilizer, means of drainage, and agricultural instruction of any kind beyond the obsolete father-to-son kind—all of which combined to drag them closer to the wretched level of the scrawny cattle that foraged on their scraps of pastureland. Only if they labored doggedly, their landlords were generous, and the seasons were favorable could they manage to override those difficulties.

The landlords also were becoming victims of a past out of accord with the present. For generations, they had been beneficiaries of rulers who had lavishly endowed them with land and serfs. In the early years of the country's growth, their military and administrative services to the government had been consistently rewarded in such coin. Later, a run-of-the-mill favorite might confidently expect a sizable estate and a hundred or more serfs as a token of appreciation from his imperial patron. Others profited still more handsomely as successive rulers distributed the lands and the millions of souls subjected to imperial rule and serfdom as a result of territorial expansion or the confiscation of Church properties (Elizabeth handed out something like 100,000 souls to her favorites; Paul, 600,000; and Catherine, 800,000). It was not to be expected that, given their easy advantages, the nobles would develop either enterprise or a sense of thrift—and they did not. Consequently, they came to lack two essentials for their continued prosperity, skill as agriculturists and capital.

Further difficulties had grown out of the fact that the holdings of the average noble-landlord had tended, generation by generation, to be decreased in acreage by the practice of subdividing estates among heirs; his returns, of course, had decreased accordingly. At the same time, his rising standard of living was requiring increased spending: for lengthened social seasons, more extravagant entertainment, foreign travel, imported tutors, and the ever more numerous amenities of the fashionable cult of culture. For all this he needed cash, often more of it than he was able to realize from his holdings. Although the government in recent years had supplemented its other generosities by providing means whereby such needy landlords could borrow money in a painless manner from state funds, the problems of the countryside were not thus solved.

The situation was not yet dire, but each year it was growing more precarious. Official records showed that government credit agencies had been lending money to the nobles since the middle of the preceding century and taking, in return, mortgages on their serfs, and that by the end of the war nearly one-fifth of all Russian serfs had been pledged as security for such loans. Since indications were that the loans were being used to balance the nobles' budgets rather than to improve the condition of holdings, chances were that the proportion would continue to rise. Moreover, landlords, still unable to meet their financial obligations, were now demanding from their serfs more and more cash in lieu of dues-in-kind or labor. Here was the point at which the system's tolerance of strain was about to meet a critical test.

The serfs were already being subjected to almost insupportable pressures before they were faced by this last imposition. The government was exacting from them more taxes than ever to meet the high cost of the military establishment; their "rights" were still being belied by "manorial justice," too often measured out in strokes of the rod or days of miserable confinement, and certain customary and legal dispensations essential to their very existence were being violated. Just when their obligations were being increased, the size of the land plots alloted to them was being decreased. One reason for this, of course, was that the serf population was multiplying: over 90 percent of the 600,000 persons added annually to the population of Russia were of the peasant class—and over half of the peasants were serfs. Another reason was that the landlords, maneuvering for more returns, were on occasion withdrawing serf-allotted lands to their own holdings. Even the few laws designed to protect the serfs from landlord abuse were being frequently flouted or evaded. Although masters were forbidden by law to offer serfs at public sales without the land they tilled and newspapers were forbidden to publish advertisements offering serfs for sale, masters and publishers were finding ways to bypass both restrictions. The government itself violated the law on sales through its public disposition of the serfs of bankrupt nobles. Any astute buyer could properly misread a published notice that the "services" of a serf were "available," understanding well enough that the serf himself was for sale and that land was no part of the proffered bargain. Adding misery to injustice, some unprincipled masters ignored directives about leniency to sick or disabled serfs and still included such persons at will among those punished by exile, without adequate provisions and without family, to Siberia.

As things were going, it seemed to be a toss-up between the inevitability of the nobles becoming bankrupt and that of the serfs rebelling. For the time being, however, the incidence of bankruptcy and uprising was so low that the inevitable seemed quite remote. The serfs continued to labor quietly, their hours too full for idle complaints. The lords continued to indulge themselves, "to keep no accounts and to drink champagne," making no particular effort to change the circumstances in which they found themselves. Even the richest of them, Count Dmitri Sheremetev, owner of 200,000 serfs, lived so far beyond his means that he spent annually about 600,000 rubles ($300,000) over and above what his estates brought in. That there would some day be a fearful reckoning occurred neither to the irresponsible members of the upper class nor to Alexander.

Still further removed from their thoughts was the likely advent of some day when there would be a questioning not only of the serf-noble relationship but also of Russian dominion over non-Russians and even the very institution of autocracy itself. On these matters, Napoleon, in his enforced leisure on St. Helena, was more discerning than either Alexander or the majority of his advisers when he declared: "I fought Europe to support monarchical rule; the monarchs who defeated me did so in the name of the freedom of the people; they will bitterly regret it." [2] It was true—though few recognized it at the time—that when Alexander, in 1813, appealed for his people's support on behalf of national liberation rather than simply invoking their loyalty to the throne, he was providing a stimulant for both the spirit of nationalism and the spirit of liberalism among them.

It was easy enough at the end of the war, however, for the tsar to consider the ten million or so of the non-Russians among his subjects —Letts, Esths, Finns, Baltic Germans, Georgians, Bashkirs, Jews,

Poles, Yakuts, Buryats, and others—with a feeling of confidence in their continued tranquility under Russian rule. Even the Poles, he confidently expected, would come peaceably to heel, once the newly established government of the kingdom of Poland was understood and accepted, as he assured himself it would be.

In support of his confidence that the various nationalities could live harmoniously under a single state, Alexander could cite extended evidence that, even in the close organization of the imperial administration, men from every corner of Europe could serve Russia and the tsar with mutually satisfying results. To name a prominent scattering: the Greek Giovanni Capo d'Istria and the German Karl Nesselrode, who, with some assistance from the Corsican Carlo Pozzo di Borgo, now ran the ministry of foreign affairs; the Scotsman Sir James Wylie, personal physician to the tsar; another Scotsman, Samuel Greig, commander of the Russian Black Sea fleet; the Russian-born, Italian-trained Carlo Rossi, architect of important public buildings; and the noted Italian officer Marquis Philippe Paulucci, now a general in the Russian army. Then there was the splendid French representation: Marquis Jean-François de Traversé, a former admiral in the French navy and now minister of the Russian navy; Armand, Duc de Richelieu, who had served as governor general of New Russia until his return to France, in 1814; Jean-Paul Marat's brother, David de Boudry,* teaching French at the Tsarskoe Selo Lycée. The Germans were so numerous as to be almost omnipresent in some areas. Among them, the native-born Baltic Germans were the most numerous, and their names—Benckendorff, Lieven, Meyendorff, Korff, Adlerberg, Stackelberg, Pahlen, von der Pahlen—were common among men holding responsible positions in the armed forces, the civil service, and the imperial court. In addition there were hundreds of immigrant Germans to be found throughout the educational system and in government service, and thousands who had accepted naturalization (in St. Petersburg alone, 23,000 of the city's 35,000 naturalized foreigners were German).

Admittedly not all persons were legally equal in Russia. Religion alone set some of them apart from others: members of the Orthodox Church had some substantial privileges, while Old Believers, Jews, and certain other religious groups were subject to discriminatory legislation. For the most part, however, people of every background lived in peace as subjects of the tsar, their way of life and their form

---

* De Boudry had changed his name from Marat, with the permission of Catherine II, in order to disassociate himself from his notorious brother.

of worship unobstructed as long as they performed their civic duties and paid their taxes.

Though there were no evidences of imminent disturbances from nationalism in Russia at the end of the war, there were evidences of two types of concerned disquiet, either of which might upset the calm if it should spread. The conservative Russian nationalism which simmered in the minds of such men as Admiral Shishkov, with his passion for defending Russian language and tradition against foreign influence, could develop to the point that it would equate the Russian state with Russian nationality and require that minorities either be assimilated or treated as second-class subjects, thus opening the way for domestic discord. Likewise, the growth of a consciousness of national identity among the minorities under Russian rule (such as that now faintly recognizable among the Letts) could lead to a call for the right of self-determination among the hitherto submerged nationalities—a right which, if exercised, would spell the end of empire. Such contingencies deserved attention, but just now their significance, like that of the problems of the countryside, seemed minor.

The calm of 1815 in Russia did not, in fact, represent contentment. One indication that the status quo was at least being thoughtfully questioned lay in the fact that liberal sentiment, which had been renewed at the time of Alexander's return from the Congress of Vienna, continued to grow. It soon became clear that a mild contagion of independent thinking was spreading both among the educated young men of the country and among those in the process of becoming educated. Easily identifiable because they made no secret of their views, they might be found anywhere. They could be recognized among university students purposefully studying philosophy and science, among the new generation of poets, among the serious young men in such organizations as the Free Economic Society [3] and the ministry of education, and among the military personnel, including the tsar's own aides and the junior ranks of the guards officers.

The young guards officers, in particular, were markedly concerned with liberal ideas. Educated in the spirit of the French Enlightenment and stimulated by their participation in the War of Liberation, they had returned to Russia with visions of imminent reforms by the tsar, who, they had reason to believe, shared their ideals and enthusiasm.

In no regiment were discussions more spirited than in the tsar's own old regiment, the time-honored Semenovsky Guards. In it were a number who shared a precocious interest in politics and economics. An earnest lot, they were further bound together by a highminded code of conduct embodying their avowed disapproval of the practices of administering corporal punishment to members of the lower ranks, using tobacco, and consorting with whores. Near the end of 1815, they instituted the practice of dining together regularly in order to discuss "Russia's present and her future." There was nothing subversive in either their manner or their purpose at these gatherings. They often had as a guest their commanding officer, the easygoing, slightly foppish but highly respected General Jacob Potemkin; in the future that they planned, Tsar Alexander was assigned a role as heroic as the one he had carried in the war.

Considered together, these young thinkers represented a vigorous new development which deserved attention. At the time, however, only a very few recognized it as such, and the tsar was not among them. During Prince Adam Czartoryski's first visit to St. Petersburg, when Alexander was the nineteen-year-old tsesarevich,* Russian society had seemed to him "only a reflection of the Court, . . . the vestibule of a temple where no one has eyes or ears for anything but the divinity within." [4] To Alexander, now the tsar with nearly fifteen years of experience behind him, as well as to most of those who served him, things were still the same. They looked patronizingly upon these young liberals—most of them nobles by birth—as members of the family who, while admittedly chattering of things unsuited to their "weak intellectual stomachs," were wholly unlikely to experience any upset or to cause any trouble.

It was easy to write off the young liberals as chatterers, particularly if they were guards officers. For all their highmindedness, many of them were so extremely affected and dandified that seriousness would appear to be an alien quality in them. It was unexpected, to say the least, among the qualities of those whose devotion to personal elegance was carried to the point of narcissism; yet some combined the two qualities handily. One such, Hussar Guards officer Peter Chaadaev, was known to spend hours at his toilette in the pictured presence of his idols: Napoleon, Byron—and himself. But he was nonetheless a thoughtful young man whose work was to stimulate and influence the thought of thousands in later years. The education of these young officers, in many cases, was another thing that set them

* Tsesarevich was the title of the heir to the Russian throne.

apart as exotic and caused their ideas to be unwisely dismissed at first as not seriously applicable to anything Russian. Paul Pestel, for example, aide to Field Marshal Peter Wittgenstein and, later, one of the first to die for his liberal views, had received a French education in Russia and a German education abroad. Scores who would become influential leaders—young nobles, like the several Muravevs presently serving in the guards—had been educated in France.

Historian Vasily Klyuchevsky wrote of such young men that, while *their fathers* had been Russians trying to be Frenchmen (referring to the obsession with the "Frenchified culture" which animated society during Catherine's reign), *they* were Frenchmen trying to be Russians. Time proved them to be, in fact, important members of the first generation of educated Russians who sought to give expression to their country's needs and to seek ways of meeting them, with or without the help of the tsar—in short, the first generation that was not content to wait in "the vestibule."

Among the activities of these young Russians, the first practical measure, undramatic but historic, was undertaken shortly after Alexander's lackluster peace manifesto. On February 9, 1816, the guards officers Prince Sergei Trubetskoi and Ivan Yakushkin, along with the cousins Alexander and Nikita Muravev, called on the brothers Matvei and Sergei Muravev-Apostol at their quarters in the Semenovsky Guards barracks. The red-haired Trubetskoi, at twenty-five, was the oldest of the six; Sergei Muravev-Apostol, a stripling of nineteen who had just entered the regiment, was the youngest. They were mutually acquainted—four of them linked by ties of blood, four by regimental affiliation, all by the memory of participation in the Battle of Borodino—and they shared much the same liberal views. Their talk on that day led from one subject to another: the excessive influence of the Germans in government service, the generally deplorable state of things in Russia, and the need for action. Finally, Yakushkin suggested that they form themselves into a secret political society * "for the welfare of Russia," and the others agreed. Thus simply was initiated the Union of Salvation.

Soviet historians refer to these six and those who joined them in

---

* So-called secret societies in Russia at this time were not clandestine organizations but more nearly what would be, in modern terminology, private associations—not hidden from the public or the government, but generally separated from both by the limiting of participation in their meetings and activities to chosen members, and by the use of "secret" rituals.

the Union as "noblemen-revolutionaries." It is true that they were nobles—"repentant nobles," as some called them—but they were not revolutionaries at first. Those who began the formulation of the organization's program were romantic idealists, passionate devotees of liberty and reason—nothing more. What they wanted for their fatherland was that it be ruled by a constitutional monarchy and that it be freed from the odious system of serfdom. They looked to the tsar to grant the one and abolish the other. But if he should demur, they were willing to speed the wheels of history by recruiting men in places of importance to help them and by preparing the public for change through the example of kind treatment for their own serfs, through the establishment of schools for the people, and through widespread philanthropic activities. What if all this should fail? They were not quite ready to cross that bridge; but they hinted that, if Alexander should die without having granted reforms, they would refuse to swear allegiance to his successor.

Before the year was up, the original members had won a dozen or so partisans of various types and diversified talents. Their differences were, in fact, too great: there could be few interests in common for such men as the religious, public-spirited Major General Michael Orlov, of the tsar's suite; Michael Lunin, millionaire nobleman, toper, duelist, libertine; and Paul Pestel, deeply devoted admirer of the Jacobins. Finally it became clear that in gaining numbers, the Union had lost cohesion. The new members promoted discord and led the group to fritter away time and strength without getting at the practical particulars of either their destination or their route.

Through a combination of omissions and commissions that served to dissipate the nimbus of liberalism that had surrounded him and replace it by one of reaction, Alexander himself unwittingly helped to set the course for the Union of Salvation. Since he did nothing in the postwar years to give tangible expression to his views on constitutionalism and serfdom (except to permit the Baltic landlords to free their serfs under terms that promptly turned them into wage slaves) and since he did not choose to say anything of his continuing but fruitless private efforts, he appeared to his recent liberal admirers to be deserting their cause. The outcome of the domestic changes he undertook to make, nobly conceived as those changes were, eventually had the adverse effect of confirming them in their fear that their champion was turning into an enemy of liberty and progress.

III

"My Caprice and My Command"

ALEXANDER I, 1815–1825

T H E first of Alexander's ill-starred domestic efforts, after his
return from abroad in 1815, was a scheme that he had been considering for some time and by which he hoped to improve at one
stroke conditions in the regular army, among the peasants, and in the
national economy.

It was to be carried out through the integration of men in selected
army units and their families into certain peasant communities on
state lands where, in so-called military colonies, all would participate
in a carefully prescribed program including military training, agriculture, and such other activities as were necessary in a well-rounded
community. Alexander saw it primarily as a reform project that,
administered with "paternal solicitude," would benefit the underprivileged without disturbing the privileged to any serious degree;
that would provide homes where soldiers might live with their
families during times of peace in a well-ordered, beneficent environment; and that, by transforming unproductive soldiers into self-
supporting subjects, would make it possible for Russia to maintain
the largest army in Europe at virtually no cost to her treasury.

To set his plan in motion and administer the new establishments,
he instituted the Special Corps of Military Colonies, with himself as
chief and General Alexis Arakcheev as his second-in-command (in

actual practice, Arakcheev was from the beginning the chief administrator).

Though the tsar made no effort to inform the public of his concepts, many liberals believed at first that the colonies represented a philanthropic endeavor and that the intention was to make a break in the system of serfdom; they therefore looked on with renewed hope while the scheme got under way.

When a regiment was chosen to be installed in a military colony, all the men would be ordered to report with their families to a certain district and, assisted by the peasants living there, to establish a new settlement according to specified plans. The existing peasant homes would be swept away and replaced by uniformly planned living quarters and public buildings all constructed on well-laid-out streets and fitted with government-approved accommodations. Thereafter soldiers, their families, and peasants shared duties and benefits equally as legal and permanent residents of the military colony thus formed. Their lives were made subject to strict regulations from that time until death; and the lives of their subsequent offspring, from birth to death.

All males eighteen years of age or older when the colony was established were put directly into the regiment, and boys between the ages of six and eighteen (later, all who came of age) were enrolled as "cantonists." Outfitted with special uniforms, the cantonists were subjected to approved education and military training until they reached the age of eighteen and exchanged their cantonist uniforms for regimentals, which would constitute their apparel from that time until death or physical incapacity relieved them of colonist duties. Men remained active in the regiment until their forty-sixth year, dividing their peacetime working hours between military training and farming or between military training and the learning and practice of skills necessary to the operation and upkeep of the community; in wartime, they went into combat-ready service if called. At forty-six, their military obligations ended, and they spent the remaining years in the colony as supervised wards of the government.

All residents—male and female, young and old—were under the command of specially appointed officers, who dictated not only the nature of their employment through every hour of the day but also, by bugle calls, the times of their rising, their assigned duties, and their retiring. To insure the punctual and perfect functioning of the program through the years, the names of marriageable individuals were publicly listed, weddings arranged with military dispatch, and every couple expected to reproduce according to prescribed schedule: any married woman capable of childbearing who did not bear a son each year was fined, and her husband discountenanced.

For five years the establishment of such colonies was pushed ahead with vigor, most of them in areas specially chosen as needing rehabilitation—four areas in the southern part of the country, one in the north. Thereafter the momentum of the project subsided as difficulties in direction arose and opposition widened. At the peak of settlement, 25 percent of Russia's standing army were participating colonists, and some of the colonies were active forty years after the plan was initiated.

The military orderliness of the operation had a particular appeal for Alexander, and he believed in the colonies as he believed in little else on earth. Moreover, his feeling for them, unlike that for his early reform attempts, never waned. It was one of his greatest pleasures to visit Arakcheev's Gruzino estate, where he always felt a personal welcome, and to drive from there with the general to inspect military colonies. He liked what he saw: clean streets, neat houses, well-kept drill fields, proper equipment on improved acres, and industrious inhabitants with good shoes on their feet, good uniforms on their backs. What a contrast to the squalor and lethargy of the typical Russian village! To him this integration of the military and the domestic suggested nothing of the irony recognized by the perceptive German traveler J. G. Kohl when he visited one of the southern colonies and observed ". . . hussars and cuirassiers in full uniform, with their sabers at their sides, laboring behind the plough or driving their wild herds over the grassy steppes—the sons of wild Mars engaged in the service of the gentle Ceres." [1]

Alexander was so anxious to accept surface appearances that, for a long time, he was unaware that they hid serious faults and inadequacies. Observant liberals, however, soon began to recognize shortcomings, and their disillusionment grew accordingly.

The peasants involved, conditioned as they were to the dull rhythm of their accustomed toil and tenacious of the grain of individuality allowed them as members of a class below society's concern, resented the uprooting and replanting of their lives and chafed under the ordered routine imposed upon them. When designated for colonies, whole villages often united in begging exemption, wanting permission to retain the meager personal liberties they called their freedom. Some, with the boldness of desperation, petitioned the tsar's mother, Dowager Empress Marie Fedorovna, to intercede for them. One group halted the carriage of his brother the Grand Duke Nicholas and implored his help. Though inexorably the selected peasants were torn from their mean huts, made to exchange their familiar garb for uniforms, and broken to colony life, their conversion was rarely more than enforced conformity. The original colonists longed for the old village life they remembered, and the younger ones proved to be laggard students of the new.

Likewise the members of the selected military units made reluctant colonists. They resented the unfamiliar routine, grumbled at the unmilitary duties ("Are we herdsmen or hussars?"), and accepted with sullen dislike their life in a semi-householding community when they longed for the camaraderie and the occasional roistering of the conventional barracks. Often, discontent grew into active resentment or resistance and, since military procedure prevailed, the officers in charge met it with punishment that was both summary and harsh. Still, revolts continued to develop in every area, sometimes on such a large scale that whole colonies would be drawn up for judgment, some of the inhabitants put to the knout, some imprisoned, some assigned to punishing physical labor—but all subdued by means designed to discourage repetition. None of this was overlooked by the concerned public.

Yet another aspect of the public response to the operation of the military colonies was beyond the comprehension of Alexander: the growing notoriety of the man whose shadow spread over all—the planning, the establishment, and the administration—his personal appointee, his intimate and trusted friend, General Arakcheev. For his hopeful attempt to turn the base metal of his empire into gold, the tsar had chosen a most unlikely alchemist. When appointed to administer the colonies, at the age of forty-six, Arakcheev was chief of the department of military affairs of the State Council. Before that, he had served in various military posts: under Tsar Paul until he fell from favor, then under Alexander, part of the time as his minister of war. He had made such a name for himself as a brutal martinet—this, in a country where martinets were as common as salted cucumbers—that few doubted the popular accounts of how he had once bitten off a soldier's ear in a fit of anger and how he had ordered men flogged to the point of permanent injury, sometimes death. Even among fellow officers, where rigid discipline was highly respected, he was known as a man with a sinister coldness of heart and a "purely German" passion for efficiency and exceptionally harsh discipline. These were hardly the specifications of a humanitarian who could share the spirit of Alexander's idealism. Moreover, Arakcheev's nature was flawed by a paradoxical twist that often led him to turn his most commendable virtues (he had some, ill repute notwithstanding) into vices.

The tsar recognized the virtues and was apparently unaware of their inversion. He admired Arakcheev's zeal for military discipline and the perfection of results achieved through it, the tenacity with which he held to any assigned course despite all obstacles, the seemingly miraculous touch he had with the most unpromising human material, and, above all, his complete trustworthiness. He could not have attached any importance to the popular sobriquets—probably he never knew them—by which Arakcheev was becoming known among those who saw, or experienced, the results when those virtues, overcharged and unrelenting, were turned into vices: the "Cruel Corporal of Gatchina," whose zeal for discipline had made him the terrorizing drillmaster of the private army maintained by Paul before he became tsar; the "Bulldog," who frequently carried tenacity into violent obduracy; the "Vampire," whose "miraculous touch," a slash with the saber or a fist in the face for those he was "improving," was likely to be bloodstained; and the "Vice-Emperor," apparently the most trusted man in the imperial government.

Alexander, with his unfortunate propensity for unintentionally contributing to situations he would prefer to avoid, did much to establish the appropriateness of the vice-emperor concept. Always loath to handle details of administration, he used Arakcheev increasingly as his intermediary in dealing with ministers and committees. Observing this, gossips were quick to advance the general's status to that of imperial confidant and next-in-command. The liberals, to whom Arakcheev was becoming a symbol of all that was amiss in Russia as well as a counterforce to progress, encouraged the notion that he was, in fact, the Mephistopheles of reaction. Instead of resenting this evaluation, Arakcheev appeared to nourish it, delighted perhaps to be considered so important and so close to the source of power. Actually, the evaluation was a faulty one. Alexander did not delegate power; he was, as the shrewd Speransky said, "too weak to rule, too strong to let others rule." Although he appeared to do so, he did not rely solely on Arakcheev's advice. The impression overrode the facts, however, and the myth was carried on.

A project almost as close to the tsar's heart as the military colonies —and almost as self-defeating—involved the country's educational system, which he had so encouraged during the early years of his reign. Now he wanted to cleanse the system, to see that the instruction of Russian youth was brought into line with the good life as he envisioned it for all of mankind. Since the only proper standard by which to be guided, he now felt, was a religious one, he wanted an understanding and trustworthy man of God to supervise the undertaking. Accordingly, when the aging Count Alexis Razumovsky, in August 1816, asked to be relieved of his post as head of the ministry of popular enlightenment, which carried responsibility for the educational system, the tsar was glad to assent: here was the perfect opportunity to institute the project.

He appointed as Razumovsky's successor the man to whom he owed his own initiation into the religious life, Prince Alexander Golitsyn. With that appointment, the tsar was adding scope to the prince's already extraordinarily wide responsibilities. When he accepted the new post, Golitsyn was not only the over-procurator of the Holy Synod but also head of the Russian Bible Society, established in St. Petersburg four years earlier as a branch of the British Bible Society. Neither organization, however, was entirely dissociated from the work to which the tsar was now assigning him. The religious aspect would be underscored by the over-procuratorship; both the religious and the educational, by the Bible Society.

Although the chief aim of the society, like that of the mother organization, was to translate the Bible into various languages (with the unprecedented addition of Russian) and to publish and distribute it as widely as possible, another had gradually evolved. The Russians who approved of the organization and whose generous contributions sustained it soon began to anticipate a very important secondary benefit from its operation: if people in the far reaches of the empire were to profit from the distribution of the Bible, they would have to be provided with an education sufficient at least to give them the ability to read it. Golitsyn supported that corollary, and while provincial branches of the society were distributing Bibles by the thousands, they were concerning themselves also with the establishment and development of provincial schools. This educational aspect of the society's work was already, in 1816, drawing criticism from the Russian Orthodox Church, whose prelates disapproved the encouragement of this popular, direct approach to the Scriptures and attributed the conception of the whole undesirable situation to the "believing mystic" Golitsyn.

Any hope for the immediate effectiveness of this criticism went glimmering when, in October 1817, Alexander broadened the authority of Golitsyn's ministry to incorporate all religious bodies, including the Russian Orthodox Church. At the same time he changed its name to the ministry of spiritual affairs and education and declared his expectation that thereafter "Christian piety be for all time the basis of true education." [2] To further insure that all sources contributing anything to education be under a central authority, he transferred from the police to the enlarged ministry most of the responsibility for censorship.

Unlike Arakcheev, who displayed an unpopular excess of strength in the administration of the military colonies, Golitsyn lacked the strength necessary for the direction of his new omnibus office. He was a good man, venerated for his saintliness (mothers brought their children for his blessing) and respected for his many unselfish acts of philanthropy. He was quite in accord with the purpose of the project, to infuse education with Christian piety, but he was simply not able to take hold of the task. Indeed it would have been difficult for anyone to convert Golitsyn's principles systematically into practical measures for carrying out the duties he had undertaken. He believed in the Scriptures as the source of all truth; he felt kindly toward members of the Orthodox Church and, to the dismay of the Orthodox prelates, toward Lutherans, Catholics, Old Believers, Quakers— in fact, toward almost every variety of Christianity; he wanted as many people as possible to read the Bible; and he abhorred both Voltaireans (though he himself had been one) and freethinkers, since he now believed that skepticism and rationalism were at the root of Europe's current troubles.

Once Golitsyn's new ministry began to exercise its commissioned functions, parceled out to hundreds of assistant administrators, inspectors, supervisors, and censors, there was ample evidence that he was a lamb among wolves. The reactionary policies pronounced in the name of the ministry, the religiosity of rules invoked, and the absurd rationalization frequently employed seemed to many observers —including even such conservatives as Karamzin—to justify the irreverent name "ministry of darkness," under which the liberals were soon lumping the whole enterprise.

In almost any phase of the ministry's activity they could point to enormities bearing out their indictment. A frequently cited one was the directive of censors Alexander Birukov and Alexander Krasovsky prohibiting the publication of information on poisonous mushrooms: since mushrooms were "Lenten food of the Orthodox" and hence "sacred," to characterize them as poisonous was sacrilegious. Another was a protracted program of harassment meted out to Kazan University by Michael Magnitsky, a ranking member of the chief administration of schools. A liberal-turned-reactionary, Magnitsky was convinced through a personal investigation in 1819 that free-thinking was rife in the university. He proceeded, therefore, to lay about him with a heavy hand, dismissing suspect professors, ordering recreant students to walk about with signs proclaiming them to be sinners, prohibiting the use of "Christian bodies" in anatomical in-struction, and requiring that textbooks be used as vehicles of Chris-tian piety (the triangle in geometry, for instance, was surely a symbol of the Trinity).

Soon it appeared that no public word or deed was to be exempt from scrutiny and classification as either sacred or altogether pro-fane. All literature, of course, became suspect. The theater, being under government supervision for the most part, was constantly sub-jected to "paternal concern" that it be free from what Admiral Shishkov would term "corrupting influence," particularly that emanating from France. Small wonder that the liberals, remember-ing the first promising years of Alexander's reign, saw reason to pro-claim that the country was now falling into the grip of obscurantists and that the domestic policy of the tsar, as it was being translated by such men as Arakcheev and Golitsyn, clearly indicated reaction to be the new order of the day.

Their disillusionment was made the more acute by the fact that, while he was pursuing what appeared to be reactionary policies within his own country, Alexander was following a very different line abroad. He gave his blessing to the German princes of Baden, Bavaria, Nassau, and Württemberg when they granted moderate con-stitutions to their subjects. He supported the Greek nationalists, who were conspiring to free Greece from Turkish rule. And he vigorously encouraged the constitutional development of the kingdom of Poland, prompting its legislature to show the world that "free in-stitutions, whose sacred principles some seek to confuse with destruc-tive teachings, are not a dangerous dream . . ." but are "in perfect accord with social order and confirm the well-being of nations." [3] Such acts disturbed also the staunch European monarchists and in-dicated to them that Alexander was still the unchanged "Son of the Enlightenment." Metternich considered them pure Jacobinism. But to the Russian liberals they indicated only that the tsar preferred foreigners to Russians. While he had been paying tribute to the nationalist sentiment of the Poles, bestowing a constitution on them, and encouraging liberalism elsewhere, he had shown no recognition of the fact that other peoples within the Russian empire had nationalist aspirations, nor had he done anything constructive for his own people. It might be, so gossip ran, that he would soon be moving his capital to Warsaw!

As the mood of frustration and indignation grew among the young liberals, they became more daring (Ivan Yakushkin, of the Union of Salvation, offered to assassinate Alexander), more critical, and more vocal. They still lacked prominent spokesmen but were finding common expression through the distribution and repetition of the words of bold-spirited young writers. Alexander Pushkin, with his fresh and biting style, was a particular favorite. His irreverent jibes at the powers of oppression were highly quotable and easily memorized—the latter being an important quality, since their political rashness made impossible their passing censorship and reaching publication. Hand-copied, his poems circulated widely and were repeated until certain passages came to have the currency of fraternal passwords among liberals. When vodka glasses were raised at convivial gatherings, pledges were likely to be made in words that Pushkin had made popular: *tirany mira* ("tyrants of the world"), to end the "down-with" toasts; and *volnost i pokoi* ("freedom and peace"), to end the "up-with" toasts. His "Ode to Freedom," written with special reference to the despotism of Louis XVI and Tsar Paul, was interpreted as an everlasting admonition to all despots and quoted so often that its substance became for a while the unofficial text of Russian liberalism:

> Rulers! Your crown and throne were given you
> By law—and not by nature:
> You stand above the people,
> But eternally higher than you is the law.
>
> . . . .
>
> And learn this, O rulers:
> Neither punishment nor reward,
> Neither bloody dungeon nor altar
> Will provide you with secure protection.
> First place yourselves
> Under the protection of trustworthy laws;
> And freedom and peace will
> Forever stand guard
> Over throne and people.[4]

The most frustrated and indignant of the liberals were drawn to the one body that seemed to offer them an opportunity for collective expression, the Union of Salvation—or, as it was renamed after its reorganization, in 1818, the Union of Welfare. By 1820 the Union's membership had risen to two hundred: a significant showing from a comparatively small educated class. It was, to be sure, an organization with a generally youthful complexion; aside from a few colonels, major generals, and civilians in their late twenties, it was composed of junior guards officers. Yet its purpose was serious and the breadth of its representation impressive. It included members from families of distinguished name—Trubetskoi, Lopukhin, Obolensky, Shakhovskoi, Sheremetev, Muravev, Orlov, Bestuzhev-Ryumin, Volkonsky; members from almost all the guards regiments, the army general staff, and the guards general staff; and members who were, or had been, adjutants to such highly placed persons as the commander of the Second Army, the governor general of St. Petersburg, the Grand Duke Michael, the commander of the guards, Empress Elizabeth, and even Arakcheev. Although the liberalism of the Union was still more a manifestation of anger than of faith, the fact that representatives of so many influential elements had united for the consideration of liberal ideas could not be dismissed simply as evidence of casual dissatisfaction. Serious alienation was certainly becoming a possibility.

The feelings of the liberals might have been tempered by an understanding either of the obstacles Alexander had encountered in his original course or of the results he expected from his present one, but he made no effort to explain. Instead, leaving his new programs in the hands of Arakcheev and Golitsyn, he virtually abandoned the active duties of administration and gave himself to an apparently aimless restiveness in which doubts and spiritual sloth seemed to have displaced his earlier assurance and vigor. His most constant companion became his coachman, Ilya Baikov, as he began a series of extended trips to acquaint himself with the various parts of his empire, to inspect military colonies, to open sessions of the Polish legislature, to visit abroad with other heads of state. In one way or another, he managed to stay away from St. Petersburg for about eight months of every year between 1816 and 1820.

Unlike the travels of Peter the Great, which fired him with a demonic urge to begin changing things, Alexander's seemed not to inspire him in any way. On occasions when he returned to his capital, he concerned himself with little beyond routine duties, habitual diversions, and social gestures. He read and signed the thousands of papers that Arakcheev relayed to him, attended balls, received diplomats, went for daily walks along the English Quay, and presided at military reviews, discharging each act with the appropriate accompaniment—cheerful talk, amiable smiles, or lordly disapproval. Then, after some private conferences with Arakcheev, he would become anxious to be away again.

From time to time, he responded briefly to pangs of contrition for abandoned dreams or unfulfilled pledges by quietly ordering that a new, but always unpublished, plan for the abolition of serfdom or a new constitutional draft be drawn up. But the effort lagged. The men he chose for the tasks—Arakcheev, for example, to deal with serfdom—had little enthusiasm for their assignments, and the tsar himself supplied neither spirit nor a sense of urgency. His one commission during this period that promised results was to his old liberal friend, Nicholas Novosiltsev: to draft another constitutional charter. The finished draft, which he received early in 1820, provided for a limited form of representative government and for guarantees of basic civil rights (without, however, stipulating freedom for serfs). Limited as it was, it could have served as a sound beginning for government reform; if there had been no distraction just then, Alexander might have signed the charter and put it into effect. Unfortunately, the possibility was never tested. Once again he put aside domestic problems to take up foreign ones.

This time the foreign problems were revolutions, three of them cropping up unexpectedly and in quick succession in 1820. They started in January, when Colonel Rafael del Riego led a successful revolt that subjected the incompetent Spanish despot Ferdinand VII to revolutionary dictation. Then, in July, General Guglielmo Pepe, a member of the *Carbonari*, took inspiration from events in Spain and, with a small band of men, forced King Ferdinand I of Naples to grant a constitution. A month later, in Portugal, army officers ousted the incumbent government and invited King John VI to return from his Brazilian exile and rule as a constitutional monarch.

Alexander's attitude toward these developments was far from the permissiveness he had displayed only recently in his support of liberal developments in Germany, Greece, and Poland. He saw these revolutions, not as beneficial displays of liberalism, but as potential threats to the stability of Europe. Though he apparently did not fear the possibility of any reverberations in Russia, the depth of his concern for other monarchies was indicated by the quickness with which he adopted a militant attitude toward the revolutions as well as the emphatic and scathing nature of his pronouncements against them. They were the work, he declared, of an international conspiracy against Christianity and monarchism by a pack of "revolutionaries, liberals, radical levelers, and *Carbonari*," whose intellectual inspiration was the "so-called philosophy of Voltaire and his like"; [5] if they could overthrow three governments in six months, they could soon move on through all of Europe if not stopped. This was a strange position for a pupil of La Harpe, and Alexander knew that when he cast a stone at the intellectual progeny of "Voltaire and his like," he was opposing men who were now invoking the same "truths" he had once invoked. He admitted as much to Metternich: "From 1813 to 1820 is seven years, and these seven years are like a century to me. In 1820 I will at no price do what I did in 1813. You are not altered, but I am. You have nothing to regret, but I have." [6]

The tsar had made an about-face and was ready to prove that fact. At the October congress of great powers meeting in Troppau, in Austrian Silesia, for the purpose of devising measures to oppose the revolutionary threat, he eagerly aligned himself with Metternich on the proposed policy of intervention in support of governments beset by revolution. The Austrian was frankly delighted that the tsar was finally opening his eyes to what he himself had perceived as early as 1789.

Had Alexander known of the existence of the Union of Walfare, he might have been even more vehement in his new role. But so far he had no misgivings about the basic loyalty of his own subjects. Of course, he was aware that many of his young officers talked radicalism and recited Pushkin's "shocking verses." But after he had taken the precaution of banishing the poet to the southern town of Ekaterinoslav, in the spring of 1820, he had put the matter aside as of minor consequence.

He was therefore unprepared for the shock he received when, on November 2, there arrived in Troppau three couriers from St. Petersburg, bringing him reports from General Ilarion Vasilchikov, commander of the guards, that there had been a mutiny in the tsar's favorite regiment, the Semenovsky Guards. For Alexander, it was as if the curtain had risen unexpectedly on a monstrous farce: only some fantastic conceit could represent his beloved guardsmen as mutineers. They were all men of long and honorable service, much decorated for valor and heroism, most of them known to him personally; he would have staked his crown on their loyalty. After all, these were not ordinary soldiers. At that time the guards were the elite of arms, a virtually self-contained military organization with its own general staff and superb units of infantry, cavalry, and artillery that were the mainstay of the country's fighting forces (collectively, in official terminology, "the guards and the army"), the pride of every parade, and the trusted warders of the imperial palaces. Any serious irregularity among them was wholly unthinkable to the tsar.

But there was no mistake: for the first time in the history of the guards, enlisted men had mutinied. With bitter reluctance, Alexander reviewed again and again the most circumstantial of the three reports, that of General Vasilchikov's aide Peter Chaadaev. It was a straightforward statement of an audacious act of insubordination. On October 16, the men of the First Company (His Majesty's Company) of the First Battalion, having assembled at roll call, had presented complaints against regimental commander Colonel Gregory Schwarz and asked that they be relayed to him. Their request had been refused, and, when they had been ordered to return to quarters, they had disobeyed the order and accepted the consequent arrest. On the following day, after the mutineers had been imprisoned overnight in the Fortress of SS. Peter and Paul, most of the other enlisted men of the regiment had demonstrated in sympathy for them and defiantly ignored the directives of authority, including those of the governor general of St. Petersburg and the Grand Duke Michael, who had been summoned to make personal appeals for discipline. Finally this group also had been arrested and marched off, without resistance, to the fortress. For several days Schwarz had remained in his quarters, and St. Petersburg had been placed on the alert against extension of the mutiny; but all had remained quiet.

Vasilchikov, in the report, assigned the principal blame for the whole incident to Schwarz. As regimental commander, he had imposed an almost frenzied discipline on the men, who had been accustomed to the easygoing discipline of his predecessor, General Jacob Potemkin. He had gone so far as to subject even cavaliers of the Order of St. George to floggings, in violation of their legal exemption from such punishment. Still, his superior felt, the men should be punished for their insubordination.

Vasilchikov did not believe that the insubordination had been politically inspired, but Alexander was in a mood to think otherwise: he could not think that such action would have been taken by the men if they had not been prompted by their officers. His conclusion was that the mutiny was further proof of an international revolutionary conspiracy and that radical officers in the regiment had inspired the mutinous behavior of the men in order to raise an alarm, thus goading him into returning home and abandoning the crusade against revolution abroad. To show that he was not to be so easily duped or frightened, he declared that the disorder was well in hand, that judgment would be forthcoming, and that he would not return to Russia until the deliberations of the Troppau congress were ended.

Privately, as his subsequent acts showed, Alexander did not interpret the situation with such complacency. It was no light thing to consider the significance of defiance at the level of the distinguished Semenovsky Guards or the fact that men accounted the most dependable of the country's defenders now sat comfortless in the cold cells of the fortress like common enemies of the crown.

The old Fortress of SS. Peter and Paul (commonly called the Peter-Paul fortress) was itself a symbol of things that any Russian tsar would have preferred not to dwell on, things that must have come unwelcomed to Alexander's already disturbed mind. Built by the forced labor of 20,000 men to serve Peter the Great against the Swedes, it was still a grim reminder that disquiet of one kind or another had always walked with Romanovs. Though no hostile shot had ever been fired from it, it remained an armed fort. And within its granite-faced walls there were, on the one hand, the dark prison that had served for the restriction and punishment of hundreds who had challenged the autocratic rule; on the other, the great Cathedral of SS. Peter and Paul, in which were seven white marble sarcophaguses marked by gilt representations of the imperial eagle, the resting places of Romanov tsars who had faced their challengers before Alexander's time.

Whether Alexander was spurred by the averted crisis or a renewed intimation of his mortality, a subject now often in his thoughts, is not known; but, after the Semenovsky disturbance, he was no longer hesitant about his choice of political courses. He remained abroad until May 1821, helping to work out an informal—but, as it turned out, a reasonably effective—antiliberal and antirevolutionary alliance of Russia, Austria, and Prussia. When he returned to Russia, it was as a ruler whose foreign and domestic policies were no longer at odds with each other. He was an integrated, consistently conservative autocrat.

Alexander continued to use his influence abroad, with no equivocation as to aims; he intended to support his fellow monarchs regardless of the cost or of his previous attitude toward the forces threatening them. He supported Austrian suppression of the revolution in Italy. In preparation for intervention in Spain, he increased Russia's conscription levies and moved Russian troops to the western frontiers; though in the end he withheld them (deferring to the French, who insisted on the privilege of intervening there), he did so reluctantly. He turned his back on the Greek revolution that began in 1821, though the act cost him the services of one of his trusted ministers, the Greek patriot Capo d'Istria. He virtually ignored his traditional role as protector of the Orthodox in the Ottoman empire: when the Turks hanged the Greek Orthodox Patriarch Gregory as well as several of his bishops, the tsar did no more than express displeasure. When the Orthodox Serbs rose against the Turks in 1821, he flatly refused to support them. This was the Alexander lampooned by Byron as the "coxcomb Czar" and "somewhat aged youth," whom he saw

> Now half dissolving to a liberal thaw
> But harden'd back whene'er the morning's raw.[7]

This newfound definiteness in the political policy of the tsar was matched by a new decisiveness in certain areas of domestic affairs, especially where subversion was a real, or imagined, problem. He approved such excessively harsh punishment as running the gauntlet and life sentences of hard labor in the mines for the ringleaders of the Semenovsky Guards mutiny, ordered that the other enlisted men be transferred to service in remote and undesirable regions, and had the officers transferred to line regiments.

In addition, he began to pay increased attention to the policing of thought. To the office of the governor general of St. Petersburg he gave the task of winnowing the population of the capital. That was an assignment that happened to be particularly suited to the personal capabilities of the current holder of that office, Count Michael Miloradovich. As governor general of St. Petersburg, he was one of the most powerful officials in the country, his post giving him broad authority over both military and civilian affairs of the city. He was also a socially popular war hero, whose tolerance and spendthrift

habits made friends for him in various circles and to whose talkative-
ness (he was known as the "Garrulous Knight") others were likely to
respond unwittingly with confidences about matters under the secret
surveillance of his office.

As other instruments of detection, the tsar relied upon the special
chancellery of the ministry of interior, a newly instituted corps of
secret military police in the guards, a special gendarme regiment, and
the informal network of agents in Arakcheev's special corps of military colonies. With their aid, reaction began in earnest. All secret
societies, including Masonic lodges, were prohibited. All military
officers and civil servants were required to swear that they were not
members of prohibited societies. And all guards units were ordered
away from St. Petersburg for an extended period in Lithuania—a
step intended not only as a means of breaking the routine in which
radicalism had grown up but also as a precaution against the possibility of a *coup d'état* led by the guards.

Any hope for reform now seemed effectively smothered. It had become dangerous even to suggest the need for reform. Reason itself
might be considered an instrument of subversion, a fact illustrated
by the case of law professor Alexander Kunitsyn, of the St. Petersburg University faculty. When his book *Natural Law* appeared, in
1820, expressing the fairly common contemporary view that there
existed a natural law which could be discovered through reason,
both he and the university came under investigation by Dmitri
Runich, a member of the chief administration of schools in Golitsyn's ministry. Runich deftly reviewed the case, denounced the work
as a subversion of religion, and obtained Golitsyn's agreement to
both the suppression of the book and the dismissal of the author.
Then, having been named acting curator of the university, he instituted a prolonged inquisition aimed at "cleansing" the whole
institution, which he regarded as a hotbed of liberalism and free
thought. The result was the dismissal of four liberal professors—
two of them "dangerous foreigners"—and the replacement of all university personnel, including the rector, who objected to the curator's
tactics. Meanwhile, Magnitsky was stepping up his activities in "rehabilitating" Kazan University, bringing it to the point where, as he
put it, instruction was based squarely on "loyalty to the heavenly and
earthly Tsars." [8] Others were rooting out undesirable courses at
Kharkov University and purging from the faculty all who were found
undesirable. In all universities, the autonomy for which Alexander
had provided early in his reign was now a thing of the past.

In this campaign aimed at policing thought, the general public was by no means forgotten. Golitsyn's censors issued orders that no reference to governmental activities was to appear in print without the approval of the agencies concerned, and further orders made printed matter of all kinds liable to censorship. In enforcing their orders, the censors adhered to regulations so rigidly that their judgments often carried caution to the point of captiousness. Printed news of the St. Petersburg flood of 1824, the worst in recorded history, was prohibited. When the respected poet Vasily Zhukovsky submitted his translation of Scott's "The Eve of St. John," it was denied publication on two counts: it served no moral purpose, and it was not fit material for Russian Orthodox observers of the sacred St. John's Day. A book on Russian grammar issued by the Academy of Sciences was rejected as an attack on the government. The text of Goethe's *Egmont* was condemned for scenes involving discussions of popular rights, and the German Theater was therefore refused permission to present it. Inspector Bronevsky of the Alexander Military Institute in Tula was forbidden to publish a weekly gazette on the grounds that the Tula area had no official censor, that the Moscow and St. Petersburg papers provided all the needed news, and that the projected paper might be deemed in violation of the rights of publishers in the two capitals. Even the faultfinders were liable to find themselves among the damned, as Michael Magnitsky learned to his chagrin when an article he submitted anonymously was refused publication. Though his article, titled "Some Thoughts Concerning Constitutions," was an attack on constitutions, it was rejected on the grounds that no appraisal of constitutions, pro or con, was needed in Russia and that, if material regarding any aspect of government were needed, it should be prepared by the authorities themselves.

Occasionally the government's intrusion was met with some opposition, but usually these instances proved only mild annoyances to the officials. Such a situation developed in 1822, when Alexander advocated, as nominees for honorary membership in the Academy of Sciences, three of his favorite officials: Arakcheev, Minister of Interior Kochubei, and Minister of Finance Gurev. Their claim to this honor, it was pointed out in answer to a protest from the academy's vice-president, Alexander Labzin, was their proximity to the "person of the Sovereign Emperor." In that case, replied Labzin, he wished to nominate someone even closer, one whose intimacy gave him the right to "sit with his back to the Emperor"—the royal coach-

man, Ilya Baikov.[9] Such brashness was futile, of course; the outspoken Labzin was ordered into exile for his "insolence," and the
issue was not affected in the slightest degree.

Strong as the wall of reaction appeared to be, there were weaknesses in it, some of them easily recognizable as threatening to the
whole structure. Golitsyn, though an agent of reaction, remained an
anomaly among reactionaries because he retained his tolerance
toward, and his interest in, many varieties of Christianity. Elsewhere
in post-Napoleonic Europe where reaction reigned, it was based on
loyalty not only to the throne but also to the established church. A
case in point could be observed in Austria, where Catholicism was
the national religion and there was no hint of benevolence toward
sects or toleration of Bible Societies. But in reactionary Russia some
benevolence was to be observed because Alexander could not bring
himself to question his friend's attitude.

As the darkness of the 1820's became more pervasive, however, the
contradictions between political reaction and religious latitudi-
narianism became more insupportable. Golitsyn became the target
of a number of influential enemies: two extremists among his own
assistants, Magnitsky and Runich; the clergy of the Russian Orthodox Church (in particular, its ranking prelate, Metropolitan Seraphim of St. Petersburg); and Arakcheev. Providentially it seemed,
they were provided with an unparalleled spokesman, the monk
Photius, who, after failing in an attempt to make Golitsyn see the
error of his ways, turned his efforts to protecting the Church and
the country from the "iniquitous influence of this impenitent mis-
creant." He was an implacable opponent. His friends claimed that
he was possessed of the "tongue of an angel" and the "sword of
saintliness." Others agreed with Pushkin that he was a pious scourge,
wielding indiscriminately "the anathema, the sword, the cross, the
knout." In reality, despite some of his apparently ruthless acts,
Photius was not a Russian Torquemada; he was more nearly a Savon-
arola, a man of passionate convictions, who saw visions, heard divine
calls, and was personally dedicated to revealing the incarnate Satan
he saw in anyone recognizing a faith outside the established church.

Golitsyn, the ever-trusting, helped to introduce Photius to Alexander. The latter, deeply impressed by the monk's religious passion,
came to look upon him as a man with a divinely revealed mission.
Photius lost no time in pressing his attack, denouncing the teachings
of certain men and groups viewed tolerantly by Golitsyn (mystics

like Jacob Boehme and religious bodies like the Moravian Brethren) as the instruments of Antichrist, "who, inspired by the satanic spirit of revolt and hate," were busily promoting a "bloodthirsty revolution." [10] This farfetched linking of mysticism, sectism, and revolution carried an implied reproof of the tsar, whose disposition toward mysticism and sects was as kindly as that of Golitsyn; Alexander could well have construed the strictures as "insolence." But, fearful of revolution and uncertain of himself, he listened to Photius and soon began to defer to the authority of the Church. Yet he clung to Golitsyn, trying to make peace between him and Seraphim, until the prince himself finally provided evidence that the Church could use to damn him.

The crisis came when censors under Golitsyn's supervision permitted the publication of a pamphlet prepared by the Bible Society, of which he was head, asserting that the Virgin Mary had given birth to children begotten by Joseph.[11] That incident broke the stalemate. When the Church denounced the pamphlet, Alexander at once ordered the arrest and imprisonment of the censors involved and reviewed the situation at length with Photius. The upshot was that, in April 1824, Photius publicly declared Golitsyn to be a heretic and anathemized him; Golitsyn asked to be relieved of his posts, and the tsar granted his request. Then Alexander clarified his own position still further by a series of acts tantamount to unconditional surrender to the Church. He appointed as minister to succeed Golitsyn the seventy-year-old Admiral Shishkov, whose definitely reactionary leaning made his selection for the post a safe one. He removed the Church from the jurisdiction of the ministry, and he named Metropolitan Seraphim president of the Bible Society—an act comparable to appointing a Jesuit as head of a Lutheran seminary.

With these acts Alexander repaired a near-breach in the wall of reaction, but there were still weaknesses in it. He was fated, it seemed, to be no more effective as a reactionary than he had been as a liberal. Even if all else had been auspicious, the lack of able men to give his government strength would have impeded his current program. His officials were far from being the "good" administrators that Karamzin had prescribed for the continued health of autocracy.

The condition of the bureaucracy upon which Alexander had to depend was exemplified in the 1824 membership of the Committee of Ministers, the body that, in the early years of his reign, had reflected the vigor of his liberal young friends Kochubei, Stroganov,

Czartoryski, and Novosiltsev—each then holding a ministerial or a deputy-ministerial post. Now, aside from the minister of finance, Egor Kankrin, and the minister of foreign affairs, Karl Nesselrode (both comparative youths in their forties), the committee was a group of tired old men, most of them nonentities despite their years of government service. The chairman, septuagenarian Prince Peter Lopukhin, was not only deaf but also too worn and tired for capable leadership, and those who sat around him were unlikely to disturb his lassitude. Shishkov, minister of education, and Traversé, minister of the navy, were in their seventies; Lobanov-Rostovsky, minister of justice, and Tatishchev, minister of war, were in their sixties. Collectively—and, except for Kankrin, individually—they lacked vitality and were quite unlikely to entertain any new ideas.

To avoid action and responsibility, the majority of the ministers were content to defer to Arakcheev, who, in most cases, was their sole connection with the tsar. Such procedure served only to compound incompetence, for Arakcheev himself lacked both vision and any practical conception of a national program. He was a faithful servant, doing his work honestly and earnestly, but he was dependent on direction from established authority. Success to him was fulfilling assignments and receiving credit and honor in high places. He cherished the tsar's approval and gloried in such distinctions as being granted an honorary appointment at Kazan University for his contribution to artillery instruction and sharing with the tsar a commendation from Metropolitan Seraphim, who pronounced the military colonies "an eternal monument" to Arakcheev and Alexander.[12] In short, he was a willing and enthusiastic associate of leaders, but he was no leader.

Another impediment to the proper functioning of the machinery of reaction was the lack of efficiency among operators at the lower levels. The agents whose business it was to detect and handle subversion, for example, were mutually uncooperative. They spied not only in their assigned fields but also on one another, producing instead of a reign of terror a reign of confusion and uncertainty. Consequently their efforts at eliminating subversion were just as ineffective as were the efforts of the agents of the ministry of education at producing loyalty. In fact, the whole reactionary program of the post-Troppau period was more irritating than intimidating, more nearly a spur to revolution than a deterrent.

The remarkable thing is that there was no revolution. For this,

Alexander could thank the autocratic traditions established by his predecessors. Members of the older generation whose maturity, position, or influence might have given them strength as an opposition force were either conservative and willing to support the tsar as a matter of course or, if liberal, too well-trained in obedience to the throne to think of revolution. As for the younger generation, they were still too immature and too ineffectually organized for revolutionary leadership.

The young men with dissident views were, nevertheless, far from quiescent. Though the tsar's policy of reaction had blighted their hopes for his direction of reform, other things had sparked their enthusiasm and given them incentive to become more purposefully active. From the vicarious thrills provided by the acts of liberals abroad, especially those of the Spanish revolutionaries in 1820, they had developed a fever of admiration for positive action. That a small band of Spanish officers with a few men could win the support of the army and bring a constitution to their country had been particularly inspiring to Russia's would-be revolutionaries. Nicholas Turgenev had saluted them in his diary: "Hail to thee, glorious army of Spain, hail to the people of Spain!" [13] Peter Chaadaev had written to his brother Michael: "Revolution has been carried out . . . without the spilling of a drop of blood, without butchery, without destruction, with complete absence of violence, in short, with nothing to stain this glorious deed. How do you like that?" [14] And Michael Orlov had been moved to boast that he could lead a division into the field against the government. Yet a willing spirit had sufficed to carry none of them to the point of action, even when the Semenovsky soldiers mutinied.

Shortly after the Semenovsky disorder, however, leaders of the Union of Welfare began to act more seriously than the drawing-room revolutionaries of past years. Anxious lest the authorities ferret them out and fearful—rightly so—that there were informers among Union members, they decided on a complex ruse. They would dissolve the Union in order to throw the government off the scent, rid themselves of members whom they considered untrustworthy, and later organize anew. It worked. Informers reported the dissolution to guards commander Vasilchikov and he, in one communication, was able to make two reports to the tsar: that there had indeed been a Union and that it was no more. Though the Union leaders may not have known it, with this report Alexander's interest in the "young trouble-makers" subsided. They were made still safer from his concern by a report he received from General Benckendorff, now chief of staff of the guards, assuring him that, except for a few addlepated young officers, the Russian nobility was too keenly aware of its self-interest to "support any kind of revolution," while the masses remained unworthy of a moment's concern.[15]

It was more than four years before the tsar became aware that the Union of Welfare had been a hydra, that from the original there had issued two secret political organization: the Northern Society, based in St. Petersburg, and the Southern Society, based in Tulchin, headquarters of the Second Army.

Until 1824, the two societies were relatively inactive, each occupied with the protracted consideration of means for approaching the goals to which it aspired. The Northern Society saw the best solution of the country's ills in a liberal constitutional monarchy permitting a maximum of local autonomy, the abolition of serfdom, and the distribution of land requisitioned, with pay, from the landlords. The Southern Society, on the other hand, pursued the idea of an eventual republic and the distribution of land to freed serfs without payment to former owners. In short, the Northern group were in the Girondist tradition; the Southern, in the Jacobin.

The growth of reaction following Golitsyn's replacement by Shishkov helped to pump life into the societies. Arakcheev and Photius became the symbols of a tyranny that threatened both body and mind, and the clearer it became that the people's choice was between compliance and constraint, the more urgently the societies applied themselves to planning.

Liberals throughout the country, finding themselves coughing and choking in what was currently described as a "psychological fog," were seeking escape. Some found intellectual relief in the daring works of writers who had followed Pushkin onto the contemporary scene. Alexander Griboedov's comedy *The Trouble With Reason* was among the most popular. Since it could not pass censorship either for publication or for performance, this play, later considered by many to be Russia's finest, was copied, studied, passed from hand to hand in manuscript, and read to interested listeners. A play with a message, set in Moscow about 1820, its high points are the argumentative brushes between a young idealistic believer in honor and freedom (Chatsky) and an unprincipled old bureaucrat (Famusov). Chatsky speaks the language of liberal youth:

Nowadays the world. is changed. . . .
[Men] serve a cause and not a master.

. . . .

But who're the judges? Because of their antiquity,
Their hostility toward a freer life is implacable;
They dig their opinions up out of old, forgotten papers
On the Conquest of Crimea and the Ochakov Siege.
Always ready for nagging,
They sing the same old song:
Not noticing about themselves
That whatever gets older gets worse.[16]

And Famusov mouths the code of the obscurantists:

Study—that's the plague; learning—that's the reason
That nowadays there are more madmen
And crazy things and thoughts than there ever were before.

. . . .

If the evil is to be undone
The books must all be gathered up and burned.[17]

The liberals who felt a need to be doing something more active and profitable sought out the secret societies.

In St. Petersburg, the apartment of Conrad Ryleev, in the headquarters of the Russian-American Company, became an open house for the Northern Society. The dissatisfied came there by the dozens: officers from all the guard units stationed in the capital as well as other concerned and courageous young men of their inclination, mostly writers and minor government officials. Though Nikita Muravev and Nicholas Turgenev were the society's duly chosen leaders, Ryleev, a relative newcomer to the organization, soon gained a commanding position in it. He was a well-known poet, a former army officer, and now head of the Russian-American Company's chancellery. Like many of his contemporaries, he was Byronic in both intellectual cast and dress. His poetic fervor and revolutionary ardor combined to give him particular appeal. The gatherings in his apartment were given over mostly to debate, the tenor of which indicated the evolution of the Northern Society's position: it was gradually moving away from the moderate ideas of such members as Sergei Trubetskoi and Nikita Muravev, who favored change through a constitutional monarchy, toward the more extreme ones supported by Ryleev, who felt that the "psychological fog" would be dissipated only by desperate means.

The Southern Society was encouraged by the changing mood in the northern group. From the beginning its members had followed the more aggressive line of thought, under the leadership of the brilliant young army officer Paul Pestel, working closely with Sergei Muravev-Apostol and Michael Bestuzhev-Ryumin. A rigorous thinker and effective strategist, Pestel was hard at work on a constitution for the Russian republic which his group anticipated; he hoped that, by the time it was ready, a workable plan for a *coup d'état* would be ready also. He and Muravev-Apostol agreed, and they easily convinced the officers associated with them, that effective action required cooperation between the Northern and Southern planners. In 1824, such cooperation seemed nearer than at any previous time since the societies were formed, two years earlier.

During that year and most of the following, the two groups debated various methods for making the break away from the old government, since it was now conceded by both that the old must be supplanted. Finally, a general plan was agreed upon: during the summer of 1826, they would carry out a *coup*, for which the signal—they had at last made the critical decision—would be the assassination of Tsar Alexander, a task for which the Northern Society had at least one eager volunteer, Peter Kakhovsky. Details were to be hammered out later.

This was hardly a firm commitment, but it was an important one. The societies had now gone in their thinking beyond their Spanish models and accepted the legitimacy of regicide as well as revolution. They based their plans on the assumption that the officers in each society could easily persuade their men to follow them and that other units would either join the revolt or refrain from opposing it. They expected to set up, after the victory, a provisional administration that would work out details for giving Russia a constitutional government—whether republican or monarchical in form was yet to be determined.

While the threat that had so recently disturbed Alexander was thus increasing, his concern with it continued to decrease, and his interest turned to other matters. When Arakcheev, who had received from informers a report concerning the existence of the Southern Society, passed the information on to the tsar, he had not bothered to take any action on it. The fact was that he was unusually tired of of what he had called the "burden of rule." Morose and despondent, he now openly complained of the weight of his office, comparing himself unfavorably with the common soldier, who could look forward to release from service at the end of twenty-five years while he, who would soon have completed twenty-five years of service, could expect release only with death. In addition, he was worried about the ill health of Empress Elizabeth, to whom he had become more closely devoted since he had broken off relations with Marie Naryshkin six years earlier; he was contemplating going with her to some place in the south before the hard northern winter set in.

Even as Alexander planned to leave St. Petersburg, further intimations of his mortality, more poignant than those he had recognized four years earlier, were forced upon him: the end of his reign was a subject now needing consideration, and the matter of the succession required his attention. Karamzin had just reminded him that, if the end of his reign was to be "worthy of the beginning," there was still much that he should do. To that, he had been able only to reply lamely that he still had it in mind to grant his subjects constitutional laws—honestly hopeful perhaps that he might in time find the strength of will to test the constitutional charter that Novosiltsev had drafted for him in 1820. Golitsyn, whose loyalty rose above the fact that he had suffered disfavor as a minister of reaction, added the further reminder that arrangements for the succession had not been satisfactorily defined.

The matter of the succession was one of those questions which, having been brought up, had occupied Alexander's mind only until some kind of resolution of it had been consigned to paper, and then had been abandoned. Yet, in this case, as Golitsyn wisely indicated, further action was in order, and to neglect it was to bequeath confusion to the concerned principals, the grand dukes Constantine and Nicholas.

For years, Alexander's oldest brother, Constantine, being legally next in succession because the tsar's marriage had produced no son, had been the heir presumptive. Then circumstances had changed. Constantine had persisted in his request for permission to end the marriage with his German wife, who had refused to live with him, and to marry a woman of non-royal lineage, the Polish countess Jeannette Grudzinska, though he knew that no child of the proposed union would be eligible to succeed him as ruler of Russia. Alexander had finally consented to the divorce—but on the specific condition that Constantine renounce his right to the throne. In a written statement to the tsar in 1822, Constantine had agreed to the condition; and Alexander had proceeded, in the following year, to sign a special manifesto naming as heir the next in line of succession, Nicholas.

Just why he had chosen to impose the condition of renunciation on Constantine and to name Nicholas as his successor is not definitely known, though it may be conjectured that he was considering the continuity of the dynasty: Nicholas had a son, Alexander, then five years of age—a more definite promise of Romanov succession than could be expected if Constantine should come to the throne. His decision made and recorded, the tsar quietly locked away sealed copies of the important document in Moscow (in the Cathedral of the Assumption) and in St. Petersburg (in the vaults of the State Council and the Senate) with instructions that the contents be disclosed on the occasion of his death.

Neither Constantine's renunciation of the throne nor the tsar's final disposition of the matter of the succession had been made public. The burden of the manifesto was officially known to only a few persons beside the tsar; they included his wife, his mother, Constantine, Metropolitan Philaret of Moscow, Golitsyn, and Arakcheev. Nicholas had been informed that he would succeed to the throne but he had not been proclaimed heir. He had continued therefore to give his chief attention to his command of the Second Guards Infantry Division and to the court and social activities expected of a grand duke. Everyone except the privileged few had continued to believe that Constantine, still serving as commander of the Polish army, was heir.

When Golitsyn brought up the matter of the inconclusive arrangement, he was showing more awareness of its critical importance than the tsar himself had shown. Alexander had neglected both the psychological preparation and the training of the Grand Duke Nicholas for his future role. The reason was as obscure as the one that had prompted him to change the succession.

It was as if he hesitated to afflict his brother with the kind of life that he himself had found so onerous. He could see, of course, that Nicholas was getting from life something that he had never experienced—contentment. Like other members of the imperial family, the grand duke had a generous income, because of provision made by his father; in addition, his lot as one of the younger sons included many privileges and few responsibilities. Alexander had seen him rise to the rank of general while most of his brother officers of the same age, with excellent wartime records, were still captains or even lieutenants. He had observed Nicholas' great enjoyment of his military life, which now included the special duties of inspector general of the army corps of engineers and close association with a number of devoted army men such as his beloved regimental commander, General Ivan Paskevich. To the tsar's mind, it was the ideal life, ideally lived (he judged it no discredit that Nicholas' firmness in matters of discipline and orderliness were considered excessive by his men). Furthermore, his brother's home life reflected much that was missing in the imperial household. Whereas Alexander and Elizabeth had no children about them, Nicholas and his wife, the Grand Duchess Alexandra Fedorovna, enjoyed a lively family, consisting now of three daughters and a son. Though the life of a grand duke was not as private as the tsar would have preferred his own life to be, Nicholas' St. Petersburg home, the Anitchkov Palace, was known to be a haven where the seriousness and severity of the military man's public manner were discarded and, with his family, he enjoyed literature (Scott's novels in particular), good music, and his collection of prints and maps. It was, as Nicholas said, the "corner of the world" where he could find "true happiness."

Alexander's reasons for not disturbing the normal pattern of the grand duke's life by acquainting him with imperial responsibilities apparently suggested no doubts about the propriety of what he was doing when he set out from the capital, on September 1, 1825, leaving matters as they were.

The tsar had chosen Taganrog as the place where he and Elizabeth should spend the winter. It was an odd choice: the doctors had recommended a warm climate and a season of rest, but this location, on the Sea of Azov, by no means met the requirements. It was, in fact, quite an unpleasant place. Peter the Great had laid out ambitious plans for it, but they had not been realized. It was now a neglected little city of 5,000, hot in summer, cold in winter, and subject to the recurrence of very unhealthful periods brought about by tidal changes.

Despite the unpromising nature of Taganrog as a resort, Elizabeth's health soon began to improve, and it appeared that the imperial couple were to have a comfortable respite from the routine of court society and the cares of state. That advantage, however, was not to last. Three weeks after he left St. Petersburg, Alexander received word from grief-stricken Arakcheev that his mistress, Nastasya Minkin, had been murdered by her household serfs and that his distress had led him to put the command of the military colonies temporarily into the hands of General Alexander Eiler. Less than a month later, General Ivan Witt, commander of the military colonies in the south, arrived with a circumstantial, though incomplete, report on the activities of the Southern Society along with a list of its members, including the name of Paul Pestel.

The significance of these two items, which earlier could have been expected to stir the tsar to action, did not impress him deeply enough now to cause him to return to the capital or to alter his plans. He sent a letter of sympathy to Arakcheev, decided against moving to arrest the known motivators of the Southern Society, and again turned his back on cares by embarking on a strenuous trip. He visited the Crimea, then poorly developed, and the naval base at Sebastopol. His customary enthusiasm for travel raised his spirits, and his enchantment with the Crimean countryside awakened his old dreams of leaving his imperial duties and retiring to some peaceful retreat. Near the end of the planned trip, however, he developed a nervousness and, finally, a fever which smothered his enthusiasm and made him anxious to get back to Taganrog.

After his return, on November 5, Alexander's physical condition deteriorated rapidly. The attending doctors, who diagnosed malaria, soon realized that his strength was not sufficient to withstand it. When it became evident that he was growing critically weaker, a report of his condition was sent by courier to St. Petersburg. On the fifteenth, at his request, he received the last rites of the Church. Four days later, he died.

The chief of general staff, General Ivan Diebitsch, who had accompanied the tsar to Taganrog, at once put official death notices into the hands of couriers, who left for the hard journey of more than a thousand miles to carry them to members of the imperial family: Dowager Empress Marie Fedorovna and Nicholas, in St. Petersburg; Constantine and Michael, in Warsaw. Then arrangements were made in Taganrog for the necessarily long period before the final formalities of the state funeral in the capital would be completed. The imperium was again in the north.

The shadow of the paradox that had marked Alexander's reign, however, was not dispelled. Even today, some believe—as did many at that time—that his death was a contrived illusion. They contend that he chose remote Taganrog as a safe point from which quietly to disappear into some retreat where, divesting himself of imperial identity, he could live out his last years as a private individual. As the story goes, when he fell ill, he arranged to be spirited away from

Taganrog and to have the corpse of some other man passed off as his. Some say that he was taken by ship to Palestine; others, that he was transported by cart to Siberia. Most of them agree that he recovered and found at last the peace he had so vainly sought in the earlier years of his life. In support of their case, they point to contradictions in the depositions of those who allegedly witnessed the death and climax their defense by relating how, more than half a century later, Alexander III opened the sarcophagus of Alexander I in the Cathedral of SS. Peter and Paul—and found it empty.[18] No one, however, has yet been able to supply evidence sufficient to substantiate any of these arguments.

Whatever the contradictions in the record, the fact remains that on November 19, 1825, the "burden of rule" was lifted from Alexander I, the tsar who had carried the Romanov name to heights of international fame but could not justify respect for it among his Russian subjects, who had wanted to clarify and simplify the basis of man's relation to man but managed only to remain himself an enigma to all.

IV

Challenge

NICHOLAS I, 1825-1826

ALTHOUGH many of Alexander's derelictions have remained difficult to evaluate, two of them became the focus of definite, and deservedly harsh, judgments immediately after his death: his inconclusive arrangements for the succession and his failure to restrict the known members of the secret societies. What he did in the one instance generated confusion for everyone concerned; what he failed to do in the other left the throne itself exposed to menace.

When it was learned in St. Petersburg that Alexander's death was imminent, his manifesto was duly opened and the change in succession made known to the inner circle of court officials. Nicholas at once decided that, when the expected death notice should arrive, he would publish the manifesto naming him heir and proclaim himself tsar. That, he felt, would be the right way to handle the matter, for the succession laws did not provide for an interregnum. When a ruler died, his heir succeeded immediately to the throne, made his accession known by a manifesto published throughout the empire, and ordered all his free male subjects over the age of twelve to take the oath of allegiance to him.

Before he had occasion to take his first proper step as planned, however, Nicholas took an improper one—as he realized too late— by confiding his intentions to Michael Miloradovich, the governor general of St. Petersburg. That also seemed the proper thing to do since, Arakcheev still being off the scene, the governor general was the most highly placed official to whom he could turn. Miloradovich was flattered by the confidence and immediately, with a great show of avuncular solicitude, took the situation in hand. He warned Nicholas that to proclaim himself tsar in the proposed manner would be basically illegal because, according to the law, Constantine was the heir; and, in view of Nicholas' unpopularity with the guards, it would be foolhardy to give them any excuse to oppose him in the name of legality. The wise course, he advised, would be to acknowledge Constantine as tsar, then prevail on him to come to the capital and renounce the throne. When Miloradovich went on to emphasize the "praetorian" inclination of the guards, Nicholas was won over.[1] He had only to recall the experiences of his predecessors to understand the importance of this consideration: five times, in the last hundred years, the guards had intervened to decide the succession. While he valued the guards as the backbone of the country's military strength and as protectors of the throne, he also recognized the danger they could present at certain critical times. Realizing that this could be one of such times, he accepted Miloradovich's plan and held himself in readiness to put it into effect.

Meanwhile, since the couriers from Taganrog were able to make the trip to Warsaw more quickly—by two days in this instance—than the trip to St. Petersburg, Constantine had learned of Alexander's death and had decided on a course that was to frustrate Nicholas' plan. Knowing that his brother, not he, was now the tsar, he felt that it was Nicholas' obligation to make the fact known. Since the relevant documents were in St. Petersburg, he reasoned that Nicholas had only to publish them and issue a manifesto announcing his accession. He himself would remain in Warsaw, hands off and uninvolved. This was his determined position even though he knew of the revolutionary spirit among the guards, suspected that any irregularity might stir them to action, and had expressed his belief that an incident in even one regiment would be enough to incite an uprising.[2]

Having set his course, self-willed Constantine would consider no other. He ordered his aides, who, like the public, believed him to be the heir and who were the only ones besides himself privy to the news of Alexander's death, to say nothing of the situation and to give no indication of mourning. He placed Warsaw under what amounted to a state of siege, allowing private individuals neither to communicate with, nor to receive newspapers from, St. Petersburg.[3]

Then, on November 26, he hurried his brother Michael off to the capital with letters for Nicholas and his mother, reaffirming his renunciation. So far as he was concerned, that settled the matter of his involvement.

The day after the Grand Duke Michael, carrying Constantine's messages, left Warsaw for his long journey (he was seven days en route), the news of Alexander's death finally reached St. Petersburg. Nicholas, following Miloradovich's advice, thereupon proclaimed Constantine the succeeding tsar, took the oath of allegiance to him, and ordered others to do the same. Then he dispatched his aide General Nicholas Lazarev posthaste to Warsaw with a letter imploring Constantine to come at once to the capital.

So began a series of maladroit efforts to clarify a muddle that too many hands had helped to make. What took place during the following two weeks seemed more like some seriocomic act of mummery than the conduct of men involved in the disposition of an imperial throne. Under the conditions, that was inevitable: Nicholas and Constantine felt equally committed to different courses, and physical distance made impossible any effective communication between them. Messages had to be carried by couriers, and the most hardened of them, using the fastest horses, required five days to make the seven-hundred-mile run between Warsaw and St. Petersburg; others took longer.

Lazarev, carrying Nicholas' appeal, reached Warsaw on December 2. Constantine promptly sent him back with an unequivocal reply: he would not go to the capital; rather, he would "retire" westward if Nicholas continued to annoy him. While this reply was on its way, Constantine's first letter was delivered to Nicholas by the Grand Duke Michael. To it, Nicholas replied at once and with passion: "It is at your feet, as a brother, as a subject, that I beg your pardon, your blessing: dear, dear Constantine, decide my fate, give your orders to your faithful subject. . . . In God's name, come!" [4]

Other exchanges followed, all of them futile. Constantine would not budge from his position (though he did not carry out his threat to retire westward), nor would Nicholas budge from his until forced to do so.

While the brothers were thus engaged in passing the crown back and forth, the danger that Nicholas had sought to avert was increasing. The secret societies, though not at first aware of the full extent of the advantage that had fallen to them, were being favored by each succeeding day of official confusion. When they learned of Alexander's death, the members accepted the succession as a regular one and, as a matter of course, took the oath of allegiance to Constantine. Then, since their plans called for a *coup* at the time of Alexander's death—earlier if they could manage it—leaders in both north and south began to appraise their positions. Many details had yet to be worked out. Not having anticipated the tsar's early death, they had set the year 1826 as the time when they expected to have ready their plans to dispose of him and appropriate his authority. Though Pestel liked to boast that his Southern Society, like his regiment, was "battle-ready," the fact was that neither of the societies was ready to act in December 1825.

Pestel and his comrades, nevertheless, decided to proceed with the *coup* at the earliest possible time—in cooperation with the Northern Society if possible, without it if necessary. Since sending an emissary to St. Petersburg to consult the Northern conspirators would consume an inordinate amount of precious time, it was decided to wait until the leaders of the Northern Society had time to send word that they had raised the flag of revolt in the capital. If there were no such word by New Year's Day, the Southern Society would take the initiative. That was a day on which Pestel's regiment was to mount guard at Second Army headquarters, in Tulchin, and the time would be propitious. He would call on his men to follow him in revolt, link forces with other rebel units (the support of 70,000 men was expected), and march them north to Kiev, perhaps on to Moscow. By that time, if all went well, the Northern group would have seized control of St. Petersburg, and the *coup* would be a certainty. It was all very stirring and serious—and irresponsible.

In the north, the fever of anticipation mounted just as rapidly as in the south; decisions about procedure, not so rapidly. Impassioned meetings at Conrad Ryleev's apartment ran on through day and night, many of the would-be revolutionaries being carried away by their own grandiloquence. Ryleev was in his element as he reminded them that they could not afford to let their "passionate souls waste away under the heavy yoke of tyranny."

The comings and goings at Ryleev's were duly reported to Governor General Miloradovich, and he knew that the young men meeting there were up to no good; yet he could not see them as a serious revolutionary aggregate. He was not completely wrong in his judgment of them, but he was sufficiently wide of the mark to be dangerously mistaken.

For a time, it appeared that action might indeed be submerged in words, for many who talked bravely shied away from the reality of revolt. But those ready for action were numerous enough to commit the society, and the central question soon became, "How shall the deed be done?"

Proposals ranged from fantastic to brilliant, but all suffered from the lack of important detail. There was not time either to determine the exact support to be expected or to provide for possible adversities. One hotheaded officer, Alexander Yakubovich, just back from years of fighting in the Caucasus, proposed that they start by breaking open the taverns, inviting soldiers and civilians to help themselves, and then, with a flourish of church banners to strike the right religious note, lead the aroused mob on to the Winter Palace. Such plans had appeal, but more sober ones came gradually to command the serious attention of committed members.

Finally Prince Trubetskoi brought information that helped to speed up the planning. As an intimate member of St. Petersburg social circles, whose members usually knew more of the developments at court than they had any business to know, he had learned that Nicholas was the rightful heir and that the suspended succession was now at a point of critical development. On December 10, Nicholas, a victim of frustration and apprehension, had begun quietly to make preparations for assuming the crown, whether or not Constantine deigned to come to his help. That fact, as Trubetskoi pointed out, suggested a schedule for the revolt: it should take place before Nicholas became firmly established on the throne, and the appropriate time would be the day he proclaimed himself tsar.

Supported by other aroused leaders, Trubetskoi went to work on definite plans. With an aggressiveness that belied his physical aspect —in looks and manners he was more nearly a Cyrano de Bergerac than a fiery rebel—he set the tone for a plan both daring and complex. The conspirators would convince as many as possible of the lower ranks—at least 7,000 of them, it was expected—that Constantine was the legitimate ruler, that Nicholas was a usurper, and that they should join their officers in opposing his accession. Some of the rebels would take the Peter-Paul fortress, with its guns commanding the city; some would surround the Winter Palace and take prisoner the members of the imperial family; and the bulk of them would march on Senate Square, ready to use force if the Senate refused to take the action that would be demanded of it. The demand (not to be made known to the lower ranks at this time) would be that the Senate issue a manifesto establishing a provisional government to administer the country until a constitutionally elected government could be installed.

Exactly what would be done with the imperial family and what kind of government would be installed were matters that would be decided later. For the time being, provision for immediate requirements would have to suffice. Trubetskoi would serve as dictator. Assisted by Colonel Alexander Bulatov, he would direct military operations and, after their success, would serve as head of the provisional government, with Prince Eugene Obolensky, of the Finnish Guards, as his chief of staff.

The planners optimistically assumed that the St. Petersburg troops who did not join them would at least refrain from interfering with them, that their scheme would readily give them control of the capital, and that the rest of the country would forthwith fall into line under their banner, particularly if given the expected encouragement from the Southern Society. They were not disturbed by the fact that they lacked—indeed, had made no effort to gain—support in the upper ranks of either military or governmental officials, among the masses, or even among the enlisted men whom they expected to deceive into launching the revolution. Nor did they concern themselves with the possibility of foreign intervention, such as that which had frustrated the rebels in Spain and Italy not so long before.

The Northern Society's leaders were now ready to put into effect their interpretation of what organized liberals had been talking about for nearly a decade. They were waiting only for Nicholas to act.

Nicholas was still afflicted by indecision, however, and continued to torment himself and exasperate those about him by waiting for some gesture of assistance from Constantine. He had the manifesto of accession at hand but hesitated to set the date for its publication. Yet the walls of obligation were unmistakably closing in. Early on the morning of December 12, he was roused from sleep to read dispatches sent from Taganrog by General Diebitsch (who had addressed them to "Tsar Constantine" or, if he were not in the capital, "the Grand Duke Nicholas"), which would have spurred most men in his position to immediate action. They confirmed the revolutionary nature of the Southern Society with full and circumstantial details, supplied by two official informers and Captain Arkady Maiboroda, of Pestel's regiment, and they provided general information concerning the Northern Society. Later on the same day, he was given more specific information about the Northern Society by Lieutenant Jacob Rostovtsev, who, though not a member of the society, had been present at discussions of plans for revolt.*

Miloradovich persisted in overlooking the significance of such information and assured Nicholas that all was under control: the gatherings in Ryleev's apartment were under strict surveillance, and all guardsmen were on good and loyal behavior. Grateful for any assuring word, Nicholas ostensibly accepted the governor general's judgment and put on a bold front. He sent Diebitsch a communication defending the honor of the guards: "I am convinced that there are few or no participants in the conspiracy here." [5] But privately he was uneasy and aware of the folly of continued inaction.

When Nicholas finally came to accept the duty he could not escape, he took it up with the desperation of a man facing his destiny. Putting aside his hope of any assistance from the unyielding Constantine, he declared his intention to publish the manifesto of accession and gave orders that the oath of allegiance be administered to all military and civil personnel in the capital on Monday, December 14; to others, as soon as possible thereafter.

It would take more than one positive step, however, to bring him relief from tension. He was torn between the bland assurances of Miloradovich and the disquieting news from Diebitsch and Rostovtsev, but he still leaned toward the belief that it would be imprudent to do anything that might upset the delicate balance on which his future rested. When Minister of War Tatishchev learned of the revolutionary conspiracy and asked permission to arrest the suspected officers, Nicholas refused to grant it on the pretext of being reluctant to mar the "festive" spirit of his accession day. Festive was hardly the word for the actual prospect in his ambivalent mind. He wanted the day to come, but he dreaded it because he could not dispel the thought that the fourteenth of December might be his last day on earth: it might be his fate—as it had been his father's and his grandfather's—to be murdered by drunken guards officers. On the eve of that day, he prayed with deeply felt emotion.

The conspirators themselves found the eve of the great day an unsettling one. Rostovtsev had let them know that he had informed the tsar of their plans, and a number of officers took that as sufficient excuse for withdrawing their promise of cooperation in the society's

---

* Rostovtsev displayed his duty as a loyal subject by thus informing Nicholas of the plans; his deference to the code of gentlemanly honor, by declining to reveal the names of the conspirators; and his possession of a clear conscience, by later acknowledging to the conspirators his partial betrayal of them.

program for the next day. With that, a few of the leaders began to lose their assurance, to see that they had perhaps exaggerated the extent of true partisanship among their fellow officers. Even Trubetskoi, one of the most dedicated and deeply involved, began to have misgivings, and it was evident that his ardor was cooling. Yet most of them dismissed both Rostovtsev's act and the defections as trifling and continued in their determination, echoing Ryleev's heroic declaration that, though they perished on the morrow, it would be for the "future of the fatherland" and, therefore, in a noble cause. They saw themselves not as praetorians but as Bolivars, Del Riegos, and Cola di Rienzis. Most of them spent the night making calls on friendly officers and counting over the dependable pledges of support.

Meanwhile, Governor General Miloradovich was doing nothing to forestall any possible disruption of the official plans for the succession ceremonies. The stage was set for a confrontation of amateurs.

Monday, December 14, began as just another day in the natural order of things in St. Petersburg—usual in its raw, bone-chilling wintriness, usual in its atmosphere of readiness for prescribed procedures.

At six o'clock in the morning, in the dozens of barracks throughout the city, 60,000 privates and noncommissioned officers in parade uniform stood in formation, waiting in the near darkness to take the oath of allegiance to Nicholas I. Their platoon and company commanders, who were to administer the oath, were waiting also—for orders from higher ranks. Superior officers, in turn, were waiting for the supreme signal as they faced Nicholas in the Winter Palace, listening to his explanation of the circumstances of his accession and his reminder that it was their present duty to insure the safety of the capital. When they had taken the oath and been dismissed, they hurried to the barracks to swear in the junior officers who would attend to a like ceremony with their waiting men. They themselves were expected to be at the Winter Palace again by eleven o'clock to attend the traditional *Te Deum* celebrating the accession. Everything went smoothly for them except in one instance. When the officers of the Horse Artillery Guards were assembled to take the oath, they stood silent in repudiation of it. This was an unexpected and quite irritating disruption of order, but, at the moment, their commander did not have time to consider its significance. He simply ordered arrest for the refractory officers, assigned others to their duties, and turned to his own further obligations.

These matters of official routine were taking place against the quietly stirring background of the Northern Society's final arrangements. When the leaders met to compare notes that morning, they found that they had some serious new problems. The officers of the Naval Guards, who had agreed to lead the storming of the Winter Palace, were now refusing to act, belatedly struck by the enormity of using force against the imperial family. Reports from other units that had been counted on were likewise studded with second thoughts and irresolution. Still, most of the planners kept up their spirits. Trubetskoi was an important exception, but he tried to keep his feelings to himself and joined the others as they turned their energies to improvising wherever they saw their original plans breaking down. If the Naval Guards would not attack the Winter Palace, would they agree to march to Senate Square? Naval officer Nicholas Bestuzhev went off to inquire. His brother Alexander, a captain in the Dragoon Guards, undertook to help raise the Moscow Guards, for it was understood that some resistance might be expected there. Among the officers of that unit, however, was another brother, Captain Michael Bestuzhev, a faithful member of the Northern Society; it was hoped that his word would carry weight with the reluctant ones. Trubetskoi left for the Senate, where, according to the plan, he was expected to present the demands of the rebels. Ryleev and others went their separate ways, first to see how the revolt was developing in the various units, then to meet in Senate Square. By nine o'clock, everyone had his assignment: there was now no turning back.

Soon the strength of the revolutionary leaven was under realistic test. In the Moscow Guards barracks, when regimental commander Baron Peter Fredericks ordered his officers to proceed with the formalities of having their men swear allegiance to Nicholas, the conspirators who hoped to enlist the support of this important unit knew that the critical hour had arrived. The task was quickly to reach the men, "reveal the plot" against Constantine, rouse them to patriotic fervor, and lead them out in a show of militant rebellion in the name of the "legal tsar," Constantine. Michael Bestuzhev, with the aid of his brother Alexander, prevailed on the men of his company not to take the oath to Nicholas, and Prince Dmitri Shchepin-Rostovsky, a friend of Michael but not a member of the society, won over the company of which he was captain. But all efforts to rouse the other companies failed. A stir of disbelief and alarm ran through the ranks as the two rebel companies prepared to leave the barracks. General Fredericks moved to block their way, and Captain Shchepin-Rostovsky, compounding his insubordination, struck him aside with the flat of his saber.

So the initial detachment of the first Russian revolutionaries got under way. Eight hundred guardsmen, with loaded muskets on their shoulders, their regimental flag flying above them, and their drums beating, marched over to Gorokhovaya Street and down to Senate Square. On the way, their drums and their occasional shouts for "Tsar Constantine" quickly drew public attention, and they were followed into the square by a throng of curious and ill-informed people anxious to witness whatever was in store. The rebels reached their destination at eleven o'clock. Seeing that they were the first on the scene, that not even Trubetskoi was there, Captain Bestuzhev and Captain Shchepin-Rostovsky ordered a battle square to be formed around the central feature of the area, the Falconet statue of Peter the Great. The response was orderly and spirited, for the men were now warming to their daring demonstration.

It was a brave show, an unprecedented display on this venerable stage. History had been made here, and all about were solid reminders of imperial achievement. The great bronze statue, about which the men were ranked, rose above them to five times their height and pointed proudly toward the harbor, the "window" through which Russia first breathed the heady air of progress. Those on the south side of it faced the massive pattern of unfinished St. Isaac's Cathedral; on the west, the old buildings of the Holy Synod and the Senate; on the east, the Admiralty, with its lofty gilded spire; on the north, the Neva River, now silent under the winter ice, and beyond it, Vasilevsky Island, where the university stood, promise of an enlightened future.

Less than half a mile away, even as the rebels were approaching their station in the square, a colorful and dignified procession of court and civilian officials, military leaders, and diplomats was entering the Winter Palace, where the *Te Deum* was to be celebrated. The service was to be the expression of solemn homage to Nicholas Romanov, whom this handful of guardsmen understood to be a usurper and whom their leaders were ready to defy as the symbol of a culpable and irredeemable dynasty.

As the hour appointed for the service neared, the tsar sat apart, hearing successive reports on the progress of the oath-taking among the guards. He anticipated each one with private anxiety, knowing that he was facing what might be his fate, though still unwilling to make it a matter of official concern. For a time, the reports were routine and satisfactory, and he was beginning to feel relief. Then came the blow: General Alexander Neidhardt hurried in with the news that the Moscow Guards had repudiated Nicholas and were even then flaunting their mutiny in Senate Square.

Much as he had feared such a development, Nicholas had made no preparation for it. His first thought was to extinguish this flicker of hostility before it could burst into the flame of revolution. With the fervent hope that he was not too late, he directed Governor General Miloradovich to go at once to the nearby Horse Guards barracks, call out the necessary forces, and rush them to the square in order to subdue the rebels and prevent their being joined by reinforcements. For good measure, he ordered additional guards regiments to follow; then, while his aides scurried around, postponing the *Te Deum* and alerting those responsible for other parts of day's schedule, he himself prepared to go to Senate Square.

Miloradovich, out of countenance because his calculations and sanguine predictions had gone so ingloriously amiss, welcomed the chance to busy himself. Commandeering the first sleigh he could find, he dashed off to the barracks and relayed the rush order for men and horses to regimental commander Count Alexis Orlov. Then, painfully conscious of every precious minute and too impatient to wait for the necessary preparations, he lost his self-possession completely and shouted at the commander a few abusive words about the Horse Guards, adding, "And what's more, I don't want to stain the day with blood. I'll finish this business myself." [6] Mounting an already saddled horse, he made for Senate Square at a headlong gallop—the "Garrulous Knight" going to reprimand some unruly boys and set things straight again.

By the time he arrived, the rebels were becoming a bit anxious, though he could not know that. Their battle square about the base of the statue had lost some of its military starch and their hurrahs for Constantine were less frequent, for they were growing uneasy about the delay in the arrival of reinforcements. The only additions to their number had been a few individuals—among them Ryleev, Peter Kakhovsky, and Eugene Obolensky. Their leaders were wondering particularly about Trubetskoi. According to the plan, he should have been there with a manifesto from the Senate, but he had not appeared; nor had his second-in-command, Bulatov.

Miloradovich approached the rebels as if he were dealing with a misunderstanding, not a revolt. Recalling how he and they had fought together against Napoleon, he assured them that they could trust his words: Nicholas was their tsar. As he talked on, embroidering his appeal until it became a florid speech, he realized that he was not making the desired impression. The men were simply enduring his words in sullen silence. Finally, his desperation giving way to anger, he shouted at them: "There isn't a single officer, not a single soldier here. No, here there are hoodlums, ruffians, brigands, scoundrels, besmirching the Russian uniform, military honor, the very word 'soldier.' You are a blot on the name of Russia!" [7]

The patience of the rebel leaders also was becoming overtaxed. Obolensky, now acting in Trubetskoi's place, ordered Miloradovich to leave and punctuated the order by giving his horse a jab with a bayonet. That might have ended this encounter with authority had the rebel throng not included Peter Kakhovsky, the young man who had volunteered to assassinate Alexander I and who was convinced that only terror was an effective weapon against tyranny. Unwilling to see a deputy of tyranny let off so easily after such a wordy assault, he stepped forward and, at point blank range, shot Miloradovich just as he was gathering his reins to turn away. The rebel soldiers, more shocked than aroused, lifted the fatally wounded governor general from his horse and placed him on a sleigh, whose driver took him at once to the barracks of the Horse Guards. He died later in the day, the first casualty of the rebellion.

The incident served no purpose. Obolensky could only suggest further waiting, and the men accepted the necessity. From time to time they sportively shot off their muskets well over the heads of the bystanders, accepted vodka from friendly hands to ward off the cold (in leaving the barracks, they had neglected to take their greatcoats), and gave an occasional shout of "Long live Constantine!" All around the square and on the rooftops of surrounding buildings, sympathetic crowds watched and called out words of encouragement. The officers and other leaders did what they could to bolster morale, still clinging to their faith in a plan that had already foundered. Trubetskoi was the one whose report they needed most critically—and were not to receive. He had gone to the Senate, as planned, only to find that the members had taken the oath of allegiance before eight o'clock that morning and had then adjourned their session. Thereupon, he had washed his hands of the revolt and, without informing anyone of his intentions, had quietly withdrawn to the General Staff building. There he had taken the oath of allegiance to Nicholas and spent the remainder of the morning apart from his involved comrades.*

The next effort to deal with the assembled rebels was under Nicholas' personal direction.[8] Years of familiarity with military affairs cautioned him against anything like Miloradovich's folly of facing the rebels alone, but he had no hesitancy about his duty in the matter. After issuing emergency directives for the bringing up of supplementary troops, he immediately placed himself at the head of the nearest unit of still loyal men, the First Battalion of the Preobrazhensky Guards, and rode out, as general and tsar, to the scene of trouble. Reaching Senate Square at one o'clock, he deployed his battalion and took up his position of command at their rear.

Within the hour, 10,000 loyal guardsmen streamed in and took up their positions about the battle square of the mutineers and in the adjacent streets, apparently cutting off both escape and help. Though all was done with dispatch and precision, by the time the opposing forces were drawn up and settled, over 2,000 men and a number of officers from the Grenadier Guards and the Naval Guards had managed to make their way to the ranks of the rebel units of the Moscow Guards. At last, the issue was up for judgment.

For Nicholas, this was a tragic situation, however viewed. As interpreted by some contemporary critics and some judges with the wisdom of hindsight, it should have been treated more lightly, as a "comedy" perhaps, or a "mere display of high spirits." But it could not be interpreted as an insignificant show by one who understood it as Nicholas did. He knew that many of the officers commanding loyal troops were members of the Northern Society, and he could only gamble on the hope that the strength of their commitment to it was weaker than their loyalty to him. Moreover, he could not be sure that the loyal enlisted men would obey an order to attack their comrades. Yet to do nothing would be not only to suffer insubordination but also to risk the danger of additional defections.

Believing that a limited but impressive attack would disperse the rebels, he ordered the Horse Guards, those magnificent cuirassiers protected by heavy breastplate and helmet, to charge. The result was a fiasco: in drill-perfect order the horsemen moved out toward the unmounted ranks, reined up for the charge—and their horses began skidding wildly on the icy pavement. Some of the rebels opened fire

---

* Later, Trubetskoi would cross Senate Square, careful not to draw attention to himself, and take refuge in the residence of his brother-in-law, Count Ludwig Lebzeltern, the Austrian envoy.

and, while doing little damage, brought the charge to an inglorious halt. Onlookers, enjoying the show, hooted and threw stones as the Horse Guards retreated.

Nicholas next tried persuasion. In the hope that mutinous spirits might be calmed by understanding, he chose three men and sent them out, one by one, to try to clear up the misunderstanding he now knew to be behind the attitude of the enlisted men, to explain that Constantine had renounced the throne of his own accord and that he himself had been duly named the heir, and to make personal appeals. The first, Metropolitan Seraphim, was given respectful attention by the men, but he made no conversions. The next, the Grand Duke Michael, honorary chief of the Moscow Guards, was expected to be more effective since he was popular with the men. Indeed he was more effective, so much so that the rebel leaders ordered him away; one, William Küchelbecker, made an effort, fortunately deflected by a guardsman, to shoot him. Finally, the commander of the guards artillery, General Ivan Sukhozanet, appealed to the men with a promise of pardon if they would disperse. But the rebels, feeling by now that even the authorities did not expect their brother guardsmen to attack them (how else explain all these milder efforts?), shouted the general down and, as he left, fired over his head.

To continue such efforts was ludicrous and becoming dangerous as well: it was past four o'clock, and the light of the short winter day was fading. Unwillingly, Nicholas accepted the advice of General Sukhozanet and others pressing for effective action. Remarking on the bitterness of beginning his reign in this way, he made the decision to use the means against which the rebels were known to have no defense at hand—cannon fire.

The first volley was high; it lit up the square and frightened the men as nothing else had, but it did not rout them. The succeeding volleys were on target. Within seconds, the rebels were in a pitiable state of disorganization, and the square had become a nightmare of horror. The dead and wounded—civilians as well as soldiers—who dropped before each volley were overrun as panic set in and thousands struggled to flee the scene. The Bestuzhev brothers tried gallantly to reform ranks and find a new position from which to fight, but the men were too demoralized to respond. Discipline was doomed, and the men made off frantically in all directions, many of them toward the frozen Neva, in an attempt to get out of range of the artillery.

Within an hour, the main part of the incident was over, and many of the rebels who had managed to save their lives had been overtaken and put under arrest. For those who escaped, it was now every man for himself. Finally, as if ending routine maneuvers, the assembled loyal units returned to quarters, while special squads and police details hurriedly removed bodies—between sixty and seventy persons had been killed—and disposed of the gory evidence that autocracy was still impervious to defiance. During the night, a few of the rebels who had avoided arrest gave themselves up, and a few were picked up at their homes. For those who still eluded the authorities, the hunt was on, and retribution was only being delayed.

The brother effort of the Southern Society was more realistically anticipated and so effectively obstructed, at the direction of General Diebitsch, that it turned out to be a mere flash in the darkening world of the revolutionaries.

Paul Pestel was arrested in Tulchin on December 13, and orders for the arrest of the other leaders in the south soon followed. Before they could be carried out, however, Sergei Muravev-Apostol, loyally seconded by Michael Bestuzhev-Ryumin, took the desperate chance of trying to raise and lead a quick rebellion to supplement the activity of which they had received reports from the north. Even as the government forces closed in, these two, as courageous as they were foolhardy, managed to evade their pursuers for more than a week. They enlisted the support of other officers and about 1,000 soldiers (most of them from the ranks of the Chernigovsky Regiment) and somehow got under way the first phase of Pestel's plan for a march to Kiev. As they moved from village to village, they also won a fair showing of sympathy from civilians, for whom they promised to provide the blessings of a future under a heavenly ruler, "the Universal Tsar." Finally, on January 3, 1826, they were intercepted and forced to stand for battle with the loyal forces, against whose cannon fire and cavalry they had no shadow of a chance. Both Muravev-Apostol, badly wounded, and Bestuzhev-Ryumin were taken prisoner; two of their fellow officers committed suicide; the other insurgents were either killed in the fighting or taken prisoner.

Nicholas I was safe on his throne. The mutiny that would go down in history as the Decembrist Revolt had given way before the first flourish of the authority it protested. And a new category of Russians, the Decembrists, was entered on the record of the Romanov dynasty.

V

Magnificent Dream

NICHOLAS I, 1826–1850

IN affirming his succession, Nicholas, like Alexander before him, assumed a responsibility that he would have preferred to avoid. As he wrote in his memoirs, looking back after ten years, he was a man "who had to sacrifice all that was dear to him in order to submit to another's will." But when he made the decision to submit, he did so as a strong man, without qualifications. Accepting the bitter truth that the ones who might have eased his way—Alexander, Constantine, and Miloradovich—had been the very ones whose personal judgments had made it difficult, he steeled himself to the fact that at this juncture he was "alone, entirely alone," and proceeded from that premise. Accordingly, on December 14, 1825, he acknowledged the translation of the Grand Duke Nicholas Pavlovich, the individual, into Tsar Nicholas I, the embodiment of imperial authority. Thereafter, his personal sentiments were Russian policy; his judgment, the standard of administration; and his aspirations, the goal of all the country's undertakings.

His first task, as he saw it, was the disposition of the problems connected with the revolt. He immediately ordered the apprehension not only of the rebels but also of any others who were suspected of membership in the "evil-minded" societies. In all, about 2,500 enlisted men and 600 officers and civilians were brought in, so over-running the cells of the Peter-Paul fortress that most of the enlisted men had to be shifted to other prisons.[1] The detention of the arch-offenders became the special responsibility of tough old General Alexander Sukin, who, as commandant of the fortress, had become notorious for the heartlessness of the iron discipline he imposed on those unfortunate enough to fall out of imperial favor and into his custody.

As to the guilt of those in the lower ranks, Nicholas felt that it was clearly the guilt of insubordination encouraged by superiors: the men, incapable of independent thought, had evidently been "seduced and swept off their feet." They would be punished, of course, and would have to be kept in prison until their punishment was determined; but they were not to be condemned as revolutionaries. The members of the societies were the ones in whom he was interested. He hoped to learn from them the nature and extent of the conspiracy behind the revolt, and he expected to have them judged and punished in accordance with their complicity in what he considered the most reprehensible crime conceivable, defiance of autocratic authority.

Three days after the revolt, he assembled a committee of investigation, placed Minister of War Tatishchev in charge, and set it to collecting evidence. He himself was often present at committee sessions, when the men, blindfolded and dragged from their cells for the ordeal, were questioned and cross-questioned mercilessly—nearly 600 of them in all. He sincerely wanted to know why these young men, most of them from noble families distinguished for generations of service to the dynasty, had decided to turn their hand against it.

As they responded to the probing of the committee, the majority admitted their involvement, whether deep or superficial; but, even while declaring their repentance, they usually made some attempt to justify themselves by citing the evil conditions that had turned them to rebellion. A few, like Pestel, tried first to absolve themselves of any guilty connection with it; then, being confronted with confessed collaborators or overcome by the mental strain of the repeated interrogations, they broke down in extravagant confession or accusation of others. A few proudly called themselves revolutionaries and continued to maintain the justness of their effort; among them were the fiery Kakhovsky, as might be expected, and Michael Lunin, who had taken no part in the revolt and was no longer even connected with either society. Others accepted their lot with reasoned courage, hoping that their effort, though ill-timed and unsuccessful, would ultimately produce some good: these included such deeply dedicated men as Obolensky, Ryleev, and Nikita Muravev.

The investigation ground on for six months while almost every night from six to midnight—sometimes during the day as well—the committee kept up the relentless questioning. After the first few weeks, time itself began to take a toll. As the great clock in the spire of the nearby Cathedral of SS. Peter and Paul marked the passage of each dragging hour with the somber notes of a hymn, hopes grew dimmer and spirits sank. Some of the prisoners went mad; some died; one, Alexander Bulatov, committed suicide by dashing himself head-first against the wall of his cell. Even among those who stood up best, some found themselves strangely changing. When, on March 26, the muffled drums of the funeral cortege carrying Alexander I's body into the cathedral were heard in the fortress, many, tempered by recent experience, were touched with a feeling for him that would have been incredible a few years earlier.

At the end of May, the committee handed to the tsar its final report, along with a list of those recommended for trial.[2] While he endorsed every step taken so far in the inquisitional process, Nicholas welcomed the end of this phase of it: now the action could be speeded up. He had only hatred and contempt for the recognized leaders and responsible participants in the revolt; he felt that the sooner these "villains and lunatics" faced their punishment, the sooner justice would be certified and his subjects be given an understanding of his uncompromising will. He was determined that the worst offenders should pay with their lives regardless of the fact that they were nobles and the fact that capital punishment had not been inflicted in Russia since 1775, when the rebel leader Pugachev was hanged.[3]

At the tsar's direction, a specially appointed court of seventy-two judges reviewed the cases of those recommended for trial, and handed down egregiously severe sentences (expecting, no doubt, that the tsar would mitigate them in the end). They decreed death by quartering for Ryleev, Kakhovsky, Pestel, Michael Bestuzhev-Ryumin, and Sergei Muravev-Apostol; death by decapitation for Trubetskoi, Obolensky, Nikita Muravev, the brothers Michael and Alexander Bestuzhev, Shchepin-Rostovsky, Küchelbecker, and twenty-four others; exile in Siberia for eighty-five; and lesser punishments for one hundred thirty-four who were found to be active, but not leading, members of the societies. Nicholas approved this classification according to individual guilt, but, as expected, was willing to be "merciful." In the case of the five supreme offenders, he substituted hanging for quartering, and he spared the thirty-one in the next group by substituting for decapitation the obligation to expiate their crimes by hard labor in Siberia for the rest of their lives.

In the half-light of the pre-dawn of July 13, 1826, just outside the walls of the fortress, the five were hanged. Later that day, the first of those destined for Siberia, stripped of noble status and military rank, began their long journey into exile (others would follow at short intervals), to face years of wretchedness as state criminals under strict police surveillance. Then Nicholas, having administered what he conceived as justice, announced to a shocked public what he had done.

In the final reckoning with the other Decembrists, punishment varied in degree and duration. Even before the fate of the leaders was decided, the soldiers of lower rank in both the Moscow and the Chernigovsky regiments, severely reprimanded and in some instances subjected to corporal punishment, had been posted to other units in remote areas. Their convicted superiors not included in the Siberian exile were now deprived of rank and either assigned for discipline to scattered units or retired from service and banished beyond the sphere of their former associations.

Thereafter the publication of any writings of the Decembrists, reproduction of their likenesses, and even mention of their names were prohibited by imperial order. Officially, the Decembrists, like the black sheep of a family, were to be remembered henceforth, if at all, in silent shame. As long as he lived, Nicholas kept close at hand a copy of the investigators' report and the names of the condemned, a constant and painful reminder of his "friends of the fourteenth"; the memory of them would never leave him.

Nicholas had insisted on postponing the coronation until the Decembrists had been dealt with. Though duly held, beginning near the end of August, with all the pomp and magnificence invariably associated with the occasion, it seemed something of an anticlimax.

The old capital, Moscow, was always the host city for throngs of participants and observers during the days devoted to this periodic revival of time-honored traditions, some of which dated back to imperial Rome. There, the new tsar found himself in an atmosphere wholly different from that in which he had begun his reign. Everything was planned to honor and glorify him, and each detail was carried out to near-perfection: endless salutes from his respectful subjects; religious services dedicated to him in the splendor of the great cathedrals; and, for his sharing, the social pageantry of balls, receptions, dinners, gala theater performances, and popular entertainments. Eclipsing all else, of course, was the solemn ceremony in the Cathedral of the Assumption, within the Kremlin, when Nicholas enacted the symbolic self-crowning (no hand but his own was empowered to place the crown on a tsar's head). This was the tradition-approved substantiation of himself as the "viceroy of God on earth"; in Nicholas' case, it was only a formal recognition of the prerogative he had been exercising for more than eight months. For him, the most significant feature of the occasion—even surpassing Constantine's willingness to attend—was provided by Metropolitan Philaret, who, during the consecrational part of the ceremony, designated him as the tsar who had saved the fatherland. That was a recognition he would cherish.

The coronation out of the way, Nicholas was impatient to put into operation the sovereign imperatives he had accepted as his personal responsibility on December 14. Although he felt himself to be "young at twenty-nine," and although he admitted that he knew little about his new position, he looked to the future with great confidence. Like many military men, he thought of army life as the quintessence of human capabilities, and a good officer as the quintessence of human virtues. If a man performed well as an officer, he could perform well in any other capacity when given the opportunity to make the necessary adjustments. He had long believed himself to be a good officer and his performance on December 14 had strengthened that belief; he had no doubt that through personal courage and decisiveness he had saved the throne. Now it was his task to show his subjects and the world that absolute monarchy could be brought to a state of order, tactical perfection, and enduring robustness in an age when too many were beginning to question absolute monarchy.

He had no intention of taking his late brother as a model. He had observed too many of Alexander's shortcomings as a ruler ever to be in awe of him, and his experience with the Decembrists confirmed his conclusions about what was fundamental to those shortcomings. While that experience was still fresh in his mind, he made a written summary of his conclusions, using terms that indicated quite clearly the direction of some of his own intentions. Alexander, he noted, had countenanced both political and religious heterodoxy through a permissiveness that had made it possible for the universities to become bad "imitations" of foreign ones with all their defects and none of their virtues, for Tsarskoe Selo Lycée to develop into a haven for "subversive" professors, for Russian youths to become "republican and atheist" as a result of study in Geneva or "liberal and deist" as a result of study in France, and for the Bible Society to addle Russian minds by distributing Bibles in "ridiculous number" despite the fact that the clergy itself found it difficult to understand or explain Holy Writ. The ultimate delinquency, in Nicholas' estimation, was Alexander's persistence in looking through his fingers at the subversive secret societies.

The traditions of the monarchy, based as they were on the acceptance of tsarist infallibility, prevented Nicholas from publicly impugning Alexander and required him, on the contrary, to profess himself nothing more than an instrument divinely selected for the purpose of continuing the policies of his "august predecessor." He had already acquiesced by dutifully and solemnly declaring himself "determined" to take Alexander as his model and Alexander's "principles as rules of conduct." But no Romanov had ever felt himself bound by the formal embellishments of routine professions; Nicholas was not to be an exception. He saw the Decembrist Revolt not only as visible proof of his brother's maladministration but also as a timely warning of what Providence held in store for monarchs who neglected their business; and he firmly intended to face Judgment with the record of a well-ordered realm to his credit.

The fact that hundreds of young men from the most respected families of the country had conspired against the government did not suggest to Nicholas that there was anything inherently wrong with the autocracy. It did, however, suggest other wrongs. He believed—as Alexander had come to believe—that there was something wrong with the educational system which had allowed "alien and pernicious" ideas to breed in the minds of young men (of the 121 condemned Decembrist leaders, 109 were under thirty-five years of age, and most of them had developed their liberal attitudes in their late teens or early twenties). He believed, furthermore, that there was much amiss in the administration of the country. Even the Decembrists, he privately admitted, had pointed to real defects in that area: corruption among members of the bureaucracy, inequity in the legal system, practices conducive to the further oppression of the serfs and the deterioration of the nobility, stupidity in the establishment of the military colonies, and inadequacy in the ministrations of the clergy. His acceptance of these as correct evaluations, however, in no way affected his condemnation of the Decembrists for using them to support the criminally incorrect conclusion that it was the business of subjects to rectify the faults of administration.

Providing good administration for his people was the obligation of the tsar, and Nicholas had no misgivings about his ability to meet this obligation, to succeed where his late brother had failed. Whereas Alexander had been equivocal and had finally given way to inertia, he would be positive and undeviating. Whereas Alexander had begun his reign under the influence of liberal notions contrary to the basic idea of autocracy, he recognized both the fallacies and the dangers of such notions and would lose no time in providing his subjects still further protection from exposure to them. Whereas Alexander had failed to improve the lot of the people, he would see to it that every class and every area in Russia recognize and profit by the paternal interest of the ruling autocrat. This was his "magnificent dream" or, as more impersonally appraised, the "Nicholas system," which for twenty-nine years was to be rigidly imposed on Russia and felt throughout Europe.

The Nicholas system was not planned as a reactionary one. In fact, Nicholas deliberately reduced the influence of, and ultimately removed, a number of the extremists left over from Alexander's ten years of reaction; among them, Arakcheev, Magnitsky, Runich, and Photius. He retained two who had been closely associated with the woeful aspects of those years, Minister of Education Shishkov and Count Peter Kleinmichel, a staunch Arakcheev aide: the one on the ground that the obliquity of his ministry would be cleared away with the departure of Magnitsky and Runich, the other on the ground that he was an extraordinarily capable military man. But most of those he chose to carry over were, while conservative, of a generally moderate and reasonable temper. He did not see any of them as reactionaries.

Certainly reaction would not be the chief concern of those be retained as officials with whom he planned to work most intimately: Minister of Finance Egor Kankrin, who was signally qualified for his duties and restricted himself to them; the patriarch-historian Karamzin, the uncompromising spokesman of the kind of level-headed autocratic rule to which Nicholas aspired; Golitsyn, a loyal and experienced supporter of that kind of rule; the generals Diebitsch, Vasilchikov, Benckendorff, and Paskevich, men of proven military ability who had demonstrated their agreement with his assessment of the revolutionary threat; Kochubei and Speransky, both now safely beyond their liberal periods, who were thinkers of extraordinary talents which he respected and needed; and Nesselrode, a man willing to lend his diplomatic skill wholeheartedly for the good of the empire.

None of the men around Nicholas, so far as he knew, held any views that would compromise his aim: "We must move in step with the century, but we must do so prudently." [4] He wanted Russia to profit from contemporary knowledge and technology, but without succumbing to novel political ideas. He adhered to autocracy because he believed that it was "in keeping with the character" of his people, while constitutional monarchy was "a government of lies, of fraud and corruption." He made it clear that he would not equivocate: he would "withdraw as far as China" rather than ever adopt a constitution.[5]

This attitude was not an unusual one in nineteenth century Europe, where dozens of rulers were absorbed in the effort to hold back the tide of constitutionalism. What distinguished Nicholas from the others was the personal stamp he put on his reign, a stamp that some have interpreted as that of an "educated Peter the Great." No one ever became better acquainted with the personal attributes that Nicholas believed himself to possess and the manner in which he proposed to use them in discharging his obligations than Alexander Benckendorff, who, after he had risen to a post of importance in the government, made a cogent evaluation of them in one of his reports— shaded perhaps by his wish to please but nonetheless basically accurate:

The Russian emperor needs only intellect, firmness, and will, and our sovereign possesses these qualities in abundance. . . .

In the eyes of the educated classes and of the people, the most appreciated qualities of the sovereign are: his aptitude for administration, his devotion to justice, his determination to see everything for himself, to know all, and to end abuses, to punish the guilty, and to reward good deeds . . . demonstrating to the bureaucrats and to the people, as the latter put it, that *the eye of the earthly god watches over them like God Himself.*[6]

Because he felt himself to be in the position of a general operating in unfamiliar territory where many of the widespread operations were in the hands of untested subordinates, Nicholas intended that headquarters be the source of all directives and that he be kept intimately aware of all conditions and every maneuver in every sector under his command. Headquarters, it soon became evident, was to be His Majesty's Imperial Chancellery. Originally established as a bureau to deal with matters of the tsar's immediate and personal concerns, the chancellery had been a relatively inconsequential body until Nicholas came to power; but he soon saw advantages in making it a kind of superministry through which he could exercise command personally and directly, conveniently disregarding established channels.

As no good general would condone imprecision or confusion in the regulations under which his forces operate, so Nicholas felt that he could not condone the irregularities to be found in the Russian laws under which his government was to operate. One of his first acts was to establish the Second Section of His Majesty's Imperial Chancellery for the specific purpose of putting the rules of government on a sound and equitable basis. This he expected to be accomplished not by the making of new laws but by the placing of "the old ones on a firm foundation"; that is, by a thorough analysis and proper codification—tasks at which ten commissions had failed since the last codification, in 1649. At his order, the Second Section began the work with vigor and spirit under the direction and close supervision of Michael Speransky. It was an arduous undertaking: in the nearly two centuries since the last codification, some laws had fallen into disuse, some had been promulgated in flagrant contradiction to existing laws, and some had never been published even though enforced. With the tsar pressing for results, the work proceeded with remarkable speed (Speransky being favored, of course, by his experience with Alexander's abortive efforts at such reform). The first volume of the new collection of laws was issued in 1828; five years later, the last of the forty-eight volumes appeared, along with a fifteen-volume digest of the laws in force.

While Speransky's work was under way, Nicholas proceeded with further plans in support of the command he had undertaken. To be sure that his personal mandate be carried out exactly where and how he chose, he knew that he needed a large body of men unhampered by red tape and directly responsible to him.

The practicality of such an executive force, especially for the detection of subversion, appealed to General Benckendorff, who, as chief of staff of the guards under Alexander, had been one of the first to recognize and warn of the revolutionary danger; he was glad to propose a scheme. He would have the tsar create a new ministry to administer all the operations of his special emissaries, for a ministry, he pointed out, would provide the centralization necessary to put an end to the fragmented and inefficient police system that Alexander had permitted to exist. Benckendorff had a further suggestion for improvement: since the police, especially the political police, had been attracting men of low character both as officials and agents and had therefore earned an unsavory reputation for "interesting" activities unbecoming to public protectors, some reform was needed, a general grooming of the whole system to insure that it command public respect and trust. This, he proposed, could be achieved through a corps of gendarmes organized in military fashion, provided with distinguishing uniforms and directed by former military officers selected for their good character and fidelity to regulations.

Nicholas was not taken by the idea of establishing a ministry of police—he was not partial to any kind of ministries—and he rejected it. But he accepted the idea of a corps and set about making it a very important part of his magnificent dream. He saw such a body as a personal instrument of firm and enlightened autocracy, a group of dedicated men who would protect the throne from subversion and the people from abuse—a combination of political police and inspectors. Eager to get his program under way and mindful of the difficulties he would encounter if he should attempt to initiate it through existing agencies, he acted directly and without delay: on his birthday, June 26, 1826, he decreed the establishment of the new arm of administration—the Corps of Gendarmes. To administer it, he added another section to his chancellery, then placed both this "Third Section" and the Corps under Benckendorff's command.

Paradoxically enough, in this position, which the tsar conceived as the center of authoritarian administration, Benckendorff's almost complete lack of authoritarian qualities proved to be the essence of his effectiveness. A typical aristocratic guards officer whose good manners and good French were more noteworthy than either his mental acumen or his alertness, he seemed the opposite of the popularly conceived "brutal" political police officer (his second-in-command, Leonty Dubbelt, was a more faithful version). Yet he proved to be the very man to do what Nicholas wanted done. He understood the significance of the gesture when the tsar, counseling him on his new duties, gave him a handkerchief and advised, "Wipe away as many tears as possible with this handkerchief. There—you have my directive!" [7] Moreover, he had an almost reverential attitude toward autocracy, and he was anxious to invest his talents in its service. Like Nicholas himself, Benckendorff had a gift for orderly planning and a passion for painstakingly detailed work. He would be undaunted by the intricacies of the machine under his control, and he would use it as directed. He would also give the arbitrary authority of the Third Section a soft-gloved aspect that would be of some advantage in getting people to accept what the autocrat intended for their common good.

Allowed to put his own proposal into effect, Benckendorff organized the corps as a military body. With the authority of the tsar behind him, he soon had its officers chosen, most of them formerly guards officers and all from respected families. Its units of enlisted men were promptly instructed in routine, drilled, and prepared for immediate action in cases of public disturbances, and all of them fitted out in trim sky-blue uniforms—which, in due course, won for them the ironic sobriquet "blue archangels."

Nicholas now had the instrument for his personal command. Through its regional offices in the major cities, the corps was expected to act as the eyes, the ears, and the good right hand of the tsar. To his subjects, its functions were readily seen to be virtually unlimited. It sampled public opinion, received petitions, examined complaints, prepared cases against dishonest officials and brutal landlords, harried judges to make decisions on long-pending cases, intervened in judicial proceedings if there seemed to be reason to do so, kept watch on persons suspected of subversion or religious heresy, supervised the operation of political prisons, and arrested and exiled "suspicious and dangerous persons." All information on these matters was collected from the gendarme offices and collated by the Third Section, supplemented by information from its own agents, and periodically reported to the tsar so that he would be always up-to-date on the tone of public opinion and the state of the empire.

Within three years of its establishment, the corps, according to Benckendorff, was fulfilling its promise. He reported to the tsar: *"The gendarmerie has become moral physician to the people. To it each comes with his ailments and despair."* [8] His hyperbole had some basis in fact: the corps was ministering to certain needs of the people through its arrests of some corrupt officials and its actions against some brutal landlords. Soon, however, its service was found by many to be provided at an unconscionable price—their submission to intrusion on privacy and their forfeit of a number of customary privileges.

The concept of the corps of gendarmes as a "moral physician" fitted well into Nicholas' dream, as did also a corollary concept provided in a statement by Dubbelt, that "men of learning should function like pharmacists . . . and dispense learning only according to the prescription of the government." [9] With that, the figure of speech was neatly completed: the corps was the "moral physician"; other agencies, the "pharmacists."

That Dubbelt singled out education as an agency that should "dispense . . . according to the prescription of the government" was not fortuitous; like all in the circle close to the tsar, he knew that education was a subject of official concern and that he was stating the approved view of it. In fact, Nicholas believed that education was a *primary* concern of a "wise and enlightened government," and that a country's "prosperity" as well as its "tranquility" was determined by the direction given to education.[10]

Much as the tsar would have liked to begin giving that direction at once, he was delayed because there was at hand no suitable man to take over the ministry of education and carry out his anticipated program. The incumbent minister, aging Admiral Alexander Shishkov, lacked the necessary vigor. When he finally bowed out, in 1828, the tsar replaced him with General Paul Lieven, a man with likely qualifications for the work but who, being ill at ease with new ideas and having none of his own, proved a disappointment. Fortune finally favored the tsar, however, through the man he chose to succeed Lieven, in 1833: Sergei Uvarov, president of the Academy of Sciences and a recent assistant in the ministry of education.

Uvarov was just the man to make education an ordered adjunct of the other elements of the magnificent dream despite his not being a military man, as were most of Nicholas' choices for high position, and despite his having shown intellectual interests of a distinctly cosmopolitan, rather than national, bent. He was brilliant, enterprising and—to the particular advantage of Nicholas' program—not overcritical about ends or means, once he took up a course that offered the personal rewards he required. His vanity was sufficient to support his conviction that, through education, he could accomplish what the tsar wanted: the improvement of Russian youth through methods that would insure their resistance to "improper ideas" in a world beset by political upheavals. He readily adopted the attitude of those who believed Russia to be "young and virginal," resilient enough to repulse revolution if properly directed. And he gratuitously proposed the strategy for the whole undertaking. It would be necessary, he declared, not only to safeguard both the youth and their elders from the pernicious influence of alien ideas but also to reinforce throughout society "the truly Russian conservative principles of Orthodoxy, autocracy, and nationality." [11]

With those words, "Orthodoxy, autocracy, and nationality," Uvarov touched the heart of the tsar. What a slogan to counter the despicable "liberty, fraternity, and equality"! True, as the distinguished Russian historian Sergei Solovev has pointed out, there was a bit of duplicity in each item of Uvarov's triplicity: "Orthodoxy—being himself an atheist, not believing in Christ even in the Protestant manner; autocracy—being himself a liberal; nationality—not having read a single Russian book in his life and always writing in either French or German." [12] Yet Uvarov's words came to symbolize the impulse of Russian autocratic rule.

That his expressions were of such significance was accepted as a matter of course by Uvarov, who saw himself watching not only over education but also over the very "soul of the age." [13] Nicholas approved and abetted this self-satisfaction, later bestowing the title of count on Uvarov and permitting him to adopt "Orthodoxy, autocracy, and nationality" as his family motto.

Caught up in his new minister's patriotic fervor, Nicholas was moved to add to the imperial idiom by giving the country a new national anthem. The one he adopted—its words by Vasily Zhukovsky and its stirring music by Alexis Lvov—was to serve to the end of the empire:

> God save the Tsar!
> Mighty and powerful,
> May he in glory reign over us,
> Reign that our foes may quake.
> O Orthodox Tsar!
> God save the Tsar!

Uvarov's conversion to the imperial dream was so apparently wholehearted that, for sixteen years, he was able to retain the favor of the tsar and his commission as tutelary of the "soul of the age." To insure that the prescriptions of the government be administered properly to the youth of the land, he increased the already considerable central authority over the entire educational system and increased the number of curators and inspectors. The aim was to turn out ideally prepared young Russians untouched by "misleading" thoughts, and there was no phase of the process outside the strict authority of his ministry.

Soon ambitious activities were under way, particularly in the area of higher education, and some of them resulted in favorably changed conditions. Professors judged incompetent were pensioned off; the salaries of those retained were raised—in some cases, tripled; new professional chairs were established; new scholarly societies were created. Able young scholars and scientists were encouraged in many ways; some of them were sent to study in Germany in order that they might avail themselves of the best in enlightened education and return to share it in the homeland; some were given hitherto unavailable advantages at home—in the first advanced school of technology (the Technological Institute of St. Petersburg) and other new professional schools; others were favored with new research facilities, such as the modern astronomical observatory built at Pulkovo, outside the capital.

Along with the provision for such progressive developments in the field of education went the requirement that all of them be made to contribute in some way to the advancement of "Orthodoxy, autocracy, and nationality." On the whole, it was considered unnecessary to specify separate courses of study for these essential concerns, since they were so overlapped and interdependent as now interpreted that, strictly speaking, they could not be considered separately; every subject was expected to take them into account. However, certain courses were understood to be more effective in emphasizing one or another of them.

Teachers of Russian history were to use the evidence of the country's past as proof that the Russian Orthodox Church and the autocratic monarchy—particularly as represented by the Romanovs—had been the basic elements of Russian greatness and that the Romanovs alone could now guarantee future greatness for the fatherland. The approach was to be direct and unequivocal. The Moscow University professor Michael Pogodin, zealous champion of the Nicholas system, was following the approved formula when he pronounced Russia a unique country, heir to vast physical and spiritual forces combined in a "gigantic machine . . . directed by the hand of a single man, the Russian Tsar . . . the earthly god." All literary fields were considered perfect areas for the proper analysis of Russian life. The sciences, it was pointed out, could be given purpose by assigning them their proper places in the achievement of the national aims.

As for "nationality," it came to be understood as such an all-encompassing idea that it was not expected to *be included* anywhere; rather it *included*—not just courses, but the whole educational process, the whole country, and, to some, the whole Slavic world. The idea of nationality became a magnification of the tsar, the Russian cultural heritage, and a utopian future. Encouraged in the schools, through the press, and by public word, it was taken up rapidly and spread widely. Everywhere, for a time, it seemed to breed extravagant expressions of faith and dedication: patriots became poets, and poets became patriots. Few could match the flourishes of Michael Pogodin—whose reputation for cleverness with words, after all, antedated his present prestige as the first *bona fide* professor of Russian history—but many approved his sentiment: "Russia, a miracle! The Russian people, a miracle! The Russian language, a miracle! The Russian stove which bakes bread in its own manner, a miracle! Russian history, a miracle! . . . One can only stand in awe at the wonder of it all and cross oneself!" [14]

Nicholas Gogol rhapsodized on Russian wit as "the purest virgin gold"; on a chance Russian word of personal description, as a "passport to be carried throughout eternity." [15] There seemed no end to fervent laudation. Large or small, if a thing was Russian, it was marvelous.

Small wonder that Nicholas was encouraged for a time to believe that he was succeeding where Alexander had failed, in winning over the minds of his educated public, and that he could anticipate the realization of his dream. Wherever he went, he was cheered; when he spoke, he was favored by rapt attention. Patriotic operas such as Glinka's *A Life for the Tsar* drew enthusiastic audiences. Newspapers vied with one another in their adulation of the present representative of the House of Romanov. It was seriously proposed that all Russians be designated as "Romanovites." The Third Section's reports, although noting the persistence of attitudes that had produced the Decembrists, indicated that the battle for the educated mind was going well. Uvarov reported the devotion he found in teachers and students alike, the "exaltation" he evoked by mentioning in university classrooms "the person of the Monarch" or commenting on the need for "loyalty to Throne and Church." [16]

That there be no question of overlooking the basic and immutable elements of the Russian Orthodox religion in the educational process, the study of it was made compulsory and supplemented by required courses in Russian Orthodox Church history and canon law in the universities—all designed to sanctify "the entire temple of popular education."

Under the leadership of Seraphim, the Metropolitan of St. Petersburg, the Orthodox Church itself, ever the supporter of tsar and fatherland, lent its strength to that of Uvarov's organization in anticipation of a new day for Russia, now guided by "the most Orthodox sovereign . . . since the days of Fedor Alexeievich." [17] Encouraged to reassert its authority, it stirred once more with militancy in a coordinated effort to counteract what its leaders considered undesirable developments that had been condoned during Alexander's reign. The results were far-reaching: the Russian Bible Society was closed; permission to translate the Bible from Church Slavonic into vernacular Russian was denied; and, in order to safeguard "the Orthodox faith of our forefathers," an end was put to the semilegal tolerance of sects and groups, such as the Old Believers and Dukhobors, that had once been in the Church. In addition, missionary efforts were intensified, particularly among the Jews, whom Nicholas viewed as a "harmful element," and among the people of the western provinces, where the Uniats (who for more than two centuries had been recognizing the headship of the Pope while they still used the Orthodox ritual and Church Slavonic) were looked upon as possibly redeemable excommunicants.

The link between the Church and the ministry of education was strengthened when, three years after Uvarov's appointment, one of his assistants, Nicholas Protasov, was appointed over-procurator of the Holy Synod. In him, the tsar had both another sympathetic supporter and another military man in a powerful office; Protasov was a colonel in the hussars and would soon be promoted to general. It appeared that the elements of the magnificent dream were coalescing auspiciously.

The tendrils of Uvarov's influence reached out into yet another area: censorship. His ministry's chief censorship administration was charged with barring the appearance in domestic publication of anything that seemed politically or morally objectionable as well as prohibiting the importation of foreign books deemed subversive. The diligence and vigilance of its personnel, easily matching that of Alexander's censors, resulted in denial of entry to works of such "undesirables" as Thomas Jefferson, Ralph Waldo Emerson, Lamartine, Stendhal, Balzac, Sand, Hugo, Gautier, Heine, Fourier, and Cabet, as well as all works dealing with "those non-Russian fraternities," the Jesuits and Masons. For some time, the busy censors did not realize that "they shall not enter!" was actually a challenge to some potential readers and that official lists and figures were not the final evidence on what all Russians were reading: smuggling was as fine an art as censoring.

As the three concepts—Orthodoxy, autocracy, and nationality—were translated into measures that touched virtually every phase of Russian life, there was no doubt that they expressed the official political doctrine of Nicholas' reign. That doctrine, which has gone into historical record as "official nationalism," remained the guiding light of tsarism as long as the Romanov dynasty lasted, barring a brief obscurity immediately after Nicholas' death and a limited shading after 1905.

Though Nicholas trusted the chief administrators he chose to get his system under way—Speransky to sift and sort the laws, Uvarov to wrestle with the "soul of the age," and Benckendorff to oversee the disposition of everything caught in the net of the Third Section—he did not at any time resign his personal responsibilities. Rather, like the "earthly god" he strove to be, he assumed responsibilities never before assumed by a tsar, apparently trying to be omnipresent; continually on the move, continually probing in likely and unlikely places, he succeeded at creating the desired impression. He might arrive unexpectedly in any office, school, hospital, barracks, or construction site and subject it to the "dragoon survey": without waiting for formalities, he would order a quick marshaling of details or explanations, observe the proceedings, and be on his way again, leaving a number of sobered—and probably shaken—subjects in the wake of a critical inspection. Wherever there was trouble of any kind, from official polemics to riot or epidemic, the tsar was likely to be on hand. When the cholera epidemic of 1830–31 was at its height in Moscow, he hurried to the city and for ten days worked to organize facilities and provide help for the victims. Later, in St. Petersburg, when the epidemic drove thousands of frightened and desperate people to riot in the streets, he rode into the thick of the crowds and, as if by the very force of his presence, restored order.

Throughout the country, his six-foot-three figure became a familiar, if not always welcome, sight: in the cities, striding along the streets, acquainting himself with the commonplaces of life; elsewhere, driving at breakneck speed ("breakneck" being all but literal when one carriage upset cost him a broken collarbone) along the miserable roads of the provincial countryside or stopping here and there to question, advise, and judge. Welcome or not, his presence was always impressive. In the words of Andrew D. White, attaché of the American legation in St. Petersburg: "He overawed all men by his presence. . . . Whenever I saw him . . . there was forced to my lips the thought 'You are the most majestic being ever created.' Colossal in stature; with a face such as one finds on a Greek coin, but overcast with a shadow of Muscovite melancholy; with a bearing dignified, but a manner not unkind, he bore himself like a god." [18]

As Nicholas made himself known to his subjects, they came to understand—and many came to respect—the guiding philosophy of his administration: a place for everyone and everyone in his place; to each his merited reward or his deserved punishment. He rewarded the loyal and efficient by praise, gifts of money and land, titles (to deserving nobles), or chivalric honors such as the Order of St. Vladimir. The disloyal or inefficient he rebuked, dismissed, or ordered into the guardhouse, prison, or exile.

He recognized no exceptions in his scheme of orderliness, not even in his own family, where each, as a member of the House of Romanov, had a select and exacting duty. The names of his four sons were ordered repetitions of his father's four sons': Alexander, Constantine, Nicholas, Michael. He planned their lives in all details that he considered essential to the propriety of their positions as grand dukes. He did not expect, of course, to control the destiny of Alexander, his oldest son—who would, by the law of succession, become the next tsar—but he could and did see that his preparation was consonant with the prospect. When the heir was six, his routine activities and physical training were put into the hands of Colonel Karl Merder. A staff of personal tutors and instructors was gradually assembled to direct him in all phases of what Nicholas considered the proper education of a tsar-to-be. Alexander, somewhat emotional and erratic in his attention to work, was never more than average in his studies, nor did he ever develop the perfection expected in his military exercises. But Nicholas insisted that the tutors get the best possible effort from him and was reasonably satisfied with the results. For the three other sons, the tsar made choices. Constantine would represent the family in the navy: in his fourth year, he was given officially the rank of general admiral, which predetermined for him an adult life of responsibility for all imperial naval operations. Nicholas would follow his father in the military engineers. Michael would take the artillery as his field.

As his reign advanced, the tsar's obsession with the notion that the rules and regulations of military life were universal guides to proper administration became ever stronger. Explaining it to the eminent German journalist Louis Schneider, he said: "Among soldiers and in the midst of their activities, I feel completely and totally happy. . . . Here there is order; strict, complete legality; no impertinence or contradicting; here all things fit together properly. Here no one commands before he has learned to obey. Here no one gets ahead of any-one without justification, and everything is subordinated to a specified goal." [19]

He favored uniforms over mufti because they were neat and because they clearly identified a man's status, rank, and branch of service. He therefore ordered most of the country's civil servants and students into uniforms and issued elaborate new regulations on the dress of court officials, making green the predominant color and carefully distinguishing one grade from another. His passion for the regulated appearance extended also to personal grooming: he required all military officers to grow mustaches and to fashion them after the handsome and luxuriant one he had grown since becoming tsar, forbade them to wear beards, and denied to civil servants and court officials the right to wear either.

To insure the desired tone in the conduct of affairs with which he was most closely involved, he created a personal military suite, to which he gave the rather grand name of "Imperial Headquarters." Its personnel included, at first, generals adjutant (full generals designated for honorary rank by the tsar) and aides-de-camp (subalterns selected from members of the imperial family and the upper nobility); later, an additional category, generals *à la suite*. All were to attend the tsar on ceremonial occasions; at other times, they might pursue their regular duties or be assigned to special ones. The various aides-de-camp served periodic terms as personal attendants of the tsar, and any member of the suite might expect, as a confidant of the tsar, to be sent on private missions, collecting information for him perhaps or carrying secret communications. The generals might be given command of important task forces, such as punitive expeditions, or be appointed to governor-generalships. Thus, its members serving him in their several capacities, the Imperial Headquarters became a vital part of Nicholas' highly personal government. And, like so many features of tsarist administration, once established, it could be expected to become an accepted feature in succeeding reigns.

Since Nicholas valued the qualities of military men—toughness, commitment to duty, and self-confidence—over those he recognized in most civilians, he chose as many of his government officials as possible from the military services. At one time, ten of his thirteen ministers were generals. Even the minister of the navy, Prince Alexander Menshikov, was a cavalry general. In fact, it would have been difficult to avoid generals in official circles. With General Kleinmichel as the powerful chief of communications, General Volkonsky as chief of the recently formed ministry of the imperial court, General Vasilchikov as chairman of the State Council, and General Protasov as over-procurator of the Holy Synod, popular reference to the central government as "the general command" was understandable. The same might have been applied to provincial governments and educational districts, where dozens of generals were to be found among the governors and curators.

To a man like Nicholas, there could be no question of postponing attention to the military strength of the country. Recognizing the need for certain improvements, he got them under way forthwith and, in a surprisingly short time, began to see encouraging results.

Sometimes the results were achieved under the direction of men who, to any judge besides the tsar, might have appeared quite unqualified for their assignments. The work of Prince Menshikov as minister of the navy was a case in point. He was well known among aristocrats and diplomats for his social polish and caustic wit, and he was respected as a cavalry general. But he was wholly unfamiliar with ships and sailors and possessed no obvious talents that would qualify him to restore a navy that had been drifting for years in the wake of contemporary standards. Yet Nicholas recognized in him many of his own characteristics and, knowing him personally as a man of integrity and enterprise, assigned him to the task. He was not disappointed: within a few months, the new minister had made himself sufficiently conversant with naval affairs to have started a program of repair and reform that extended through the whole navy.

Menshikov took as much pride as the tsar himself in seeing the fleet brought back to full strength; ships of the line, frigates, corvettes, or brigs—he admired "every trim hull and every gallant sail." He even went beyond restoration, having several small ships fitted with steam, naval fortifications strengthened, and a number of useful voyages undertaken. Under his direction, the navy finally provided an attractive career for able and energetic men.

The army, much the senior service, seemed to the tsar to require only reinvigoration. Reviewing its performance against the enemy forces it had met during the first five years of his reign, neither he nor his advisers saw anything inherently wrong with it. Its general organization and training programs were functioning smoothly. He had approved certain features of the military colonies inherited from Alexander I and, after some serious riots among the colonists during the cholera epidemic of the early 1830's, had ordered reforms that would make them, he hoped, satisfactory adjuncts of the units under conventional training.

All that he asked of any system was that it produce genuine soldiers of rigid uniformity—and, as he saw them, such soldiers he now had. In the well-trained ranks each infantryman marched with precision, each cavalryman rode as one with his splendid mount. The officers also were faithful to the standards he approved: on parade, they were a magnificent sight, a martial symphony of spruce tailoring, lustrous leather, and the traditional richness of epaulettes, aiguillettes, stars, eagles, and gleaming saber hilts—all set to the rhythmic flourish of plumes, pelisses, and proud regimental colors. When a unit moved, 2,500 men to the line, smartly and faultlessly across Palace Square, as they often did, observers could easily subscribe to the tsar's opinion: the scene was a "sight for the gods." As basic aids to the army's observable assets, brilliance and bigness, Nicholas had the Military Academy instituted for higher officers, new cadet schools opened for officer training, and a system of reserve troops begun. In this area he had no qualms about the probity of his judgment or the sufficiency of his foresight.

It was one of the chief pleasures the tsar derived from his position that he could—indeed, was expected to—give much time to military matters. There were the long conferences with agreeably punctilious Prince Alexander Chernyshev, whom he had appointed minister of war in 1832; attendance at parades, drills, and reviews; and the duty he found most exhilarating, that of inspecting the various military units. In addition there was the periodical selection of recruits for the guards regiments: for example, snub-nosed men for the Pavlovsky Guards, as specified by snub-nosed Tsar Paul; tall ones for the Preobrazhensky; handsome ones for the Semenovsky; dark-haired and light-complexioned ones for the Ismailovsky. In all this, Nicholas involved himself directly, attentive to every detail, taking over command at parades if dissatisfied with their conduct, constantly planning improvements. He was particularly proud of his ability to lend practical assistance at times—as when he designed a tunic with six instead of nine buttons or when he wrote out the steps for a military drill scene in the ballet "Revolt in the Harem" (at the same time, prudently replacing the word *revolt* by a less repugnant one, *unrest*).

Although Nicholas was constantly on the move and although he expected, and was generally given, almost filial respect and public devotion, he was no mere peripatetic paterfamilias. He made a deter-

mined effort to know and understand the problems of his realm and
to do something about them.

He kept a close check on everything published in the country, including the fifty-odd periodicals and all the new books—the latter, it
was alleged by some, being fewer in number than the official censors.
When he had any comments on the literary merits, political flavor, or
general import of what he read, he passed them on to the authors. If
he judged a work, either in print or in manuscript, to be of undesirable subject matter or suggestive of subversion, he would order what
he considered appropriate chastisement for the writer. His disapproval of Michael Lermontov's poem on the death of Pushkin, for
example, resulted in the author's being court-martialed and banished
from the St. Petersburg Hussars to a line regiment in the Caucasus.
He found particularly offensive the poet's reference to antiliberals as
the "hangmen of our freedom, genius, and renown." On the other
hand, he showed an approving interest in many men of letters; sometimes out of admiration, as in the case of Vasily Zhukovsky, whom he
chose to instruct the Grand Duke Alexander in the general virtues
and refinements lacking in the traditional military training; sometimes out of a mixture of respect and expediency, such as he had
shown in the case of men like Pushkin and Griboedov, who would be
less likely to be dispensing undesirable ideas, he hoped, if held close
to the throne with emoluments or favors. For a time, many writers
responded amicably.

Imperial favor included also those concerned with the other arts.
Directing that no expense be spared, Nicholas encouraged the production in the imperial theaters of dramatic innovations both unconventional and daring. He personally liked the new, romantically styled
plays like N. V. Kukolnik's *The Hand of the All-highest Saved the
Fatherland*, which was little more than a paean to autocracy; but he
was often willing to accept the still newer, boldly realistic ones (if adequately edited to remove "undesirable" passages), such as Griboedov's
hitherto forbidden *The Trouble with Reason* and Gogol's *The Inspector General*, as well as the realistic acting of the popular M. S.
Shchepkin. He liked the new trend in music, the effort to compose
truly Russian music, even though much of the best of it—Michael
Glinka's, for instance—drew themes and styles from folk literature
and melodies, not from imperial glories. He was willing to have the
Academy of Art encourage such painters as A. G. Venetsianov as he
turned away from traditional sources, the Bible and history, and tried
to paint realistically the subjects he found among the peasants; or,

later, Paul Fedotov, whose realistic paintings were clearly critical commentaries on men and methods understood to have imperial favor. Since he considered architecture a refinement of his favorite "creative" skill, engineering, he took a direct interest in it. Some, it is true, deplored his preference for a fussy imitation of the old Muscovite style, which he impressed on a generation by decreeing that no new churches or government buildings be designed without his approval. Others welcomed his interest and applauded his defense of the traditional.

When Nicholas observed the general swell of intellectual activity, he could not but take a personal pride in it. There had never before been anything like it in Russia, and he interpreted it as an agreeable return on his efforts to disseminate cultural advantages. He was especially pleased to learn that more people were reading books than ever before. The fact that the majority were content with translations from the French, such as Eugène Sue's *The Mysteries of Paris* and *The Wandering Jew*, or Osip Senkovsky's light, romantic fiction written under the pseudonym of Baron Brambeus, was not a matter of concern to him: after all, they were "safe" books. Wherever he turned, he could see what he believed to be evidence that his program was succeeding. More people were attending the theater; men of letters were becoming able for the first time in the country's history to maintain themselves by writing; journalists were gaining in importance, some of them advancing to the status of press lords like Nicholas Grech and Faddei Bulgarin, who enjoyed gentry incomes from their popular *Northern Bee*. Most of what he saw Nicholas was able to pronounce "good."

The tsar's assessment had the unqualified ratification of Uvarov, who stated in the report of his first ten years as minister: "Under my leadership the ministry of education has stood the test of time and circumstance, has shown itself to be the guarantor of security, the guardian of order, and the reliable physician for incidental troubles." [20]

In short, official nationalism, in the estimation of its sponsors, was proving itself to be the doctrine par excellence for Russia.

While Nicholas could take comfort in his belief that most of his upper-class subjects were now turning their minds into politically safe and beneficial channels, he knew that the country's basic problems were not being solved thereby. They were, of course, his own responsibility: he would not have wanted the situation otherwise.

Yet he understood that many of the undertakings essential to the solution of these problems had perforce to be initiated slowly, particularly if they involved deeply entrenched customs and classes— as most of them did.

He strongly believed that the provision of honest and just government was fundamental to any extensive effort at reform. That was a belief supported by the wise counsel of his late, revered mentor Nicholas Karamzin, and he intended to act on it. He decreed changes and set standards that he expected to lead directly to improvements. He increased salaries at all levels of the bureaucracy, provided training for civil servants in the universities and other higher schools, and depended on the Third Section to see that ordered corrections were carried out. In St. Petersburg and Moscow he could observe enough progress for a time to satisfy him that a good beginning was under way. In the central offices of the government, a minister or high official who took bribes or dipped into the till soon became a rarity. And the old-fashioned, underpaid, semiliterate government clerks (such as Gogol described in "The Overcoat"), with their shabby clothes smelling of cheap liquor and cheaper tobacco, who would not move a finger until receiving that "sinless revenue," a tip, were being replaced by clerks who took pride in their uniforms and their work and regarded offers of tips or bribes as insults.

He wanted also to assure his people of personal well-being, and he included both the landed nobility and the peasants in this component of his dream. Here he was hampered, of course, as others had been before him, by the imperial commitment to the traditional view of the nobility as one of the pillars on which the throne rested. But he did what he felt that he safely could do. He supported the nobles by continuing to provide them with easy credit, meanwhile admonishing them—fruitlessly—to use the borrowed money for productive ends. He made some recognition of their wish to become a closed caste by making it more difficult to achieve noble status. He increased their educational advantages, notably by the establishment of the Imperial School of Law, to which only nobles were admitted. He provided crown lands east of the Volga upon which the impoverished of their number could resettle.

At the same time Nicholas did all that he thought feasible for the serfs and other peasants. It was his belief that, for moral as well as practical reasons, serfdom had to be abolished, and the time for action would come either in his reign or in the one following. He was determined, however, to proceed with what he considered the necessary circumspection, for he believed that premature emancipation could ruin the nobles by precipitously cutting off their supply of labor. Moreover, if word got out to the serfs that a change was being considered, they might rashly try to take their freedom before the government was ready to offer it. As it was, he had been forced to deal with a number of disturbances among them; minor and scattered though they were, he shuddered at the thought of their growth and spread. He planned to prepare the way for emancipation by gradual, "imperceptible" means such as increased protection of serf rights and the encouragement of nobles to permit serfs to buy both freedom and land. Alexander had anticipated him in these ideas, but Nicholas worked with greater energy.

He successively established nine secret committees to study the problem of serfs and other peasants, and he issued more legislation on behalf of them than all his predecessors put together. To lessen their personal hardships, he forbade such practices as the exile of serfs to Siberia, the sale of serfs without land, and the breaking up of serf families by sale. But he was not ready to make any basic changes in the system by which they were bound.

With the state peasants, he could proceed with less restraint and perhaps set an example for the serf-owning nobles. As in other instances when he wanted to keep his hand directly on developments, he at first created another section of his chancellery and assigned it the duty of handling the affairs of the state peasants. Then, a year later, in 1837, he reorganized it as the ministry of state lands, which he placed under the direction of Count Paul Kiselev.

The new minister was faced by problems of staggering number and variety, involving as they did some twenty million peasants and nearly five hundred million acres of state lands. But he was a genuinely concerned man who throve on practical problems, a man Nicholas could admire in spite of his former association with such liberals as Pestel. Kiselev set out at once to do something that had not been seriously attempted before: to improve the life of the state peasants as much as possible, not merely to squeeze revenue from them. The initial activity he managed to stir up among them suggested that he might be successful. With government encouragement and assistance, thousands of peasants began moving to more fertile areas, some began trying out new crops (potatoes, in particular), young peasants enrolled in newly established schools to learn new methods of farming and handicraft, and some began moving from overcrowded rural areas to the cities to find work and improve their lot. Nicholas had reason to believe that he was finally "admitting some light into the dark chamber of serfdom."

At the same time, he was taking action on conditions affecting others among his subjects who—by their own standards, at least—were disadvantaged. To provide improvement for certain individuals between the established upper and lower levels of society and to make amends for his putting noble status out of reach of those who might have aspired to it, he had ordered that a class of "honorary citizens" be legally recognized. It would include some men of learning, merchants, scientists, and children of clergymen—all of them qualified by their new classification for relief from such onerous liabilities as the payment of poll tax, corporal punishment, and recruitment for military service.

In the one field where he did not trust his own competence at first, the national economy, Nicholas felt that he had chosen an outstanding deputy, Minister of Finance Kankrin. For seventeen years he judged that official's excellence sufficient reason for suffering his eccentricities. If Kankrin could keep the currency sound and the imperial budget in balance, the tsar could tolerate even his distressingly "undisciplined" attire, which in winter gave him the appearance of a *farceur* in motley—a voluminous gray cape, flapping green scarf, plumed hat, and bulky felt boots. He particularly appreciated the fact that no general disarrangement of the country's economy was suggested in Kankrin's program. Industry, for instance, was not to be pushed, juggled, patterned, or pampered. The minister's theory was that it should expand only in response to market demands. Since Russian industry was meeting demands, it should not be artificially stimulated, that is, supported by such means as government loans and government underwriting of frequent industrial exhibitions.

Nicholas applauded also Kankrin's personal attention to the details of administration, which could descend to the miserliness of requiring clerks to reuse old envelopes; he even accepted, without becoming unduly ruffled, Kankrin's judgment that 11,000 rubles was an excessive salary for one of Tsesarevich Alexander's teachers.

One of the tsar's rare disagreements with Kankrin's judgment came in 1835, when the Austrian promotor Franz von Gerstner requested permission to build a railroad network in Russia. Kankrin, speaking for the majority of the Committee of Ministers, opposed the request on the grounds that railroads would serve no economic purpose and that, moreover, they would not only encourage unnecessary travel but also actually undermine society by bringing the classes into close contact. The tsar accepted the majority view, but with misgivings. His fondness for engineering experiment was stirred by the idea of building railroads; in fact, he and General Kleinmichel had already discussed it on several occasions. He could see that railroads might expedite his plans for Russia's future, possibly being of some military value as well as providing general convenience. So, while denying Gerstner's request, he permitted him, under the supervision of General Kleinmichel, to build an experimental sixteen-mile line from St. Petersburg to Tsarskoe Selo. Then, so pleased was he with the result that, over Kankrin's further objection, he ordered a line built between the two capitals. When this one was completed (in 1851), he directed the construction of yet another, to extend from St. Petersburg to Warsaw.

Nicholas supplemented these steps in the development of communications by promoting two further noteworthy achievements: the setting up of the first Russian electric telegraph line and the construction of many new highways. Thus he made at least a beginning in shortening the distances that made the administration of his sprawling empire so difficult.

To expend so much energy on such a variety of domestic activities and still to keep firm control of a watchful, vigorous, and sometimes enterprising program of foreign affairs was a prodigious feat. But Nicholas, who was fast earning the epithet "The Iron Autocrat," had the stamina for it almost to the end of his reign. He saw no reason that the principles on which he based his plans for the ordered development of Russia could not be applied elsewhere; to that end, he did not hesitate to offer his services—or to impose them if he felt the need to do so.

His position on European affairs was little different from that taken by Alexander I in his later years. Though he was at times more aggressive and less tactful than Alexander in support of it, he maintained it in much the same way: through personal direction, personal deputies, or extraordinary missions operating outside regular channels.

His path was smoothed immeasurably by Count Karl Nesselrode, who had served in Alexander's intimate diplomatic corps and whom Nicholas had invited to continue in charge of foreign relations. Nesselrode, whose modesty, unobtrusiveness, and slight physical build —Metternich dubbed him "the little minister"—set him in striking contrast to the tsar, proved to be the perfect negotiant for Nicholas, who was determined to manage the empire's foreign affairs personally. In both experience and ability, he was well fitted for the task of steering the tsar's diplomatic dealings, too often inconsiderately blunt and peremptory, in such a way as to relieve their offensiveness without changing their intent.

Though ostensibly Nicholas' policy was to support abroad the same principles to which he was pledged domestically in his program of "Orthodoxy, autocracy, and nationality," he had no scruples, in foreign affairs, about changing the evaluation of those elements or adjusting their definition to suit the actions he chose to take, actions that almost always put the maintenance of the existing order above all else. When "nationality" in Western Europe was seen in the 1820's and 1830's to be prompting liberal movements threatening to the old conservative and reactionary regimes, he denounced it unequivocally. Whether it was producing native efforts to unify Italy, to reorganize Germany, to break up the traditional rule in Austria, to free the Belgians from the Dutch, or to restore Poland to the Poles, Nicholas could see it only as a threat to autocracy, which he equated with legitimism in Europe, and he unhesitatingly championed its suppression.

The results were such that, for a time, the empire's foreign relations fitted fairly comfortably into the magnificent dream. In one instance where Russian military measures actually aided the cause of liberalism, the aid was in Nicholas' estimation only an unfortunate by-product: the Greek War for Independence, begun during the preceding reign, was indeed helped by Russia's involvement with the Turks, the oppressors of the Greeks. But Nicholas made it clear that the Russian action did not originate in any liking for the rebels, but in his country's traditional position with respect to the Ottoman empire.

In instances where liberalism triumphed despite the inimical attitude of Russia, Nicholas allowed himself the satisfaction of demonstrative disapproval. When Louis Philippe accepted the authority esablished by the July Revolution (1830) in France, displacing Russia's friend Charles X, the tsar for four months refused to admit the very existence of a French government, expressed open contempt for this "so-called sovereign" who had forsaken his heritage and, after that, continued to behave toward him and his emissaries as if to force the whole situation into inconsequence by his imperial disdain. When Belgian independence of Holland was recognized by other European heads of state, he acknowledged it with reluctance after an extended delay, then for two decades held back final arrangements for regular diplomatic relations with the new state.

The handling of one challenge of the old order, the Polish revolt of 1830–31, fell legitimately within the tsar's authority, and he used every possible means to make his treatment of it an impressive example of how such irregularities should be handled—as well as a reproach, he hoped, to England and France, whose sympathies were with the Poles. Following his futile attempts to reason with the insurgents and the anguish of the early months of military operation against them—the exposure of appalling shortcomings in the equipment and conditioning of the Russian forces, the ignominy of reverses, the death of his beloved brother Constantine and that of campaign leader Field Marshal Diebitsch of cholera—Nicholas set his face toward a direct, fast, and complete purge of this "mutinous insanity." When the Russian forces, under the driving direction of Diebitsch's replacement, Field Marshal Ivan Paskevich, had finally forced the Poles to yield, he personally handled the settlement.

Declaring the nationalistic outburst a "nullification" of all arrangements between Russia and the kingdom of Poland, he abrogated the Polish constitution of 1815, subjugated the country to "Russification" by incorporating it as an "indivisible part" of the Russian empire, and placed it under the viceroyship of Paskevich. At the same time, he ordered that everything possibly contributory to Polish nationalism be confiscated, destroyed, or made subject to imperial surveillance. His agents confiscated books (including whole libraries from institutions of study and research), all personal trappings of former royalty, standards and trophies of the former Polish army, and even such national treasures as the sword of Kosciuszko. The Russian stamp was placed firmly on the revised educational system, local government administration, and all Polish publications. The lands of the Catholic Church were secularized, and its clergy made salaried employees of the state. All of this, according to Nicholas, should be construed as the work, not of an avenger, but of a concerned sovereign: he was simply initiating the Poles directly into the Nicholas system, whereby all imperial subjects were to profit and prosper.

While most of the adversities Nicholas encountered through his European policy during the first part of his reign were temporary and recently incurred irritants, those he encountered in upholding Russia's irregular and still unsettled policy in Eastern affairs were the same old twinges that had plagued the Romanovs from the time of

Tsar Alexis. He recognized little that was new with respect to the time-tattered Eastern Question, that congeries of problems which had accrued to Russia—to all the great powers, in fact—as a result of the progressive decay of the Ottoman empire. He understood that the Western powers were concerned over Russian expansion in Transcaucasia, Central Asia, and the Far East; but, while appreciating the necessity to handle affairs diplomatically in those important areas, he saw nothing alarming.

On the contrary, he could see actual gain and promise of gain almost everywhere, not excepting the Far East, still on the periphery of Russian influence but alive with possibilities. Even when opposition developed, he could for a time count the outcome of practically every encounter as a Russian advantage.

The contest over Georgia, renewed by Persia within six months of his accession, was checked again after a nine-months' war. The resulting Treaty of Turkmanchai gave Russia, in addition to indemnity and commercial concessions, the right to put a fleet on the Caspian Sea and to annex a slice of Armenia as well as the city of Erivan. The Russo-Turkish War of 1828–29, that conflict which in an ostensibly offhand way finally rescued the Greeks from Ottoman tyranny, was at first disheartening to Nicholas, especially so since he was trying personally to advise his high command just when the enemy forces were prevailing; but when General Diebitsch, by a desperate and bold bluff, finally brought the Turks to terms, he forgot the dark days. Russian gains by the Treaty of Adrianople (which ended that war) were extensive: control of the Danube delta and territories in the Caucasus, including a portion of the Black Sea coast; the reaffirmed right of commercial passage through the Straits and of navigation on the Black Sea; and certain rights over the Danubian principalities of Moldavia and Wallachia which, for two decades, made them virtual protectorates of Russia. Then, when relations with the Ottoman empire were reversed four years later by the sultan's reluctant call for Russian aid against his rebellious Egyptian subjects and Russia's eager response, still further advantages were gained at the cost of little effort and less actual assistance. The Treaty of Unkiar Skelessi put Russia in an enviable position—by means of admittedly undiplomatic action on the part of Russia's envoy, Count Alexis Orlov, who attributed the favorable terms to his "caressing them [the Turks] with one hand while crushing them with the other." It bound the two parties to an extravagant pledge of "everlasting" friendship (in impetuous disregard of the fact that the duration of the treaty was specified as eight years) and, by secret clause, assured Russia of Turkey's undertaking to prohibit the entrance of "any foreign vessel of war" into the Straits "under any pretext whatever." Those advantages, though from the outset viewed unfavorably by the Western powers, were enjoyed for eight years. Even when they were reduced—by the Straits Convention of 1841—Russia, being a party to the action, did not need to admit any diplomatic reversal. Rather, as Nicholas was pleased to point out, Russia was now standing with the other powers in regard to the Eastern Question: the convention provided for the *collective defense* of Turkey by Russia, Great Britain, France, Austria, and Prussia. Russia had allies.

Nicholas knew that he was still criticized by certain Western diplomats, particularly in England and France, for being constantly on the cry against any who threatened the old order in the West, though he himself was always ready to violate the status quo in the East. Yet he did not admit to any impropriety in his position: as he reasoned, his Western policy was the same as that he followed in Russia; and if his Eastern policy differed somewhat, that was because it was unavoidably influenced by particular circumstances— not of his making—which affected Russia's future as a great power. In any case, was he guilty of any excesses? Had he not restrained his hand when he might have destroyed Persia in 1828? Had he not asked only for the "key to Russia's door" in 1829 and 1833, when he might have forced greater concessions from the Turks? And now, had he not shown a generous willingness to cooperate with all the other powers—even, against his judgment, with France? Of course, if the infidel Ottoman empire continued to give evidence of expiring in the path of Christian progress—well, that was a possibility that could not be disregarded. He would handle it in due course.

All things considered, by the midpoint of his reign, Nicholas could feel reasonably confident that he would achieve the goal he had set himself: to pass on to his son Alexander an empire in good order, well placed in international affairs, and internally progressive.

The tsesarevich on his sixteenth birthday (in 1834) had acquitted himself well in the symbolic coming-of-age ceremonies, the first public activity in which he had assumed a responsible part. Since then, he had been introduced to some of the adult duties expected of him and had become acquainted with many of the people to whom, as the future tsar, he must dedicate his interests. Aside from evidence that no amount of training would ever make him more than medi-ocre as a military man and the fact that he faced the health hazard of a developing bronchial disorder, there was every reason to ex-pect his future progress to be as the tsar planned it. When he was just past his eighteenth year, he had made a seven-months' tour of Russia. The next year, he had begun an extended tour of Europe—the traditional exposure to royal courts and a review of eligible young princesses.

On his European circuit, Alexander had shown a troublesome streak of stubbornness when, having fallen in love with Marie, the fifteen-year-old daughter of the Grand Duke Louis II of Hesse-Darmstadt, he refused to look further even though both his father and his mother disapproved of the choice he had made. This ob-stinacy became a popular subject of amusement among members of court society, to whom overt opposition to the will of the tsar was a notable phenomenon. One story that went the rounds originated with the Russian envoy to Darmstadt and concerned the response he received on informing the young lover that Marie was known to be the natural daughter of the grand duke's master of the horse. Alexander, he said, at once asked if she were listed in the *Almanach de Gotha* as the grand duke's daughter; and being told that she was, he snapped, *"Alors, de quoi vous mêlez-vous, imbécile!"*

Before the discord between parents and son became publicly em-barrassing, Nicholas and Alexandra, seeing that nothing diverted the tsesarevich from his attachment, not even a visit to England with its attendant gaiety, finally consented to the union.

Once Alexander and Marie were married, in 1841, and their resi-dence established in the Anitchkov Palace, the tsar appeared satisfied that the best possible arrangment had been made, that he had now discharged his duty with respect to the future of the dynasty in a regular and proper manner. He could be sure that his heir would be spared such bitter experience as he himself had suffered because his late brother had been less faithful to that duty.

VI

Magnificent Failure

NICHOLAS I, 1826–1855

A LTHOUGH Nicholas I accomplished much in his nearly three
decades on the throne, he was too closely involved in contemporary affairs to recognize fully that his country's problems were
far larger than his accomplishments and were likely to prove far
more enduring. He began to detect that fact only when it was too
late for change or compensation—both of which were, in any case,
foreign to his nature. Time, however, has provided the perspective
and discrimination that he lacked. Now even a cursory accounting
will bear out the retrospective judgment of Alexander Nikitenko, a
St. Petersburg University professor who served for twenty years as
one of the tsar's censors: "The chief shortcoming of the reign of
Nicholas Pavlovich was that it was all a mistake." By any standard,
the effort to better Russia by means of the Nicholas system, based
with such careful deliberation and comprehensive planning on
official nationalism, was a failure—one of the greatest failures in
history.

The tsar himself was chargeable for the results insofar as they
were due to his personal interpretation of the autocrat's duty, the
obsessively fear-ridden periods of his administration, and his pervasive conservatism. But a number of other factors were involved
as well.

Nicholas' initial reform effort, to provide basic justice for his people by having Speransky codify the laws and Benckendorff jog the courts into action, was effectual only up to a point. The codification was needed, and it was accomplished speedily and efficiently. The gendarmes, by literally standing over the judges and forcing them to make quick decisions, brought the courts temporarily out of the morass of the two million pending cases in which they had been bogged for years. But such measures could not assure justice through Russia's old legal and judicial system with its secret judicial proceedings, its exclusive reliance on written evidence, its assumption that the higher the social status of a witness the more reliable his testimony, its amateur—sometimes illiterate—judges taken largely from local nobility, and its subordination to the police. Nicholas allowed that system to continue and thereby left unchanged the justifiable popular evaluation of so-called justice, that it was in reality a danger to both honest and dishonest men. Even the extraordinary policing he provided did not remove from it the venality that had long been proverbial: "If you have a hundred rubles, the law is on your side." His effort to speed up court action was likewise ultimately futile; as soon as the gendarmes relaxed their pressure, the inherent clumsiness of the system reappeared, and the number of pending cases passed the old mark and continued to climb.

As for the changes that were to transform the bureaucracy and convert all officials into stewards of honest and efficient government, they proved all too soon to be only surface scratches. While Nicholas could look about him—among his high-ranking officials, in administrative departments of the two capitals, in committee rooms where chosen men were devising plans for carrying out his will—and observe heartening changes within a few months of his accession, he could only hope that similar changes were taking place in the further reaches of his government. What did not come within the scope of the imperial eye, however, by no means measured up to that hope.

Even in the two capitals, the odor of jobbery and boodle remained strong. Advancement was still dependent on *protektsiya* ("protection"—through which one's interests were looked after by someone more highly placed), and the use of position for self-enrichment was recognized as a fine art. Though prominent officials ordinarily took no bribes, they often accepted thinly veiled approximations. Benckendorff, for one, an extravagant gallant in his off-hours, lived far beyond his means, eking out his excellent salary with fees he received as director of various companies engaged in business with the government. The practice was common among ministers. Lesser officials reasonably enough felt that, if such as Benckendorff could accept directorships, there was no impropriety in their accepting small favors, perhaps dining at the expense of men who needed their goodwill or receiving small tokens of appreciation. As the reign advanced, infractions of this nature were dwarfed into virtual insignificance by practices at superior levels. Even General Kleinmichel, favored by the tsar as a highly competent aide, became known to the public as a man who not only obtained results through brutality reminiscent of Arakcheev's but also used his official prerogatives to achieve undeserved prosperity. While he may not have been the thief that his numerous enemies believed him to be, there could be no doubt that, as head of the administration of ways and communications, he helped his relatives at government expense.

Beyond the capitals, in the great spread of the empire, where bureaucrats had for generations been dissembling with impunity, neither Nicholas' dream nor his directives made any significant impression. Many of the governors, living like proconsuls, continued to enrich themselves and enjoy their power, setting the examples followed in varying degrees by their underlings. Distant capitals and out-of-the-way villages were not within effective reach of the central government. The great distances that had defeated invaders from abroad defeated the Third Section's emissaries as well. Benckendorff did not admit that his efforts were unavailing, though he knew that for every dishonest official apprehended, dozens went undetected. He did admit, however, that it was a rare thing to find "decent men" among either the bureaucrats or the clergy and that, when the dishonest were brought to trial, they usually escaped punishment.[1]

An instance of the corruption that was possible in the byways of the bureaucracy was recorded by Alexander Herzen, who, as a young independent thinker, had run afoul of the political police and been exiled to Vyatka, where he was assigned to the service of the governor, Cyril Tyufaev. This man, under the *protektsiya* of Arakcheev and Kleinmichel, had advanced from minor clerk to secretary, to department head in a secretariat, to deputy governor, and finally to governor—of Perm, then Tver, then Vyatka. Herzen found him an unprincipled sycophant, "coarse in nature and intolerant of the slightest contradiction," who governed by brutality and the pernicious abuse of authority. Once, threatened by the brother of a girl he had seduced, he had the young man certified as insane and thrown into a madhouse, where he soon died. Still, experienced bureaucrat that he was, Tyufaev easily foiled Benckendorff's investigators by lies and devious tricks and continued in safety to live luxuriously, maintain a "polygamous household," and add to his personal substance by extorting money from the people of Vyatka. When he finally faced the "misfortune of justice," it was through a weakness in one of his routine subterfuges. In preparation for a visit by the Grand Duke Alexander, he locked up not only the musicians for the occasion (to keep them sober) but also those who threatened to complain against him. But somehow one of the prisoners managed to slip a statement of the situation past his jailor to Alexander; when eventually it reached the tsar, Tyufaev was replaced by a decent man. By that time, however, he was sixty-two years of age and apparently resigned to a retirement in comfort on his Kazan estates.[2]

Such cases—and they were common enough—not only kept the majority of Russians from respecting the bureaucracy as Nicholas wished but also, year by year, added to the arsenal of those who were beginning frequently to point out that most bureaucrats were little more than scoundrels indulging their ruthless and greedy souls at the expense of the people.

Nicholas' economic program was affected by the same insufficiency that beset his efforts to provide good government in his realm: it stopped short of the heart of the problem. Neither the tsar nor Kankrin was an enemy of economic progress, but both suffered from fears and fancies that impeded it. Nicholas worried more about the growth of an urban proletariat—a class that in his mind corresponded to the French revolutionaries—than about the country's relative economic status among the great powers. He deplored economic changes that upset the traditional Russian ways. He was quite explicit about the innovations he disapproved, as this criticism of progressive Moscow merchants illustrates: "[They] cut their beards off, wear frenchified clothes, drink champagne, and drive around in fine carriages; their wives take in the *Journal des Modes*; that is not how honest Russian merchants should behave; they should be like their fathers, modest, sober, and saving." [3]

Kankrin, who wholeheartedly seconded the tsar's conservatism, confused a balanced budget and solvency with a sound economy and often drew his unsound arguments across the path of progress. His position, upheld by other ministers, helped retard Russia's entry into the railroad age; for, though Nicholas overrode his objections to the extent of giving the country its first public railroads, he did not give it a railroad system (that undertaking was postponed until the 1870's). Without adequate railroads and without the stimulus of large-scale investment, also opposed by Kankrin, the economy expanded at about the same rate as the population during Nicholas' reign. From Kankrin's point of view, that was as it should be: industry and agriculture were in balance, and Russia was not plagued by the ills of speculative and excessive investment as were the industrialized nations of western Europe.

But all was not well. The economic condition of those responsible for the agricultural output, the peasantry and the lesser nobility in particular, continued its gradual decline. Moreover, Russian industry was rapidly falling behind that of the West. Iron ore production, for instance, which had been nearly equal to that of England in 1800, showed little expansion during the next fifty years, while England's increased twelvefold. Coal production remained so negligible, since foundries still used charcoal for fuel instead of the newfangled coke used in the West, that by the end of Nicholas' reign the total Russian output equaled only a thousandth part of England's.

Still Kankrin, complacent in his belief that all was as it should be because supply was meeting demand, failed to recognize the problems his position was inviting, and Nicholas trusted his acuity. Neither foresaw the prospect that without iron and coal there could be no large industries; that without large industries, the Russian people were condemned to a low standard of living, and the military force, the mainstay of empire, was condemned to inadequate support.

Unfortunately, since there seemed to be nothing unusual taking place among the people and since the economy and the military services had continued thus far into the nineteenth century in undisturbed eighteenth century serviceability, Nicholas could easily overlook situations that would eventually prove critical. One such was fast developing in the area of his most cherished service, the army.

Impressive as it appeared in the second quarter of the century, the Russian army was beleaguered by tradition and hampered by its leadership. It represented in many ways the legacy of the preceding century's greatest Russian general, Alexander Suvorov, whose military precepts had included contempt for the musket and reverence for the bayonet. His reasoning was straightforward and unqualified: "The bullet misses, the bayonet doesn't miss; the bullet's a fool, the bayonet's a fine lad." Many of the men who influenced contemporary standards and methods—men like Paskevich, now a field marshal, and Minister of War Chernyshev—were themselves products of the late eighteenth century, trained according to the Prussian military tradition with its concept of the army as a mechanism consisting of men reduced to automatons by the repetition of drill and punishment. Under their influence most of the army training was based strictly on the manual of arms. They had little use for the adornments of military science; wars, they believed, could be won without it, but not without discipline.

It is true that some officers, notably Swiss-born General Antoine Henri Jomini, took the heretical view that the Napoleonic wars had taught the need for tactical flexibility and individual initiative, two qualities lacking in the Russian army. After the esablishment of the Military Academy, in 1832, there was a brief tug-of-war between the old views and the new. However, even without the tsar's prejudices, the odds in favor of the old views were high; predictably, they prevailed.

Had the new views won the day, and had technical skills been improved sufficiently to provide the soldiers with more arms and better ones, many difficulties would have been forestalled. As it was, both Nicholas and his generals continued to favor a drill-master's army, indulging their enthusiasm for parade-ground display at the expense of battle readiness. The fact that Russia could field the largest army in the world and that none outshone its brilliance on parade could never compensate for the fact that neither its men nor its horses were properly trained for warfare. Obsolete field equipment was used in training, out-of-date arms were common issue, maneuvers were unrealistically planned, and marksmanship was often neglected or inadequately taught. The cavalry horses, though superb beasts well fed, well groomed, and painstakingly trained to the drill figures and the slow, graceful parade gait, were underexercised and wholly unfitted for the grueling long-distance marches or the driving charges required of them under conditions of warfare. When on the move, the infantrymen proved themselves faster and more enduring than the horses often enough to prompt the wry observation that the army would make better time if the men carried the horses.

As for the navy, Menshikov's commission was to restore it to its former condition, and that he did well. However, the improvements he made—fitting a few ships with steam and remodeling some naval fortifications—by no means brought it up to date. While navies of other great powers were being converted to steam and armed with new and more efficient guns, most of Russia's ships still moved under sail and were annually becoming less battleworthy because of their lack of comparable maneuverability, protected hulls, and guns of adequate range and firepower.

Nicholas was not entirely blind to the country's military short-comings. But he had allowed the satisfaction of repeated victory to overshadow them (bearing out a remark of one of his generals, "Victors cannot be expected to judge themselves"); consequently this area of his dream continued to build toward a nightmare.

In yet another matter of deep concern to Nicholas, the nature of his subjects' thinking, appearances belied actuality. He had, so he believed, set up a more efficient barrier to "pernicious ideas" than Alexander's had been, and his program of "Orthodoxy, autocracy, and nationality" continued to produce widespread and satisfying results; yet, as was the case with the military services, successes obscured shortcomings. While his gendarmes, censors, inspectors, professors, and priests were quite effective in producing loyal behavior, they were not as effective in producing loyal thoughts.

Nothing in the new program could guarantee to exorcise the "pernicious ideas" that were already in the minds of many Russians. Moreover, by some oversight, no provision was made to strip private libraries of "pernicious" books. Consequently, it was possible to grow up in a home in which the spirit was either hostile or indifferent to the spirit of "Orthodoxy, autocracy, and nationality," and many were reaching their teens well acquainted with the thoughts of proscribed writers. Alexander Herzen was one of them: tutored by a French revolutionary emigré and a Russian liberal and given access to the many forbidden books in the library of his nobleman father, he came to university age knowing Voltaire, Schiller, and Goethe but not having read the catechism.

Nor could official vigilance, extensive as it was, guarantee that no unapproved books entered the country. The border was too long to be effectively policed, and no great risk was required to smuggle the forbidden volumes into Russia. In fact, some booksellers searched the official lists of banned foreign books for titles likely to be in demand, ordered them from smugglers, and quietly sold them. When the police finally began to check the stocks of St. Petersburg dealers, in 1849, they found substantial supplies of such books; one dealer had more than 2,500 in his possession. Thereafter, when established outlets were raided, the sales simply retreated further into the black market.

There was also an unforeseen development in the plan to protect young men from the "liberal and deist" influence of education in France and the "republican and atheist" influence of education in Switzerland by sending a select number of them to study in the presumably conservative atmosphere of German universities. Many of them developed ideas in complete disaccord with Nicholas' program. Some—outstanding among them, Timothy Granovsky—devoted their energies thereafter to the steady leadership and encouragement of the country's questioning or disaffected youth. Others became direct and vigorous opponents of the regime; among these was the progenitor of revolutionary anarchism, Michael Bakunin, whose harassment of the autocracy was to reach two decades into the next reign.

Still others, without the stimulus of foreign study, entertained ideas that the tsar would have considered dangerous. Despite apparent evidence to the contrary, intellectual restiveness had not disappeared after the Decembrist Revolt. Most of the older generation remained silent for a few years thereafter, some appalled by what the Decembrists had tried to do, others numbed by the severity with which the new tsar had handled them; but their silence did not always mean approval. Among the more thoughtful of the younger generation, intellectual restiveness was quietly nourished.

Of these younger thinkers, a significant number were to be found in Moscow during the first decade of Nicholas' reign, most of them at one time or another enrolled or attending lectures at Moscow University. Outstanding among them were Herzen, Bakunin, Vissarion Belinsky, the brothers Ivan and Peter Kireevsky, Constantine Aksakov, Ivan Turgenev, Michael Lermontov, Ivan Goncharov, and Nicholas Stankevich—all belonging to the category of students said to derive more from university life than from university lectures. Like the young men of the previous decade's Northern and Southern Societies, they had the urge to analyze and reason. Though they were not, strictly speaking, intellectual heirs of the Decembrists, most of them had been old enough—near their teens—in 1825 to be consciously touched by the revolt and its aftermath; most of them had retained their youthful outrage on behalf of the condemned.

They and their associates among the students of the university, full of questions about life and its problems, were not satisfied with the answers of professors, priests, and officials. They liked rather the answers to be found in the writings of currently popular German philosophers such as Schilling, Fichte, and Hegel. In their pursuit of understanding, any group of like-minded young men might form a "circle," a kind of informal assembly then to be found here and there among intellectuals of all ages and reminiscent of the earlier unions and societies. One of the most influential of the student circles met in the Moscow quarters of Nicholas Stankevich, a gentle, idealistic young man highly respected by most of his contemporaries. Though his manner and his refined features, framed by the currently popular long hair, suggested one who would favor pastorals over philosophy, young Stankevich's mind mixed neither fancy nor sentiment with what he considered serious problems. Though he was the son of a rich landowner, he heartily approved the growing disregard of social status among those who called themselves thinkers: in his circle, Belinsky, the son of an impoverished provincial doctor, was as acceptable as the young nobleman Bakunin. The concern of such groups as this was certainly not consonant with Uvarov's "soul of the age." Yet it was not what the Third Section could condemn as politics. To the participants, young men who were to dominate the literary and intellectual world for the next generation, theirs was simply an effort to understand. In that spirit, they gave themselves earnestly to hour on hour of talk on a mélange of subjects—poetry, the meaning of God, morality, man's future—and often probed into areas that under the Nicholas system were sacrosanct preserves of the autocrat, thus quietly circumventing the wall that the tsar was trying to erect for their "protection."

There were other circles in Moscow, and intellectuals and men of letters were welcomed into the salons of a number of the city's distinguished families. It was possible for those who had the time and inclination to follow a lively schedule. On Sundays, Madame Avdotya Elagin was "at home," and her sons Ivan and Peter Kireevsky were usually on hand to provoke a discussion of their favorite topic, the nature of Russian culture. On Mondays, the popular assembly point was Peter Chaadaev's bachelor quarters. Chaadaev, who had resigned his commission in the guards in 1821 and thereafter spent a number of years traveling abroad (thus missing involvement with his friends in the Decembrist Revolt), belonged to the older school of restive intellectuals. But both the youthful and the mature found him a stimulating host: a handsome, would-be dilettante with a keen mind, an ironic wit, and a provocative air of aloofness. Another host with another manner, Dmitri Sverbeev, received on Tuesdays. And so on, through the week: there was no dearth of opportunity for intellectual exercise in Moscow.

In St. Petersburg, where people were more intimately involved with the viewpoint of officialdom, discussions were likely to be less lively and irreverent in tone. But the capital had its regular salons; prominent among them was one in the home of the tsar's brother Michael, where the highly cultivated, German-born Grand Duchess Helen was hostess to a variety of musicians, men of letters, and interested young men, including Tsesarevich Alexander. There were circles here also, many, like the earlier societies, made up of well-born officials and officers who talked freely among themselves without any fear of judgment by higher authority.

The Third Section was not disturbed by the existence of these gatherings; in fact, many gendarme officers were welcome guests at some salons. The Third Section had much better sources of information: its employed informers were efficient; its agents sometimes visited the homes of those under surveillance to look over libraries, even opened private mail whenever expedient. As long as they learned of nothing more noteworthy than philosophical and literary talk fests—"bird talk" to the Third Section—there was no inclination to intrude. Their concern was with those who demonstrated an interest in politics, who expressed some desire to see political change in the country.

When the near-quiet that marked Nicholas' first decade as a ruler was finally broken, it was by way of the printed, not the spoken, word. In September 1836, the Moscow periodical *Telescope* published an anonymous essay entitled "Philosophical Letter," written as from "Necropolis" (City of the Dead), and for a while reverberations from it filled the air and upset the calm as nothing had done since Pushkin's pen inveighed against autocracy and Griboedov's satirized bureaucracy. The essay was composed as a reproachful exposé of the comparative backwardness of the Russian people and a declaration of how improvement had to be achieved:

We have never progressed in keeping with other peoples of the world [but] exist as if in banishment outside the times, untouched by the universal education of mankind. . . .

[In Europe] each person is fully possessed of his rights and easily gathers the ideas that have spread throughout society and uses them for his advantage. .... They are the concepts of duty, justice, law, and order. . . .

Despite the fact that we were called Christians, we did not move when Christianity, leaving the past behind it, progressed along the path solemnly indicated by the Divine Founder. While the world entirely rebuilt itself, we built nothing, but continued in our thatched huts. . . .

Though our limited mental habits, traditions, and memories do not link us to any peoples of the world, . . . we still belong to the Western world. This link still makes our destiny dependent on European society. Therefore the more we try to affiliate ourselves with it, the better off we shall be. . . .[4]

It was read eagerly and widely, not so much because people agreed with it—although some did—as because it was so daring. When it was learned that the author was one of the bright figures of Moscow's intellectual forums, Peter Chaadaev, the thrill of personal involvement through acquaintance heightened the interest.

Somehow Nicholas, avid reader though he was, failed to discover this shocking diatribe for himself. Metropolitan Seraphim, who read the press carefully for signs of heresy, noted it and called it to the tsar's attention as a "critical libel against the fatherland, the faith, and the government." [5] Once apprised of it, Nicholas reacted with predictable vigor. He ordered that the responsible censor be dismissed for his carelessnesss in passing the essay; that the *Telescope* be closed down, its publisher exiled; and that Chaadaev be declared insane and confined to his home, under a doctor's care, to protect him from Moscow's "raw and cold air." At Nicholas' further direction, all the publishers in St. Petersburg were herded together like schoolboys and required to hear the reading of the order suppressing the *Telescope*—a warning to the wise. Then Benckendorff, for the edification of his officers, gave this view of the subject that Chaadaev had chosen to examine: "Russia's past has been admirable; her present is more than magnificent; and as for her future, it is beyond the conception of the most vivid imagination; this . . . is the point of view from which Russian history should be conceived and written." [6]

While the gust of official reaction lasted, some among the country's intellectuals, recognizing it as typical of the enduring force against which serious liberals needed to brace themselves and take the offensive, began to consider the futility of limiting themselves to occasional outbursts such as Chaadaev's; others interpreted it as just another titillating diversion. Each point of view had some justification, based on the erratic nature of the government's response to manifestations of liberalism during the past two decades. More often than not, official disapproval, when aroused, had been direct and immediately suppressive; in some instances, it had led to outrageous reaction and personal injustice. On the other hand, there had been

ebb and flow in the government's vigilance, and rebuke and restraint
had by no means proved to be either lastingly intimidating or dis-
piriting. Often, offenders had merely been subjected to some kind
of social quarantine, inconvenient but in the main inconsequential:
placed under "genteel arrest" (in their own homes perhaps, as in
the case of Chaadaev), exiled to the provinces and given some minor
government post (as in the case of Pushkin and Herzen), or temporarily silenced by the proscription of their writings and freedom
of speech and association. To many potential supporters of change,
such restrictions were not particularly disquieting, for they had been
seen to be, in many cases, more stimulating than inhibitive to the
"victims." The outcome of the "Philosophical Letter" incident appeared for a time to justify continued complacence. Before long, the
shock had passed, and Chaadaev became again a familiar figure, cool
and sardonic, at Moscow salons: to some, the apotheosis of intellectual courage; to others, an interesting, though still a somewhat
patronizing, confederate.

Gradually, the question of Russia's place in the civilized world, so
unceremoniously broached by Chaadaev, began to disturb a growing
number of the more seriously thoughtful among the younger generation. They took it up in their customary way, adopting viewpoints
and starting debates—freely in their private groups, guardedly in
print. Some of them were inclined, with various reservations, toward
the direction indicated by Chaadaev. Among the young leaders with
this viewpoint were Belinsky, Herzen, and Stankevich. Their general
contention was that Russian improvement depended upon further
learning from the West: that sound models were to be found in
Western laws, political institutions, and technology. As they, along
with other like-minded individuals, became more widely known, they
were designated as *Zapadniki* ("Westernizers" or "Occidentophiles").

Those who opposed the Westernizers' point of view, who sought
to defend the national individuality of Russia, became known as
Slavophiles because they saw Russia's future development governed
by Slavic, as opposed to Western, tradition and achievement. This
position, first brought to the minds of the younger men by the writings of Alexis Khomyakov, was enthusiastically passed on by the
Kireevsky and the Aksakov brothers. Like the Westernizers, the
Slavophiles deplored many things in the country's present, pointing
out particularly serfdom, censorship, the debasement of the Church,
and the abuse of bureaucratic power; however, they believed that

to improve the present and ensure a healthy future, Russia should turn, not to Europe, but to the spirit of the old Muscovy days, when the Orthodox Church, working with the favorable material of the "Slavic soul," infused all society with the quality of *sobornost* (an almost untranslatable term meaning something like "sense of community"). This quality, they affirmed, was to be found in traditional institutions such as the still functioning *mir,* the village commune of the peasantry; the *artel,* a form of producer-cooperative found among some artisans; and the *zemsky sobor,* an early assembly of representatives of the people, which they believed to have linked tsar and people effectively in the fifteenth, sixteenth, and seventeenth centuries. The more conservative among the Slavophiles concentrated on the redemption of their own country and its duties as a leader among Slavic peoples. Others, like the poet Fedor Tyutchev, took a more ambitiously sweeping view:

Seven inland seas and seven mighty rivers,
From the Nile to the Neva, from the Elbe to China,
From the Volga to the Euphrates, from the Ganges to the Danube . . .
This is the Russian Empire.[7]

Whatever their position, the "Young Russians" were again making themselves heard, and the authorities were no longer able to ignore them.

Nicholas could not fathom the nature of the debate, nor could Benckendorff or Uvarov. They recognized certain immediate results as untoward: when, for example, Ivan Aksakov wrote a historical article exalting Moscow over St. Petersburg, they agreed that it was an "unsuitable" interpretation. But they did not recognize that these educated youths were arguing from premises that denied the Nicholas system, that they were hailing as their leaders men who were completely out of tune with that system.

One of their favorites was Timothy Granovsky, whose lectures on history at Moscow University drew them in throngs. Granovsky, who had been among the promising young men chosen to study in Germany, had returned hostile to the ideas of the tsar and sympathetic to those of the Westernizers. At the university, where he began to teach in 1839, at the age of twenty-six, he was one of the few popular professors. Disparagers liked to attribute his attraction to his youthful good looks and quiet eloquence, neglecting to note the same qualities in some of his unpopular colleagues. The fact was that the students, as well as many of their educated elders, recognized and approved his subtle treatment of what they considered serious problems. They could understand his discussion of a seemingly exotic subject such as the legal systems of medieval France and England as an indirect attack on the Russian legal system, and that was precious support for their own thinking. It was not to be expected that Granovsky's popularity would go completely unchallenged. As he explained his situation in a letter to a friend: "The authorities look disapprovingly on my relations with the students. . . . [Metropolitan Philaret] demanded my explanation why I do not mention in my history lectures 'the will of God,' which governs the events and the destiny of the nations. 'I am informed,' he said, 'that you are a harmful professor, that you darken the minds of the loyal sons of our Sovereign.' " [8]

Even when Granovsky lectured to the public, large audiences acclaimed him and admirers crowded around him as if he were an opera star. Such popular regard was in decided contrast to the attention accorded Stepan Shevyrev, another professor at the university, whose public lectures were poorly attended, though he was one of the most eloquent spokesmen of official nationalism.

Encouraged by a few men like Granovsky and recognizing the potentialities of the printed word, the young intellectuals began to turn to writing with greater confidence and purpose. Beyond offering an opportunity to display literary talent, publication offered a challenge: to test just how far one could go in presenting unconventional thought without attracting official censure. As a result, the same public who read the purely literary works of the period's ablest men of letters—Dostoevsky, Goncharov, Turgenev, Lermontov, Gogol— soon became acquainted also, through the periodicals, with such purposeful thinkers as Khomyakov, the Aksakovs, the Kireevskys, Herzen, and that young firebrand who stirred the Moscow group as no one else could, Vissarion Belinsky.

Belinsky was a striking example of the generation of disaffected young men who followed the Decembrists—the "mixed breed," the non-class, whose number was not limited to the scions of privileged families. Coming from a family of slender means, he had been forced into independence at an early age, and had developed accordingly. He entered Moscow University on a scholarship in 1829, managed to be expelled three years later, and took up the unavoidable burden of earning a free-lance livelihood. The course he followed thereafter —as he developed a sense of literary appreciation, a faith, and a political philosophy—was as erratic as what had gone before. But he became one of the best-known figures in Russian journalism, an influential literary critic and a stimulating writer who inspired the liberal-minded to idolization, the conservative to frustration and animus.

"Nature," Belinsky claimed, "destined me to bark like a dog and howl like a jackal, but circumstances compel me to mew like a cat and wave my tail like a fox." His words may have been mews to him, but they were brave roars to his admirers. His literary criticism, written in a spirit of boldness, contemptuous of tradition, and imbued with hope for a new and better world, caught the imagination of young men to whom a wink was as good as a nod, and they read him assiduously. His point of view made him an unequaled publicist for the Westernizers. Slavophile Ivan Aksakov admitted unhappily that in the provinces "Belinsky's name is known to every youth who is at all intellectual, who seeks a breath of fresh air amidst the stinking mire of provincial life." [9] What he wrote, no matter what the subject, usually reflected his view of Russia as a harbor too long undisturbed, "where only the mold is green, where the frogs are croaking under the soft mire," where the great need was for awakening action. Before long, he had started some undercurrents moving.

The effect of this intellectual agitation, however, did not suggest to Benckendorff any cause for alarm. And when he died, in 1844, the official attitude remained unchanged, for the man who succeeded to the leadership of the Third Section, Alexis Orlov, had been schooled to the same viewpoint as his predecessor. He was a stickler for formality, the letter of the law, and documentation; he did not seek hidden meanings nor consider it necessary to supplement his own diplomacy in handling run-of-the-mill recalcitrants. So the Third Section's 1844 report to the tsar simply deplored the "coarseness" of Belinsky's literary criticism, but found his writing innocent of "politics" and explained his coarseness as a misguided effort to attract impressionable readers by shocking them.[10]

Three years later, the Third Section itself was shocked into attention. The occasion was the circulation in Russia of copies of an excoriating letter that Belinsky, then in Germany seeking to heal his consumptive lungs, had written to Gogol explaining why he had written an unfavorable review of Gogol's *Choice Passages from Correspondence with Friends*. Belinsky, who had previously praised Gogol's social satire in *The Inspector General* and *Dead Souls* and called the author a true artist, interpreted this last work both as a renunciation of all that he had admired in Gogol and as a plea for serfdom, the Orthodox religion, and the political status quo. As Gogol's complaint about his review had aroused Belinsky, so the temper of the rebuttal aroused the censors:

. . . [Russia] presents the dire spectacle of a country where men traffic in men . . . a country where there are not only no guarantees for individuality, honour and property, but even no police order, and where there is nothing but vast corporations of thieves and robbers of various descriptions!

The Church . . . remains a champion of inequality, a flatterer of authority, an enemy and persecutor of brotherhood among men. . . . According to you the Russian people is the most religious in the world. That is a lie! The basis of religiousness is pietism, reverence, fear of God. Whereas the Russian man utters the name of the Lord while scratching himself somewhere. He says of the icon: *if it isn't good for praying it's good for covering the pots.* . . . Religiousness has not even taken root among the clergy . . . [The majority of them] has always been distinguished for their fat bellies, scholastic pedantry, and savage ignorance. . . .

Only literature, despite the Tatar censorship, shows signs of life and progressive movement. . . . [The public] looks upon Russian writers as its only leaders, defenders and saviors against Russian autocracy, orthodoxy, and nationality. . . .[11]

Before the storm created by these caustic words had blown itself out, Belinsky returned from abroad. He would surely have been arrested and made to pay for his audacity (no one could now doubt his having stepped into the forbidden field of politics) if his disease had not worsened and forced asylum upon him—death, in May, 1848.

After that, the Third Section and the ministry of education settled down again, on guard as usual against political sentiment or activity, but still unaware that, in the battle for the "soul of the age," the Belinsky forces were quietly outmaneuvering the Uvarov forces.

If conditions had been improving according to plan throughout the country, developments within this small minority of the population would have been less noteworthy. But, while Nicholas continued to believe that orders from St. Petersburg could effect either change or stability wherever and however his understanding indicated the need, there was constantly accumulating evidence that the lot of the majority of his subjects was deteriorating and that the state of their morale was not promising.

Against the remorseless forces of decay operating in the countryside, Nicholas' efforts were flimsy indeed. Circumstances continued to press in on the poorer nobles: 10,000 of them lost their land during the reign, reducing the number of the landed nobility to 100,000. Many of the nobles endured by going ever more deeply into debt; by 1842, 50 percent of their serfs were mortgaged to government banks, and each year the percentage grew. Yet those who survived the ravages clung to their way of life, justified serfdom as a means whereby they discharged a paternal and beneficent duty to the less fortunate, and watched fearfully for any indication that the government planned to tamper with what security they had left. Emancipation, they warned, would ruin the nobility and the rest of the country as well; for, if the serfs were freed, they would first bathe the country in blood by their violence, then starve it to death by their idleness.

The efforts of the gendarmes to enforce the claimed paternal and beneficent duties of the landlords were as generally ineffective as the government's efforts to aid them financially. Deplorable practices continued. In one year, the agents on the Borisovo estate of Prince Radziwill beat to death forty-four serfs, blinded forty-two, and otherwise mutilated thirteen. There were countless cases of the illegal sale of serfs as substitutes in army service. Owners whose holdings were being depleted and whose serfs were being mortgaged away kept adding greater burdens of both labor and dues to those who remained. Yet the landlords complained that the government, by trying to stop these abuses, was fomenting discontent among their serfs and inviting trouble.[12]

In still another respect Nicholas failed to please the nobility, whom he sought particularly to help. They remained dissatisfied with the action he had taken on their wish that noble status be made unattainable by those in the lower social strata. Though he had set a stricter standard for any who might aspire to that status, it remained accessible to civil servants who reached Rank Five in the bureaucracy. The more class-conscious and ambitious nobles felt that, as long as that concession continued, not only would the "refined strain" of the aristocracy be exposed to debasement by "common dross," but also the political power of the nobility would be endangered by the possibly uncongenial additions to its ranks.

Even the state peasants, for whom the Kiselev project had promised seemingly achievable benefits, became more and more disillusioned as the project proceeded. Its administrators, incompetent bureaucrats (few able and trained men were available for the novel undertaking) smothered by the welter of some 4,000 legal articles regulating their work, soon fell into the common pattern of unconcern and corruption. The plan to equalize holdings through resettlement and redistribution did not reach all peasants, and the inequalities that persisted were the more galling in contrast. The young farmers found that they could not profit from the improved farming methods they learned, since they could not afford to hire the labor necessary to use them. The agricultural schools fell into disuse because of this impracticability, and other schools declined because of a general lack of appreciation. The peasants objected to having their communal funds used to provide improvements and services that they did not consider necessary. Moreover, the whole project was opposed by many landowners, who realized that this planned improvement was expected to be an example to them—might, in fact, be interpreted as a prod.

These problems of the countryside were supplemented during Nicholas' reign by the fact that the peasants were picking up the scent of *volya* ("freedom" or "emancipation") despite official efforts to seal the idea up in committee rooms. Benckendorff, who had flatly declared to Alexander that the *chern* were changeless, warned Nicholas in his report for 1839 that the "common people of today are not what they were twenty-five years ago." The blame for their change, he said, could be laid to their association with government clerks, merchants, and soldiers—all of whom were now themselves changed by their increasing degree of literacy:

[These persons], having a common interest with the people, are making them accustomed to new ideas and are fanning a spark in their hearts which may burst into flame some day.

Incessantly they say among the people that . . . Orthodox Russians are enslaved, in violation of Holy Writ; that their masters—that is, the nobility—are the cause of all the evil; . . . that the masters conceal the truth from the tsar and belittle his Orthodox people to him. . . . The entire concern of the people is being directed toward one goal, emancipation. . . . Serfdom is a powder keg beneath the state, all the more dangerous because the army is made up of peasants.[13]

As Benckendorff said, the peasants still went to Holy Writ for their arguments; they did not go to Rousseau or Locke. Western political notions were, as an official report stated, "ideas which at the moment are, thank God, completely alien to them." [14] But unrest was unrest, whatever its rationale, and it was duly noted. Defining an outbreak, *volnenie*, as any illegal collective action, whether refusal to perform services for a landlord or armed attack on superiors, government records showed that the number of these disturbances was on the rise in the first half of the ninteenth century * and that, in the last two decades of the period, the number of attacks on the lives of landlords or their agents increased from eighty-six to a hundred and one.[15]

Peasant unrest, however, was still localized, unorganized, and sporadic. Its target was the landowners, not the Little Father. A hundred outbreaks in a year, even though more than half of them were so serious that they had to be quelled by the use of troops, seemed relatively inconsequential against the great expanse that was Russia. Most of Nicholas' high officials, serf owners themselves, were therefore able to take an optimistic view of the situation; even if serfdom were a "powder keg," any possible explosion, they believed, would be delayed for at least another generation or two.

Had Nicholas been less stubborn, he might have despaired and dropped his efforts to deal with the problems of his underprivileged and dissatisfied subjects after years of little accomplishment. But he continued to summon committees and issue legislation on their behalf until he was caught up by an overwhelming and, to him, unavoidable involvement elsewhere.

When the revolutionary waves began to roll from Paris, in February 1848, Nicholas' attention was at once drawn almost exclusively to the impending peril. It was his abiding passion to defend his own throne and the principle of established authority everywhere against any and all revolutionaries.

His chief immediate concern was with his Polish subjects. After they had rebelled in 1830 and he had punished them by nullifying the constitution of the kingdom of Poland, he had made up his mind to prevent for all time the restoration of the Polish nation. His conservative allies, Austria and Prussia, were committed to him and he to them to prevent that restoration and to act together against revolution anywhere. But as the outer defenses of the Nicholas system, those states were not as dependable as they once were. Prussia now had the weak-willed Frederick William IV on the throne; Austria still had Metternich but he was aging, and the emperor, Ferdinand I, was feebleminded. That was the situation which prompted Nicholas'

---

* The increase was not year by year (for instance, the number shot up to more than a hundred in 1826 and went down to thirty-three in 1827) but decade by decade.

remark to a Danish diplomat in 1846: "Once we were three, but now we are one and a half. I don't count Prussia, and Austria counts for only a half." [16]

The first revolutionary wave brought appalling results: Frederick William was demonstrated as a dangerous compromiser with his "dear Berliners"; Metternich was ousted and Austria left in the hands of the liberals; Italy was torn by insurgence. "What is still standing in Europe?" Nicholas asked in a letter to Queen Victoria, and answered his own question: "Great Britain and Russia." [17] Would Victoria join him in the struggle against revolution? She would not. Russia stood alone.

The tsar was beside himself with anxiety and rage, but he never for a moment questioned the validity of his position. He could not see the revolutions as a commentary on the defects of monarchism. The reason he sat strong on his throne while others toppled was clear enough to him: he had never compromised the integrity of monarchism as they had. Anyway, this was no time for self-criticism and questioning. Revolution was no chimera; it was the palpable embodiment of the ideas he had been fighting all his life; this was yet another time when he needed to strengthen defenses against them.

By way of setting his own house in order and assuring himself of important moral support in defense of the domestic status quo, he made a point of putting the nobles' minds at ease about emancipation. He publicly affirmed the imperial respect for the nobles' property rights, among them their rights over their serfs. Before a special deputation of nobles in St. Petersburg, he extended the hand of friendship without equivocation: "Let us forget all unpleasantness between us. . . . Be assured that under my leadership no earthly power will trouble us." [18]

As a first precautionary military measure, Nicholas deployed over 400,000 troops along his western borders, holding them in readiness to fight for "God, tsar, and fatherland" against the infiltration of "anarchy." When a liberal nationalist rising in the Danubian principalities of Wallachia and Moldavia seemed likely to spread across the border into the Russian province of Bessarabia, he did not hesitate to send Russian forces into the principalities and scotch the rising. This was his demonstration that the display of military readiness was no mere gesture.

To make doubly sure of internal safety, he undertook to raise still higher the barriers against seditious ideas. At Menshikov's suggestion, he appointed a secret committee, headed by Count Dmitri Buturlin, to supervise and tighten up the work of existing censorship authorities. Under the committee's directives, it was no longer sufficient for censors to check and sample; they must now pick, probe, and analyze. Before long, their files were bulging with cases and their stamp was likely to be found on anything within their reach. They rooted out of textbooks such as phrases as "sovereign remedy," "Caesarian operation," and "forces of nature." They reassessed Gogol's works, objected to his *Dead Souls* on the grounds that "a human soul is immortal," and banned the republication of his writings, which extolled the virtues of common man and bred pride—surely to be followed by arrogance—in the lower classes. They denied entry into Russia of such "questionable" fiction as *Uncle Tom's Cabin,* Hawthorne's *The Scarlet Letter,* and Andersen's fairy tales. The members of the Buturlin Committee read the press carefully to make sure that it exercised no unofficial influence. Official publications were scrutinized as closely as any others: when the war ministry's newspaper, the *Russian Invalid,* noted that insurgent troops were fighting "bravely" against loyal Austrian forces, its editors were reprimanded and advised to remember that their paper was being read in taverns and market places by minor civil servants and lackeys who should be protected against wrong impressions. The printed word was powerful, and the autocrat intended that it serve only official nationalism.

The ministry of education, of course, was alert to the expanded effort to direct the thinking of the people into proper channels. Instructions went out to all university officials to increase their surveillance over what was being taught and to bear in mind certain essential "facts": that autocracy could not be questioned nor serfdom criticized, that submission to temporal authority was required by Holy Writ, and that Russia could never be anything but an autocratic monarchy "in which the sovereign is the protector of the Church and the father of the country and, as such, unites in himself the entire state." [19] Yet Uvarov's own philosophy of education was questioned by the Buturlin Committee, and the prestige of his position waned somewhat. When rumor began to spread that powers beyond his ministry were considering the closing of the universities, Uvarov was moved to defend the institutions. Being now overshadowed by the dark wing of the current obscurantism, however, he chose to let another speak for him. He arranged that an article expounding the "harmlessness" of higher education, written by

Professor I. Davydov, be passed by the censors and published anonymously in the *Contemporary*. But the scheme went awry: the article
stirred not only the Buturlin Committee but also the tsar himself,
and Uvarov was severely reprimanded for allowing the dissemination of what amounted to a criticism of "superior judgment." The
outcome was Uvarov's resignation and his replacement by his reactionary assistant, Prince Platon Shirinsky-Shikhmatov. The universities were not closed, but their enrollment was curtailed. With their
curricula cleansed of offerings in philosophy and metaphysics, they
became acceptable for a time as the latest models of ideological
nurseries.

Such reinforcement of protection against sedition seemed excessive
to a number of the tsar's admirers, but they did not feel free to
speak—nor would they have found him of a mind to listen. Any
resilience that might have remained in his attitude hardened, in
April 1849, with an affair that called back for him the agony of
December 1825. It was the culmination of an extended investigation
of a circle of young men who held a weekly meeting under the leadership of Michael Butashevich-Petrashevsky, a subordinate in the
ministry of foreign affairs. The group was a heterogeneous lot: writers (Dostoevsky among them), guards officers, teachers, civil servants,
businessmen, and nonmatriculated students; but they had a common urge to consider causes and possible solutions of contemporary
problems. When sufficient evidence had finally been assembled
against thirty-nine of them to prompt their arrest as members of
what the Third Section interpreted as a far-flung revolutionary conspiracy, the tsar felt that he was faced by a return bout with destiny.

Five succeeding months of investigation by a special committee
which Nicholas had appointed failed to prove the allegation of
revolutionary conspiracy. It was found only that the Petrashevsky
Circle gathered regularly and discussed ideas both heretical and subversive, that Dostoevsky had read to the others a copy of Belinsky's
letter to Gogol—at that time, a criminal act—and that some of them
favored revolution. It all added up merely to a conspiracy of ideas,
but in the overheated atmosphere of the time, that was enough. A
military court sentenced twenty-one of them, including Butashevich-
Petrashevsky and Dostoevsky, to death; others, to lesser punishments.

The climax featured a version of Nicholas' ostensible mercy—
again, reminiscent of the Decembrist affair. Those condemned to
death were taken from the Peter-Paul fortress on a bleak day in
December and marched to Semenovsky Square, where they were to

face the firing squad. Then, by prearrangement, just as the order for execution was being given, one of the tsar's aides galloped up to announce that the tsar had "mercifully" spared their lives and that their sentences were changed to extended terms of hard labor in exile.

Important as Nicholas had considered the case of the Petrashevsky Circle, he had not been able to give it the kind of attention he had given the Decembrists. The aftermath of 1848 in Europe had been occupying much of his attention, and it was not yet cleared away.

He had reconciled himself to the new French republic, whose president had shown enough good, conservative sense to draw his admission, "I have faith in the conduct of Louis Napoleon." In the spring of 1849, Austria's hard-pressed young emperor, Francis Joseph (who had succeeded the figurehead emperor, Ferdinand I, in the previous year), also began to show "good sense" by inviting Nicholas to assist in the suppression of the Hungarian revolutionaries under Louis Kossuth. The tsar sent Field Marshal Paskevich with more than 150,000 men, who, by two months of hard fighting, earned him Austria's gratitude for making possible the restoration of Hapsburg control over Hungary as well as for providing the military relief necessary for the country to get its possessions in Italy well in hand again. One of the by-products of that neighborly act was less propitious. When Russia joined Austria in demanding that Turkey surrender certain Hungarian and Polish revolutionaries who had sought asylum there, England and France approved Turkey's refusal and threatened to support it with force—not so much because of concern for the refugees as because of the possibility that Russia was about to gain a further advantage in Turkey. But Nicholas maneuvered out of this diplomatic corner by withdrawing his support of the demand.

That left him time for more active opposition to the growth of German nationalism and the efforts of his troublesome brother-in-law, Frederick William IV, to upset the organization that for three decades had held the German states in a relationship agreeable to Russia.

Nicholas had already voiced contempt for Frederick Williams' willingness to accept a constitution, his "fatherly" attitude toward the rebellious duchies of Schleswig and Holstein when they sought to exchange Danish control for a place in the German confederation, and his audacity in trying to unite the purely German states under Prussian leadership as a counterbalance to Austria. Now, with a

combination of renewed diplomatic effort, intimations of belligerence, and personal insistence, he set about to manipulate the disturbed and disturbing elements in a way acceptable to himself—that
is, in a way to restore legitimacy in the near-West and to settle the
German states again in the arrangement set by the Congress of
Vienna. By mid-1850, Prussia agreed to end the squabble with Denmark and to stand aside while Schleswig and Holstein were reunited
with that state. In September, Austria revived the old Germanic
Confederation, to which Nicholas hastened to give Russia's official
recognition. Two months later, Prussia renounced the ill-conceived
German "union" and joined Austria in the confederation.

The revolutionary storm had passed at last. Things would never
again be quite as they had been before 1848, but most of the work
of the revolutions had been undone: in the central, and much of
the southern, part of Europe, the legitimate political structure had
been reestablished, and the continent now bore a fair resemblance to
that which had been approved in 1815. For this, Nicholas justifiably
took much of the credit. Russia appeared to be the strongest power
in Europe again. To be sure, the means the tsar had used along the
way left some unfavorable aftereffects: many persons—particularly in
Hungary, France, and England—nursed a deep bitterness toward this
victorious "gendarme of Europe"; the frustration that Russia had
virtually forced upon Prussia still rankled; even Hapsburg gratitude
was tinged with wariness of the ultimate intentions of the champion.

For the tsar, such considerations were offset by the fact that the
foreign revolutions had caused hardly a tremor in Russia. While the
reading public had followed the news of developments with such
interest that newsdealers found it necessary to exact fees from the
great numbers who read the newspapers at the stands without buying
them, while many were excited—and some delighted—by the initial
revolutionary successes, there had been no responsive outbreaks.
Young Russian liberals did not try to imitate their counterparts in
Berlin, Vienna, and Paris. The urban proletariat, such as it was,
speculated about events abroad but only as something exotic. In some
parts of the country, during 1848, there were periods of tension, easily
attributed to the spread of cholera in the spring and the unusually
large number of fires in the summer. Among the Bessarabians as well
as among the peasantry and some of the Polish nobility in the western
provinces, there was restiveness, but, being of a familiar nature, it was
not considered alarming. A retrospective report of the Third Section
in later years included a statement of how officialdom saw the situa-

tion: "In Russia itself there were no grounds to fear uprisings or disorders. The general mood of Russian society was characterized not only by complete quiet, but even by a certain inertia." [20]

The sense of national strength and the confirmation of official belief that Russia had been made resistant to revolution added glory to the celebration, in December 1850, of the twenty-fifth anniversary of Nicholas' accession. The same conditions made it possible for the tsar to overlook much of what he had failed to accomplish and to accept as justified his ministers' effulgent twenty-five-year reports. What he wrote on Nesselrode's report, which he passed along to the Grand Duke Alexander, indicated his satisfaction: "God grant that I succeed in handing Russia over to you as I have tried to make her: strong, independent, and beneficent; the best for all of us at no one's expense." [21]

The words were not intended to suggest that Nicholas was foreseeing the end of his reign, only to keep the tsesarevich aware of the heritage for which he was being prepared. The Grand Duke Alexander was now thirty-two years old and sufficiently well acquainted with the problems and processes of the present government to understand what "strong, independent, and beneficent" meant to his father. Nicholas had allowed him to "sit in the seat of power" on various occasions—when he himself made an official visit to England in 1844, when he took his hurried trips through the provinces, when he accompanied the ailing Empress Alexandra on her trips to the German spas or Italy. He had been about as successful in preparing Alexander as he judged himself to be in his other projects: the results were not perfect, but they represented his utmost efforts. He knew that he could not leave Russia a ruler who promised to be either particularly strong of character or accomplished as a soldier. "My son Sasha," he once declared in a moment of despair, "is a *baba* ['old woman']; there will be nothing great done in his time." [22] However, he was visibly pleased to see that, of late, Alexander had shown himself willing, even anxious at times, to overcome his emotional instability, square his shoulders, and accept his duties in a manner becoming a future autocrat. The change was due in part to the fact that, as his family grew—the oldest of his three sons, Nicholas, was now seven years of age—he became more aware that he had inescapable dynastic resposibilities, that his own accomplishments would determine ultimately what he would pass on to his heir.

Particularly encouraging had been the active and interested part Alexander had taken in the work of the committees studying the problem of serfdom. With the education he had received and the pre-training he was now receiving, he should be as prepared for his heritage as it was possible to make him. True, he had for a while shown a disquieting interest in a kind of liberalism akin to that of his late uncle Alexander I and had been a frequent participant in the popular salons of his aunt the Grand Duchess Helen. But the events of 1848 had given him such a chilling realization of the dangers of liberalism in political matters that he could now be safely trusted, Nicholas felt, to confine his reforming zeal to social problems—with more success, he earnestly wished, than he himself had been granted.

Since he believed that what he had accomplished was reasonably satisfactory and that his methods had been proven effective, Nicholas planned no immediate changes. Foreign policy would flow as usual from the fountainhead and be converted into suitable action as occasion demanded. Domestic policy would provide that the minds of his subjects be protected and directed with no relaxation of official effort, and that interrupted phases of the magnificent dream be revived when possible. One area the tsar recognized as still seriously in need of renovation and change was the judiciary, and in 1850 he appointed a committee under Count Dmitri Bludov to study conditions and draft appropriate legislation; but he did not press it for action as he would have in his earlier years. Those who had expected a change, a post-crisis relaxation, were due for a disappointment. Censors continued to censor. The Buturlin Committee censured censors. The Third Section, now under Count Orlov, ably assisted by the strong gendarme chief, Dubbelt, continued to be the official omnipresence, concentrating more than ever before on the surveillance of possible subversives. Shirinsky-Shikhmatov continued to set on education the stamp of his and the tsar's belief that its basis should be "religious truth," not "philosophy."

Officialdom seemed wholly unaware that while these persistent repressions and denials were "protecting" the majority, they were driving the young liberals close to alienation. Granovsky wrote to Herzen, who had escaped the last tightening of vigilance by going abroad in 1847: "Our situation becomes more and more intolerable. . . . Many decent people have become despondent"; three years later he wrote in desperation, "It is hard, brother, but there is no escape for the living." [23]

It was true that, by 1850, the country seemed to have settled into a changeless mold. Although Nicholas was aging—paunchy, almost bald, morose—he was still hard-working and unrelenting. He might

become weary on occasion, but never lax. Contemporaries felt
that he still showed promise of a long life. And after him? The
Grand Duke Alexander was seen to be emulating his father's military bearing and severe manner, sharing the same views. The
Nicholas system could go on forever.

Up to this time, neither the Nicholas system nor Russian strength
under Nicholas' administration had ever been tested against major
opposition. That test was now in the offing—the Crimean War.
Though Nicholas himself unwittingly brought it about, he had not
seriously conceived of the possibility of war during the two decades he
had been shaping the elements from which it developed.

From the beginning of his reign, he had recognized the need for
dealing diplomatically with the major powers on the old Eastern
Question, but he intended that Russia's position be one of such fairness and generosity as to be both inoffensive and unassailable. Knowing that other powers, England and Austria in particular, had vital
interests in the Near East just as Russia had, he understood the prudence of working in concert with them in order to safeguard the
interests of all. Since the main issues would arise, as a matter of
course, from the final disintegration of the crumbling Ottoman
empire, he took that anticipated event as his point of departure. He
was willing to allot generous portions of the empire to other powers;
foregoing Constantinople (permitting it to be a free city even though
Russians believed that sooner or later it must be theirs), he asked for
Russia only the territory of Bulgaria and the Danubian principalities,
Wallachia and Moldavia, along with the right to maintain a Russian
garrison on the Bosporus. Moreover, convinced that the Ottoman
empire, long accepted as the "Sick Man of Europe," was well along
in terminal illness and that efforts to prolong it would serve no
purpose, he was willing at any time to discuss the ultimate arrangements, the parceling out of the territory and the allocation of advantages to which the powers might look forward. He tried repeatedly
—and unsuccessfully—to get commitments from Austria, Prussia, and
England on his views. In his notorious insensitiveness to the attitude
of others, he failed to note not only that the suspicions of the other
powers were aroused by his dwelling on the imminent demise but
also that the general inclination among them was to provide therapy
rather than to make a premature distribution of effects. As early as
1833, he asked Metternich his opinion of the Sick Man's condition
and was asked in return whether his interest was that of a doctor or

an heir. Later, Metternich reportedly alerted the English to the Russian view that the Sick Man was on his deathbed and that the time had come for the settlement of his estate.

When positions were finally declared, the result was what had been called one of the silliest wars ever fought, touched off by "a quarrel between two packs of monks about a key and a silver star." The likelihood of war resulting from a drawn-out discord between the Roman Catholic and Eastern Orthodox clergy over the care and use of the holy places in Palestine seemed remote until two ranking monarchs became stubbornly involved. The chief demands of the Roman Catholic monks were for possession of the key to the main door of Bethlehem's Church of the Nativity (at that time in the hands of the Orthodox), an understanding about the responsibility for the upkeep of the holy places, and the return of the silver star which they claimed had been stolen by the Eastern Orthodox monks from its place at the Grotto of the Nativity. Louis Napoleon, wanting to insure as much support as possible from the Catholics, pressed Sultan Abdul-Mejid to comply with their demands, while Nicholas, for political as well as religious reasons, rose to the defense of the Orthodox. The sultan was able to equivocate for a time, assuring both factions of compliance to come; but when a French squadron steamed into the Bay of Tripoli in the summer of 1852, ostensibly on a minor mission unrelated to the religious controversy, he rightly construed it as a threat and ordered that the Catholic demands be met.

Nicholas took that development in bad part and, before the end of the year, was faced with a situation he could not abide. France had finally intruded on, not just one, but two sensitive areas: French diplomatic force had subjected Orthodox monks to foreign orders, and Louis Napoleon, disregarding the intent of the 1815 arrangements so dear to Nicholas' heart, had just asserted the continuation of the Napoleonic dynasty by assuming the title of Emperor Napoleon III.

A show of firm intent on Russia's part—force, if necessary—was in order. Accordingly, Nicholas dispatched two army corps to his southern borders and made ready not only to reiterate the earlier Russian demands of the sultan but also to add some more comprehensive ones. He was not planning to start a war nor to enhance his own power over the hapless sultan. But he was convinced that his position with respect to the sultan's Orthodox subjects was defensible and that the recent presumptions of the French should not go unchallenged. After all, he was the senior autocrat, and considered himself the chief arbiter of international problems in the Near East.

Even if he were compelled to use force, any opposition the Ottoman empire could offer, he was sure, would be inconsequential. Continuing his old refrain, he had only recently said to the English ambassador Seymour, "The bear is dying; you may give him musk, but even musk will not long keep him alive." [24] Furthermore, he felt confident of ample support, whatever the outcome of his next move. That England would cooperate he had no doubt, though Nesselrode reminded him that Anglo-Russian relations had become somewhat strained because of England's uneasiness about the Treaty of Unkiar Skelessi and her disapproval of Russia's attitude toward the recent liberal movements in Europe. He did not question Austria's position: surely Francis Joseph would be anxious to return the favors accorded him after 1848 and, more recently, in his conflict with Turkey over Montenegro. Frederick William IV, he felt sure, would follow his lead. As for Napoleon III, though he would be hostile, he would be isolated and therefore impotent. All things, then, were propitious for a showdown.

In January 1853, Nicholas sent his trusted minister Prince Menshikov to Constantinople to "bring the sultan to his senses" on the matters involving the Orthodox monks, to get an affirmation of Russia's rights with respect to his Orthodox subjects, and, by way of demonstrating the strength of Russia's position, to mobilize the support of the foreign ambassadors in residence there. The results were not what the tsar had expected. Menshikov was promised redress in connection with the Orthodox use of the holy places as well as recognition of certain Russian rights regarding the Orthodox under Turkish rule, but he met firm resistance to the Russian demands for affirmation of the tsar's rights as protector of all Orthodox laymen in the Ottoman empire. Abdul-Mejid was shrewd enough to see that if he recognized the Russian right to oversee the well-being of his twelve million Orthodox subjects, his own authority could easily be eclipsed by that of the tsar.

Menshikov's orders were to stand firm, and the longer he did so, the dimmer grew Nicholas' chances of victory in his diplomatic campaign. The major powers were quick to interpret the Russian demands as a planned step toward the subversion of Turkish sovereignty. The English government alone among them seemed willing, despite its considerable commercial interest in the Near East and its seasoned understanding of the need to appraise every Russian move in the area, to reserve judgment in the hope that Russia would trim the extreme demands. But after three months, that hope seemed futile to everyone; England, France, Austria, and Prussia united diplomatically behind the sultan.

In May, the lines were at last clearly and openly drawn. Menshikov returned to St. Petersburg; Nesselrode sent Nicholas' ultimatum to Abdul-Mejid, giving him eight days to accept the Russian demands or to expect Russian forces to occupy the Danubian principalities of Moldavia and Wallachia ("not to make war" on him but to hold "material guarantees" that the demands would be met); and the British government ordered its Mediterranean fleet to join a French squadron in eastern waters.

War had not come, but its shadow was advancing. By the end of the next two months, the Anglo-French naval force had proceeded to the entrance of the Dardanelles, while Nicholas had recalled the Russian legation from Constantinople and sent a Russian force of 80,000, under Prince Michael Gorchakov, to occupy the Danubian principalities "peacefully." Then followed three months of heightened activity in diplomatic circles: England, France, Austria, and Prussia united in a protest against the occupation of the principalities; Nicholas held personal conferences with both Francis Joseph and Frederick William; a dozen plans for keeping the peace were proposed and rejected—some by Russia, some by the other powers. Meanwhile, dispatches came to Nicholas from far and wide, each of them further proof that forbearance was weakening abroad. Turkish nationalists and religious zealots came out in angry demonstrations; the press and public in England and France heatedly protested Russian occupation of the principalities; the sultan welcomed the arrival of standby naval and military aid from Egypt and invited four armed vessels (British and French) into the Straits; Napoleon III became increasingly impatient for action as he envisioned French prestige rising above the shambles of the Holy Alliance. It was clear that the diplomatic treadmill was to be abandoned.

The first to step off was Abdul-Mejid. On September 27, 1853, he threatened war if Russia did not remove her troops from the principalities within eighteen days. Nicholas finally had to face what he had inadvertently invited. On October 20, he issued a war manifesto to his people declaring that Russia was being forced to military action in order to protect "the sacred rights of the Orthodox Church." Then he threw himself wholeheartedly into the now more desperate effort to vindicate his position and retrieve Russian prestige. It was a complicated undertaking: on the one hand, he had to keep up the attempt to gain sympathetic consideration from the Western powers individually or collectively and, on the other, to guide developments in the areas where Russia was sure to be challenged if fighting broke out.

Though somewhat dismayed by the turn of events, Nicholas was not intimidated by it. He believed that the Russian cause was just and that the Russian forces were adequate to uphold it. He had no misgivings about the support of his subjects: traditionally both their patriotism and their religious zeal were readily quickened when challenged by foreigners. In addition, he was soon made aware of special support "on principles," which the Slavophiles were at first gratified to offer. The issues seemed ready-made for them. Sergei Aksakov (father of Ivan and Constantine) saw the war as one that would liberate the Slavs from the "Turkish and Germanic [Austrian] yoke" and arouse Russians to a higher pitch of fervor than had the war of 1812. Fedor Tyutchev was exultant:

> And beneath the ancient vault of St. Sophia, in reborn
>   Byzantium, will stand once more Christ's altar.
> Kneel down before it, O tsar of Russia, and arise
>   tsar of all the Slavs.[25]

The tsar's judgment about Russia's military strength was tested first at sea. While the Anglo-French squadron was poised at the entrance to the Bosporus, Russia's Black Sea fleet, under Admiral Paul Nakhimov, met and destroyed a poorly armed Turkish flotilla in November 1853. But when the superior Anglo-French vessels pushed on through the strait, under orders to protect the Turkish shores, all Russian vessels of the Black Sea fleet were ordered into harbor at Sebastopol. The one victory was soon seen to be of slight consequence except as the breach of peace that hardened the hostile alignments. It was followed shortly by St. Petersburg's breaking diplomatic relations with both London and Paris, the formal alliance of France and England with Turkey, and an Anglo-French ultimatum that Russia leave Moldavia and Wallachia. When Russia ignored the ultimatum, war became a reality, in March 1854.

After that, Russian naval power was shown up for what it was, an obsolete array of ships, mostly sail-propelled and armed with obsolete guns, outclassed wherever it was threatened or engaged—on the White Sea, in the Pacific (on both sides of which Russian possessions were defenseless against the Anglo-French forces), and in the Gulf of Finland. If Admiral Charles Napier had been more confident when, in the spring of 1854, he was cautiously advancing an Anglo-French squadron through the Gulf of Finland, he might have been surprised at the ease with which he could have effected a strategic landing. His maneuver brought him within sight of highly important points: Peterhof, where Nicholas and his court were at the time, and Kronstadt, fortress and base of the Russian Baltic fleet as well as the chief defense of St. Petersburg, only twenty miles distant. It also threw the Russians into a state of consternation: troops were rushed to guard the shores, and the tsar, in desperation, sent out a call to the four nearby northern provinces—St. Petersburg, Olonets, Novgorod, and Tver—for civilians to man a reserve flotilla of oar-propelled ships to assist the regular navy against an enemy landing. The Grand Duke Constantine, ranking officer in the navy, urged that the Baltic fleet be sent out to the attack. But the more experienced admirals, knowing the limitations of their equipment, prevailed upon him to accept a safer measure: to hold the fleet in readiness, in a passive-defensive attitude, and await developments. Fortunately Napier, who considered his own ships "ill-manned and ill-disciplined," decided not to attempt a landing and ultimately withdrew.

With that relief in the north, more attention could be turned to the south, where developments were far from promising. It had become evident that not only was Russia to fight the war alone but also that she was to be denied even the moral support she expected of Austria and Prussia. They had set themselves apart in an offensive-defensive alliance and joined England and France in proclaiming the integrity of the Ottoman empire and demanding that Russian forces be removed from the principalities. Both remained neutral; but Austria, disturbed by the prospect of Russian encroachment on her eastern border, moved closer to Turkey and, now bound by convention to occupy and hold Moldavia and Wallachia once they were cleared of Russians, was massing troops in Translyvania. To try to hold the principalities under the circumstances was clearly unwise, if not impossible. Gorchakov's troops, already weakened by cholera and fever, had failed to get under way a plan to strike across Bulgaria toward Constantinople, having been halted by the Turks at Silistra in their strongest attempt; and to invite the additional hazard of drawing Austria into the war was not to be considered. So, after holding the "material guarantees" for a year, Nicholas had to face the double ignominy of his unfulfilled threat and his misplaced trust in the friendship of Francis Joseph. That setback, though disheartening, was somewhat offset by the reports he received from the Caucasus, where Russian forces were making some headway against the Turks and local insurgents.

The heart of the war, however, was clearly to be in the Crimea, where the enemy, the Black Sea now open to them, could concentrate on the destruction of Russia's strongest foothold in the Near East. Their initial objective, in all likelihood, would be the naval base at Sebastopol. To command its defense, by both land and sea, Nicholas again put his confidence in Minister of the Navy Menshikov. His earlier gamble on the ability of the prince to overcome his lack of experience for work assigned to him had, in his judgment (wrong, as others could see more readily than he), paid off, and he would try again. Menshikov, unfortunately for Russia, accepted the tsar's estimation of his ability—"unfortunately" because Russia had officers who could have handled the Crimean operations so much better than he. His thirty years in charge of the navy had added little to his limited knowledge of warfare, and it was now too late for him to learn.

Menshikov expected the enemy to attack at Sebastopol, and he reasoned correctly that, knowing its seaward fortifications to be formidable, they would not depend on a naval attack to reduce it. He was quite mistaken, however, in his judgment of when they would attack. At the end of August, he declared, "A landing at this late date is impossible." [26] Two days later, an Anglo-French-Turkish force of more than 60,000 men landed just south of Eupatoria, about thirty miles north of Sebastopol. This was the first time since 1812 that enemy troops had set foot on Russian soil. The only resistance they met was verbal: a local official angrily informed them that it was forbidden to enter Russia without first going through quarantine (an entirely relevant quibble, it proved, for there was cholera among the invaders).

While the enemy marched south toward Sebastopol, Menshikov temporized for five days before setting out to intercept them. In the meeting, at the Alma River, his 35,000 Russians halted the allied forces, of almost twice their number, only long enough for one disastrous battle. Though his men fought bravely, in the end Menshikov had no choice but to retreat.

If the Crimea were not to be lost, Sebastopol must be held. Circumstances, such as the enemy's two-day delay to recoup after the battle of the Alma and their critical lack of health services, provisions, and heavy artillery during the first weeks, provided the

Russians with time to push ahead, under the direction of military engineer Colonel Edward Totleben, with preparations for the city's defense. That was accomplished by sinking part of the Black Sea fleet in the harbor to protect the northern side of the city from approach, ringing the inland sides with redoubts and gun emplacements, setting heavy artillery into place, and trying to arrange for supplying an extended stand. Menshikov drew his force away from the city to insure against encirclement, to keep supply and communication lines open, and to direct the offensive against the allies, leaving Admirals Kornilov, Istomin, and Nakhimov to direct the defense of the city. Before Menshikov felt it safe to relinquish any men from his field army to the defenders and before reinforcements could come from the interior, the fortifications were manned chiefly by a few thousand sailors from the inactive or destroyed vessels of the fleet.

The siege of Sebastopol, which began in October 1854, when the allies had made their way around to the southern, and most vulnerable, side of the city, was to last for eleven months.

Outside the beleaguered city, the world's largest military force, more than a million strong, was able to do little for its relief. The Russian army had not fought a major power for forty years, and the defects concealed by its reputation had reduced it to a second-rate fighting force. Those defects, already shown up in the relatively minor test of the Danubian occupation, were now revealed with terrible clarity. Its superior officers were, on the whole, unqualified for the extraordinary commands of this mid-nineteenth century war. The men on whom the burden of leadership in the field now fell— Menshikov, Gorchakov, and Paskevich—each of whom had shared in the glory of Russian arms during the Napoleonic wars, remained satisfied with the methods that had produced that glory, having used them satisfactorily in the intervening years against such weak opponents as the Poles, the Hungarians, and the Turks. The senior officer who differed was a rarity; most of them were equally lacking in up-to-date knowledge of military science. Likewise rare were the ones who commanded either the respect or the affection of their subordinates.

Even with better leadership, the men could not have repeated the distinquished record of the Russian army's former years. What they had been trained to do in the field—to make bayonet charges—they did well, often to good advantage. Beyond that, they were severely handicapped. They were completely outclassed in firepower.

Whereas nearly half of the enemy were equipped with rifles having a range of twelve hundred paces, only 5 percent of the Russians were so equipped; the rest had muskets with a range of three hundred paces. And to the inadequacy of their arms, a personal inadequacy had been added through a neglect of marksmanship. In practice their average at two hundred paces was one hit in ten tries at a two-yard target; in battle, tension and the required speed, of course, lowered even that average.

Notwithstanding such conditions, Menshikov, like many of the Russian high command, had faith in numbers: it seemed to him that Russia should be able to overcome the allies, if by no other means, by crowding them into the sea. After the Alma defeat, he sent dispatch after pleading dispatch to St. Petersburg, asking for reinforcements and excusing his reverses on the grounds of bad luck. Nicholas responded by asking whether or not the enemy had a monopoly on good luck and indicating that reinforcements were in limited supply. The somber fact was that most of the Russian army was committed elsewhere. Paskevich was holding the bulk of it in the western provinces, for use if Austria should bestow "a donkey's kick" on Russia; over 200,000 men were deployed to protect St. Petersburg and its environs; 150,000 were engaged against the Turks on the Caucasian front; and 100,000 of the least able were manning the internal security units for contingencies such as peasant outbreaks.

It was recognized that, without strong reinforcements, the Crimean field army could do little more than keep the way to the interior open; the widening disparity between its size and that of the continually increasing allied force discouraged engagements. Though the call-up of recruits was increased, the Crimean army's needs could not be adequately met. Moreover, getting any kind of aid to the Crimea was a slow, miserable business. Communications were slow: between Sebastopol and Kiev and between Moscow and St. Petersburg, there were electrical telegraph lines; but between Kiev and Moscow—over five hundred miles—there was only an optical telegraph, the use of which was limited to clear days. With the enemy blocking the sea approaches to the Crimea, the one route for men and supplies was overland, more than a thousand difficult miles in length. There was no railroad south of Moscow, only dirt roads that, even in good weather, were inadequate for the heavy transport they were now expected to carry. As they became clogged with broken-down supply wagons, disabled horses, and the sick and dead left by the troops in transit, traffic was slowed and critically delayed. Such conditions worsened, rather than improved, as the weeks passed. With the lack of medical and sanitary services, disease spread: of the men sent to the peninsula during the war, more than half died on the way. No supply schedule could be maintained; so food spoiled, material was ruined, lost or—at best—two months in transit.

These conditions dampened Menshikov's early optimism and, in his discouragement, he was soon blaming the central authorities while overlooking his own and his officers' errors when he was able to do so little on the offensive or to draw the enemy strength away from the siege of Sebastopol. His intentions were respectable, but he was no tactician. His forces failed in an effort to displace the enemy from the landing place the British established at Balaklava, eight miles southeast of Sebastopol; two weeks later, when they engaged an enemy force of less than half their number at Inkerman, they had to retire again without honor. Unable to rise above such reverses, the Russian offensive gradually deteriorated into a kind of slow-motion byplay; the enemy forces, though themselves beset by divided command, epidemic, supply shortages, and criticism from the home fronts, were benefited by a field less obstructed than they had any reason to expect.

The final defense of the Crimea lay with the forces at Sebastopol, desperately holding out against continual bombardment. Under attack by both the land and the naval forces of the allies, their position had been an uneasy one from the beginning of the siege. But their resistance was dogged, heroic, and endured in misery. Rations and ammunition were frequently in short supply. Medical services were inadequate in every respect. Though the efforts of the distinguished Doctor Nicholas Pirogov, his medical staff, and scores of "sisters of mercy" were never relaxed, they could relieve or save only a very limited number of the sick and wounded who overflowed their ill-equipped and irregularly supplied hospitals—a number which declined as the inevitable typhus, scurvy, and gangrene increased. The fighting men themselves had no regular rest or respite, for the reinforcements were never sufficient to justify relaxation.

Hope for any relief from these conditions waned when Menshikov's growing passivity and the onset of winter made it possible for the enemy to call in forces from the field and concentrate on the siege. Now, both sides faced months of unrelieved struggle to determine the verdict in the Crimea.

Nicholas, absorbed in his efforts to understand why his diplomacy had gone awry in the West, to justify his present position, and to retrieve some of Russia's prestige, did not recognize completely the evidence that, within his own country, his regime was under critical strain. Circumstances, he knew, made it necessary here and there to draw the controls tighter, but that was not unusual in wartime. He was satisfied to postpone judgments and adjustments, if called for, until later.

One of his own acts had given rise to disturbance in an area that he himself admitted to be potentially dangerous—among the peasantry. When he issued the call for a reserve flotilla, at the time of the Anglo-French naval threat in the spring of 1854, he made it clear that serfs could join only with the written permission of their owners and on the understanding that they return to their owners at the end of their service. However, imaginative serfs—and occasionally members of the local clergy—put a different construction on the call: that serfs could volunteer at will and that volunteers would be emancipated at the end of their service. The good news spread rapidly by way of the countryside's own system of communication, *slukh* ("rumor"), and was received with an uncontrolled surge of response. Hundreds of serfs in the four designated northern provinces left their estates without permission and hurried away to register their names.

Soon the word had reached as far south as Ryazan, over five hundred miles from St. Petersburg. There, in the center of old Russia where the population was denser, serfs by the thousands took to the road, heading to Moscow to sign up for the flotilla. When the Third Section informed Nicholas of what was happening, he immediately ordered that those illegally on their way be peacefully turned back, that those who had reached Moscow be returned in chains, and that those known to have led the venture be arrested. The response was an angry one in many of the villages from which the volunteers had come. In some, anger burst out in attacks by serfs on local officials. The upshot was the usual suppression: troops were sent in, and by late summer things were quiet again.[27] But the word emancipation still rode the *slukh* southward, and anticipation stirred warningly through the serf villages in Kiev and nearby provinces.

This restiveness among the serfs aroused little public concern—the censors saw to that. But in a number of highly placed officials and other men of influence it revived a fear that had lurked among the peripheral thoughts of responsible upper-class Russians for generations, the fear of a widespread serf uprising. It also reinforced the doubts that had been developing in their minds about the soundness of the Nicholas system itself. Had its emphasis been judiciously placed? Had the tsar, in fact, been "protecting" Russia from non-existent dangers and exposing her to real ones? Many who had been among the enthusiastic supporters of "Orthodoxy, autocracy, and nationality" began to feel that this animation of the native specter was indeed more threatening than the foreign dangers that the tsar had been busy sealing out. In the words of the historian Pogodin: "We need have no fear of a Mirabeau, but of a Emelka Pugachev. . . . No one goes over to the side of Mazzini, but a Stenka Razin rouses the people. This is where our revolution is arising; it is from this quarter that danger threatens." [28]

Aside from the peasant unrest, enough irregularities and misfortunes had been piling up since the spring of 1853 to shake the confidence of many. The tsar's policy had drawn the country into foreign disfavor, his initial intransigence in dealing with Turkey had merely accommodated the Western nations by providing them with a cause for taking a stand against his conduct in international affairs, and many of his chosen agents had proved undeniably incompetent and dishonorable. It was not the record of "an earthly god," whose will was invincible and whose judgments were inviolable.

Putting together the debacle of Russian arms, the stories of officers appropriating the rations of their men, and the reports of army contractors fattening on corruption, thoughtful Russians were humiliated and appalled. Those already hostile to Nicholas became harsher than ever in their denunciation. A change of sentiment among some of the Slavophiles, now disturbingly different from Tyutchev's expression of patriotism in 1853, came to his attention through a letter written by Ivan Aksakov to a friend and intercepted by the Third Section. It characterized the regime as beyond both hope and sympathy:

. . . The old order passes; the terrible despotic power that presumptuously imagined itself capable of changing the current of life by its own strength now stands fully revealed in all its bankruptcy. Let it go bankrupt! The only pity is for the poor Russian soldiers! . . . Petersburg patriotism will not regenerate Russian life; it is wholly foreign, politically created, another Western importation. . . . All that Petersburg can do is *to repent*, but that is the last thing it will do . . .[29]

Although Nicholas was aware of the change in atmosphere, there was no indication that he comprehended either its nature or its cause. His mind was too set to admit any self-questioning. The turnabout in foreign affairs was, to him, a clear case of betrayal of trust, not of mishandling on his part. He had to accept it, he would endure it, but he would not be broken by it. As he wrote to Frederick William IV in the summer of 1854: "Nothing remains for me now but to fight, but to conquer or perish with honor, like a martyr of our holy faith . . ." [30] Nor would he be broken by the painful knowledge that many shocking defects were being revealed in the current military operations and even in the upper levels of his government. Observers marveled at his ability to maintain the majestic image when beset by so much manifest adversity.

It was all the more remarkable in view of the problems and stresses of his personal life, to which court gossip gave wide circulation as well as varied and often distorted interpretations. For ten years, during which the health of the Empress Alexandra had been declining and she was seen only infrequently at social affairs, the tsar's name had been persistently associated with that of the empress' lady-in-waiting Mlle. Varinka (Barbara) Nelidov, whose company he openly favored at every ball or reception he attended without his consort. Though sorely distresed by the tone of the rumors, Nicholas had done little to indicate his disapproval except, on one occasion, to demand—futilely—the return from France of a Russian writer who had published an offensive satire on the subject. Few troubled to reason that he might be able to cherish both his wife and the lovely young Nelidov. So the relationship continued, a source of lively interest to his disparagers, another personally justifiable situation that put him on the defensive in an ever more critical and unsympathetic world.

As his cares accumulated, Nicholas became quieter, apparently more absorbed in his own thoughts; yet his back remained straight, his manner unyielding.[31] He sought no respite from his duties. Little problems as well as big ones were still passed up to him, and he continued as usual to judge them individually. When Leo Tolstoy, then serving in the Crimea, asked permission to start a popular newspaper for soldiers, the tsar appraised his request just as he had for years been appraising similar civilian requests: his answer was an emphatic "no."

However, he could not hide the fact that he was hurt, deeply and acutely, by every report of military reversal or official improbity. Each failure of the Crimean field army and the shock of enemy fire on each redoubt defending Sebastopol racked him personally. When he learned that Alexander Politkovsky, director of the Fund for Disabled Soldiers, had stolen more than a million rubles from the fund, he sadly observed that even Ryleev, the Decembrist, and his friends would not have behaved so badly. For him, there could have been no more poignant comparison. Perhaps the most painful duty he ever performed as a military man was his last one: signing over Menshikov's command to Gorchakov after Menshikov had failed, early in 1855, to dislodge the allied defenders of Eupatoria, which had been occupied and held as a landing place for Turkish forces.

All these burdens were the heavier for the tsar because, just now, he found himself more nearly alone than he had been at any time since that terrible day of decision in December 1825. He was also, for the first time, on the defensive, both in diplomacy and at arms. It was a situation particularly heartsickening for a man who, for three decades, had felt power growing in him as he had "saved Russia from revolution"; who had gone on to suppress revolution in Poland, Hungary, and the Danubian principalities; who had rescued from dissolution both the Austrian empire and the Germanic Confederation; who had imposed his displeasure on every political move unsatisfactory to him anywhere in Europe; and who had been able to take pride in the triumphs of his armies each time he had sent them out—against Persians, Turks, his own unruly subjects, or those of neighboring states.

Had that power, then, been a mere chimera? Certainly the hand he had extended in friendship toward the West was now empty. Austria had been the last power to emphasize that fact, late in 1854, by entering into an offensive and defensive alliance with England and France; it had been underscored a month later when little Sardinia ostentatiously joined the coalition. Moreover, he understood that in England, where there had been some pacifistic voices under Lord Aberdeen's government, his name was now nothing more than "the enemy" as the avowedly anti-Russian Palmerston was coming into favor. Even when he had agreed to consider the "Four Points," the allies' demands for humiliating assurances from him, he had received no gesture of goodwill in return. Likewise, close about him, the old evidences of power were fading. His military forces, except in the Caucasus where conditions were favorable, had their backs to the wall, and the spark of patriotism that had cheered him in 1853 had flickered out. He was still the autocrat: his throne had been neither shaken nor threatened by recent reverses. But there was no denying that the apparatus of the Nicholas system had been severely buffeted.

There was a rumor abroad, which probably never reached Nicholas, that he would be forced to abdicate. That, of course, he could never have credited: he still expected of his people the infinite loyalty that he sincerely believed to be his due.

A bit of tragicomic relief was provided when, in January 1855, at one of the gatherings celebrating the centennial of Moscow University, the speech of Professor Stepan Shevyrev was found to be composed in the spirit of earlier years when praise of the tsar was *de rigueur* on such occasions. The professor's words somehow lacked the proper ring (his private thoughts were not in exactly the same key), and the listeners could hardly be expected to respond as they might have formerly to his remarks that the "light of knowledge" had been shed "over all classes" in Russia, that education had kept pace with the "superior aspects of progressive scholarship in the West," and that all the country's important educational problems had been "solved during the last thirty years in the history of education of our fatherland, under the guidance of our tireless monarch." [32] The tsar may have been grateful for the effort, but no amount of such timeworn sentiment could now affect the state of affairs that was closing in on him.

In the raw days of early February 1855, Nicholas contracted the indisposition to which all St. Petersburg residents were involuntary heirs, the grippe. And though his concerned physician, Doctor Martin Mandt, advised rest and nursing care, the tsar disregarded both the advice and the wintry chill as he continued to meet his engagements and carry out his self-imposed duties. Within a week, it was clear that he had finally overestimated his strength and overtaxed his reserve, for his illness grew seriously worse, and his suffering became acute. Finally, he demanded a definite statement of his condition, and the doctors gave it; there was no hope. He was near death.

Orderly to the end, he made his final confession and faced the inevitable with courage and with consideration for those he held dearest. Characteristically, he asked Alexander to thank the guards for saving Russia on December 14, 1825, and to assure the army that he had loved it with all his heart, that if he had not succeeded in all that he had sought to do, it was only because he had not been given "strength or time." Then, with his family and close friends around him, he made his brief farewells.

Even at court, only a few knew how close the tsar was to death. When it came, on February 18, 1855, the official announcement was so unexpected to the public that speculations about various unnatural causes of death—suicide, in particular—began to circulate.[33] But the fact uppermost in the minds of thoughtful Russians was that they again faced change of one kind or another. Some, sincerely grieved, would have agreed with Dubbelt's reaction: "No one can believe that this oak with a body and soul, this giant, has so suddenly toppled." [34] Others, quietly relieved, looked hopefully to the future as the Grand Duke Alexander became Tsar Alexander II. Some made no effort to conceal their belief that the tsar's death was a timely blessing, coming while there was still time perhaps to make the changes necessary to save Russia; they felt, however, as the self-exiled Alexander Herzen indicated in his first appeal to the new tsar, that it was necessary to "make haste."

However accepted, Nicholas' legacy to Russia was weighted with problems far in excess of those he had inherited: the pressing ones connected with the recent diplomatic imbroglio and the Crimean War; the many old ones that he had put aside because he found no solution that would accord with the principles of autocracy; and the new ones inherent in his most pernicious bequest, the nucleus of a police state. His dying admission, that he was handing over "the command" in bad condition, was an egregious understatement.

The magnificent dream had passed, its brightest images lost in the twilight of the magnificent failure; but the alienation brought about by the Nicholas system would not be uprooted nor its growth again successfully checked as long as the Romanovs ruled Russia.

VII

New Policies

ALEXANDER II, 1855–1865

THAT Tsar Alexander II took up his imperial duties with apparent willingness and resolution was evidence that his father had succeeded in imposing upon him a form of behavior that at least concealed the reluctance and irresolution he so often displayed in earlier years when confronted with difficult tasks. He was the product, for better or worse, of thirty-seven years of vigilance and planning, drilling and discipline, urging and conditioning administered by the "Iron Autocrat." And he sought to be the model successor. He copied his father's habits even to the length of sleeping on a hard camp bed, forced his kindly face into a look of imperious majesty, and affected the manner of a grand seigneur. Unfortunately, the result did not always redound to his credit: to some he appeared only a blurred copy of his father, his imperious countenance "a mask and a caricature of a mask at that, stripping his face of its pleasant, natural expression, often giving him a repellent rather than a majestic look." [1] However, like Nicholas I, he was animated by a sincere sense of duty, could give commands, and was capable of effective insistence on what he considered proper. While he was neither a leader of men as his father had been nor a figure commanding respect or awe, he was quite capable of inspiring responses of affection and of fear—both functional tools of administration.

What lay ahead for the new tsar did not invite a diffident approach; yet Alexander could not deny the misgivings he felt in accepting the responsibility for doing something about the bitter truths he had reluctantly come to know during his father's last years. He knew that the system so painstakingly built up by Nicholas was now a shambles; that not since the days of Peter the Great had Russia been in such need of renovation. The country was without friends, the monarchy was without support in very important areas of society, the armed forces were a discredit to a nation calling itself a world power, and the fuse to the "powder keg" of serfdom was growing shorter with every day that the system continued. Though he recognized all this, Alexander, not being a rebel at heart, dreaded the institution of the new policies necessary to cope with the country's problems. He had definite ideas about the policies needed, however, and only one course was open to him: he had to bring them to test—and that as soon as possible.

He was favored by having, in the imperial family itself, some very competent and strong support. His oldest brother, the Grand Duke Constantine, who had inherited Nicholas' powerful drive for action but not his narrow outlook, could be depended upon to encourage vigorously and back up any progressive efforts looking toward emancipation, economic growth, and the overhauling of the machinery of government. Along with Constantine—and having much the same attitude toward Russia's problems and their solution—were the German-born Empress Marie Alexandrovna, warmly interested in her adopted country's life, and the Grand Duchess Helen.

Support, of course, had to be sought from many sources, the public being an important one of them. Some of the steps Alexander took during the first year of his reign helped to ease the apprehension of many of his subjects and arouse hopeful anticipation in others. To nearly everyone's approval, he dismissed Kleinmichel and instructed his successor, General Constantine Chevkin, to begin work on plans for new railroads. He replaced the chief of the Third Section, Count Orlov, unpleasantly associated in the public mind with the repressive controls of the post-1848 period, by the amiable and somewhat liberal Prince Vasily Dolgorukov. That Orlov was to remain close to the throne, a man of significance in the Committee of Ministers as well as the State Council, was at the time remote from popular concern. He appointed General Alexander Timashev as replacement for the objectionable Dubbelt as chief of staff of the gendarmes—another instance when the public responded favorably to change without ques-

tioning intention, for they were unaware that the tsar had offered
to make Dubbelt chief of the Third Section. In addition, he took
some needed direct measures to ease the tensions produced by the
late tsar's pervasive efforts to "police the minds" of his subjects: he
dissolved the Buturlin Committee, lifted the restrictions on the universities, and removed many of the bars to foreign travel; he also as-
sented to the translation of the Bible into Russian and removed
press controls that had barred the republication of works of popular
authors such as Gogol.

For the time being, however, Alexander's aim was to indicate imperial leniency and to stimulate, not to upset. He had a war to finish
before he could undertake any critical domestic change. For that
reason, he made no immediate effort to renovate the bureaucracy or
disrupt the customary routines of government. Though the plight of
the millions of enserfed Russians had weighed heavily on his conscience and occupied his mind for years, he would not consider emancipation in the midst of war. Nor would he risk, in any way, the loss
of the goodwill of the nobles, whose aid would be necessary to win
the war. Rather, following the example set by his father in 1848, he
took particular care to solicit their moral support at this time. Believing their interests to be ill-served by the policies of Dmitri Bibi-
kov, Nicholas' appointee as minister of interior, Alexander replaced
him by Sergei Lanskoi, who hastened to assure them that the government was resolutely committed to safeguarding "the rights conferred
on the nobility." And he underwrote that commitment personally: "I
have faith and confidence in you. I believe that the nobility will be
the well-born estate in the full sense of the term, and at the basis of
all that is good. Do not lose heart! I am with you, and you are with
me." [2]

To despair of winning the war, Alexander felt, would be to dis-
honor the name of Russia. Heedless of the dismal outlook in the
Crimea, he ordered Menshikov's successor, Prince Michael Gorchakov, to hold Sebastopol at all costs. It was a futile order: the country
could not provide the men and materiel needed, and Gorchakov, a
typical product of Russia's traditional army training, a disciplinarian
rather than a strategist, could not provide the leadership. The tsar's
order staggered most of the army's high command. Gorchakov considered obedience to be nothing less than suicidal, and Field Marshal
Paskevich admonished him that it would be also morally indefensible.
The military code made no provision for disobedience to an imperial order, however; so the defense continued.

At first, the odds against the Russians mounted discouragingly: the intensity of the siege was redoubled, and the defense was weakened by the death of Admiral Istomin. But, surprisingly enough, by the middle of 1855 the defenders had overcome some of their disadvantages and were better off than they had been three months earlier, now able at least to rebuild their fortifications as rapidly as the enemy cannonades and assaults could reduce them. Consequently Alexander felt justified in the resistance he had shown to the attempts at negotiating peace which had been going on in Vienna. Briefly encouraged, Gorchakov resumed attack on the British and French positions. The encounters went so disastrously against him, however, that he again gave way to desperation. He could see no way of effectively deterring or even interrupting the siege, which was again building up ominously as still more men and munitions were being assembled by the enemy. As he reported the position to the minister of war, his men had now "accomplished the extreme limits of the possible."

Even so, the order to continue the defense remained, though by this time it was virtually a death sentence for the defenders of Sebastopol. They were beset not only by the enlarged enemy forces but also by demoralization, having just lost from their remaining leaders Admiral Nakhimov, who had been mortally wounded at the height of the recent surge of effective resistance, and the engineering genius Colonel Totleben, incapacitated by injuries. The tide had turned for the last time. On August 27, the enemy stormed and held the Malakhov redoubt, a fortified height considered by both sides to be the most nearly impregnable of the city's outer defenses, and their entry could no longer be contested.

Thus faced by necessity, Gorchakov ordered the defending garrison to march out under cover of night toward the north, having blown up their powder stores and set the ruined city aflame. After 349 days of siege, Sebastopol was lost.

Still Alexander would not yield. His position was precarious, but he clung desperately to every shred of hope. He made much of the fact that operations in Transcaucasia were still favoring the Russian forces and that a second allied armada had just withdrawn from a foray into the Baltic and been repulsed by the Russian defenses at Sveaborg. He braced Gorchakov with patriotic tradition by sending him words of encouragement from the ancient capital, Moscow: "Do not lose heart; remember 1812 and put your trust in God. Sebastopol is not Moscow and the Crimea is not Russia. Two years after the Moscow fire, our victorious troops were in Paris. We are the same Russians and God is with us." [3]

A few weeks later, at Bakhchisarai, once the proud capital of the Crimean Tartars and now the headquarters of Russia's Crimean army, Alexander considered plans for the continuing campaign with every indication of confidence. When, in November, the Russian forces occupied the strategic fortified city of Kars after a hard, two-months' siege, he used that fact in an effort to build up dwindling hope both at home and in the camps of war.

Seeing the tsar bent on continuing the fight, Francis Joseph, the most provokingly incalculable of the Western heads of state, finally brought matters to a resolution. In the middle of December, he announced that Austria would go to war with Russia at the beginning of 1856 unless, by that time, Alexander had agreed to join in peace negotiations on the basis of certain conditions, including the four that had been presented to Nicholas I and two new ones that Austria now saw fit to impose.

Even that threat might not have altered the tsar's vision of himself as another Alexander I had it not been reinforced by evidence of weakening support within his own government. His ministers were now braving his displeasure to point out that to fight on without allies, without money in the treasury, without credit, and without the support of the increasingly war-distressed populace was to insure disaster. No longer able to disregard these hazards, he at last ordered the Russian forces to disengage, protesting as he did so that he was committing an act of cowardice. He responded to the Austria ultimatum one day before his time would have run out.

In February 1856, an international congress (representing England, France, Austria, Turkey, Sardinia, and Russia) assembled in Paris and, within a month, had ready the terms of settlement—on the whole, a foregone one. Alexander accepted the resulting Treaty of Paris out of bitter necessity, but privately he was far from acquiescing to its provisions. For the time being, he could only allow Russia to endure the restraints it inflicted and take what comfort there was in the fact that it might have been worse. There had been no choice but to cede the mouth of the Danube as well as part of Bessarabia and to accept the humiliating conditions that Russia must never again maintain naval forces on the Black Sea or interfere in Turkish affairs. On the other hand, Sebastopol had been restored to Russia in return for the Turkish city of Kars, and the powers had agreed that all would take a responsible interest in protecting Turkish Christians. Moreover, the negotiating sessions of the congress had uncovered the beginning of a rift in the Western bloc that had been so solidly antagonistic to Russia: Napoleon III, satisfied with the restoration of French prestige on the continent, had, by flaunting it, earned England's disapproval.

There was no denying that Russia's standing among the powers remained gravely low, but Alexander did not consider the losses irretrievable. He was confident that strategy could be devised to form new alliances, regain status for his country, and overcome the restrictions imposed by the Treaty of Paris. In this campaign, to the winning of which he became as dedicated as he had been to victory in the recent military operations, he would have a dependable agent in his new foreign minister, Prince Alexander Gorchakov (a cousin of the Crimean commander, Prince Michael Gorchakov), who had held the painful position of ambassador to Austria during the war and was eager to see a readjustment of relationships that would put "perfidious" Francis Joseph in his proper place.

At the war's end, Alexander was free, in the sense that there was no longer a sword at his throat, to undertake the troublous tasks that waited—and grew more urgent as they waited—on the domestic front. On the premise that there was a close connection between the shortcomings of the armed forces and those of civilian society, he felt that he should carry out reforms in the two areas simultaneously. That, of course, would be an ambitious undertaking for him, for he was a reluctant reformer. But, prompted by official urgings, family advice, and what he interpreted as public trust, he set himself resolutely to make a virtue of the necessity to improve the insupportable conditions of the realm he had inherited.

Since the day of his accession, the very atmosphere had seemed charged with anticipation of change, and, war or no war, some of his subjects had been unwilling to wait for legal procedures to that end.

As had happened many times before when a new ruler came to the throne, *slukh* at once began to carry the magic word emancipation through the countryside. The serfs were stirred to hope when they learned that, just before his death, Nicholas had signed a manifesto summoning a temporary militia for auxiliary service—for which service, they reasoned, volunteers would be rewarded with freedom. They were also encouraged when some officials permitted them to take the oath of allegiance to the new tsar—a privilege they understood to be restricted to free men.

In a number of provinces, the credulous serfs began to stream out of their villages as if by prearrangement, illegally headed to the places of enlistment for the militia, and had to be forcibly turned back. In the province of Kiev, however, they made a more direct and disquieting approach to what they believed was due them. There, where the serfs numbered more than a million, feelings were easily aroused by recall of the days when the region had been ruled by free Cossacks and there had been no serfdom. Now, elaborating on current rumors, they convinced themselves that their priests had hidden from them a manifesto of Nicholas I permitting them to enroll as free Cossacks in the army; to right the situation, they simply declared their freedom and demonstrated it by laying down their tools and refusing to work further for their lords.[4]

Since their overseers could not move them either by persuasion or by coercion, the landlords called for help from the internal security and gendarme units, expecting that the usual public flogging of a few ringleaders would be sufficient to restore the accustomed servility of all. But the matter was not so easily settled: in some villages, the serfs refused to be driven to work and took to the offensive with clubs, even bare hands. In the end, of course, authority, speaking with musket fire, prevailed; but the effort required weeks instead of the usual few days. Following the Kiev disorder, serf outbreaks had to be subdued in the neighboring provinces of Chernigov and Voronezh; and from these, unrest crept eastward to the Volga region, where the great revolts of the past had erupted.

For a while the prevalence of unrest appeared uncommonly threatening. But when all had been quieted, some officials were inclined to shrug their shoulders at what was to them a historically familiar pattern: false rumors among the serfs, accusations against those imagined to be obstructing the beneficences which the Little Father intended for his people, and unorganized resistance that collapsed quickly in the face of energetic use of force. Alexander, on the other hand, though giving priority to the war at the time, did not shrug his shoulders in the belief that the serf problem was what it had always been. His service on his father's committees devoted to its study as well as his private consideration and observation had convinced him that the abolition of serfdom could no longer be left to another generation. He understood quite well the validity of Alexander

Gorchakov's argument that serfdom was "the source of all evil," [5] and resolution of the problem was high on his list of pressing duties.

Shortly after the signing of peace, Alexander received still another reminder that time was running out—this one from the area of the Black Sea coast. There, the serfs became aroused by a fanciful rumor that Napoleon III had agreed to a peace settlement only on the condition that the Russian serfs be freed and that, to meet this condition, the tsar had established himself in a gilded tent in Perekop, at the gateway to the Crimea, ready to grant freedom to all who presented themselves before an appointed day. So enticing was the prospect that thousands of families shouldered their belongings and began the trek to Perekop. Most of them were intercepted and forcibly returned to their villages; a few, to their grief, reached their destination, to find neither tsar nor freedom. Their failure, however, did not lessen the import of their undertaking. What they had done dramatically reinforced the fact that agrarian unrest was becoming more easily stirred, was involving ever larger numbers, and was directed more often than formerly toward emancipation, not just toward the alleviation of specific conditions or inequities of serfdom.

Those who hoped that Alexander would act on the problem of serfdom without delay sensed an encouraging note in certain phrases of his manifesto announcing the conclusion of peace: "With the help of Divine Providence, which has always been kind to Russia, may her internal well-being become firmly established and perfected . . . and may everyone enjoy the fruits of his honest labor, safeguarded by laws equally just and protective for all." [6] Was it not possible that these benign and ambiguous phrases referred especially to the "dark people" and indicated his intention to end serfdom?

While some cherished the belief that they might be so interpreted, others carried their doubts to the point of derision. Among the doubters were a number of students in Kharkov, who composed and distributed a mocking version of the manifesto, in which they compressed a lack of faith and a distrust that were common not only among the politically minded youth but also among many of their elders who had, over the years, succumbed to disillusionment. Their recast of the tsar's words was an exercise in acrimony:

We are grateful to you, dear Russians, for your blindness toward all of Our abuses. We are grateful to you, you veritable sheep, for the patience with which you have borne all the disasters, all the injustices, all the evil proceeding from Our despotic power. . . . We are grateful that you do not seek true enlightenment, but have faith in Our slaves who

fleece you, the clergy. . . . Sleep, dear Russians, as long as We have not
stolen your last shirt, shed the last drop of your blood. . . . Be assured
that there has never been, nor will there ever be, a single word of truth
in Our promises of reform. Remain forever exactly as you have always
been. We are ineffably pleased with you! [7]

The noble-landlords welcomed the ambiguity of the tsar's words
and waited hopefully for some assurance that they did not im-
ply any intention to change the present status of the serfs. They
were the first to have a direct explication. At a meeting of Moscow
nobles, Alexander gave them to understand that emancipation was
precisely what he had in mind:

I understand, gentlemen, that rumors have spread among you about my
plans to abolish serfdom. To forestall a lot of idle talk about such an
important subject, I think I should inform you that I do not plan to do
this at once; yet you understand, of course, that the present practice of
owning souls cannot continue unchanged. It is better to start the abolition of serfdom from above than to wait until the serfs begin to liberate
themselves from below. I request you, gentlemen, to work out means by
which this can best be accomplished.[8]

He asked further that his position on serfdom and his request for
cooperation be made known to all nobles. Thereafter, to open an
approach to the problem from the opposite end also, he followed his
father's example by setting up a central, and secret, committee in
St. Petersburg.

To carry out a change as widely significant as emancipation would
require wide cooperation, and Alexander sought it not only among
the nobles but also among enlightened groups of every kind. He took
the trouble to visit the grand duchy of Finland, the kingdom of Poland, and the Baltic provinces to convince their upper classes of his
goodwill. (Lest the Poles expect too much, however, he gently warned
a group of their notables: "No dreams, gentlemen, no dreams.") As
a further token of goodwill toward all, he used the occasion of his
coronation, in August 1856, to announce the amnesty of a number
of political prisoners and exiles, including the surviving Decembrists
and some members of the Petrashevsky Circle, and to suspend the
summoning of new recruits for the next three years.

The desired response from the nobles was slow in coming. For
months, most of them refrained from any indication that they had
altered their position on emancipation or that they intended to respond to Alexander's request for their cooperation in devising means
to bring it about. His secret committee, most of its members being

landowning nobles opposed to emancipation, was equally unhelpful in getting the project under way. All seemed to believe that if they simply marked time and disregarded the issue, Alexander, like his predecessors, would let the matter sink into the morass of imperial business, and nothing would come of it.

They were mistaken. During 1857, the tsar intensified the official pressure at all points. He made the energetic Grand Duke Constantine chairman of the central committee—a sure way of stirring up action of some kind—and finally won from it a general plan of procedure. Then he pointedly reminded the governors and the provincial nobility that he was becoming impatient with inaction and let it be widely known that he was actively considering emancipation, even allowing newspapers for the first time to carry items on the subject. He felt certain that the nobles would quickly see the wisdom of cooperation, once their easily roused serfs knew that the prospect of freedom was no longer a will-o'-the-wisp. To make doubly sure of local action, he ordered his governors to see that the nobility within their provinces organize committees for preparing and submitting emancipation plans; and to provide for the coordination of plans and the preparation of legislation, he publicly designated the central committee as the government's Chief Committee on Peasant Affairs.

This show of determination on the part of the tsar moved the nobles, as he intended that it should, to begin making their unhappy peace with the thought of emancipation. Countless others welcomed it with warm expectancy. In Moscow particularly, the winter of 1858–59 was one of unparalleled ebullience, when among the educated residents the discussions were, in the words of Slavophile Alexander Koshelev, "of only one subject—the opening of an era of beneficent reconstruction in Russia," with "dear old Moscow almost turned into a parliament." [9] Herzen, embittered enemy of the Romanovs though he was, relented enough to proclaim that Alexander was a standard-bearer of progress who would transform Russia as King Charles Albert had recently transformed Sardinia. Even some of the clergy, not given to spontaneous support of this kind of progress, joined in the paean. The rector of Kazan Theological Academy, Ioann Sokolov, sweepingly declared: "Russia is striving to be born again. The hour has come! . . . Oh, the Church must be and, in fact is, ready . . . to summon all sons of the fatherland to take part and cooperate in this great undertaking of rebirth in the name of Christian truth and love." [10]

Soon the idea of progress, spilling over in every direction, began

to take on definition for many. Some nobles, even though still opposed to emancipation, were affected by the idea and looked hopefully to the possibility of the government's becoming a limited monarchy that would guarantee civil rights and give them a share of political power. Professors and students looked for academic freedom;
writers, for freedom of expression; Jews for legal equality; and Poles,
though they had been warned not to dream, for national liberty.
Religious leaders renewed their faith that the Church would finally
be released from the iron control of the state. Their mood showed
up in expressions such as that of one prelate's pronouncement about
the late Nicholas Protasov, the hussar officer whom Nicholas I had
appointed over-procurator of the Holy Synod: *"Sic transit gloria
mundi! Est Deus, qui ad Suum terribile judicium appelat homines
usurpantes sanctae ecclesiae jura."*[11] Appanage peasants saw reason to
expect early improvement in their lot, since the tsar, personally responsible for the imperial properties to which they were attached,
would surely lead the way as an exemplary landlord. State peasants
hoped for a change that would remove their obligations to the government before the recently appointed minister of state lands, General
Michael Muravev, had a chance to begin imposing new methods of
administration upon them. The serfs, knowing themselves to be at
last the center of imperial concern, now looked hungrily to St. Petersburg for the blessing of freedom, which had so often seemed, from
their depths, more distant than the skies above.

Alexander himself, while impressed by the enthusiasm he had
aroused, did not like the liberal ring of the word progress now being
so widely bandied about. "What is this progress! ! !" he wrote in the
margin of a report in which the word appeared, and promptly ordered that the baleful term be thereafter prohibited in official communications.[12] Regardless of his scruples about the word, however, he
accepted its spirit. Therein lay his appeal to those who were to be
the strength behind the throne on some of the most important issues
of his reign.

Among them, his brother Constantine stood first, not only because
he was a capable leader personally related to the tsar but also because
he was so fired with belief in the need for change that he was capable
of disregarding obstructive tradition and virtually overriding opposition. The use to which his residence, the Marble Palace, was now
often put as the center of the reform-minded among the capital's
aristocracy and upper bureaucracy was, in itself, an unspoken and
quietly ironic reflection on tradition: the elegant structure had been

conceived and built at the order of his great-grandmother Catherine
II as a token for her lover Count Orlov. Here, Constantine welcomed
men who would help Alexander's government to take action that had
been evaded for generations.

His guests often included Minister of Interior Lanskoi, a frail
septuagenarian with a lively mind, who, despite his early pacifying
words to the nobility on behalf of the tsar, was clearly of the anti-
nobility, as the proponents of emancipation were currently called. In
his ministry, where the great files on the subject of serfdom were now
being mined for helpful information and where new files were growing, he was happily and usefully situated. An important footnote to
Lanskoi's interest in reform was his choice for assistant minister:
confuting the popular jest that Russia would one day be ruled by
idiots because ministers invariably favored men inferior to themselves
as assistants, he persuaded the tsar to appoint as his deputy the
nephew of Count Paul Kiselev, Nicholas Milyutin, an able young
noble well known as an ardent reformer with much respect for the
Slavophiles and none for the nobility. Milyutin was one of the so-
called reds among Constantine's colleagues in reform, men whose attitudes were considered revolutionary by the more conservative of
those outside the circle.

Another of the "reds," perhaps more extreme than his brother
Nicholas, was Dmitri Milyutin, a brilliant and well-educated staff
officer, whose ideas about the country's tradition-ridden armed services were, to say the least, radical. Then there was the jovial Jacob
Rostovtsev (who, it will be recalled, was moved to split his loyalties
by informing Nicholas I of the Decembrist plot and then admitting
his act to the rebels themselves), now one of the tsar's generals adjutant and a staunch supporter of emancipation on terms generous
to the peasants. Another was Peter Valuev, whose appearance, suggestive of a mannered milord—muttonchop whiskers and all—obscured for some his personal competence and practicality in many
areas. He had written a memorandum on the state of the nation which
Constantine so admired that he had distributed copies of it among
his staff in the ministry of the navy. The gist of his views, as stated
in the memorandum, was that Russia, while brilliant on the surface,
was decadent underneath. To alter the condition, it was necessary
to compel the bureaucracy, which now concealed the decadence, to
serve under the searchlight of public scrutiny and, in recognition of
the fact that "the mind needs elbowroom," to permit the educated
people, freed from excessive surveillance and regimentation, to con-

tribute to the life of the fatherland.[13] It was, in effect, a summary of what Constantine and many other reformers believed. Converting their beliefs into practice would mean setting the government on a course quite inconsistent with that established under official nationalism in the preceding reign, but it was an undertaking that most of them anticipated with relish.

Often, while such men were personally at grips with the problems of reform, trying to meet the arguments or outmaneuver the obstructionist tactics of the opposition, the tsar seemed to be standing aside, holding the initiative in the autocratic manner but wisely doling out the duties of execution to others and demanding from them the energy and effectiveness at strategy lacking in his own makeup. It was evident that he preferred the company of men like Count Alexander Adlerberg, a friend of long standing and now a general in his suite, an elegant aristocrat with whom he played piquet and escaped from talk of politics. If imperial involvements were particularly oppressive, he might, like his illustrious uncle Alexander I, seek assistance through spiritualism. When the preparations for emancipation were at their most frustrating, he attended a number of séances presided over by the popular Scottish spiritualist Daniel Home, and was impressed by the demonstrations he witnessed: the levitation of tables, their movement to the rhythm of "God Save the Tsar," and the summoning of the spirit of Nicholas I to answer questions by definable rappings. Despite the Empress Marie's depreciation of both Home and these manifestations, Alexander accepted them as authentic and credited the séances with providing the reassurance he needed in order patiently to keep up the fight for the reforms he had undertaken.

The preparation of emancipation legislation demanded an extraordinary measure of patience and determination not only from the tsar but also from those who advised him and those who undertook to carry out his instructions. That almost five years were required to complete the task was not surprising under the circumstances. There was much more involved than simply granting liberty. Reason advised against a repetition of the mistaken measures that had been taken in dealing with serfdom in the Baltic provinces. There, during the reign of Alexander I, the serfs had been granted liberty without practical provisions for their ensuing condition, and their plight had been nowise improved thereby: they had simply become farm laborers helplessly under the economic control of their former masters.

Alexander II and his most practical advisers accepted the reasoning that, if emancipation were to be the desired boon to people and country, if it were to bring stability to Russia through a secure peasantry and a secure nobility, certain conditions must be met. Freed serfs would be allotted enough land to sustain them; they would be required to compensate their former landlords for the land received, but not for their personal liberty. To ease the shock of transition for the landlords, the freed serfs would be required to perform customary labor and pay customary dues for a specified period after emancipation. They would receive their land allotments not as individuals but as members of the village commune, a conservative and stabilizing institution without whose influence the serfs would be dangerously at a loss in a world beyond the limits of their experience.

These conditions were not immediately accepted as imperial dicta. The majority of the noble-landowners—the so-called planters—were determined to fight every step of the way for emancipation on terms more favorable to themselves. The minority—the emancipators or *muzhikophiles* ("peasant-lovers")—were, on the other hand, just as determined to create a self-sustaining peasantry by the most direct means possible. The contest between the two factions raged in the provincial committees and in the Chief Committee on Peasant Affairs, where, but for the domineering of Constantine, the whole scheme might have foundered before the opposition of influential "planters" like Minister of Justice Victor Panin and the strong-willed Prince Paul Gagarin. The issue was joined with uncompromising desperation in the two commissions set up to assist the chief committee by editing the recommendations and plans submitted by the provincial committees and drafting the emancipation statute—both under the direction of Rostovtsev, assisted by Nicholas Milyutin. By the end of 1859, when the provincial committees had completed their work and sent representatives of St. Petersburg to take part in the final work of framing the emancipation legislation, it was clear that the obduracy of the "planters" was forcing the undertaking into a virtual stalemate. It was a situation that could be resolved only by the tsar.

Alexander met the test—unwillingly perhaps, but with the needed directness. He had asked for reasonable assistance from the nobility, and it had not been given in the degree and manner expected. His patience had finally run out. Although he had promised the provincial representatives a share in the framing of the statute, he now arbitrarily limited their participation to the giving of opinions. To all involved, he let it be known that he expected the preparations for emancipation, based on the conditions he had approved, to proceed without further delay.

The momentum picked up at once. Those who had felt that emancipation was being talked away—and their number had come to include such men as the redoubtable Constantine himself—took courage again. Even the death of Rostovtsev, early in 1860, and the tsar's appointment of the anti-emancipationist Count Panin to replace him did not retard the final work as demanded. Still, the drafting and revising of the legislation by the commissions was a laborious business, and the results were not ready for the Chief Committee until the fall of 1860. Then four more months were required for the final study and revision by the committee and the State Council.

While the condition of the serfs was the chief subject of concern in this drive for new legislation, Alexander was not neglecting his other unfree subjects. He had appointed a commission in 1858 to determine the best arrangement, consonant with the accepted conditions for serf emancipation, for making the appanage peasants a part of a secure rural class; and within a year, he had granted them their personal freedom. In addition, he had instructed the ministry of state lands that the millions of state peasants also were to be brought into line with the new conception. Measures to effect changes for both groups were now under consideration.

The Emancipation Act was ready for Alexander's signature on February 19, 1861, the sixth anniversary of his accession.* As he signed the lengthy document and the manifesto which would introduce it to the public (at a date to be decided upon), he could hardly have avoided the sin of satisfaction that is said to accompany the heaping of coals of fire on appropriate heads, for the manifesto, laced with the grandiloquent phraseology of Metropolitan Philaret, included these words: "Russia will not forget that it [the nobility], prompted only by respect for the dignity of man and Christian love of neighbor, voluntarily renounced serfdom and established the basis of a new economic future for the peasantry." [14]

The legislation was far from perfect, but Alexander was satisfied that it provided as nearly as possible under the circumstances the conditions he had laid down for emancipation. None would doubt that it was based on a bold and generous conception or that it was the century's most far-reaching piece of legislation, marking as it did the

* Although he became tsar on his father's death, which occurred on February 18, 1855, Alexander dated his accession from February 19, when he issued the manifesto announcing his assumption of the throne.

end of the ancient institution with which almost every phase of Russian life had been entwined.

If carried out as intended, it would within a short time bring beneficial, though not obviously drastic, changes to the countryside. The landlords would release to the emancipated serfs that portion of their estates which they had not previously set aside for their own use—in most cases, about 50 percent—and it would become the property not of individual farmers but of the peasant village commune, which would be required to apportion it to the village families and assess them for payment. Though different plans for payment were provided, the government expected usually to recompense the landlords for the land, at assessed value, with interest-bearing bonds and allow the former serfs to settle their indebtedness directly with the government by annual payment of "redemption dues" extending over a period of forty-nine years. The village commune, retained as the convenient liaison device between government and peasant, was to make provision for collecting these dues from the individual families as well as for insuring that each discharge the customary obligations to the landlords for a period of two years, as required by the new legislation. In addition, it was to assume certain communal duties of a self-governing nature, such as the selection of recruits required by the army, the collection of taxes, the supervision of planting, and the maintenance of law and order.

The tsar realized that the landowners were being asked to pay a considerable price, in many cases a ruinous one, to make emancipation possible under these terms. He expected from most of them only dutiful acquiescence, not willing acceptance. He realized also that the serfs would consider their liberation incomplete and their dreams unfulfilled in view of the limitations imposed by the provisions of emancipation. They would be dissatisfied with the two-year postponement of their release from obligations to the landlords, with the limited amount of land they would receive, with the requirement of redemption payments that possibly for forty-nine years would stand between them and clear title to their land allotments, and with the fact that they were still financially tied to the village commune, unable to escape legal responsibility for communal taxes and dues even by a change of residence.

Whatever its reception, the act was now law, and the complex task of putting it into effect must be begun. Alexander did not share his nobles' fears that the liberated serfs would indulge in an orgy of violence and then relapse into a state of idle drunkenness; yet he thought it wise to withhold from them the fact of emancipation until after Butter Week, the Orthodox pre-Lenten carnival, when the consumption of alcohol was known to be at its highest. And he approved the idea of taking precautionary measures against the predictable local outbursts among disappointed serfs. Accordingly, he dispatched ranking officers from his own suite to the provincial capitals with orders to oversee the publicizing of the act as well as the imperial manifesto and, if any disorder should result, to take whatever measures were necessary to handle it.

In Moscow and St. Petersburg, the documents were made public on March 5, 1861. Two days later, the emissaries sent couriers out from the provincial capitals with copies to be given publicity in the other cities and towns. On the same day, there came the first announcement of new laws under which the appanage peasants would be given tenure of the holdings they occupied, subject to a forty-nine-year obligation to pay for what they received, and the minister of state lands was directed to devise a plan whereby the new legislation for serf emancipation could be applied also to the state peasants.

This official announcement of emancipation for Russia's serfs and other unfree people would, in years to come, be celebrated with glowing pride; but at the time it was received with a striking lack of emotion. What the main statute provided was viewed by leading proponents of reform as too little, too slow, and too deviously designed; by leading nobles, as too much, too soon, and too unadaptable to their own needs. In the two capitals, officials were able to muster a fair show of enthusiasm; in the Michael Riding School particularly, where Alexander himself read the manifesto to a fashionable St. Petersburg crowd gathered for the changing of the guard, the reception was quite jubilant. Elsewhere, during the following weeks, as the manifesto was read and the act explained to provincial assemblies in churches, in market squares, or on the steps of manor houses, the mood was somber and the occasional cheers were subdued ones. In Kazan, university students whipped up the mood of dissatisfaction and promoted such disorder that police were called to quell it. Their sentiments remained unchanged, however; and when the tsar, on the advice of those who blamed the student "lawlessness" on leniency in the central administration, was led to replace Minister of Education Kovalevsky by the strict disciplinarian Admiral Efim Putyatin and to order tighter controls, they simply became more firmly settled.

As was expected, the explanation of the terms of emancipation stirred dissatisfaction and resentment in the serfs. Reluctant to give up their naïve belief that the Little Father had been preparing a glorious release for them, they invented an explanation: the "real manifesto" providing for "real freedom" had been kept from the people and would one day be brought to light. Most of them, inured to disappointment and accustomed to obedience, accepted what was proffered and returned to the old pattern, enduring each day in the hope of a better tomorrow.

In a few localities where the feeling of the serfs broke into open defiance, there was nothing particularly new about the resulting incidents. The worst of them occurred on the estate of Count Michael Musin-Pushkin, in the village of Bezdna, province of Kazan. There, a literate and imaginative peasant, Anton Petrov, enlivened the *slukh* channels with a most provocative story. His theme was old, but the details timely: the landlords having foisted upon the people a spurious emancipation manifesto, the tsar had secretly informed Petrov that he was to receive a copy of the real manifesto; it was on its way in the custody of a youth wearing on his left shoulder a silver medal and on his right a gold one. Petrov let it be known that, until the arrival of the imperial courier, he would need personal protection; and from villages near and far, credulous peasants flocked to his side, ignoring the remonstrances of priests and officials. By the time armed authority arrived to set the matter straight, 5,000 peasants had formed a thick cordon around Petrov's hut. When they ignored the command to yield and permit the arrest of Petrov, the troops were ordered to open fire. Still they stood, fervor against fire, until repeated salvoes had killed at least fifty of them and wounded seventy-five more. The effort had failed, as was usual with such spontaneous acts of defiance, and Petrov was wrested from the throng of peasants, later to be executed. But the legend of a "real manifesto" lived on.[15]

Alexander was justly proud of his handling of emancipation, feeling that he had approached it in such a way as to forestall agrarian revolution without unduly disturbing the supports of autocracy and that he had saved intact the institution that would insure future rural stability, the village commune. He had no doubt that the nobility would adjust itself to the new life; that in the future, as in the past, it would continue the functions of the "well-born estate," providing officers and civil servants, administering local affairs, and upholding the social importance of country squires. Though he expected the development of new enterprises—a foregone certainty since the indefatigable Constantine was already astir about the coal and iron in the Donets River basin—and the growth of cities as his planned railroads fanned out across the land, he did not expect urban centers ever to become anything but insignificant islands in the sea of rural Russia. As long as the countryside remained under the capable management of the nobility and the properly directed husbandry of the peasantry, the regime rested solidly on bedrock: that was his satisfying belief.

Emancipation was unquestionably a golden milestone, and perhaps others lay ahead for Alexander. Yet his approach to succeeding ones would not be easy since, in establishing himself as an accessory to change and a somewhat obstinate taskmaster, he had invited responses for which he was unprepared and followers for some of whom he had no affinity.

Unlike Nicholas, who surrounded himself with men who shared his views, obeyed his orders, and were blindly devoted to him, Alexander evoked little enthusiasm after the bright dawn of his reforms and could count on little personal loyalty beyond a very limited circle. On the eve of emancipation, the chief of staff of gendarmes, General Timashev, confided to Peter Valuev, who was at that time moving up the ladder of the St. Petersburg bureaucracy:

To remain in service at this time requires boundless personal devotion. This I had for Emperor Nicholas. I do not have it for Emperor Alexander. For his principles, yes; for his person, no.

The Emperor deludes himself about what is happening. Deep in his soul he is a despot.[16]

Timashev did not leave the service, but neither he nor the scores who shared his sentiments could give the support that Alexander needed.

Among those who served him, bitterly antagonistic factions soon developed. At one extreme were the brothers Dmitri and Nicholas Milyutin, in the vanguard of the reform-minded; at the other, a number of unreconstructed reactionaries such as Minister of Justice Panin, all of them veteran bureaucrats whom Alexander was at first reluctant to dismiss from government service. Between were various shifting factions made up of men who, although critical of those features of emancipation that were disadvantageous to the nobility, thought of themselves as mildly liberal, deplored both extremes, and approved certain reforms favored by the tsar. Such a man was Alexander's choice to head the Third Section, Prince Vasily Dolgorukov, whose enemies maliciously accused him of transforming the organization into a "temple of mirth" by his easygoing ways. But even he, reformer though he was, did not share his views with the tsar; in his conception of Russia's future was a constitutional monarchy on the Prussian model, and he knew better than to bring the word *constitution* into discussions with an autocrat.

In this political disharmony, when the establishment of a position and adherence to it were so essential, Alexander was often at a loss. Unfortunately he was unable to conceal that fact: as one observer recalled: "When he talked to a man of spirit he seemed like a rheumatic caught in a draft." [17] Sometimes his reactions appeared to be reversals of his own principles. Two months after he signed the Emancipation Act, he removed from the government two of the staunchest supporters of emancipation in order to appease the "planters." He replaced Minister of Interior Lanskoi (making him a count in consolation) by Peter Valuev, whose liberal views had not prevented him from giving adroit support to the "planters," and he dismissed Nicholas Milyutin and removed him temporarily from the scene by granting him "permission" to travel abroad. He explained his action with the reluctant "I must, for the nobility describe you as one of the reds."

This apparent disloyalty to reformers, however, did not mean that Alexander was disloyal to the idea of reform. He finally replaced Panin, in the ministry of justice, by reform-minded Dmitri Zamyatin. Also, when a band of daring students happened to afford him the opportunity, he demonstrated that he was still willing to become personally and directly involved in a liberal cause. While he was away from the capital on one occasion, in the Crimea seeking relief from his asthma, students of St. Petersburg University overrode authority by an act never before witnessed in the capital, a public protest in defiance of their superiors. Critical of the provisions of the emancipation legislation and restive under recent restrictions placed upon them within the university (for which the tsar himself was responsible, having just recently appointed the reactionary Putyatin as minister of education to suppress student dissension), they marched demonstratively through the streets and distributed leaflets until the police interfered, arrested 200, and dragged them off to the Peter-Paul fortress. Informed of the incident, the tsar returned at once, to find a mood of general uneasiness among his officials. The student disorder had reminded them of the student uprisings in Vienna and Berlin in 1848; many of them, even some who had welcomed reforms, saw in it an indication that the tsar had loosened the reins of authority too much, had waited too long before putting a restraining hand in the ministry of education, and that outright anarchy could follow unless he disowned the cause of reform. But Alexander did not respond with severity, as Putyatin advised and as many others hoped he would. He had stronger criticism for officials because of their gratuitous harshness toward the students than for the students because of their misbehavior. Though he approved of disciplinary measures for the leaders of the demonstration, he instructed that the other students involved simply be given a stern reprimand and released on trust. Then, as if to emphasize his attitude, he ousted a number of reactionary officials and appointed recognized reformers to their posts. Outstanding among the new appointees were Alexander Golovnin as minister of education and Dmitri Milyutin as minister of war. Both were considered by the reactionaries to be dangerously liberal, and Golovnin was believed by gendarme chief of staff Timashev actually to be in treasonable communication with Herzen.[18]

The Russian government was taking on a character that intrigued observers throughout Europe. In foreign capitals, bets were being taken on the outcome: would the empire fall prey to revolution or would the tsar find it expedient to follow the path of his predecessors and, in the end, turn reactionary? Alexander proclaimed through his foreign ministry: "Our motto is: *neither weakness nor reaction.*" To uphold that motto, of course, was going to be a strain for one whose nature rebelled against complications and difficulties. But the tsar allowed himself to be convinced that, by the use of rewards and incentives rather than punishment and repression, such loyalty could be bred in his subjects that their forbearance and cooperation would be assured and the course of his reforms therefore made easy.

Entranced by the notion of benevolent autocracy, Alexander accepted Constantine's view that a little kindness would work wonders with the Poles and dispel the anti-Russian feelings that, for generations, had made it necessary to keep the storm warnings up in that area. Recently the Polish opposition had been almost out of hand again, and something had to be done. Though Prince Michael Gorchakov, who succeeded Paskevich as viceroy in 1856, had kept the opposition fairly quiet for five years while relieving some of the pressure of Nicholas' last suppressive Russification measures, Polish nationalism had continued to thrive. After his death, in May 1861, it had become demonstratively revolutionary—so troublesome, in fact, that for a while neither Polish conciliators nor Russian arms could establish tenable order. The governor general of Warsaw had committed suicide, Gorchakov's successor had resigned, and another Russian martinet, General Alexander Lüders, had taken over the viceroyship. Still the opposition seethed, unrepentant and unreconciled. Finally Alexander, sincerely committed to reform and trusting Constantine's view of the situation to be a practical one, agreed to a tempering of Russia's arbitrary domination by a program of "re-Polonization" for the kingdom of Poland. In 1862, to emphasize the imperial goodwill, he appointed Constantine to replace General Lüders as viceroy.

From the tsar's point of view, the steps laid out for the re-Polonization program were genuinely lenient: liberalization in state administration, in local government, and in regulations governing the use of the Polish language and Polish educational institutions. But they did not satisfy the Polish nationalists, who sought both a broadening and an acceleration. Their goal was Polish independence. Unfortunately for all concerned, their impatience overrode their reason, and they attempted to force the pace. Beginning with a slaughter of sleeping Russian soldiers in their Warsaw barracks, in January 1863, the nationalist resistance grew quickly into a general uprising, releasing again a flood of passions distilled and redistilled through years of hope, frustration, and harsh repression.

From Warsaw, the rebellion surged through the kingdom of Poland and into the nine formerly Polish provinces known as Russia's Western Region (Lithuania, White Russia, and Little Russia), where the still powerful Polish landlords and Catholic clergy were ever ready to whip up anti-Russian feeling. For a time, England, France, and Austria gave their diplomatic blessings to the rebels and stirred with an air of moral indignation. A scattering of supporters from Russian radical and liberal circles, fired by the distant urgings of such kindred souls as Herzen and Bakunin, spoke up in defense of the revolt. France even talked threateningly of giving military aid. But neither readiness and willingness to fight nor any realistic support they were likely to get could give the rebels the ghost of a chance against Russian arms. With only Prussia's support, the imperial forces were more than a match for the ineffectually organized rebels in the skirmishes, guerrilla forays, and poorly planned risings they could manage. The Poles nevertheless dragged out their effort for more than a year.

Within Russia proper, the regime was for a time actually strengthened by the revolt. There was, as usual, an outburst of chauvinism when it was learned that foreigners were censuring the homeland. Most liberals disavowed their confidence in Herzen and neglected or temporarily abandoned their anti-regime activities. Before long both the Westernizers and the Slavophiles were claiming the government's position as their own.

When the insurrection was finally quelled (in May 1864), the rebellious areas being put under strict martial law and another harsh administrator, Count Theodore Berg, sent in to replace Constantine as viceroy and direct the pacification, Alexander became anxious to get back to his plans for domestic reforms. Perhaps now he would have the added advantage of greater support among his subjects. The working out of a new Polish policy would require extensive planning, and there was no reason that other projects could not be developing at the same time.

The return to the business of reform was by no means unopposed. Its detractors were now ready with the argument that this last Polish revolt was another warning sign that reform had gone beyond the margin of safety.

None mirrored this attitude as well or encouraged it as ably as Michael Katkov, the clever and sometimes unscrupulous publisher of the daily *Moscow News*. Though in his student days Katkov had been a Westernizer and something of a radical, he gradually moved to the right during the following two decades. He had not opposed Alexander's first reform measures, but student unrest had made him increasingly disenchanted with reform and increasingly concerned over what he took to be the weakening of authority. In 1863, he adopted, and thereafter maintained, a vigorously anti-Polish, sharply Russian chauvinistic, highly conservative position. He was morally convinced that political unrest in Russia was the work of an international conspiracy in which Polish nationalists, Mazzini and other European revolutionaries, Palmerston and other English leaders, and various domestic "traitors" had a hand. Privately he believed that Minister of Education Golovnin, a close friend of Constantine, was one of the archtraitors, that he had duped the grand duke into a defense of pro-Polish policies and was therefore responsible for the resulting trouble. The publisher's anti-Polish position helped to raise the circulation of his *Moscow News* to 12,000, a remarkably high figure for those days, making it the most widely read and most influential paper in Russia—a position it was able to maintain for the next twenty-five years.

Katkov's reactionary views coincided with the views of many in the government, but they did not change those of the tsar. Alexander was disappointed in the Polish response, but he could not adopt the tenet that reforms in themselves were undesirable.

He had a most compatible supporter in Minister of Interior Peter Valuev, who, while accepting the need for reform, understood the necessity to guard against encroaching on the prerogatives of the autocrat. When he took over his ministry, Valuev took over also a most important and long overdue reform task in which Nicholas Milyutin, as assistant minister, had been engaged—that of supervising the committee drafting legislation to establish new provincial and district administrative bodies. Now that the state, through the changes accompanying emancipation, had practically displaced the nobility in rural government, adjustment was called for, and there was the promise of something new in the legislation now in preparation.

By the end of the Polish revolt, his committee had almost completed its draft, and throughout the country people were waiting anxiously to hear the results. The liberals hoped that this would be a reform making up somewhat for their disappointment with the emancipation act by giving the peasants their rightful share in the handling of their own affairs; the large landowners hoped that it would be a measure restoring their privileged position in all affairs of the countryside; the older bureaucrats hoped that, whatever its nature, it would not interfere with established practices.

The committee's recommendations provided some features agreeable from each point of view. Qualification for membership in the new bodies of local government, zemstvos, would be based on property, not on social class, as in the pre-emancipation period (since property owners included peasants as well as nobles, the innovation was significant). The zemstvos' authorized functions would include the building and maintenance of roads, primary schools, hospitals, and clinics as well as the provision of assistance to farmers and the carrying out of welfare work.

Many liberals looked to the zemstvos as a step toward representative government, but Alexander interpreted them differently. He accepted Valuev's explanation that the new bodies could never undermine the prerogatives of the crown because they would have neither legislative power nor police authority, and that, furthermore, besides promoting the commonweal, they would harness the energies of people whose urge to be useful led them to "make a lot of noise and kick up a fuss because they have nothing to do," and would thus prevent the growth of political discontent.[19]

In regard to the zemstvos, Valuev was presenting an argument that he knew to be agreeable. He was wise enough, however, not to indicate to the tsar what he would personally have liked to see established as the succeeding level in government: an imperial legislature something like the Prussian *Landtag*. Being realistic about the matter, he suggested something less: an imperial congress consisting of delegates from provincial zemstvos and municipal councils that would sit as an advisory body with the State Council. Alexander allowed this timid proposal to be considered secretly by several of his other officials, who, with the exception of Dolgorukov and Dmitri Milyutin, professed to be horrified by the idea of such a body. One of them even accused Valuev of trying to smuggle in "a constitution and a bicameral system." [20] The tsar pigeonholed Valuev's proposal with considerable relief but held fast to the planned zemstvos. They would, after all, be safely limited organs of local self-government; their introduction would not be as threatening to the established system as feared by the bureaucrats of the old order nor as innovational as imagined by the landowners—nor, he had to admit, as promising of change as hoped by some liberals.

The Law on the Zemstvos received the imperial approval on January 1, 1864, and shortly provoked a lively response. The majority of liberals, who had expected the new organizations to be democratic and of some political significance, were disappointed when they learned that the election of members was to be based on indirect and unequal suffrage and that the zemstvo functions were to be limited mainly to local economic needs. Herzen, despite the fact that by this time he had lost his popularity among the liberals, reflected their mood when he stated in his newspaper, *The Bell*, that the provisions of the law were "mean, insincere, and niggardly." [21] A few liberals, however, pleased that even this had been provided, called the law "one of the highest achievements of contemporary Russian legislation." [22] Strict conservatives and reactionaries could look forward only to resigned endurance or the possibility of revision.

Reform was just as urgently needed in urban local government as in the rural, and it was under active consideration in Valuev's ministry. But to reorganize the municipal institutions, that for time out of mind had been developing haphazardly and independently, was a more difficult undertaking than the establishment of the zemstvos.

Just now, hundreds of local committees were trying to analyze the needs of the municipalities, and Valuev's workers were struggling through the welter of their reports and recommendations. Six more years would be required for the task.

Though some postponements were necessary, there was as yet no noticeable recession in the tsar's drive for reform. The country's laws and judicial system were next in line. The drafting of legislation for their reform had been under way since 1850, when Nicholas I appointed the Bludov Committee to begin the work. After Alexander reorganized the committee, in 1861, it took three more years to complete the work. The promulgation of the resulting new statute was a lengthy step toward fulfilling the promise of Alexander's first post-war manifesto to provide "the protection of law equally just to all." With it, he scrapped the ancient courts and codes and substituted for them courts and codes founded on the institutions and principles of Anglo-Saxon and continental systems. The new codes, based on the principles that all were equal before the law and that there should be no punishment except for violation of existing law, provided for trial by jury, an independent judiciary, tenure for competent and principled judges, and an organized and self-governing bar. The scope of this reform prompted the suggestion that for a time very few— probably not even the tsar himself—wholly comprehended it.*

One change, sought with particular eagerness by the liberals, was approached grudgingly and handled somewhat equivocally in Alexander's program of reform. That was the change in censorship regulations. A new law, issued in 1865, relieved the severity of censorship without lessening in any material way the government's control over what was written and read. Foreign publications were admitted, but their sale made subject to official approval. Publishers and editors were granted more freedom of judgment in choosing or rejecting materials, and provision was made for more judicial consideration and less arbitrary suppression of questioned material. Yet, though censorship was ostensibly to be controlled by the ministry of interior, the law did not forestall the likelihood that in practice its exercise would remain generally disorganized, and that those concerned would sometimes still find it necessary to deal with various agencies whose interpretation of the law would vary and the quality of whose enforcement would be unpredictable. Luckily, experienced Russian

---

* This suggestion was borne out a few years later when, on being reminded that he could not dismiss a certain judge on grounds of personal dislike since he had signed a law making judges irremovable except for misconduct, Alexander asked in astonishment, "Did I sign such nonsense?"

publishers, editors, authors, importers, and salesmen had by this time
learned to operate as an informal fraternity of subtle, and generally
effective, circumventors: they would make the most of the new law.

In addition to the most publicized reforms, an impressive catalog
of others was accumulated during the first eventful decade of Alexander's reign. Autonomy was restored to the universities. Legal measures were taken to improve primary education, a field in which the
zemstvos had begun at once to translate legal provisions into active
betterment, and to promote secondary education, now being extended
to include children of the lower classes. The autonomous administration of the grand duchy of Finland was placed on a firm basis. The
assimilation of the Jews was encouraged, and some laws discriminating against them were abolished. The economy was stimulated by the
authorization of ambitious plans for railroad construction and the
encouragement of growth in corporations and private banks. Corporal
punishment was abolished for almost all persons—the peasants excepted as not being "advanced" enough to be spared the rod. And, as
a body to consider overall questions of policy, Alexander established
the Council of Ministers, with himself as presiding officer.

In the great range of his reforms touching practically every phase
of Russian life, none, with the possible exception of emancipation,
was nearer to the tsar's heart than the prodigious one that had been
under way since the end of the Crimean War and was still far from
completion—further reform of the military services. Here he was concerned with what had long been recognized as one of the mainstays of
autocracy; tampering with it was not to be taken lightly. Emancipation, of course, had involved another of the mainstays, the nobility;
but Alexander's feelings in that case had been of a different nature.
While he valued the support of the upper class, he heartily disapproved of those aspects of its development that he sought to reform.
In the case of the armed services, he was not moved by disapproval
but by a desire to improve effectiveness. Yet he was torn, particularly
in the consideration of army reform, between sentiment and practicality, between cherished tradition and the unquestionable need
for modernization. It was not easy for him to direct changes that
would detract from the parade perfection of the army or to face the
reaction of most of the senior officers, who fought reform with the
courage of lions and the protectiveness of doting mothers. But, in his
judgment, reform could not be postponed; personal feelings had to
give way to exigency.

Committed to change and improvement whatever the cost, Alex-

ander accepted the fact that it involved far more than adopting improved weapons and different training methods for the fighting units,
important as those steps were. It involved also the development of a
new system of recruitment (now that serfdom, the former major
source of conscripts, was gone) and an extensive corollary program of
economic development adequate for the support of modern military
services. He profited from the fact that he could entrust the final
planning and carrying out of the military reforms to two men of
proven ability: the Grand Duke Constantine, who took over the direction of naval modernization, and General Dmitri Milyutin, minister
of war after 1861, who took over the preponderant task, the reform
of the army.

Milyutin stood far above the level of Russian officialdom: gifted,
dynamic, and unfettered by tradition, he was probably the best man
that could have been found to complete the basic measures of military
reform. The task was to bring efficiency and economy into an unwieldy, ill-equipped, ill-trained, and staggeringly expensive organization that, with its ranks made up of men drawn arbitrarily from the
lower classes and subjected to tyrannical discipline, resembled more
nearly a medieval army than a modern one. Anyone undertaking a
renovation would have a long way to go before he could produce
evidence of a reformed army.

Milyutin had changes under way by 1865. Within another decade
his undertakings would make an impressive array: the final abolition
of the military colonies; the reorganization of personnel, from the
level of the war ministry to that of the remotest line regiment; the
training of officers in humanized discipline; the preparation of
soldiers for fighting rather than parade; the improvement of special
services such as engineering, provisioning, medical aid, and military
justice; the modernization of equipment, including the belated replacement of muskets by rifles and of cast-iron cannon by steel ones;
the introduction of educational innovations from the highest ranks
down to the lowest, where, in the opinion of veteran generals, literacy
was to be equated with uselessness; and—of fundamental significance
—the adoption of universal conscription, making "defense of the
Throne and Fatherland" by military service the duty of all classes.

Impressive as were the efforts to make such changes, they could not
transform the Russian army unless the changes were endorsed and
pursued cooperatively by all concerned; that was a condition which,
unfortunately, did not prevail. To accomplish what he did, Milyutin
often had to depend on reluctant assistance, and of necessity he made

enemies. To many of the old school, he was a combination of Arak-cheev and Robespierre. Even Alexander sometimes blocked his efforts; for instance, being unwilling to see the parade-ground spirit eliminated from all military activity, he would not acquiesce to Milyutin's wish to integrate the guards with the army. In the end, however, opposition gave way sufficiently to allow the promise of effective change, and the tsar was generally well pleased with what was accomplished.

During the first decade of his reign, Alexander could make but little progress toward the disposition of two of the special problems he had inherited: the basic restiveness among his liberal-minded subjects (paradoxically, often stirred, rather than quieted, by his liberal acts) and his country's standing among the powers. These matters were not neglected, but, being of such a nature that they could not be handled by directives and exhortations, they would continue for some time in the category of the unfinished.

So far, the liberals' attitude had been dealt with as its relatively infrequent expression seemed to demand. There had been the students' disorderly reaction to emancipation; the organization and brief functioning of a revolutionary society known as Land and Freedom, which had tried to rouse active discontent among students, peasants, and soldiers; and some sharp denunciations of the government's Polish policy. The leaders of the restiveness—notably Michael Mikhailov, Dmitri Pisarev, and Nicholas Chernyshevsky—had been as ardent and dedicated as earlier leaders of discontent. But they had found themselves doubly impeded, at first by the difficulty of rekindling a fire that had been smothered by police measures and later by the willingness of Minister of Education Golovnin to remove from students and faculties many of the restraints that had actuated earlier rebelliousness. Of the most deeply involved spokesmen of discontent, the majority were now either abroad, in Siberia, or in the Peter-Paul fortress, paying the usual penalty of "subversion." The time was advantageous for the tsar to seek popular support for the regime. But he continued to listen to the contrary arguments of the liberals and conservatives among his advisers and took no positive steps toward winning the minds of his people.

In the matter of Russia's position among the nations, though a great deal had been done in the only way it could be done, quietly and slowly, the West remained an unpredictable camp, preponderantly hostile. Prussian friendship endured, had even taken firmer root during Bismarck's ambassadorship to St. Petersburg (1859–62) and after the tsar's uncle became King William I, in 1861. But there remained the uncertain and the unfriendly—Austria, France, and England.

Relations with Austria would have to surmount a wall of hatred, which Alexander's policies so far had done more to heighten than to reduce. He had massed Russian troops in a gesture of support for France at the time of the Franco-Austrian war. He had disregarded the Austrian protest (along with that of England and France) concerning his treatment of Poland. And he had favored Prussia in the Austro-Prussian tug-of-war.

As for French willingness to let bygones be bygones, Alexander had learned that he could count on it only when the occasion appealed to Napoleon III. He might have French support or neutrality on some of his plans to relieve Russia of the restrictive bonds of the Treaty of Paris (1856), but was sure of vehement opposition to every act enforcing his Polish policy. So far, however, Franco-Russian relations had included an occasional exchange of diplomatic amenities, among which were some he could count as *de bon augure*. Napoleon III had appeared willing to see Russia regain the Bessarabian territory lost in 1856, had joined the tsar in support of the Montenegrins against the Turks, and had agreed that the treatment of Christians under Turkish rule had to be more strictly policed by outsiders (the French, as it turned out). He had also approved the establishment of a coaling station at Villefranche, near Nice, for Russian merchant and naval ships.

England, on the other hand, still adhered to the Palmerston rule: if it's Russian, distrust it. Relations were particularly strained because of Russia's continued territorial expansion in central Asia, toward the perimeter of that region monitored by the British empire, whose rulers were always mindful of any possible threat to India or the Eastern trade routes, and in the Far East, where the Western states were maneuvering for commercial advantage. England's attitude was overcautious, but understandable: Alexander had allowed his emissaries to proceed almost at will in these sensitive areas, and, by 1865, Russia's growing strength and influence in the East appeared to be well on the way toward offsetting her loss of status in the West. By strength of arms and the energy of ambitious governors, Russian rule had been pushed relentlessly into the southeastern border areas. The last native resistance in the Caucasus had been broken; the integration of the rich subtropical area of Transcaucasia was under way; and imperial forces, having completed the conquest of Kazakhstan, were biting deep into Turkestan, the area now known as Russian Central Asia.

In the Far East also, Russia was gainfully following her own course, profiting by a situation inadvertently provided by England and France—the weakening of Chinese resistance to foreign encroachment. Nicholas Muravev, governor general of Eastern Siberia, with a virtually unrestricted hand, unrestrained ambition, and high disregard for existing Russo-Chinese treaties, had probed for advantages in Chinese territory, secured them easily by small armed forces, and invited traders and settlers into a new annex to his domain, which he had thus highhandedly extended south to the Amur River. For these achievements, Alexander II later made him a count and, to give him the honor of continued association with the name of the Amur, permitted the change of his surname to Muravev-Amursky. Another ambitious man devoted to his country's pursuit of influence and trade, Admiral Efim Putyatin, Russia's diplomatic representative in China just before his appointment as minister of education, had prevailed upon the Chinese to grant to Russia trade rights equaling those that had been established in the area by England and France. Then his successor, Count Nicholas Ignatev, by a bit of diplomatic artifice, gained from China the Treaty of Peking, acknowledging Russia's previously staked-out claims and recognizing Russian rule over some 350,000 additional square miles of strategically located territory on the western coast of the Sea of Japan, stretching south to Korea.

Putyatin had also brought Russia into contention with Japan by defending Russia's appropriation of all the Kurile Islands and claiming Sakhalin as Russian territory. Though Japan continued to protest, the first treaty ever negotiated between the two countries (in 1855) recognized the Russian title to all but the southernmost of the Kuriles and—somewhat equivocally—a dual interest in the large island: "Sakhalin remains undivided between Russia and Japan . . ." Two years later Russia began the establishment of a large penal colony on Sakhalin.

It is true that these advantages and the acquisitions along the Amur River and the coast (now divided into two provinces, the Amur and the Maritime) remained an unrealized asset. But one newly established city at the lower tip of the Maritime Province had been given a name suggestive of hope for some coming day: Vladivostok, "Ruler of the East."

Imperial duties had left Alexander little time for his family during the ten years since he became tsar. However, a relatively quiet interim in 1864 gave him a chance to make a journey with his daughter Marie and his sons Nicholas, Alexander, Vladimir, and Alexis to see German relatives (of whom there were now a bewildering number, for the Romanovs were related to almost all the ruling families of Germany). It was not a family visit, strictly speaking, for the Empress Marie could not interrupt one of her "cures," now be-becoming more frequent as her health declined and she was less actively involved with issues of the day, to accompany them; and the younger sons, seven-year-old Sergei and four-year-old Paul, were too young to travel without the supervision of their mother. It was nevertheless a pleasant visit. The official and social display of interest in the Grand Duke Nicholas and his coming marriage to Princess Dagmar of Denmark were all that could be asked. Even if he had not been heir apparent, Nicholas among members of his family would have drawn personal attention; slender, elegant, and handsome, he was quite unlike his less courtly and more rugged brothers. Recurring lapses into ill health had so often separated him from them and their energetic exercises and training that now, at twenty-one, he appeared to be of a completely different fiber. This contrast might have reminded the tsar of his own early years alongside his more vigorous brother Constantine, but it did not lead him to adopt his father's impatient attitude. He had a tender love for Nicholas and no doubt whatsoever regarding the excellence of his personal qualities.

After the return from abroad, Alexander's freedom from urgent problems continued for a brief season. He could look forward to the marriage of young Nicholas and the Princess Dagmar, scheduled to take place in the spring of 1865, and feel satisfied about the establishment of the next household in the dynastic order of the Romanovs. He could, if he chose, look about him and take satisfaction from the evidence that, in the first decade of his rule, he had belied his father's prediction that he would be "an old woman" of a tsar who would accomplish nothing. Domestically in particular, he had already achieved much. Indeed, whereas Nicholas had taken a prudent walk with the century, Alexander had moved—or allowed himself to be moved—at a brisk trot. The future, while not rosy with promise, offered at least a prospect of stability.

VIII

Old Practices

ALEXANDER II, 1865-1881

A FTER a decade of drive for reform, Alexander was becoming less inclined toward change. In his judgment, all the necessary reforms were now either completed or about to be completed. Though he believed—and admitted confidentially—that eventually Russia would have a constitution,[1] he felt that for the time being, and as far as he could see into the future, the country's needs could be met only by what it had, a strong monarchy, without which it would unquestionably "disintegrate."[2]

As the sense of urgency passed, so did his responsiveness to most of the reformers close about him (Dmitri Milyutin, still busy with the program of army reforms, was among the few exceptions). Even the liberal members of the imperial family were now feeling his remoteness. The Grand Duke Constantine, the practicality of whose advice had been disproved in the case of the last Polish revolt, found it increasingly difficult to get his brother's ear. The Grand Duchess Helen also had lost some of his trust during the same period: she had shown too lenient an attitude toward the Poles for a while, and her leanings had made it possible for a fanatic official to discredit her among some people by accusing her of being in secret correspondence with Herzen. Empress Marie, once an energetic supporter of reforms, no longer exerted any influence—nor, in fact, tried to do so. Her social consciousness seemed to have been gradually eclipsed by personal concerns: her own failing health, her religious devotions, her six sons, and her daughter.

One of the things that had helped Alexander to endure his duties and given him special purpose in planning for the future of the country, one that had also held him emotionally close to his family despite the distance growing between him and the empress, was a special affection for his son Nicholas, heir to the throne. The unexpected death of Nicholas, from cerebrospinal tuberculosis, in the spring of 1865, left the tsar so disconsolate that he withdrew even further into his personal loneliness and, for a time, appeared almost a stranger to those closest about him.

The death of Nicholas affected far more than the emotions of the imperial family, for the one now to be groomed for future leadership was the twenty-year-old Grand Duke Alexander, whose temperament and interests were so different from those of his late brother as to suggest changes in the future expectations of the country. He was of a generally coarser mold than the gentle Nicholas and of a less promising turn of mind. Tall, well-muscled, but somewhat ponderous in movement and manner, he was ill at ease in situations beyond the conventional formalities in which he had been schooled as a grand duke whose expectancy was a military career. Whatever his potential abilities as a future tsar, they had yet to be developed. As heir apparent, he would have to make many adjustments, but his character was unlikely to be changed by them. He and Princess Dagmar, his brother's fiancée, had agreed to respect Nicholas' deathbed request that they marry; and in the eighteen months before the date set for their wedding, he had to rearrange his personal life. That would not be easy for him, nor immediately agreeable. The princess was a lively and charming girl and, being the sister of the Princess of Wales (the future Queen Alexandra), she might have impressed a future tsar as at least of some diplomatic worth; but, under other circumstances, the Tsesarevich Alexander would probably not have chosen her as consort. At the time, his feelings were engaged elsewhere. Besides, Dagmar's personality and interests were of a kind that had never attracted him. (Later, observers could cite the "affinity of opposites" when his respect for her developed into warm devotion.)

To provide the special training appropriate to young Alexander's new status as tsesarevich, his father introduced him, as onlooker or minor participant, into official sessions and encouraged his closer association with those who could help him to an understanding of what lay in his future. Of the teachers who had been concerned with his earlier education, two in particular could be trusted to continue their influence, now in a more purposeful way: the historian Sergei Solovev would give him a solidly nationalistic view of the country's past as background for its prospects, and the able jurist Constantine Pobedonostsev would convince him of his duty to respect and defend his autocratic inheritance. The tsesarevich accepted these arrangements—he had no practical alternative—and, before long, had turned his face to the course from which he would deviate but little in the next thirty years.

Meanwhile, the family crisis was changing the outlook of the tsar himself. He was beginning to realize the futility of his hoping for a relaxation of pressures, to understand the inescapable truth that problems were his imperial birthright.

No longer able to find the old relief of mind among his family, he began to give his attention more frequently, and ever more agreeably, to the lovely Princess Catherine Dolgoruky. She was the daughter of the late Michael Dolgoruky, whose children, at his death, had come under the guardianship of the tsar. Now in her teens, graduated from Russia's most fashionable finishing school for aristocratic young ladies, the Smolny Institute, she was living in the St. Petersburg home of her brother Michael. While many young men sought to attract the interest of the dark-eyed, ash-blonde beauty, she was flatteringly deferential to the courtly attentiveness of her imperial guardian, thirty years her senior. As time passed and adversities, both personal and official, grew more burdensome to Alexander, Catherine became his most prized friend and confidant. Ironically, she became also one of his most fateful problems.

Try as he might to steer clear of adversities by holding to a steady political course along the route he had already laid out, Alexander could not continue to disregard the two strong political currents that, each year, were increasing in pressure—the one toward the left, the other toward the right.

He had been made specifically conscious of a pressure to the left early in 1865, when delegates to the Moscow provincial assembly of the nobility adopted an address congratulating him on the creation of the zemstvos and calling on him to "complete the state structure by convening a general assembly of men elected from all Russia to discuss the common needs of the entire state." Outraged by the "in-

solence" of the nobles and infuriated by the highhandedness of the
official newspaper that published the text of the address in defiance
of the censors, he soundly rebuked the lot of them. Then, to emphasize the enormity of such presumption, he reminded the provincial
governors, who were responsible for the acts of all persons—noble or
otherwise—under their jurisdiction, that the right to consider and
initiate reforms was reserved "exclusively" to him, the autocrat,
whose power derived from "God Himself."

Despite his imperious reaction, however, the assemblies of the
nobility in St. Petersburg, Tver, Ryazan, and Vladimir added their
voices to the clamor for an imperial representative body. Zemstvos
did likewise. The St. Petersburg zemstvo, newly organized and holding its first meeting before a fashionable audience assembled to observe the novelty, called openly for an imperial zemstvo. As other
zemstvos came into being, many of them followed the St. Petersburg
example. No relaxation of the pressure toward the left was in sight.

Those pressing for a rightward shift were just as persistent. They
were the ones who dismissed as pernicious the notion that "the mind
needs elbowroom" and argued that to relax controls was to invite
chaos. The strict reactionaries among them—and there were many—
believed that the tsar had already gone too far in relaxing controls.
For an example they could point to Poland, where the policy of concession had so manifestly failed; until the Polish situation was satisfactorily adjusted, they needed no further evidence.

After the Polish revolt, Alexander had realized that these reactionary voices had the prior claim on his attention: a new Polish policy
was necessary and urgent, however trying the ordeal of devising one.

Preliminary to any planning, of course, was the need to define the
spirit in which the rebels were to be handled. It was understood that
the focus of all considerations would be on the Poles since, even in
the Western Region, where non-Poles had joined the revolt, upper-
class Poles living in that area were judged responsible for promoting
the insurrection. Leniency toward them was out of the question, according to Michael Muravev, governor general of the Lithuanian
provinces of Vilna, Kovno, and Grodno in the Western Region:
"It is high time that Russia and all Russians finally convince
themselves that it is neither possible nor desirable to come to
terms with the Polish spirit. . . . Humanitarianism in this respect
would be the essence of crime against Russia." [3] Those were remarkable words from a man who had been associated with the Decembrists, a member of an outstanding old family known for the solid

and level-headed leadership it had contributed. But his was no abstract observation: the governor general practiced what he advocated, publicly hanging so many Polish rebels that he became known as "The Hangman," the object of a fierce and unrelenting hatred. Muravev's point of view had the wholehearted support of the tsar's other agent now at grips with the problem, Viceroy Berg, in Warsaw. But what, Alexander wanted to know, was the alternative to humanitarianism? Certainly not destruction. There must be some kind of compromise. Pacification and the enforcement of a few changes had begun as soon as the insurgence was crushed, but official policy had yet to be worked out.

It was difficult for Alexander to accept the approach being urged upon him, particularly in view of the success he had achieved with a very different approach in the grand duchy of Finland. He had shown an interest in both the economic and political progress of the Finns, had permitted them many of the blessings of autonomous life including the meeting of their Diet for the first time since the annexation of the grand duchy, in 1809, and had thereby won their loyalty and high regard. He would have preferred to extend goodwill to Poland also.

This was another instance when his crown prevailed over his heart, however, and he finally accepted with reluctance a plan that, though harsh in many of its features, seemed to promise viability. It rested on the reasoning that the Polish revolts had always been the product of "Polonism," an attitude born of the "malicious" striving by the Polish nobility and clergy for an independent state, and that, once the political and ideological influence of these two classes was destroyed, Polonism would disappear and the formerly rebellious region would become a stable and placid part of the Russian empire. These changes, it was argued, could be achieved through a new kind of Russification, carried out in accordance with a two-part plan—one part applicable to the kingdom of Poland, the other to the Western Region.

The aim for the kingdom was, in brief, to make it a politically integrated part of the empire, henceforth to be administered by Russian-speaking officials and known as the Vistula Region (in fact, it continued to be called the kingdom of Poland). Its Polonism would be uprooted by restricting the Catholic Church to purely religious functions and by debarring the nobility from all administrative positions. Then, if all went as planned, the lower classes, freed from the influence of Polonism but permitted to use the Polish language, exposed to Russian history and culture in the schools, and generously provided with land at the expense of the nobility, would come to appreciate the tsar as their friend and legitimate ruler. While this scheme was not expected to convert the inhabitants of the kingdom, predominately Polish and Catholic, into Orthodox Russians, it was expected to eradicate once and for all the idea carried over from the time of Alexander I that a quasi-Polish state was a political possibility.

In the Western Region, long a battleground between Russia and Poland, Russification would be guided by the assumption that the area was historically and ethnically Russian and would be directed toward strengthening its Russian Orthodox character.[4] Here, it was argued, the process would be relatively simple because, while admittedly most of the upper class and the clergy were Polish and the middle class was Jewish, the great majority of the population, the peasantry, was Russian and Orthodox. The non-Russian influence would be expunged by hobbling the Catholic Church, dismissing Polish teachers and civil servants, and proceeding to expel those Polish landowners who had supported the recent revolt and escaped Muravev's heavy hand (about 10,000) and to confiscate their land. At the same time, Russian influence would be strengthened by increasing the religious and educational efforts of the Orthodox Church, encouraging Russian civil servants, teachers, and peasants to settle in the area, and transferring the confiscated estates to Russian nobles. It was expected that these measures would, in time, dissipate whatever Polish flavor there was; though it could be expected that there would still be Polish Catholics in the area, they would probably speak Russian and would be of little consequence.

The new Polish policy ran counter to the principles that had guided Alexander's most significant measures to date, and its administration promised enduring difficulties, many of which, it should be noted in fairness to the tsar, he either did not recognize or did not appreciate.

The very assumption on which the policy was based—that it was possible, by the means proposed, to transform attitudes, beliefs, and institutions—was subject to question. In addition to reflecting an antiquated view of the nature of Polish nationalism, it blithely ignored the ethnic complexity of the Western Region; the fact was that its northern, central, and southern provinces were respectively Lithuanian, White Russian, and Little Russian (now known as Ukrainian). The Lithuanians, though long subjected to Polish domination, were expected simply to adopt the Russian language, if not the Orthodox faith, and become contented subjects of the tsar, while the Little and White Russians, considered merely backward Russians, were expected to be even more readily integrated. As for the Jews, whether those in the kingdom of Poland (where they constituted more than a third of the urban population) or those in the Western Region (where they constituted nearly half of the urban population), the policy took little recognition of them. Russian officials hoped, of course, that the Jews could ultimately be assimilated; but, considering their slow rate of conversion and the tenacity with which they clung to their ancient ways, little progress toward that end could be expected in the near future. The only special effort to deal with them would be to encourage their enrollment in Russian-language schools.

It soon became evident that, in acquiescing to the new Polish policy, Alexander was taking a significant step to the political right and, regardless of his intention, endorsing a course that would serve as a brake on reform. There was clearly an affinity between reaction and Russification, the essential feature of the policy—not an irresistible affinity, but a common one, easily detected among his government officials. Exceptions were to be found in a few like Minister of War Milyutin, who remained a dedicated reformer even though he was an avowed Polonophobe and a Russifier. But reaction was moving toward the heart of the government with the advance of a number of men disposed toward the Muravev attitude and favoring the tightening of controls. Among them, Count Dmitri Tolstoy, whom Alexander had appointed to the post of over-procurator of the Holy Synod in 1865, was just now establishing himself as a leading proponent of reaction. In the ministry of education, where he had recently served, he had proved to be a single-minded, hard-driving Polonophobe. It could be expected that he would not only give vigorous direction to Orthodoxy in its battle with Polonism in the Western Region but also oppose the policy of his former superior, Minister of Education Golovnin, whom he considered both a Polonophile and a dangerous liberal with deplorable ideas about the advantages of academic freedom and university autonomy.

The first opportunity for the reactionaries to take steps of any real political consequences resulted from a plan devised and translated into action by a slightly unbalanced young man whose aim was to bring about the exact opposite of reaction. He was Dmitri Karakozov, the scion of an impoverished noble family, who had left two universities, Kazan and Moscow, under conditions of mutual dissatisfaction and was currently a member of "Hell," a self-styled terrorist cell within a student revolutionary organization. Even in this company, he was a misfit, impatient with the wont of his fellow members to put more hellfire into words than into deeds. He wanted action. Having seen the masses unmoved by exhortation, he wanted to stir them by means they could not disregard; when he could not get the cooperation of his group, he resolved to act independently. He would carry out the most violently stirring deed conceivable, the assassination of the tsar.

Karakozov's chance came on April 4, 1866, when he joined a curious crowd waiting outside the Summer Garden, a formal park near the Winter Palace, to catch a glimpse of Tsar Alexander returning from a walk in the garden. He managed to get into an advantageous position (he expected one unobstructed shot to serve his purpose) without attracting undue attention; then, when the tsar appeared, he made his attempt. It failed. According to onlookers, as he had pointed his gun, his arm had been struck aside by one of the crowd, Osip Komissarov. Immediately seized and turned over to the Third Section, Karakozov identified himself for the record as a peasant by the name of Petrov, and rumor, reflecting the sentiment of the hour, identified him as a Pole on the grounds that only a Pole would attempt such an appalling deed. To the Third Section, of course, the problem was not identification but the strict and speedy process of judgment and execution.

Reverberations from Karakozov's misguided shot rolled in from near and far. For weeks, fervent Russians crowded into churches to give thanks for the tsar's deliverance; theater audiences halted performances to demand the playing of "God Save the Tsar"; zemstvos and assemblies of the nobility sent messages of jubilance. The public contributed lavishly for the construction of a chapel on the spot where the tsar had stood at the moment of peril, and the designers interpreted the current spirit through the words to be inscribed over its entrance, "Touch not Mine Anointed." From all over the world came words of official concern. The United States, where memory of the assassination of its own emancipator was still fresh, sent a special mission to express gratification that the danger to Alexander's life had been "averted by Providence." The hero of the day, Komissarov, a young artisan of peasant origin, was ennobled by a grateful tsar, acclaimed by press and public, even wined and dined in the exclusive English Club.

The Russian response, during these weeks, was an overwhelming demonstration of traditional monarchist sentiment. That was no indication, however, that the Karakozov episode need have any political consequences. In fact, it would have had no such consequences if the Grand Duke Constantine, Milyutin, Valuev, Golovnin, and others like them had had their way. But the reactionaries, among the most outspoken of whom were Gagarin (now chairman of the Committee of Ministers), Katkov, Muravev, and Tolstoy, seized avidly upon the attempted assassination as further proof of what they had been arguing—that reforms had been carried too far and that the government was now threatened by anarchy. They pointed out to the tsar that, to handle the situation, he needed to strengthen the police, tighten censorship, overhaul the educational system, and intensify Russification. In addition, having learned that certain peasants believed the Karakozov incident to be the outcome of a conspiracy among disgruntled landlords to kill the tsar as a preliminary to undoing his emancipation measures, the reactionaries began agitating against "peasant-lovers" in high places, who, they charged, were now inciting the peasants against the nobility.

Alexander, who had been wavering between liberal and reactionary viewpoints, was now drawn toward the reactionary. Of course, to interpret the Karakozov attempt on his life as his father had interpreted the Decembrist Revolt, as a warning and a reminder that the welfare of the country depended upon the direction of a strong autocratic hand, would be to deny the unspoken premise of the reforms —that is, that Nicholas I had been mistaken. But Alexander was tired of stress, tired of turbulence, tired of being sniped at literally and figuratively. He longed for protection from it all. So once again, the specter of Mazzini led a Russian autocrat to turn his back upon the specter of Pugachev.

Accepting the validity of the charge that Golovnin's laxness had allowed certain students to develop seditious ideas and that Dolgorukov had failed to keep the Third Section sufficiently alert to what was happening, Alexander agreed that their responsibilities should be in firmer hands. He assigned Golovnin's post to Dmitri Tolstoy, whom he allowed to continue as head of the Holy Synod, where the severity of his administration had already led clergymen to the feeling that he so confused requisition with inquisition as to deserve the name

Gogmagog. He replaced Dolgorukov with Count Peter Shuvalov, a general in the imperial suite, who had proved his administrative strength and decisiveness when appointed, a year earlier, to the governor-generalship of Riga. Under the direction of these two men, both the ministry of education and the Third Section could be expected to undergo pronounced changes.

Alexander indicated that the nature of any changes would be determined by the conclusions of the commission now investigating the recent attempt on his life. Those conclusions were virtually predetermined by his appointing Michael Muravev as chairman of the commission and designating reactionaries—including Shuvalov and Tolstoy—to make up the majority of its membership.

The Muravev Commission expected to uncover a major revolutionary conspiracy but managed only to find a loose association among a few malcontents, chiefly students or ex-students. Their organization functioned irregularly through scattered groups and devoted itself mainly to propaganda and economic improvement among the underprivileged. The small cell that called itself "Hell" was the only one with pretensions even suggestive of danger, and it had not developed beyond the pretext. This was flimsy support for the commission's preconceived views, but, for want of something better, it was made to serve the purpose.

In the report to Alexander, the commission deduced two "facts" from their wide-ranging investigation. One was that the country's institutions of higher learning were producing seditious elements devoid of respect for God, tsar, fatherland, and the social order; the other, that the people at large, though deeply and eternally devoted to their tsar, had become distressed by the evident decline in authority and were insisting that the government reassert its authority by strengthening the police and requiring the educational institutions to develop "useful," not "harmful," Russian subjects. Speaking in its own name, the commission added yet another item for consideration: in view of the peasants' willingness to believe the absurd story that disgruntled nobles had inspired the Karakozov act, there could be no doubt of the necessity "to support and regenerate the nobility and the landlords, because without these conservative and healthy elements no properly organized society can exist." [5]

Thus there was placed into Alexander's willing hands the prescription for a new course. And in May 1866 he proclaimed the new course in a florid rescript introduced by thanking Providence for providing Karakozov as a warning of the evil consequences arising from hostility toward religion, private property, and the family. To provide safeguards for the future, he ordered that youth be taught henceforth "in the spirit of religious truth, respect for property rights, and regard for the basic principles of public order" and forbade all government schools to permit either the secret or the open dissemination "of those destructive ideas that undermine the bases of the material and spiritual well-being of the people." Then, as if in consideration of the commission's concern about peasant-noble relations, he demanded that there be no further incitement to hostility of class against class.[6]

While arrangements for the enforcement of the new policy were under way, the Grand Duke Constantine and Dmitri Milyutin made an effort to convince Alexander that there was more to be feared from stifling public opinion, curtailing reforms, and tightening controls than from a handful of revolutionaries. They might as well have saved their energy; the tsar gave no indication of being impressed by the argument. Rather, by way of emphasizing his position, he received Katkov, the journalistic spokesman of reaction, and said to him: "I know you, believe in you, and consider you as my own. Preserve the sacred fire within you." [7]

A season that had begun in the spirit of reform was ended. The pressure from the political right had prevailed, and the regime had settled itself firmly in the course from which it had given promise of venturing, official nationalism.

Alexander proclaimed the new course, but he did not direct it. Once the preliminaries were over—Karakozov having paid with his life for his misdeed, a few of his associates having begun their penal terms, and the outspoken press of the opposition having been quieted by the closing of a number of extreme leftist publications— the tsar seemed to feel justified in laying aside the champion's banner. Willing simply to preside rather than to lead or initiate, he let the authority for the new drive pass to the two men who were anxious to accept it, Shuvalov and Tolstoy, and to his minister of interior, the loyal but no longer personally sympathetic Valuev.

Peter Shuvalov's character was appropriately suggested by one of his nicknames, "Peter the Fourth." An ambitious and able politician as well as a sophisticated courtier, he had the qualifications to do what he chose to do as head of the Third Section. To keep alive Alexander's interest in the policing of the country, he stressed the continued threat of revolution; to encourage the imperial favor for himself, he often joined the tsar in the hunt, at cards, or in the wider social life of the capital. As a reward, he soon had Alexander's dependence upon him both for reports on the morale of the nation and for a trusted analysis of that morale.

Shuvalov's enterprising activity, however, was not merely to gain personal recognition. He was seriously intent on improving the Third Section and the corps of gendarmes, on making them serviceable agents of the government's new policy. Under his direction, they became more efficient and more diligent than they had been in over a decade. He required that his men intensify their undercover work within the country and extend it beyond the borders, particularly among Russian students in foreign universities. He subsidized a number of "loyal" newspapers and secretly published monarchist pamphlets. He improved security measures in St. Petersburg with the abolition of the office of governor general for that city and the transfer of police responsibility to a prefect serving under the direct supervision of the Third Section. Meanwhile, as his officers brought in groups of young revolutionaries from time to time, he was able to show sufficient evidence—for the reactionaries, at least—that the "revolutionary threat" was a reality.

One of the largest groups brought in consisted of members of an organization calling itself the Russian Revolutionary Committee and made up mostly of students. They had been rounded up after the body of a murdered youth, Ivan Ivanov, had been found and informants had revealed his membership in the organization as well as evidence that his death had been planned to prevent his threatened withdrawal from it. The young man who had contrived the murder and executed it with the connivance of three fellow revolutionaries was Sergei Nechaev, a fanatic disciple of the émigré Bakunin and one of the first so-called professional revolutionaries to attempt to operate within Russia. However, the ministry of justice, not knowing his identity at first (in any case, he had fled the country before the group's arrest) and being more particularly concerned with exposing the organization's revolutionary nature, put on trial those who were found to be connected with it in any way, in all about eighty. Each was charged with conspiracy to overthrow the government, and those identified as ringleaders were charged with the murder of Ivanov.

Their trial, beginning in July 1871 and lasting three months, was presented as a show trial, open to the public. No proceedings with such overtones of crisis had been held in Russia since the Petrashevsky trial, and it had been secret. The prosecution directed the mood by the dramatic way it introduced evidence relating to the "cold-blooded murder" and presented sensational excerpts from the clandestine paper *The People's Revenge* concerning the proposal that the organization, whose fraternal symbol was the terrorist's axe, execute an uprising against the authorities on the ninth anniversary of emancipation. The lack of actual proof that any of the accused had murdered Ivanov, or had helped to organize a revolutionary attempt, or had done anything more culpable than to distribute revolutionary propaganda was easily overlooked. So the court, a special tribunal that dispensed with the services of a jury, found them all guilty of subversive complicity, released some under police supervision, and sentenced the others to terms of hard labor, varying according to the degree of their involvement. In the following year, Nechaev was arrested in Switzerland and released to the Russian authorities. He was brought to trial with less fanfare, convicted, and sentenced to life imprisonment.

The trial was grist for the mills of those already convinced of the revolutionary danger. The reactionaries in the government made the most of it as they worked to reduce the influence of the liberals remaining in office. Others kept the fear of revolution fresh in the public mind; among them was Dostoevsky, who used Nechaev as the model for the principal figure in his novel *The Possessed*. A new cell block in the Peter-Paul fortress, the Trubetskoi Bastion, was opened for occupancy in 1872—a visible sign that preparations were being made to handle the challengers of authority.

While Shuvalov was doing his part in initiating the new policy, Dmitri Tolstoy was equally busy. For one thing, he was seeking means for carrying out the Muravev's Commission's suggestion that the country's educational institutions be made to produce "useful," not "harmful," Russian subjects.

By this time there was no difficulty in recognizing the harmful subject. Ivan Turgenev had typified him a decade earlier in Eugene Bazarov, the chief character in his *Fathers and Sons*. Since the novel's publication, through serialization in Katkov's *Russian Herald*, the character had continued to stir intense feeling, the political left at first objecting to the "unfair caricature" and the political right approving the literary portrayal while damning even more emphatically the original. Bazarov was the archetype of those who were called nihilists. Turgenev presented him as a brash young medical student despising the nobility, interested in the cure of bodies but not of souls, and accepting as true only what could be verified by observation or experiment. Bazarov's female counterpart was Vera Rozalsky, a character in Chernyshevsky's didactic novel *What Is To Be Done?*, written while he was imprisoned in the fortress. She quickly became the popular representation of the emancipated woman, of whom the official opinion, as reflected by the Third Section, was far from flattering: "[She is an individual] with hair cut short, wearing blue glasses, slovenly dressed, loath to use comb and soap, and living in common law matrimony with one or more members of the male sex, who are equally repelling." [8]

The reactionary press, led by Katkov, had found the apotheosis of the nihilist in Nicholas Nekrasov's *Contemporary*, which had been one of the leading "thick" magazines favored by certain writers and readers contemptuously called the intelligentsia. And others of its kind were now suspect.

Tolstoy was particularly concerned about those who constituted the so-called intelligentsia both because of the nature of their influence and because of its extent in significant areas. Though the intelligentsia looked to John Stuart Mill, Comte, Buckle, and Darwin for inspiration rather than to Hegel, Schelling, or Fichte, they were continuing the intellectual tradition of Herzen, Belinsky, and Granovsky. They were also displaying the same mood of independence and iconoclasm, and putting the same emphasis on freedom. In his campaign for the minds of the country's youth, Tolstoy recognized them as the front line of the enemy; he understood that their position was already strong. Too often, in his opinion, students who left the gymnasium (the classical secondary school) with good records and an innocence of alien ideas were likely, under the influence of older students in the university or professional institute, to become acquainted with the ideas of the intelligentsia and be won into their ranks. Though most of them could be expected to abandon the extreme views that had beguiled them for a while and go on to become staid bureaucrats or professionals, they usually retained a trace of liberalism, sometimes more than a trace. If they became journalists or teachers in gymnasiums or primary schools, their influence would soon be predisposing yet another generation toward the thinking of the intelligentsia. It was a situation that Tolstoy would do all within his power to alter. He was well aware, however, that it involved highly elusive elements that would be difficult to detect; even in his own alma mater, the Tsarskoe Selo Lycée, where close supervision and tight controls permitted few lambs to stray, it had not been possible to keep out "advanced" ideas.

The task that Tolstoy was undertaking was much like that undertaken by Uvarov for Nicholas I, but it would be more arduous: now there were more students, more of them came from the lower classes and the national minorities, censorship was milder, and the educated public was more sophisticated. Nevertheless, he was determined to break the self-perpetuating tradition of intellectual dissent. That Uvarov, working under more favorable conditions, had failed in a similar undertaking would have deterred a man with a broader mind; but Tolstoy's was a narrow mind (some called him the "statesman with ear-flaps") and a firm one.

"Often in error, but never in doubt," he was convinced that the place to start was in the gymnasium, where young people improperly instructed in history, science, and modern literature were acquiring slipshod habits of thinking, mistaking mental frivolity and indolence for serious thought and consequently becoming potential victims of the infection of mischievous ideas which they would encounter when they went on to the higher schools. To correct this weakness, he proposed to require in the gymnasium a basic and thorough education in Greek, Latin, and mathematics, which would serve to habituate the student to work hard, to do things in an orderly way, and to think logically. So equipped, he would be ready for study in any field. Moreover—and here was the salient point—he would be immune to the "spurious" ideas that lurked in his future. The scheme was not a novel one: a number of educators had considered it, but none believed in it as firmly and passionately as did Tolstoy.

At the heart of the proposal that Tolstoy presented for official consideration were two items that met with dissent: the requirement that all students in gymnasiums spend a large part of their time —about half—in the study of Latin and Greek, and the requirement that graduation from a gymnasium be made prerequisite for admission to a university. Many in the ministry of education itself disapproved of the proposal. A majority of the normally complacent State Council voted against it, some of them pointedly recalling French revolutionaries trained in the classics, others maintaining that Russia was more in need of engineers and chemists than of philologists and jurists. No matter: the tsar, then in Bad Ems taking the waters, sent his approval, and the proposal became law in June 1871. The promulgation of the new statute came while the public was aroused by the arrest and accusation of the members of the Russian Revolu-

tionary Committee, most of them students who "had been led astray"
—a decidedly propitious coincidence.

Reforming the gymnasium by no means exhausted Tolstoy's
ample energy. He set about with determination also to rehabilitate
the universities and to make an even better job of it than his most
ambitious predecessors had. Accordingly, he prohibited university
students from engaging in any kind of group activities, used expul-
sion freely to "purify" their ranks, denied them the privilege of
studying abroad, and began a slow but purposeful campaign to end
university autonomy. In addition, at the other limit of his educational preserve, he encouraged the establishment of church-operated
primary schools, which were to serve as defenders of the "Orthodox
folk-soul." Farther afield, he zealously promoted the Russification of
the Western Region and the kingdom of Poland and achieved a
modest beginning in the Russification of the Baltic provinces. His
great pride, however, remained the reformed gymnasium; there, he
felt, with time on his side, he was laying a solid foundation for the
future.

Unlike functionaries of Tolstoy's dedication, who could find both
pleasure and satisfaction in their duties as official tools of reaction,
liberal-minded Valuev was a misfit who could ill conceal his dissatisfaction. Because he wanted to remain in the government, however,
he tried dutifully to keep the ministry of interior in line with the
new policy, and for a few months he seemed to be holding his own.
From his office a steady flow of directives urging the preservation of
order and the prevention of "insolence" went out to provincial administrators, municipal administrators, peasant elders, and censors.
Manfully he tried to "support and regenerate the nobility and the
landlords," as the Muravev Commission had recommended.

However, since tenure of office so often depended on the ability to
assert and demonstrate personal importance to the tsar, Valuev, still
the unregenerate liberal, now lacked the assurance of the strong
position he had held during the period of Alexander's reforms. His
disadvantage grew when, in 1867, another attempt was made on the
life of the tsar. The attempt, by an émigré Pole in Paris, where Alexander had gone on the invitation of Napoleon III to attend the Paris
Exhibition, could not, of course, be attributed to any condition for
which Valuev was responsible; but it did further the ascendancy for
those crying for a tightening of controls, and they were his detractors. Charging him with dereliction of duty that had allowed severe
suffering and near-disaster to develop in widespread areas affected by

a recent famine, they successfully urged that he be replaced. To be rid of Valuev's influence would be "good fortune for the government," declared the tsesarevich,[9] whose political awareness was beginning to show the effect of careful sharpening by his astute tutor Pobedonostsev; his viewpoint was the one generally prevailing among government officials.

The result was that Valuev remained in service under the new program for only two years. The tsar's replacing him with General Timashev, hardened by ten years of experience as gendarme chief of staff, indicated the direction that the ministry of interior was now expected to take. That change followed closely a similar readjustment in the ministry of justice, where the wholly unqualified and ultraconservative Count Constantine Pahlen had replaced Dmitri Zamyatin, liberal exponent of judicial reforms.

At last, the policy of reaction was for all practical political purposes in the hands of approving officials. Of the important liberals whom Alexander had originally called to office, only two remained: Minister of Finance Michael Reutern and Minister of War Dmitri Milyutin, who not only retained their positions but also remained relatively free to continue their work as planned during the first years of the reign.

Discouraged liberals saw this last shift to the right as further indication that Alexander had come to the point where, instead of leading, he was resigned to being led. And there was an accumulation of undeniable evidence that his attention to personal matters was gradually superseding his concern with the imperial.

After the marriage, in 1866, of the tsesarevich to Princess Dagmar (thereafter known by the Russian name Marie Fedorovna), the tsar had shown less and less interest in arranging that the heir be given experience in the practices of government and an understanding of his future responsibilities. In fact, he soon weakened still further not only the ties with his son but also his other close personal connections by openly affirming the growing intimacy of his friendship with Catherine Dolgoruky. He met her privately during his Paris visit in 1867 and shortly thereafter established her in a St. Petersburg residence, where neither his family nor the public could any longer ignore their liaison. As his attention to Catherine increased, the alienation between himself and the empress developed into a bitterness that finally involved his daughter and his sons, most of them sympathizing with their mother. His relationship with the tsesarevich in particular became so strained that, for a time, each appeared to seek reasons for opposing the other. This was a situation that unfortunately made it easier for the ambitious Pobedonostsev to draw the heir into his own conservative way of thinking and direct him toward the future arrest of Alexander's hard-won reforms.

The tsar's attitude was softened temporarily as the tsesarevich's family grew and he found himself unable to resist a grandfatherly pride in the young grand dukes Nicholas and George.* But even that nearness was threatened when a child was born (1872) in his extramarital household—a son, the first of three children born to him and Catherine Dolgoruky, whom he now called his "wife before God." Two years later, the marriage of his beloved daughter, Marie, to the Duke of Edinburgh and her departure for England loosened still further the ties with the older family.

The unseemliness and stresses of his private life did not deter Alexander from observing the public proprieties, maintaining appearances with the Empress Marie, taking his place as the head of society at balls and the theater, attending the parade activities of the guard, and always taking care not to draw undue attention to Catherine. At times, his racking asthmatic cough and his burdened eyes told of the personal cost of these efforts, but he regarded them as part of his ordained and irrevocable duty as tsar.

Furthermore he expected all who represented the House of Romanov to deport themselves in a manner befitting the eminence of their name. Two of his brothers were among those who failed to measure up to his standard in this respect. The Grand Duke Constantine drew reproof for indecorum which linked his name in public gossip with that of a certain popular ballerina and invited added attention to the indignity of his wife's withdrawing from St. Petersburg to their palace in Pavlovsk because she found the capital "too advanced" since the reforms. When the Grand Duke Nicholas, his interest absorbed by a sentimental affair, neglected his wife so shamefully that she was forced to near-poverty, the tsar not only scolded

---

* After Nicholas, born on May 6, 1868, a second son, Alexander, had been born on May 26, 1869, and had died just short of his first birthday. The date of his birth may be easily verified—e.g., in *Almanach de Gotha*, 1871 ed., and *The Times* (London), June 8, 1869 (N.S.). Yet a number of writers in English persist in repeating the inaccurate story appearing in the English-language version of the Grand Duke Alexander Michaelovich's memoirs, *Once a Grand Duke* (New York, 1932): that Alexander was the first-born and that "an ignorant nurse and a negligent physician were responsible for Nicholas II wearing the crown, having overlooked the illness that attacked his elder brother. . . ." It is noteworthy that this story does not appear in the Russian-language version of the grand duke's memoirs, *Kniga Vospominanii* (Paris, 1933).

him and sent him off to the Caucasus to cool his ardor but also ordered his inamorata to remove her residence from the capital.

Regardless of Alexander's efforts, the activities of the imperial family continued to attract public interest, and there could be no assurance that observers would be either sympathetic or circumspect in their reactions. Count Peter Shuvalov, for one, finally expressed too freely his disapproval of Catherine Dolgoruky and therefore, after eight years of personal and official closeness to the tsar, was replaced as head of the Third Section by Alexander Potapov and straightway sent off as ambassador to London. Even a trusted adviser—and Shuvalov remained that—could not be allowed to disregard protocol.

Alexander may have felt justified in turning so much of his attention from imperial to personal matters during the first years of the post-Karakozov period. From his point of view, the affairs of the empire were by then well in hand, and the reports he was receiving indicated an auspicious future. Indeed, it seemed quite likely that Russia could look forward to years of tranquility and progress: the first, assured by his readjustments in the administration of education and the handling of political subversion; the second, by his continued support of certain forward-looking programs in both domestic and foreign affairs.

There was heartening reassurance in the fact that dissent was declining in all quarters. The kingdom of Poland and the Western Region had become peaceful enough so that martial law could be ended there and amnesty offered to many of the former rebels. Zemstvos and assemblies of the nobility had quieted down. Tolstoy affirmed that students were becoming more serious and diligent. The records of the Third Section indicated that subversion was safely under control.

Meanwhile the processes of change were promising a healthy recovery from the general depression of spirits that had settled over the land during the last years of Nicholas I's reign, and people were being stirred from conditions that many had come to accept as immutable. In the countryside, the cumbersome administrative procedures were gradually producing a realization of emancipation. The zemstvos, already established in thirty-three provinces of European Russia, were enlivening their localities by making travel and transport possible over new or improved roads, introducing hitherto unavailable health services, awakening some peasant interest in better methods of farming, and opening more primary schools. For the cities, though administrative reforms had been delayed both by the tightening up following the Karakozov incident and by the changes in the ministry of interior when Valuev was replaced by the more reactionary Timashev, a new law promulgated in 1870 brought some uniformity and order, if not satisfactory liberalization, to their government.

Many other improvements, Alexander was always glad to point out, would affect all his subjects. whether of urban or rural residence, high or low estate. The army reforms, for instance, would not only increase the country's military efficiency at less cost but also, with the introduction of universal military training, place the responsibility for service fairly on all classes. Education, too, was finally reaching all classes to some degree. Aside from the enthusiastic zemstvo workers, there were countless others striving to make the most of the present tsar's favor for education, and even Tolstoy's restrictive measures were no brake on the growth of the system as a whole. Literacy was increasing among the urban lower classes as never before, and facilities were gradually expanding for all. Enrollment in institutions of higher learning was becoming more representative of the population and, at the same time, growing at an unprecedented rate. The growth was particularly striking in St. Petersburg, which, with 10,000 enrollees in the university and other civilian higher schools by the mid-1870's, was leaving Moscow far behind as the educational center of the country.

Many were being reached in even greater degree by changes affecting the courts and the general economy. Practices introduced through the new courts and the new laws were bringing justice nearer to all and improving the legal profession: trial by jury, improvements in the university training of lawyers, and the formation of self-governing bar associations. Likewise the ambitious reforms of Minister of Finance Reutern were working a revolution that was already affecting millions. He was diligently promoting the development of manufacturing and mining industries by the use of both public and private funds, encouraging the establishment of private banks, and slowly but surely balancing the national budget.

At the same time, Reutern was making provision for greatly increased railroad construction. From the first sixteen-mile line authorized by Nicholas thirty years earlier, Russian railroads were extended to over 3,000 miles in the 1860's and, in the next decade, to 13,000 miles. Planned as a system stretching from Moscow into all parts of European Russia, rail lines were now bringing unrivaled changes as they linked major cities and areas of production with one another and with distant ports. One immediate result was an acceleration in the growth of industrial cities and seaports: St. Petersburg and Moscow were soon approaching the million mark in population, while other well-located centers—Riga, Odessa, Kharkov, Kiev, and Warsaw—were becoming booming metropolises. Industrial capitalism was taking root in Russia.

Many individuals, most of them wholly unrelated to the business of government but interested nonetheless, added to the merits of this period. None of them provided more of genuine worth than did those engaged in the arts and letters. Their number included men whose greatness would become, in time, universally recognized: Leo Tolstoy, Dostoevsky, Turgenev (though now living abroad, still an important contributor to Russian letters), Ostrovsky, Tchaikovsky, Borodin, Rimsky-Korsakov, Moussorgsky, Rubinstein, and Repin. Many of their works would memorialize Alexander's reign—not always, of course, as he would have preferred it to be remembered.

Socially the country had just entered a gilded age reflecting the increase in general prosperity. The upper aristocracy set the pace. Although some of the great landowners among the nobles were now in reduced circumstances as a result of the ending of serfdom, most of them continued to live on the grand scale of the past. At the fine clubs of St. Petersburg, such as the Yacht Club, where the spirit accorded with the conviviality of its many members from the fashionable guards regiments, there were to be found scores of generals, ministers, counts, and princes—even some grand dukes—who serenely defied apoplexy by their indulgence in fine food, and ruin by their indulgence in gambling. Further flamboyance was to be observed among the newly rich, their ranks including not only Russian families but also many of Welsh, Scottish, English, Belgian, German, and Jewish origin. Their wealth, derived for the most part from railroad building, textiles, iron, steel, sugar, and banking, did not buy their acceptance in established society; nevertheless, they spent their substance freely and cheerfully, apparently untroubled by the fact that much of it found its way into the pockets of the bureaucracy and aristocracy.

Alexander himself saw to it that social standards at the imperial level were kept high and that court life was in no way neglected. Functions such as the major court ball, held each January in the Nicholas Hall of the Winter Palace, gave him particular pleasure.

As host, he took delight in being able to greet by name many of the 3,000 guests. The men—grand dukes, court officials, senior civil servants, diplomats, senior guards officers, a few junior guards officers selected for their good looks and dancing ability—were part of his workaday life; and most of the women—Romanov relatives, other members of Russian upper-class society, wives or daughters of visiting dignitaries—were well known to him. He rarely failed to take part in all the activities of the occasion. They usually included, in addition to a succession of dances such as the polonaise, the mazurka, and the waltz, tête-à-têtes over champagne and pastries, pleasant intermission strolls through the brilliant galleries, and at midnight— sometimes later—an elaborate supper at tables so arranged that the tsar, seated on an elevation with his most distinguished guests, remained the central figure of the festivities.

The social activities, though supported wholeheartedly by Alexander, absorbed only a small part of the attention he found time to allot to the imperial court. He gave careful direction to the administration of the family's great property holdings and added to them as he saw fit. Because he liked the subtropical climate of the Crimea, he bought a thousand-acre estate, including a large vineyard, near Livadia and thus brought into prominence an area that became an upper-class resort; members of the imperial family and some of the higher nobility, following his example, bought land and built villas there. Also, in the fashion of the earlier Russian rulers, he distributed valuable tracts of state lands to his favorites at court. By such acts, he soon appeared well on the way toward reestablishing the grandeur he coveted for the imperial court. True, there were some individuals in his government who, observing the brilliant display of riches and sumptuous living and having been made oversensitive by the reading of history, shudderingly felt themselves to be reliving the times of Marie Antoinette; but their premature fears did little to dampen the mood of exuberance among the well-placed and personally satisfied.

Auspicious domestic manifestations notwithstanding, Alexander did not lose sight of the need to balance them with some evidence of progress toward regaining status for Russia among the great powers. Yet, although he and foreign minister Gorchakov had aimed purposefully at the two goals they considered basic, the renewal of ties with European states and the expunging of the shame of the Crimean War, the results for more than a decade were insignificant:

continued "family friendliness" from Prussia, ambivalence from France, and animosity from Austria* and England.

Finally, at the time of the Franco-Prussian War of 1870–71, Russia could begin to see the first indications of returning respect. Prussia was grateful for the Rusian promise of "benevolent neutrality," translating it as "help if needed"; Austria prudently avoided testing it, therefore refrained from attacking Prussia; and Italy interpreted it as good reason to reject overtures from France. Gambling on this tenuous improvement in standing. Alexander approved Gorchakov's bold diplomatic gesture of sending to all the great powers an unequivocal denunciation of those clauses in the Treaty of Paris requiring the demilitarization of the Black Sea. When this boldness not only met no strong challenge but actually resulted in the powers' agreeing to abrogate the humiliating clauses, Russia was no longer an outsider. A great obstacle to recovery from Nicholas I's last mistake had been removed; to secure the gain, Alexander directed Constantine to accelerate the reestablishment of the Black Sea fleet. Soon there followed a revival of the old conservative alliance in the form of the Three Emperors' League, in which Alexander aligned himself with Francis Joseph and William I, who was now head of the newly established German empire. With that, Russia was able to recall at least the attitude of a great power among the European states. To be sure, England was still "the enemy" notwithstanding her acquiescence to the abrogation of the Black Sea clauses; the recent war had made Prussia the heart of a powerful empire; and Austrian interest in the Balkans was still disquieting. But those were conditions that could be left for future consideration.

In the Far East. Russia had been holding her own, having sold Alaska to the United States and concentrated all attention on the near side of the Pacific. By encouraging settlers through financial assistance, she had increased the population of her holdings to about 100,000—still a negligible number, but a 70 percent increase in the past decade. When, by a treaty with Japan in 1875, she gained sole possession of Sakhalin in exchange for the islands she claimed in the Kurile chain, there was promise of a somewhat improved position in the East.

It was in Turkestan, however, that the greatest strides were made. Although Alexander gave orders against further penetration and

* After 1867, a dual monarchy, Austria-Hungary, was created from the Austrian empire and the kingdom of Hungary; but, since the Austrian emperor (at this time Francis Joseph) remained ruler of the new state, in general parlance it continued to be called Austria.

foreign minister Gorchakov assured other countries that Russia did not intend to annex additional territory there, aggressive leaders of the Russian forces already in the area kept up the advance, occupying new territory whenever possible. And the ambivalent tsar, more pleased with their achievement than angered by their independence, accepted the fruits of their efforts. In 1866, he approved the formal incorporation of those parts of Turkestan that had fallen to Russian conquest during the past two decades. Then, to insure the strict pacification and administration of the new addition, he put it under the control of General Constantine von Kaufmann, who had just served two years in Lithuania as successor to Michael Muravev ("The Hangman") and had developed an adeptness equal to Muravev's in the application of ruthless policies of pacification.

Kaufmann not only showed himself to be a merciless administrator in Turkestan but also exploited every opportunity for adding still more territory. The move by which he served imperial expansion most notably was against the rebelling khanate of Kokand, then a protectorate of Russia. In 1873, he personally led a punitive expedition against the khanate, battered its forces into temporary inaction, and sealed its fate by the shrewd act of turning over to Colonel Michael Skobelev the task of completing its subjugation.

Skobelev, though only thirty-two years of age at the time, had already won distinction through his service with the rugged southern forces, first against the guerrilla bands of the mountain tribes in the Caucasus, then at the head of a hard-riding, savage-fighting Cossack regiment in Turkestan. He was known as a man whose personal extravagance and wild dissipation were such as had ruined many promising young officers, and whose record was studded with spectacular military exploits that had succeeded because of what appeared to some of his superiors to be only his daring and recklessness. He might, in fact, have been dismissed as just another very lucky swashbuckler, had not the results of his unconventional tactics been so extraordinarily valuable as well as successful. In Kokand, he added to his reputation as an officer who could drive his men relentlessly, demand perfection and unqualified bravery, yet at critical times inspire them to face death willingly at his command. Hard as he was, he was a hero to the rank and file, who saw in him a "human being"—in their catalog, a rarity among officers. They accepted without complaint the knowledge that he put victory above all else and "used men's lives liberally," for they saw that he counted his life no more valuable than theirs. He never hesitated to join in the thick of combat—always conspicuous in his light uniform and mounted on a white charger—if he saw them hard pressed. When they were not on the battlefield, he made their comfort and welfare a matter of personal concern: they knew that, on occasion, he used his own funds, even defied superiors, to supply their needs.

Such leadership paid off consistently in the Kokand campaign. Within a few months, with a ferocity that annihilated where it could not subdue, Skobelev's forces had completely overrun the resistance. A grateful government recognized the accomplishment, through which 50,000 square miles and more than a million inhabitants were added to the empire, by heaping honors upon Skobelev: medals, promotion to the rank of major general and, finally, assignment to the governorship of the conquered khanate, now made a Russian province.

After the annexation of Kokand, most of Turkestan was under direct or indirect Russian dominion, the rest certain to fall in time. By these accessions, along with recently annexed Kazakhstan, the southern border of the empire was pushed out to include new territory half the size of the United States. Yet, aside from increasing Russia's expanse to one-sixth of the world's surface and her Asiatic possessions to one-third of that continent's area, the additions were not immediately of any great importance to her, being chiefly arid lands, sparsely settled. There was a possibility, of course, that their value would increase. The trade routes through Turkestan that tied Russia with China, Persia, and India by way of the fabled, but, faded, cities of Bokhara, Samarkand, and Tashkent were not to be overlooked; nor were the cotton-growing areas where mountain rivers and oases supplied water for irrigation.

For the time being, however, the consideration of potentialities was secondary to that of the immediate costs of conquest. Both the pacification and the administration of the new areas were problem-ridden and expensive. The predominantly Moslem population, which increased the number of non-Russians in the empire to one-third of the total population, was hostile. Moreover, the farther Russia drove into Turkestan, coming closer to the northwest frontier of India, the more inflamed became English fears of her "threat to India." Although there were some Russians—the audacious Skobelev among them—who would have been glad to "threaten" India, there was actually no justification for the English fears. Nevertheless, they were frequently revived by jingoists and, when the Russophobe Disraeli returned to the office of prime minister, in 1874, he was able to play on them to enhance Anglo-Russian tension.

Regardless of these minor difficulties and vexations, the international standing of Alexander's empire appeared in no way precarious, and, since he did not expect a condition of world harmony or perpetual amity, he was reasonably satisfied with it.

When the Slavic inhabitants of Bosnia and Herzegovina rose against Turkish rule in 1875, Alexander saw no reason to become involved. Nor was he moved to intercede when, within a few months, the Bulgarians precipitated a crisis with the Turks and were savagely beaten into submission, or when a surge of nationalistic feeling among the Slavs of Serbia and Montenegro led to their declaration of war on Turkey. Even when the Russian General Michael Chernyaev accepted command of the Serbian forces and Count Nicholas Ignatev, the Russian ambassador to Constantinople, insistently pleaded the cause of the Slavs, Alexander still objected to Russia's becoming implicated except as one of the community of neutral European states seeking to mediate. He had the strong support of Reutern, who pointed out that the economy, already strained by railroad and industrial expansion, would again be thrown into imbalance if required to accommodate the expenses of a war. Minister of Foreign Affairs Gorchakov agreed that, after years of waiting for the present reasonably satisfactory situation in international affairs, it would be folly to hazard it in an imbroglio that would revive the now fortunately quiescent Eastern Question.

Moreover, Alexander was not sympathetic with those of his subjects who were encouraging the Slavs in this war and urging Russian participation, the so-called Pan-Slavs. To his mind, they were troublesome visionaries. They organized societies and dedicated themselves to the unreasonable mission of liberating all Slavs from non-Slav domination and establishing them in some kind of federation—a goal no autocrat could be expected to approve. They lacked even the saving grace of the early Slavophiles, who had generally limited their concern to Russian Slavs and were not political reformers; but now even the older ones were beginning to make common cause with the Pan-Slavs.

Yet as the months passed and the war progressed—on the whole. unfavorably for the Slavic forces—the tsar found it increasingly difficult to stand aloof. He could not escape the accusing voice of the aroused Pan-Slavs around him, unendingly protesting the government's inaction in the face of the excess of the "infidel Turks bent, not on the defeat, but on the destruction of the Russians' brother Slavs." It came from the press (Katkov was a passionate proponent of intervention); from zemstvos and churches, busily raising funds, organizing hospital units, and recruiting men to help the Balkan Slavs; from the army, so affected by the appeals that thousands of privates and hundreds of officers were volunteering for the fighting front; from the inner circle of the imperial court itself, where the tsesarevich, the empress, and Pobedonostsev were promoting relief projects; and from the professional Pan-Slavs of the country, inspired by their vision of the Slavic destiny, which Ivan Aksakov and others of their leaders could now so easily vivify.

This was something new for a Russian autocrat to face. Most of the members of Alexander's government were shocked, some of them disgusted, by such untowardness: Valuev branded it "Slavophile onanism." [10] The Pan-Slavs, on the other hand, were elated. Evaluating the situation later, Aksakov declared, "Public opinion, unsupported by the government and without any national organization, was carrying on a war in a foreign country." Strictly speaking. this expression of concern for the embattled Slavs did not constitute public opinion; the majority of the people remained unmoved by the "war in a foreign country." But it was indisputably a swell of influential opinion publicly expressed in disregard, even censure, of the government's position—and that was worth remarking.

After more than a year, during which Russian volunteers continued to fight along with the Balkan peoples while Alexander and the heads of other neutral states tried futilely to find terms of settlement agreeable to Turkey, the tsar was converted to the belief that only a more direct approach could be expected to insure any kind of just conclusion to the conflict. Accordingly, in the autumn of 1876, he authorized Ignatev to issue an ultimatum to Turkey demanding a cease-fire under threat of Russian severance of diplomatic relations, then began to make ready for the expected involvement. Ordering partial mobilization and development of plans, he himself attended to the appointment of the military leadership. For important commands, his choice fell on grand dukes. For the Balkan-Danube front, where the main action would be, he appointed his brother Nicholas; for Transcaucasia, the second front, his brother Michael; for a strategically important wing of two corps, the heir, Alexander; for a single corps, his son Vladimir; and for a crucial naval operation on the Danube, his son Alexis.

When there followed the deadlock of an international conference to devise peace plans and, later the Turkish rejection of both a Russian proposal for simultaneous demobilization and a six-power plan for peace with some guarantees for the Balkan peoples, Alexander felt that he must at last take the step he had tried for two years to avoid. He came to a mutually satisfactory agreement with Francis Joseph (who had his imperial eye on Bosnia and Herzegovina) about future arrangements in the Balkan area, received Germany's ambivalent approval of his intended step, and accepted the inevitability of England's opposition to it. Then, on April 12, 1877, he declared Russia to be at war with Turkey.

Russian operations, presently under way on both fronts, were encouragingly successful for about three months. The problem of Rumania's allowing a passage to Russian troops was solved when Turkey's highhanded interference led Prince Charles to declare his people's independence and offer aid to Russia. The crossing of the Danube, though difficult and costly in lives, was completed, and the Russian command expected soon to control the important Shipka pass in the Balkan Mountains and the crossroads at Plevna; from these points they hoped to proceed across the Balkans and head toward Constantinople (any thought of coastal advance had been ruled out because of the superior strength of the Turkish navy on the Black Sea). The tsar had taken up quarters near the front to give counsel and observe the operations. In the meantime, the Transcaucasian campaign of the Grand Duke Michael moved on to Kars.

Then weaknesses began to show up. The army, though improved by Milyutin's reforms, was not yet first-class in any respect. Arms were inferior to those of the Turks, who were using late models of Krupp artillery and American and English rifles. Transport services were inadequate to bring up forces as rapidly as needed to equal those of the enemy. Medical and supply services were still shot through with corruption and inefficiency. The command was still top-heavy with officers whose titles were more distinguished than their military abilities.

Soon the front ranks were reflecting these deficiencies. On the second front, the assault on Kars had to be abandoned and the Grand Duke Michael's forces withdrawn to safety for reconditioning. In the Balkan-Danube region also, frustrations mounted. Though General Joseph Gurko had made a spectacular beginning in the campaign to take the Shipka pass, the Turks had rallied and held against him. At Plevna, which had been under extended siege by some of the best Russian units, even the intrepid Skobelev finally admitted the futility of spending additional thousands of Russian lives against the heavily fortified stronghold. In a single assault, he had lost more than 8,000 men, including his entire staff except one colonel, Alexis Kuropatkin. Reverses at all points were of such proportions that the Grand Duke Nicholas advised retreat. But the tsar, faced thus for the second time in his reign with an agonizing back-to-the-wall military situation, responded just as he had toward the end of the Crimean War—by ordering that the effort be continued at all costs.

This time, the results justified his desperate decision. Guards units and reserves were brought up as reinforcements; demands on the country's resources were doubled to provision the forces and supply materiel; General Totleben, "the genius of Sebastopol," was called to take charge of strategy in the Balkan area. Early in November, reports from Transcaucasia began to improve. General Michael Loris-Melikov took Kars, and all operations were moving again. Experience and practical tactics regained advantages for the Russians at Plevna and at the Shipka pass. Then the drive toward Constantinople was begun and carried forward with a determination that became the glory of the war, much of it credited to the skill and perseverance of three generals: Radetsky, Gurko, and Skobelev. The Balkan Mountains were formidable in winter, but the Russians, paying the appalling price of a slow and difficult advance—thousands of deaths from freezing and exposure—made their way over. In January, Skobelev led a triumphant force into Adrianople, and the Grand Duke Nicholas established advance headquarters there.

The outlook was now so unquestionably good that the tsar, who had returned to St. Petersburg in the previous month, was led to approve measures explicable only as diplomatic bravado. When the sultan called for cessation of hostilities, Alexander succumbed to over-enthusiastic counsel and offered an armistice with peace terms attached, thus opening the door for enduring trouble. Francis Joseph sharply protested this presumptuous consideration of peace plans without consulting Austria—and there went the rapprochement achieved in the Three Emperors' League. Great Britain, interpreting the act as clear evidence of Russian perfidy laced with ulterior motives, probably including the seizure of Constantinople and the

Straits, ordered the British fleet to proceed into Turkish waters—
and there was the old Eastern Question come to life again.

Much as he wanted to avoid turmoil, Alexander was never able
to get far away from it. For three months after the armistice, while
diplomacy boiled outside his realm, Pan-Slavism and old-fashioned
Russian nationalism boiled within it, demanding that Russia push
on to Constantinople and the Bosporus. The tsar, caught up in the
fever and now attending more indulgently to enthusiastic Ignatev
than his more conservative old foreign minister, Gorchakov, urged
the Grand Duke Nicholas to press on from Adrianople. But, after
an advance, with the sultan's consent, to San Stefano, "a short march
from Constantinople," the commander pleaded the impracticality
of further action.

Peace negotiations were handled by Ignatev, who met Turkish
representatives at San Stefano in February and imperiously dictated
terms to them. Embodied in the Treaty of San Stefano, the terms
provided for political and territorial rearrangements that would
achieve primarily, not satisfaction for the Slavic peoples for whose
defense the war was undertaken, but significant advantages for imperial Russia. Serbia, Montenegro, and Rumania were to be independent of Turkey but, with the exception of Montenegro, under
conditions that either fell far short of their aspirations or were
wholly unacceptable. Bulgaria was to appear as a large autonomous
principality, which, Ignatev anticipated, would gratefully accept the
direction of its benefactor and become a center for Russian domination of the Balkans. In addition, Turkey was to pay Russia indemnity amounting to over a billion rubles, most of it in territory along
the Black Sea coast and in Transcaucasia.

It was a treaty doomed even before it was ratified. Great Britain
attacked it as a Russian power play; Austria, as an invalid document
concocted in violation of a prewar agreement. Alexander soon recognized that defense of its terms put Russia in a precarious position,
on the brink of another conflict that might well result even more
disastrously than had the Crimean War. For four months, however,
stubbornly set on the course into which he had been drawn, he
sought some glimmer of hope in the dark prospect.

But again he was entrapped: while he was being denounced
abroad for going too far, at home he was still being reproved for not
going far enough. The Pan-Slavs sought the liberation and organized
association of all Slavs; yet, as they pointed out, he had already
thrown those living in Bosnia and Herzegovina to the Austrian wolf

and had left the others to become victims of power diplomacy. They had dreamed of Orthodoxy triumphant over the "infidel Turk"; yet, when the goal was in sight, he was not forcing the Russian advantage. Their leaders often deepened the perplexity of the tsar by reiterating their trust in him while condemning the situation he was condoning. Aksakov, a master of the trick, could conclude a denunciation of current Russian diplomacy as unforgivable "folly" with words of the most extravagant flattery: "Our trust in our Tsar cannot be subverted. He has given his word that the holy work shall be carried to the end, and his word cannot be broken."

In fact, Alexander had not abandoned the possibility of taking Constantinople and establishing the Russian advantage once for all. But the Grand Duke Nicholas would not move; and when he was replaced (on pretext of his impaired health) by Totleben, the situation remained unchanged: the new commander in chief also disapproved the undertaking. The international outlook did not remain unchanged, however; it worsened. Great Britain, whose preparations for war now had Parliament's approval, asserted her determination to "protect" Turkey, taking Cyprus in return for the service, and formally contracted with Austria for mutual defense of interests.

What appeared to be a stalemate was resolved only when, after the retirement of Ignatev, who had proved himself a definite diplomatic handicap, Alexander began to rely on Ambassador Shuvalov's efforts at easing tension in London. Gradually diplomacy managed to cool passions; by June, all parties were willing to accept Bismarck's offer of Berlin's hospitality to a congress of the powers "to consider in conference" the infamous Treaty of San Stefano.

The resulting Treaty of Berlin nullified the San Stefano arrangements and left Russia in the ignominious position of a military victor whose gains had been parceled out by others. The majority of the powers represented at the congress, more intent on containing Russia than on establishing justice for the politically underprivileged Balkan peoples, not only rejected all proposals bearing any hint of enhancement of Russian influence in the peninsula and the Black Sea area but also reduced Russian gains generally. Ignatev's plan for a large, Russian-dominated Bulgaria was summarily upset by the recognition of an autonomous principality limited to the Bulgarian region north of the Balkan Mountains and the provision that the people's choice of their prince and their representatives in the government be confirmed by Turkey "with the consent of the powers." (Russian troops were allowed to remain in limited occupation, however; so all was not expected to be lost in that area.) The chief dividends allocated to Gorchakov and Shuvalov, Russia's representatives at the congress, were the return of southern Bessarabia and the continued possession of Ardahan, Kars, and Batum in Transcaucasia.

In view of this outcome, the Russo-Turkish War now seemed to many Russians to have been a futile and disappointing undertaking. Officials felt that losses had not been justified. Pan-Slavs and liberals —usually, but not necessarily, set apart from one another in their ideological pursuits—were equally disturbed by the Treaty of Berlin.

The acquisitions, though territorially valuable to the empire, could not compensate for the fact that the war had left Russia in serious financial straits. Minister of Finance Reutern, who had struggled for sixteen years to put the finances of the country into respectable order and who had warned that the war would upset it, simply resigned rather than undertake the same task again. His successor, Samuel Greig, admitted that the postwar imbalance was awesome. Others saw it as proof of the need for further and more drastic reforms.

To the Pan-Slavs, the treaty was a document fraught with disquieting prospects. It accepted Austrian occupation of Bosnia and Herzegovina, thereby putting Slavs under non-Slav domination; reflecting the pressure of foreign Jewish financiers, it guaranteed the civil rights of Jews in Serbia, Rumania, and Bulgaria. These results, they contended, were sufficient proof of the West's contempt for the Slavs and of the growing power of the Jews—neither condition tolerable to conscientious Russians seeking the emancipation of the Slavs and the ascendancy of Orthodox Christians. The Pan-Slavs were not a unified political force, but, since they were well represented in the Church, the army, and the landed nobility, their attitude could not fail to be of moment.

The liberals were discontented chiefly with that provision of the treaty which permitted the new principality of Bulgaria, temporarily occupied by Russian troops, to choose its own prince, who would rule in accordance with an organic statute, a constitution. When the Bulgarians actually availed themselves of that liberal arrangement while the occupying troops were still present, the Russian liberals were bitterly reminded of the first Alexander, who had allowed the Poles a constitution while he was denying the Russians a voice in their government. They easily ignored the fact that Alexander II had been in no position in 1878 either to grant or to deny the Bulgarians a constitution; also the fact that the document, so far, seemed a tenuous blessing since the first prince chosen, young Alexander of Battenberg, a nephew of Empress Marie, was personally recommended by the tsar and would probably be inclined to attend more diligently to advice from his imperial uncle than to the provisions of a constitution. Regardless of pros and cons, the liberals saw here an opportunity to renew the agitation begun by the assemblies of the nobility and the zemstvos in 1865—and peremptorily silenced by the tsar—for popular representation in the government; and they began at once to renew it.

By this time, Alexander had grown accustomed to the rise and fall in the expression of discontent among his subjects, and he was not unduly disturbed by the current complaints of the Pan-Slavs and liberals: his established agencies seemed capable of keeping them safely within bounds. Since his return from the Balkan front, however, he had become seriously concerned about the reappearance of a domestic problem that the war had temporarily obscured for him—the cut-and-come-again revolutionary movement.

Though the movement had declined after the government's precautionary arrangements following the Karakozov assassination attempt, it had been revived, in the years just prior to the war, in the form of populism—its revival assisted, ironically, by the very measures that Alexander had accepted as the enduring means of repressing it. Tolstoy's approval of wholesale expulsions of undesirables from the universities and of calling home Russian students from abroad had turned hundreds of young people, including a growing number of women, toward the active ranks of the discontented intelligentsia. Those ranks, fed from many sources touched by the government's latest reactionary measures, had accepted the current rallying cry of the socialist leaders, echoing Herzen's "To the People!" Thus the populists (narodniki) had come into being.

In the beginning the populists had adopted a program—and they still adhered to its fundamentals—aimed directly at freeing the country from tsarism in order that it might be reorganized as a self-governing, cooperative commonwealth. They accepted the view that it would take a revolution to overthrow tsarism; but they believed that it would be a simple, perhaps bloodless, one if the "dark people" could be led to understand their true interests and to demonstrate their wishes in a general uprising. With burning zeal and unwarranted confidence, the young populists, assuming the dress and attempting the activities of peasants and workers, had invaded the countryside and the factories to preach their gospel. Most of them, however, having naïvely accepted the Bakunin view that the masses were ready to rise against tsarism, had soon become disillusioned. They had found few workers and even fewer peasants responsive to their campaign; the gendarmerie, drastically responsive.

This initial failure, though discouraging, had by no means destroyed the populist movement. On the eve of the war, they were still active—but they were changing. Some were beginning to neglect persuasion and seek new approaches to revolution. Leading proponents of change, meeting in St. Petersburg in 1876, set up principles for a secret society (which, two years later, revived the name Land and Freedom and adopted it) to provide tighter organization and new procedures. A few of their number undertook a bold demonstration in the capital, but it proved to be a dismal failure for them, a brief exercise for the police who halted it. The leaders, arrested and tried, quickly found themselves in the Peter-Paul fortress, and it was decided that such old methods were becoming too dangerously familiar to their official adversaries. When they had adopted a new method, the occasion for its public introduction would be provided, inadvertently, by one of the imprisoned leaders, Alexis Bogolyubov. But that would come only after an interval of "prudent preparation."

During the war years, after a second campaign to win the masses had failed, the more completely political-minded of the populists began to adopt what was basically a policy of frustration—terrorism. Their reasoning was that, if they were to help the masses who had proved so reluctant to help themselves, it must be through some direct method; and terror was the one they considered themselves most capable of employing. They believed that, by a terroristic campaign devoted to the systematic assassination of unpopular men in the tsarist government—police officials, governors, prosecutors—the regime could be forced to capitulate and the way opened for a new order. Theirs was not a novel idea: it had been voiced sporadically among Russia's serious young revolutionaries for a quarter of a century. It had led Ivan Yakushkin and Peter Kakhovsky to offer to kill Alexander I; it had led Kakhovsky, under stress, to murder Miloradovich; it had been Karakozov's personal reason for attempting to kill Alexander II; it had provided the enthusiasm for the Russian Revolutionary Committee. Regardless of its history, terrorism now appealed to the romantic minds of a number of revolutionaries as an appropriate instrument for their current crusade.

The year 1878 saw the beginning of a period of sustained terrorism. It was opened by one of the emancipated women, Vera
Zasulich, who had become convinced of the urgent need to rid the
country of malevolent officials. When she learned that the St. Petersburg prefect, General Fedor Trepov, had ordered the flogging of the
imprisoned revolutionary Bogolyubov, she straightway attempted
to mete out retribution by shooting the prefect. Like many terrorists, she was unskilled in the use of weapons and merely wounded
her quarry; but neither that fact nor the fact that her deed had
not been directed by any organized group stood in the way of
her becoming a heroine to the terrorists as soon as she was arrested.
Officials, expecting her case to serve as a public warning against such
outlandish behavior, allowed her a trial by jury. To their consternation—and the open approval of the public—she was released; before she could be reapprehended, she escaped abroad.

Other expressions of the new lawlessness followed at such unpredictable places and in such unpatterned sequence that the terrorist
threat, which at first seemed negligible, began to take on an aspect
of seriousness. In various cities, terrorists resisted arrest, one group
in Odessa boldly shooting it out with police who came to raid their
quarters. They flaunted their defiance in leaflets prepared by their
underground presses. As their popularity spread, students began to
disregard authority and demonstrate in support of their acts. Some
students in Kiev, after an unsuccessful attempt on the life of a court
official, killed a gendarme captain.

Seeing arrests and trials increasing in number, the tsar called for
an accounting by the Third Section. The incumbent chief, General
Nicholas Mezentsev, pleaded lack of funds for sufficient undercover
work, and he was allotted an increase. But he did not live to use it:
he was assassinated, in the summer of 1878, by a former army officer,
Sergei Kravchinsky, better known as Stepniak. To find a replacement
for Mezentsev, the tsar looked beyond the corps of gendarmes and
chose, as he often did, a military man familiar to him: the tough,
thick-necked General Alexander Drenteln. He impressed on the new
chief the need for unrelenting vigilance and firm control in order to
achieve what was now required: quick results in the struggle against
what was coming to be known as *kramola* ("sedition").

It was not easy to define the offense indicated by the term *kramola*,
which suggested something both palpable and impalpable, both
corporeal and invisible. Moreover, Drenteln had scant information
on which to rely in his attempts to detect it. He believed, for in-

stance, that a group known as the Russian Social-Revolutionary
Party was one of the major terrorist organizations, though the fact
was that, while the group ostentatiously displayed crossed revolvers,
daggers, and axes on leaflets and rightly claimed credit for terrorist
actions in Odessa, it had fewer than two dozen members. Like it,
most terrorist groups were of quite limited size. Yet, even with a collective membership not exceeding 1,000, they were able to create
the impression of being a small army because their recklessness and
often spectacular successes seemed to reflect confidence based on extensive support.

Alexander's notion of the critical significance of *kramola,* exaggerated by ignorance as well as the fear always induced by anything
suggestive of revolutionary activity against the tsarist government,
led him to excesses in combating it. Oblivious of what some of his
practical officials recognized, that a physical attack on *kramola* was as
useless a gesture as "slashing at the water with your sword," he
ordered Drenteln to undertake an absurdly massive drive against
both the terrorists and any others suspected of connection with revolutionary organizations. And it was carried out with unblinking
solemnity. To three of the chief centers of terroristic activity were
sent temporary governors general with extraordinary authority, each
of them a general who had distinguished himself in the late war: to
St. Petersburg, Joseph Gurko; to Kharkov, Michael Loris-Melikov;
and to Odessa, Edward Totleben. They were granted both civil and
military authority, including the right to expel undesirable persons,
exile persons considered dangerous, close periodicals, use military
courts to try civilians accused of terrorist acts—in short, to take whatever action they deemed necessary for the preservation of order and
the eradication of political resistance. Similar rights were temporarily extended to the permanent governors general of Moscow,
Kiev, and Warsaw.

These "associate autocrats" carried out their commissions to the
full extent of their authority: the areas were shaken, searched, and
purged in a relentless program of raids, arrests, expulsions, imprison-
ments, and executions. Totleben alone, during his first four months
in office, consigned thirty-one civilians to trial in military courts,
which condemned five to death, eighteen to long periods of hard
labor, and eight to resettlement in Siberia; he rid Odessa of other
"ill-meaning persons" by expelling fourteen from the country and
exiling dozens to distant parts of the empire. The city, he assured the
tsar, was changed beyond recognition. Reports from every quarter

indicated that, if activity could produce the desired results, the cleansing campaign would shortly be over and the tsar would be able to celebrate the silver anniversary of his accession, which would fall on February 19, 1880, in peace.

This indiscriminate sweep, however, too often netted the innocent and missed the guilty, many of whom were left to strike again. Moreover, such tactics only aggravated the terrorists' hatred of officials, and before the end of spring, 1879, they were reacting with ever more disturbing exploits: the assassination in Kharkov of Prince Dmitri Kropotkin, singled out for his brutality in the treatment of political prisoners, and attempts on the life of both Drenteln and the tsar.

The inclusion of the tsar among the targets of terrorism shocked and distressed some of the heretofore active workers in the Land and Freedom society and, within a few months, caused a split in the membership and led to the abandonment of the revered party name. The larger group, adopting the name People's Will, endorsed a program that now unequivocally included regicide on the ground that the tsar was "the embodiment of despotism, hypocritical, cowardly, bloodthirsty, and all-corrupting." The other, led by George Plekhanov, tried for a couple of years to continue the original populist program, but gradually disintegrated, its adherents going their various ways.

Members of the People's Will, however, were young men and women of remarkable intensity and industry; they continued to give a disturbing account of themselves under the leadership of the party's Executive Committee, a small, self-appointed group that planned strategy and directed operations. In November, they dynamited a train in which they expected, mistakenly, that the tsar would be traveling. Then they turned to what they thought would be a more dependable scheme for the assassination: they furnished dynamite to a willing young revolutionary, Stepan Khalturin, employed as a carpenter in the Winter Palace, and trusted him to see that it served its intended purpose.

Although Drenteln had tightened security at the Winter Palace, Khalturin was able to take in the hundred or so pounds of dynamite he planned to use and to place it safely in a basement two floors below the tsar's dining room (the area immediately below the dining room was a guardroom, rarely empty and thus inconvenient for his purpose). On February 5, 1880, just before the scheduled hour of a state dinner, he set the deadly charge and quietly left the building.

The explosion was on time, but, fortunately for the intended victims, the dinner was not: the guests had been delayed. The actual victims were eleven Finnish guardsmen who were killed, and fifty-six others wounded, as walls collapsed and floors gave way. The would-be regicides had again failed.

The explosion, however, served some purpose for the plotters; it shattered morale even more effectively than it shattered walls. The Grand Duke Constantine wrote in his diary: "We are reliving the Terror, but with this difference: the Parisians during the revolution saw their enemies face to face. We neither see them nor do we know them." [11]

No one could anticipate what lay ahead. Police quickly put St. Petersburg under regulations that suggested a state of siege. Armed guards patrolled the streets, curfew was imposed, and every movement was suspect. Some residents, fearing more violence despite the precautions, left the city. Alexander secretly moved his second family, Catherine Dolgoruky and her three children, into the Winter Palace for such safety as that residence could provide. In another part of the building, the unhappy Empress Marie lay ill, distraught but insistent on spending her last days at home near her sympathetic sons.

Not being a reflective man, Alexander did not analyze the predicament with any degree of thoroughness. He admitted that some of the policies adopted in 1866 might be judged unwise; but the crying need now was not for regretting past action but for immediate and effective means of eradicating *kramola*. Drenteln's methods had been temporarily discredited since the recent emergency measures had not prevented this last, and most daring, of the terrorists' acts. What were the alternatives?

The tsesarevich, inspired by Katkov, suggested that the tsar appoint a commission, give it dictatorial power over all government agencies, and entrust it with the task of working out and enforcing a general policy throughout the country. That an autocrat would be attracted by the thought of handing over so much power was not to be expected, and no one was surprised that Alexander found it difficult to accept. As the mood of panic continued, however, and the supporters of the idea came to include many whose judgment he trusted, he gave in and agreed to form such a body. After all, he would be delegating authority, not relinquishing it, and the head of the commission would be responsible directly to him.

Having made up his mind, Alexander considered suggestions and accepted certain plans for the drastic scheme. The commission would be composed of nine men, collectively to be known as the Supreme Executive Commission, empowered to proceed unrestrained with measures considered necessary to root out sedition and directed to consider ways of improving the government's relationship with the people. It would administer St. Petersburg directly as well as the entire area comprising the St. Petersburg Military District. From that base it would supervise and direct the work of all civil and military authorities elsewhere in the country. To serve as chairman of the commission and make suggestions for its membership, Alexander appointed the fifty-five-year-old General Michael Loris-Melikov.

The appointment came as a decided surprise to many, particularly in St. Petersburg. Loris-Melikov was well known in the capital, but as an outsider, not a sharer. Though technically a noble (a shrewd ancestor having gained admission to the Georgian nobility) who had begun his career in the guards and had recently been made a count for service to the empire, he was not generally considered acceptable in aristocratic circles. Some referred to him as "the Armenian," in snobbish allusion to the fact that his father was an Armenian merchant, and resorted to sly ridicule in describing him: swarthy, dumpy, full of smiles, oozing charm, and familiar on short acquaintance.

But the tsar had no time for the punctilios of the aristocracy just now. Encouraged by his son Alexander and Minister of War Milyutin, he had come to consider his choice the man of the hour. As temporary governor general of Kharkov, Loris-Melikov had proved himself efficient and even-handed, a far better administrator than either Gurko or Totleben, each of whom had abused his temporary authority, irritated the local bureaucracy, and made little distinction between the innocent and the guilty. Moreover, he was a popular hero, credited with the capture of Kars in the recent war and, later, with courageous and humanitarian leadership in Astrakhan when it was ravaged by the black plague. To his further credit, he had won the confidence and trust of all who had worked closely with him.

Politically, Loris-Melikov was different from most of the others who, in past years, had been called to the task of dealing with antigovernment manifestations: he was no reactionary. He had been friendly with the favorite poet and publisher of the radical intelligentsia, Nicholas Nekrasov, and sympathized with what Nekrasov called the burden of his poetry, "the suffering of the people." In agreement with those who thought the size and importance of the terrorist movement exaggerated, he had not liked the post-Karakozov course. He believed that, once terrorism had been eradicated, the tsar would be well advised to adopt a more liberal policy. However, convinced that Alexander was "more fearful of specters than of facts," he kept his views to himself as he prepared to undertake the initial task of exorcising the specter of terrorism. In the hope of gaining the support he would need to carry out the program he had in mind, he suggested as candidates for the tsar's appointments to the Supreme Executive Commission men who could be expected to give him their confidence—among them, the tsesarevich and his political mentor, Pobedonostsev—and the tsar favored him by accepting his choices. He was further favored, indirectly as well as directly, by an unsuccessful terrorist attempt on his life only a few days after he took office. His assailant, Ippolit Mledecki, a converted Jew connected with the People's Will, was arrested, tried, and hanged within forty-eight hours after the attempt—a timely instance of the dispatch Alexander approved. Thereafter, so far as the tsar was concerned, he could proceed with virtually unquestioned license: whatever his ideas, he was free to test them.

Meanwhile, the routine affairs of life and government must go on as usual—that was the tsar's will. Though Alexander appreciated the apprehension of those about him and though he himself was under great mental strain and almost unbearably beset by the discomfort of his asthma, he refused to cancel the accession anniversary celebration. It was held as planned—the traditional brilliant display. There were parades, concerts, banquets, and receptions. Alexander was assured of the boundless loyalty of his subjects and glorified as the Tsar-Liberator. But the brilliance of it all was darkly overcast for him. He could not but recognize the insincerity of some of the public adulation; though he knew that he had done much in the twenty-five years of his reign, he could take no joy in it now. The continued progress of the many programs he had begun could not sustain the sense of accomplishment he had felt during the first ten years. That sense had gradually given way to frustration as his diplomatic efforts brought more disappointment than satisfaction, the promising youth of the country swelled the political opposition, members of his own family turned away from him, and his enemies began hunting him down. The Tsar-Liberator was himself under duress. It was now up to the Supreme Executive Commission, guided by whatever wisdom and ability its chairman possessed, to find the means for his deliverance.

Rarely had anyone but a tsar wielded as much power in Russia as did Loris-Melikov. He was the chief administrator of the capital and the surrounding provinces; he determined the privileges and powers of governors and governors general. When, at his suggestion, the tsar removed Drenteln from his post, the Third Section came under his control.

He did not abuse his power, but he used it freely to the full extent of the need as he saw it. His aim was first to distinguish between the nonviolent liberals and the terrorists—a change from recent methods —and to deal with the active offenders speedily and decisively. He soon had sufficient information about the members of the People's Will to help him round up many of them (though he failed to take the most wanted, Khalturin). Within a few weeks, conditions were clearly in his favor: an increase in the number of terrorists under arrest, an accumulation of usable evidence from their confessions, and a decrease in terrorist activity. With that, tension began to subside, and the picture of "Loris-Melikov, the savior" began to emerge.

As his position became more secure, he undertook, in his reports to the tsar, to express his views about the general state of the country and to emphasize the need for a serious change in domestic policy. Subversion, he indicated, was a diseased outgrowth of widespread dissatisfaction among the people: the peasants did not believe that the Emancipation Act had been fairly executed, zemstvo officials were frustrated by administrative interference, students were embittered by the Tolstoy programs and regulations, the clergy was in a miserable state, loyal subjects resented officials who treated them as if they were disloyal. In short, morale was at a low ebb, much as it had been at the end of the Crimean War. But, in his opinion, it could be restored by a renewal of beneficent effort and an indication that the tsar was attentive to the voice of his people. The tsar might begin by ridding his government of the unpopular Tolstoy, punishing officials who abused their power, mitigating censorship and, in general, living up to the spirit of the reforms. He would thus not only regain the goodwill of his people but also forestall further agitation for an imperial zemstvo and a constitution. This advice was laced with flattery, but its meaning, not altogether flattering, was clear: the tsar had been taking the wrong advice for fourteen years. Alexander, apparently not offended by the judgment, responded to it by declaring himself "almost in agreement." [12]

The extent of the tsar's agreement was dramatically suggested by the first changes he made. He dismissed Tolstoy from both of his posts, in the ministry of education and in the Holy Synod, and relegated him to the State Council, where he could meditate harmlessly on the uses of authority. To replace him as minister of education, he appointed Andrei Saburov, a ready supporter of Loris-Melikov; and, at the chairman's suggestion, he appointed Pobedonostsev as over-procurator of the Holy Synod. In suggesting this appointment, Loris-Melikov was intending to assure himself of the support of the tsesarevich, known to be a steadfast follower of Pobedonostsev; and, for a time, he had that support, wholehearted and eagerly helpful. Support came also from many others as he was seen to be achieving a relaxation in censorship and in the harassment of the liberals. And when Alexander Abaza, his choice for a successor to the reactionary Minister of Finance Greig, removed the heavy salt tax and showed interest in other changes, Loris-Melikov was blessed as father of the ideas.

Before Alexander had time fully to appreciate the lessening of the terrorist threat and to evaluate the stir created by this beginning of liberalization in the government, his attention was claimed again by that abiding source of disquiet, his personal problems. They became most demanding soon after the death of the Empress Marie, which occurred late in May 1880. It was then that, being free at last to make legitimate his relations with his "wife before God," he started on a private course that only a few could approve.

Even those who expected him to marry Catherine Dolgoruky were astonished at the unseemly haste with which he did it. She herself urged that there be no delay. During the summer, bowing to her persistence and justifying his act in the light of "honor, conscience, and religion," he secretly married her. Then, by personal decree, he conferred upon her the title "Most Serene Highness Princess Yurevsky," expecting to confer the title of empress at a later date.[13]

This crowning of a fourteen-year liaison with imperial honor and sanction met with the unqualified disapproval of the tsar's family. The tsesarevich in particular was quite open in denouncing "the outsider," whom he considered both designing and immature (thirty-five years of age at that time, he was two years older than his stepmother); he even talked of moving with his wife and four children from the capital to Denmark.[14] While many tried to avoid commitment to one attitude or another by social aloofness, some politely

accepted the marriage, and a few, like Loris-Melikov, recognized the
importance of Princess Yurevsky's favor and actively sought it.

The distress of this period was gradually tempered for Alexander
by two conditions. He had the personal comfort of security in being
with his second family, to whom he was deeply devoted. He seemed
always to be in good spirits after an hour with the oldest child, eight-
year-old George (Gogo); and if he resented society's initial lack of
courtesy to Princess Yurevsky, he was not unduly depressed by it. In
addition, he had the pleasure of seeing an improvement in his political standing among some of his subjects—not all of them by any
means, but many who had, for some time, seemed irretrievably
alienated.

The agreeable aspect of the changing political climate, and unfortunately an offsetting discordant aspect, could be credited to Loris-
Melikov. While he continued energetically to hunt down terrorists,
he did not neglect the cultivating of public opinion, and he soon
managed to stir up response. His ascent and Tolstoy's fall inspired
an open debate between two groups of the politically concerned, the
one viewing-with-pleasure and the other viewing-with-alarm. Their
debate became unusually loud and bitter both because of the issues
involved and because of the growing sophistication and assertiveness
of the educated public.

The viewers-with-pleasure were generally those who thought of
themselves as liberals, who cherished a belief in progress, in the spirit
of reform, and in a political course providing that policy be guided
to some degree by the views of society—meaning, to them, the educated class. Some of them thought Loris-Melikov's goals too limited,
but the majority approved his "dictatorship of the heart" and sub-
scribed to the view expressed by the Tver liberals, that he was bringing "honesty and goodwill into the relations between the government and the people." [15]

The viewers-with-alarm, politically conservative, doggedly insisted
that to listen to those professing to speak for society was to listen to
an unrepresentative minority, not the people, and to act on their
advice was to invite disaster. Dostoevsky, in an eloquent expression
of this view, suggested that Loris-Melikov was mistaking the temper
of the St. Petersburg liberals for the temper of the nation, which
was something quite different: "To the people, the Tsar is the in-
carnation of themselves, their whole ideology, their hopes and beliefs. . . . Let them speak about their needs, let them tell the whole

truth about them. But, I repeat, first let them speak alone, while we, 'the people's intelligentsia,' for the time being, humbly stand aside and look at them, listening to what they have to say." [16]

Many conservatives believed that the liberals were inspired by alien forces, among them the Jews, who in recent years had been receiving increased attention. At the time of the Russo-Turkish War, anti-Semitic feelings were fed by the stories of Jewish profiteering at the expense of the army supply services and the use of Jewish influence in the peace settlements to force the guarantee of civil rights for Jews in the Balkan areas. Of late there had been a revival of the medieval myth that Jews used Christian blood in making unleavened bread for Passover, some arguing that it was no myth.[17] While he was chief of the Third Section, Drenteln had encouraged the view that Jews constituted a dangerous element.

In the absence of elections or public opinion polls, no one could say with certainty which of the sides commanded the greater support. The conservatives had been profiting by the support of such influential publications as Katkov's *Moscow News* while the liberal press was under restriction. Yet the liberals appeared to have the larger following—an impression reinforced by the conservatives' concern lest liberal views be taken as representative.

Unperturbed by these political contentions, Loris-Melikov held to his course. At the end of July, he informed Alexander that the peak of terrorism had been passed and the time had come to return to normal procedures. On his advice, the tsar abolished the Supreme Executive Commission and made some changes which, it soon became evident, would determine the nature of future "normal procedures." In order to unify the police administration, he abolished the Third Section, transferring the corps of gendarmes to the jurisdiction of the recently established department of state police, under the ministry of interior and entrusted that department, headed by Vyacheslav Plehve, with the functions formerly exercised by the Third Section. Then, not unexpectedly, he named Loris-Melikov as minister of interior. These changes climaxed one of Loris-Melikov's shrewdest maneuvers: to end the mood of crisis and dictatorship, to act in what seemed a liberal manner, and yet to retain, and even regularize, his power—in short, deftly to exchange one hat for another.

As head of the newly strengthened ministry of interior, Loris-Melikov was the most powerful official in the government. Other ministers were either beholden to him or in sympathy with his views, and the tsar was almost completely dependent upon him. In his own estimation, he could count on the favorable influence of Princess Yurevsky and of the tsesarevich. He confidently believed that, under these conditions, he would have no difficulty in holding his own by keeping the terrorists down and forestalling any gains by society that might effectively threaten the autocratic authority.

To make certain of its goodwill, Loris-Melikov proposed to give society a modest portion at the legislative table, assuming that the tsar would approve the portion and that society's appetite would not grow with the eating.

Accordingly, in the latter part of 1880, while Alexander was in Livadia, Loris-Melikov dusted off some proposals once made by Valuev and the Grand Duke Constantine and overhauled them for the tsar's consideration. In the scheme he offered, it was provided that the tsar invite representatives of such groups as zemstvos, assemblies of the nobility, and municipal councils to participate in drafting legislation on subjects approved by the ministry of interior, and that he enlarge the State Council by the addition of representatives from the same groups. The State Council would consider the legislative drafts and make recommendations concerning them to the tsar. This proposed arrangement, modest as it was, had been rejected, in one form or another, by Alexander before this time; but Loris-Melikov trusted his power of persuasion to win approval for it now.

When Alexander returned to St. Petersburg, in January 1881, Loris-Melikov put the proposal before him, taking care to reassure him that it was wholly innocuous: it had "nothing in common with Western constitutional forms," and it would in no way limit the autocratic prerogatives.[18] If the tsar adopted the proposal, his minister pointed out, he could be sure of the cooperation of the educated class in the continuing struggle against *kramola*; if he did not, that class would drift into political indifference, thus providing an environment favorable to *kramola*. Again the tsar was "almost in agreement." He did not like the idea of enlarging the State Council; but, when that condition was dropped, he approved the remainder of the proposal and authorized Loris-Melikov to edit it for publication.

Having made his decision, the tsar did not trouble himself about its possible consequences but turned his mind again to private affairs. Now that the period of mourning for Empress Marie was officially over, he was beginning to appear with Princess Yurevsky in public and to find pleasure once more in court life. As in 1866, so now fifteen years later, he was recovering his optimism, looking ahead to a season of calmness.

His mind thus engaged, Alexander managed to stay aloof from the quiet but significant agitation that was stirring through his government because of the legislation under preparation, which finally came to be overstated as the "Loris-Melikov Constitution." While it had some prominent champions, including the Grand Duke Constantine, Milyutin, and two of the new ministers, Saburov and Abaza, it excited unqualified hostility in others. Many were beginning to suspect Loris-Melikov of attempting to subvert the principles of autocracy and insinuate constitutionalism into the Russian government. Among them was the tsesarevich, now privately disavowing his advocacy of Loris-Melikov for reasons both personal and political. Personally, he disapproved of the minister's acceptance of Princess Yurevsky as the respected consort of the tsar and his apparent willingness to discuss matters of state with her. Politically, he shared Pobedonostsev's serious distrust of the so-called contitution as well as the calculations of its sponsor. As the future tsar, he was at this point particularly attentive to his mentor's pronouncements on the nature of tsarism, its appropriateness to the country he would rule, and the expediency of being on the alert in its behalf.

Like Katkov, Pobedonostsev had welcomed Alexander's early reforms but had come to feel that of late he was being led, in the name of reform, to put his country into jeopardy. Not being given to equivocation, he did not hesitate to lead the tsesarevich directly to the heart of his own political philosophy, regardless of its conflict with that which appeared to be guiding the tsar. He was morally certain that ordinary human beings, particularly Russians, although not without redeeming qualities, were not fit to govern themselves; therefore Russia needed a strong, autocratic tsar, assisted by able bureaucrats—such as himself. Ideally, the country should have one ruler; one faith, the Orthodox; and one nationality, the Russian.

Such ideas appealed to the slow-thinking but strong-willed tsesarevich, as did most of the ideas of his political counselor. But neither he nor Pobedonostsev felt that speaking up at this time would gain anything but the tsar's displeasure. Rumors were spread that his residence, the Anitchkov Palace, had become the center of opposition, even that he was under house arrest because of his attitude. But they were groundless; he wisely refrained from attempting what he knew was impossible—effectively to oppose his father. Most of the others who had misgivings about the direction of Loris-Melikov's leadership followed his example.

One, however, the tsar's uncle William I of Germany, could afford to express himself as others dared not. Mistakenly believing a constitution to be the intended outcome of his nephew's proposed measure, he sent what he considered a timely dispatch in which he warned, on the basis of his own experience, against any traffic whatsoever with constitutionalism. Alexander gave no evidence of being troubled by it.

At the end of February, Loris-Melikov submitted his final draft of the new project and, along with it, the draft of a manifesto proclaiming it still another "sign of the monarch's confidence in his most loyal subjects." Privately, Alexander must have pondered on the deception of such phrases as "the monarch's confidence" and "most loyal subjects" when he was brought the intelligence that the terrorist Andrei Zhelyabov had just been arrested and would give the police only one statement about the active members of the People's Will: that they intended to kill the tsar regardless of any precautions taken to guard him. But, as if with a mind single only to the matter in hand, the tsar proceeded with Loris-Melikov's proposals.

On the morning of Sunday, March 1, Alexander ordered that the Council of Ministers plan to meet on the following Wednesday for the final consideration and editing of the announcement of the new project. After discussing business with his minister of interior, he attended religious services in the palace chapel and lunched with his family. Later he set off for his customary observation of the guards ceremonies at the Michael Riding School. As he watched the display of superb horsemanship, he appeared more animated than usual, enjoying particularly the wild riding of the Caucasian tribesmen who formed his ceremonial bodyguard. After leaving the Riding School, he paid a short call at the residence of his cousin the Grand Duchess Catherine. Then, apparently well satisfied with the day, he ordered his coachman to drive him directly back to the Winter Palace.

The handful of terrorists contriving his fate were, for the time being, satisfied also. They had just completed their plans to insure that, whatever route he chose for his return to the palace on this occasion (he had recently been varying his approaches), they would be on the alert for him. On the route he now chose, Sophie Perovsky, lieutenant to the imprisoned leader Zhelyabov, had stationed four so-called throwers, each carrying a bomb, and had taken her place at a vantage point from which to give a signal as the tsar approached.

If the first thrower failed, the second would follow up—and so on. The four potential assassins—Ivan Emelyanov, Ignatius Grinevitsky, Timothy Mikhailov, and Nicholas Rysakov—were known to be fanatically daring; they had volunteered for this service which, if successful, would in all likelihood claim the life of the thrower as well as that of the tsar. The bombs, ingeniously designed by a former engineering student turned terrorist, Nicholas Kibalchich, were so constructed that they had to be thrown at close range, and the user's body therefore became virtually a part of the infernal apparatus. As the tragedy was played out, only two of the volunteers were called upon to act: Rysakov, a mining student, and Grinevitsky, an aristocratic young Polish graduate of the Technological Institute.

When Alexander's carriage and its escort, returning at its usual dashing speed, neared Rysakov's station, Perovsky signaled and he threw his bomb just as the imperial carriage passed. The explosion damaged the carriage and wounded a number of the escort but barely touched the tsar. Shaken but ignoring pleas that he consider his own safety, Alexander hurried from the carriage to inquire after the wounded and take a look at Rysakov, who had at once been seized. Then, as he turned to enter a police sleigh to leave the scene, Grinevitsky darted up and hurled the second bomb—this one, at the tsar's feet. The instant explosion achieved its fearful purpose—as the terrorists expected, a double execution. Alexander, mangled and bleeding, was rushed to the Winter Palace, where he died about an hour later. Grinevitsky, willing victim of his own violence, died of his wounds on the same day.

The Grand Duke Alexander had now become Tsar Alexander III. His oldest son, Nicholas, within three months of his thirteenth birthday, had become the tsesarevich. Neither would ever escape the memory, or free himself of the terrible foreboding, of March 1, 1881.

IX

Status Quo

ALEXANDER III, 1881-1894

THE Executive Committee of the People's Will had finally
reached the ultimate target of their terror. In their overcon-
fident enthusiasm, they proceeded at once to act on the premature
conclusion that they had brought autocracy to its knees and that the
new tsar would accept their stipulations in order to avoid a fore-
doomed future. Declaring themselves in the spirit of generous victors
to have "discarded all prejudices" and "suppressed the distrust
created by the actions of the government throughout the century,"
they advised Alexander III, in an open letter, of the situation he now
faced and the courses open to him: "There can be only two ways to
escape from such a situation: either revolution . . . which no death
sentence can stop; or the voluntary transference of supreme power
to the people. . . . Your Majesty must decide!" [1]

It was a futile address; they had already deafened the ears to which
they spoke. They had revived and intensified for Alexander the horrible dread that had gripped the heart of the government a year
earlier, after the explosion arranged by Khalturin in the Winter
Palace. He was beset by fear, and he was determined to rid himself
of its source by the most direct means within his autocratic power.

The tsar's apprehension was shared by many, particularly in the
capital. On every hand were evidences of defense against the in-

visible enemy—the nihilists, as some chose to call the terrorists. There were hurriedly erected barriers, guards moving continually at the alert around the Winter and Anitchkov Palaces, riflemen posted at the entrances of government buildings, armed and mounted patrols in the streets. The police were redoubling their efforts to round up suspects.

The imperial family was, of course, the center of concern. Alexander and Empress Marie Fedorovna stayed within doors as much as possible, and their four children were safeguarded by a twenty-four-hour watch. Over-procurator Pobedonostsev, now taking his guardianship more seriously than ever, personally cautioned the tsar to lock all doors leading to his bedroom and to lock himself in it before retiring.[2]

Unavoidably, the anticipation of prolonged danger spread. Bismarck ordered the German ambassador in St. Petersburg to telegraph him "morning and night about what happened or did not happen" and added that, if he received no telegram, he would assume that the telegraph was "no longer functioning."[3] In every quarter of the city there were some who expected the worst and suffered the desperation of waiting for undefined trouble from an unidentified source. Even after calm days had grown into weeks and the special guards had become bored in their waiting for the enemy, the shock of March 1 continued to keep many in a state of tension.

Loris-Melikov was not among them. Although he had failed lamentably in his efforts to protect the late tsar, he was still of the opinion that the number of terrorists was small and that they could be handled by ordinary police methods. His anxiety was focused on the possibility that, if the granting of reforms was delayed, the many educated and responsible Russians who sympathized with the revolutionaries would be further drawn toward them. However, not having the tsar's agreement on this point of view, he had to face the fact that, for the time being, he could do nothing to forestall the possibility. Since his sanguine appraisal of the terrorist problem was so clearly unacceptable, some officials expected that he would at once be replaced. But the tsar was reluctant to part with him; his competency might yet be needed in the ministry of interior.

Alexander had no intention, however, of postponing what he considered the necessary attention to the terrorists. He took care of that matter by choosing General Nicholas Baranov as prefect of St. Petersburg. It was in this office, charged with the maintenance of law and order in the capital, that he wanted action, immediate and forceful.

Baranov met the tsar's requirements for the assignment despite a somewhat blemished past, during which he had impressed some observers mainly as "an adroit rogue and a liar." He had even been drummed out of the imperial navy by order of the Grand Duke Constantine for fraudulently claiming a victory over a Turkish battleship in the recent war.[4] But such discredit had not stood in the way of his immediately setting out on a new service career—in the army, where he had the special endorsement of Alexander, then tsesarevich, who had welcomed the opportunity to discountenance his uncle Constantine. More recently, he had held a governorship for a short time, though disapproved by Loris-Melikov, and had served on the Supreme Executive Commission in a spirit favored by both the tsesarevich and the over-procurator. Now he was accepted by Alexander, with the hearty approval of Pobedonostsev, as one of the "true Russians" needed to replace liberals in crucial positions.

With Baranov in charge, St. Petersburg was soon saturated with emergency vigilance. He surrounded the city with Cossack patrols to intercept and search all who entered or left. To protect the tsar and hunt out revolutionaries, he established an elaborate organization of volunteers, the Committee of Public Safety (which some called the "Baranov Parliament"—a tacit play on the word baran, "sheep"). Its members watched over the comings and goings of the tsar and all activities involving members of the imperial family, stood guard at railroad stations and palaces, and reported anything they interpreted as suspicious. To supplement such measures, the prefect enlisted a veritable army of informers by requiring that cab drivers report the addresses to which they took their fares, that landlords divulge the actions of their tenants, and that servants inform against their masters and their fellow-servants. The drama of all this was heightened, from time to time, by announcement from the office of the prefect that a plot against the tsar or the state had just been discovered.

Most of Baranov's efforts proved, in the end, to be mere stage effects. The announced plots were mares' nests. The Cossack patrols so interfered with the supply of food and goods that they had to be withdrawn. The information collected from informers proved more embarrassing than useful; ministers, for instance, could not be expected to welcome a revelation of what servants observed in their households. Yet the general effect was salutary: somebody was doing something, and that was what mattered.

At the end of March, the formalities of his father's funeral having been observed in safety and other matters now pressing for attention,

Alexander was glad to accept Baranov's advice that he move with his family from St. Petersburg to the imperial palace in Gatchina, where he could be more easily protected.

This residence would have been his preference in any case. In the suburban town of Gatchina, thirty miles southwest of the capital, it offered, in addition to safety, escape from the official and social proprieties of the court life in which he could never feel at ease. Though the six-hundred-room palace, set in an immense park, impressed some as an architectural monument to Gloom and was feared by the servants as the haunt of Tsar Paul's ghost, Alexander had liked to visit the place when he was younger, free to enjoy its lake, its kennels, and its stables. He looked upon his enforced return as a kind of homecoming. Here he could get down to the grim business ahead of him without undue interference. Above all, however, he now appreciated Gatchina as a haven for his family. For himself, it had to be imperial headquarters, and there was no lightening of the burden he had brought with him.

In the capital, the plot behind the assassination of his father had been laid open by a month of businesslike, round-the-clock police investigation, aided by the confession of Nicholas Rysakov and information supplied by other terrorists under arrest. On April 3, five of those found most closely implicated were hanged: Kibalchich, Mikhailov, Perovsky, Rysakov, and Zhelyabov. Thousands of witnesses, their feelings ranging from approval to barely suppressed indignation, were present at the execution, the last ever to be held publicly in St. Petersburg.[5]

The five terrorists who died on that day epitomized the opposition that Alexander faced. Four of them were students or former students; one was a simple metal worker. They represented families from both high and low station. Zhelyabov was of peasant origin, a fact that reminded the tsar of the continued need to forestall the filtering down of disturbing ideas to the masses. Kibalchich, the son of a priest, would remain in his memory as the bold author of what he then regarded as the "fantasy of a diseased imagination," a letter written on the eve of the execution and specifying three measures by which the tsar could end the terror: the amnesty of political prisoners, the abolition of the death penalty, and the granting of freedom of speech.[6] Though these representatives of the opposition impressed Alexander, they neither evoked any sympathetic understanding in him nor altered his autocratic convictions.

After the executions, tension in St. Petersburg relaxed somewhat;

The strain of World War I: Military losses—such as shown in this photograph
of Russian soldiers taken prisoner by Germans in Galicia. *The Bettmann
Archive*

Scene in Winter Palace when Nicholas II, in 1906, presided over ceremonial opening of first Russian legislature, which Revolution of 1905 had forced him to grant. *Culver Pictures, Inc.*

Typical workers, whose struggle against inequities imposed upon them during the years of Russia's industrial growth helped to precipitate the Revolution of 1905. *Tass from Sovfoto*

St. Petersburg street scene in 1905, typical of those in many Russian cities, where workers, students, and professionals joined in demonstrative antigovernment protest.

Cartoon depicting confidence in the superiority of the Russian navy over the Japanese before outbreak of the Russo-Japanese War, in 1904. *The Bettmann Archive*

Tsar Nicholas II and Romanov grand dukes marching in parade at Peterhof. At the tsar's right, the Grand Duke Nicholas Nicholaievich, who became commander in chief of Russian forces at beginning of World War I. *Underwood & Underwood*

Tsesarevich Nicholas, shortly before he came to the throne, inexperienced and unprepared for the problems that, as last of the 300-year line of Romanov rulers, he was to inherit.

Tsar Nicholas II and his wife, Alexandra, in the early years of his reign. *The Bettmann Archive*

Death of the plotters. Contemporary sketch of scene as terrorists implicated in assassination of the tsar were about to be hanged.

Tsar Alexander III and family, about mid-point of his reign. Back row: Empress Marie Fedorovna, Tsesarevich Nicholas, the Grand Duchess Xenia. Front row: the Grand Duke Michael, Alexander III, the Grand Duchess Olga, the Grand Duke George. *Underwood & Underwood*

Tsesarevich Alexander (the future Alexander II), of whom his father said, "My son Sasha is a *baba* [old woman]; there will be nothing great done in his time." *The Bettmann Archive*

Tsar Alexander II, near the end of his reign, after he had belied his father's prediction by liberal reforms, including emancipation of the serfs; then, by reactionary measures, had nullified much of the good he had done. *Culver Pictures, Inc.*

Death of Alexander II. Contemporary sketch of scene when terrorist Grinevitsky threw fatal bomb. *Historical Pictures Service—Chicago*

Contemporary sketch of French assault on Malakhov redoubt, immediately preceding Russian surrender of Sebastopol during Crimean War—grim consequence of the "magnificent failure" of the Nicholas system. *The Bettmann Archive*

Tsar Nicholas I, as the vigorous young tsar who expected to make reality of his "magnificent dream" for Russia. From portrait by G. Stodurt. *The Bettmann Archive*

In St. Petersburg during the cholera epidemic of 1831: Nicholas I demonstrating his willingness to go "out among the people." From a French lithograph. *The Bettmann Archive*

Scene in town of western Siberia. *Soviet Life from Sovfoto*

Senate Square, in St. Petersburg, at time of Decembrist Revolt, 1825. From a contemporary sketch. *Sovfoto*

The Imperial Palace (*background*), with its famous fountains and cascades, in Peterhof.

Scene in peasant village. *Culver Pictures, Inc.*

The Winter Palace, in St. Petersburg. *Tass from Sovfoto*

Tsar Alexander I, head of the House of Romanov when it reached the zenith of its distinction among the ruling houses of Europe. From a portrait by F. Krüger. *The Bettmann Archive*

The strain of World War I: Food shortage—leading at first to scenes like the above, a food line in Petrograd; later, to hunger and rioting. *Sovfoto*

Revolution! Drawing shows mounted Cossack, representative of traditional defenders of monarchy, supporting revolutionaries against police in Znamensky Square.

Former Tsar Nicholas II under arrest at Tsarskoe Selo, 1917. The Russian monarchy and the Romanov dynasty had collapsed. *Culver Pictures, Inc.*

but in the countryside, where news came late and in garbled form, it was actually on the increase. As invariably happened at a change of rulers, *slukh* was revived, and sensational versions of the happenings in the capital passed from village to village. In some areas, peasants understood that the landed nobility had killed the Tsar-Liberator because of his kindness to the peasantry, and they rose in personal retribution against local landlords. In others, hope was stirred by rumors that the new tsar intended to announce at his coronation a plan for distributing the lords' lands, and peasants became restive with the waiting.

In the southern provinces, rumormongers amplified the fact that one of the convicted terrorists (not among the five executed) was a Jew by spreading the inflammatory fiction that the tsar had ordered his loyal subjects to "beat the Yids" (*bei Zhidov*) for having murdered his father. In scores of villages, towns, and cities, peasants and persons of peasant origin began to do just that—beat the Jews. Thus aroused, the spirit of the pogrom was to sweep back and forth through the southern provinces for three years, while most of the aggressors forgot the original impulse but continued to vent their hatred on the person and property of those they traditionally reviled as "exploiters" and "anti-Christians." As these disturbances were reported to Alexander at the time, he accepted the likelihood that they were being incited by the revolutionaries, but that was not the case, as he learned later.

Encumbered though he was by the accumulation of immediate problems, the strain of unaccustomed responsibility, and the fear of unknown enemies, Alexander had not been able to postpone the task of setting his political course.

While he did not begin, as he might have, by asserting his own convictions, the essence of them was generally understood by those who had observed his development over the past years: autocracy was divinely ordained; nationalism, based on the fact that "real Russians" were Russian Orthodox by birth and monarchist by conviction, was an essential policy of government; and both the intelligentsia and the press were, for the most part, "rotten." [7] Had he at once proclaimed his intention to be guided by these convictions, it would have been necessary, of course, for him to disavow out of hand the "Loris-Melikov Constitution," now the most urgent issue confronting him. Privately, he was averse to the Loris-Melikov principles and believed that his "constitution" would be dangerous for

Russia; yet, being unsure of his own untested strength, he agreed to set a date for the further consideration of the project, March 8.

He knew well enough who the principals of the defense would be: the Grand Duke Constantine, Milyutin, and Abaza. Next to Loris-Melikov, they were the ranking figures in the government he had inherited. Collectively they represented for him a very real problem, since the record of each was clearly marked by the sinister impress of liberalism. A difficult confrontation was inevitable.

Alexander did not lack support for his point of view, however. Many conservative officials were fervently hoping that the customary accession declaration of intention to continue the policies of the preceding reign would prove, in this case, to be nothing more than verbal obeisance to tradition; for that reign represented for them far too much that was liberal. The press also, despite Alexander's general condemnation of it, was not to be overlooked—certainly not the publications originating in the offices of Michael Katkov and Prince Vladimir Meshchersky. No one could conceive of Katkov's nationalistic *Moscow News* forsaking the attack against its chosen dragon, liberalism. As for Meshchersky, publisher of the newspaper *The Citizen,* he had once been a close personal friend of Alexander, and, having fallen out of favor, was now anxious to prove his support for the new tsar and revive the former friendship. Yet another generally sympathetic voice in the press—and this one widely respected—would be that of the Slavophile and ultranationalistic Ivan Aksakov, whom Alexander as tsesarevich had helped to gain influential backing when he was leading the drive to succor the Balkan Slavs in the last war.

Then, of course, there was Pobedonostsev, the self-appointed guardian of autocracy and keeper of the imperial conscience, who was never reticent about making his position known. Many had learned to their sorrow that, when roused, he belied his appearance of a desiccated pre-reform clerk and burned with the righteous fire of a prophet. He was the first to give Alexander a reason for resisting the inclination to take a trial step on the road his father had opened to him. Recognizing Alexander's willingness to give the "constitution" a hearing and sensing a threat to both authority and the doctrines he held sacred, Pobedonostsev rushed to assail Loris-Melikov in an impassioned letter to the tsar:

I do not believe him. He is a prestidigitator and may even be playing a double game. . . . He is not a Russian patriot. . . .

If they sing you the old siren song that it is necessary to calm down, to continue the liberal tendency, to yield to so-called public opinion, for God's sake, Your Majesty, do not listen, do not believe. It is as clear to me as the light of day that to do so would be the ruin of Russia and of you.[8]

Then, at the meeting of the Council of Ministers on March 8, after hearing Loris-Melikov's defense of the project, which the majority supported, he beseeched the tsar to consider the dire significance of it:

And when, Sire, are you being asked to establish a new, supreme talking-shop on a foreign model? Now, only a few days after the execution of the most terrible crime. . . . In such a dreadful time, Sire, we do not need to think of creating a new talking-shop where new, corrupt speeches will be given, but we need to think of business. It is time to act.[9]

When Alexander did not commit himself to the one view or the other, Pobedonostsev grew anxious, but no less determined to turn his former pupil in the right direction. He felt that the appointment of Baranov, which occurred on the day of the critical meeting, was a good omen; but he had his heart set on a much more important appointment, that of a "proper" minister of interior. Accordingly, while he continued to denigrate Loris-Melikov, he began to extol the virtues of Count Nicholas Ignatev, whom he considered a suitable candidate. Here, he told the tsar, was a man of "healthy instincts and a Russian soul," who enjoyed a "good name with the sound part of the Russian population—the common people." [10]

Ignatev's popularity was, in fact, not limited to the common people. Of well-established Russian noble stock, he had graduated from the Corps of Pages and the General Staff Academy with highest honors and had then made a dazzling career in the diplomatic service. He had confidently and successfully promoted Russian interests in China, Central Asia, and the Near East; while so doing, he had managed to impress both his peers and his superiors. In recent years, he had become widely known, along with General Michael Skobelev, as one of the more glamorous figures connected with the Russo-Turkish War. From seeing his likeness so often reproduced, almost everyone recognized him at sight: military bearing becoming to a man of prowess, distinguished features framed by dark hair and given dash by a splendid sweep of mustache, an air of boundless energy. He was a man to command attention and respect; there could be little doubt that he would be a popular choice. Even more important, so far as Pobedonostsev was privately concerned, was the fact that he disapproved of the liberalism inherent in the Loris-

Melikov program. Ignatev's attitude, as he himself presented it in a communication to Alexander, was based on his belief that the liberals were pawns of a "powerful Polish-Yiddish group" in St. Petersburg that exercised "direct control over the banks, the stock exchange, the bar, a good part of the press." He accused this group of the secret promotion of revolutionary disturbances as a means of forcing the government to accept its demands for "the broadest rights for the Poles and the Jews and for representative institutions on the Western model." In fact, he charged, "every decent voice in the Russian land is assiduously drowned out by Polish-Yiddish cries, repeating over and over that one should listen only to the 'intelligent' class and that, consequently, one should reject Russian demands as backward and unenlightened." [11]

Though such sentiments were appealing to Alexander, he had to weigh against them certain aspects of Ignatev's reputation as he knew it. Like Baranov, he was well known as a cheerful, compulsive liar; but the tsar thought that could be ignored since he "lied only in little things." [12] More important, as a Slavophile he had made no secret of his belief in the need for a *zemsky sobor*; but even that could be overlooked by an autocrat who had no intention of allowing belief in anything akin to a consultative assembly to get out of hand. So, after a brief hesitation, Alexander agreed with Pobedonostsev that Ignatev was a "true Russian," deserving of responsibility in the government, and at the end of March he appointed him minister of state lands. Pobedonostsev had to be patient: the ministry of interior was not yet available.

During the succeeding four weeks, the new direction was finally determined. Loris-Melikov belatedly recognized that Pobedonostsev's star was on the rise and, also belatedly, he began to assess the nature of the over-procurator's views and openly to criticize him as a relic of the sixteenth century. If he saw promise in the fact that the tsar's mind was not yet set and, therefore, might be influenced by his efforts, he was heading for disappointment.

It was quite apparent to the more discerning that Alexander was steadily gaining self-confidence as each day brought him evidence that his position was less precarious than he had believed it to be. Although he viewed the public as no kind of guide, he was pleased with any favorable report from that source. One such was brought to him by Ignatev, along with a copy of Ivan Aksakov's address to a meeting of the St. Petersburg Slavonic Benevolent Committee held in memory of Alexander II. It was reassuring to learn that Aksakov, speaking to an agreeably responsive audience of 2,000, had charged the tragedy of regicide to Russia's whoring after the false gods of Western liberalism: here was evidence that not all of the educated class was corrupted by ideas of liberalism.[13] He was further assured of the public's "sanity" by reports that no new cases of terrorism were appearing and that the peasant disturbances were obviously not being stirred up by revolutionaries. Gradually, as the heartening evidence accumulated, he gathered the courage to act: he would jettison Loris-Melikov and declare his personal intentions. To that end, he secretly authorized Pobedonostsev to draft a manifesto expressing a firm commitment to autocracy.

The manifesto was published on April 29. Through it, the tsar asserted his intention to respect God's will that he govern "with faith in the power and truth of autocracy" and never to permit any "limitation on the autocratic power," which was "both necessary and beneficial to Russia." [14]

His meaning was easily interpreted by both friend and foe. Katkov euphorically editorialized in his *Moscow News*: "Now we can breathe freely. . . . The people have waited for these royal words as if for manna from heaven. They are our salvation: they give back a Russian, autocratic tsar to the Russian people." [15]

Bitterly, Loris-Melikov offered his resignation, and Alexander, who was not given to sentimentality, promptly accepted it. With the same promptness, he appointed the succeeding minister of interior —Pobedonostsev's choice, Count Nicholas Ignatev.

Other changes were now inevitable. Abaza added his resignation to Loris-Melikov's, and the ministry of finance passed to Nicholas Bunge, an economist with an academic background. Minister of War Milyutin withdrew, and the conservative General Peter Vannovsky replaced him. Then, after an exchange of recriminations with his imperial nephew, the Grand Duke Constantine renounced his posts in the government. He was succeeded as general admiral by Alexander's favored brother, the Grank Duke Alexis, and as chairman of the State Council by his own brother the Grand Duke Michael.

Clearly, conservatism had won the day, and there would be little official hospitality in St. Petersburg for those most prominently associated with the liberalism of the preceding reign. Loris-Melikov left as soon as possible, to spend most of his remaining years, an ailing and forgotten man, in Nice. Princess Yurevsky vacated the Winter Palace, at the tsar's request. She finally chose Nice as her permanent home and, supported in comfort by imperial funds, followed a life of quiet retirement, which was to outlast the monarchy by five years. The Grand Duke Constantine moved his residence to Paris and, with his mistress and their children, took up the usual life of émigré royalty. Milyutin chose retirement within his homeland, where he was to find that he had yet thirty-one years in which to observe the consequences, in others' hands, of his two decades of service to the empire.

Alexander filed away the Loris-Melikov project with a final note: "Thank God, this criminal and precipitous step toward a constitution was not taken." [16]

While the manifesto of April 29 implied a new course, Alexander still had but a general notion of what that course was to be. He expected it to be based on the principles of "Orthodoxy, autocracy, and nationality"; to be adequate to the task of ending *kramola*; and, by way of restoring Russia's place among the great powers, to aim at the renewal of the conservative alliance with Germany and Austria. With those ends in view, he meant to be a vigorous chief executive, to hold the reins of government firmly in his own hands, and to work assiduously. But on most issues, domestic ones in particular, it would be for his ministers to suggest specific policies; for him to judge their merits. To keep their association in proper balance, he would depend on Pobedonostsev.

The over-procurator already had his extraordinary commission well in hand, the primary subject of his hopeful concentration being Minister of Interior Ignatev. He did not share the minister's devotion to Slavophile doctrine completely; but, in his enthusiasm, he chose to discount the differences between them and to dwell on their common purpose. It was the same choice he had made, a year earlier, in the case of Loris-Melikov. Now, he was urging Ignatev to "go forward with the great task," admonishing him never to confuse "light with darkness" or "Jesus with Satan" and exhorting him to "act in the spirit of Jesus Christ driving the money-changers from the temple." [17]

Ignatev responded eagerly, anxious to be about the business of ridding the country of its "unhealthy elements" and so rehabilitating it that both the tsar and his subjects would be assured of a safe and rewarding future. His aim was not reaction, as he interpreted reaction, but simply repair and readjustment.

His first objective was the eradication of *kramola*, which he, like the tsar, defined as including not only terrorism but also any threat to the political and social order.

Of all the threatening manifestations, terrorism was the most readily suppressed. Within the year, most of the known terrorists were under arrest or in flight, and the desperate handful still at large were finding few opportunities to act. But putting an end to other activities recognized as seditious was a more complicated task. Ignatev, taking Alexander II's temporary anti-*kramola* measures as a guide and working closely with Baranov, spent months of intensive effort in the preparation of a law to deal with sedition. Also participating in the undertaking was the director of the department of state police, Vyacheslav Plehve, a rising young bureaucrat of East Prussian origin, who was destined to follow it further than either of his seniors. Although appointed to his post by Loris-Melikov, he adroitly identified himself with Ignatev's crusade against liberalism, for he saw this as an opportunity to secure his future.

The result of the collaborative effort, published in August 1881, was officially known as the Statute Concerning Measures for the Protection of State Security and Social Order but generally as the Law on Exceptional Measures. It prescribed conditions for the exercise of extraordinary license by local authorities and, indirectly, by the minister of interior, under whom they functioned. Customary legal regulations and administrative practices might be suspended in any area for any period during which there was, in the judgment of the central authorities, a need for so-called protection against terrorism, peasant outbreaks, strikes, student demonstrations, or other indications of abnormal conditions. A locality might be designated for either "reinforced protection," the civil equivalent of limited martial law, or "extraordinary protection," the equivalent of complete martial law. Officials in such areas were given exceptional powers, varying with their rank and function and with the degree of "protection" they were required to enforce. They might forbid meetings of any kind, even in private homes. They might search and arrest on their own authority; suspend the operation of schools, zemstvos, municipal councils, and assemblies of the nobility; close business establishments; impose limited sentences without trial; expel from their jurisdiction any person guilty, or suspected, of political offense or violation of security regulations. The law provided, in addition, that an interministerial committee, acting on the recommendation of police or gendarme authorities, might sentence persons considered to be political criminals to terms of exile up to five years and might do so without judicial trial.

The potency of the new legal weapon was tested at once as a number of cities, districts, and provinces (including the vital provinces of Moscow and St. Petersburg) were placed under reinforced protection. The results, to the minds of Ignatev and his supporters, substantiated the argument that such a measure was needed. Though the law had been enacted for administrative convenience as a temporary measure subject to triennial renewal, the monarchy never allowed it to lapse; and some of the designated areas were to be held permanently in the fetters of its "protection."

As a further check on *kramola*, Ignatev proposed, and easily won the tsar's approval for, the enactment of more stringent press controls. Their enforcement was entrusted to a special interministerial commission empowered to suspend or close down any offending publication and to the minister of interior himself, who might, after three warnings, subject to preliminary censorship any publication in the two capitals, where Alexander II had removed such censorship.

From *kramola* in general, Ignatev turned to what he judged unequivocally as a particular source of it, the Jews. Along with the Poles, they stood high on his list of unhealthy elements; since the Poles were already under the restriction of existing legislation, he could concentrate on the Jews. Here again, he had the nod of assent from Alexander, who, though admitting that the lot of the Jews was a hard one, was wont to recall that they had crucified Christ and that their plight was "preordained by the Gospels." "In my heart," he once said, "I am very happy when they beat the Jews, even though the practice cannot be permitted." [18]

Using the current wave of pogroms in the southern provinces as justification, Ignatev urged a prompt change in government policy regarding the Jews. His reasoning was that they exploited the peasants, fomented sedition, and hated the Christian world; that pogroms were therefore expressions of justified hostility; and that the first obligation of the state in the matter was to protect the Christians from the Jews. He would not credit the evidence that, while the hostility behind the recent attacks was of both economic and religious origin, the encouragement of its display had come from local officials not from revolutionaries, as some had charged. Nor would he consider the arguments of other, more coolly practical members of the government, who pointed out the advantages of providing a more normal economic life for the Jews by removing some of their

legal disabilities, such as the generally imposed restriction to residence in the western part of the empire (the Pale), and of resuming
the recent policy of encouragement to assimilation. He was not impressed by warnings such as that given by Michael Reutern, now
chairman of the Committee of Ministers, behind whose judgment
lay sixteen years of experience as Alexander II's minister of finance:
"It is necessary to protect everyone from any kind of illegal encroachment. Today they hound and rob Jews. Tomorrow they will go after
the so-called kulaks [well-to-do peasants], who are morally the same
as Jews, but of the Orthodox Christian faith. Then will come the
turn of the merchants and landlords. . . . We can expect the most terrible kind of socialism in the not too distant future." [19]

Ignatev's view prevailed, as was to be expected, considering his impressive support: the tsar, Pobedonostsev, Plehve, Aksakov, and the
nationalist press. While it was being formally legalized, the government adopted provisional measures indicating future policy. They
included two important new restrictions: Jews were not to engage in
business on Sundays, and Jews might not, henceforth, take up residence or acquire real estate in rural areas. In these measures, and in
others to follow, there was the clear implication that, unless the
Jews chose to become part of the Russian Orthodox world by conversion, they were not welcome in Russia, and that, if they remained,
they could expect to be hemmed in and further restricted. Already,
Ignatev was encouraging their emigration, then in full swing, by announcing that the western frontier was "open" to them. Later, Pobedonostsev emphasized the situation by his remark that the Jewish
question would be solved only by the emigration of one-third of the
Jews, the conversion of one-third, and the disappearance of the rest.

Busy though he was with repressive measures, Ignatev did not for
a moment forget his positive program. His fondest dream was to get
it under way by the establishment of that body for which all good
Slavophiles yearned—a *zemsky sobor*, a great consultative assembly
elected by the peasants, the landed nobles, and the merchants.
Though in his conception the membership would be widely representative, the non-Russians would be swallowed up in a Russian
Orthodox sea, and the body would provide a true opportunity for a
meeting between the tsar and his people. When called upon, the
delegates would share their hopes and sorrows with the tsar, confident that his divinely guided conscience would lead him to do whatever was best for them. Such a nobly conceived institution, Ignatev
believed, should be dramatically inaugurated on an auspicious oc-

casion, and he could think of none more fitting that the coronation, scheduled for May 1883. He fancied that, by opening a *zemsky sobor* at that time, in the Moscow Kremlin, the heart of Russia, Alexander could once and for all show himself a true father of his people, erase any fears that he was a reactionary, and call forth a loyalty that would glorify his reign.

Ignatev fancied also that he could gain Alexander's approval for the project. So far as he knew, the tsar had not taken a categorical position for or against a *zemsky sobor*. As for Pobedonostsev's certain opposition to it, Ignatev had a plan for circumventing that: he would ally himself with the influential minister of the court, Count Ilarion Vorontsov-Dashkov. The count's family was known to be in high favor with the imperial family. His children, collectively known among their intimates as the "Potatoes," were playmates of the young grand dukes Nicholas and George and their sister Xenia, and the count himself was not only on close terms with the tsar but also was charged with making the coronation arrangements.

Ignatev proposed to enlist Vorontsov-Dashkov's support by winking at, instead of obstructing as he might, a volunteer patriotic association that the count had recently organized, the Holy Guard. Inspired by Baranov's Committee of Public Safety, the organization was dedicated to the serious purpose of protecting the tsar and fighting revolutionaries; but there had been a distinct touch of comic opera in its activities thus far—for example, its negotiations in Paris with revolutionary representatives, promising them certain political reforms in return for a "cease-fire" in Russia until after the coronation. Moreover, the association was in an obviously ambiguous position: though it had the tsar's approval, it was operating extralegally and duplicating—thereby presumptuously belittling—the work of Ignatev's ministry. Understandably, with Ignatev willing to tolerate the Holy Guard, Vorontsov-Dashkov prudently lent his support to the proposal for a *zemsky sobor*.

But Ignatev had yet to learn that there was no way of circumventing Pobedonostsev. Although Alexander lent a friendly ear to Vorontsov-Dashkov's words and permitted Ignatev to press confidently ahead with the preparation of a proposal for a *zemsky sobor*, he did so without consulting his mentor; for that matter, without yet making up his own mind about it. When Pobedonostsev finally learned what was afoot, he lost no time in making a readjustment. He sent the tsar a crackling communication advising him that to permit a *zemsky sobor* would mean *"revolution, the ruin of government, and the ruin of Russia."* [20]

Alexander did not take offense at the implication that he had given consideration to a foolhardy scheme. He was usually impressed by those—they were few—who dared to be direct with him, and he knew that Pobedonostsev's directness was backed by astuteness and loyalty. In this case, he was ready to accept the need to reconsider his whole attitude toward Ignatev. He had already admitted the truth of his brother Alexis' assertion that the minister lied in big things as well as in small ones, and now he admitted also the reasonableness of Pobedonostsev's argument regarding this latest project.

The outcome was not delayed. Being incapable of the subtle approach, Alexander curtly informed Ignatev that there would be no *zemsky sobor* and followed that blow by a note expressing his judgment that the two of them could not serve Russia together. Thus, after one ambitious and strenuous year, Ignatev's ministerial venture was over. As he had while representing Russia at Constantinople and at San Stefano, he had allowed enthusiasm to outrun discretion. Now, though only fifty years of age, he was willing to take a safer course: retirement to one of his estates in Kiev, where secret visits from Bulgarian friends kept him reminded of his colorful past and assured him that some of his accomplishments were remembered with gratitude.*

To replace Ignatev, the tsar chose Dmitri Tolstoy, who, when he was minister of education and over-procurator under Alexander II, had proved himself a severe judge of that "handmaiden of revolution," liberalism. He could not be expected to be either popular or glamorous, as Ignatev had been; but he would be safe, tough, predictable and on most matters in agreement with Pobedonostsev. There would be no more talk of a *zemsky sobor.* Nor would the ministry of interior be likely to condone any further free-lancing from the public, such as Ignatev had accepted from Vorontsov-Dashkov's volunteer guards. Tolstoy readily agreed with Pobedonostsev

---

* Shortly after Ignatev's retirement, Russians were to feel the loss of another colorful and popular hero, Michael Skobelev. He died in 1882, having established a reputation in his short lifetime—he was thirty-nine at the time of his death—as the most valorous, and perhaps the ablest, general of his day. Although, like Ignatev. Skobelev had sometimes embarrassed his superiors and even the tsar (he had loudly prophesied a war between Slavs and Teutons when Alexander III was striving to maintain peace), no one could gainsay the value of his achievements. He was given the funeral of a national hero.

that the Holy Guard represented not only more swagger than security but also a politically dangerous nuisance, and they cooperated in persuading the tsar to order it disbanded. Theirs would be a strong combination, one that would encourage Alexander, now that the air was cleared of emergency, to accept and pursue definite policies.

Alexander's personality being what it was, he needed little encouragement toward firmness. He had felt his way cautiously during the first year of his reign, but that did not indicate either a weakness of character or a lack of determination to be his own master.

By the time of the coronation, in the spring of 1883, Alexander appeared to be the wholly self-confident autocrat. Much as he disliked the formulas of ceremony and the trappings of royalty, he seemed actually to relish his part in this elaborate confirmation of enthroned power. Minister of Court Vorontsov-Dashkov, in charge of arrangements, made sure that everything was carried out with due respect to all traditional details. Moscow welcomed the tsar with the splendor of public displays, religious services in his honor, and high society's extravagant program of social affairs and entertainments—the usual animated setting for the main event in the Kremlin, the ceremonial crowning. Almost everything interested Alexander, even some of the sophisticated functions, the diplomatic receptions, and the high point of the public entertainment, the popular festival. At the festival, held on Khodynka Field, a military training area just outside the city, thousands of his peasant subjects gathered to pay him homage and to receive the simple tokens of his paternal regard for them—sweets, *kolbasa* ("salami"), drink, and souvenirs decorated with a representation of the imperial double-headed eagle. Never again would Alexander be so close to so many of his people.

Through it all, wherever he went, the tsar responded as if he were satisfied with the order of things as they were and as if he expected that it would continue unchanged. To the peasant elders who came to take part in the ceremonies, he said:

. . . When you return home, give my hearty thanks to all; follow the counsel and leadership of your marshals of the nobility; and do not believe the absurd and ridiculous rumors and stories about partitions of the land, free gifts of land, and the like. These rumors are spread by your enemies. All property, including yours, must be inviolable. May God grant you happiness and health! [21]

And to the marshals of the nobility:

I thank you for your loyalty. I have always been confident of the sincere feelings of the nobility; and I sincerely hope that the nobility will continue to be, as it has been, the support of all that is good for the throne and the fatherland. May God grant that you live in peace and serenity.[22]

Such directness left little doubt of his determination to hold firmly to what he had called, in his manifesto of the past year, his "faith in the power and truth of autocracy." He could be confidently expected to uphold what he had inherited: the traditional relationship of the Russian Orthodox Church, the autocracy, the nobility, and the peasantry. Official nationalism was to be the *mot d'ordre* of his reign.

Alexander's course, though differing from both his father's and his grandfathter's, bore some resemblance to each.

In his strong-mindedness, vigor, and directness, he was a throwback to Nicholas I. He spoke with the voice of a sergeant-major and issued his orders in a manner that discouraged argument and even discussion. Yet he was not unapproachable or lacking in humane understanding. One of his generals adjutant liked to relate how once, when belatedly sending congratulations on the occasion of the tsar's birthday, a group of officers attempted to mask their delay by wiring, "We are drinking Your Majesty's health for the fifth day in succession," and received the good-natured reply, "Time to stop!" But Alexander rationed such affability with care. He guarded his autocratic prerogatives jealously and acted the part of a true chief executive. In practice, he dispensed with the Council of Ministers (in which he saw the making of a cabinet) and dealt directly with the individual ministers. Being a man of strong character—again like Nicholas—he admired strength in others and appointed many strong ministers, but he permitted no one in his government, not even Pobedonostsev, to dominate him, to exceed stipulated authority, or to organize factions. In short, he was, as the Russians like to say, the *khozyain*, "the boss."

While Alexander was an able, and often aggressive, *khozyain* in the field of political affairs, the role being consonant both with the tradition of the autocrat and with his personality, he appeared reluctant to impose his will elsewhere. He disapproved of much that was associated with the splendor of the court and the activities of high society, both of which had been encouraged by his immediate predecessors; yet he made only limited changes affecting either. Throughout his reign, the Russian court continued to be, as it had been for more than a century, the most ceremonious and sumptuous in Europe, retaining the traditional and keeping pace with the modern. The number of titled court officials such as marshals, masters and mistresses of ceremonies, gentlemen and ladies in waiting, chamberlains, maids of honor, cupbearers, huntsmen, and masters of the horse grew to more than a thousand. Scores of generals adjutant, generals *à la suite*, and aides-de-camp were added to the tsar's military suite. On the whole, these members of the court had few duties, and they were not often officially assembled; nonetheless, the imperial establishment flourished.

Like the burgeoning court, its satellite society was as lively as ever. The polished, the well-born, and the extravagant—those among whom Alexander was never wholly at ease—still dominated court society. Their way of life remained pleasantly secure in the shadow of the throne, and their activities continued to reflect the elegant and frivolous manners affected by the officers of the more fashionable guards regiments.

On only one group associated with the court, the members of the imperial family, did Alexander impose any significant restraints. In his treatment of them he was more heavy-handed than even Nicholas had seen fit to be; he went so far as to make adjustments involving the most valued of their extraordinary privileges—their titles and their incomes. When Paul had decreed that grand ducal titles and munificent allowances be bestowed on children, grandchildren, great-grandchildren, and great-great-grandchildren of Russian tsars, there were only a few eligible beneficiaries. By the 1880's, however, some two score grand dukes and grand duchesses were claiming their imperial rewards, and the number was steadily increasing. That circumstance suggested to Alexander the need for enforcing among them the kind of practical retrenchment that he would have liked to see further extended in and around his court. Five years after he came to power, he satisfied that need by issuing a law that earned him the resentment of many a Romanov. It provided that, thereafter, only the children of a tsar and children of his sons might receive the title of grand duke or grand duchess; other imperial descendants were restricted to the title of prince or princess of the imperial blood, and their allowances were to be considerably less than those of grand dukes and grand duchesses.

Although Alexander III's court might appear to be a continuation of his father's in most respects, the general tone of his reign came to resemble that of his grandfather's, keyed to peace and stability. To maintain that tone in domestic affairs required continued resort to such arbitrary measures as the new curbs on the Jews, the new restrictions on the press, and the Law on Exceptional Measures. It required also that the corps of gendarmes be supplemented; that was achieved by the establishment of a new division of the department of police, the *Okhrannoe Otdelenie* ("Security Division"), commonly known as the *Okhrana*.

Beginning its operation in Moscow, St. Petersburg, and Warsaw, the *Okhrana* was extended to the principal centers of population throughout the country. Through it, the government was able to reach further than ever before, and by more subtle means, into the personal activities and thoughts of those who might harbor the virus of *kramola*. Its members were truly undercover agents. Its function was to keep political suspects under close observation, respecting no debarment from private matters—even personal mail; and its functionaries were plainclothesmen specially trained for covert investigation, infiltration, and assembling of evidence. They and the gendarmerie were expected to tighten the net ineluctably about all manifestations of *kramola*.

This increased vigilance on the part of the government, combined with the weakened and dispirited state of the opposition resulting from the drastic tactics of Baranov and Ignatev, gave the antirevolutionary campaign a general appearance of success. Radicalism seemed to have been almost rooted out. A few revolutionary groups were exposed, and a few plots by youths still clinging grimly to belief in political terror were uncovered, but their threat was usually considered slight. The most sensational of the plots, involving fifteen university students set on the assassination of Alexander early in 1887, was safely foiled; all of its originators were speedily brought to judgment, and five of them were executed. In addition, there were occasional strikes among the growing number of workers in industry. Aside from the conspiracy against the tsar, however, none of these events seriously ruffled the surface tranquility.

That such results were produced through increased firmness of control justifies, to some extent, the comparison of Alexander's rule with that of Nicholas I. Yet his manner of rule differed strikingly in one important respect: he did not attempt to supervise and direct the entire political and cultural life of the empire, to mix indiscriminately with his subjects, or to seek intimate knowledge of their problems. Even if he had been prepared to attempt that, the elaborate security measures devised to protect him from assassination would have prevented it. His movements rarely exceeded a limited schedule, carried out usually in the company of Empress Marie Fedorovna and their five children (the last of whom, Olga, was born in the spring of 1882). At the end of the winter social season, which they spent in St. Petersburg, living in the simplicity of the Anitchkov Palace rather than in the royal magnificence of the Winter Palace, they would return to Gatchina. There they remained until summer, when the period of their most varied recreation began. The imperial summer residence being at Peterhof, other pleasant areas were conveniently accessible to them: Krasnoe Selo, site of the guards' summer exercises and the foregathering of St. Petersburg society, also the inviting waters off Finland, where the family occasionally enjoyed a week or two aboard the imperial yacht "Polar Star." As summer gave way to autumn, they liked to attend the annual army maneuvers, usually held in one of the southwestern provinces. Then they might be hosts to a limited number of guests in one of the lodges in the imperial hunting preserves laid out in areas formerly under Polish ownership—in Skierniewice perhaps, or Spala, or Belovezha, where a preserve of a quarter of a million acres, once favored by Polish kings, had recently been acquired. Finally, as the schedule customarily ran, they would return to Gatchina again for the last weeks of the year.

These seasonal excursions, with an occasional trip to the family's Crimean estate, in Livadia, determined the limits of the tsar's acquaintance with his realm. And every foot of every journey, every minute of every day, was scrupulously screened by the troops and police who guarded him. Other tsars had relied on personal guards for protection, but none before Alexander had seen the need for such an extensive security establishment.

The chief responsibility for the tsar's security rested on the palace commandant, who held the rank of general and discharged his duties through three carefully selected military units and a special detail of police. Of the military units, the one designated as the Personal Escort guarded the grounds of the palaces Alexander occupied and provided a detachment of Cossacks to accompany him whenever he traveled; the Joint Battalion of Guards attended to the routine of palace security, both inside and out; and the Railroad Battalion checked and guarded all routes over which he passed (as an added precaution, two imperial trains identical in appearance were used on each trip, no one except the guards knowing which one carried the tsar and his party). Further security was maintained by the Palace Police, a group of highly dependable plainclothes agents with close ties to the secret police; they not only kept under close surveillance all persons in areas adjacent to the palaces but also discreetly checked on all who came to the court on business, the personnel of the ministry of the court, and those who guarded the palaces.

Thus shielded, Alexander was perforce a man apart, living in a manner that would have been unbearable to the strenuously active and outgoing Nicholas I. Yet, though he sometimes spoke of his life as an "imprisonment," the degree of privacy he was assured was altogether to his liking.

Even under other circumstances, Alexander could never have followed in his grandfather's steps "out among the people." Most of his subjects knew him only as the bearded giant (he stood six-feet-three) whose published likeness they sometimes saw and whose word was handed down to them as law. Even the Romanovs serving as responsible government officials or military leaders—and there were many of them among his brothers, uncles, and cousins—learned to respect his privacy, to accept the fact that there were to be no unscheduled visits and no casual discussions with him.

Measured against his father, Alexander was unquestionably a different kind of man; because of that, important similarities of their reigns were easily overlooked or misinterpreted. Whereas Alexander II was to be remembered chiefly as the Tsar-Liberator, whose main character fault was the leniently regarded one of irresolution in domestic affairs, his son was soon to earn, and make no effort to overcome, the name of Tsar-Persecutor, whose outstanding character fault was the reprehensible one of bullheadedness. However, the implication of this facile comparison notwithstanding, Alexander III was not a reactionary. His program was by no means conceived as a return to pre-reform days.

In fact, at the beginning of his reign, there were some intimations of continued reform. Ignatev, as has been noted, was committed to the creation of a *zemsky sobor*. In addition, Nicholas Bunge, who served as minister of finance for five years after Abaza's resignation, took some realistic steps toward the general improvement of every level of society. They included: for the peasants, reduction of their redemption payments, measures to make more land available to them, establishment of a national bank to provide means for their purchase of land, and initial measures for unburdening them of the poll tax; for the financially pressed landlords, establishment of the Nobles Land Bank to provide government loans; for industrial workers, provision of a system of inspection intended to insure the protections legally due them as well as some betterment of working conditions for women and children in factories. During the same period, a committee appointed by Alexander to serve with Michael Kakhanov, a prominent member of the State Council, was working diligently on suggestions for the improvement of local government, using data assembled through Loris-Melikov's investigations; its final report, in 1885, included recommendations worthy of any enlightened group of reformers.

Unfortunately, such promising measures were either nullified or lost to view among succeeding ones resulting from the nature of what soon came to be recognized as the dominant policy of the reign, strict conservatism.

The spirit of Alexander's conservatism, animated by distrust and fear, as was the government policy during the period 1866 to 1880, was not long in question. It was easily recognized through the prominence and influence of such men as Pobedonostsev, Tolstoy, and Katkov—all now sedulously upholding for the new tsar the same principles they had upheld for his father prior to the Loris-Melikov "dictatorship of the heart." Expressed in measures directed especially toward the curbing of disruptive elements and making no allowance for social and political change, it led toward the freezing of the order as it had come to be under Alexander II; and unavoidably, being alien to reform, it gave a reactionary tone to his reign.

Most officials quickly learned that the basis of Alexander's evaluation of any measure or procedure was the answer to the question, "Is it Russian?" He himself was "Russian" to the core—notwithstanding his Germanic bloodline and his inclination to express his nationalistic views in French. His passion for "Russianizing" extended from the personal to the imperial. Russian foods being his choice, he had them included on all menus for the imperial household and encouraged others to eat them often. He wanted his daughters to choose Russian husbands and was pleased when their taste agreed with his. He liked Russian wines, especially the excellent ones now being provided from the imperial vineyards in Crimea; so he ordered that, at court and in the officers' mess of the guards regiments, no foreign wines be served except on the occasion of honoring foreign diplomats or rulers. Because he wanted to see Russian character, practicality, and simplicity in military dress, he directed a general restyling of uniforms to free them from much of their "foreign frippery." New features including typically Russian top boots and the black lambskin shapka as part of parade dress were introduced at his direction, and objections to such changes from traditional wear proved useless. One noble-guardsman's response, that he would be damned before he would dress like a peasant, brought him an example of the quick chastening to be expected by the uncooperative, an unwelcome assignment as a military attaché. In his all-encompassing and enthusiastic regard for everything Russian, Alexander recognized no inappropriateness in imposing Russian culture on his non-Russian subjects: to him, the imposition was not just a political expedient but a moral good. He could not see that the experiences of the last half-century had in any way disproved the validity of "Orthodoxy, autocracy, and nationality" as principles of government appropriate to the whole of the Russian empire. His subordinates had no difficulty in determining the limits to be observed.

Minister of Interior Tolstoy was particularly pleased to observe them in the various areas of his authority. They gave him assurance, for instance, in obstructing the Kakhanov Committee's proposals for reforming local government; reform, as he could point out, had already made local governing bodies so independent of central authority that they were endangering the very basis of Russian autocracy. So he dissolved the committee in 1885, disregarded most of its recommendations, and set about making readjustments where he felt that they were needed.

In the four years before his death, in 1889, Tolstoy worked out proposals (converted into law under his successor, Ivan Durnovo) for virtually destroying the effectiveness of zemstvos and municipal councils as organs of local self-government. When enacted, they provided almost unsurmountable bars to any popular questioning of central authority from those sources. The zemstvos were made subject to strict control by governors, direct interference by the minister of interior, and an increase in the proportionate representation of the nobility in their membership. The municipal councils were devitalized by the tightening of bureaucratic authority over them and by making them less representative; this was done by restricting the urban electorate through increased property qualifications.

Additional measures served to kill hopes for further improvement among the peasants. The most revolutionary one rescinded many of the self-governing privileges accorded the village commune in 1861 and restored much of the administrative and judicial power in the countryside to the nobles. It was to be exercised through the offices of land captains, usually members of the landed nobility, who were appointed by the minister of interior and empowered to determine local election procedures and court appointments, to arrest and fine peasants without trial, and to annul at will any decision made by any peasant assembly in the rural communities under their jurisdiction. Peasant "self-government," never a reality, was at last officially acknowledged as a meaningless form. Furthermore, the advantages expected from the abolition of the poll tax were denied to the peasants. They were still held, by new legislation, to the group responsibility associated with the tax. In the end, the peasants themselves were the chief ones to reimburse the treasury for the tax loss, as all of them paid increased tax on such things as matches, spirits, and tobacco, and some, the former state peasants, were required to make increased allotment payments. Again, conditions in the countryside were frozen *in status quo*.

Other measures continuing the spirit of 1866–1880 were aimed at restraining the growth of the youthful intelligentsia; these were directed by Minister of Education Ivan Delyanov, who had served in the previous reign under Tolstoy and was anxious to carry out his earlier unfinished plans. When his favorite project, a new university charter, was approved by Alexander and legalized, he was well on his way. The universities, their autonomy again disallowed, were placed under the direct authority of the ministry of education. University students were categorically denied the right to act collectively, even the right to assemble in groups of more than five. The education of women was handled as a special problem: to forestall any increase in the ranks of the emancipated ones, opportunities for higher education, already limited, were further restricted for women. As for education among the lower classes, circumscription became the watchword. Acting on the theory that individuals should not be educated above their station, the ministry of education advised its officials that children of "coachmen, servants, laundresses, small shopkeepers, and the like" were to be discouraged from attending secondary schools, and tuition fees were raised to reinforce the discouragement. Of course, under these conditions, fewer were enrolled in the higher institutions, and that fact only made it easier to guide students' development into acceptably trained, Orthodox Russians.

But what of those whose background presented special obstacles to their being made "good Russians" through conventional means? For them there were the guidelines of Russification, which Alexander's reign saw tightened on Poland, the Baltic provinces, Finland, and

Russian Central Asia. Aimed at the realization of "Russia for the Russians," what amounted to a quiet reconquest was effected in those areas as their schools, press, and civil administrations were subjected to regulations of reinforced stringency requiring the use of the Russian language and the adoption of Russian modes of operation. At the same time, that auxiliary of Russification, the Russian Orthodox Church, was redoubling its missionary efforts and laboring ceaselessly to force perverse nonaffiliates—wherever found, in the heart of the empire or on its fringes—either into conformity or into oblivion: Jews, Uniats, Stundists, Dukhobors, Lutherans (in the Baltic provinces), and Moslems (in Central Asia).

The surface calm which was produced in Russia by enforced compliance with the official domestic policy and which endured to the end of the reign was matched by the condition maintained in the country's foreign relations. Notwithstanding a few periods of disquiet, there was justification for the popular observation that Alexander was one tsar successful in keeping both the peace and the Seventh Commandment—a truly remarkable accomplishment, for few Romanovs before him had kept either and none had kept both. Just as faithfulness in personal matters was in accord with his nature, so also was his endorsement of peaceful strategies in foreign affairs; since he was another tsar who liked to act as his own foreign minister, he endeavored to keep a close check on all developments. His foreign minister, Nicholas Giers, experienced though he was, having been Gorchakov's assistant before succeeding him in 1882, rarely managed to be more than a competent assistant.

Alexander's foreign policy, however, was not determined solely on the basis of personal option. Russia's place among the great powers was of primary concern, and the tsar could overlook occasional vexations or disappointments in order to keep it in sight. For instance, when it came to lifting Russia out of the isolation brought about by the Russo-Turkish War, he was able to restrain his personal dislike of the Hapsburgs in order to join in renewing the alliance of Austria, Germany, and Russia—in effect, the old Three Emperors' League. The terms of the alliance, agreed upon in 1881 and kept secret for almost six years, gave him assurance that Russia would not stand alone on the question of keeping the Straits closed and would not be friendless in case of conflict with another power. That assurance had to be bought at the price of delimiting somewhat Russia's freedom of action in the Balkans (by the formal acknowledgment of Austria's position there) and in the Ottoman empire generally; but he accepted the price. There was the consolation that Russia might realize yet another advantage—from the three powers' agreement that the Russian-dominated principality of Bulgaria be allowed, under certain conditions, to enlarge itself by uniting with Eastern Rumelia.

Four years later, the Three Emperors' League, which had been renewed for a second three-year period, was credited by some with proving its worth in a situation that brought Russia close to conflict with England in Central Asia. Since 1880, when Anglo-Russian relations had begun to improve as a result of the antipathetic Beaconsfield being replaced by Gladstone, Russian forces in that area had been inching into questionable territory without serious challenge. In 1885, however, when their advance appeared to be threatening Herat, which England considered the key to India, Queen Victoria asked Alexander for a reckoning. He responded favorably, but before a settlement could be negotiated, a Russian force made an unauthorized attack in the area under contention, and the English, sensing bad faith on Russia's part, made ready to fight. Many observers felt that, if the British fleet had been given permission to proceed through the Straits at the time, the outcome would have been a costly war. At any rate, when Germany and Austria honored the alliance agreement on the Straits question by demanding, along with France and Italy, that Turkey refuse passage, the war fever— whether influenced by that fact or not—subsided. The border questions were settled in the next two years, and Russia's precious state of peace was preserved.

Meanwhile, developments elsewhere were beginning to expose sentiments that would overtax the new alliance. The first serious test occurred in the Balkans, where Russia's one prospect of influence now lay in Bulgaria. Shortly after the accession of Alexander III, his cousin Alexander of Battenberg, who had been ruling that principality (often in conformity with the promptings of Russian advisers and military aides) under the constitution approved by Alexander II, tired of his status and set aside the constitution. The gesture was one that the new tsar could approve, for a constitution was no more to his liking than to the prince's. But when the Bulgarian nationalists took matters in hand, forced the prince to restore the constitution and, by 1886, had his agreement to the unification of Bulgarian territory by the annexation of Turkish-controlled Eastern Rumelia, from Russia's point of view Bulgar ini-

tiative was going too far. Disregarding the fact that he had joined
the emperors Francis Joseph and William I agreeably in anticipating the union of Bulgaria and Eastern Rumelia, Alexander now
strongly protested it, compounding what was already becoming a
diplomatic complication. Serbia and Greece were beginning to demand their "equivalent" territorial rights; Austria was abetting Serbia; the uninvolved powers were restraining Greece as well as advising other participants in the confusion; and Turkey was in the
act of strengthening Bulgaria by nodding at the occupation of Eastern Rumelia. Russia's position in this predicament was unlikely to
be improved by amateur diplomacy; but Alexander, disregarding
Giers' advice, looked the other way as Bulgarian officers with the
connivance of certain Russian officers forced the prince to abdicate,
spirited him out of the country, then established a provisional pro-
Russian administration. Three days later, when Bulgarian nationalists threw out the provisional government and invited Alexander
of Battenberg to return, the tsar refused his approval. The prince
accepted the rebuff and retired to Austria, yet Russia's humiliating
status as a rejected guardian remained unchanged. In the summer
of 1887, the Bulgarians, over Russia's protest, installed as their new
ruler Prince Ferdinand of Saxe-Coburg-Gotha who was known to
be pro-Austrian. The tsar thereupon withdrew all Russian army
officers from the principality, but he could suggest no further coun-
termove short of using force—and that was out of the question. As
long as he ruled, however, Alexander would make sure that the Bul-
gars felt his disapproval and that Prince Ferdinand's government
went unrecognized by Russia.

As for Austria's attitude in the affair, the tsar recognized it as both
anti-Russian and hostile. In fact, he had already begun to appreciate
some of the reasoning behind the position of Katkov, whom he had
angrily reprimanded only a few months earlier for publicizing the
Three Emperors' League and depreciating both Austria and Germany as friends of Russia.

He had not lost the traditional Romanov regard for Hohenzollern
friendship, however. Even while refusing to commit Russia to a
renewal of the Three Emperors' League because of his disillusionment with Austria, he had been treating for an alliance with Germany (accepting Bismarck's word that a prior treaty arrangement
between Germany and Austria was strictly defensive); it had been
worked out in terms of the secret, so-called Reinsurance Treaty signed
in June 1887. But that arrangement also began to lose luster for Alex-

ander when the old Emperor William I died and William II came to the German throne. Then when Bismarck, with whom the tsar could deal confidently, was forced out of the government in 1890, Russia's reliance on accord went with him. It was no surprise that Germany, now settled to the satisfaction of William II's government in the Triple Alliance with Austria and Italy and having no further need for ties with Russia, did not renew the "Reinsurance Treaty."

It had all come to pass as Katkov had predicted. He had not lived to see his views vindicated; he died in mid-1887. But his contention that Russia, free of Germany and Austria, should cultivate the friendship of France (France, the radix of revolution!) had recently been growing in appeal. This change in attitude was not due solely to the growing distance between Russia and the neighboring monarchies: France, an excellent source of guns and money-to-loan, was becoming a practical choice. Germany provided a special urgency for a changed regard for France by signing a treaty with England, in the summer of 1890. Though the treaty was concerned only with mutually advantageous territorial arrangements, Alexander and Giers saw it as another indication of a significant shift on the international scene, one that might leave Russia facing isolation again unless she stirred herself to reestablish a place among the powers.

As the first decade of his reign drew to a close, Alexander admitted no serious doubt that he would be able, in due course, to make whatever adjustments were necessary in the country's foreign affairs. Neither did he question the adequacy of his domestic policy. There was evidence, however, that his vigilance remained acute; and, while he attended closely to what he found to be the rather baffling game of diplomacy, he did not lose sight of domestic vexations.

Understandably, he was concerned about the occasional evidence that the revolutionary fire had not been completely extinguished. He studied every report concerning Russian revolutionaries abroad: from Zurich, where they were accused of making bombs for use in Russia, and from Paris, where distance from home lent bravado to their words and plans. He followed closely every isolated incident uncovered and every trial involving chargeable *kramola*. When the imperial train was wrecked, near the little southern town of Borki, and he and his family escaped death by what appeared a near-miracle, he was for a while deeply disturbed by the sensational, though unfounded, charge that it had been bombed by revolutionaries. He never forgot the date of the incident, October 17, 1888; yet he continued to believe that the established control of lawlessness was as effective as the police could possibly make it.

What weighed more heavily on his mind was a distant prospect for which he felt personally responsible: the succession. He had misgivings about his heir, Tsesarevich Nicholas, now twenty-two years of age. Would he be able to carry on the duties that waited in his future? Nicholas' slight build (in height he reached only to his father's shoulder) and his youthful, unpretentious bearing gave him the appearance of immaturity among the Romanov men, most of whom were tall and physically impressive, capable of appropriate courtliness when it was expected of them. Moreover, the kind of life Nicholas was leading was more like that of a frivolous guards officer than of a responsible man. He was a vacillator, bright and knowledgeable one minute and seemingly indifferent to anything serious the next. His fine manners, his aversion to arguments and confrontations, his "waste of time" at art exhibitions and concerts in the company of his mother, at roistering regimental dinners, or with young friends at the opera, ballet, or theater—all were deplorable to his personally unpolished, serious-minded, and stolid father. That he was unquestionably honorable, also dutiful, respectful, and compliant—often, to be sure, out of fear of his father's harsh discipline— was commendable; but to Alexander, these qualities could not make up for the lack of firmness and vigor.

No one could say that Nicholas' preparation had been neglected. His education, especially designed to fit him for his autocratic role, had begun when he was seven years of age with the study of the Orthodox religion and the three R's. At nine, he had been put under the supervision of General Gregory Danilovich, known for devoted and up-to-date pedagogy in his previous work as director of a military gymnasium. For the next thirteen years, the general saw his charge through course after course, provided by the best talent of the empire: eminent professors, ministers of the realm, generals with honored records, ranking clergymen, and—inevitably— Over-Procurator Pobedonostsev. The program attempted was a formidable one, intended to provide the equivalent of a secondary, university, and General Staff Academy education. It ranged through many fields, including French, German, English, chemistry, economics, history, law, mathematics, and military strategy. Four years before this private tuition was concluded, it was supplemented by practical activities as Nicholas was introduced to the work of the

State Council and the Committee of Ministers and, through training in the Hussar and the Preobrazhensky Guards, to the skills of
both a junior cavalry officer and a junior infantry officer. In addition,
he was given the advantage of travel within Russia and an extended
tour through the major European countries.

When the routine of formal education came to an end, in April
1890, the occasion in the estimation of the tsesarevich merited only
a note in his diary: "Today, at last and forever, I ended my studies. . . . " [23] To Alexander it meant that the heir was now a man,
and the time was approaching when he should be ready for the responsible activities of one. Yet neither he nor the older grand dukes,
judged by their attitude toward young Nicholas, actually expected
him to be ready.

However, there was to be one more planned activity to further
his acquaintance with the world, a grand-circle tour—to the East, and
back by way of Siberia.

While it was being arranged, the heir enjoyed his first months of
freedom from scheduled duties. During the summer he met the
lovely young Polish ballerina Mathilde Kshesinsky, then dancing
with the Imperial Russian ballet. But before their acquaintance had
time to grow into what promised to be a romantic attachment, the
trip intervened.

It began in late October, when Nicholas sailed from an Adriatic
port aboard the cruiser "Pamyat Azova" with his own suite and a
number of his good friends, including his brother the Grand Duke
George and a favored cousin, Prince George of Greece. High points
of the planned tour included visits to Egypt, India, China, Japan,
and Siberia.

As it turned out, this tour became one of the most deeply impressive experiences of Nicholas' life, bringing him at times a thrilling consciousness of what it meant to be heir apparent to the Russian throne and confirming for him some of the preconceptions he
had adopted during his years of training. Everywhere hosts were concerned to give him due honor. Queen Victoria feared that, when he
was in India, he would see the country through the eyes of Anglophobe aides; so particularly careful plans, including a tiger shoot,
were ordered for his pleasure there. The queen did not realize that
the tsesarevich had already accepted the Anglophobe view that in the
East a mutually agreeable future belonged to Russians and Asiatics
and that the English could never be anything but intruders. In
Delhi, he wrote in his diary: "It is unendurable to be surrounded

by Englishmen again . . . to see redcoats everywhere." [24] He was too
well bred to betray his feelings to his hosts, but this visit fixed his
hostility toward the British raj and increased his devotion to what
he considered Russia's Asiatic mission. His father, of course, would
have been disturbed if it had been otherwise. In fact, the whole tour
went off quite as the tsar had expected, except for two untoward incidents. Before the party left India, the Grand Duke George suffered
a flare-up of his chronic bronchitis and found it necessary to abandon
the tour and return home; in Japan, a religious zealot made an irra-
tional attempt on Nicholas' life.

Having completed the foreign arc of the route and come at last
to the eastern reaches of the Russian empire, the tsesarevich, at
Vladivostok, took part in a ceremony symbolic of the progress of
Russia's Asiatic mission: the turning over of the first spade of earth
for the projected great Trans-Siberian railway to connect that city
with European Russia. The remainder of the tour was through Siberia, where he recognized for the first time the actual extent and
condition of this underdeveloped region. Here he made his first
sustained contact with the peasantry, who overwhelmed him by their
adulation and impressed him by their demonstrations of loyalty.[25]

When Nicholas returned to St. Petersburg, in August 1891, Alexander expected him to take up a life befitting his station, to perform responsibly whatever duties were assigned him, maintain a
modest grand ducal court, and, in time, marry and beget an heir.
The expectations were not fulfilled readily or perfectly, of course; a
few months away from his former life had not transformed the tsesarevich, though it appeared that they had increased his seriousness in
some matters.

Nevertheless, the tsar himself, dissatisfied though he might be as
he considered the prospects, could see that the years of preparation—
and perhaps his own example—had brought some acceptable results:
that some of his cherished principles had been accepted by Nicholas
and some of his policies would in all probability be perpetuated by
him. There was every indication that the heir was a "true Russian,"
conservative and respectful of his autocratic heritage. "My feeling,"
he wrote in his diary, "is that one should be conservative in all things
and retain the old traditions and the old ways as long as possible." [26]
It was evident that the things for which he had the deepest liking,
while not always the same as those his father chose, were similarly
"truly Russian." All who knew him understood that his assessment of
the Russians in comparison with other people was wholly in accord

with Alexander's. The Jews were despicable; the Poles, unjustifiably presumptuous; the Teutons, clean and industrious; the English, personally admirable but politically odious; the French, cultured but politically degenerate; and the Greeks, simply degenerate. The Orthodox Russians, on the other hand, particularly the "dark people," were the salt of the earth, inherently sound and infinitely loyal. But he would admit that, lacking some of the good qualities of the Teutons in consequence of the long period of Mongol rule, the Russians required to a greater degree than other peoples the guidance of a firm hand, an autocratic hand free of attempted assistance from such outlandish sources as the intelligentsia and the liberal press.

Even so, Alexander could not see how Nicholas, lacking strength of personality, afraid to take command, and generally too unassertive, would ever be able to provide that firm hand. The one subject on which he was now showing firmness—with an obstinacy that matched his father's—happened to be one thoroughly displeasing to the tsar: his growing love for Princess Alix of Hesse-Darmstadt. Family history was repeating itself here; the domineering paternalism of Nicholas I had been challenged by the same problem when his otherwise docile heir had insisted on making his own choice at the same German court. Still, Alexander protested his right to judge in this case. Though he himself was the son of a former Hessian princess (grandfather Nicholas having finally weakened) and the brother-in-law of another (the wife of his brother Sergei), he did not wish to be the father-in-law of a third. Surely, he argued, the Romanovs were already sufficiently connected, by intermarriage, with the ruling houses of the lesser German states: in addition to Hesse-Darmstadt, the states of Saxe-Altenburg, Saxe-Coburg, Mecklenburg-Schwerin, Mecklenburg-Strelitz, Baden, Oldenburg, and Württemberg. In the last thirty years, Russia had been forming dynastic ties also with England, Denmark, and Greece; and he saw no reason that Nicholas should not seek the hand of someone higher than a Hessian princess—perhaps Princess Margaret of Prussia or Princess Hélène, daughter of the Orléans pretender to the French throne.[27] This was one case, however, in which the tsar was to find invalid his belief that obedience could be compelled. He might get satisfactory results when, as he liked to boast, he beat his favorite dog for misbehavior and, if the "little beast" bit him in return, beat it some more; but a refractory son was another matter. Before long, he decided that there might be some advantage in foregoing a showdown on the question of a betrothal and returning to the older problem of Nicholas' responsibility.

With considerable reluctance and misgivings, which he did not trouble to disguise, he tentatively accepted the advice of his minister of ways and communications, Sergei Witte, and began to take a few practical and more positive steps toward helping Nicholas to achieve the maturity he expected of him. He made him chairman of the Siberian Committee, one of whose chief concerns was the ambitious plan for the Trans-Siberian railway, and of a committee to aid the victims of a prolonged and devastating famine that had stricken twenty of the central grain-growing provinces in 1891. In addition, he arranged that Nicholas be promoted to the rank of colonel and given command of the First Battalion of the Preobrazhensky Guards. None of these was either a high honor or a duty entailing much responsibility. Other tsesareviches, at a like age, had been given major commands and entrusted with more significant duties. But Nicholas, though deeply aggrieved by his father's lack of trust in his ability, made no protest, only withdrew into himself and let appearances further confirm the derogatory opinion.*

Having done, or made provisions for, all that he considered feasible in the preparation of his successor, Alexander put the problem aside. Others were more immediate and, he thought, more manageable.

The critical conditions in the central provinces were just now drawing widespread attention. Famine was no novelty in this black-earth region: though the land was exceedingly fertile, rainfall was only adequate in normal times and disastrously inadequate on an average of once a decade. So close to the margin of existence were the peasant inhabitants that a meager harvest was almost certain to bring famine, for they never had any reserve of supplies. A drought in 1891 and an epidemic that followed it were now taking the customary toll. Peasants were dying by the thousands, starved or overcome by cholera, and neither Russian efforts nor those of foreign sympathizers, who sent ton after ton of provisions, could do much to stay the ravages. By the next planting time, there would be an appalling lack of able farm workers, animals, and seed; for the effects of famine always carried over into the second season.

* Even after he came to the throne, Nicholas refused to take a rank higher than colonel. By that time, however, his attitude was influenced not by self-pity but by respectful memory of his father.

This famine, in addition, had some unusual results, reaching beyond the physical and the economic to the political. For this, the
government itself was partly responsible. It had been encouraging,
through its fiscal and economic policies, the export of grain without
practical consideration of home needs. In the widely quoted words
of Minister of Finance Ivan Vyshnegradsky, who had succeeded
Bunge four years earlier and was intent on balancing the national
budget, "We ourselves may not eat, but we shall export grain."
Although exports were curbed, once the famine began, critics of the
government had already begun pointing out the injustice and the
inhumanity of what had been done. The government's guilt, in their
view, was now compounded by the fact that, its fiscal capacities
strained to the limit, it had no resources to use in overcoming the
famine—nor, as many knew, any profound interest in doing so, for
traditionally famines were considered part of the natural order. Of
necessity, emergency relief in this instance became for the most part
a privately sponsored undertaking. Its leading proponent was the
novelist Leo Tolstoy, whose passionate appeal for action was readily
answered by individual philanthropists and by zemstvos all over the
country. But open purses and willing hands did not make the task
easy: at first, local authorities, suspicious of private initiative generally and the zemstvos in particular, hampered the relief in many
frustrating ways. That, of course, stirred anew the animus of those
already hostile to the regime, and soon open protest was being heard
again. Some now went so far as to argue with conviction that the
famine itself was basically the fault of the tsarist regime, which was,
after all, both "archaic" and "inhumane."

No great political storms followed the famine, but there was a
significant break in the political quiet that had prevailed since Alexander came to power. Moderate liberals as well as the quiescent rem-
nant of the populists were impelled to resume the drive for political
change that had been abandoned since 1881. Of those now recognized as dissidents, the extremists were dealt with readily enough
while others, less conspicuous, had a measure of lasting influence. In
particular, zemstvo leaders, long silent, and leaders of the Committees for the Advancement of Literacy in the two capitals again began
considering means to improve the conditions with which they continued to struggle. The result for the time being was only a modest
drive, for there were no headstrong agitators among these men, and
the government still maintained effective restraints on political activity. Yet any renewal of concerned political thought indicated, if

nothing else, that the general air of serenity was somewhat deceptive.

The new stirrings were soon to be reinforced from a source that had been of little consequence in earlier movements—the working class. It had been growing since the government came to realize, as a result of the Crimean War, that modernization of the economy was a necessity if Russia was to compete effectively with other countries, and that modernization called for industrial development. During the tenure of Alexander's first two ministers of finance. Bunge and Vyshnegradsky, who had pushed ahead with industry—manufacturing, mining, metallurgy—through government sponsorship as well as the encouragement of foreign investment in Russia, the number of workers had increased to about a million and a half. The beginning of construction on the Trans-Siberian railway, in 1891, promised a continued increase. By the next year, when Vyshnegradsky retired and the tsar advanced Sergei Witte to the post of minister of finance, what may properly be called an industrial revolution was getting well under way in Russia, and the workers were approaching their competence as a class—a fact not yet fully recognized by the government or by the workers themselves.

Before long, as Witte became the moving spirit in the country's development, planning and directing a sweeping, and in many ways new, economic program, he was not only stimulating these changes already in progress but also instituting others that were to prove far more broadly influential than even he intended. Alexander had chosen him, as he had chosen other ministers, because he liked what he observed about him: his ambition, his rough-hewn ways, his bluntness, and his energy. It was a choice approved by many who had observed Witte's dedicated work in various positions connected with provincial railroads and, recently, in the ministry of way and communications, where he was the enthusiastic head of the Trans-Siberian project. Prince Meshchersky's paper, *The Citizen,* had praised him as one of Alexander's "great" appointees. But neither the tsar nor most of Witte's other admirers had actually understood the ambitions of the man or foreseen the extent to which his personal qualities would determine the direction of Russia's future.

Two features of Witte's policy soon became unmistakably evident: it encompassed the whole of Russian life, and its keystone was one enterprise, railroad construction. He saw the construction of railroads contributing the needed incentives for a sound industrial growth, which would in turn regulate all other aspects of the national economic development. That consummation would be brought about by a simple chain of reactions: as extensive railroad construction proceeded, heavy industry would have to keep pace, and its growth would naturally stimulate light industry. Both developments would lead to expansion and prosperity in urban centers, and the requirements of the increased urban population would promote still greater production in light industry as well as an increase of production in rural areas. Thus prosperity would be passed down through every class and into every region while the national economy, modernized, steadied, and thriving, would put Russia abreast of the leading nations of the world. Witte himself, it was understood, would be the sensitive guide through every phase of the process.

Through no intention of either Witte or Alexander, the new program involved, in addition to economic changes, significant social and political changes which, if they had been recognized at the time, would have brought immediate protest from some quarters. Inevitably, the program would further the creation of new social relationships; in so doing, it would hasten the doom of political beliefs based on the assumption that the old relationships remained unchanged. Witte realized that there would be no place of pride for the landed nobility in the Russia he planned and that the peasantry would become numerically less important while the urban classes became correspondingly more important. But he believed that these changes could be achieved within the political structure of an autocratic monarchy, and he recognized no danger in digression from old social patterns. The tsar, not given to abstractions and complex thought, did not follow the implications of the new program even as far as his minister. He expected the new industrialization to be incorporated into the life of his realm without changing either the social or the political order, and others throughout the country continued in the same complacency.

Pobedonostsev was one who could not conceive of unwanted change. Once, on hearing Witte speak of a Russian working class, he replied in great heat:

Workers? A working class? I know of no such class in Russia. And I do not understand, Sergei Yulevich, what you are talking about. There are peasants. They constitute 90 percent of the population. And among them are a comparatively small number who work in mills and factories, but who, nonetheless, remain peasants. You are seeking artificially to create some kind of new class, some sort of new social relations, all completely alien to Russia. In this respect you, Sergei Yulevich, are a dangerous socialist.[28]

Appearances, to be sure, supported the over-procurator's view. Russia still had the marks of a peasant country, and census figures showed it to be one; they indicated that even in St. Petersburg the majority of the inhabitants were still legally of the peasant class. But appearances were deceiving. The law itself contributed to the deception by making it extremely difficult for an individual to free himself of peasant classification. Many who were in fact workers and permanent city dwellers were still legally on the rolls of the village communes from which they had come, still required to pay their share in taxes and redemption dues owed by the commune.

None of this, however, could alter the fact that a Russian working class was in process of development or that, regardless of official intention, its development would be advanced by Witte's new economic program. Though its members might resemble the peasantry in appearance and even be legally recorded in that class, they were beginning to develop characteristics very different from those of the peasants. Some of them were literate. Some of them, overcoming traditional restraints, were losing their servility and acceptance of authority. Meanwhile, in far-off Geneva, Russian political émigrés were laying the foundations of a Marxist socialist party that would enlist their support. In fact, in the big factories and mills of the two capitals, resentment of miserable working conditions was already prompting a few of the workers to accept the guidance of revolutionary student propagandists in the secret study of Marxist and other socialist writings. Elsewhere also, according to reports from the department of police, the number of propagandists trying to appeal to workers was growing, and the gendarmerie were finding themselves overtaxed in their efforts to cope with them.

More than ever before, Russia's domestic and foreign policies were now being drawn with realistic consideration for their interrelationship. As Witte, in his plan centered on the projected construction of the great Trans-Siberian railway line, was envisioning an East-West trade route that would appeal to European countries as a means of economical transit and thereby bring profit to Russia, so diplomats were finding consideration for domestic needs to have relevance to international political moves.

The diplomatic problems brought about by the disintegration of Russia's alliance with Germany and Austria, symbolic bulwark of conservative monarchism since the end of the Napoleonic wars, and the end of the "Reinsurance Treaty" with Germany were finally resolved in a way that coincided with the new concept. When German tariff discriminations grew so flagrant and onerous as virtually to close the German frontier to Russia economically, neither Emperor William II's continued amiability nor Giers' reluctance to give up hope for accord with Germany could alter the evidence that reliable and beneficial friendship no longer lay in that direction. Russia had to look elsewhere. And the yearly increase in French loans, which were the main sustenance of Russia's developing industrial program, provided tangible arguments for an alignment with France.

It began to develop in 1891, following a dramatic indication by Alexander of his willingness to return French goodwill in kind. When he welcomed a unit of the French navy at Kronstadt, having approved arrangements to have national banners flying side by side and a band playing "The Marseillaise" (ordinarily forbidden in Russia), a page of history was about to be turned. The Franco-Russian understanding got under way directly with secret negotiations and, despite Giers' remonstrances, passed on to a military convention, ratified early in 1894, that united the two countries in a defensive alliance. At each step, specific terms were kept secret, but the general arrangements were obvious to all.

Though dictated by circumstances and qualified by drawbacks, the Franco-Russian alliance had some significant values beyond the economic. It gave Russia a chance at respectable participation in the shifting of the balance of power in Europe. It relieved in some measure the feeling of segregation that she had endured since 1882, when Germany, Austria, and Italy formed the Triple Alliance. It insured against such military isolation as she had suffered in the Crimean War, and it allayed her fear of having to confront, without an ally, an attack by Germany or by the combined forces of Germany and Austria.

On the other hand, the potential dangers in this realignment of powers could not be overlooked. Russia might have to support the French against the Germans on issues that did not involve Russian interests—a disquieting prospect in view of the strength of the new German empire, whose economic and military power now surpassed Russia's. The cause of monarchism, a common concern in the former alliance of the three emperors, now stood in danger of being weakened if the monarchies should come to the point of war among themselves. Furthermore, the separate monarchies, instead of attempting as they had in the past to keep down the aspirations of national minorities—particularly, in Russia's interest, the Poles—by common

action, would now find it more logical, in competition, to encourage
the minorities of opposing states. The Austrians, for instance, might
find it advantageous to encourage nationalism among the Ukrainians
in Russia; though the Russians might retaliate by encouraging nationalism among the Austrian Slavs, the eventualities were equally
repugnant to the peace-loving Alexander. Neither he nor his practical advisers, however, saw any choice but to accept these drawbacks
and try to make the best of them.

Significant as were the changes taking place in and around Russia,
the tsar did not find it expedient to give Tsesarevich Nicholas an
opportunity to obtain first-hand acquaintance with them through
active participation in the affairs of government. Rather, he practically ignored the heir during this important period and kept imperial matters, as usual, strictly in his own hands.

While Nicholas accepted the prescribed life in the shadow of his
father, he did not abandon his stubborn insistence on being allowed
to declare his love for Princess Alix of Hesse-Darmstadt. But the
deadlock continued: the tsar remained unyielding, the heir remained
determined. With no other immediate course open to him, Nicholas
turned again to the pleasant and accepted activities of a young guards
officer. He resumed his interest in the beautiful ballerina Kshesinsky
and, following royal example, established her in the residence formerly occupied by the mistress of his great-uncle the Grand Duke
Constantine, next door to the quarters of his uncle the Grand Duke
Alexis, who had foresworn marriage for a succession of charming
mistresses. Thus settled, he continued with a social life differing
little from that of any other highborn young Russian in the capital.

By the spring of 1894, Nicholas' apparent satisfaction with his state
and, more particularly, the indications that his liaison with Kshesinsky was likely to be an enduring one, had brought Alexander and
Empress Marie Fedorovna to recognize the advisability of putting
an end to this idyll of bachelorhood. So, his parents agreeing, the
tsesarevich at last became the victor in a contest of wills with his
father: he was granted his wish to present his sentiments to Princess
Alix.

Nicholas went at once to Germany, where he found the princess
as affectionately inclined as himself, but hesitant about accepting his
marriage proposal. She was loath to give up the Lutheran faith, into
which she had been born, and her background encouraged caution.
Her mother, the former Princess Alice of England, had died when

Alix was six; her early training under the supervision of English governesses chosen by her grandmother Queen Victoria, as well as her later visits to England, had introduced her to the English wariness of things Russian. However, at twenty-two she was old enough to have a mind of her own, and she was in love. Finally she yielded.

Nicholas dutifully reported the event to his mother: "The whole world is changed for me: nature, mankind, everything; and all seems to be good and lovable and happy." [29] The engagement was announced forthwith, the wedding date was set for the coming spring, and elaborate preparations were begun for the kind of event expected only once in a generation. Public reaction to the betrothal was reserved, for the princess was barely known in Russia. She had appeared there first when, as a girl of twelve, she attended the wedding of her sister Elizabeth to Nicholas' uncle the Grand Duke Sergei. Five years later, she made a visit to her sister—the memorable occasion on which she and the tsesarevich recognized their mutual love—but she had not been widely introduced. Abroad, the announcement was of little interest except to a few diplomatically-minded individuals among the English and French. Queen Victoria accepted her granddaughter's love for Nicholas as sufficient reason to give her blessing, while the French consoled themselves with the thoughts that in all likelihood her good looks, not her nationality, had prompted the tsesarevich's choice and that, in any case, Alexander, whose reign would probably continue for many years, was unlikely to be influenced by his daughter-in-law's Germanic origin. To one person, the ballerina Kshesinsky, the betrothal meant personal bitterness; but after Nicholas returned and quietly terminated their relationship she accepted the irrevocable and soon replaced him with another Romanov lover, the Grand Duke Sergei Michaelovich.

For the tsar, there was comfort in seeing that, once again, the incidence of distractions seemed on the decline and that public affairs were settling down to the relatively peaceful normality that he believed to be the proper condition in a properly ruled empire. Still, he himself was not at peace: he was disturbed by an uncommon worry, a feeling of ill health that, try as he might, he could not throw off. By the summer of 1894, when his daughter Xenia was married to the Grand Duke Alexander Michaelovich, he could not summon the energy to take more than his required part in the magnificent celebration. He was beginning to lose weight and to find himself annoyingly at the mercy of quick fatigue.

His medical advisers, though not regarding the condition as serious, urged him to take a rest in a milder climate. But strong-willed Alexander, disdaining the idea of pampering himself no less than that of pampering others, insisted on going to the imperial preserves in Poland as he usually did at the hunting season. This time, however, he could not dictate the results of his obstinacy. His condition deteriorated until, at the urging of his brother the Grand Duke Vladimir, he grudgingly agreed to permit the calling of the famous German specialist Dr. Ernst Leyden to examine him and consult with the doctors in attendance. Dr. Leyden, then in Warsaw, was able to come at once. His diagnosis was nephritis; his prognosis, probable recovery after an extended and vigilant convalescence. The tsar, it was decided, must leave at once for the south, where he should have complete rest and the needed medical attention.

The country house that was the retreat for the imperial family in Livadia now became Alexander's gethsemane. Once he and Marie Fedorovna were settled there, he began to chafe at the ignominy of thus succumbing to physical weakness, unable except at rare intervals to rally any of his customary exhilaration at being in this lovely Crimean garden spot. He was comforted only by the anticipation of a return trip to the north.

Though no one admitted that his condition was critical, the tsar was obviously extremely ill, and it was understood that, under the best of circumstances, it would be a long time before he could resume his duties. Yet he neither took the tsesarevich into his confidence about the affairs of state nor delegated any authority to him. His final concessions to the reality of the situation were limited to summoning the members of the immediate family to Livadia and agreeing that Princess Alix be invited and informed of his willingness to advance the date for her marriage to Nicholas. The tsar was not alone in his refusal to look ahead more practically to the imminence of his reign's end. His brothers, as if themselves the beneficiaries of authority, assumed the duty of dealing with matters needing imperial attention while, as usual, ignoring the tsesarevich. When Princess Alix arrived, none of the family except Nicholas gave her more than perfunctory notice.

The situation changed only for the tsar. He grew weaker as the autumn days passed, and the family finally had to accept the fact that there was no longer any hope for his recovery. Princess Alix, sensing the crisis and pained by the obvious and disrespectful neglect of Nicholas by the Romanovs who now thronged Livadia, wrote on a page of his diary: "You are Father dear's son and must be told and asked about everything. Show your own mind and don't let others forget who you are." [30] Her plea failed. Nicholas remained a hesitant bystander until destiny thrust him forward.

Tsar Alexander III died on October 20, 1894. The twenty-six-year-old tsesarevich, sustained by the confidence of few besides his mother and Princess Alix, succeeded to the headship of the House of Romanov as Nicholas II.

X

Hesitant Autocrat

NICHOLAS II, 1894–1898

THE death of Alexander III, whose thirteen years as tsar had been virtually a personal reign, left a prodigious void that would have been a challenge to any successor. Nicholas was unreservedly dismayed by it: his knowledge, he felt, was insufficient and his preparation inadequate.[1] He found little in those close around him to encourage confidence. As his Romanov kinsmen took the oath of allegiance to him as Nicholas II, most of them still regarded him as an inexperienced junior member of the family.

Nicholas' first attempt to assert himself only emphasized his insecurity. When, as arrangements were being made to leave Livadia, he announced that he would marry Princess Alix without delay, his uncles loudly and firmly objected on the grounds of what they interpreted as unseemly haste. Reconsidering, he acquiesced to their advice that the marriage be postponed until after the funeral. It was a characteristic reaction, but hardly an imperial one.

The distressing duty immediately ahead for Nicholas was to make the return journey to St. Petersburg, along with other members of the family, accompanying Alexander's body. After the first lap, by ship at half-speed to Sebastopol, there were repeated stops for local expressions of condolence as the cortege proceeded overland by train, and an overnight halt in Moscow for services in the Kremlin, a depressing reminder of his father's coronation and the burden that had now become his own.² With the arrival in St. Petersburg, his depression deepened as the procession from the station crawled along for four hours through drizzle, mud, slush, and ice to the Cathedral of SS. Peter and Paul. To consider these first days as an "elevation" to power seemed ironic indeed.

Realization of the change in his life was almost beyond the ability of Nicholas to grasp. Even at the burial service, on November 7, as he looked at Alexander's bier beneath the canopy of silver cloth embroidered with the imperial eagle and listened to the mesmeric tones of the clergy and the choirs, he felt that he must be experiencing an intensified nightmare, that his father "could suddenly appear" to end it.³

Finally, of course, Nicholas had to face reality and recognize that prolonged hesitation was an indulgence that the Autocrat of All the Russias could not allow himself.

His heaviness of heart was lightened somewhat by the whole-hearted support of the one he had chosen as consort, Princess Alix, who had already been received into the Orthodox Church and taken the Russian name Alexandra Fedorovna. Their marriage took place a week after the funeral, in a simple ceremony performed in the Winter Palace church. Under the circumstances, however, they had to forego both a honeymoon and the immediate establishment of a home. Since imperial obligations required Nicholas' presence in the capital, his suite in the Anitchkov Palace, residence of Dowager Empress Marie Fedorovna, became their temporary home while quarters were being redecorated for them in the Winter Palace and at Tsarskoe Selo. Yet their life together began in such a way that, according to entries in Nicholas' diary, no one could ask for "greater or more beautiful happiness on earth."

As he took up his imperial duties, Nicholas still did not feel any sense of vocation to be a ruler. Nor did he impress others as a ruler, for his appearance, despite his recently grown beard, suggested more readily a youthful and slightly abashed subaltern. For one thing, it was difficult for him to avoid being overshadowed by others of the Romanov family, particularly his ubiquitous uncles, who held eminent positions in the government and military services. The senior uncle with whom he would be closely associated as tsar, the sixty-two-year-old Grand Duke Michael, fourth son of Nicholas I, had been active in the military service since his youth and, for the past twelve years, had been chairman of the State Council. Despite his age and extensive experience, however, he was less likely to aggravate Nicholas' sense of insecurity than were three of the younger grand dukes who, as Alexander III's brothers, had known him intimately when he was the callow tsesarevich. The oldest of them, the big, ruddy-faced Vladimir, now commander in chief of the guards and of the St. Petersburg Military District, was by far the most officious. Twenty-one years older than Nicholas, he had felt free in years long past to haul him around by the ear for childish pranks, and he had no intention of being deferential to him now. The two others were so situated that they also could, if so inclined, put an inexperienced nephew out of countenance: Alexis, who as general admiral administered the naval affairs of the empire, and Sergei, who held the highly important governor-generalship of Moscow. Then there were his uncles of the second degree,* in less important stations but, by virtue of birth, influential among those who mattered in government and society: the grand dukes Nicholas Nicholaievich, commanding officer of the Second Guards Cavalry Division; Constantine Constantinovich, president of the Academy of Sciences and commanding officer of the Preobrazhensky Guards; and Alexander Michaelovich, an officer in the imperial navy.

But Nicholas was determined to do his best, and a training that had equipped him to make the right gestures and choose the right words helped him to hold his own well enough as long as there were no crises to face.

On the improbability of imminent crises, he had the unsolicited word of the Grand Duke Vladimir, who assured him of his good fortune to be ascending the throne at a time when the country was so much more stable and peaceful than it had been when either his grandfather or his father had come to power. That state of affairs, the grand duke pointedly reminded him, was a dividend from Alexander III's sound policy of "Russia for the Russians"; if he would just model his reign after his father's, all would be well.[4] Since that was Nicholas' inclination in any case, he found the advice easy to follow in many instances. One of his first opportunities to indicate the continuity of policy was presented when General de Boisdeffre, chief of the French general staff, came to offer words of sympathy and delicately turned the conversation to the Franco-Russian alliance. Nicholas impressed him by the immediate and polite assurance that no policy of the previous reign, either domestic or foreign, was to be changed; within a few days, he reaffirmed that position by having the

---

* By English reckoning of kinship, these men would be termed cousins of the tsar.

foreign affairs ministry send the general an official statement that the alliance was "guaranteed for the duration of the reign." [5]

That he would resolve all categories of problems so simply, according to the rigid pattern of what had gone before, was neither Nicholas' expectation nor his intention. Every tsar in the past hundred years had veered from the course set by his predecessor, and in minor matters he also would follow his own bent. But, as he had already learned, he could expect his every deviation, however slight, to be watched and interpreted. When he had been conspicuously friendly towards the Polish delegation attending his father's funeral and again, on his wedding day, when he had withdrawn the troops guarding the route from the Anitchkov to the Winter Palace and permitted spectators in open windows and on balconies, he had provoked immediate public reaction. People, he was told, had been astonished and, sensing a mood of relaxation, had begun hopefully to recall the early days of Alexander I and Alexander II. Yet he had intended no intimation of liberalism; he was merely acting the part of the "ideal" ruler, identified in his mind since childhood with Scotland's King James as Walter Scott portrayed him, so personally at ease with his devoted subjects that they acclaimed him "The Common's King." [6] He loved the Russian people and wanted them to love him, but he understood no relationship besides that between an autocrat and his subjects.

It was soon evident that, regardless of his intention, liberal hopes were now becoming fairly widespread among some of those who had carried the liberal banner in the mid-1860's and late 1870's and among their spiritual children, all beginning to appeal for a resumption of reform. The *European Herald,* a somewhat liberal magazine which Nicholas occasionally read, timidly ventured the suggestion that, since conditions responsible for the repressive policies of the preceding reign no longer existed, the new reign might introduce new policies. At St. Petersburg University, students began circulating a petition for the restoration of university autonomy. A group of writers, editors, and artists petitioned for the abolition of preliminary censorship. Several zemstvos, in framing addresses of loyalty, expressed the hope that the tsar would extend their functions. The Tver zemstvo, true to its tradition of boldness, went so far as to indicate hope that he would permit the zemstvos to inform him of their opinions concerning matters within their competence.

Nicholas reacted to these suggestions just as his father would have. When the university students attempted to present their petition, he

allowed the police to drive them away. He referred the petition concerning censorship to an *ad hoc* committee which, after one meeting,
recommended rejection, to which he concurred. As for the Tver
address, he instructed the minister of interior to convey his displeasure to its authors and to punish the chief culprit by excluding
him from St. Petersburg for a year.

These early liberal manifestations showed Nicholas that he must
do more than simply follow the policies of the preceding reign: he
must demonstratively affirm them as the guiding rules of his own
course. The advice his mother had given before his first military
maneuvers was even more to the point in this situation: "Never forget that everyone's eyes are turned on you now, waiting to see what
your own first independent steps in life will be." [7] Again his action
duplicated that of his father: he authorized Pobedonostsev to prepare
a suitable statement of his intention to rule according to the established principles of autocracy. The over-procurator, anxious to secure
his position with the new tsar and gratified that he was not listening
to any liberal "siren songs," welcomed the opportunity to write the
political credo for the son as he had for the father.

Using the statement as Pobedonostsev had drafted it, except for
minor changes to make it more emphatic, Nicholas presented it on
January 17, 1895. That was the day when representatives of the
zemstvos, assemblies of the nobility, and municipal councils came to
the Winter Palace to offer wedding congratulations and present gifts.
It was hardly an appropriate occasion for a political statement, but
he chose it because it provided a signal opportunity to address important representatives of the educated public, men on whom he
particularly wanted to impress his position. This was his political
debut.

The speech was brief, but it served Nicholas' purpose. Through
it, he satisfied the proprieties by acknowledging his gratitude for the
loyalty of those present and, by informing them clearly and unequivocally of his political position, he specified the limits to be respected
by them and all his other subjects. To lay such "senseless dreams" as
those of the zemstvos about participation "in matters of internal
administration," he gave them to understand that the public welfare
was his concern and that, in providing it, he intended to "support
the principles of autocracy . . . firmly and steadfastly." There it was:
he had taken his first important "independent step." In doing so, he
had not only blocked the objectives of many of his listeners but also
declared the policy that would subdue the hopes of millions. Yet the

act was to him only an essential defense of an essential Russian tradition, not in any sense calculated to preclude, thwart, or oppose anything that was good for his subjects. When he said that public welfare was his concern, he was speaking from conviction; he sincerely believed that it could be best served through the processes of autocracy.

Having affirmed the nature of his course, Nicholas felt that he could now turn more single-mindedly to the details of government, with which his twenty-six years had provided him such distressingly inadequate acquaintance. Also, he could give some attention to the establishment of a residence befitting his station.

In the spring of 1895, with the coronation still a year in the future, Nicholas and Alexandra were able to leave Anitchkov Palace for their first home. It was in Tsarskoe Selo, a little town enough like Gatchina, where Nicholas had spent much of his youth, to restore in him some of the serenity of former days. Since both he and Alexandra preferred simplicity to ostentation, they chose to live, not in the Grand Imperial Palace, but in the smaller, neoclassic Alexander Palace, set apart in its own enclosed grounds, which Catherine II had provided for the grand-ducal court of her grandson Alexander. The apartments they had selected for their personal use had just been refurnished to their taste—exceedingly *bourgeois,* according to the *beau monde* of the day—and they were well pleased with the results.

The days at Alexander Palace soon fell into a pattern as agreeable as any could be to a man of Nicholas' makeup, a pattern based on the principle to which he adhered throughout his reign, that *"l'exactitude est la politesse des rois."* He rose regularly at seven-thirty and was ready, dressed in military uniform (the Cossack Guards uniform was one of his favorites), for his simple breakfast of tea, biscuits, and rolls at eight-thirty. His working day began at nine o'clock. By that time, a *valet de chambre* was already at his study door and an aide-de-camp, familiarizing himself with the day's appointments, was in the adjacent reception room with the first visitor. Precisely at the appointed time, the *valet de chambre* would announce to the waiting visitor, "His majesty invites you," and the business of the day would begin.

Ordinarily, mornings were reserved for conferences with the tsar's chief administrators and advisers. Since Tsarskoe Selo was only half an hour by train from St. Petersburg, these official callers were not unduly inconvenienced in keeping appointments with him; many even welcomed the opportunity to escape from the atmosphere of the capital. His ministers came weekly with their interminable and prob-lem-ridden reports. Almost every day, Count Vorontsov-Dashkov and lesser court officials came for conferences. Pobedonostsev sent un-solicited opinions, admonitions, and words of advice whenever he felt the urge to do so. A number of grand dukes, particularly those who had assumed the office of avuncular counselors, were frequent callers—welcome or not.

In the afternoon, there were usually others to consult, appoint-ments to make, diplomats and generals to receive, medals to confer, parades to review.

If possible, the early evening hours were left free of official duties. That was the time when Nicholas and Alexandra liked to read aloud to each other, stroll in their park or, after November of that year, when their first child, Olga, was born, to enjoy the homey pleasures of devoted parents. Later in the evening came the desk work. The foreign ministry, the Senate, the State Council, the Committee of Ministers, the Holy Synod, standing committees, *ad hoc* committees —all sent him their reports and journals regularly, and he had not only to read them but also to review and affirm or reject each sugges-tion or recommendation they contained. In addition, as titular com-mander of the armed forces, he had much military and naval busi-ness to review; also seemingly limitless numbers of petitions and complaints sent on from his Chancery of Petitions, each of which he wanted to consider, for they represented the response of his subjects to the rulings and actions of his administrators. To do all this was a stupendous task, but Nicholas liked to work at it alone. He had no private secretary and, since he preferred to make his responses in brief written communications, he refused even to have a telephone in his study. He was willing to delegate the drafting of the state papers and speeches to the appropriate officials, but he wrote his own notes.

Such a schedule, of course, kept private time at a premium; yet Nicholas usually managed somehow to take an hour or so each day for fresh air and exercise. And he still returned to some of the favored activities of his bachelor days: an occasional regimental dinner perhaps, or attendance at a French play that Alexandra, who was primly English in her moral standards, might consider racy.

For the court social season that opened on New Year's Day of

1896, the imperial couple returned to St. Petersburg—this time, to occupy their own apartments in the Winter Palace. There, as was expected of them, they took part in the traditional round of balls, banquets, and entertainments that followed one another in tiring succession and reached their climax on Mad Day, the last Sunday before Lent. Following that, they had only a brief respite at Tsarskoe Selo before leaving for Moscow: the time for the coronation had arrived.

The program for this coronation was in charge of Minister of Court Vorontsov-Dashkov, who had directed the preceding one; and he required strict observance of the rule that it could be changed only by adding features, never by omitting any. His army of assistants, ranging from high officials to laborers, had begun preparations months ahead, and the prospect was for unprecedented splendor. The Grand Duke Sergei, governor general of Moscow, had introduced the novelty of electrical illumination, and Vorontsov-Dashkov had given his personal attention to the main events.

When the official observance got under way, on May 9, it was favored by the brilliance of the day and the spirit of the throngs who cheered the arrival of the imperial party, bared their heads and crossed themselves as the tsar passed, and filled the city with their jubilance. Everything went as planned: the bells of Moscow's "forty times forty" churches pealed out, cannon boomed, massed choirs sang "God Save the Tsar," and regimental bands played stirring marches. It was a demonstration that Nicholas would often recall, a show of feeling that, whenever repeated, strengthened his faith in the immutable devotion of his people to himself, the Little Father, a man touched with divinity.

Following five days of traditional preliminaries, the coronation ceremony was held before an august gathering in the Cathedral of the Assumption. As usual, it began with an extended and magnificent ritual conducted by the clergy and concluded with that for which all else was setting, the act of coronation. Nicholas received the imperial crown from the hands of Metropolitan Palladius and, in the time-honored gesture epitomizing autocracy, placed it on his own head while the metropolitan intoned the ancient formula affirming the God-given nature of the autocratic power. Once more, the right of the unbroken Romanov line to the throne of Russia had been ceremonially recognized.

To celebrate the enthronement, festivities were in order for everyone—a week of receptions. balls, opera, and ballet for the elite, popular entertainment of various kinds for others. And history might have recorded another familiar coronation sequence had it not been for the conclusion of the popular festival planned for May 18.

The event was to be held at the usual place, Khodynka Field, and conducted in the same way as the one included in the celebration honoring Nicholas' father. By sunrise of the festival day, half a million expectant people, mostly peasants, had gathered at the field, all of them animated by the sight of row on row of tables and booths piled high with refreshments and gifts expected to be distributed at ten o'clock. The captain in charge of the one detachment of sixty men detailed to patrol the area had realized, as the crowd increased, that to control it, reinforcements were needed; hours earlier, he had begun sending to the Moscow police headquarters frantic requests for them. But, so far, only one squadron of Cossacks had shown up. Clearly, so few men could not be expected to keep in check for hours a crowd as large as that now massed, shoulder to shoulder, at Khodynka Field. Consequently, when the pervading air of expectancy was seen to be developing into impatience and restiveness, the order was given that distribution would begin at once.

With that, the waiting throng surged forward toward the tables and booths, deaf to shouted instructions, heedless of the fact that they had to cross an area which, because it had been used for military training exercises, was slashed by a ravine and a number of ditches, and unaware that before them were also some partially covered pits and an abandoned well. Once started, the movement accelerated and promptly became an uncontrollable press. In seconds, hundreds of men, women, and children in the vanguard, reaching the first breaks in their course, began to lose their footing. But their cries of panic and pain were lost in the clamor of the orderless thousands behind them, and the human wave swept on. There was no possible way to stop the headlong rush as bodies piled on bodies, and the more fortunate were driven helplessly over them; it had to run its course.

The frenzy ebbed and the crush subsided in less than an hour, but the tragic evidence remained. Emergency squads, belatedly hurried to the scene, began separating the wounded from the dead and taking them to hospitals. The dead were piled into carts and carried away to Vagankovsky Cemetery for burial in mass graves. The officials—police, civil, and military—who had been given responsibility for the festival directed the clearing away of all other reminders of their indefensible negligence. The official tabulation set the number of dead or dying at 1,429; the wounded, at "thousands."

Nicholas' first thought, when he learned of the tragedy, was to cancel the remaining festivities, conduct services for the dead at Khodynka Field, and then retire to a nearby monastery for a few weeks (as tsars had done in the past at times of extraordinary grief). This was the spontaneous impulse of the compassionate man who, in his heart, wanted to be the "Commons' King." But, lacking the inner strength to act the part, he allowed his impulse to give way before the cold, insistent argument of his uncles: that, although he owed the victims some consideration, he owed his guests the courtesy of carrying on. So, improper though he felt the action to be, he carried on. Later in the day, as scheduled, he appeared at Khodynka Field, now cleared, where he was enthusiastically received by a new crowd. In the evening, he attended a ball given by the French ambassador, a function which diplomatic expediency required him to attend, so the grand dukes insisted, in order to avoid offending the French.

During the succeeding days, the imperial family attended services for the dead, Marie Fedorovna sent bottles of Madeira to the wounded, and Nicholas visited those in hospitals, bringing them "indescribable joy," according to the official account.[8] Later, gifts of money or modest annual pensions of twenty-four to sixty rubles were provided for those bereft of breadwinners. As if definitely to settle responsibility for the disaster, several secret investigations were instituted. In their findings, the investigators were critical of Moscow's governor general, the Grand Duke Sergei, as well as Count Vorontsov-Dashkov, and they recommended the prosecution of a number of men—including Moscow Police Superintendent Vlasovsky—who failed to provide and carry out adequate plans for directing and controlling the festival crowd. But practically no redress followed: the Grand Duke Sergei was not even officially censured; the tsar refused Vorontsov-Dashkov's request to be relieved of his post as minister of court; and no one was prosecuted. Of all the officials involved, only Vlasovsky was dismissed—with an annual pension of three thousand rubles.[9]

Contrary to what some had expected, there was no immediate display of popular criticism or indignation following the event—not even in Moscow. Some workers went on strike at the time, but their complaint concerned wages lost during the coronation festivities, not what happened at Khodynka Field. Students seemed to be about the only ones really aroused, and it was almost six months before there was any public indication of feelings. In early November, when the Grand Duke Sergei was returning to Moscow from a trip, some daring individuals decked the city's lampposts with placards reading: "The Duke of Khodynka is returning to protect Vagankovsky Cemetery." [10] On November 18, university students organized memorial services at the cemetery, and when that gathering was dispersed by the police, efforts to recall the tragedy appeared to have been abandoned.

The consequences of Khodynka, however, were actually both enduring and significant. The memory remained, not among the common people particularly but among thoughtful Russians of the political opposition. To them, the incident was yet another black mark against the bureaucracy, another item of proof that, while the police were efficient enough in protecting their masters, they were indifferent to the lives of others. They saw in it also further evidence of the antipathetic nature of the tsar himself. As his reference to "senseless dreams" had been interpreted a few months earlier as a manifestation of his contemptuousness for "society" (that is, his politically concerned educated subjects), his behavior with respect to Khodynka was now taken as a manifestation of his insensitiveness to the woes of "the people." Indeed, the facts seemed to support censure: instead of acting spontaneously and warmly, Nicholas had contented himself with formal and not overly generous gestures; and, instead of punishing irresponsible and inefficient officials, he had let them off either scot-free or very lightly reprimanded. He had, in short, timidly yielded to the worst traditions of the bureaucracy.

Khodynka was to have a lasting influence on Nicholas. In addition to imposing on him the onus of the opposition's reinforced disrespect for the autocratic authority he exercised, it strengthened in him a sense of fatalism which would lead him, at times, to accept difficulties that, with effort, he might have overcome. Already inclined to attribute joys and sorrows to God's will, he now became increasingly convinced that, while a man's heart might aspire toward certain goals, God would direct his steps. As he reviewed his life to date, conscious of the prophetic incidence of his birth—he was born on the day of St. Job the Sufferer—he felt that unquestionably his steps were being directed down a tortuous path.

Yet, while the experience he had just undergone encouraged his fatalism, it also produced in him a change that would, to some extent, compensate for it: it made him more self-willed. Although he recognized that he had often cut a poor figure and that others had often traded on his timidity or ignorance, he regretted the one and resented the other. Khodynka proved to him that "others" could be grievously wrong, that it behooved him to be less docile.

To change his relationship to those about him was not easy. Members of the numerous and vocal imperial family, in particular, remained unimpressed by his authority, and he was never able to bring them to heel as his father had done. Fortunately, he was usually able, in dealing with them, to avoid crises. He had learned, during his years as tsesarevich, to stifle anger, curb his temper, and exercise tact with such skill that, as one of his relatives commented, he appeared to be "the most polite man in Europe." Now he began to accept the necessity to be also direct and emphatic in indicating that there was a point beyond which even members of the family might not trespass on his sphere. Six months after Khodynka, when his uncle the Grand Duke Vladimir persisted in ignoring his wishes in making guards appointments, Nicholas lost his patience and wrote to him: ". . . My *kindness* is responsible for this whole incident— yes, I insist on this—my stupid kindness. Only in order not to quarrel and not to disturb family relationships, I have constantly given in . . . a blockhead, without will and without character. Now I do not simply ask, I command you to carry out my *previously expressed will.*" [11]

Such declarations of independence brought about at least a semblance of respect among the older grand dukes in their official capacities; but, in private circles, many members of the Romanov family maintained an attitude that was less than respectful. Some of them, often abetted by their wives, aggravated Nicholas' difficulties by encouraging petty intrigue, gossiping, and at times exerting behind-the-scenes influence. The Grand Duke Vladimir and his wife, Marie Pavlovna, provided one of the most consequential centers of gossip and intrafamily scheming. Others joined them or sponsored rival centers. Even Dowager Empress Marie Fedorovna drew a special following. By law and tradition the dowager took precedence over the reigning empress, but this was an advantage that few had pressed. Marie Fedorovna, however, in good health and youthful in spirit, was of no mind to become a respected but ignored relic. It was soon clear that she was to be the most popular member of the imperial family, sought after by those who professed great respect for her judgment and relied on her influence with the tsar in political matters and those who simply enjoyed the royal touch and the lively atmosphere at her court.

These various Romanov "sub-courts" flourished the more easily because Empress Alexandra was outshone by her mother-in-law and because she did not aspire to leadership in the life of the capital. She was ill at ease in society and stiff, her face flushed when things went wrong, and she found it difficult to engage in small talk or pay compliments. At court, where little mercy was shown the unsuccessful, the ladies marked her down as a dull combination of English gentlewoman and minor German princess—too lacking in chic, too prim, too religious, too much the *Hausfrau.* The men also, regardless of her good looks and fine figure, responded to her with no more than the socially required attention; somehow she seemed always to make them feel ill at ease and unwelcome. It was as well that she found it agreeable to join Nicholas in what amounted to virtual retirement from social relationship, except as a formal duty, with other members of the imperial family.

This disunity among the Romanovs, which had been growing since the time of Alexander II, unquestionably weakened the dynasty and, therefore, jeopardized the throne; but, for the time, it was little more than a fascinating and challenging game to the principals below the tsar.

Like the imperial family, Nicholas' ministers also found it expedient to adjust themselves to his temperament and his personal manner of leadership. Gradually, as opportunities appeared, he replaced the ministers remaining in the government after the death of Alexander III, and by 1898, he was surrounded by men of his own choice—with the conspicuous exception of Pobedonostsev and Witte. Some found it easy to serve him; others had difficulties. The ones who at first misjudged the laxness of his inexperienced hand and assumed too great a degree of independence soon felt his disapproval. He did not castigate such offenders as his father had done; he quietly obstructed their plans, ignored their advice, or, if they pressed him too hard, cautioned them to keep within the bounds of the authority delegated to them. Under this treatment, even Pobedonostsev finally learned to restrain his presumption and began to confine himself to matters concerning the Holy Synod unless otherwise directed. Witte also found it prudent (though at times impossible, it appeared) to subdue his overactive propensity for offering opinions on matters outside his jurisdiction. At length, all the ministers came to understand that, while Nicholas was "gentle," he was also stubborn; that his mind could be changed on superficial things, but not on things he considered fundamental; that he preferred men who were frank yet not disputatious, energetic yet conservative; that he bridled at outright flattery but could be flattered by being made to feel the warmth of loyalty; that he favored ministers who attended strictly to their duties and did not talk politics.

Not all who served him measured up to his requirements, of course; his reign was marked by the usual conflicts of judgments, aims, and personalities. In making some of his earliest appointments, he had been reluctant to impose his judgment and had listened to the insistent voices of the more experienced. One instance in the first year of his reign, when he was choosing the successor to Ivan Durnovo for the ministry of interior, proved instructive. He omitted from consideration two men he would later choose, Dmitri Sipyagin and Vyacheslav Plehve, on the advice on Pobedonostsev, who labeled one "an imbecile" and the other "a scoundrel," and appointed Ivan Goremykin, a man who would blend effortlessly into the bureaucratic background. He soon saw, however, that by being thus passed from one "safe" man to another, this critical ministry was neither gaining respect nor serving the regime with distinction (Durnovo had been known derisively as "Tête de Veau;" Goremykin was dubbed "His High Indifference"), and he thereafter began gradually to gain confidence in his own ability to match men with what he judged to be his government's needs.

Two of his later appointees, in 1897 and 1898, whose qualities accorded nicely with his personal judgment of what made good officials were Baron Vladimir Fredericks, who succeeded Count Vorontsov-Dashkov as his minister of court, and General Alexis Kuropatkin, who became his minister of war on the resignation of General Vannovsky.

Fredericks was a descendant of Baron Peter Fredericks, who, as commander of the Moscow Guards in 1825, had tried vainly to restrain the guardsmen who had joined in the Decembrist Revolt; like his ancestor, he was a loyal supporter of the tsarist regime. He had been commander of the Horse Guards and, later, chief of the imperial stables. Alexander III had held that he should never be allowed to rise above the latter post, but Nicholas had high regard for him. He knew him as an honorable and responsible man, one who was not afflicted with the curse of presumption and who would be unlikely to meddle in politics. Moreover, he seemed to have the diversified capabilities demanded in a ministry where he would be expected, in addition to handling the tsar's personal property and the daily routine of the court, to supervise the administration of the municipalities of Tsarskoe Selo, Peterhof, and Gatchina; to direct the management of the imperial palaces, hunting preserves, museums, theaters, stables, factories, and the Imperial Academy of Art; and to see to the special financial affairs of the members of the imperial family. His manifest talent for tact and diplomacy would be a decided advantage in dealing with the highly individualistic Romanovs whose properties—land, palaces, mines—were under the supervision of the minister of court, as was also the source of part of their income, the crown properties—twenty million acres of cultivated and timbered land, providing annually about five million rubles. The unlikelihood of his dealing in family gossip and intrigue with members of this group, now some fifty in number, was yet another item in his favor. To round out his suitability to serve as chief court official, Baron Fredericks looked the part: in his late fifties at the time of his appointment, he had the bearing of quiet authority, yet retained the impressive appearance of a gentleman guardsman of sophisticated taste and gallantry.

General Kuropatkin, though of a very different stamp, impressed Nicholas as an equally good man for his post. With his strong, heavily bearded face and thickset body, he had the appearance of a stolid peasant, the tsar's favorite type of subject; and, on the empire's battle fronts, he had shown himself to be a "truly Russian soldier." He had earned honors as Skobelev's chief of staff in the Russo-Turkish War and had continued to be creditably active thereafter, becoming commander in chief in the Caucasus just before his appointment to the ministry of war. To have advanced to the rank of general before he was fifty, his present age, was in itself noteworthy. Nicholas was impressed by this record, though he knew that some judged Kuropatkin, regardless of his well-rewarded past, to be of limited stature as an officer. A former minister, while admitting that he was a brave man, said of him: "He will go far; but one will be disappointed in him. He has the soul of a regimental clerk." [12] Nicholas could not read the stars, however; and he was confident that Kuropatkin could help him do for the country the things he was incorporating in his modest plans for it. He only wished he had more like him.

XI

Clouded Vision

NICHOLAS II, 1898–1903

ALTHOUGH Nicholas II, in his early statement of intention to "support the principles of autocracy," was using words put together by Pobedonostsev, he was nonetheless asserting his own basic position, unqualified and already fixed. His preparation and experience had allowed him to recognize no other. His predecessors had maintained the autocratic principles, and he expected to do the same. The manner of his administration might differ from theirs, but he intended that whatever measures he undertook would be strictly in keeping with his tsarist heritage.

He did not recognize that, by the time of his accession, the conditions maintained by his predecessors had become incompatible with reality, that a clash between circumstances and policy could be avoided only by some kind of accommodation on the part of the government. It was a state of affairs easy to overlook because, after the reforms of Alexander II, which had provided only partial solutions to the country's most critical problems, Alexander III had closed the door to any new reforms and imposed a temporary and deceiving air of calm that was to last for a brief period after his death. During that time, Nicholas, as well as responsible men at all levels of the bureaucracy, accepted as reality the illusion that his father had bequeathed him a well-ordered realm.

It was an optimistic evaluation, but by no means a groundless one: for a few years, much continued to go well for Russia because of programs continued from the previous reign. The one undertaken by Minister of Finance Witte, by far the most ambitious, was producing a particularly impressive lot of benefits. Although Nicholas knew that many officials disapproved of Witte's methods and though he himself found it difficult to excuse his aggressiveness, he could not but look with favor on the country's growing financial stability, dependent in great part on Witte's monetary reforms, including the establishment of the gold standard. He could even take personal pride in the fact that some of the measures, unacceptable to conservative members of the State Council, owed their inauguration to imperial approval alone. Moreover, certain accomplishments of the program, he could see, were putting Russia safely into the ranks of the world's most progressive states. In railroad construction, no country was making greater advances. Industry was booming. Textile centers such as Moscow, St. Petersburg, and Lodz were stirring with unequaled enterprise. The richness of the country's natural resources was finally being realized: coal in the Donets basin, oil in the Caucasus, and iron in the Ukraine. Both foreign and domestic trade were showing a healthy increase. The long-sought favorable import-export balance was being achieved, and great ports like Odessa were no longer mere calling stations in world commerce. To crown all, a balanced national budget was again in sight.

Admittedly, there were still problems and occasional untoward incidents: road building was as slow as ever, some peasants continued to resist such progressive measures as inspection of cattle for communicable disease, students were still circulating petitions for the restoration of university autonomy, the influence of the Catholic clergy was still too high in the Western Region. Such matters, however, did not suggest to the tsar or his advisers any basic fault in policy, only the need for continued effort, vigilance, and perhaps some new planning. It was generally agreed that, in certain areas, a few changes in policy—some of them already begun by Alexander III— might be needed. But only minor changes would be involved. They would include, perhaps, making alterations in the administration of Finland, introducing zemstvos in a number of provinces where there were none, and ending the system of exile, which, though financially inexpensive, was now recognized as politically costly since political exiles were able to influence the free population of the regions to which they were sent. These and kindred matters, according to Minister of Interior Goremykin, could be handled through a simple program of "completion and repair"—a soothing suggestion that there needed to be no changes made in the basic structure of the state.

As with domestic affairs, so with the foreign: until the turn of the century, all looked fair for the regime. There was no threat of a major war, and it was the opinion of most officials that, if one should develop, it would be between either France and England or Germany and England.

Nicholas, personally averse to war, was eager to believe Kuropatkin's beguiling explanation of how he could enjoy the fruits of power without the risk of conflict. It was a tidy view of Russia's future relations with Europe. At a suitable moment, when international opposition could be expected to be slight, Russia would seize the Bosporus, thus attaining her major goal in that region, control of the Straits. This act, by stirring up the Slavs throughout the area, would speed up the "inevitable" disintegration of Austria, the Slavic parts of which could join in a Slavic confederation, while the Germanic parts could be absorbed by Germany. Later, when the "inevitable" war between Germany and England should break out, Russia would abet France in holding a pistol to Germany's head and forcing her to return Alsace-Lorraine. And with that, Europe would settle down to a gratifying state of stability.[1]

At that time, Nicholas had no good reason to doubt Kuropatkin's prowess as a prophet. His own chief problem in connection with the foreign ministry seemed to be the matter of keeping it provided with officials. In the first six years of his reign, three successive ministers of foreign affairs died in office—the aged Giers, Prince Alexis Lobanov-Rostovsky, and Count Michael Muravev.* By the time of Muravev's death, however, the tsar was becoming less assured about Russia's relations abroad.

While Nicholas chose to dwell principally on the favorable conditions within his realm, trusting in the sufficiency of Goremykin's "completion and repair" policy, undeniably detrimental and disruptive forces were developing behind the façade of progress and quiescence.

The very success of Witte's great new industrial program as it harnessed forces to promote the general economy stimulated conditions hazardous to the status quo and brought disparagement that

* Not to be confused with Michael Muravev, "The Hangman," a distant relative.

would have intimidated a man less determined than Witte. What he envisioned was, to many influential conservatives, a new Russia rising too rapidly and with too little regard for the old. Pobedonostsev found various occasions to criticize him to the tsar. The landed nobility blamed him for their financial losses due to the devaluation of the ruble in order to stabilize the currency. Government officials complained that he often bypassed them, ignored the established bureaucratic procedures, and went directly to the tsar in seeking to initiate measures properly falling within their authority. Others raised cries that he was burdening everyone with rising costs by maintaining high import duties on manufactured goods in order to achieve a favorable balance of trade, that he was stifling individual enterprise by making the state everyone's banker, and that he was driving Russia into irredeemable debt by his excessive borrowing from other countries.

Even those who approved and supported Witte's program had to admit that, while achieving its aim of increasing the country's wealth, it brought certain immediate financial disadvantages. The requirements of accelerated industrialization were so great that, although the national funds were apportioned in what appeared to be a practical manner, some of the traditionally preeminent needs of the state were not being satisfactorily met. Chief among them was the need to keep militarily abreast of the other great powers. Russia was approaching the turn of the century with outdated armament that would be wholly inadequate if her pretensions to great-power status were seriously challenged. France and Germany had adopted new, rapid-firing rifles and artillery, and Austria was reported ready to follow suit. Russia would need more than a hundred million rubles to modernize her weaponry.[2] This was a fantastic amount at a time when the ministry of finance appeared unable to squeeze another kopeck out of the taxpayers. To avoid the hazard, Kuropatkin and others proposed that Nicholas take the lead in an effort to get agreement among the European powers on the limitation of armament in such a way as to preserve the balance of power. He complied, and out of his effort came the first international peace conference, which met at The Hague in 1899. But when the conference rejected the arms proposal—practically a foregone response—Russia was back with her problem, forced to seek more and more sources of revenue for the armed forces and still unable to overtake France and Germany.

A variety of other problems followed closely in the wake of almost all the innovations accompanying the Witte program. Industry was not all profit and progress. As industrial enterprises developed and workers were gathered to man them, urban population figures soared. Cities that had been able in fair measure to meet the needs of their populations during the last three decades despite noticeable increases now began to feel unwonted pressure. By the end of the century, a million and a quarter persons were crowded into St. Petersburg, and Moscow counted a million—in both cases, tens of thousands more than could be properly cared for, even at the lowest standards of health and comfort. In St. Petersburg, for instance, the flood of new workers was pushed out to the poorly developed outskirts, for military barracks had already taken up such a great amount of space in the inner city that room for new housing was at a premium. Even there, the quarters available were comfortless and insufficient in number. Worse yet, because of the lack of sanitation and the impurity of the water in these outer districts (some private water works had been taken over by the municipal administration, but they supplied only part of the inner city), there were frequent outbursts of dysentery and typhoid fever. In lesser cities, where the growth of population was even faster, the conditions were proportionately worse: Warsaw, where the population had tripled; Kiev and Odessa, where it had quadrupled; and Lodz, the Polish textile center, where there had been a ten-fold increase. The wretchedness of living conditions in such centers was, in most cases, equaled by that of working conditions in the industrial establishments and the misery was aggravated by the long hours imposed on the workers.

It was inevitable that the workers, hoping to improve their lot, began to take advantage of the circumstances which, for the first time in the history of the country, had created a proletarian class and provided it with the opportunity for group expression of discontent. Thus, "labor trouble" came to Russia. In the textile factories of St. Petersburg, illegal strike followed illegal strike from the time of the coronation until well into 1897, when the government finally agreed to shorten the working day to eleven and a half hours. The idea of the strike was gaining favor in other areas also; in Moscow, it even led to the consideration of striking for an unprecedented nine-and-a-half-hour day. Though this restiveness was not revolutionary in nature (labor was not yet ready even for unionism), it suggested that the workers were awakening to the value of group action in matters of common interest.

Urban growth not only led to the gathering of workers into

larger and more intimate association but also brought together increased numbers of others whose concentration was significant. As
the extraordinary number of families moved in, more young people
had access to secondary and higher schools; the resulting increase in
literacy, while providing a basis of unity among the individuals concerned, also helped to change the intellectual tone of the cities. Additional influence came from the thousands of professionals—teachers, pharmacists, engineers, doctors, lawyers, journalists. Many of
them were already imbued with the ideas of the intelligentsia and
resentful of being denied both a voice in the government and the
right to organize for political purposes. They were becoming
markedly more interested in professional organizations and learned
societies, potential breeding places of liberalism and protest. In due
course, writers and publishers, rightly assessing the changing market,
expanded their efforts; in the 1890's, the number of periodicals available to the public was increased 100 percent—an indication that the
dissemination of ideas was to flourish again, the ranks of the discontented to be enlivened. For any such revival, there was now one
practical advantage: many of the new urban dwellers, so recently of
the countryside, retained their rural ties and would, therefore,
be able to provide a kind of liaison, hitherto lacking when liberals
of the cities tried to reach or influence the peasantry.

The changing aspect of the cities also affected members of minorities whose ethnic backgrounds gave them common interests: such
groups as the Ukrainians, Letts, Lithuanians, Finns, Estonians, and
Jews. Their leaders, with the urban advantages of education and
wider knowledge of the dissatisfaction among others, were encouraged to greater activity among the submerged nationalities throughout the country. At first, the interests of these national minorities
were, strictly speaking, more cultural than political, more concerned
with their own language, literature, and history than with the attain-
ment of national rights. But, in a sense, the very fact of their national
consciousness was political, for it was in conflict with the interests of
the state. (Ironically, this turn of events was the fruit of Russification: most of the minority leaders had received their education in
Russian schools dedicated to making them "good Russians.")

As Witte was mistaken when he predicted that the results of
urban growth would be wholly propitious, so also was he mistaken
when he predicted that the general economic benefits derived from
industry would spill over into the countryside and lift the rural
population into the mainstream of national prosperity. Not that he

was at first particularly concerned about the advancement of the rural population. He was intent on building an economy that would sustain the structure of empire; industry was the support of its keystone, railroad construction, and all else was subordinate. Those persons employed on the land, though about 80 percent of the population and though still a convenient source of cheap industrial labor, were to him no longer basic factors in the economy. They were simply, for all practical purposes, provisioners of the imperial larder; surely they could be expected, out of concern for their own stomachs, to keep to their duties and provide as they had in the past.

But the situation was not so simple. The new economic prosperity did not spill over as a rule, and the conditions that had made it possible for the agrarian population to sustain itself as well as the national economy in the past no longer prevailed. In fact, as Witte's critics were ready to point out, his program, instead of assisting, was one of the chief deterrents to agrarian progress because its adherence to a high tariff to protect Russian industry drove the price of needed agricultural machinery to prohibitive heights, and, without machinery, the required production could not be achieved. True, many estate owners had kept abreast of the times, had managed efficiently, and had been flexible enough to shift from less profitable crops to more profitable ones; they remained men of means with property unencumbered by debt. There were also many peasants so comfortably situated that they could afford ready-made boots and better-than-average clothes, enjoy such luxuries as glass windows for their cottages, and provide vodka for their occasionally festive tables. Yet, in a great part of rural Russia, poverty weighed heavily, the majority of both nobles and peasants were barely holding their own, and a large minority were going downhill.

In the depressed areas where, by the end of the nineteenth century, poverty was etching more deeply into the lives of more people than ever before, the familiar causes, technological backwardness and population growth, had been supplemented by a new adversity: the market competition from foreign grain, notably American. Competition had brought a drop in prices; and, with 95 percent of the arable land sown to grain, that was a serious matter. When the income from grain declined, the land-owning nobility and peasants alike suffered. This was particularly evident in the most fertile provinces, those in the black-earth region, where the land was still the only important source of income. The marks of deterioration were everywhere. Among the less prosperous nobles, there were more sales of land and an increase in their indebtedness. The peasants, already feeling the pinch of a decrease in the size of their holdings—the result of growth in population—were approaching desperate straits as, inevitably under the circumstances, they fell more deeply into debt while their arrears in taxes and dues increased.

Many Russians saw these conditions as evidence that the country was facing a serious and critical agrarian problem. But Nicholas was not willing to accept their view; to do so would raise awkward issues. He opposed making any changes in the institution that to him was so "truly Russian" as to be almost sacrosanct, the village commune, and to make improvements without such changes would be most difficult. Even after the emergency brought about by a particularly poor harvest in 1897, he would not agree to a general review of agrarian conditions. From time to time, he appointed committees to investigate limited aspects of the rural situation, but they accomplished little beyond filing reports, though they found that in regions where zemstvos had been established, the zemstvo workers were usually ready to expose the need for social, political, and economic reforms—considerations outside the limits of the committee directive. As for the general restiveness, Witte had a facile explanation: the peasant's appetite had increased.[3] In fairness to the minister of finance, it must be noted that he did advise the tsar to call a conference to consider the problems of the agricultural industry and that, when Nicholas finally convened such a conference—in 1902, four years and another near-famine later—Witte struggled manfully to get practical results from it.

As the pressures of various problems built up, the conflict between the circumstances he faced and the principles he defended was forced upon Nicholas in many instances, and the practicality of his program of "completion and repair" was often challenged.

For instance, in the matter of completing the introduction of zemstvos, he had to consider ramifications he had not anticipated in the beginning. By the time Goremykin had ready his proposals for the provision of zemstvo services in provinces where zemstvos had not been organized, the tsar had developed misgivings about the undertaking, even on a limited basis, for his committees investigating rural conditions had opened his eyes to the fact that many leaders in the existing zemstvos were suspiciously liberal in their thinking. When Witte rushed to declare that the very idea of zemstvos, a form of local self-government, was wholly incompatible with autocracy, the decisive word had been spoken. Nicholas simply removed Goremykin from the ministry of interior to the State Council, replaced him by Dmitri Sipyagin, and left the question of extending zemstvos unresolved. Sipyagin, a self-assured nobleman whom the tsar knew to be highly respectful of imperial prestige and power as well as intolerant of any change in the established order, would be a "safe" man. In fourteen years of government service, he had come to enjoy the exercise of authority (even more than fine food, some said, though he was known to be a discriminating gourmet); he took over the ministry of interior with relish, assuming his new authority to be second only to that of the tsar. He ignored Goremykin's plans and began at once to limit the operation of existing zemstvos by such measures as restricting their right of taxation to provide necessary operating funds and rescinding their power to supervise provisioning in the countryside.

Another operation begun earlier and left for Nicholas to complete was made difficult by precedents reaching back to the time of Alexander I. It involved the administration of the autonomous grand duchy of Finland, which had enjoyed constitutional privileges and a degree of cultural entity that for years had made it an exceptionally contented and trouble-free part of the empire. Russification could be expected to be galling to the Finns, but Alexander III, with his concept of "Russia for the Russians," had not been deterred by that fact; he had left far-reaching plans for bringing the grand duchy into what he considered its proper place in the empire. Nicholas' task was to carry on, and he had anticipated no difficulty in doing so.

In 1898, he undertook to extend Russian military conscription to the grand duchy. The number of men that this measure would add to the million in the imperial army—about 20,000—would be trifling, but the tsar felt that, as a matter of principle, the Finns should contribute to the defense of the state. While waiting for the Finnish diet to enact legislation to meet the requirement, he was strongly supported on that position by the newly appointed governor general of the grand duchy, tough-minded General Nicholas Bobrikov. The nationalist press approved it wholeheartedly, as did Minister of War Kuropatkin. It was further endorsed by Vyacheslav Plehve, who, through his driving ambition and vigorous support of official nationalism, had kept the favor of two tsars, advanced to the post of state secretary, and made himself highly acceptable for the leadership of the State Council's section on Finnish affairs.

The applause was entirely one-sided, however; the Finnish diet refused to consider the enabling legislation on conscription. When, early in the following year, Nicholas declared his right to issue legislation for Finland without its consent, he met unexpected defiance. Five hundred thousand Finns—one of every five inhabitants—signed a petition against the new policy; pictures of their earlier "friend" Alexander II were draped in black, and no head was bowed to the "intruder" on Finnish constitutional rights. Still, Nicholas let his military training guide his statesmanship: once engaged, he would not retreat. Witte and Marie Fedorovna advised against his stand; the foreign press and Russian liberals criticized it; but he stood firm beside Bobrikov in the belief that "a strong and steady hand" would restore order and proper respect among the Finns. He was wrong; when he would finally be forced to admit that fact, Russo-Finnish relations would have been dangerously impaired.

Nicholas was due for many more revelations concerning the nearly one hundred and thirty million people for whom destiny had given him responsibility without realistic understanding.

One serious prospect for which he was unprepared was the revival of political unrest, unobtrusively begun at the time of the famine in 1891. Considering the last restraints imposed by Alexander III—the "protection" of the Law on Exceptional Measures, the covert activity of the *Okhrana* in the large cities, the limitations set on education, and the various arbitrary curbs applied to press and public, it seemed hardly possible that any substantial sources of *kramola* should have survived. Yet many persons had eluded the restraints by leaving the country, others by becoming more secretive and less active. *Kramola* had declined, but it had not died.

George Plekhanov, leader of the young revolutionaries who had refused to approve the terroristic tactics employed by the People's Will, had gone abroad, become converted to Marxian socialism, and in 1883 helped to found among fellow émigrés in Geneva the first Russian social democratic organization, Emancipation of Labor. With that, he had become one of the ideological leaders in another phase of activity among students and older intellectuals within Russia. It was now to be observed in all the leading cities, where "legal Marxism"—that is, the economic aspect of Marxian doctrine—was a familiar subject of discussion and published articles, pamphlets dealing with the political aspect were passing from hand to hand, and small Marxist groups were growing in number. This new enthusiasm was suggestive of the circles organized by the restive youth of the country half a century earlier, but it was directed toward more immediate and practical ends.

At first the meetings of the segregate groups were little more than talkfests, given to extolling the advantages of Marxism over the old populist dogmas, and analyzing the exciting new theory that revolution was to be realized through a working-class party, and socialism approached by way of capitalism. But, by the time of Nicholas' accession, members were beginning to feel the need for union; and in 1895, about twenty of the St. Petersburg groups undertook to organize a union, guided by Vladimir Ulyanov (better known by his revolutionary name, Lenin) and Julius Martov. They named it the Fighting Union for the Emancipation of the Working Class and dedicated it to agitation among workers as a step toward translating theory into practice. Their boldness, however, exceeded their finesse, and the alerted authorities soon had all of the actively involved leaders—most of them political suspects in any case—in prison, the first step on the way into Siberian exile.

Nevertheless, the example of their effort prompted young Marxists in other cities to try to unite and begin carrying their revolutionary message to the workers—usually with the same frustrating results. Then, three years later, at a congress in Minsk, a handful of delegates from the depleted ranks founded the Russian Social Democratic Party. At the time, the party was in reality only a sketched gesture accompanied by a statement of the idea for a nationwide organization. It was not formally organized with charter and program, until five years later. After 1898, however, the scattered groups could call themselves the affiliates of a party, and the associated individuals began to identify themselves as party members, the SD's—that in itself gave them a sense of strength.

The arguments of those who supported the Social Democratic doctrine had not turned the more dedicated populists from their basic beliefs. The spirit of populism, revived at the time of the 1891 famine, had inspired the surreptitious organization of many groups among like-minded individuals, especially students, by the beginning of Nicholas' reign, and, like the groups of the Social Democrats, they strove toward some kind of united effort. For a decade, however, the diligence of informers and the alertness of the police were sufficient to nullify all efforts to establish populist unity. It was not until late in 1901 that representatives of a number of groups were able to meet, in Kharkov, and establish the core of a national organization, the Socialist Revolutionary Party. Again, as in the case of the SD's, five more years were required for working out a charter and a program agreeable to the scattered leadership. Meanwhile, those who accepted the general aims of the party, calling themselves Socialist Revolutionaries—soon to be popularly known as the SR's—joined exuberantly in the great underground debate on how to make a revolution. Their contention was that the revolution should be of, and for, the majority, the peasants. It should lead directly to socialism for Russia, not into some such "political purgatory" as that planned by the Social Democrats with their notion of a capitalist transition period. A sufficient number of the Socialist Revolutionaries favored the terrorist aspect of the old People's Will to win the party's acceptance of terror as a supplement to propaganda in its revolutionary efforts. It would be the responsibility of a special section, the Fighting Organization, which would continue the earlier program of assassinating selected government officials in order to frighten and debilitate the autocracy.

Between the two ideological extremes, the revolutionary and the autocratic, stood the liberals—the less flamboyant thousands of Nicholas' educated subjects who admitted imperfections in the system under which they lived, recognized needs, and sought improvement without upheaval. Like the populists, the liberal leaders felt their conscience stirred by the part they had taken in the relief work of 1891, and they were quietly urging a revival of concern when the new regime was getting under way. Some of the most dedicated and outspoken of them were to be found where they had intimate knowledge of the greatest economic and social hardships of the greatest number: in the zemstvos, which were the forcing-beds of various types of dissatisfaction, and in the Committees for the Advancement of Literacy. Others were scattered throughout the upper and middle classes of society. In political conviction, they were divided between those who hoped to see the reforms that had been begun by Alexander II extended until representative, constitutional government should be achieved and those who looked for reforms without changes in government. Whatever their position and however they were inclined to present it, the liberals were to be another disturbing factor which the tsar would not continue indefinitely to disregard with impunity.

While political concern was quietly taking hold of a greater number of Russian minds than ever before, and while some were sufficiently single-minded about one or another of the definable programs to be struggling toward effective organization, there was still no antigovernment force of any significant strength before the turn of the century. The membership of every evolving group, whether inclined toward the Social Democratic, Socialist Revolutionary, liberal, or some other kind of doctrine, usually had to overcome, in addition to the vigilance of the authorities, its own lack of experience, inner discord, and sometimes diffidence or vacillation as well.

The one type of malcontent seemingly irrepressible in spite of impediments, but subject to all of them, was the student.

The schemes by which different ministers of education—Uvarov, Dmitri Tolstoy, and Delyanov, in particular—had sought to mold Russian youth into amenable subjects in an authoritarian state had missed their goals. While the educational system showed the effects of the specially designed regimen that had been in force for more than three decades as the nineteenth century drew to a close, the effects were not what had been intended. The application of the classical discipline, the winnowing out of "undesirables," and the dispensing of all authority from the ministry of education had by no means made the students more immune to "pernicious" ideas than their predecessors. Rather it had turned their minds more purposefully toward that which promised escape from their condition. Their gods were not those stipulated in the curricula, but men whom they considered "contemporary realists." They were men like Leo Tolstoy, in whose Christian anarchism they saw a denunciation of traditional beliefs such as those imposed so painfully upon themselves and in whose defense of communism and conscientious objection to military service they saw support for their resentment of the ways of the world into which they were being arbitrarily turned; George Plekhanov, whose Marxian socialism impressed them as intellectuals and as dissidents; Nicholas Mikhailovsky, with his convincing journalistic appeal for a socialist, agrarian commonwealth; and the late Semyon Nadson, one of the so-called civic poets, who lamented the evils of despotism and the inequities of society—with both of which afflictions they claimed personal experience.

Inevitably, students were drawn to outside protest groups and brought back to institutional life their modes of protest, almost all of them illegal: demonstrations, strikes, and organization for the purpose of considering political issues or planning purposeful action against authority. During the academic year 1897–98 there was a noticeable increase of political activity in the institutions of higher learning and a beginning of illegal organization in the secondary schools. These manifestations, however, were not sufficient to suggest the need for change, and, after the death of Minister of Education Delyanov, in 1897, the old policies were given an insured extension by the appointment of the safely reactionary educator Nicholas Bogolepov as his successor.

It took a bit of sensation to bring the mood of the students into any kind of prominence. In February 1899, following the annual celebration of the founding of St. Petersburg University, mounted police barred students from the use of a bridge leading from the university location, on Vasilevsky Island, to the heart of the city, where it was thought they might stage an unofficial celebration. In the skirmish provoked by the act, the students jeered and threw stones, and the police charged their ranks (whether using whips or not was a matter of later argument).[4] The consequences of the incident were out of all proportion to its gravity. As interpreted by the students, many of the faculty, and some of the public, the police charge was unjustified brutality, an illustration of the relationship between government and society, and it served to break the dam that was holding back student resentment throughout the country.

In the capital, the students of the university, the other higher schools, and even of one gymnasium demonstrated their feelings by going on strike against all educational routine. At Moscow University 3,000 of the 4,000 enrolled students refused to attend classes or take examinations. Within a few weeks, their defiance had become so obstructive that the entire student body was dismissed and the university closed while the police made a thorough investigation. Three thousand of the students were finally found to be "politically reliable," and they were permitted to continue their studies. Meanwhile strikes had developed at other universities, but on a smaller scale. Everywhere students endured suspension and often parental and official reprimand as well in order to release their pent-up feelings in public protest.

When the upsurge had at last worn itself out, assisted somewhat by the tsar's approval of rules permitting the conscription of suspended students for military service during the period of their suspension, an uneasy peace returned to most of the student bodies. Turbulence sank most slowly in Kiev, where the threat of conscription was protested so vigorously that, in 1900, hundreds of students were expelled and, under orders from the new minister of interior, Sipyagin, about 200 were marched away to military service. Still the prevailing mood there and elsewhere remained so combative that a militant minority in any group could easily stir up trouble.

The following year, the government was moved to action again when an expelled student, Peter Karpovich, a professed Socialist Revolutionary, shot and fatally wounded Minister of Education Bogolepov. This was the first assassination of a high official since that of Alexander II, and Nicholas took it as an indication of the immediate need for still more stringent control over the youth of the country. To provide that control, he selected the former war minister General Peter Vannovsky to replace Bogolepov.

Few could see in Vannovsky the agent of strength the tsar expected him to be. He was not a well educated man and, now seventy-nine years of age, he was so infirm that two strong men were required to assist him at stairways. His selection was an illustration of Nicholas' lack of acquaintance with men who might be considered for high posts, a lack that limited him often and seriously. At least, he knew Vannovsky and liked his qualifications. He was loyal, he was a general (the tsar was coming to feel that more generals were needed in civilian posts), he had a reputation for firmness, and he had some claim to knowledge of the student mentality, having once administered a cadet school and having helped in the investigation of recent student disorders. Perhaps he could succeed where others had failed. His task, as Nicholas specified it, was to restore order, reestablish authority, continue the investigations, and submit proposals for means by which the youthful mind could be further protected from whatever was prompting the current unruliness.

If Nicholas had any misgivings about how he had been handling his imperial duties to date, he did not share them with his ministers. They knew only that he appeared to be gaining self-confidence, a fact that some attributed to the growing influence of his father's onetime friend Prince Vladimir Meshchersky. On coming to the throne, Nicholas had pointedly rebuffed Meshchersky, a disreputable individual popularly known as the "Prince of Sodom," by denying further government subsidy for his paper, *The Citizen*, and personally ignoring him; recently, however, he had begun showing him decided favor. The prince had been publishing his recollections of the reign of Alexander III and featuring in *The Citizen* some laudatory articles about Nicholas' policies. As Sipyagin, a cousin of Princess Meshchersky, had pointed out, the friendly editor could be a valuable friend. Whatever the reason, he was added to the tsar's limited circle of confidants, soon to win from him an intimate encomium: ". . . I am pleased to recognize that our contact is not due to chance.

It is a direct result of the training given me by my dear Father, and the heritage of all that was dear to him. . . . You appeared and at once revived and reinforced that legacy. Somehow I have grown up in my own eyes." [5]

While Meshchersky was giving Nicholas reassuring support on his policies and Sipyagin was affirming the proficiency of his enforcement agents, another man was trying to warn him of conditions that were far from reassuring. Leo Tolstoy, whose influence among the people at this time was so great that he was sometimes called "Russia's other ruler," sensed foretokens of trouble and tried to impart his feelings to the tsar. Addressing him as "kind brother," he urged him to consider the strain under which his subjects were existing when one-third of them were being administered under the Law on Exceptional Measures, to see that both church and state were faltering, and to recognize that disaster was inevitable unless changes were made. It was another of those warnings that Nicholas chose to ignore: he did not agree with the interpretation and, in any case, following public advice on policy would have been unbecoming to an autocrat.

The tsar could not long ignore the fact that his measures to solve the problem of student turbulence were far from effective. In January 1902, the students of Moscow University renewed their campaign of protest in a public demonstration that was quelled only after nearly seven hundred demonstrators were arrested. Then the spirit of revolt seized St. Petersburg University again. When the authorities retaliated by an announcement that the institution was to be closed, some of the students locked themselves in the classrooms and defied the gendarmes until driven out by force. In other university cities, students, sometimes joined by workers, surged into the streets, flaunting red flags, singing and shouting for rights and improved conditions.

Unarmed demonstrators were easily subdued, of course, but they tallied every instance of the use of force against themselves as demerits against brutal and unjust authority. They had a very real complaint when, in March, the Law on Exceptional Measures was invoked against the arrested Moscow students with the result that sixty-seven of them were exiled into Siberia for terms of up to five years and over 500 were sentenced to short jail terms.

At this point the spirit of revolt broke through whatever hesitation had stayed those young Socialist Revolutionaries who swore by terror as a tool of revolution. Among students and workers in all parts of Russia, they began to make extensive plans for the death of hated officials. Minister of Interior Sipyagin, whom they blamed for the severe Moscow sentences, headed the list of those they marked for immediate assassination. They planned the deed carefully and carried it out with dispatch. As executioner, they chose tall, blond Stepan Balmashev, a twenty-one-year-old party member, who could look and act the part of an imperial aide-de-camp. On April 2, dressed in military uniform, he approached the minister unchallenged and calmly shot him. Sipyagin died before the end of the day.

The news of the occurrence shook the tsar, but it did not change his mind. On the very day of the assassination, he wrote to Meshchersky, "Now we need not only determination but also severity, and believe me, it is in my soul." [6] Two days later, he named Vyacheslav Plehve as minister of interior and instructed him to continue Sipyagin's policies. There was no mistaking the meaning of this appointment. Nicholas knew Plehve's record as the strong-handed director of the police department of the ministry of interior under Alexander III, then as a major official in the State Council and a supporter of Bobrikov's rigorous policy in Finland. He knew also that, although Plehve was of German origin, he considered himself wholly Russian, and that he supported official nationalism with every fiber of his very tough being. He was the kind of man to impress on the country the fact that the tsar had no intention of yielding to pressure of any kind. There would likely be friction between him and the other strong man in the government, Witte, but that would be welcomed by many who had come to resent Witte's arrogation of ever-widening authority.

Shortly after appointing Plehve, Nicholas relieved General Vannovsky of his post as minister of education. He reasoned that, because the general had not been able to bring the stormy students under control, he was essentially responsible for Sipyagin's death. Furthermore, though he had been asked to suggest plans for educational reorganization, his response had been unsatisfactory. To replace him, the imperial choice fell on Gregory Zenger, a classical scholar then serving in the ministry of education, who had the support—with some reservations—of Pobedonostsev. As Zenger took over the ministry, he had the advantage of having already a thorough acquaintance with Nicholas' ideas, some of them inspired by Meshchersky, about shoring up the unsound spots in the educational system. The tsar had become convinced that still further changes were necessary if student unrest was to be eradicated, and he now proposed specific revisions at the secondary and higher levels. They included restricting university enrollment, admitting to classical gymnasiums only those students preparing for a university education, converting most of the secondary schools into terminal technical institutions organized where possible as boarding schools and staffed insofar as possible by retired army officers or members of the army reserve, and providing "proper" study material for all. He would have curricula changed in whatever way necessary to suit the over-all purpose of education as he conceived it—to instill religious faith, honor, and respect for the family along with devotion to throne and fatherland. Thirty-six years had passed since Alexander II, with the Karakozov episode fresh in his mind, had issued a rescript in similar vein. Obviously the formula had not effected a lasting cure of the seditious infection, and many responsible men would have advised the tsar against prescribing it again if he had given them the chance.

During the period when heightened student disorder was most pressing, developments outside the country began to demand an uncommon amount of attention also.

In this area of his obligation, Nicholas soon found not only that precedent was lacking in some of the situations he had to face but also that, in what had gone before, the government's foreign policy had always been more involved and less clear-cut than its domestic policy. However, like his father, he insisted on being intimately involved in all foreign affairs. The course he followed, unfortunately, was too often charted by a number of hands—the unavoidable consequence of his taking advice from various sources, frequently disparate and conflicting ones. His procedures were therefore at times erratic to the point of confusion and apparently dictated by expedience rather than principle.

Witte, for one, was ever ready with advice, for he considered himself an indispensable aide in foreign affairs, whether as a maker and preserver of imperial status or as an empire builder. Just as he nonchalantly intruded in domestic matters, he unhesitatingly stepped into foreign matters, sometimes ahead of the foreign minister, and shouldered his way whenever possible to the side of the tsar in order to "guide" him. Even when Nicholas had tired of Witte's rough ways and become resentful of his patronizing manner, he was often won over by the very assurance and vigor of the man.

The problem that faced the tsar just now involved Russia's interests in the Far East, on which, as on everything else, Witte tried to be in the forefront of advisers. But it happened that the tsar already had a kind of guide in this instance: his own notion of Russia's "Asiatic mission," though so far he had followed it in a decidedly muddled fashion. His previous direction of relations with China, where the trouble was now coming to a head, was typical. He had approved Witte's turning the Chinese predicament at the end of the Sino-Japanese War of 1894–95 to Russian advantage by a number of "generous" acts: extending loans, arranging for the establishment of the Russo-Chinese Bank, and offering Russian "protection from attack" through a scheme based on China's conceding to Russia the right to build the Chinese Eastern railway from west to east across Manchuria.* Yet he had allowed his foreign minister Muravev to take some conspicuously ungenerous steps: to endorse the Open Door policy and to involve Russia in the great-power scramble for territory and concessions in China, from which he had emerged, in 1898, with a twenty-five-year lease on the Liaotung Peninsula with its two coveted ports, Dalny and Port Arthur, as well as a concession to build another advantageous railroad line, the South Manchurian, which would connect Harbin, on the Chinese Eastern, with Dalny. Then, within a year, in another twist of diplomatic illogic, he was to support Count Vladimir Lamsdorf (whom he had made minister of foreign affairs on the death of Muravev) in a declaration of Russia's "deep concern" for China's national integrity.

In 1900, Nicholas took a significant position when members of a Chinese nationalist society, the Boxers, broke out in a frenzied counterblast against aggressive foreigners. On learning that they were attacking the foreign legations in Peking, he did not hesitate to add Russian troops to the quickly organized international "defense" force. Nor did he hesitate to order troops into Manchuria when the insurgents threatened the Chinese Eastern railway and the South Manchurian line, still under construction. This move into Manchuria was a brave display of assurance—and, some would say, a declaration of intention—on Russia's part. It could be interpreted both as an invasion of Chinese territory and as a warning-off to Japan, in whose dream of empire Manchuria figured prominently—particularly the Liaotung Peninsula, on which in recent years she

---

* This concession not only gave Russia a shortcut for the Trans-Siberian route to Vladivostok but also put a sizable strip of Chinese territory under Russian administration for a period that might extend to eighty years.

had been constrained to relinquish a foothold and had seen her advantage transferred to Russia. The implication had no influence on what appeared to be Nicholas' rule-of-thumb policy. After the Boxer Rebellion had been quelled and peace negotiations with China begun, he simply added to its ambiguity through two further measures. On the one hand, he approved the holding of a Russian occupation force in Manchuria to induce compliance with demands he had put to the Chinese government, though a few weeks earlier he had agreed to the withdrawal of all troops as soon as danger had passed; on the other hand, he made it known that Russia would firmly oppose any peace terms imposing harsh conditions on China.

While the Russian negotiators were involved with those of other powers in what proved to be an unusually prolonged session of give-and-take at China's expense after the rebellion, two enterprising Russians were busily contriving another Far Eastern involvement for their country. Former guards officers Alexander Bezobrazov and Vladimir Vonlyarlyarsky had devised a scheme which they now represented as a means whereby Russia, through the financing and handling of operations on an extensive timber concession in northern Korea, could establish a foothood that would serve as an invaluable outpost for later development of political influence in that area. Their scheme, shrewdly advanced by Bezobrazov through his friends in court and high society circles, had fascination for many, including the tsar, members of the imperial family, government officials, and ranking military men. They were attracted to it not only because of its alleged potentialities for the empire but also because of its promise of immediate gain for those willing to become involved. Others, however, interpreted it as a foolhardy enterprise and a dishonorable retraction of a Russian agreement guaranteeing Japanese economic preponderance in Korea. Witte was an outspoken opponent of the undertaking; practical as he was, he had yet to accept the fact that it was usually futile to protest against the imperial will—which, in this case, was strongly underwritten by his arch-opponent, Plehve.

Again, Russia's course was up to Nicholas. The differences among his advisers were irreconcilable.

However compelling the tsar's interest in the Far East, he could not keep it focused there in order to see any development through to its conclusion just then; the near-at-hand was crowding out the remote.

In addition to the student unrest, still by no means expunged, continuing uneasiness was reported from many quarters. An industrial
depression was throttling down the new prosperity, idling some of
the factories, and disturbing workers, who could see their recent
gains beginning to disappear. Another bad harvest was inflicting
widespread suffering on the peasantry. There was further evidence of
Finnish defiance as Russian conscription was introduced in the
grand duchy. These matters troubled Nicholas, of course, but he
could not see that they required any reconsideration of policy. Most
of the people were blaming Witte for both the depression and the
bad harvest, and the tsar was inclined to let him handle the problems
and face alone the resentment that was so obviously building up
against him. As for the Finns, he continued to think that they would
settle down when they recognized the cost of doing otherwise.

Just after Plehve's appointment, when the tsar was anticipating
the effective control of disturbances among his youthful subjects, he
learned that rebelliousness was erupting at another level. By the
summer of 1902, the black-earth region was experiencing an outbreak of the worst peasant violence since the 1880's. In the provinces
of Kharkov and Poltava, angry peasants in organized groups descended upon dozens of estates, drove the owners away, and began
looting and burning. As with past disorders, the turbulence subsided
when troops were rushed in and the peasant leaders hauled out before their followers and flogged, but the scar remained. Plehve
charged the trouble to the SR's, who were known to be organizing
peasant brotherhoods in some provinces. Nicholas was anxious to
believe it to have been instigated by "outside, pernicious" forces, for
he never liked to think that the peasant heart, uninfluenced, harbored any insubordination or violence.

He had hitherto considered the rural economic problems chiefly
from the point of view of the nobles, but he could no longer ignore
the fact that peasants also had to be taken into account: obviously
economic distress was making them more susceptible to "outside,
pernicious" guidance. It was a deplorable situation but, as he saw it,
not yet portentous. It required his attention, but it did not lead him
to consider tampering with existing institutions, either the village
commune of the peasants or the established position of the landed
nobles. Plehve would have to study the matter and work out some
viable solution that would not alter the social structure. The tsar's
only immediate duty was to make sure that the concerned parties,
nobles as well as peasants, understood his position. Accordingly,

when attending maneuvers that summer in the heart of the black-earth region, he called together the local nobility and, separately, the peasant elders, and addressed them plainly and directly. His remarks, though prepared by Meshchersky, reflected his considered attitude toward those concerned. He assured the nobles that he was sensitive to their problems and that it would be his "constant concern" to strengthen their class, the "traditional bastion of order and of the moral strength of Russia." Then, speaking to the peasants, he warned them that the authorities would deal harshly with any new disorders. He reminded them of his father's advice not to heed false rumors about redistribution of land but to obey the marshals of the nobility and admonished them: "Remember that one does not get rich by stealing from others, but from honest work, thrift, and obedience to God's commandments." [7]

Nicholas' regard for the autocratic mandate and his belief that the pattern of his life was preordained led him to accept final responsibility for all the difficulties that plagued Russia. Still, during the first eight years of his reign, he left their handling, for the most part, to his appointed agents and failed to come to grips effectively with any of the basic problems. He always appeared to welcome any freedom from the continuous pressures of the official milieu.

In the fall of 1902, he found a few weeks of such freedom by accompanying his family to their villa in Livadia, where life at least seemed calmer. Although his routine work followed him (twice-a-week couriers provided the liaison with St. Petersburg), the immediacy of it did not. Here he could take long hikes, play tennis, and give some time to reading in his favorite fields, Russian history and literature.

Distance from the center of court life seemed also to relax the stress of certain unsettling personal matters. Recently, there had been a plethora of them: the obvious discord that had developed between his mother and Alexandra, the state of disunity within the imperial family, his own growing impatience with the domineering Witte, the recent disgraceful behavior of his uncle the Grand Duke Paul, who had willfully married the former wife of a brother officer after explicitly promising that he would not do so. There were other things, of course, that could not be dismissed from the mind as readily as these; the death of his beloved brother George was one of them. Although more than three years had passed since the grand duke died—of a lung hemorrhage, alone in Transcaucasia, where he had gone for his health—the pain of personal loss remained with the tsar.

The death of George, the older of his brothers, had made it necessary that, in obedience to imperial law, Nicholas name his other brother, Michael, as heir presumptive since he himself had no son; but he had not felt it necessary to make plans for the eventuality of Michael's succession. It was true that Alexandra had borne only daughters (the fourth, Anastasia, in May of the preceding year), but she was only thirty years old and there was no reason to doubt that she would yet bear a son.

His chief worry, just now, concerned Alexandra herself. The problem of the succession had become deeply distressing to her, and her anxiety for a son, for the fulfilling of her "duty" to provide an heir, had become so intense that she was losing interest in all unrelated matters. When they were in Livadia two years earlier, she had suffered the unfortunate experience of a false pregnancy, which both indicated a neurotic tendency and proved a stimulus to its intensification. Since then, it had expressed itself in her deepening attachment to religion, in her growing sensitivity to social slights and animosities, and in her desire to restrict her personal contacts to those with whom she felt secure.

As she had become absorbed in this mood, Alexandra had accepted the friendship of those she found agreeable to it. Among them were two women, now favored as her "dear" Militsa and Anastasia, who impressed her as particularly understanding. Known in court circles as the "Montenegrin princesses" (being daughters of Prince Nicholas of Montenegro), they were members of the imperial family by virtue of marriage—Militsa to the Grand Duke Peter Nicholaievich, Anastasia to Prince George Romanovsky. They were friendly and spirited women who, when not dabbling in Balkan politics, devoted much of their time and attention to mysticism and spiritualism. Alexandra found them sympathetic confidants, and since their belief in the "powers beyond man" coincided with her own, she respected their counsel. Through them, she became acquainted with the French faith healer known in their circle simply as Philippe, who assured her that faith fortified by prayer would bring the realization of her desire for the birth of a son.[8] With his encouragement, she hit upon the notion of sponsoring the canonization of the early-nineteenth-century ascetic monk Seraphim as an expression of spiritual dedication and veneration that would hasten the answer to her prayer for a son.

During this stay in Livadia, she seemed content, looking forward to the canonization of Seraphim, which had been set for the following summer, though she was not yet altogether convinced that it had been necessary to set it so far ahead. She had asked that the ceremony be held in the summer of 1902; but, when Over-Procurator Pobedonostsev demurred at the thought of speeding up the formal arrangements for such an important event, Nicholas had quietly given him a year in which to make preparations. It was the first significant matter in which the tsar had to stand between Alexandra's determination and official opposition to it. Having appeased those concerned on each side of the issue, he could now put it aside along with the countless others that he hoped would remain quiescent.

All in all, so far as Nicholas could judge, the problems that faced him as he approached the end of his eighth year of rule were neither extraordinary nor critical. If, for the coming years, his destiny should provide no heavier burdens, perhaps he could yet achieve the comfortable grasp of his imperial duties that he usually managed to display but all too rarely felt.

XII

Last Warning

NICHOLAS II, 1903–1906

B Y 1903, there was no escaping the fact that some of Nicholas' ministers, by their demonstrative confidence, had led him to unrealistic expectations. Foremost among the misleaders was Minister of Interior Plehve.

It had been easy for the tsar, given his inclination toward complacency, to overlook the real trouble underlying the assassination of Sipyagin, for instance, when his successor displayed such apparent understanding of both cause and cure. From the time Plehve was given the direction of the department of state police, in 1880, through thirteen years of other service in the ministry of interior and eight years as imperial state secretary, he had not deviated from his conviction that a farsighted program under resolute administration —both of which he could supply—would bring a state of lasting tranquility to Russia. When he was given the comprehensive authority necessary to test that conviction, he promised the tsar a greatly improved future. He would insure it by a series of concurrent accomplishments: he would conciliate the "dark people," labor as well as the peasantry, conciliate the "sensible" elements among the educated, and uproot the revolutionary movement. He would do all this and yet adhere to Sipyagin's administrative policies.

While feeling his way in the matter of conciliating labor, Plehve learned something of the rough and precarious terrain between theory and practice. He wanted to follow a course of reform that would reinstate some of the practices initiated by Bunge, but abandoned early in the reign of Alexander III, and continue with plans of his own. However, one of his first steps—and, as it proved, a most injudicious one—was not of his own planning: he tacitly approved a project conceived by Sergei Zubatov, chief of the Moscow secret police, and begun in that city during the ministry of Sipyagin. Known as "police socialism," it was a scheme whereby the secret police were to counter the influence of revolutionaries among workers by providing legally some of the things that the revolutionary agitators were urging them to seek illegally. The workers would be permitted to organize, set up meeting places with limited facilities for recreation and self-improvement, and openly discuss their needs and aspirations. At the same time police agents would undertake to protect the workers' legal rights, insure the proper monitoring of working conditions by factory inspectors, and see that factory owners grant needed improvements, including even the gradual reduction of daily working hours. The purpose was to convince the workers that the tsar's relationship to them was a personally concerned and beneficent one, like that of a father to his children, and that any suggestions to the contrary were misleading and unsound. As a means of subverting the subverters, police socialism was judged by Moscow officials to be a promising undertaking, and Plehve allowed it to be extended to other industrial cities.

To him it was worth a trial—to score a point against Witte, if for no other reason. Witte naturally objected to interference in his ministry's affairs by police agents serving the ministry of interior; that, as he saw it, was exactly what police socialism sanctioned when police agents were allowed to concern themselves with factory inspection, legally under the ministry of finance, and with such matters as working hours and factory conditions, which he regarded as strictly within the domain of the factory owners, the stalwarts of his economic program. He objected in vain; the project was continued, and Plehve was planning other reforms that would vex him still more.

Labor, however, was no longer passively waiting for the government to act in its behalf. Agitators, finding workers' organizations ready-made forums, were infiltrating them almost at will and, despite police vigilance, promoting an increase in strike activity. The workers were responding, not because of any particular interest in the distant political advantages set forth by the agitators but because of their hope for more immediate ones such as better wages and working conditions. The proletarian giant was waking to self-identity.

Some men in the government had become convinced of that fact as early as the fall of 1902, when the Rostov-on-Don workers had joined in a three-weeks' general strike, demanding political as well as economic changes and offering more than token resistance to the troops who contested their action. During the few weeks of relative calm following that strike, Plehve had prepared, and the tsar had approved, measures to give workers a limited means of legal expression (through so-called factory elders, who might represent them before employers) and to increase the employers' responsibility for their well-being. Still, "conciliation" was not achieved during that period.

In the summer of 1903, tens of thousands of workers in the industrial centers of southern Russia and Transcaucasia went on strike, demanding shorter hours, higher wages, better working conditions, and—what was becoming more significant—political reforms. Though they repeated the slogans they had been taught, these strikers were not revolutionaries. Neither were they yesteryear's loyal monarchists. Many of them rallied around the socialist agitators, rioted, destroyed property, fought police and troops. The change in their mood was beginning to impress the authorities.

The new leader of workers, as the police saw him, was "a special type of semiliterate *intelligent,* who feels obliged to spurn religion and family, to disregard the law, and to defy and scoff at constituted authority." [1] When it was learned that those who led one of the major strikes that summer, in Odessa, were members of a police-sponsored organization, the dangers of police socialism were finally recognized; then that experiment, along with other unproven means of handling the growing labor problem, was abandoned. The old methods must be shored up, it was decided, and made to serve; with them, Plehve had a comfortable familiarity.

As for the peasant problem, the new minister had in mind a special approach. He began by trying diligently to win the cooperation of Dmitri Shipov, the highly respected and influential chairman of the Moscow zemstvo board. If anyone among the educated were "sensible," by Plehve's standards, it was Shipov, who believed fervently in the monarchy and its traditional institutions. He also feared for the future of the monarchy unless the people were protected from the arbitrary power of the bureaucracy and unless they had some means of reaching the ear of the tsar with their complaints and aspirations. To win him would be to gain a hand in two of the problem areas: among the peasants, who constituted the majority of the "dark people," and among the educated.

Plehve was hopeful that Shipov and those who looked to his leadership would be one with the government when they became acquainted with the direct measures he was planning for the countryside, aimed at giving the peasants a more satisfactory sense of personal freedom and closeness to the hands that governed them. He intended to relieve them of collective responsibility for communal indebtedness, to make it easier for them to leave their communes, and to make financial assistance more accessible to them. He intended also to provide that much of peasant legislation originate in the provinces, where there was a close understanding of local problems, rather than in the central government. All these plans, it seemed to him, should appeal to the zemstvos.

But even as the preparation of the new legislation progressed, he was discrediting himself with the zemstvo leaders by his official acts. One of his first ministerial tasks had been to deal with the aftermath of the peasant riots in the provinces of Kharkov and Poltava, and he had proceeded in the traditional high-handed and impersonal manner, giving priority to insurance against repetition, whereas the zemstvos sought immediate consideration for what lay behind the outbreaks. In addition, they soon saw that the countryside was becoming another area for the acrimonious sparring between him and Witte, each having a special commission from the tsar to study rural problems. Then, early in 1903, he lost the confidence of the zemstvos completely by supporting measures to increase the power of the provincial governors and strengthen the district police forces. Neither Shipov nor any other leader would become allies of his ministry when it was in the process of providing for them more government interference and bureaucratic obstructions.

Another man Plehve chose to woo as part of his plan to conciliate the educated was the liberal Paul Milyukov, the last volume of whose *Studies in the History of Russian Culture* had been published to wide acclaim in 1901. Though Milyukov, who believed in democratic, constitutional government, was hardly "sensible" by the minister's standards, he was a man of prestige and learning, whose goodwill would be invaluable to the government. To win him would justify overlooking certain aspects of his past. Beginning in his stu-

dent days at Moscow University, the talented Milyukov had consistently divided his time between studies and politics. As a student, he
participated in liberal demonstrations; later, as a professor at his
alma mater, he encouraged young liberals in political action; and,
since Nicholas' accession, he had shown no willingness to abandon
his involvements inimical to the government. Even while he was being plied with inducements by Plehve—including, unbelievably, the
post of minister of education—he harbored the satisfying knowledge
that Peter Struve's journal *Liberation,* which at the time enjoyed
both his favor and his collaboration, was to be smuggled into Russia
from Stuttgart as an organ of opposition to the very government that
Plehve was trying so unconventionally to reinforce. Still, Milyukov
was willing to cooperate if given evidence of square-dealing on the
part of the government. Until that evidence was forthcoming, however, he would be moved neither by Plehve's persuasion nor by his
threat, "If you do not make peace with us, at least do not enter into
open conflict with us. If you do, we will sweep you away." [2]

As Plehve failed with Shipov and Milyukov, so he failed with other
men who might have helped to set the government on a safer course.
The reason was two-fold. He could not pursue the repressive policies
of Sipyagin and still convince dissidents of the government's goodwill. Being a man inordinately interested in operational details (as
an associate saw him, a "superlative clerk"), he confounded his own
most commendable efforts by reducing all social and political problems to administrative challenges. The prospect was not appealing
to those who sought tangible improvements.

A year after Plehve had become minister of interior, liberals were
beginning to discuss the idea of organization among themselves as
the only means for achieving practical reforms. In the summer of
1903 a group of zemstvo leaders, university professors, lawyers, and
other professionals meeting abroad gave serious consideration to a
plan for a secret coalition of local liberal groups in Russia to work
for political liberty, a necessary precondition for the improvement
of the masses. Six months would be required to bring the plan to its
conclusion (in the establishment of the Union of Liberation), but
there was no longer any defensible hope that the type of men who
conceived it were going to assemble in Plehve's camp.

Unable to win the friends he needed, Plehve relied increasingly on
the weapons of coercion: censorship, the Law on Exceptional Measures, the political police, and the Cossacks, most feared of the troops
employed in punitive actions against domestic disturbances. To keep

his eye on the revolutionary movement, he increased the use of secret agents to such an extent that the government became an important silent partner in revolutionary activities. One who served the government thus secretly, Evno Azef, served also as chief of the SR's terrorist arm, the Fighting Organization. Before long, both the opposition and, significantly, many supporters of the throne began to charge Plehve with deliberately callous misdeeds as he used more and more arbitrary authority to harass liberals, interfere with zemstvo work, accelerate Russification, and persecute the Jews.

When a violent, two-day pogrom occurred in the Jewish section of the Bessarabian town of Kishinev during the Easter season of 1903, resulting in the death of forty-five Jews as well as the beating of hundreds and the plundering of homes and shops, Plehve was accused of having instigated the atrocity. Though the accusation was unjustified, it could not be denied that his anti-Semitic policy encouraged such outrageous acts. Like many of his colleagues—the tsar also—he had accepted as true the charge that the Jews were "leading the revolutionary movement" and "putting on airs"; he was not averse to their being taught "a lesson." [3] His defensive interpretation of individual cases, however, could not alter the accumulating evidence that the tightening of controls was neither weakening nor intimidating the opposition. In May, the governor of Ufa, General Nicholas Bogdanovich, was assassinated by an SR member in retribution for his having ordered troops to fire on strikers. As the weeks passed, the number of persons accused of political crimes mounted as never before.

Whatever his personal blame or lack of it, Plehve had worked himself into an unenviable position by the middle of 1903. He was not the monster that some of his critics pictured him as being, but he was the willing executor of harsh and hateful policies that had returned little good either to him or to his country. And it was becoming evident to practical men that he could force those policies no further; he had reached a dead end. The predicament of Nicholas II's Russia was now strikingly like that which Peter Valuev had observed in the Russia of nearly four decades earlier: "All our troubles are in fact caused by the current need for new forms, but we seek to preserve the old ones. We demand obedience, but in the name of what? Only in the name of duty to obey and the right to command. . . . We move in a vicious circle from which we cannot escape." [4]

Still, Plehve did not experience the sense of alarm and dread that a more sensitive man might have felt. He admitted privately that the government would have to make concessions sooner or later, but he felt that for the time being the situation was reasonably well in hand.[5] Though he viewed the immediate future with equanimity, he had no objection to a "short, victorious war" as a means of rallying the people behind the tsar; however, he did not think of war as an imperious need.[6]

When Plehve spoke of war, he had in mind a war with Japan. Russia's future in the Far East had been a popular subject of speculation and debate in and around the imperial court since the time of the Boxer Rebellion; because Japan was known to be an ambitious competitor, the likelihood of trouble with her had been an unavoidable consideration.

Even before the rebellion, the Japanese had come to regard Russia as a dangerous and inimical rival for power in southern Manchuria and Korea, particularly after she had begun the construction of the South Manchurian railway and the fortification of Port Arthur as a strong naval base. Afterwards, their apprehension was stirred by two additional circumstances: Russia's continued occupation of Manchuria, which suggested that she was laying claim to that area as a Russian sphere of influence; and the development of the Bezobrazov scheme for a Russian-held timber concession in northern Korea, an obvious screen for extending Russian influence there. So the Japanese government, recognizing the necessity for a confrontation before Russia should become too well established to be dislodged, decided in mid-1903 to broach the problem and offer to negotiate. Basically its position was one of willingness to recognize Russian preponderance in the northern part of Manchuria—but not in the southern—in return for Russian acceptance of Japanese preponderance in Korea. Details, of course, would have to be worked out.

Being pacific by nature, Nicholas agreed to negotiations, but without the intention of allowing any but minor Russian concessians. To him Japan was, after all, an insignificant "barbarian" power, and what she wanted or did not want was of little moment. His lofty unconcern was based on a wholly unrealistic evaluation, which underrated Japan's potential strength and overrated Russia's. The fact was that his country had again become as diplomatically isolated as it had been on the eve of the Crimean War. England and the United States were outspoken opponents of Russia's Far Eastern policies; Germany's William II, while pretending to support Russia against the "Yellow Peril," was secretly assuring Japan that Germany would be a benevolent neutral if war should come; France, now forming an entente with England, could not be expected to support Russia.

Japan, on the other hand, had built up some practical advantages by posing both as a friend of the Open Door in China and as the sloe-eyed innocent confronting the wicked Russian giant. The international press had responded favorably and, better yet, England had been moved, early in 1902, to forsake her "splendid isolation" and enter into an alliance with Japan. In addition, the Japanese people, their feelings whipped up by the patriotic Black Dragon Society, were ready to fight the encroaching giant.

Within the ranks of Nicholas' advisers, the conflict of opinion on the whole Far Eastern question gradually grew sharper as proposals and counterproposals traveled between Tokyo and St. Petersburg. The key problem came to be Russia's position in Manchuria. Minister of Foreign Affairs Lamsdorf, of whom it was said that he was prudent to the point of imprudence, advised the evacuation of Manchuria by gradual stages in order neither to give the appearance of hastening to appease the Japanese nor to continue offending them. Minister of War Kuropatkin, though favoring Far Eastern expansion, pointed out the strategic inconvenience of trying to hold all of Manchuria. Sharp-tongued Witte declared it foolhardy to continue gratuitously alarming the Japanese when there was no profit, either general or economic, in doing so. Others urged aggressiveness, among them Plehve, as a matter of course favoring the opposite of whatever Witte favored. Bezobrazov and his clique of influential supporters in St. Petersburg argued that the Japanese understood only the language of power and that the tsar should therefore be bold; Admiral Eugene Alexeev, Russia's aggressive naval commander in the Far East, impatiently called for preparation and action.

The arguments raging about the sensitive tsar were almost more than he could bear, yet he dreaded making the decisions necessary to end them. He got away from them briefly in the summer of 1903, to attend the ceremony that meant so much to Alexandra, the canonization of Seraphim. By the time he returned, in August, he had steeled himself to take a firm position on the Far East.

Nicholas' first steps were incisive and surprisingly drastic. He named Admiral Alexeev viceroy over all Russian holdings east of Lake Baikal and, to the dismay of the ministers of foreign affairs, finance, and war, gave him complete authority over all diplomatic, economic, and military matters in that region. To lay down policy for Viceroy Alexeev, he formed a central committee with himself as chairman, by that act taking personal leadership in all matters pertaining to the critical area. Then he climaxed his new firmness by ridding himself of the vexing Witte, who was by then involved in practically every ramification of the Far Eastern problem, by the neat trick of "advancing" him to the "highest post in the empire," the chairmanship of the Committee of Ministers, actually an honorary retirement post. His choice as successor in the ministry of finance, Edward Pleske, was a capable man, but one whose ill health made it impossible for him even to approach Witte's personal engrossment in imperial affairs—a fact that eased tensions in some quarters while leading to difficulties in others.

As negotiations with the Japanese continued, neither power being satisfied with the progress and each growing daily more distrustful of the other, the war fever rose in the military circles on both sides; Nicholas, however, remained firmly pacifistic. Admiral Alexeev grumbled at the inaction, declaring that if Alexander III were alive, he would give the Japanese a thrashing that they would not quickly forget; [7] Kuropatkin counseled the starting of troop reinforcements to the Far East. But the tsar maintained that, though Russia had no reason to fear war, she should avoid precipitating one by any untoward move that might provoke the Japanese. He was still unable to see that Russia had already provoked the Japanese by establishing herself so firmly on the Liaotung Peninsula and by probing into Korea. And he was leaving out of consideration one highly important fact: that Russia's having the largest army in the world and one of the largest navies could not be counted on to intimidate an enemy who could see the prospect of a war begun and ended before Russia, 6,000 miles away, could send effective forces to the fighting zone. In the fall of 1903, he was sufficiently confident of a peaceful settlement that he accompanied Alexandra to Darmstadt to attend a funeral, ignoring widespread rumors of Japan's preparations for war as well as Minister of the Court Fredericks' argument that his presence was needed in St. Petersburg to allay public concern. He insisted that he must act according to his conscience and that, anyway, the rumors were probably misguidance inspired by the English.

The tsar was away for a month, during which he spent some time at his Polish hunting preserves, apparently unworried, since the Far Eastern matter still remained a "paper problem." Each week, he felt, was adding to the justification of his contention that, even if war with Japan was inevitable, time was Russia's best ally. The delay thus far had made it possible for Kuropatkin to consider means for getting reinforcements to the troops already in Manchuria and for the Grand Duke Alexis to examine plans for sending auxiliary naval assistance, if the need should arise, to strengthen the squadron based at Port Arthur.

When he had held out against his war-minded advisers until the end of the year and had just finished a revised proposal of settlement (Russia's fourth) to be considered by Japan, he saw no reason to re-study his tactics; rather he felt a resurgence of confidence. At the official reception on New Year's Day, 1904, he sought out the Japanese envoy, Shinchiro Kurino, and talked to him like a Dutch uncle, im-pressing on him that Russia was "quite conscious of her own strength," though there was a limit to her patience.[8]

As it happened, the patience on the other side was approaching a nearer limit. On January 24, 1904, the Japanese government broke off negotiations and recalled Kurino. Even then, Nicholas was re-luctant to change his attitude. He tried anxiously to reopen nego-tiations, though he admitted the likelihood of war and agreed to some active preliminary preparations. He went so far as to order all Russian forces in the Far East on the alert and give Admiral Alexeev permission to assemble supplies and transport facilities. But he made it clear that there was to be no unprovoked gesture of hostility: if war came, it would be the doing of the Japanese, not the Russians.

The Japanese obliged. Without troubling to declare war, they made their first strike on the night of January 26—against the ships of Russia's Pacific Squadron lying at anchor before Port Arthur, dis-abling three of them. It was a wholly unexpected attack. In fact, the ease with which the Japanese torpedo boats sighted their targets was due to the festive illumination in the town behind the Russian ships: a celebration honoring the name day of the port admiral's wife was under way.

None of Nicholas' advisers, not even Alexeev, had expected the Japanese to begin action at this heavily fortified point, nor had they properly anticipated the Japanese strategy. The next day brought a belated reassessment. The Japanese fleet, under Admiral Togo, en-gaged the Russian squadron at mid-morning and, in less than an hour, had it under such fire that every able vessel put about and made for the protection of the inner harbor. Thus, within twenty-four hours, the Russians had been driven into an unfavorable posi-tion, their ships faced with returning to the unequal fight or risking a blockade that would hold them helpless, unable to prevent the Japanese from undertaking to reduce Port Arthur by land assault.

There was also the possibility—which the Russians discounted and their opponents hoped to realize—that, their offshore movements now virtually unimpeded, the Japanese would be able to land sufficient numbers in southern Manchuria not only to prohibit relief for the port but also to take the offensive against the Russians in the north before they could strengthen their forces.

Nicholas had blundered into his first war. He recognized that the Port Arthur incident was a humiliation for Russia and that, to his sorrow, he would now have to order men to risk their lives in retaliation; but his confidence in Russia's incontestable advantages remained unshaken. He had simply to assign the proper men to handle the unexpected developments, he felt, and the contretemps would soon be cleared up. Viceroy Alexeev, without question, was already in his element; his only fear was understood to be that Russia would let the Japanese off too easily, before they had received the thrashing they deserved. To command the army, the tsar chose General Kuropatkin (replacing him as minister of war by General Victor Sakharov) and sent him off with the assurance that he would return with the aureole of the valiant Skobelev. He knew that many military men disparaged Kuropatkin's ability, but the choice would have popular support, and Nicholas believed that there would be few difficulties to be faced in this brief war. The problem of the unfortunate Pacific Squadron he turned over to competent Admiral Stepan Makarov. General naval operations, of course, would remain the responsibility of the Grand Duke Alexis. The tsar had no doubt that he now had the right men in the right places and that accounts with Japan would soon be squared.

As reports of the Japanese "perfidy" were relayed from place to place throughout the country and the preparations for action came to public attention—troop trains being assembled, reservists marching through the streets, supplies being loaded—there seemed to be a promise that Plehve's evaluation of the public response to a war would prove correct. The tsar was particularly pleased to see "the generally sleepy nature" of his people roused to patriotic enthusiasm.[9] Even the students of St. Petersburg University were so caught up in the exhilaration that they joined the spirited crowds that made their way to the Winter Palace, sang "God Save the Tsar" with them, and cheered when the tsar appeared.

However, when no official effort was made to sustain the early fervor, much of it gradually disappeared in the unchanged routine of workaday lives. The war was, after all, a remote one, begun for reasons that most people did not understand or, if understood, they were not concerned about. As enthusiasm died down, there came into prominence a fact that had been temporarily overshadowed: not all of the people had rallied for tsar and fatherland. From the beginning, all socialists and some liberals had been antipathetic to Russia's position in the Far East, and there had been no hiatus in their expressed opposition.

The majority of the people did not share the views of the extremists, but few could regard the war complacently when reports of developments began to reach them. The news during the first months of 1904 set the tone: the sinking of the Pacific Squadron's flagship, the "Petropavlovsk," with Admiral Makarov and more than eight hundred of the ship's company aboard, a major Japanese victory on the Yalu River, Viceroy Alexeev's expectation that Port Arthur was doomed to a costly siege, accumulating evidence that many leaders in the Far East were guilty of irresponsibility and lack of alertness, Kuropatkin's continued delay in taking the offensive while the Japanese pushed across Manchuria, inadequate transportation facilities delaying reinforcements and supplies for the fighting men, disagreement on critical problems among military tacticians—none of it encouraging, all of it reinforcing the arguments of anti-war propagandists.

Another development to impress itself on the people as the months passed was the war's adverse effect on the domestic economy, which had just begun to recover from the recent depression when the Far Eastern crisis arose. A few industries, notably the metallurgical and leather, provided military supplies and therefore profited from the war. But the textile industry, the country's largest, was greatly slowed down because, as the call-up of reservists continued, the general home-front income was so reduced that civilian demand for textiles fell; and while the military services' demand grew somewhat, it was not sufficient to offset the decline. Consequently, manufacturers reduced their output, employment in textile centers dropped, and thousands of laborers were added to the ranks of those who saw reason to decry the war. When they joined their dissatisfied voices to those of students, professionals, and others who had come to oppose the war, the effect was that of restrained mutiny on the home front.

Nicholas still believed that general agitation of this nature could be toned down if the boldest and liveliest of the dissidents, the students, were properly restrained. To that end, he now appointed a new minister of education, General Vladimir Glazov, an experienced disciplinarian with a solid record as administrator of the General Staff Academy, and commissioned him to do something about the chaotic state of the schools. Student response to arbitrary control, however, grew steadily more resentful, more actively revolutionary, and it continued to be an important part of the public clamor.

By the beginning of summer, the belief that Russia, under the guidance of unfit officials, was drifting into dangerous waters was being expressed openly and with increasing frequency among the educated of the country and sometimes, to the chagrin of the officials implicated, diffused through foreign publications. One Russian, published anonymously—though identified as a responsible and highly placed man—in the July issue of the English *Quarterly Review,* denounced Plehve as a "Muscovite Grand Vizier," Pobedonotsev as a "Torquemada," and Meshchersky as a "Cagliostro," adding:

All that broad-minded monarchists like the present writer desire is to save our people without injuring the Tsar. Against monarchical institutions, without which our nation could not work out its high destinies, we have nothing to urge. Even the dynasty we accept as a fact. But we strongly hold that the affairs of the nation . . . should be conducted by competent and moderately honest men independently of Court influence and on ordinary business principles.[10]

These sentiments had the personal approval of many Russians who did not speak out so boldly. One of them, Alexis Suvorin, who published the popular jingoistic and ultramonarchistic daily newspaper *New Times,* recorded in his diary intimate thoughts very different from those he expressed publicly:

Under autocracy God himself rules. . . . The emperor receives instructions only from God. . . . But, since He is invisible, the emperor takes counsel with the first, best thing he meets—his wife, his mother, his stomach, his entire nature, and accepts all this as divine guidance. . . . [Absolutism] attracts whole swarms of idle, superfluous men who create offices for themselves.[11]

Among intellectuals generally, the mood of desperation was much as it had been during the Crimean War. The liberals, who had finally achieved the formal organization of their underground Union of Liberation, were quietly enlisting supporters throughout the country. As an organized body, they were now firmly dedicated to the belief that, to get results, action had to be initiated by the people.

In some quarters, particularly in areas where people were moved by nationalistic feelings, despair was approaching grim proportions. A few Finns and Poles showed no qualms about accepting from Japanese agents funds and arms to use in their fight against tsarism. One consequence of this growing alienation might have been expected to alert the tsar. Less than four months after the opening of hostilities in the Far East, a Finnish student murdered General Nicholas Bobrikov, harsh administrator of Russification in Finland; then, to dramatize his countrymen's despair, he committed suicide. But the tsar did not respond as expected. He wept for Bobrikov, but not for Finland or the political miscalculations and mistakes of his regime. To the vacant post he straightway sent Prince Ivan Obolensky, a man who could be trusted to make no concessions to the disaffected.

On July 15, however, distress came closer to the imperial doorstep. While Nicholas was waiting in his study at Peterhof for the arrival of Plehve to deliver the weekly report from the ministry of interior, he received the news that his minister, who had only two years earlier succeeded to his position on the assassination of Sipyagin, had just been killed by a bomb thrown at his carriage as he drove through the capital. Plehve's death, coming so soon after Bobrikov's, struck hard. That night the tsar wrote in his diary: "In the person of dear Plehve, I have lost a friend and irreplaceable minister of interior. The Lord visits us sternly with His wrath. To have lost two such loyal and devoted servants in so short a time! But such is His holy will."

The assassin, it was learned shortly, was Egor Sazonov, a twenty-five-year-old Socialist Revolutionary, who had been expelled from the university for his radical activities.* He was given a life sentence to hard labor, a punishment befitting the gravity of his crime as the tsar saw it, but disproportionately severe as many others saw it. Baron Aehrenthal, Austrian ambassador to St. Petersburg at the time, reported his amazement at the indifference he observed in the highest circles and the apathy, even hostility, with which "all strata" of the educated class viewed the "government's struggle against the revolutionary opposition." [12]

Many saw in Plehve's death an opportunity for the government to change its course, and Count Nicholas Muravev, the able minister of justice, undertook to do something about it. He pleaded with the tsar to understand that Plehve had misrepresented conditions, that things could not continue as they had been, and that the safe course was for him to be guided by the collective wisdom of his ministers.

---

* Much later, it was learned that Sazonov had been under the direction of the police agent Azef, who was also chief of the SR's Fighting Organization.

The tsar's reply was a pointed rebuff: "Would you have me form a cabinet with Witte?" [13] He was sure that he judged the situation better than those who advocated change: as he remarked on one occasion to Peter Stolypin, governor of Saratov, "If the intellectuals only knew with what enthusiasm the people receive me, they would fall in a faint." [14] He fully intended his next minister of interior to continue the policies of Sipyagin and Plehve.

For more than a month, however, the question of a successor remained open. Part of that time, the tsar's concern was with matters relating to an event of dynastic importance: the birth of a son, on July 30. Nothing could have brought more satisfaction to either Nicholas or Alexandra. At last, Russia had its tsesarevich, and the imperial couple had the answer to their prayers. The elaborate preparations for the ceremonial christening of the child—he was given the name Alexis—occupied the tsar for more than a week. After that, until late August, he allowed routine duties, including a trip south to review Cossack divisions, to take precedence over the appointment of a new minister of interior.

In the tsar's favor among limited choices, Boris Stürmer, who had served under Plehve and shared his views, stood highest. While the appointment was still under consideration, however, a number of influential men who knew Stürmer as a man of great pretensions and little moral courage, in disfavor with both the general public and zemstvo leaders, sought the help of Dowager Empress Marie Fedorovna in presenting an alternative. Through her, they recommended Prince Svyatopolk-Mirsky on the grounds that he had opposed the unpopular policies of the last two ministers; that, as a soldier and as governor general of Vilna, he had earned a reputation for loyalty, honesty, and moderation; and that he would be able to restore public confidence in the ministry of interior. Finally, at his mother's urging, Nicholas agreed—but with no great degree of enthusiasm—to offer Svyatopolk-Mirsky the post.

The prince accepted it, though he esteemed neither the tsar nor the position. He was willing to serve as a duty to his country, but he would not do so under false colors: he would first express his feelings about what lay ahead. His statement approximated what Loris-Melikov had pointed out to Alexander II. The government, he said, must come to terms with the people by distinguishing between subversives and critics, mitigating restrictions on the national and religious minorities, modifying press controls, and giving the educated a channel of communication with their tsar, perhaps through elected representatives in the State Council. It was his belief that, if these requirements were not met, the rift between government and people would inevitably become so wide that all the tsar's subjects would "either be under surveillance or engaged in surveillance." [15] He was particularly conscious of the trouble building up in areas at the mercy of overbearing administrators. Among them was one he did not specify to the tsar, the Grand Duke Sergei, who, as governor general of Moscow, was widely accused of treating the city as if it were his personal fief.

Nicholas appeared to agree in substance, if not in detail, with Syvatopolk-Mirsky's evaluation, and the prince took up his work in the belief that he had been accorded a mandate to change domestic policy and follow a new course.

While Svyatopolk-Mirsky was laying out his program for relieving the somberness on the home front, the clouds were thickening in the East as reverse followed reverse for the Russians. Port Arthur, invested and unrelieved, fought on against odds that mounted every day. The remaining vessels of the Pacific Squadron, under the command of Admiral Alexis Birilev since the death of Admiral Makarov, made their final attempt to break out, aiming at a run for the port of Vladivostok, and met inglorious and utter defeat by the Japanese fleet. The Grand Duke Alexis' only plan for reconstituting Russia's naval strength in that area was now to send out, as the Second Pacific Squadron, a number of reconditioned ships from the Baltic fleet, and it stirred little enthusiasm. Yet he could do no more, for the better warships, in the Black Sea fleet, were restricted to those waters under terms of the Straits convention of 1871. In Manchuria, General Kuropatkin, after responding to the pressures of impatience in St. Petersburg and finally abandoning his retreat-and-delay tactics in August, had made one stand (a losing one, at Liaoyang) and one thrust (a losing one, at the Sha Ho River), then pulled clear to settle down at Mukden—still without bringing credit to Russian arms.

Svyatopolk-Mirsky's first steps as minister of interior indicated that he might offer something to compensate for the continuing misfortunes of war. He rid himself of Plehve's close associates, including Stürmer; he announced that he believed in the good sense of the public and would seek its confidence. As if to prove the sincerity of his intentions, he permitted Shipov, chairman of the Moscow zemstvo board, to begin arranging for a congress of zemstvo officials.

Such measures suggested to many that, after a generation of chill inaction, the country was breaking free into a "political spring," a season of warmth and promising activity—perhaps a new era.

The beginning of Svyatopolk-Mirsky's ministry did, in fact, coincide with the beginning of a new era; but, despite the minister's personal expectations, it was not one inaugurated through his official accomplishments. He soon awoke to the fact that he was hoping to mediate between two parties—the tsarist government and the articulate public—neither of which he had properly understood when he set out. He had taken for granted both that he had the tsar's mandate for change and that the people would wait patiently while the change was being made; he would be dealing with a controversy among gentlemen and would be able to handle it accordingly. He was wrong on each count. The tsar honestly agreed with his new minister up to a point: he felt that some controls could safely be relaxed, and he admitted that it was high time to lift certain disabilities (such as those retained against religious dissenters merely to keep from offending crusty old Pobedonostsev); but he did not agree that the country faced an internal crisis. Consequently his mandate was quite limited. So also was the patience of the organized forces seeking change. Some individual leaders—Shipov, for example—behaved patiently, but they were in the minority. Others, observing officials seemingly in retreat on some issues, became the more intent on pressing for concessions that the government was not expected to grant of its own free will. These, organized to represent national minorities and the deprived or disadvantaged of all classes, were the ones who were leading the way into the new era.

The extent of the forces organized for action was indicated at a secret meeting of their representatives in Paris in October 1904. To that meeting came members of the Polish National League, the Finnish Party of Active Resistance, the Socialist Revolutionary Party, the Lettish Social Democratic Party, the Georgian Socialist-Federalists, the Armenian Revolutionary Federation, and the liberals' growing Union of Liberation. The goals on which they agreed at that time were explicit enough: to supplant Russian autocracy by democracy, and to gain the guarantee of rights for national minorities. The means by which these goals were to be reached had yet to be worked out.

Among those seeking action, the socialists spoke in the most resounding terms—of propaganda, recruiting, political strikes, and armed uprisings. However, while growing in number, they still resembled an enthusiastic guerrilla band more closely than an army of revolution. The liberals, on the other hand, who put their trust in peaceful—although illegal—pressure, had behind them enough solid support from the middle classes and the nobility to give them strength to act.

The liberals in the militant Union of Liberation had also the will to act. They had not agreed on a detailed program at this time, but they had agreed on principles. Their goal was liberation from tsarism; their tactic was to provide, through the mobilization of zemstvos, assemblies of the nobility, municipal councils, and professional groups, a demonstrative and unqualified demand for a constituent assembly. They were now ready to begin the open conflict against which Plehve had warned Milyukov.

The union scored its first victory—a partial one—at the zemstvo congress that Svyatopolk-Mirsky had allowed Shipov to assemble. Shipov had hoped that the congress, when it met in St. Petersburg in November, would celebrate the alleged spirit of amity now existing between government and society by asking for little more than the moderate reforms that the new minister was already drafting; but the majority, spurred on by the Union of Liberation, insisted on going further. They adopted resolutions calling for measures guaranteeing complete legal justice for all without discrimination and for an *elective legislature,* not an *advisory body,* thus overstepping their leader's advice and throwing down a provocative challenge to the government.

For the educated world this was a call to arms. There had not been a similar act of defiance in a generation. All over the country, zemstvos, municipal councils, and assemblies of the nobility began illegally and defiantly petitioning the tsar for representative government. Professional groups—doctors, lawyers, engineers, and teachers —began the practice of assembling at "political banquets," where they discussed the shortcomings of tsarism and daringly called for a constituent assembly.

This public waywardness brought Svyatopolk-Mirsky to the point of despair. Clearly the dialogue he had hoped to hold with society must be renounced before it could begin, and he expected therefore that the tsar would dismiss him out of hand.

But Nicholas had on his mind matters that he considered more pressing. The Second Pacific Squadron, the ragtag armada recently sent off on its 18,000-mile run to the relief of Port Arthur, had nearly involved Russia in war with England by mistakenly firing on some

English fishing boats in the North Sea; though the crisis had sub-sided, the settlement had not yet been made. Minister of Justice Muravev, sensing the hazardous drift of matters within the country, was asking to be relieved of his post. The Grand Duke Sergei, who furiously disapproved of Svyatopolk-Mirsky's course, was insisting on withdrawing from the governor-generalship of Moscow. Until the urgency of these problems was reduced, the tsar preferred not to look for a new minister of interior.

So Svyatopolk-Mirsky stayed on, feeling himself redundant but hopeful of somehow seeing his proposed reforms through. If he should fail, he feared, the outcome would be catastrophe for Russia. But the going was hard. Jealous subordinates were quietly sabotag-ing his efforts; most of the ministers were opposing him; Witte, while posing as his ally, was hoping to use him as a stepping-stone to power. The Grand Duke Sergei was pointedly calling him *Svyatopolk Okayanni* ("Svyatopolk the Damned")—an obvious reference to the eleventh-century ruler of that name who had been forced from the throne and killed in flight. At the Yacht Club, members were betting that the victor to come out of the melee would be a "Sergei": either Sergei Witte or the Grand Duke Sergei—certainly not Svyatopolk-Mirsky.

A self-deluded Sisyphus, Svyatopolk-Mirsky went on about his business. He prepared for the tsar's signature the draft of a ukase that would announce plans for the reforms he had been urging. The item on which he placed his chief hope of underwriting a reform program was the one promising the addition of elected members to the State Council. That, predictably, was the one about which the tsar wavered and about which, at the insistence of his uncle Sergei and Pobedonostsev, he finally balked. Like Alexander III, closing his ear to the "old siren song" of liberalism, he cut that item from the draft. He was still standing steadfast in the defense of autocracy.

Nicholas signed the bobtailed ukase on December 12 and sent it out as representative of the government's goodwill. It fell far short of that, as interpreted by the thousands who had been so energeti-cally informing the government of what was needed. The ukase delineated in stilted terms what the state would offer by way of im-proving the "social order": it would limit the application of the Law on Exceptional Measures, provide government insurance for work-ers, and ease the legal position of national and religious minorities. There was no word in it indicating that there would be any provision of means whereby the people might communicate their desires to the tsar. Rather, as if to emphasize the continuation of the old relationship betwen society and government, on the very day the ukase was issued, the tsar directed the police to greater vigilance and stricter enforcement of rules forbidding unlawful meetings, and ordered zemstvos, municipal councils, and assemblies of the nobility to confine themselves to their proper business.

By these acts Nicholas expected to end the hubbub that had been raging since his appointment of Svyatopolk-Mirsky. Yet he was not at ease about all the undertakings of his idea-ridden minister. His view of the man was loyally seconded by Alexandra, who always showed a personal interest in her husband's problems. She later made a fair statement of it in a letter to her sister Princess Victoria of Battenberg: "The Minister of Interior is doing the greatest harm— he proclaims grand things without having prepared them. It's like a horse that has been held very tight in hand, and then suddenly one lets the reins go. It bolts, falls, and it is more than difficult to pull it up again. . . . He won't believe what Nicky tells him, does not agree with his point of view." [16]

When he observed the public response to the ukase, expressions of bitter disappointment and accusations of betrayal, Svyatopolk-Mirsky found that he could take no more satisfaction than anyone else in what he had accomplished during the partial turnabout since Plehve's death. Seeing nothing ahead except the necessity to build more jails, he pleaded to be removed from the ministry. He even suggested to the tsar the names of men among whom he might find a replacement. One whom he recommended as a "decent" sort, Alexander Bulygin, assistant to the governor general of Moscow, was already under consideration by the tsar as a successor to the Grand Duke Sergei, who was still demanding to be relieved of his post. But Nicholas was faced by his usual quandary: he knew personally few able men from whom to choose officials. Moreover, in this instance as when Svyatopolk-Mirsky had previously expected to be relieved, he felt that he could not afford to concentrate on the problem, which could be temporarily disregarded—as others could not.

Nicholas was again becoming sadly conscious of his self-assumed kinship to St. Job the Sufferer. The most intimate reason was that the joy which he and Alexandra had found in the young Tsesarevich Alexis was now turning to ashes. The doctors had found the child to be afflicted with a rare and incurable ailment, hemophilia, and warned that he was liable to uncontrollable bleeding, internally from any slight blow or externally from even the smallest cut. The tragic implications of the diagnosis were exaggerated for the parents not only because of their love for their only son, now doomed—if he lived—to the limitations imposed by the painful and unpredictable disability, but also because of Alexandra's feeling of personal guilt: hemophilia was known to be hereditary in her family. Though they were determined to keep their sorrow a secret as long as they could, it was soon visibly affecting them. Alexandra, already a neurasthenic by contemporary definition, was becoming more unfavorably inclined toward those about her—colder to the many she disliked, more devoted to and possessive of her family, more given to weeping, more invalidic. Nicholas did not react so obviously, but his soft eyes could not conceal the fact that some inner sadness had settled on him.

Adding to the tsar's woe was the fact that, as the end of 1904 approached, his country's accumulation of misfortune seemed greater than at any time in the past.

Reports from the Far East continued to be disheartening. Kuropatkin remained at Mukden, his army still formidable but yet to be proved in battle. Viceroy Alexeev's officiousness had so interfered with effective action in the war theater that it had been necessary to recall him. In late December, Port Arthur, after one hundred and forty-eight days of desperate defense, had been surrendered (as great a blow to Nicholas as the fall of Sebastopol had been to his grandfather); with that, the Japanese siege force of thousands was released to join the inland forces against Kuropatkin. When news of this adversity overtook the Second Pacific Squadron, which had reached Madagascar on its way to the intended relief of the beleaguered port, its commander had questioned the tsar about the usefulness of continuing after the surrender. Nicholas had no answer but "Proceed." Everything possible would be done to reinforce the admittedly mediocre squadron, but, as soon as feasible, it should continue to the zone of action. The tsar's fatalism led him to see God's will in Port Arthur's fall, but not an indication that he should admit defeat for his country. On the contrary, he believed that, until God decreed otherwise, his duty was to fight on with every man and every kopeck at his disposal.

The reversals of the distant war were matched by other distressing considerations. Recently, for the first time, reservists called up for duty became defiant and had to be forcibly entrained. The liberals were stepping up their attack on what they considered the inadequacies of his ukase of December 12. The socialists were talking of

political strikes and dreaming of armed uprisings. Warsaw was unsettled as a result of the first armed act of Polish resistance in forty
years and a campaign of terror that the Polish Socialist Party had
organized in its wake. In Baku, 50,000 workers, almost the whole
labor force of that oil center, had gone out on strike, calling for better working conditions and a constituent assembly, and were holding
out doggedly against the authorities. In Moscow, university students
on strike were planning to organize armed political demonstrations
after the Christmas holidays.

Oddly enough, St. Petersburg and its environs appeared particularly free of disorder and active discontent before and during the
holidays. The prefect of the city, General Ivan Fullon, and a few
other officials knew that there was some tension in the factory districts, but they understood it to be well under control. They were
placing their confidence in the Assembly of St. Petersburg Factory
Workers, an organization of a few months' standing embodying the
principle of the ill-fated attempts at police socialism, which had
fallen into official disfavor two years earlier. Established among the
workers of the capital by the young priest Father George Gapon,
with the approval of Plehve and the secret cooperation of local police
officials, it had thus far seemed to serve its stated and approved purpose: to immunize workers against socialist influence by allowing
them, in their carefully supervised organization, to pass their time
pleasantly and talk about their problems in an Orthodox and monarchist atmosphere.

Those who were leaving the problem of worker discontent in the
hands of Father Gapon were doing so without a full understanding
of the man. He was not the tool his superiors thought him to be. He
saw himself as a prophet sent to aid the oppressed and cast down the
barrier by which the tsar's evil ministers had separated him from his
people and obstructed his view of their needs. He expected to take
an emphatic step toward that goal soon after the coming New Year.
He planned that on February 19, 1905, the anniversary of emancipation, he would lead his workers in an impressive march to the Winter
Palace and on their behalf place into the hands of the tsar a petition
beseeching him to end the war, grant representative government, and
bestow social justice upon his subjects. This was to be a token pil-
grimage under his personal leadership; Fullon knew nothing about
it at first.

The undertaking was quickened by circumstances. On January 3, workers who were members of the assembly brought the entire work force of the Putilov ironworks, 13,000 men, out on strike over a minor dispute. Within five days the strike spread to virtually all plants and factories in the city, idling some 150,000 workers. When Gapon saw the workers' utter indifference to their employers' appeals to resume work, it was his duty, if he was to abide by his understanding with the authorities, to help stop the strike. Instead, he took charge of it and made it an adjunct to the realization of his own scheme. He changed the date of the planned march to January 9 and began circulating the petition which he hoped to present to the tsar. Then he gave himself wholeheartedly to drawing the workers into the magic of his conception. He pictured for them the thrilling scene as they and their families would assemble in the square facing the palace, a calm sea of loyal subjects waiting to be given what had so long been denied them. When the tsar had received and read their petition, he would appear before them on the balcony, Father Gapon at his side, to include them in a great and wonderful moment of history: he would greet them as their Little Father and *grant them what they had asked*. What if the tsar should not respond as expected? Said Gapon: "If the tsar does not fulfill our request, it will mean that there is no tsar." [17]

There was no doubt in Gapon's fevered mind that the tsar would be at the palace, as he usually was during January. But this year was exceptional; because the court social season had been curtailed in deference to the war, Nicholas had chosen to remain in Tsarskoe Selo, going to the capital only when the occasion required him to do so. Recent reports about unrest in the industrial districts had not changed his routine. Whereas Nicholas I would have rushed to deal with the strike personally, Nicholas II, who usually eschewed precipitous action was not inclined to become involved. Anyway, he anticipated no crisis, and he trusted Fullon to maintain order.

Fullon likewise foresaw no crisis. He watched the strike spread with some misgivings, but he was reluctant to use force against the workers; moreover, he still deluded himself that Gapon would take whatever action might be necessary to forestall trouble. However, on the seventh, when he learned of the planned march, he was moved to do something himself, knowing that to permit such a march would mean the end of his career. First, through the Metropolitan of St. Petersburg and others, he sought to persuade the wayward priest to cancel the march. Gapon contumaciously refused. Then the prefect, with the tsar's consent, undertook to handle the matter from without. Acting in concert with Svyatopolk-Mirsky and the Grand Duke Vladimir, commander of the St. Petersburg Military District, he made plans to stop the march by force. He arranged for some 20,000 soldiers to join the full police force of the city, gave orders for their deployment, and waited.

On the ninth, a Sunday, the strikers and their families assembled in the various districts as planned and, in ordered throngs of thousands, singing hymns and carrying icons and portraits of the tsar, moved through the icy streets leading from the shabby factory districts toward the Winter Palace, where all were to meet. As the van of each aggregation reached the point on its march designated by the authorities as the limit of their approach toward the center of the city, they were ordered by the police to disperse. When they refused, as each line of march did, their ranks were charged and broken by cavalrymen and mounted police. They re-formed, however, and the rear lines unhesitatingly pressed forward. Then the soldiers opened fire on them. At that point the organized part of the venture was concluded.

Those who could, Gapon among them, fled, leaving behind on the bloodied snow and ice hundreds of dead and wounded. Some of the workers continued, by various routes, to Palace Square and nearby points on Nevsky Prospect. There, along with crowds of supporters and well-wishers, they drew the fire of the second line of defense, the forces guarding the public buildings, only to yield additional victims to what would be recorded as one of the government's most infamous triumphs.

Thus, within a few hours, another damning entry had been made against Russian autocracy—"Bloody Sunday." The Grand Duke Vladimir footnoted it indelibly with his laconic summation for the press: "We prevented the assemblage." [18]

At the end of the day, the tsar wrote in his diary, "Lord, how painful and grim." He was deeply affected, but he could not assign any blame for the occurrence either to himself or to the officers who had given the order to fire. Blame, in his estimation, rested on Svyatopolk-Mirsky, for the "unpardonable folly" of creating a climate favorable to dangerous license; on Gapon, the "socialist priest," for misleading the naïve workers; on Fullon, for his reluctance to proceed against the planners in time to forestall their final act of insubordination; and, regrettably, on the workers themselves, for being disobedient and defiant of constituted authority.

To Nicholas the lesson of Bloody Sunday was an obvious one; the reins had again to be tightened. The means to be used were familiar: changes in official personnel. He replaced Svyatopolk-Mirsky by Alexander Bulygin, who had proved his mettle as assistant in the administration of the Grand Duke Sergei in Moscow. He transferred Prefect Fullon to a distant post and changed the administration of St. Petersburg back to a governor-generalship. To head the new administration, he appointed General Dmitri Trepov, whose father had distinguished himself as Alexander II's firm opponent of lawlessness. That Trepov, as governor general, would put the capital under the kind of restraint that Nicholas felt necessary could be judged from his past nine years, when he had earned notoriety as the iron-handed superintendent of police in Moscow and, like Bulygin, had helped to enforce the harsh rule of the Grand Duke Sergei.

The tsar, by his own standards, had now done all that was necessary, or reasonably to be expected of him, as a result of the experience of January 9.

Tidying up Bloody Sunday as just another episode to be obliterated by reinforced authority was far from acceptable to the public. The Union of Liberation, with some exaggeration, exemplified popular reaction with the declaration:

[The tsar has] revealed himself as the enemy and butcher of the people. We will say no more about him, nor shall we speak of him henceforth. . . .

Yesterday there were still divisions and parties. Today the Russian liberation movement must have one body and one soul, one unifying thought: retribution and freedom at all costs. . . .

It is impossible to live thus any longer.[19]

There was indeed abundant evidence of a loosely organized "liberation movement" with support that ranged, as enthusiasts judged it, "from the revolutionary to the conservative strata" of educated Russians.[20] Its champions spoke with great unanimity on the need for political change as they now gathered in the palaces of the ancient families such as the outspoken Dolgorukovs, in the mansions of the newly rich, in the august halls of the Academy of Sciences, in the faculty rooms of secondary and higher schools, in the editorial rooms of newspapers, in club rooms, and in the assembly halls of the nobility. Yet, speech, never a mover of mountains, was unlikely to force any concessions from the tsar; the liberationists needed auxiliary forces. Shortly after Bloody Sunday, those forces began to appear—from the ranks of labor.

Most of the St. Petersburg workers had, for the time being, lost the stimulus to political action when they had lost Gapon (a hunted man, he stayed in hiding for a few days, then fled the country), but they had not lost their determination to continue their strike. Within a matter of days, workers all over Russia—500,000 of them, more than had been on strike during the whole of the preceding decade—had abandoned their work. They were still not revolutionaries. Most of them were not even conscious supporters of the liberation movement, though their potentiality as reinforcements was not to be overlooked. Regardless of the fact that they were primarily concerned with economic betterment, they were so embittered both toward their employers and toward the tsar that, unless appreciable changes were forthcoming for them, they could be counted on to strike again and again on little provocation—for freedom as well as for bread.

Of course, the workers made up only a small part of the "dark people," for whose ultimate benefit political changes were being sought; the rest, the peasants in the countryside, were still silent. But how long they would remain so, no one knew. Many at court and among the ministers were considering that question with a growing fear in their hearts. Speculation about the outcome of a conflict between the masses and the throne was far from cheerful. Almost every day brought new rumors. One was that, if the tsar failed to take more effective action soon to secure the throne, the guards officers would depose him and install Alexander's illegitimate son Prince George Yurevsky as tsar.

Ministers tried to advise Nicholas, to convince him of the urgency of the situation. Some suggested the possibility of undoing the harm of Bloody Sunday by a dramatic act of benevolence. The one who would have qualified as the most reticent of them, Minister of Agriculture Alexis Ermolov, surprisingly proved the most courageous in approaching him and spoke with a bluntness that few would have dared:

Today Russia finds herself in a grave situation, unparalleled in her history, the outcome of which is impossible to predict. . . .

You cannot depend on armed force, on the army, alone. On January 9, the army performed the harsh duty imposed on it—that of shooting at an unarmed crowd. Disorders, which have been restricted to St. Petersburg, are now spreading to many cities, and in each of them it has been necessary to pacify by armed force. Thus far, it has been successful. But

. . . what will happen when disorders spread from the cities into the villages, when the peasantry rises and carnage begins in the countryside? With what forces and what units can this new *Pugachevshchina* be pacified? . . . The army, which in the past has been obeying its officers and shooting the people from whom it derives, is now in constant contact with the populace, hearing the cries and curses hurled at it by those who have suffered at his hands. Will it behave in the same manner under similar circumstances in the future? [21]

The tsar listened to all this and was impressed; yet for a time, like a blind man led along the brink of an abyss by guides he distrusted, he shrank from taking any action. However, when he was finally convinced that there was no alternative, he agreed to take a very decisive step. He would give substance to that which, a decade earlier, he had decried as a "senseless dream," the establishment of an elective, consultative assembly, a *duma*; and he would grant to his subjects the right of petition. What more benevolent measures could be expected of an autocrat?

Before Nicholas could announce his intention, the immediacy of the menace he faced was emphasized by the assassination, in Moscow, of the unpopular Grand Duke Sergei. Killed by a bomb from the hand of ex-student Ivan Kalyaev, a member of the SR's Fighting Organization, the grand duke was the first Romanov victim of terrorism since 1881, when his father met a similar death. The tragedy was doubly grievous to Nicholas. He had lost his favorite uncle, the one he liked to consult, believing him to be a true friend. And, because of the implied threat to the whole imperial family, he had to accept the ignominy of such reinforced personal protection that, for a time, he was virtually isolated from his people, living in Tsarskoe Selo under heavy guard and avoiding all public appearances, even in St. Petersburg, the seat of his imperial authority. To private pain was added public mortification, for he felt degraded in the eyes of the world since it must now appear that he was making concessions under duress. But the fact remained: he had no choice. As usual, he was resigned to doing what had to be done.

On February 18, 1905, the tsar publicly directed his new minister of interior, Bulygin, to draft a law establishing a consultative assembly, announced the right of petition, and called on all "decent" men to support the throne. He was not happy about what he had done but hoped that it would have the desired effect—ease tension among his people and bring a return to important matters, such as the war with Japan.

To many monarchists the tsar's expectations seemed wholly justified. They confidently predicted that February 18 would be a date of prime significance in Russian history, that it would be remembered as the day on which the monarchy saved itself.

The opposition took a different view. A decade earlier—even a year earlier—the concessions would have been dramatic; now they were regarded as paltry, for aspirations had expanded and the willingness to resist authority had become manifest. Moreover, now that the barricades had been breached, most opposition leaders felt, new demands and new attacks were in order. Consequently, in the succeeding months, the government found itself faced by an increase rather than a subsidence of disorders.

During that time, dissidence spread like an epidemic. Almost every industry in Russia was idled on one or more occasions as workers went on strike. In some cities—Riga, Lodz, and Warsaw were outstanding examples—strikers battled troops and police. Resistance to discipline in the higher schools forced the closing of most of them. Membership in the socialist parties increased as never before. The Union of Liberation began to organize political unions. Feminists came into prominence again, demanding equal rights for women. National minorities made bolder demands for national rights. Even the Church, silent for half a century, again asked for freedom from state control. Then, what Ermolov feared, the extension of dissidence from the cities to the villages, started. Peasants began to help themselves to the landlords' grain and timber, to burn manor houses and other properties, to take the uncommon step of joining political organizations. And soon the spirit of the countryside was being given a voice through popular rhymes and new words set to old folk tunes:

> Ah, rat-tattoo, boom-boom!
> All the *muzhiks* are aroused.
> They are cutting down the forests and
>   burning out the threshing floors,
> While waiting for the day when they'll be free.

Never since the Time of Troubles had there been such turbulence in Russia. The socialists proclaimed it the beginning of the long-expected revolution, and in some places the evidence was convincing. But the actual outbreaks were sporadic and diffuse. The army still obeyed orders. Most of the time, the police were able to control the streets and maintain a semblance of order.

Nicholas, characteristically, having agreed to procedures for handling the current unrest, left details to the designated officials while he turned his concentration to something else—this time, back to the war with Japan.

Since the capitulation of Port Arthur, both sides had been grouping forces in the Mukden area. By the middle of February, when they finally joined battle, they were two of the largest forces ever to become engaged—the Russians with over 300,000 men, the Japanese with only a few thousand less. Their eight-day battle, one of the bloodiest in history, ended in a costly defeat for the Russians, who suffered nearly 100,000 casualties. It was also a great humiliation, not only for the abased empire but also for Commander in Chief Kuropatkin. Nicholas, as if to make amends for what now appeared his misplaced dependence on Kuropatkin, immediately transferred him to a subordinate post—a welcome relief to the general —and put the more aggressive General Nicholas Linevich in command. Though a serious setback, Mukden had not been a rout; and while the outlook for the exhausted forces was not promising just now, the tsar expected Linevich at least to regain some prestige for Russian arms. Meanwhile, he followed attentively the progress of the Second Pacific Squadron, which he was trusting to limit the enemy's control of the sea (admittedly, its capability was not sufficient to defeat the Japanese navy). But even that hope went by the board with heartbreaking finality in mid-May, when the squadron, intercepted by the Japanese off Tsushima Island, was mercilessly battered and defeated. In all its history, Russia had never before been subjected to such an inglorious experience.

Yet, when the Japanese let it be known later that month, through President Theodore Roosevelt of the United States, that they were ready to negotiate, Nicholas' feelings were mixed. He preferred that Russia fight on; but he was not sure of the troops' willingness to continue. And he feared that the loss of another battle would so weaken the government in the eyes of the people as to open the door for revolution. However, when he found that with few exceptions his military advisers favored negotiating, he reluctantly agreed to it. At the end of May, the president invited the two powers to hold their peace conference in the United States.

Looking around for someone to appoint as emissary to meet the Japanese, Nicholas intended to choose almost any good man besides Witte, whom he had removed from active prominence in the hope of avoiding his further unwanted assistance. But when suitable candidates found excuses for evading the disagreeable task, he resigned himself to the painful obligation. On receiving the appointment, Witte characteristically took little trouble to conceal his overweening sense of vindication.

Two months elapsed between the agreement to negotiate and the opening of the peace conference, in Portsmouth, New Hampshire. Since no armistice was declared, fighting continued in the Far East, but intermittently and on a small scale. The Japanese, bustling about the Sea of Japan with little opposition, occupied northeastern Korea, "repossessed" Sakhalin Island (which they had been practically forced to share with Russia in 1855 and to cede to her in 1875), and threatened Vladivostok. On the major battleground, Manchuria, there was little activity, none of significance.

In all considerations pertaining to the coming settlement, one problem was uppermost in the mind of Nicholas: how to extricate his empire from the diplomatic predicament into which it had again slipped. While attending to that monumental task, however, he could not allow himself to forget that there was a yet unresolved domestic problem. In that respect, his situation was roughly the same as that faced by Alexander II fifty years earlier when, at the end of the Crimean War, Russia was beset by the loss of prestige, by diplomatic isolation, by the unhappy knowledge of military and naval inferiority, and by domestic unrest.

Personally, Nicholas was in a situation even more unfavorable than Alexander's had been. Whereas Alexander had a sound source of guidance in his brother Constantine, who understood something of what lay behind the unpalatable facts with which the government had to deal, Nicholas found, among the Romanovs about him, no one of comparable stature or insight whom he trusted.

Certainly Constantine's sons were no support. One of them, Constantine Constantinovich, held various important positions in the government but, finding the work connected with them too often "boring and incomprehensible," gave most of his serious attention to the writing of poetry. Another, Nicholas Constantinovich, somewhat unbalanced, had been exiled to Tashkent as punishment for stealing his mother's jewels. And a third, Dmitri Constantinovich, taking the view that only grand dukes of ability should accept important posts, devoted his time to horses.

Even the avuncular combine of grand dukes, made up of his father's brothers, was now broken. Sergei had been assassinated. Alexis, his self-esteem and his reputation as general admiral shattered by Tsushima, had requested, and been granted, release from his naval responsibilities and was now living abroad with his current mistress. Paul was still enjoying his role as the family outcast because of his unacceptable marriage. The oldest and most responsible, Vladimir, was sulking, out of patience with Nicholas on two counts. He scorned the recent political concessions: the duma—"a congress of chatterers!" And he resented the fact that his son Cyril had not only been denied imperial permission to marry Victoria, the former wife of Empress Alexandra's brother, the Hessian Grand Duke Ernest, but had also been warned that disregard of the tsar's will in the matter would cost him his grand ducal title and the right to reside in Russia.

The sons of Nicholas' granduncle Michael Nicholaievich were prominent and socially influential members of the family, but they also failed to provide the kind of cooperation he needed. Of them, the Grand Duke Alexander Michaelovich, who had married the tsar's sister Xenia, was willing enough to mix in the affairs of state, but was poorly qualified, afflicted as he was by a vanity unmatched by either ability or energy. His brother Nicholas Michaelovich, a well-known and highly intelligent historian, was on friendly terms with the tsar; but his political views, so liberal that he was given the nickname "Égalité," led him more often to intrigue than to assistance. Another brother, Sergei Michaelovich, then living openly with the tsar's former mistress, Kshesinsky, had no political interests of note.

The tsar's Romanov kin were indeed a weak bulwark for the throne. Even his only surviving brother, Michael, was a boyish young man whose chief concern was to escape his mother's control and achieve manhood.

Of the active members of the imperial family, the bachelor Grand Duke Nicholas Nicholaievich was the most able. He had been continually in military service since his youth and had advanced steadily by virtue of skill and diligence. Twelve years Nicholas' senior, he had been his commanding officer in the Hussar Guards and had never lost the respect of his former subaltern, now tsar. To his credit, he had accepted the change in the authority of their respective positions with good grace, always treating Nicholas with proper formality and addressing him as "Your Majesty." The grand duke's father, Nicholas Nicholaievich the elder, who had been Alexander III's highly respected inspector general of cavalry, had died in 1891, and Alexander had chosen to leave the office vacant thereafter. But

Nicholas, soon after his accession, had passed it on to Nicholas Nicholaievich the younger.

He still considered that appointment a good one, and the grand duke as one of his most dependable leaders; he had recently considered giving him the Manchurian command. Now he was turning to him for aid in rebuilding the armed forces, an assignment he could be expected to handle adequately. Most officials in the higher levels of government regarded Nicholas Nicholaievich as an honorable and serious soldier. Though he was often criticized as too rigid a disciplinarian (his subordinates were said to be kept in fighting tone by their lively fear of the six-foot-six martinet), he had a reputation for the successful achievement of whatever he undertook.

Unfortunately, the judgment of the Grand Duke Nicholas Nicholaievich would be most unlikely to enlarge the tsar's vision concerning any matters, whether military or civilian. He was a politically unsophisticated cavalryman who liked soldiering, hunting, and horses, but not abstruse thought or probing contemplation. In fact, when urged to thought or action not consonant with his mood of the moment, he was likely to give way to flaming temper—a mark, some called it, of the "hereditary hysteria of the Oldenburgs," passed on through his German mother. The best that could be said for the grand duke's attributes as a political adviser was that he knew enough to be afraid—something that could not be said for the tsar.

Next on the short list of men to whom the tsar felt that he could turn for advice was honest, hard-working General Trepov. As governor general of St. Petersburg, he had taken that area firmly in hand after Bloody Sunday, and Nicholas had confidently extended his reach by assigning him the additional post of assistant minister of interior with authority over the country's entire police system. He was a dependable official, but politically he was even less sophisticated than the grand duke.

Unquestionably, Nicholas was more alone, more dependent on his limited devices in political matters, than he had been at any of the other critical points in his reign. Determination, however, had not deserted him: if he had to make his decisions unaided, he was willing to accept the responsibility. For a time, he took heart in the belief that he was overcoming in some measure both Russia's loss of prestige abroad and his government's unpopularity at home.

In late August, when the Portsmouth peace conference was concluded, Nicholas saw that, under his direction, the tenacious Witte had gained better terms for Russia than she had earned. The Treaty of Portsmouth, while providing some advantages to the victor, did not exact any great redress from the loser. Russia would cede to Japan the rights she had acquired in Port Arthur and Dalny, turn over to her the South Manchurian railway, recognize the preponderance of her interests in Korea, and relinquish to her the southern part of Sakhalin. But those losses were minor in view of the fact that Russia still held northern Sakhalin as well as most of her other considerable holdings and advantageous developments in the Far East, and that she was not required to pay the cash indemnity about which Japan had at first been threateningly insistent. As for future designs in Manchuria, where each now had railroad interests, consideration was postponed by a gentlemanly bow from each side: Manchuria was recognized as China's territory, not to be subjected to any kind of foreign intrusion that could impair Chinese sovereignty.

With that settlement behind him, Nicholas looked to the early subsidence of domestic unease. That, he confidently believed, would follow his issuance of the new legislation for the establishment of a duma. Presiding over the sessions during which details were worked, out, he had taken care, however, that the law present no loopholes to tempt those who might want to read into it more than was inended: "to provide preliminary consideration and discussion of legislative proposals, to be transmitted through the State Council up to the supreme autocratic authority." He had insisted that provisions for the election of deputies insure a representation predominantly Russian and rural, and that the peasants, whose political sense he judged to be commendably "sound," be granted sufficiently broad suffrage to make possible their serving as a salutary counterforce to the nobility, which had been behaving so defiantly in recent months. Whatever the ultimate effect of his granting to a limited representation of his subjects the exceptional privilege of meeting in an elective consultative body, it was not subject to immediate test: though he signed the law on the duma in August, the date for the election of delegates was still undecided. As a measure of interim appeasement, on the recommendation of Trepov and a number of ministers, he restored autonomy to the universities. That, he was willing to believe, would calm some of the "educated" and the overzealous youth.

All things considered, the prospects from the government's viewpoint was fairly favorable as the tsar left his routine duties early in September for a brief rest, sailing with his family off the Finnish coast. The change for him was so generally pleasing that it swept him into a feeling of benevolence such as he had not enjoyed for many months. It extended momentarily even to Witte, whom he proceeded to reward for his recent services by conferring on him the title of count.

Hopefulness among officials at this time was ill-founded. They were able to overlook danger signs because they could see no significant weakening in the framework of the Russia that had proved its strength in the time of Alexander I. It appeared to be the same Russia, resting on autocracy, the established Church, and the dominant Russian nationality; the Russia committed to the imbalance between an underprivileged majority and a minority rewarded with "distinction and benefits, respect and comfort." But that Russia was, in fact, facing an extremely precarious situation: the revolutionary surge that had begun earlier in the year had not reached its crest. Most of the opposition remained unimpressed by such minor leniencies as the restoration of university autonomy and were bitterly disappointed with the promise of a duma that would have the right to speak but not to act.

In their determination to achieve some basic changes, the opposition leaders continued the drive to organize for strength. The socialists were tightening their party organizations and, profiting from experience, improving the effectiveness of their efforts among the workers. The liberals, who now made up the tactical leadership of the opposition, having formed unions along professional lines, had now brought those unions together in the Union of Unions, under the presidency of Paul Milyukov. Its aim was to induce the government to convoke a constituent assembly on the basis of universal, equal, direct, and secret suffrage—a far hark from the consultative assembly of the new law. One element recently incorporated into the Union of Unions was evidence of an important change among the peasants: the All-Russian Peasants Union, organized at mid-year in a conference promoted by SR's and left-wing liberals. Its members were willing to add their voice to the call for a constituent assembly, though it was understood that their reason was more economic than political, since the peasants still sought land above all else. The zemstvos also were now strengthened by a central organization, which worked closely with various municipal councils—all demanding, if not a constituent assembly, at least a legislative assembly in which the entire population would be fairly represented.

Though the late-summer activities of the opposition were not flagrant, they broke into local prominence in hundreds of places, and they were significant. There were open expressions of minority nationalism in Lodz, Helsingfors, Riga, Vilna, Kiev, and Tiflis; of agrarian discontent in the black-earth provinces as well as in the borderlands; of labor rebellions in dozens of industrial cities. Discontent in the navy had been quietly spreading since June, when the crew of the battleship "Potemkin," of the Black Sea fleet, had made history by mutiny, the first that service had ever known. While the Black Sea fleet had been temporarily inactivated and elaborate precautions taken against repetition of trouble in that region, the seed of mutiny was beginning to grow among the sailors of the naval bases of Kronstadt and Sebastopol. In the army also, insubordination was becoming more common, especially among the reservists in Manchuria, anxious to get home and impatient with unexplained delays. Students, as usual, were busy with propaganda and anxious to prepare for action. A congress of student representatives had just met in Vyborg, Finland, and vowed to continue the struggle for a constituent assembly by revolutionary means. Some socialist leaders, Lenin among them, were convinced that an armed uprising was possible and, looking ahead to practical action, were planning both a boycott of the coming election of duma deputies and disruptive strikes.

None of this, however, was unusual enough to appear alarming to Nicholas when he returned to Peterhof, on September 1. Neither he nor Trepov expected the coming months to be free of disorder, but they assumed that they could cope with whatever occurred. Not even the instances of insubordination in the armed forces suggested any great problem, for the Cossack units, the ever-reliable troops, were expected to arrive soon from the Manchurian front. They were a consideration because Nicholas was now convinced that strong measures were both justifiable and necessary in handling any kind of protest against authority. Yet he was just as confirmed in his belief that the majority of the people were loyal to him and that the sources of trouble were easily definable—the intellectuals, the Jews, the Poles, the Finns, the English, and (as he was becoming persuaded through his reading of pamphlets provided by one of his aides) the European Masonic movement.

Renewed trouble of a more immediate nature, again involving the Grand Duke Vladimir's troublesome son Cyril, was thrust upon Nicholas soon after his return. Combining defiance of imperial injunction with impertinence, Cyril not only married the divorced Victoria, in Germany, but also straightway came boldly back to Russia.

Nicholas, no longer the "gentle cousin," was true to his previous words of warning. He reaffirmed his intention to take away Cyril's grand ducal title and rights and ordered him to leave Russia immediately, never to return. There followed a bitter scene with the Grand Duke Vladimir. When the tsar refused to temper the severity of his judgment, his uncle asked, and was granted, permission to resign his official duties.

The tsar finally relented on the matter of Cyril's title, but he stood firm on the summary imposition of the other harsh penalties. His attitude impressed many in the imperial family as spiteful and cruel, and some of them came to the facile conclusion that he had acted at the insistence of Alexandra, who simply sought to discommode her former sister-in-law.

This new rift in family relations could not have come at a worse time.

The next crisis was not long delayed. When it came, in October, it provided an appalling test of Nicholas' convictions, a stupefying kaleidoscope of experiences that shook his faith and led him to the brink of desperation. He poured out his feelings in a letter to Marie Fedorovna, then in Copenhagen:

All sorts of conferences took place in Moscow. . . . Everything was being prepared for the ry. strike. The first one began in and around Moscow, and then spread all over Russia practically at once. . . .

God knows what happened in the universities. *Every kind* of riff-raff walked in from the streets, riot was loudly proclaimed—nobody seemed to care. . . .

It makes me sick to read the news! Nothing but new strikes in schools and factories, murdered policemen, Cossacks and soldiers, riots, disorder, mutinies. But the ministers, instead of acting with quick decision, only assemble in council like a lot of frightened hens and cackle about providing united ministerial action.[22]

He was picturing, from his coign of vantage, the October General Strike, the great strike of which revolutionaries had so long dreamed but which they had not really expected. It was unplanned (Nicholas mistakenly thought otherwise); however, it was made possible by prior preparation—not preparation for a general strike necessarily, but for some kind of pandemic display of the general unrelieved discontent. Conditions favoring it had been developing since the days of the Decembrists and had been improved immeasurably by what had been happening since the death of Plehve, the aggravation of unrest, and the coalescing of opposition groups.

The period of serious disorders followed the outbreak of a succession of small strikes and supporting demonstrations in Moscow and St. Petersburg during late September and early October. On the occasion of these strikes, the university students were seen to be particularly active as agitators and organizers of protest, taking advantage of the fact that on the campuses they were legally immune from police interference now that university autonomy had been restored. When the more serious labor insurgence began, they were ready to join in the thick of it. Others, less openly animated at the time, were quietly waiting.

The general strike proper began in Moscow, during the first week of October, with a walkout of railroad workers, who were so situated that they could sever connections and disrupt schedules for long-distance rail travel in all directions. From there the strike fever, as Nicholas observed, "spread all over Russia practically at once"—not to workers alone but to the whole of the urban opposition. Moscow was the first city to be immobilized, as factory workers, office personnel, public service employees, students, and professionals of every kind abandoned their routine activities and joined forces with the original strikers, taking to the streets in demonstrations or meeting in the halls of the university and other higher schools to plan, petition, and demand. The economic aspects of the strike were soon supplemented by the political, and the brotherhood of the Moscow opposition became, for the time being at least, a reality. Opposition elsewhere, city by city, as if ignited by sparks from the central fire, began joining the strike movement, following much the same course.

The next flare-up was in Kharkov. There, the first strikers, the railroadmen, were quickly joined by hordes of collaborators whose unruliness, encouraged by a "fighting committee" of SR's and SD's, led to such disorder—street brawls, lootings, and general rowdiness—that the civil authorities were glad to accept assistance from the liberals of the city, who formed a defense committee and armed temporary militia groups to provide liaison between the rebellious citizenry and the helpless officials. As quickly as possible, the city was put under martial law. Again the liberals acted as interagents, this time to prevent bloodshed at the university, used as strikers' headquarters, where the troops sent to clear the buildings were met by armed strikers who had barricaded themselves inside. That impasse was ended without incident, but the defiance of authority continued elsewhere in the city and gave way only when military force became incontestable.

In St. Petersburg, where resentment born of recent occurrences still smoldered, the opposition was easily roused. The day after the Moscow strike began, about 10,000 workers and students assembled in the university halls to consider various approaches to the ripening opportunity for action. They made no plans for a general strike. However, on the next day, when the railroadmen, on agreement among themselves, quit work, a number of factories were closed simultaneously by walkouts. Once started, the strike spread until it included the personnel of most of the city's schools, stores, service facilities, offices, and even such government-controlled establishments as the imperial theaters, the port and customs services, and a branch of the State Bank. As thousands of strikers paraded the streets and crowded into meetings at the university, their spirits kept high by the leadership of socialists, liberals, and anarchists, it was clear that even without planning the opposition in the capital could present a formidable front.

Beginning thus in the large central cities, the strike spread quickly to the smaller urban centers. It was estimated that, by October 14, this sudden defiance of authority had drawn the support of more than half a million railroadmen, a million factory workers, 50,000 government employees, and tens of thousands of professionals, students, and clerks in offices and retail stores. They had effectively paralyzed all the activities of urban life in Russia: commerce, industry, transportation, education, municipal services, and entertainment.

What may be called Russia's first revolution was clearly in the making. Yet this ostensibly concerted display of rebelliousness was hampered by two significant conditions: it attracted only a neglible reaction from the bulk of the population, the peasantry; and it was not in fact a united action. True, the chief aims were everywhere similar—better working conditions for those employed in both privately owned and public establishments, a constituent assembly, the removal of disabilities imposed on religious and national minorities, political amnesty. But the leadership, made up of socialists, liberals, and many with no political identity, was by no means united on ultimate aims or procedures beyond the strike.

Moreover, the tsar still held the instruments of power, the police and the army; he could decide whether to crush rebelliousness or to calm it by making concessions. The resolution of the problem obviously had to be undertaken while he still held that advantage. Witte, his feeling of indispensability restored by his recent success at Portsmouth, was ready with an analysis of the situation: "The roots of unrest are to be found in the disparity between the high-minded aspirations of Russian intellectual society and the framework within which it exists. Russia has outgrown her political framework and is striving for a legal order based on civil liberty."

There were two courses, he added, sufficient to deal successfully with this unrest. One was to employ force, under the direction of a general with dictatorial powers over both civilian and military matters. The other was to grant political change: "The framework of Russian political life must be changed to make it conform to the ideas that animate the moderate majority of society. . . . We must have faith in the political sense of Russian society and believe that it does not want anarchy, with its attendant threat of the horrors of strife and political disintegration." [23]

It went without saying that, if there were to be a dictator, the tsar's choice would fall on the Grand Duke Nicholas Nicholaievich; if a cabinet were to be formed, its premier would be Witte. Nicholas' instinctive preference was for the first alternative. But neither Trepov nor General Alexander Roediger, whom he had recently appointed to succeed General Sakharov as minister of war, would so counsel him. Trepov talked boldly, even issued orders that his forces not spare the cartridges against the strikers; but he did not dare commit the police to open battle with them. Roediger feared that the soldiers would refuse to obey if it should become necessary to order that they fire on civilians.

It soon became clear that, in reality, there was no choice. When the Grand Duke Nicholas Nicholaievich was approached by Minister of Court Fredericks on the matter of accepting the role of dictator, he impatiently declared that the only course was to "support Witte" and that, if the tsar tried to force the responsibility on him, he would shoot himself. Then Trepov finally expressed the opinion that, even if the troops proved loyal, their full-scale use against the strikers might provoke a civil war that could be won only at the cost of fearful carnage.

That was the decisive consideration: though Nicholas approved authoritarian firmness, he shrank from bloodshed. It was better to accept the inevitable and make the most of it. "There was no other way out," he later wrote to his mother, "than to cross oneself and give what everyone was asking for." He had resigned himself to doing two things he found highly disagreeable: making further political concessions and allowing Witte to rise again to a place of authority in the government.

Late on the afternoon of October 17, 1905, in his study at Peterhof, with Witte and the Grand Duke Nicholas Nicholaievich among the witnesses, Nicholas signed what has come to be known as the October Manifesto, a document that, on the face of it, meant the end of the centuries-old institution of tsarism. In it was the essence of what had run through Russian dreams for generations:

> We make it the duty of the government to execute Our firm will:
>
> 1) to grant to the people the unshakeable foundations of civic freedom on the basis of genuine personal inviolability, freedom of conscience, speech, assembly, and association;
>
> 2) to admit immediately to participation in the State Duma . . . those classes of the population that are now completely deprived of electoral rights, leaving the further development of the principle of universal suffrage to the new legislative order;
>
> and 3) to establish as an inviolable rule that no law may go into force without the consent of the State Duma and that the representatives of the people must be guaranteed the opportunity of effective participation in the supervision of the legality of the actions performed by Our appointed officials.[24]

Nicholas was replacing the plans for a consultative duma with plans for a legislative duma elected by universal suffrage, thus granting his subjects representative government—the greatest political concession ever endorsed by a Russian ruler.

The next day, the tsar would appoint Witte to a post that he had himself held until now, that of Chairman of the Council of Ministers, in effect making him premier and authorizing him to seek out as ministers men who shared his views and enjoyed public support.

Nicholas II had brought Russia to the threshold of change, to an era of constitutional monarchy.

XIII

Last Reprieve

NICHOLAS II, 1906–1914

IN the October Manifesto, Nicholas II made an unprecedented statement of intention on behalf of the tsarist regime. Whether or not it was a satisfactory countermeasure to revolution would be determined through the interpretation placed upon it by the adversaries: those aligned with the throne and those in the various sectors of the opposition.

Members of the imperial family closest to Nicholas accepted the manifesto as something that could be made an instrument of salvation *if* properly handled, and they believed the condition could be met by the new premier. On the day before the signing of the manifesto, the dowager empress had written to the tsar, "I am sure that the only man who can help you now and be useful is Witte, . . . a man of genius, energetic and clear-sighted."[1] And on the evening of the signing, October 17, the Grand Duke Nicholas Nicholaievich reminded Witte that this was the anniversary of the railroad wreck near Borki, in which Alexander III had barely escaped death, adding, "This is the second time the dynasty has been saved on this date."[2]

Others, particularly among those members of the upper class whose personal dislike of Witte did not exceed their self-concern, shared this feeling for a while. To them he was a *deus ex machina* appearing at a time when the current revolutionary excesses had thrown them into such apprehension that, as the tsar bitterly recalled years later, "they thought the end was coming." They knew him to be a resolute monarchist, a strong pacesetter, and one who usually carried through whatever he undertook. Under his direction, they believed, order would be restored, the monarchy would survive, and with it their class.

Witte accepted this flattering appraisal as no more than his due. He had complete confidence in his ability to treat as well as diagnose. He had no doubt that the manifesto would end the general strike now gripping the country, and, with that obstruction out of the way, quick pacification of the revolutionary opposition would follow. He saw nothing to prevent the ensuing formation of a strong cabinet enjoying public support and the election of a moderate and cooperative Duma. Such a cabinet and such a Duma would insure that government and society could work harmoniously to reestablish stability and provide a mutually advantageous future. He would admit that, after the fundamental laws were revised to accommodate the fact of an elected legislature, the subsequent planning, rearrangements, and modifications would take time, perhaps a decade or two; and that during the required time, Russia would have to forego some great-power luxuries in order to give her resources and attention exclusively to domestic reconstruction. But all could be justified; all would be ultimately rewarding.

Unfortunately, only one of the expectations was realized according to Witte's schedule. Most of the strikers, while disappointed that the government was not responding favorably to their call for a constituent assembly, were glad to see that it at least promised them the right of "association," the right legally to form trade unions. In return for that concession, they were willing to give up the general strike, releasing the country from enforced immobility. That did not mean the ending of strike activity, however, nor the recession of revolutionary disorder and open dissidence.

As news of the manifesto swept the country, public reaction seemed at first to be unrestrained jubilation. But there was an adverse undertone. Though the majority of the opposition leaders were now willing to allow the government an opportunity to prove its goodwill and were genuinely optimistic about what they might achieve through the Duma, the extremists saw advantage in pressing on while the authorities were still off balance and before the awakened proletariat could be lulled back into a state of inaction by a few concessions. The socialists, sometimes divided on particular issues—the SD's had been divided since mid-1903 into a majority group, the Bolsheviks, and a minority group, the Mensheviks—were in general agreement that the revolutionary drive must not be relaxed.

A soviet (council) representing part of the capital's labor force had been organized at the instigation of socialist leaders a few days before the issuance of the manifesto and dedicated to keeping basic issues fresh in the minds of workers. Under the formal name St. Petersburg Soviet of Workers' Delegates, it began the publication of the news organ *Izvestia*. With the support of left-wing organizations, particularly the Mensheviks, the soviet grew at a phenomenal rate. Within a month, it was representing some 200,000 workers in St. Petersburg and serving as the model for soviets being organized in Moscow, Odessa, Kiev, and other industrial centers. With respect to established authority, the soviets adopted the policy of trusting no promise, accepting no compromise, and usurping any political power possible within their area. The mood of defiance among the workers they represented was whipped up by a barrage of revolutionary oratory and writing. All the agitators were liberal with incendiary words, but none could outdo Leon Trotsky, who kept the workers reminded, through *Izvestia*, that their duty was to reject "the police thug Trepov," "the liberal financial shark Witte," and "the police whip wrapped in the parchment of a constitution." The rank and file, as was usual in Russia, fitted the sentiments with familiar tunes, which they sang with enthusiasm. A popular stanza:

> The tsar lost his nerve,
> So he issued a manifesto—
> Freedom to the dead,
> Arrest for the living.

During the week following the issuance of the manifesto, the assertiveness of the soviets was more than matched in many places throughout the country as thousands began reveling prematurely in the liberties promised in the manifesto and undertaking to assume at once the rights that had been so long denied them or unrestrainedly displaying the hatreds they had been forced to suppress. Often the results were mob violence, directed either at established authority or the objects of personal prejudices. There were violent strikes, assassinations, appropriation of property, and acts of vengeance against officials. There were many pogroms unequaled in savagery (one, in Odessa, left 500 dead). There were outbursts in a number of rural areas, where peasants plundered grain and timber from their landlords in defiance of local authority and the priests who tried to reason with them. Lettish peasants in the Baltic provinces carried their grievances to particularly desperate ends, paying off old scores against their German landlords with bludgeon and torch.

The urge to interpret the new-found liberty as license affected the armed services also. The Kronstadt and Sebastopol naval bases were plagued by mutiny; in fact, the navy was so riddled by disaffection that for a time it was considered useless as a fighting force. The army was not so deeply affected, but there also discipline began to crack, particularly among reservists returning from the front. Some mutinous units were able to defy all control, restrain their officers, and make common cause with civilian revolutionaries along their route.

This epidemic of disorderliness spread as far as it did because civil officials responsible for order in the various infected areas were themselves at first unsure of proper procedures under the "new dispensation." By the end of the third day, however, orders were being passed down, and pacification was getting under way with no change from the traditional in manner or purpose. The only difference was in the extensiveness of the attack being mounted against the insurgence. Though public defiance had never before been so widespread or so stubborn, the government was still in control of the superior instruments of force, and the outcome was easily predictable: the revolutionary fire of 1905 would be brought under control. But nearly two years would be required to extinguish it.

To Witte, despite the incidence of disorder, the prospect appeared favorable. He looked at the masses with eyes of an earlier generation, seeing the majority of the people "always and ever the same," readily cowed, easily led. In view of their recent exposure to the notions of liberalism in general and constitutionalism in particular, he expected to have to do a lot of "leading"; but he felt himself capable of making his own version of "enlightened absolutism" more palatable than others and of proving its workability. His disillusionment was not long postponed.

His first lesson came with his attempt to form a cabinet, a new Council of Ministers that would enjoy public support. Nicholas gave him virtually a free hand in the selection of all but four ministers, whose appointment continued as before, by designation from the throne. The four who remained, under that arrangement, were General Roediger as minister of war, Admiral Birilev as minister of the navy,* Baron Fredericks as minister of the imperial court, and Count Lamsdorf as minister of foreign affairs. When the other incumbents and those who worked closely with them had vacated their offices, as they did at once either by resignation or acceptance of dismissal, Witte found himself with an extraordinary opportunity—to establish public favor through judiciously selected replacements. What an impression he could make with a publicly approved selection of successors to such unpopular men as Bulygin, Pobedonostsev, and Trepov! What a chance to win the youth of the country when he replaced the severe General Glazov as minister of education!

Witte expected to find his men among the liberals, the "moderate majority of society," who would now, he believed, be so pleased with the provisions of the October Manifesto that they would be anxious to have a hand in activating them. He was wrong. His offer of seats in his cabinet was turned down by leaders of the left wing of the liberals because they understood his position to be so favorable to the regime as to be unadaptable to their aims. Paul Milyukov indicated their attitude when he said, "Nothing has changed, the fight goes on." [3]

Something had changed, of course: Russia was entering the era of constitutional government. But the change was not sufficient for Milyukov and the many liberals who thought as he did; they intended to continue their peaceful struggle until the tsar yielded his remaining power to representatives of the people. This intention clearly precluded any useful traffic between them and Witte. More moderate liberals also rejected the premier's offer, their chief reason being simply that they did not wholly trust him in his new role. In the end, Witte was left with no alternative but to bring into his cabinet bureaucrats and outsiders with little reputation, none of them likely to inspire the hoped-for support.

He lost much of his already small following when he finally chose —though reluctantly, it appeared—Peter Durnovo as minister of interior. Durnovo was a seasoned bureaucrat who had served his government well in many ways but was publicly tarred with "police brutality" because of his years with the department of police and with self-seeking because of his reputation as an unscrupulous

---

* The minister of the navy became the chief administrator of that service after the Grand Duke Alexis retired from activity and the rank of general admiral was abolished.

climber of the political ladder. And the cabinet gained no luster by any of the other ministerial choices. Three of them were from Witte's former colleagues in the ministry of finance; one was a brother-in-law of Durnovo; and the others, though willing and competent in their separate spheres, lacked the ability to do more than administer the traditional routine of the ministries. Here was no promise of a "new order."

It was obvious that Witte's hope of establishing a friendly link between government and the people had now to be pinned on the Duma, elections for which were to be held in the spring of 1906. He still had faith, not wholly shared by Nicholas, that the electorate would listen to the "voice of moderation" and send to the Duma men who would cooperate with his administration. For that, he could only wait: the government itself was ill-prepared as well as unwilling to influence the elections by direct means.

By the beginning of 1906, the electorate was being subjected to a din of voices that had not figured greatly in Witte's calculations. Though there were no legally recognized political parties in Russia, there was by this time a plethora of politically concerned groups and organizations calling themselves parties; regardless of their legal status, they were now stirred to action. The coming elections were, after all, the first national elections in the history of the country; virtually all adult males had the right to vote in them; it was inevitable that there be countless ideas about how and for what purpose they should be used.

The socialists, the SD's and the SR's, were urging a general boycott of the coming elections, which they characterized as a government ruse to divert the proletariat from the revolution with "constitutional illusions."

The majority of the liberals, supporters of the Union of Unions and the Union of Liberation, had just formed a new political organization, the Constitutional Democratic Party, and through it were now busily soliciting support for deputies who would use their influence in the Duma to enact measures providing governmental changes and reforms beyond those included in the October Manifesto. Members of the new organization, popularly known as the Cadet Party,* envisioned for Russia a true parliamentary government somewhat like that of England; a constitution drawn up by repre-

---

* "Cadet" is English for the Russian "Kadet," formed from the name of the party, *Konstitutsionno-Demokraticheskaya*. The "Ka" represents the first two letters— pronounced "ka" though spelled "ko"—and the "det" is from letters of *Demokraticheskaya*.

sentatives of the people; far-reaching social and economic improvements including positive protection for labor, national rights for the minorities, the elimination of discrimination based on nationality or religion, and radical agrarian reforms, beginning with the expropriation—with payment—of large estates for redistribution among the peasants. The Cadet program had wide appeal among disaffected groups and brought them many votes that might have gone to the socialists had they not insisted on boycotting the elections.

The other parties that joined the campaigning were generally more moderate than the Cadets, poorly organized, and without any significant mass support. The most important of them was the Union of October 17, known popularly as the Octobrist Party, which Dmitri Shipov helped to found among right-wing liberals who felt that the people should be satisfied with the reforms granted by the October Manifesto and that Duma deputies should cooperate with the government to effect them.

One shade of political opinion, to be recognized as often in deeds as in words, was that of the extreme right, which repudiated the very concept of the change in government with which others were so seriously occupied. It represented the reaction of many of the Orthodox clergy, ultraconservative officials, and certain nobles, all of whom saw the October Manifesto as a deplorable capitulation to the revolutionaries, something that had been forced on the tsar by the poisonous work of alien elements. They were willing to assume a self-imposed responsibility as readjusters. Organized as patriotic monarchist groups and parties, many of which came to be known by the unflattering generic name of Black Hundreds, they undertook to "turn back the revolution." Outstanding among the many groups of these extreme rightists wrapped in the mantle of official nationalism was the Union of the Russian People. It managed to enlist support that ranged into the highest government circles and insured it a great deal of freedom and protection in campaigns against those it considered the enemies of the monarchy: revolutionaries, liberals, and minority groups, especially the Jews. In their efforts to protect the throne intact, these monarchist groups could be expected to impede Witte's work as well as further to estrange the moderate opposition. By the very frenzy of their activities, which often included violent physical assaults on the "enemies," they could be expected actually to aid the radical opposition; for it was easy to suspect that if these represented the true heart of the government, the October Manifesto was meaningless and, as soon as the government had the people sufficiently lulled, it would simply jettison the Duma and, with it, the promised civil liberty.

Suspicion of the government's good intentions was heightened, in February 1906, by official announcement that, according to the fundamental laws as they were then being revised by the ministers and other high-ranking persons of the dynasty and government in conference with the tsar, the Duma was not to be the sole legislative body of the empire. The State Council was to admit additional members elected by the Orthodox clergy, the nobility, the zemstvos, the universities, commerce, and industry; and, thus enlarged, it would form a second legislative chamber having equal power with the Duma in the making of laws. Although there had been an intimation as early as October 17 that the council would be changed in some way, this announcement came as a shock to the liberals. They had not expected the Duma to share legislative power with another body; now they were informed that it would share with a body that they could only expect to be a conservative one and therefore a brake on the Duma.

A number of other developments also invited interpretations that would help to drown out, long before the elections (now set for March 1906), the "voice of moderation" on which Witte was concentrating his hopes. There was Nicholas' appointment of Trepov to the post of commandant at the imperial court after he resigned his posts as governor general of St. Petersburg and head of the department of police, an indication that the tsar's personal sentiments had in fact not changed. There was the ostensible official sanction of outrages perpetrated by such reactionary groups as the Black Hundreds against whomever they chose to call revolutionaries. There was the experienced police hand of Durnovo to be seen in the intensified program of pacification then under way, the harshest that had ever been known in Russia. During the pacification, there was the use of tyrannical instrumentalities which, it had been hoped, the October Manifesto had disavowed by the grant of "civic freedom on the basis of personal inviolability, freedom of conscience, speech, assembly, and association." They included: martial law—imposed on the insurgent Baltic provinces in November; armed force—used to curb the peasant revolts through ruthless punitive campaigns in the chief agricultural provinces, to engage and overpower the supporters of a great strike begun in December under the leadership of the Moscow Soviet, to eradicate the revolutionary element in the Baltic provinces (where some 2,000 rebels were hanged or shot), and to compel discipline in mutinous units of the army and the navy; mass arrests—employed in disabling the militant St. Petersburg Soviet and in breaking up forbidden meetings; censorship—applied to publications showing overt approval or support for opposition forces; and the extensive purge—used to rid the government of employees suspected of revolutionary leanings.

The results of the elections to the epoch-marking First Duma were a shocking disappointment to the government. Over 300 of the 497 seats were won by the Cadets, who were the chief recipients of the protest and opposition vote, and the minor parties to their political left; thus the opposition came out with a safe majority. Deputies who had no political affiliation, chiefly peasants, won most of the remaining seats, while those supporting the moderate views of the Union of October 17 won only thirty-eight, and those to their political right won only seven. Clearly the Duma was to be no bridgehead between government and society; rather, a beachhead for assault on the government. Its initial move would undoubtedly be a demand for Witte's resignation and his replacement by a premier of its choice.

Witte, who, in his three decades of government service, had never been confronted with such a debacle, was dismayed. The man who had accepted the premiership with such confidence only six months ago was now at the breaking point; already burdened by the symptoms of physical decline, sleeplessness and a debilitating palsy, he found the recent succession of disappointments almost beyond endurance. He had lost even the tentative reliance of the tsar, who, while he had never wholly trusted Witte, had at least thought him strong and clever. Now Nicholas' quiet endurance of him was turning to bitterness; no one, in his opinion, except perhaps "foreign Jewish bankers," now had any confidence in the man. Alexandra, as usual, put the imperial sentiment succinctly: everyone, she said, had thought Witte very clever; yet in the end the Cossacks "once more had to save the state." [4]

Understanding that, willy-nilly, change had to come, Nicholas acted promptly in order to avoid the suspicion of acting under Duma pressure. He released Witte, along with his cabinet, on April 15, twelve days before the First Duma was to open. The man he chose to succeed as premier was sixty-seven-year-old Ivan Goremykin, a thoroughgoing monarchist. While neither Goremykin nor his cabinet could be expected to be any more palatable to the Cadet-dominated Duma than the retiring officials would have been, some of the new ministers would at least be an improvement over the retiring ones. The strongest of them—such men as Peter Stolypin, who now succeeded Durnovo as minister of interior, and Alexander Izvolsky, whom Nicholas chose to replace Lamsdorf as minister of foreign affairs—would be found to have brought valuable practical experience as well as personal ability to their posts.

Another matter of timely importance, as the opening of the First Duma approached, was the final intimation of the tsarist conception of the new order. It was embodied in the revised fundamental laws of the empire, now issued as the regime's final recognition that civil liberties had been granted and that a legislative body including representatives of the people had been incorporated into the government. It was immediately evident that, in some instances, the civil liberties defined in the new laws were a decidedly circumscribed version of those anticipated from the wording of the October Manifesto, also that the legislature was to function under definite restrictions. Yet, in the very fact of legal recognition, there was a stimulating prospect of what might follow—challenging to some, distressing to others.

In order to have the fundamental laws revised before the opening sessions of the Duma, Nicholas had summoned, and presided over, a number of conferences during the preceding two months despite the distraction of continuing strikes, assassinations, and peasant violence. The conferees had met as guardians of the old order, understanding that their commission was to protect tsarism from further erosion but holding various views on the proper manner of discharging that commission. Two among them, Witte and the aged Count Constantine Pahlen, who had been Alexander II's minister of justice, were in strong disagreement on a very important point. Witte openly insisted that the revised laws should not be constitutional in nature, hence not binding on the tsar. Pahlen, on the other hand, believed—as he privately informed the tsar— that failure to accept the constitutional form of rule would doom the monarchy.

Predictably, the gravest attention had been paid to the revision of the first article of the laws, which read: "The Emperor of All the Russias is an autocratic and unlimited monarch. Fear as well as duty commanded by God Himself is the basis of obedience to His supreme power." To the recommendation that he eliminate the word "unlimited" from the article, Nicholas had passionately replied that, although he intended to uphold the October Manifesto, he would not part with that time-honored word. He was confident, he said, that the vast majority of his subjects would approve its retention and that, if there were any outcry, it would come only from the "so-called educated element, the proletariat, the third estate." Yet, after an interval of anguished soul-searching, he had agreed to revise the article by striking the word out—in clear admission that he was no longer an unlimited monarch. He was still an autocrat, however. As he interpreted the term "autocrat," it signified that he derived his power from God, to whom alone he was responsible; that, though he had accepted limitations on his power, he could still ignore those limitations if he saw reason to do so.

As they were finally revised, the fundamental laws by no means made a figurehead of the tsar. Even as a limited monarch, he still had wide authority. He remained in complete control of the executive branch of the government with authority to issue decrees, appoint and remove officials, declare war and conclude peace, and place areas under martial law, reinforced protection, or extraordinary protection. In addition, he retained his prerogatives as the "supreme leader" of the armed forces, the source of judicial power, the "supreme defender and protector of the dogmas" of the Russian Orthodox Church, and the head of the imperial family. Significant legislative powers also were reserved to him: he was to initiate all legislation; his approval or disapproval would determine whether or not any bill became law; he had authority to issue emergency legislation when the legislature was not in session; and he had certain restraining powers over the chambers of the legislature—to prorogue either or both, to appoint half of the state council members, and to dissolve the Duma before the expiration of its five-year term.

As further safeguards for the regime, three new articles were added—these, to frustrate any attempts of national minorities to gain national rights. The first declared the Russian state to be "one and indivisible"; the second specified Finland as an "indivisible" part of the Russian state; and the third affirmed Russian as the language of the state and made its use obligatory in the armed forces and civilian administration.

To hold the line where it was now drawn and to obviate changes in the fundamental laws beyond those satisfactory to the regime, the revision specified that only the tsar might initiate a review of the laws and that no further revision might be made without his consent. The barriers around what remained of the old order had been made formidable indeed. However, regardless of Nicholas' refusal to admit that the revision of the fundamental laws made up a "constitution," Russia had, in reality, been transformed by it into a constitutional monarchy. It was of a special kind, to be sure—more like the Prussian or Japanese than the English—but a constitutional monarchy nevertheless.*

To Nicholas, the coming of representatives of the people to "help" him rule was another dark passage on his fated course as tsar. This one distressed him the more because he believed that it might have been avoided. As he looked back at the terrible events of the preceding two years, he drew sadly unjustified conclusions from them, sharing the view of many about him that the driving force of the revolution had been native demagogues clustered in St. Petersburg, working hand in hand with "international Jewry." Perhaps, he felt, if he had taken personal command in Manchuria, the war would have turned to Russia's advantage, leading the people to credit, rather than blame, him. Perhaps if he could have found a sufficient number of men capable and courageous enough to deal quickly and decisively with *kramola,* dissidence among the people would have been subdued before it became revolutionary. The next time, if there were a next time, he intended to be better served.[5]

As for the problem in hand, he accepted the fact that he must live with it. When the diehards in the government—and there were many of them—urged him to rescind the October Manifesto, he stoically resisted them, declaring that he firmly intended to implement it. But it was evident, when he made such remarks as "My autocracy remains as it was before," that his attitude towards the new order was actually one of rather dangerous ambivalence, a combination of resignation and repugnance.[6]

He agreed to open the sessions of the First Duma and the State Council, but he did it reluctantly; for he was still the autocrat who had often remarked, in rejecting the idea of a legislature, that to keep a clean house, one must not admit pigs to the table. On April 27, he received members of the two chambers with imperial formality in the Winter Palace. While his mother fought back tears and his wife stood rigid and red-faced, he addressed them briefly, his words limited to a simple acknowledgment of the occasion and an exhortation to work earnestly. That behind him, he returned immediately to his Peterhof residence, while the legislators proceeded

---

* The 1906 *Almanach de Gotha,* that sturdy handbook of European royalty, identified it, somewhat ambiguously, as a constitutional monarchy ruled by an autocrat.

to their respective meeting places—the Duma's in the Tauride Palace, the State Council's in the Marie Palace—and settled down to business.

Nicholas would not admit that it was either necessary or politic for him to become acquainted with the Duma leaders or otherwise to enlarge his political horizon in recognition of the change that was taking place in his government. Insofar as possible, he continued his old way of life, seeing the kind of people he had been accustomed to seeing, reading the kind of reports he was accustomed to reading, and looking only at those newspapers that did not "irritate" him with their political chatter. It was easy enough for him to withdraw in this manner because his new palace commandant, General Trepov, was still enforcing the restrictions that had been imposed for his personal protection fourteen months earlier, at the time of the assassination of the Grand Duke Sergei. Now that he preferred to be apart from the main current of affairs, he found it no great inconvenience to abide by the restrictions: to reside only in the well-guarded palaces in Tsarskoe Selo and Peterhof, to visit the capital only when necessary, and to refrain from traveling about the country.

Even in this physically limited world, Nicholas was not spared the effects of what went on outside. He found familiar faces less friendly, less open than they had been. He knew that his friends were frightened by what had happened, also that they were uncertain of his ability to cope with what might come. Few of the imperial family, aside from the Grand Duke Nicholas Nicholaievich and his brother Peter, gave him their full support now, and few aside from the Montenegrin princesses were on friendly terms with Alexandra. Lacking confidants and relieved of many social obligations because court life continued at the austere level imposed by the recent war, Nicholas and Alexandra became more domestic than ever, also more spiritually confined just when the tsar especially needed enlargement of spirit.

For almost three months, Nicholas endured what amounted to political siege from the forces of the First Duma. A week after his Winter Palace speech to the deputies, they replied with a statement indicating their belligerence and followed it up immediately with demands for various reforms. When Goremykin showed no intention of considering their demands or of cooperating in any practical way with the Duma, its sessions became rancorous demonstrations against the government, rife with name-calling exposés of official abuses, censure of the cabinet, and continued demands for reform, including radical changes in the electoral law. If the government had acceded to the demands of the Duma, it would in effect have been recognizing ministerial responsibility, and that it would not do. On the other hand, Nicholas might legally have dissolved the body, as soon as he recognized the stalemate, and called for new elections; but he hesitated to risk public reaction to such a step. So the siege continued until, in June, the Duma finally began concentrating on areas where the government considered its presumptuous advances too threatening. Its publicized support of the Cadets' radical agrarian program and its undertaking to determine the responsibility of local officials for a recent anti-Jewish pogrom in Bialystok were seriously irregular from the viewpoint of the government: the one because it ran counter to the official policy of the inviolability of private property, and the other because it was an arrogation of unauthorized power. And when the Duma was found to be preparing a direct appeal to the people on the issues, there was no question but that it had gone too far.

When Nicholas decided to dissolve the Duma, in July, he saw that Goremykin was reluctant to take responsibility for what might follow. But fortunately there was a man at hand, Minister of Interior Peter Stolypin, who had been recommended by Goremykin and who was willing and able to take the responsibility. So the tsar replaced the tired old premier by Stolypin, whom he allowed to retain direction of the ministry of interior, and preparations for the dissolution were begun immediately. Without alarming the deputies, the new premier had the antiriot forces strengthened in St. Petersburg and at other sensitive points in anticipation of possible public protest. Then, when all was ready, on July 9, he had the doors of the Duma chamber locked and the announcement of the dissolution published.

The "practice session" of Russia's first representative legislature was over after less than three months, though it might have been extended to five years if its aim had been cooperation with the government rather than intransigence.

Nicholas had at last found—by accident rather than design—a man who could broaden his outlook. Stolypin had come to the ministry of interior from the governorship of Saratov, where he had proved himself, in dealing with the recent turbulence there, an able and practical administrator. The embodiment of much that inspired confidence in the tsar, the new premier, now forty-three years of age, was energetic, daring, and wholly contemptuous of opposition. That he was also handsome, eloquent, "truly Russian," and of a good family well represented at court added to his acceptability.

Stolypin was more than a vigorous man with good credentials, however; he was a man of vision, with definite and realistic ideas about means for placing the monarchy on a firm and stable basis. He believed that Witte had failed because he had not interfered in the elections to insure the selection of sympathetic deputies for the First Duma and because he lacked a definite program. Unlike Witte, he would proclaim a program designed to show the people that their interests would be served by the government, not by the revolutionaries; he would take a hand in the elections to insure that the Second Duma be cooperative; and he would bring outstanding leaders of the political moderates into his cabinet. "I shall fight," he declared, "under a flag that will fly bravely in the wind, and if all do not take their stand under my colors, at least I will have supporters." [7]

He proposed to gain support from workers by providing them with government-sponsored insurance and from national and religious minorities, including the Jews, by easing the restrictions they found so onerous. But he expected the real strength of his support to come from those who would approve his proposals for agrarian reforms, which he considered the heart of his program.

Even before 1905, Stolypin as well as others had come to believe that the village commune had failed to provide peasant life with the benefits envisioned by Alexander II. But, in the present reign, since the tsar considered the commune to be sacredly "Russian" and therefore not to be questioned, all efforts at agrarian reform had dealt with peripheral matters. Stolypin had the good fortune to come onto the scene just when Nicholas, with the preceding winter of agrarian revolts fresh in his mind, was ready to change his view. He could no longer conscientiously oppose the argument of his premier and the conservative nobility that the village commune had failed to produce the desired respect for property and authority and must, for that reason if no other, give way to a new system of land tenure.

Stolypin's proposal was for a system of individual peasant proprietorship of enclosed farms with which the owners could do as they pleased—sell, lease, improve, neglect, reap the rewards of hard labor or the penalties of sloth. It was a system that would be, as Stolypin later characterized it, "a wager not on the wretched and drunken, but on the sound and the strong." Many peasants included in it could be expected to become bankrupt, perhaps join the proletariat; but those who were left would be prosperous, wedded by self-interest to private property and monarchy. Stolypin set great store by the zemstvos as adjuncts to his scheme for rural improvements; he recognized their contribution to the enrichment of peasant life and favored an increase in their authority as well as the establishment of zemstvos in provinces still lacking them.

Except for his proposals looking toward agrarian improvements, Stolypin's program did not go far beyond the timid, and still unfulfilled, promises of the ukase of December 12, 1904. Memory of that date was now revived not only by the similarity of the proposed reforms to those promised nearly two years earlier but also by the government action taken simultaneously with the official announcement of them, on August 25. On the former occasion, people remembered, Nicholas had ordered immediate and more rigid controls on public protest. This time also he ordered tighter control measures "with stronger teeth," including the creation of field courts-martial to try revolutionaries for acts of violence and to carry out sentences within no more than four days after the commission of such acts. Stolypin's flag was bravely flying.

The premier hoped that, between August 25 and the date set for the opening of the Second Duma, February 20, 1907, he could so strengthen the position of the government that its will would be the deciding factor both in the elections and in the legislative sessions to follow. It was well that he liked a good fight, for the opposition was apparently bent on holding its own at any cost. Reports of mutinies (including one in the tsar's own battalion of the Preobrazhensky Guards), strikes, peasant uprisings, and assassinations poured into his office. The newly authorized courts-martial tried and hanged terrorists by the dozen, while the political police decimated the ranks of less dangerous revolutionaries by arrest. But through it all, the premier kept up his personal efforts. He negotiated with Cadets and Octobrists about cabinet posts and took a vigorous part in the election campaign in an effort to defeat opposition candidates and insure the election of government supporters.

At the end of that six-months' period, Stolypin's flag was still flying, but not as proudly as he had hoped. He had two accomplishments to his credit, and they were by no means insignificant: the emergency pacification operation had brought Russia a reasonable degree of relief from violence and public defiance (as one minister put it, "The patient will live"); and his proposal for a new system of land tenure, embodied in a ukase issued by the tsar on November 2, was now being put into operation in the countryside. Though subsequent legislative approval would be required for the land reform, the dispatch with which he had handled the matter insured that the government, not the legislature, would have the credit for initiating it.

Weighing against these two accomplishments was the fact that in most other respects he had failed to gain his objectives. He had failed to persuade either Cadets or Octobrists to enter his cabinet, and he had failed to influence the elections sufficiently to bring a pro-government majority into the Second Duma.

In this second round of elections, though the Cadets had lost some of their numerical strength and the political right had gained some, revolutionary parties had entered the campaign and elected enough deputies to insure that the Second Duma would be even more hostile than the first. It opened with the unpleasant scene of right-wing deputies standing to sing "God Save the Tsar" and left-wing deputies sitting in defiant silence. Then the bold opposition leaders took up the attack where their predecessors had left off. Instead of approving Stolypin's land reforms, the deputies wrangled over various substitute proposals, the Cadets holding out with their usual tenacity for the expropriation and distribution of large estates. The revolutionary parties made their increased strength felt by introducing drastic measures for overriding government authority in famine control and the handling of unemployment. And few of the deputies were uninvolved in the turbulent sessions on such inflammatory subjects as the national budget and the condition of the army. Finally, the government could endure no more. Using as an excuse an alleged SD conspiracy to propagandize the armed forces, the tsar dissolved the Second Duma, on June 3, 1907, amid socialist threats of general strike and armed uprising.

Stolypin was still confident: though the Second Duma had failed him, the third would not. Like the tsar, he believed that at least 80 percent of the population—those people, particularly the "truly Russian" ones, who lived in the rural areas—were staunch monarchists, though admittedly the millions of peasants lacked the "maturity" to recognize their essential interests or to vote judiciously. It was up to the government, therefore, to see that the right of suffrage be exercised in such a way that those who could best appreciate the problems of the majority were selected to help the government operate in the interests of the majority. On June 3, the very day that the Second Duma was dissolved, the tsar issued a new electoral law that redistributed representation in the Duma in such a way as to favor Russians over non-Russians and the landowning nobility over all others. Nicholas justified the promulgation of this outrageous law on the grounds of imperial prerogative. But the opposition, rightly interpreting it as an illegal measure by which the autocrat was retaking what he had begun to relinquish, dubbed it a *coup d'état* and called the politically rearmed government the "June Third Monarchy."

The impropriety of the law notwithstanding, it served its intended purpose. When the Third Duma was convened, in November 1907, it was seen to be safely conservative. One-third of the deputies, the largest single bloc, were Octobrists, who stood squarely behind the government on the matter of putting into effect the provisions of the October Manifesto. The Cadets still led the opposition, but without sufficient support to prevent the government from getting on with its program. The extreme left was represented by only thirty-three members. The Octobrist Alexander Guchkov was elected chairman of the body, and indications were that it would endure for the allotted five years.

With the opening of the Third Duma, Russia entered a period of decided improvement marked by purpose on the part of the government and progress recognizable in many areas. The outlook, while by no means wholly bright, was more propitious than at any time since the beginning of Alexander II's reign. The legislature began to fulfill its promise of reasonable cooperation and, under Stolypin's energetic leadership, the cabinet functioned as a fairly unified body, working to prepare legislation in support of his program.

High priority was assigned to agrarian reform. The ukase giving peasants the right to withdraw from the village commune was granted legislative approval and its provisions, already being put into effect, commended. Government commissions continued to advise, assist, and sometimes cajole peasants into taking title to the allotment lands they had held as members of the commune, and then into taking the next step, consolidating their scattered strips of land into farmsteads on the Prussian style. It was a difficult undertaking, often resisted by the peasants, but it was carried forward relentlessly.

At the same time, with the tsar's approval, dozens of ameliorative measures were being taken on behalf of the peasantry. Two of them were particularly agreeable to the land-hungry peasants; despite loud protests from grand dukes, most of the six million acres of arable land held by the imperial family was put up for sale to them on easy terms, and many of them were given assistance in improving their lot by migration to virgin lands in western Siberia.

The remainder of Stolypin's program moved more slowly, but it was not neglected, for the premier was not one to be sidetracked. All in all, he was able, as none before him had been, to take real satisfaction from his accomplishments. As he began to observe the first fruits of the new order, he was justly proud of his part in helping to set it on its course. A very important supplement to his program was an undertaking of the ministry of education, to work toward the provision of universal primary education for the country. This goal, incorporated in a law adopted at the suggestion of the Third Duma, was to be achieved, according to the ministry's plan for progressive increase in the number of schools and teachers, by 1920. Meanwhile, industry and commerce were on the upswing, and almost everywhere there was evidence of productive activity. Russia might be raw and backward in many respects, but she was recognizing the practicality and profit in turning more serious attention to her great physical and human resources. Given twenty years of peace at home and abroad, Stolypin confidently predicted, Russia would be unrecognizable.

The premier's aspirations for continued peace at home and abroad were shared by the minister of foreign affairs. But, whereas Stolypin sought peace primarily to permit domestic reconstruction, Izvolsky sought it to permit Russia to regain her status as a great power. In his opinion, which was supported by many of his colleagues, if Russia were not to become "a half-forgotten Asiatic power," she must make a peaceful settlement of conflicts of interest in Asia. She needed particularly to come to terms with England in the south-central part and with Japan in the eastern in order to have freedom for concentrating on matters of decided consequence in the Near East, where things were once more astir.[8] The tsar, who had burned his fingers badly in independent forays into foreign affairs, was content to follow Izvolsky's lead.

The times were propitious for the new orientation. Japan was willing enough to discuss Far Eastern problems with a chastened Russia. England, recognizing the value of Russian friendship to help her counterbalance the growing power of Germany, was ready to compromise on issues concerning which she had been intractable. For added measure, France, already allied to Russia and having formed an entente with England just before the Russo-Japanese War, was now anxious for the development of Anglo-Russian accord as a link in a triple entente.

Izvolsky hastened to take advantage of the favorable atmosphere. In 1907, he arranged for the establishment of amicable relations with both Japan and England in the most sensitive of the Asiatic areas. A convention signed in mid-year represented a settlement in Manchuria, where both Russia and Japan had been quietly pursuing their respective courses of aggression since the war. While repeating the diplomatic gesture of recognizing China's legal sovereignty, it designated two spheres of foreign activity in Manchuria and assigned the northern one to Russia, the southern to Japan. This arrangement by no means settled all questions in the Far East, but it could be expected to reduce friction and the possibility of conflict. It was followed shortly by an Anglo-Russian convention, which served the same purpose in regard to Central Asian areas, Russia and England making mutual concessions and designating spheres of influence and activity in Persia, Afghanistan, and Tibet.

With that, relations among the powers were so altered as to produce another of those reversals in international alignments that provide many of history's highlights. Soon, in diplomatic circles, England, France, and Russia were referred to as the Triple Entente, as opposed to the Triple Alliance of Germany, Austria, and Italy; the reversal was, to all intents and purposes, an accomplished fact. The new understandings left much unspoken and still to be resolved, but they gave Russia the sense of security that Izvolsky considered necessary for the pursuit of her immediately important interests.

To emphasize Russia's Near Eastern interests just now was to ignore the advice of officials who believed, as Witte had insisted, that the changing domestic situation necessitated the foregoing of great-power aspirations for a decade or so. But neither the tsar nor Izvolsky agreed that such restraint was necessary or, for that matter, advisable. It could mean neglect of even the minimum of Russia's aspirations regarding the Straits—their opening to Russian men-of-war, which the recent war with Japan had shown to be vital—and the abandonment to Austria of all her influence in the Balkans. On the other hand, it seemed reasonable that skillful diplomacy, the clever use of opportunities and friends, could achieve modest gains and preserve fundamental interests for Russia without the risk of war or the impairment of the domestic program.

When Izvolsky set out to work his way personally through the tangle of European diplomacy, he did so with fine disregard for the wisdom of the old Russian saying that he who cannot deal with wolves should not enter the woods. He thought he had struck a clear path to the solution of the Straits problem when, in July 1908, the Young Turk revolt temporarily weakened Turkey's power to resist encroachment. The same path enticed the Austrian foreign minister, Baron Aehrenthal. Inevitably the two statesmen met and discussed the wishes of their respective countries to gain, at Turkish expense, certain advantages denied them by international agreement in 1878: for Russia, the passage of her warships through the Straits; for Austria, the annexation of the provinces of Bosnia and Herzegovina, which she had been occupying for thirty years. At a final, secret meeting in September, they considered the conditions under which they would proceed toward their goals. As Izvolsky understood their conclusions, in return for Austrian support of Russia on the Straits question, Russia would endorse Austria's wish to annex the coveted provinces—both issues, of course, to require international approval for final settlement.

Less than a month later, Aehrenthal, with no diplomatic preliminaries, proceeded to announce the annexation of Bosnia and Herzegovina in complete disregard of previous bargaining. Izvolsky felt that he had been betrayed, and when the matter was made public, Russian nationalists burned for redress of the slight. The tsar was inclined to join in military action against Austria when Serbia declared her superior claim to the ethnically Serbian provinces and threatened to fight for them. But when Germany gave notice of intention to intervene on Austria's behalf, when the Russian generals insisted that their forces were not ready to meet Germany's, and when other powers showed themselves not particularly averse to Austria's unilateral action, the tsar had no choice but to stand aside.

Again, Russia was without support on the Straits question. To other powers, the prospect of Russia's gaining military advantage through the opening of the Straits was a much more serious matter than that of Austria's annexing the provinces whose status, by virtue of the thirty-year Austrian occupation, was hardly changed by it.

Even Russia's new friend, England, maintained that the only acceptable readjustment concerning the Straits would be to open them to ships of all countries in peace as well as in war.

The Bosnian Crisis, as the aftermath of the act of Austrian annexation was called, ended quickly, but it had enduring consequences. It made war between Serbia and Austria all but inevitable. It intensified Russian ill-will toward Austria. It reminded Russian Pan-Slavs of their country's "duty" to the Slavs of the Balkan states. It prepared the way for a challenge of Russia's basic relationship with the Balkan states, since Germany was now taking the position that Austria had the right to act as she saw fit with regard to them without consultation with Russia—this, despite the fact that for nearly two centuries European diplomats had recognized that both Russia and Austria, being the two powers most closely concerned, had mutual responsibility for resolving issues in the Balkan area. That position raised the possibility of war between Russia and Germany from a highly remote to a very distinct—though presumably still distant—likelihood. The hurried display of Austro-German solidarity in the crisis even weakened the Triple Alliance, since Italy, feeling that the two powers had acted without due consultation with her and resenting Austrian growth toward the Mediterranean, now began making friendly overtures to Russia.

For Minister of Foreign Affairs Izvolsky, the results of his prolonged efforts on what he considered Russia's most important diplomatic problem were so discouraging that he was more than willing to exchange his ministerial post for the Russian ambassadorship to Paris in 1910, when the tsar understandingly offered it. His assistant in the ministry, Sergei Sazonov, took over his portfolio in the full knowledge that Russia's position with respect to her western neighbors was by no means a satisfactory one. He also understood the diplomatic significance of their current designation as the Central Powers, a recognition of their closeness and solidarity.

By the middle of 1909, though Russia's fortunes abroad had been disappointing in some respects, there was a substantial moderation of difficulties within the empire, accompanied by reassuring evidence of progress toward social and economic recovery. There was justification for the belief that the storm had been weathered and that the government was firmly in control again.

Personal tensions, no less than political ones, were now eased somewhat for Nicholas. He had smoothed relations with his uncle

Vladimir by allowing the disgraced Cyril to return to Russia, an act that had relieved him of a great deal of family criticism. After Vladimir's death, in February, he had the feeling that finally, at the age of forty, he had become the real as well as the titular head of the Romanovs. He was freed at last from the sense of subordinacy so often imposed on him by his father's brothers. The only one of them remaining, the Grand Duke Paul (Alexis had died in 1908), was still in France, an exile. And the patriarch of the family, the Grand Duke Michael Nicholaievich, only surviving son of Nicholas I, was now on the Riviera, in ill health and near death.

For the first time since Bloody Sunday, Nicholas could resume the freedom of movement that had been considered unsafe for him during the revolutionary period. The general improvement encouraged him to throw off the depression that had hung over him since the beginning of the war with Japan, and he welcomed the opportunity to travel again. In his initial excursion he chose to include a trip to Poltava to preside over the bicentennial celebration of the Battle of Poltava, in which the army of Peter the Great, in 1709, defeated the forces of Charles XII of Sweden, saving Russia and demonstrating the country's growing claim to the status of a major power.

On this occasion, as Nicholas again came physically close to his people, acquaintances were struck by the salutary change in him: he seemed to have recovered a feeling of well-being and confidence in himself. It was as if he could now dismiss the last five years as a bad dream and renew his pride in the glorious history of the Romanov dynasty when he stood surrounded by descendants of men who had fought under Peter and watched his troops parading under the same regimental colors that had flown over Russian soldiers two centuries earlier. Speaking at the Poltava cadet school after the main events of the celebration, he predicted a period of "progress and prosperity" that would bring to future generations "an easier life"; few could doubt his deep faith in what he said.

From Poltava, he went on to Kiev, "the mother of Russian cities," and worshiped in the Cathedral of Saint Sophia, "the mother church," symbol of more than eight centuries of Holy Russia's history. The enthusiasm of the Kievan crowds lifted his spirits still higher: they cheered him, sang "God Save the Tsar" at the least provocation, and pressed upon him the openheartedness of true and loving subjects. Watching the public scene with him, Stolypin was convinced that the revolution was truly over, that the past was now forgotten and that "no trace remained." [9]

Publicly, the prerevolutionary atmosphere did indeed seem to have been restored. When Rimsky-Korsakov's opera *The Golden Cockerel,* with its allegorical message of doom for complacent monarchs, opened in Moscow later that year, few thought it relevant to the contemporary situation. The censors insisted on some changes, but even they had grudgingly accepted the opera's Tsar Dadon as a wholly fanciful ruler in a fanciful empire.

Having been granted release from his "political captivity" and the distress occasioned by the revolution, Nicholas resumed his more active duties as head of state. He made frequent trips, through his own provinces and to the courts of Europe. He took an honored part in still more celebrations reviving the historic glory and achievements of the empire; in 1910, for instance, the bicentennial of the annexation of the Baltic provinces. This display of returning assurance reached something of a climax when, in January 1911, he attended the opera in St. Petersburg for the first time in six years. The monarchist press hailed the occasion as "the day of great forgiveness," suggesting that the tsar, by his appearance, was indicating his generous willingness to consider the offenses of 1905 as pardoned bygones.

Nicholas' public appearances had become quite common by September, when he made another official visit to Kiev, this time to unveil a statue of Alexander II, marking fifty years of emancipation. Preceding the day of unveiling, a number of gala events, including the grand maneuvers of the Kiev Military District and an opera performance, were to take place. To insure protection for the imperial party, which again included Stolypin, Kievan officials made elaborate precautionary arrangements for each event. They rounded up and put under lock and key every suspected terrorist, detailed picked soldiers and police as personal guards, and organized a special commission to distribute tickets for the opera.

The precautionary reckoning of the officials, unfortunately, did not allow for the deviousness of resolute terrorists. One such, Dmitri Bogrov, had marked Stoylpin as his victim and had the advantage of being able to fit his plans for assassination unobtrusively into official plans to guard against it. He was a young lawyer of Jewish origin, who, disillusioned with anarchist activities, had become a secret agent of the Kiev *Okhrana* and, finding that service still less to his liking but unable to extricate himself from it, now wanted to convince the anarchists of his second change of mind. He had decided on drastic means: he would singlehandedly kill the man whom revolutionaries particularized as the symbol of counterrevolution, Stolypin. Knowing that both the premier and the *Okhrana* chief, Colonel Kulyabko, were to attend the opera, Bogrov gained admittance to the theater on the night of the performance by claiming to have a report for Kulyabko regarding two assassins en route to Kiev to kill Stolypin (he himself had previously invented the rumor and put it about). When his superior had heard the "report" and ordered him to leave the theater, Bogrov simply disregarded the order. During the second intermission he completed his mission, shooting Stolypin under conditions that made his own escape impossible.[10]

The premier died four days later. Bogrov, who was apprehended on the spot, was hanged shortly thereafter.

The incident made it necessary for Nicholas to remind himself of a fact that he and many others realized but longed to repress: that, though the government had regained control, it could not expect to proceed unchallenged.

Stolypin had died when, in his judgment and to most outward appearances, the "June Third Monarchy" was in the ascendant. A close accounting, however, would have revealed some unmistakable indications of decline. The crowds that cheered the tsar did not cheer the government.

The calm in the countryside was the result of stern pacification and the siphoning off, by industrial expansion in the cities, of the most energetic and least docile of the peasants. Beneath the calm, the old problems and tensions continued. Most peasants still divided their world into one of "we" and "they," the latter being the landlords working hand in hand with the local administration and the clergy. It was possible that in time they would come to identify their interests with those of the government—Lenin feared that they would, thus lessening their potential worth to the revolutionary cause—but, aside from a prosperous minority, they still had little reason to do so.

Labor's attitude reflected another unrealized goal. Stolypin had been preparing, and had almost completed, the draft of legislation providing government-administered accident and sickness insurance for workers; however, even if he had lived to see it through, it would not have propitiated labor. Workers would have welcomed the insurance but would have continued their efforts to gain an eight-hour working day and higher wages, the goals for which they fought in 1905 and which now appeared as far away as ever. They still had no way to bypass management, well organized and adamant in its determination not to deal with trade unions or yield to strikes. And the government's power seemed to be used in favor of management: police closed most trade unions (for good reasons from their point of view—infiltration by revolutionaries) and harassed the few that remained open. These conditions did not make workers revolutionary, but they encouraged the acceptance of militant leadership, which came predominantly from the revolutionaries.

Other elements that remained unconvinced of the government's interest in their welfare were the national and religious minorities. Though Stolypin had made well-intentioned efforts on their behalf, the results had been paltry. His proposal to grant religious freedom to all denominations whose practices did not violate the law died quickly before the opposition of his own cabinet and the Holy Synod. His proposal to eliminate some restrictions on Jews was rejected by the tsar, responding to widespread opposition from the extreme rightists. In short, the government had earned no significant credits among the minorities during the five years of his premiership. It had earned debits instead by its continued hostility toward Jews, Finns, and Poles, by its interference with Ukrainian cultural activities, and by its obvious and emphatic assertion of the Russian and Orthodox character of the state. Such tactics, instead of killing aspirations, had the effect of widening the gap between government and the minorities, convincing the underprivileged that the government did not intend to allow any change in their status and making them therefore more assertive and determined than ever.

Stolypin's leadership could be credited with somewhat better results in attempts to narrow the political gap between the government and society in general. Though that gap was by no means closed, society had been drawn a bit nearer, as could be seen particularly in the Third Duma, where government-supporting Octobrists comprised the largest single bloc of deputies and where Cadets, although still in opposition, were losing some of their bite and showing more readiness to cooperate with Octobrists than with socialists.

390 YEARS OF THE GOLDEN COCKEREL

A very important segment of society, however, remained firmly on the side of the opposition—the majority of the educated class, whose oppositional votes (for Cadets and socialists) in the last elections had been obscured by the operation of the new electoral law. Even the Octobrists were becoming dissatisfied by the time of Stolypin's death, increasingly uncertain of the government's capacity to act effectively, and anxious that the Duma exercise more influence than the premier had allowed it.

Moreover, in the year before his death, there were signs that the reasonably normal conditions which had reappeared after 1907 were beginning to give way before the recurrence of active restiveness. In 1910, the mood of students in higher schools was seen to be changing, defiance of authority mounting again. In the following year, student disorders, occasioned in part by the heavy-handedness of Minister of Education Leo Kasso, were becoming serious. The strike movement also, which, in 1910, had reached its lowest point during the century, with no more than 47,000 workers on strike, had begun a new growth in 1911, supported by more than double that number of workers.

Stolypin had not taken these conditions as signs of failure, but had remained confident and eager to push on. If the programs in progress were to be carried forward, he had told the tsar, he was the man to direct them; if no advances were intended, if the aim was to "stand still," the minister of finance, Vladimir Kokovtsov, should be named to succeed him.

Two days after Stolypin's death, Nicholas appointed Kokovtsov as premier, permitting him to retain the finance portfolio, and appointed Alexander Makarov to fill the other vacancy left by Stolypin, the ministry of interior.

It was almost as if Fate, in making way for a new premier, had again lent a hand in the affairs of state—this time, from the autocratic viewpoint, a helpful hand. And that was precisely the point Alexandra made a few weeks later, when Kokovtsov came to Livadia, where she and Nicholas were vacationing. Calling him aside, she urged him not to invoke Stolypin's name as often as he did, and to remember that when a man dies, his destiny has been fulfilled. Her advice, as he later recalled it, was clear and direct: "You must not try to follow blindly the work of your predecessor. Remain yourself; do not look for support in political parties; they are of so little consequence in Russia. Find your support in the confidence of the Tsar—the Lord will help you. I am sure that Stolypin died to make room for you and this is all for the good of Russia." [11]

About Kokovtsov there was much that appealed to the tsar. Neither a reactionary nor a liberal, he was an honest servant of the crown whose highest aim had been to become ambassador to France. In his seven years as minister of finance, he had worked diligently, and with a great deal of success, to accumulate in the state treasury enough gold to stabilize the ruble. Furthermore, he was content to pull in bureaucratic harness; as he wrote of himself, "I have never sought popularity, I have never catered to public opinion." [12] He could certainly be expected to be a less venturesome premier than Stolypin and, in that respect, a welcome change to the tsar.

Nicholas did not intend to revoke the late premier's program, but, now that he was relieved of Stolypin's energetic persistence, he intended to excise what he considered objectionable aspects of it. Without fanfare, he let it be understood that Kokovtsov was not to renew Stolypin's effort to bring liberal leaders into the cabinet, and he quietly resumed his own superior authority in the selection of ministers, a matter in which he had allowed both Witte and Stolypin much freedom. By so doing, he was in effect bringing off another *coup d'état*. He was regaining authority, and he was blocking the major progressive effort begun by Witte and continued by Stolypin, to bring society and government together. Unfortunately he was doing so at a time when his regime was in desperate need of more, rather than less, support from society. He was unwisely burning strategically important bridges behind himself, intent only on recovering power—power that, as had been shown, he could not use well and did not want others to use.

That the reclaiming of autocratic authority by the tsar made inevitable another change of political course was not readily apparent to the public. Kokovtsov, after all, had worked closely with Stolypin and seemed to share his views; many people expected therefore that he would continue in the direction of his predecessor, and they responded to his appointment accordingly. The political leftists, anticipating nothing good from him, kept the opposition reminded of a remark he inadvertently made in an address to the Duma in 1908: "Thank God, we have no parliament as yet." Among the rightists, it was rumored briefly that Kokovtsov, a trafficker with foreign Jewish bankers, might prove less a Russian nationalist than Stolypin, but that fear was soon dispelled.

The consequences of the new appointment proved to be quite

different from what was expected. Even Stolypin's prediction that to appoint Kokovtsov was to bring the new program to a standstill, proved incorrect; as matters were handled, the result was not a standstill but a regression accompanied by subtly expanding liabilities for the regime. Under Kokovtsov, government officials soon felt a release from the sense of urgency and purpose; friendships that had meant substantial support for the government grew tenuous, and enemies came to the alert.

Responsibility for these developments, however, was only in small part Kokovtsov's. He could be blamed for little more than taking a post for which he, proficient in finance but not in politics, was ill-fitted, and, in view of the reduced power of his office, even that fault could be discounted. The responsibility rested firmly on the shoulders of Nicholas II, who continued stubbornly to misread reality, blind to the nature of the choices before him for the imperial regime—change or destruction. Yet, faced by arguments on the subject, he simply retreated again into the state of impervious independence and isolation from irritatingly practical men and their unpleasant advice. It was a position in which, as it proved, his protective love for his wife would lock him ever more firmly. Other monarchs might—and often did—work their own undoing by inconstancy, but to a degree Nicholas was led to his by constancy: his loyalty to Alexandra sometimes closed his mind completely to reason and expedience.

The circumstances that drew Nicholas more closely to the side of the empress and further away from others arose from a number of sources: Alexandra's social reticence and consequent unpopularity in court circles; her worry about the tragic outlook for her young son, Alexis, doomed by hemophilia to a life of uncertainty and recurring pain; the decline of her own health, aggravated by rheumatism and a heart disorder; her growing dependence on family and religion for her only happiness; finally, her approval and defense of the so-called man of God, Gregory Rasputin.

Rasputin had been introduced to the imperial couple in 1905 by the Montenegrin princesses, of the St. Petersburg circle devoted to mysticism and spiritualism. At that time neither Nicholas nor Alexandra had been any more impressed by him than by other such men, whom they met frequently in the course of their lives. "Men of God" —they might be monks (like Seraphim) or, more likely, aged laymen, often of the peasantry—were an informal part of Russian religious life. They were accepted by many as spiritual supplements to the organized Church, consecrated men who, in their simplicity, experienced the presence of God as other men did not.

When Rasputin was first recognized as a "holy man" in St. Petersburg, though he was relatively young for one of his calling—about the age of the tsar—he had already achieved a reputation. From his native Siberian village of Pokrovskoe, where his wife and children still lived, he had gone on long pilgrimages and accumulated a sizable following as one who had seen visions and been granted competence in divine matters. Despite the fact that he was a barely literate peasant, artless and uncouth, he had won the sponsorship of several prelates and the respect of a number of influential lay patrons. Making no particular effort to impress except as an ordinary "man of God," he nevertheless spoke with confidence that bordered on arrogance and was always ready with advice, assurance, counsel, prayer, or—if he felt it appropriate—censure. Few could remain long in his company without forming a strong impression of him. While some found him a "sly, dirty peasant," out to hoodwink the gullible, many esteemed him an especially gifted holy man. Even practical-minded Witte, who came to be one of his admirers, felt that Rasputin, better than almost anyone else, instinctively understood Russia, its people, and their feelings. Others, including people of all classes and both sexes (though women were in the majority), flocked to his modest living quarters for purposes varying with what he meant to them personally: they were the spiritually uneasy, the sick, the unhappy, and the lovelorn, along with backsliding drunkards, repentant sinners, ambitious office seekers, beggars, and ordinary curiosity seekers. Occasionally he deserted them all and returned to his family in Pokrovskoe, but he always came back to St. Petersburg, which soon became his second home, the place where he was generously cared for and given the attention he obviously liked.

One of Rasputin's admirers, young Anna Vyrubov, was a maid of honor and devoted friend of the empress; it was through her that he was finally given an entry into personal friendship with Nicholas and Alexandra. Beginning in 1908, Vyrubov often invited the imperial couple to meet the "man of God" at her small house, just outside the palace gates at Tsarskoe Selo. They began inviting him occasionally to the palace, finding in his simple discourse, apparently, some kind of key to the spiritual peace they had vainly sought in the

Church. Alexandra in particular took great comfort in his sympathetic concern with her personal problems, his "understanding" of the burdens she bore as empress of a country seething with unrest and as a mother of a future tsar with only a distressingly infirm hold on life. Soon his counsel became an important component of her increasingly spiritual life.

This is not to say that Alexandra favored Rasputin in any social sense. By custom in Russia, even the court clergy were placed socially near the bottom of the hierarchy of court attendants, below the court physician and superior only to court harbingers and *valets de chambre;* Rasputin's position was not as elevated as theirs either by tenure of any office or by the performance of any specific service. The relationship between him and the empress remained that of a *grande dame* and a superior servant who was permitted the kind of liberty of speech that might be expected of an old peasant retainer. He could not be called even her priest confessor, for, while Alexandra talked with him of spiritual problems, she did not make her confession to him.

During the first years of their acquaintance, Rasputin's association with the imperial couple consumed very little of his time or energy; it was with others that he built the reputation destined to darken that privileged association. Unlike most "men of God," whose advanced age and spiritual dedication were shields from carnal temptation, he was at this time in the prime of life, a virile man in a city where temptation abounded. He had not always resisted temptation in the past, and still did not see any surpassing virtue in resistance. The words of Father Vasilev, one of his defenders among the clergy, might have been a summary of Rasputin's rationale: "Divine gifts often reside in sinful men." Though undoubtedly there was a genuine core in the man, a belief in his benign gifts, and a sincere concern for others, rich as well as poor, the whole man was not in accord with it. He accepted the fact that he was a sinful man, a lover of wine, women, and jollity; and he indulged his nature. When he fell from grace, he "followed sin by repentance"—just as he constantly urged his followers to do—and straightway began a repetition of the same sequence.

Such a man inevitably drew both attention and criticism from the public, and when it became known that he had entrée to the imperial palace, Nicholas and Alexandra were treated to a share of the criticism. Denouncements came from many sources, including each year a greater number of disillusioned former admirers, finally even the Montenegrin princesses. By 1911, Rasputin was being looked upon as the snake in Eden by a disturbed throng of influential persons concerned with the good name of the monarchy: the dowager empress as well as practically all other members of the imperial family, most of the court, many of the ministers, a large part of the Church hierarchy, government supporters in the Duma and State Council, and the conservative press.

Some dared to tell the tsar that Rasputin was a grave liability, and the police provided him with ample evidence that the man was more sinner than saint. Yet, though Nicholas recognized the danger of scandal and more than once was almost ready to have the offender banished to Pokrovskoe, he continued to hesitate, letting private interest take precedent over public, convincing himself that "better ten Rasputins than one hysterical empress." [13] He faced the problem squarely for a brief period in 1912, when Rasputin was accused of being an active member of the *Khlysty,* an orgiastic sect illegal in Russia. He did not believe the accusation, but since it was a serious one, it could not be ignored. He ordered an investigation, which failed to prove the charge and did nothing to dislodge Rasputin from his strong position. Then, when Nicholas dismissed Minister of Interior Makarov for "lack of control over the press," the public promptly decided that his action was prompted by his disapproval of unfavorable publicity about Rasputin; it was concluded that his patience with popular criticism of the man was wearing seriously thin. That fall, Rasputin's position became a veritably unassailable one in the imperial household as the result of an incident involving the tsesarevich. Eight-year-old Alexis, stricken by a severe internal hemorrhage, which the court physicians pronounced unquestionably fatal, made an astonishing recovery after his mother received a telegram from Rasputin assuring her that the boy would live; there was no doubt in Alexandra's mind that the "man of God" should be credited with the "miraculous" cure. To her, Rasputin was now as saintly as Seraphim.

Thereafter, the tsar chose to regard the matter of Rasputin as a private one, closed to further discussion. His relations with other members of the imperial family and practically all of his old acquaintances, therefore, became more strained and more guarded. Again his outlook was narrowed to central officialdom, chiefly his ministers, on whom he relied more than ever for his view of reality (and then only if they avoided the subject of Rasputin) and to the tight little world of his wife, his four daughters, and the young tsesarevich.

The Rasputin affair was a double misfortune. Since what people believed about it went far beyond the tawdry truth, the imperial name was tarnished with scandal; since it stood between the tsar and many personal associations, he became less responsive than ever to pressures for accommodation to changing political reality.

People were finally warned off the personal matter as a subject for public discussion, but political matters were in a different category. During the period of the Third Duma, particularly after Kokovtsov came to the premiership, political discussion abounded and political reality was being changed despite the tsar's lack of response. This time the urge for change was coming from restive supporters of the throne as well as from the reviving revolutionary movement.

Just when influential men dedicated to preserving the monarchy were growing less and less confident of Nicholas II's capacity to save it, their chances of influencing the course of government were brightening. In their present ranks were many of greater political sophistication and more ambition than the monarchists of the past. Moreover, they now had the legal means for expressing themselves, the Duma, to supplement the informal forum and the press. In the Third Duma, when Kokovtsov became premier, their position was clearly exemplified by four leaders who represented the majority of the deputies: Vladimir Purishkevich, Peter Balashev, Michael Rodzyanko, and Alexander Guchkov—spokesmen respectively of the extreme rightists, the moderate rightists, and the Octobrists (Rodzyanko and Guchkov, best described as right of center).

Purishkevich, one of the founders of the monarchist Union of the Russian People, from which he had broken to establish the Union of the Archangel Michael, was really an interloper; like the deputies on the extreme political left, his intention was not to serve the Duma but to destroy it. An intensely patriotic man in his own way, he championed a purified, effulgent, incorruptible monarchy based on the principles of official nationalism.

Balashev was the leader of a loose bloc of deputies with a narrow popular base calling themselves Nationalists, short for Russion Nationalists and Moderate Right, consisting largely of landed nobles from the southwestern provinces. He and his followers considered themselves guardians of ancient monarchical traditions. Though disapproving of the October Manifesto, they were willing to accept the Duma if the electoral law be further revised to increase the representation of their class.

Rodzyanko, who had been elected chairman of the Third Duma in the spring of 1911 when Guchkov resigned because of strained relations with Stolypin, represented the mildly liberal nobility. He was a physically impressive man (his weight, two hundred and eighty pounds, prompted the tsar to introduce him to young Alexis as "the fattest man in the empire"), who had the qualifications typical of his social standing and helpful to his present interests. He had served in the guards, made good connections at court, and acquired a court title. With a somewhat exaggerated notion of his own importance, supplemented by a great booming voice, he had little difficulty, during Duma sessions, in keeping prominent the causes that he and his followers espoused: constitutionalism and monarchism.

Guchkov, the major figure among the Octobrists, represented a new political force, the capitalists. His family, descended from peasants adhering to the faith of the Old Believers, had amassed a fortune through the textile industry; using his part of it, Guchkov now controlled important publishing interests, including the conservative *New Times,* and was steadily accumulating land put up for sale by impoverished nobles. He was a vigorous man with vigorous ideas (as a matter of principle, he had fought in the Boer War against the English), wholeheartedly employed on plans for the renovation of Russia. Since he believed that the army would be an important factor in the country's future, he was making it one of his chief concerns.

These four men, representing as they did disparate elements among the electorate, were divided, as might be expected, on political philosophy. They were divided also on foreign policy: the Octobrists, like the Cadets, supported the Triple Entente, and the rightists favored a return to the conservative alliance with Germany and Austria. On one goal, however, they were in accord: the defense of the monarchy, from external enemies and from itself.

In one notable effort to purge the monarchy of what he considered detrimental elements and practices, Guchkov headed an assault on the administration of the Church and of the army, singling out as targets their respective administrators, Over-Procurator Vladimir Sabler and Minister of War Sukhomlinov.

On the face of it, Sabler had much to recommend him to friends of both Church and state. He was a man of outstanding piety as

398   YEARS OF THE GOLDEN COCKEREL

well as a fervent Russian nationalist, whose missionary zeal was in complete accord with official nationalism. But, like Pobedonostsev, whose assistant he had been, he ruled the Holy Synod with an iron hand at a time when it was trying to free itself from authority imposed by the state, and, in the opinion of Guchkov, supported by many like-minded observers, he was making "a holy mess" of it. By high-handedly transferring or promoting high churchmen with more regard for what he considered piety than for administrative ability or seniority and by bestowing honors on mere priests that archbishops had previously attained with difficulty, he earned a reputation as a man with no respect for the religious hierarchy, one who would not hesitate to turn a "boar into a bishop." [14]

For such acts alone Sabler would have been condemned both by the political right, who felt that he was destroying the dignity of the Church, and the left, who were anticlerical even when those handling Church affairs were on their best behavior. The matter did not rest there, however; there was the added charge against him, unjust but readily believed, that he was a sycophant of Rasputin. With no real foundation, that idea grew out of the fact that Sabler enjoyed the favor of the empress, who was quite absorbed in the activities of the Church, and appeared often to act on the basis of her likes and dislikes, now generally believed to be influenced by Rasputin. Alexandra saw Sabler as a model of piety, and her view was endorsed by the tsar as well as by her personal confessor, Father Vasilev. But that did not influence the critics, who saw him as an intriguer and a detriment to the monarchy.

In the spring of 1912, after Sabler had disciplined Bishop Hermogen, one of the churchmen who had renounced their former friendship with Rasputin, Guchkov daringly brought disapproval into the open. Before a demonstratively sympathetic Duma audience, he attacked both Rasputin and Sabler. Rasputin was a perfect target for sensational accusations, and Guchkov made sensation of accusations against Sabler as well, charging him with unwitting provocation of revolution and anticlericalism and, thus, with debasing the monarchy.

Next on the list for similar treatment before the Duma was the army, in the person of General Sukhomlinov. A month after Guchkov assumed the function of public prosecutor of Sabler, he took to task the minister of war. Armed with information supplied by cooperative officers, he denounced Sukhomlinov for two related acts of impropriety: the organization of a secret branch of the gendarmerie to spy on army officers for evidence of subversion and the appointment of Colonel Sergei Myasoedov, a gendarme officer suspected of having connections with Austrian intelligence, to command that branch. Again, a highly placed official was being censured as an unworthy servant of the crown and, therefore, a danger to the monarchy.

To attack such a man as Sukhomlinov was to demonstrate that freedom of speech was now more than a meaningless phrase in Russia. And to point out defects in the army was to indicate that the monarchists were aspiring to standards better than the traditional ones of the regime.

By old standards, Sukhomlinov was an unlikely subject of reproach. He had come to his high office in a traditionally approved manner, having served under Skobelev, risen by earned steps in the cavalry, held the governor-generalship of Kiev, and been appointed chief of staff the year before he became minister of war, at the age of sixty. Though he had worked hard during his three years in the ministry and had contrived to increase the army's effective strength, he had not overcome the shortcomings of his background, that of an old-fashioned cavalryman with little appreciation of the changing nature of contemporary warfare; nor had he escaped that common debility of Russian generals, complacency. Moreover, he had not kept his personal reputation unassailable. Since he had thus far proved inept and bumbling in his dealings with the Duma, the deputies were easily convinced of his personal responsibility for misconduct and weakness in a post of critical importance to the security of the monarchy. His lack of judgment in the choice of friends provided his critics with a semblance of proof: when governor general of Kiev, he had associated with a man suspected of being in the service of the Austrian intelligence; he now trusted Myasoedov, who had been virtually cashiered by the corps of gendarmes; he was more friendly than most generals with army contractors; and—an added fillip for the gossips—he had chosen for his wife an ambitious and indiscreet young woman whose previous marriage had ended scandalously.

Sukhomlinov was not in fact either an incompetent officer or, as many later insisted, a traitor and grafter; but he was obviously, in his superior post, something of a liability. Even so, Guchkov's well-aimed fire did not affect his official standing. It ricocheted and struck, instead, his assistant, General Alexis Polivanov, who was relieved of his post on suspicion of having supplied Guchkov with his information and of being a radical.[15]

These efforts in the Duma to protect the monarchy from itself, by attacking men whom Nicholas had appointed, were highly offensive to him, for he could see them only as attempts to weaken the monarchical prerogatives. As usual, he rallied to the side of his appointees, maintaining his firm confidence in both Sabler and Sukhomlinov. As for Guchkov, Nicholas regarded him as an unmitigated "scoundrel"; the more he thundered, the less the tsar listened. Even the fact that the supporters of the crown were becoming uneasy seemed not to impress him at all. He was content to leave to Kokovtsov the task of dealing directly with the Duma and the press—a task for which the premier was not equipped.

The government was not at all unhappy to see the Third Duma come to the end of its five-year term, in June 1912. And to prevent a repetition of its performance, steps were taken not only to preclude the reelection of political gadflies to the next legislative body but also to insure the election of more docile deputies. This time individuals, not parties alone, were a concern of campaigners on behalf of the government.

When the Fourth Duma was opened, in November 1912, the results were seen from the government's point of view to be mixed. On the positive side were the facts that the majority of the deputies were men who could be trusted to be favorable to the government, and that many of the Third Duma's gadflies—among them Guchkov, who vowed that he was leaving politics forever—were not elected. Detracting from these pluses, however, were some very important minuses: the representation of the left had increased slightly; the Cadets continued to hold a large share of the representation from such cities as St. Petersburg; the Social Democrats had won a significant share of the labor vote, electing fourteen deputies. Moreover, the government majority was lackluster, with a heavy leavening of the kind of landed nobles who, as some said, could be "counted on to support the monarchy if it supported them." It proved itself also an unpredictable majority when, at the opening session, it joined forces with the left, against the wishes of the government, to reelect Rodzyanko as Duma chairman.

Except on the matter of electing a chairman, the Fourth Duma gave promise of being manageable, but little more than that. Kokovtsov, with neither the will nor the capacity for playing parliamentary politics, did not win its heart. Sabler and Sukhomlinov remained under its disapproval, and to their company were now added Minister of Interior Nicholas Maklakov (whom Nicholas had recently appointed on Makarov's fall from favor) and Minister of Justice Ivan Shcheglovitov.

The tsar's appointment of Maklakov had been made over Kokovtsov's objection, a clear usurpation of the premier's privilege of selecting his ministers subject to imperial approval; but Kokovtsov had chosen to overlook it without demonstration. Nicholas believed the new minister to be a "strong" administrator, capable of dealing with the press and, in view of the fact that his political views were harmonious with those of the rightists, capable of getting along with that element in the Duma. Maklakov did not live up to expectations, however. He began at once to antagonize the right-wing deputies by his imprudence in harassing the zemstvos and thereby undermining much of Stolypin's work.

Shcheglovitov, also a dedicated monarchist, managed inadvertently to rouse the animus of many of the same group, even as he thought himself to be serving their cause. His most flagrant misdeed, in their judgment, was authorizing the prosecution of Mendel Beiliss, a Jew, on the poorly supported charge of having murdered a Christian child to obtain blood for ritual purposes. The investigation of the charge had started just before the death of Stolypin but had not become a subject of high-level concern until now. Maklakov was unwise enough to encourage Shcheglovitov; the tsar, naïve enough to accept his assurance of Beiliss' guilt; and the extreme right, represented by such men as Purishkevich, anti-Semitic enough to support the prosecution. But the Octobrists as well as many Nationalists, although themselves anti-Semitic, condemned Shcheglovitov, for they reasoned that the good name of the government, not that of the Jews, would suffer if Beiliss were brought to trial on what was generally judged to be a trumped-up charge. The minister lost an irretrievable advantage when they were proved correct. The preparation for the trial and the trial itself, which ended in Beiliss' acquittal, not only gave the government a bad name, abroad as well as in Russia, but also reduced the prestige of the ministry of justice.

By the time the trial ended, the number of disenchanted government supporters had greatly increased. Guchkov expressed their mood at an Octobrist conference in 1913: "We are forced to defend the monarchy against those who should be the natural defenders of monarchical principles, the Church against the Church hierarchy, the army against its leaders, the authority of the administrative power against the bearers of that power." [16]

The fact was that cooperation between the government and those who wanted to befriend it, begun in Stolypin's years, was almost gone. It was not being supplanted by direct opposition—so far, attacks had been mainly personal, directed against individual officials —but the earlier hopes of the government's supporters were unmistakably giving way to dispirited irritation.

As the animation of the government's friends declined, that of its enemies, particularly the revolutionaries, rose.

The strike movement, which had been revived in 1911, accelerated sharply during the following year, given impulse by what became known as the Lena Goldfields Massacre, an incident growing out of a strike that halted work in the Lena goldfields, in Siberia. When the management called in troops to break the strike, the workers stood firm, and the troops fired on them, killing more than 200. That was sufficient, for both the public and labor, to mark the day as a repetition of Bloody Sunday. The miners singled out, for vilification in a song, the captain who had led the troops:

> And they gave him a bonus for this,
> Poured out a barrel of gold for him.
> That he killed workers—that's no tragedy:
> The earth, in due time, will bear more of them.

The popular outcry aroused by the incident was intensified by the thoughtless words of Alexander Makarov, minister of interior at the time, who answered when questioned in the Duma about the incident, "Thus it has been, thus it will always be." Although his intention was only to affirm that force would always be met by force, his words were taken to mean that the government's will would always prevail and that armed force would always stand between labor and any opportunity for improving its lot.

Three hundred thousand workers in various parts of the country went on strike in protest over the massacre, and the bitterness that had been accumulating in the ranks of labor, long before the incident, began to break out into the open with greater boldness and frequency. In St. Petersburg the workers, accountable year after year for about half of the strikes in the country, were ready as usual to demonstrate on behalf of labor's cause. The significance of their attitude was not limited to this one incident, however; they were becoming a force to be reckoned with beyond the traditional bounds of labor discontent. More readily than workers elsewhere, they were willing to accept political aims, as they showed through their frequent strikes for noneconomic goals. They were likely to call a strike on the occasion of a commemoration of Bloody Sunday, a celebration of May Day (the international labor and socialist holiday), or any suitable event; in short, they were beginning to blend agreeably into the revolutionary movement.

All indications, in St. Petersburg or elsewhere, that labor was becoming a dependable revolutionary force were important, for labor could provide the power needed by the reviving revolutionary movement.

Although the police had arrested almost all major and many minor leaders of the revolutionary parties or forced them to flee the country during the pacification program begun by Stolypin late in 1906 and had later made it impossible for central party organizations to function, they had not destroyed the parties. Far from being suppressed, the revolutionary movement had continued to grow, gathering a larger following among workers, students, and even the middle class than it had before 1906, while its ideology was spread through the press, trade unions, workers' clubs and schools, evening courses, and the exceptionally convenient channel provided by the socialist deputies in the Duma, who enjoyed legislative immunity.

The revival of the strike movement, in which socialists exercised a commanding influence, gave revolutionary leaders new courage. Many felt that the lean years were finally behind them, that they could begin a purposeful drive toward their political goals, among which the chief immediate one continued to be the establishment of a democratic republic. They could overlook a few setbacks, such as the failure of mutinies planned by revolutionary sailors in the Black Sea and Baltic fleets, where failure did not obscure the important fact that the number of revolutionaries in the personnel of the fleets was sufficient to make the attempt, and they recognized no insurmountable barriers ahead of them. The Bolshevik faction of the SD's, in particular, cheered the rally. At a conference held late in the year in the Austrian city of Cracow, where Lenin was living, the delegates agreed that "Russia has once more entered the arena of open revolutionary mass struggle," and that "the new revolution, of which we are experiencing the beginning is the inevitable result of the bankruptcy of the Third of June policies of tsarism."

The Bolsheviks were premature in their judgment, as they were wont to be under Lenin's leadership, but, as 1913 wore on, it began to look as if events would support their prognosis. Before the end of the Beiliss trial, in October, unrest was again becoming general. The public, roused by the sensational trial, was openly critical of the government's part in it. The cities were harried by strikes. The Duma was restive. When the tsar, then in Livadia, asked Maklakov to report to him in person, the minister replied that it would be unwise of him to leave the capital at such a time, when any relaxation of vigilance might prove disastrous. He asked for, and was granted, the right to take two exceptional measures if they should become necessary: to dismiss the Duma if there was evidence that it intended to take advantage of the current unrest to enhance its power, and to place St. Petersburg under extraordinary protection if public or labor unrest became any more threatening. It was authority that, much to his relief, circumstances did not oblige him to exercise.

Once the Beiliss trial was over, the revolutionary threat, like many before it, began to die down of its own accord, exhausted before it became a real challenge. The decline led a Cadet writer of the period to deplore the fickleness of a public that was apparently losing its interest; he compared the current attitude unfavorably with the popular spirit that had supported the liberation front in 1904 and lamented the fact that newspapers were able to supplant it by stimulating interest in such subjects as the doings of the highly acclaimed orchestra leader Willy Ferrero and the French motion picture comic Max Linder.[17] By the end of the year, Kokovtsov was confidently reporting the weakening of the revolutionary movement and declaring that, beyond the large cities, the country was to be found in a state of absolute calm.

Though the revolution had not developed on this occasion, perceptive observers of both the right and the left remained apprehensive. The government, they felt, was at a critical crossroads: it would soon be forced either to shift somewhat to the left, by making further concessions, or to make a sharp turn to the right. They understood what unquestioning supporters of the "June Third Monarchy" did not: that it had by no means achieved a satisfactory settlement with the opposition or the degree of consensus necessary to insure stability.

They could see the futility of halfhearted efforts by the government, whether made in the interest of executing liberal concessions or of stiffening arbitrary authority. Aside from the Stolypin agrarian reforms and the movement toward universal primary education, both of which were being implemented more slowly than expected, what had actually been accomplished under the "new order"? Even the old processes of official nationalism were becalmed. Proof could be found in such areas as the Western Region, where a ruthless program of Russification had been begun by Muravev half a century earlier and where the anticipated results were still unrealized. In his 1913 report, the governor of one of the provinces (Minsk) in that region informed the tsar that, although Poles comprised only 3 percent of the province's population, they were still dominant among the landlords and still exercised such a powerful cultural influence that vigorous measures should be undertaken to prevent their "Polonizing" the peasantry.[18]

Extreme rightists, like Balashev and members of the powerful pressure group the Council of the United Nobility, insisted that all would fall into adjustment if the government would adopt a more "national" policy—that is, one that further strengthened the Russian Orthodox and rural character of the state. This, of course, was a shopworn thought that only underscored the debility of traditional assumptions about the nature of the monarchy.

Such observations seemed not to disturb the tsar, his ministers, or most of the clergy and the nobility. They had no doubt that, administered with vigor and self-confidence, the monarchy would prevail. Nicholas believed the chief problems of the day to be the occasional uproars in the Duma, the effrontery with which the press expressed itself, and the prevalence of drunkenness. Satisfying one of his recurring needs, to assert himself by putting his stamp on some policy or other without actually tampering with the social or political structure of his realm, he chose to do something about the drunkenness. It was a problem that most people had come to accept as they did the weather. They considered it unfortunate because it was responsible, they believed, for much of the peasant poverty; but they were of the opinion that nothing could be done about it.

The tsar's interest in drunkenness was not a new one, nor was it insincere, though he was rather belated in taking action. His concern was sharpened when he was traveling about the interior during the celebration of the Romanov tercentenary, in 1913, seeing so much peasant poverty, about which he held the common Russian view that it was the result of drink. As soon as possible he instructed Kokovtsov to take appropriate action for enforcing temperance in the countryside. His move met with much approval, both public and official, but not the approval of the peasants or of the premier himself. Kokovtsov, mindful of the state of the imperial treasury, could not work up any enthusiasm for an effort to impose temperance, since the sale of spirits, a government monopoly established during Witte's tenure, provided a fourth of the government's annual revenue.

This lack of enthusiasm on Kokovtsov's part was a factor in Nicholas' decision to relieve him of his official status. In addition there were the premier's troubles with the Duma and the ministers, particularly Sukhomlinov, whom the tsar had supported in regard to contested military appropriations. Finally, in consideration of the difficulties growing out of this general incompatibility with official associates, the tsar, at the end of January 1914, dismissed the man who had served him for ten years—first as minister of finance, then a minister and premier—with the simple explanation that the country now stood in need of someone "fresh for the work."

The tsar intended to replace Kokovtsov as premier with the incumbent minister of agriculture,* Alexander Krivoshein, believing that his ability, adroitness, and charm would make it possible for him to handle both the Duma and his colleagues without sacrificing the prestige or the prerogatives of the throne. But Krivoshein, having recently been ill, suggested that the honor be given again to Goremykin. So it was that, for the second time, the cynical old man was brought back from obscurity to become premier. He presented a sad picture: whereas at sixty-nine he had looked seventy-four, now at seventy-four, he was a frail and exhausted ancient, in whom the spark of life was barely discernible. Few people—himself included—expected him to remain long in office. Decrepit as he was, however, he could be depended upon for unswerving loyalty and he would be able to keep his colleagues in check.

To assume Kokovtsov's other duties, as minister of finance, Nicholas chose the experienced banker and, recently, assistant minister of commerce and industry, Peter Bark.

Again, the government was freed of a developing discomfiture. Shortly after letting Kokovtsov go, the tsar banteringly asked the Grand Duke Nicholas Michaelovich what he thought of the latest *coup d'état.* The grand duke, an ardent student of history with a particular interest in Alexander I, replied, *"Cette fois, sire, vous avez surpassé le charmeur de Tilsit."* [19]

---

* After 1905, the title of this official was Head of the Chief Administration of Land Organization and Agriculture, but the earlier designation, minister of agriculture, was commonly used.

XIV

Overdrawn Account

NICHOLAS II, 1914–1915

AT the beginning of 1914, as Nicholas II was gathering up the reins of his government, he saw no reason to doubt that he could soon have Russia back on course again, adapted to peace at home and abroad and able once more to achieve a place of pride among the nations.

Though he deplored the recent evidences of discord and defiance of authority, he found it easy to accept the rationalization of those who saw nothing excessive in these "scattered manifestations" among a vast population of 178 million. Disquiet in the agricultural areas, they pointed out, was by no means new. As for the recent increase, it merely reflected the fact that the rural population had increased from 100 million to 133 million in the last fourteen years. Labor disturbances were understandable also: when five million men had become—the mass of them within the last decade—wage-earning laborers, concentrated in new environments among new associates, it was not surprising that, naïve and credulous, they had been easily misguided by the purveyors of utopian dreams and *kramola*. In assessing these developments, the tsar was reminded, it was necessary to maintain perspective and to remember that the country's economy had continued to improve, that far-reaching and profitable reforms had been instituted in the countryside, and that industrial progress had not at any time been seriously halted. True, the productivity of Russian labor and the standard of living were low in comparison with advanced European countries and the United States, but the rate of increase in industrial production during the past five years could be shown to be far in excess of that in any country in the world, and it continued to rise.

For Russian military services also, in Nicholas' judgment, the future looked bright. Certainly, improvements had been made since 1905: the number of long-term noncommissioned officers had been built up, line-officer duty had been made more attractive by pay increases, the condition of enlisted men—most of them illiterate—had been improved through broadened instruction in reading and writing, and efforts to provide better equipment had been begun. Like many of the military experts, both in Russia and abroad, the tsar let himself be dazzled by the fact that within his realm there were 30 million men of military age—a juggernaut on call. In the standing army, there were currently 1,423,000 men, a number that could be increased each year, if the need arose, by the induction of a larger percentage of those who reached the age of twenty-one and were subject to call. The reservists numbered about 2,600,000. The militia (*opolchenie*) provided a pool of millions more: those who had not been called up for regular training when they reached twenty-one but had been assigned to the militia accounted for nearly ten million; and others were added annually, for reservists who reached the age of thirty-nine automatically became militiamen until they were forty-three. Beyond all this, there was the fact that the Duma had just approved a new three-year program for reconditioning and increasing the capacity of the armed forces, and Minister of War Sukhomlinov had assured Nicholas that all was going well.

On the diplomatic front, there was nothing disturbing. The Triple Entente was satisfactory enough as a counterbalance to the Triple Alliance. Minister of Foreign Affairs Sazonov could be trusted to offer no intentional obstruction to the peaceful continuation of things as they were. His Anglophile soul was content with the evidence that, in the same degree that the tsar's relationship with his German cousin William II was becoming strained, his regard for the goodwill of the English was increasing. In recent years, the few rough spots encountered by the ministry of foreign affairs had been smoothed over without Russia's becoming seriously involved in the process, and it now seemed possible to regard the scars simply as evidence of concluded incidents.

Caution was still required to keep relations with England free of friction, but her friendship was unquestionably worth the caution. If she appeared to be seeking a rapprochement with Germany, as the Haldane mission to Berlin in 1912 indicated, it was accepted as impolitic for Russia to protest too much. If she became concerned about William II's dream of German commercial expansion by way of rail construction in the Near East or his pointed interest in the improvement of the Turkish armed forces, it was highly agreeable to echo her concern and be able to find the narrow path of safe conduct through the maze of conflicting interests. If she took exception to the aggressive acts of Russian agents in Persia, where they were pursuing the age-old practice of encroachment on border areas, it behooved Russia to restrain them.

In the Balkans, as in Persia, Russian emissaries had often—particularly in the past two years—indulged their enthusiasms to potentially dangerous lengths, but they had stopped short of embroiling their government. They had, for instance, allowed their personal devotion to Russia's "historic mission" among the Slavic peoples sometimes to override protocol and, uninhibited by Sazonov, had supported national aspirations that had brought highly sensitive problems into international prominence again and reawakened the "Slav-conscience" of many Russians. They had done that by encouraging the creation of the Balkan League among the states whose independence from Turkish rule had already been established (Greece, Serbia, Montenegro, Rumania, and Bulgaria) and by watching with approval when it became clear that, unmindful of counter-advice from both Austria and Russia, the League intended to free by force all European territory remaining under Turkish rule. In a war beginning in 1912 the member states—Rumania excepted—had carried out that intention. When the European powers stepped in to help with the distribution of the spoils, the so-called settlement at which they arrived had only emphasized divisive interests and bared old rivalries. It established an independent Albanian state between Serbia and the sea, thus condemning Serbia to the continued payment of an onerous tariff to Austria, and it favored Bulgaria with the addition of the Macedonian territory taken from Turkey. Inevitably such an arrangement, particularly inimical as it was to the territorial dreams of Greece and Serbia, had led to a second Balkan war. This one, fought in 1913, had been a victory for those states over Bulgaria, which was forced to accept extensive losses.

In her efforts to exercise any control over these Balkan developments, Russia had not distinguished herself as a champion of the
Slavs. But she had stayed clear of dangerous involvement, and the
tsar was hopeful that the apparent calm which had finally been
achieved would hold.

That the Balkan situation contained the seeds of trouble could
not be denied, however. The unity of the states was now broken, the
Bulgarians were embittered and vindictive, and the Serbians harbored a smoldering resentment against Austria, blaming her for the
tightening of commercial restrictions and the thwarting of their
aspirations for a Greater Serbia. Moreover, these latest developments
had opened the possibility of a new phase in Austro-Russian relations with respect to the area. Austria, now backed by Germany, had
abetted Bulgaria's defiance of the other Balkan states; the Bulgarians,
who had been moving purposefully away from their Russian orientation since Alexander III's denunciation of their nationalism, now
looked to Austria as their mentor. The Serbians, on the other hand,
now looked more anxiously than ever to their powerful Slavic kin
for support against what they believed to be the Austrian intention
of engulfing, if not actually destroying, them.

Observers more diplomatically astute than Nicholas had noted
the dangerous tilt of the Austro-Russian seesaw before the outbreak
of the Balkan wars. The German military attaché Paul von Hintze
had reported to his emperor in 1910 his belief that, although the
tsar had no wish for war and would prefer to cooperate with Austria
in the Balkans, he was allowing his ministers there to pursue an anti-
Austrian policy which would one day bring him face to face with
the prospect of war, and that he could then be expected to struggle
and plead for a way out.[1]

That day became imminent—though not recognized as such at the
time—on June 15, 1914 (June 28, N.S.), when a Serbian nationalist
murdered the heir to the Austrian throne, the Archduke Francis
Ferdinand, then visiting in Sarajevo, the capital city of Bosnia.
Austria, seizing upon the deed as a pretext for further pressure
against her ambitious southern neighbor, accused the Serbian government of official complicity, and Russia was brought to the alert
on behalf of her traditional interests in any Balkan affairs involving
Austria.

For almost a month, the issue hung fire. European statesmen, of
whom only the Germans were being favored by Austrian consulta-

tion, attached no great importance to it. The tsar was not perturbed as long as the matter seemed only a disciplinary slap at Serbia, whose "pretensions" he himself had once dismissed as "negligible." Sazonov expressed no official reaction until early in July, then only directed the Russian ambassador in Vienna to caution Austria about the need to respect the "dignity of Serbia" in any action she might be contemplating. Even the Russian press, though defending Serbia as the sinned-against party, sounded no new alarums during this period.

However, when it was learned that, on July 10, Austria had presented Serbia with a forty-eight-hour ultimatum which no state could accept *in toto* without relinquishing its sovereignty, and when Germany reiterated her support of Austria's right to handle her Balkan relations without outside interference, St. Petersburg woke to the seriousness of the matter. If allowed to dominate Serbia, Austria would unquestionably become the paramount influence in the Balkans and a menace to Russia's position as a great power. She would be yet another section of the barrier separating Russia from European friends—a barrier already discernible, with the Straits closed, Bulgaria in the camp of the Central Powers, and Germany brooding over the Baltic. Yet the tsar wanted to avoid war. He instructed the foreign ministry to advise Belgrade of the need to respect the ultimatum as far as possible short of resigning Serbian sovereignty. Serbia did as advised, but her response proved unacceptable. On July 15, Austria declared war on her and launched a quick attack on Belgrade.

During the following two days the activity of foreign offices and embassies throughout Europe quickened to the threat of war, and telegraph lines hummed as diplomatic efforts were made to limit the belligerency. Nicholas, in a telegram to the German emperor, pleaded, "I beg you in the name of our old friendship to do what you can to *stop* your *allies* from *going too far*." [2] On the same day, the people of St. Petersburg came out in a great demonstration expressing the sentiment of Slavic brotherhood.

Both Minister of War Sukhomlinov and Chief of General Staff Yanushkevich were urging meanwhile that, whatever transpired, Russia should begin general mobilization; for, if she were drawn into war, a delay in readiness would give the advantage to the enemies. In a short war, such as might be expected in the present situation, victory would go to the side striking first with superior force. Considering the problems of Russian mobilization—long distances and comparatively poor transportation—delay would be not just disadvantageous but fatal.

Finally, on July 17, Nicholas received Sazonov, minister of foreign affairs, in his study at Peterhof, for a consultation on the considered conclusions of the military experts. Sazonov, tight-lipped and grave, stated them without equivocation. The tsar could avoid war only by abandoning Serbia. To do that would mean that Russia would lose all her influence in the Balkans and be reduced "to a pitiful dependence upon the arbitrary will of the Central Powers." The alternative, to support Serbia, would require that he accept war as inevitable and prepare for it by ordering general mobilization.[3] For an hour Sazonov defended the second position while Nicholas, nervously smoking cigarette after cigarette, tried vainly to resist the finality of it: he was reluctant to believe that Austria would accept no terms except such as would make Serbia an Austrian satellite—terms that neither Serbia nor Russia would consider.

The tsar knew that he could not reverse himself, once he had made his decision for general mobilization. It would, in all likelihood, precipitate Russia into war with Austria and her ally Germany, and that in turn would lead to a general war—the Triple Entente against the Central Powers. But at length he gave Sazonov the hoped-for answer, that Russia would take the risk. He was again accepting—though with obvious irritation—what Fate imposed.

The decision was relayed to the impatiently waiting General Yanushkevich, and the period of what he considered impractical inaction was ended. The next day, red mobilization notices summoning reservists to service were posted throughout the country. Recognizing the portent, Count Pourtalès, the German ambassador, called on the tsar to urge the cessation of mobilization and point out to him that military conflict among the three conservative monarchies would only weaken them and thus endanger the political structure of each. That was a prospect that Nicholas did not care to discuss: he simply replied that the matter was in God's hands. Berlin's last hope of preventing Russian involvement now rested on an ultimatum demanding cessation of mobilization within twelve hours. When it also proved ineffectual, William II followed it, on July 19, with a declaration of war.

Once the dividing line between peace and war was crossed, most of the Russian people responded with ready support for their country's position. The early wartime regulations, such as the withdrawal

from labor of the right to form unions and the prohibition of the
sale of liquor, were accepted without resistance, and the people appeared to welcome the opportunity to aid their fellow Slavs against
the Teutonic aggressors. This popular endorsement of what he was
doing cheered and encouraged the tsar, as public approval always
did. His generals—Sukhomlinov loud among them—lifted his spirits
still higher by their assurances that victory would come so easily to
Russian arms in cooperation with the French and English that, by
Christmas, Russians would be shaking hands with their allies in
Berlin. He was affected the more personally because he intended, in
this war, to do what he had failed to do at the time of the war with
Japan: he would keep himself more prominently before his people,
he would honor tradition by praying for victory in the Moscow
Kremlin, and he would take command of the fighting troops.

On July 20, in a solemn ceremony at the Winter Palace, the state
of war was officially proclaimed. The imperial manifesto, read in the
St. George Hall to a distinguished gathering of 5,000 men and
women representing royalty, officialdom, and the military leadership,
stated the cause: "We must not only help a kindred state that has
been unjustly attacked but also protect the honor and dignity of
Russia as a great power." [4] And the tsar's oath, modeled on that of
Alexander I in 1812, affirmed his resolution to honor it: "I solemnly
swear that I will never make peace so long as one of the enemy is
on the soil of the fatherland." From the formalities, Nicholas went
to a balcony overlooking the square that echoed the tragedy of
Bloody Sunday and greeted a throng of his cheering, singing subjects
who had waited for hours to see their tsar and express their enthusiastic support of the war.

The overwhelming majority of the Duma and State Council members also, when the tsar opened their session six days later—an office
he had not performed since 1906—welcomed him with heartwarming
readiness. A handful of socialist deputies, opponents of the war, remained hostile and restrained, but they were not able to affect the
general mood. In their separate meetings later that day, both chambers of the legislature voted military appropriations and members
made fervent pledges of determined loyalty. The words of the
inveterate enemy of tsarism, Paul Milyukov, outshone them all: "We
are fighting to save our fatherland from foreign invasion, to free
Europe and Slavdom from Germanic dominance. . . . We are united
in this struggle, we make no conditions, we demand nothing, we
accept the fortunes of war with a firm will to win." [5]

The spirit of those words was the spirit of what came to be known as the *Union Sacrée,* to which all but the socialist deputies adhered (and of the socialists all but the Bolsheviks were soon to give their support) in a commitment to abandon politics for the duration of the war in the interest of a common cause.

Still further demonstrations of loyalty marked Nicholas' reception in Moscow, when he went to the old capital to take his part in the religious services held traditionally at the opening of a war. Thousands thronged the city and jammed the streets, the windows, and the rooftops to hail their leader and jubilantly profess their loyalty to the fatherland. In the Kremlin, over a hundred metropolitans, archbishops, bishops, archimandrites, and abbots assisted in the ceremony invoking divine aid in the achievement of victory.

The tsar had now taken the first steps in the discharge of his resolution to handle this war in the time-honored manner of a strong Russian ruler. His next intended step had been to take over the supreme command from the Grand Duke Nicholas Nicholaievich, whom he had appointed to assume that duty until he himself should be ready; but here he had to accept frustration. When the ministers had learned of his intention, all except Sukhomlinov had entreated him to remain at the center of government, where, they insisted, his presence was indispensable. With no reasonable rebuttal to offer, Nicholas had deferred to them, taking what consolation he could from his reservation of the right to change his mind at a later date.[6] For the time being, therefore, he felt obliged to leave the opening moves of the war to his chosen proxy. The Grand Duke Nicholas Nicholaievich was already at *Stavka* (General Headquarters), which had been established at the small rail junction of Baranovichi, about five hundred miles southwest of St. Petersburg, a point roughly midway between the northern and southern extremes of what was expected to be the initial battle front.

The choice of the grand duke as commander in chief had the approval of the general public as well as the troops, and no one could have looked the part more perfectly or been more faithful to patriotic duty and the military proprieties. Unfortunately those assets did not add up to the competence needed at *Stavka*. Nicholas Nicholaievich, with his limited military skill outside the cavalry and his meager aptitude for the broad thinking required in the command of a modern fighting force, was thirty-six years removed from his last experience in active warfare, which had been during the Russo-Turkish War. The chances of his being able to handle the

command effectively were further curtailed by the detrimental fact
that he was on the most hostile of terms with Minister of War
Sukhomlinov, with whom he had for years carried on an unremitting
—and unsuccessful—battle over military organization. Almost as detrimental was the fact that most of the members of the imperial
family disliked him personally. His chief support among them came
from his brother Peter, the tsar, and the Montenegrin princesses
(one of whom, Anastasia, he had married in 1907).

Stavka lacked also the one good substitute for a strong commander, a strong chief of staff. General Yanushkevich, clever though
he was, did not have the necessary qualifications. Perhaps Sazonov's
characterization of him as a "narcissistic nincompoop" was undeserved, but it represented a typical reaction of officials who had
dealings with him. What ability Yanushkevich had was often eclipsed
by his overconfidence, his unmistakable avidity for power, and his
inexperience in the command of men, the result of having spent
most of his career with the war ministry and the general staff.

Whatever the qualities of the high command, adequate or not,
within a week after Nicholas' approval of general mobilization, the
processes of war were irrevocably under way. Germany's declaration
of war on Russia had been followed by a succession of declarations.
The Central Powers* and the Triple Entente were set squarely
against one another.

When Sukhomlinov had been challenged, on the eve of the war,
to justify his claim that Russia was ready for war, he had replied,
"We are ready for six months; the war will be short." [7] Franco-
Russian plans called for France to take the offensive in the west
against Germany while Russia attacked both Germany and Austria
from the east. The expectation was that both would move rapidly
toward a meeting on enemy soil. If England should help them (she
was known to be less than enthusiastic about getting involved in
squabbles about the Balkans), the march to victory would be stepped
up, of course.

During the first weeks of the war, operations were, in fact, accelerated beyond the planned speed, but not with the planned results at all points. Since Germany had quickly halted the developing
French offensive, and, even after England entered the field in protest

---

* Of the Central Powers, Italy remained aloof at this time. She interpreted
Austria's invasion of Serbia as an offensive operation, and, since her alignment
required her to aid only in defensive action, she remained neutral until the following
year, then chose to attack Austria.

against the invasion of neutral Belgium, had been able to continue her pressing attack, Russian aid was required to divert German strength from the west before arrangements for opening the eastern front were completed. Yet, despite the difficulties of the unexpected necessity to rush the deployment of forces, both of the planned Russian offensives were under way and driving steadily ahead before the enemy was set for them: a two-pronged thrust by the First and Second Armies against the Germans in East Prussia and a heavy campaign against the Austrians in eastern Galicia. In each area, commands were assigned to generals of distinguished experience: in the north to Samsonov and Rennenkampf; in the south, to Ivanov, Brusilov, Ruzsky, Alexeev, and Dmitriev.

By the end of August, Russian forces had encountered the extremes in the fortunes of war. The southern campaign had driven the Austrians out of the oil-rich area of Galicia and made it possible for the Russians to invest the key fortress of Przemysl and establish positions for an assault on the Carpathian passes into Hungary. But in East Prussia, after the initial Russian advances, the German forces, strengthened by the revamping of command and the addition of troops withdrawn from the western front, had brought Russia's Second Army to a jolting halt at Tannenberg and then moved on to a sweeping victory over the First Army.

The tsar and his military leaders considered the returns from the Galician front highly satisfactory, and the northern reverses far from disastrous. The idea of a short war still prevailed, sustained by the fact that, for the first time in a hundred years, Russia was fighting with the support of powerful allies. Reciprocity in arms was an unfamiliar experience to this generation of Russian leaders, but they could not overlook its advantages. To check the Russian armies in East Prussia, it had been necessary for the Germans to reduce the strength of their western offensive to such an extent that France and England were given the chance to make a stand at the Marne. As a turnabout, Russia "shared" in the successful invasions and seizures of Germany's farflung colonial possessions by England, France, and Japan (recently aligned with the Entente powers) and in Serbia's successful repulse of the first Austrian invasion of her territory.

However, in the remaining months of 1914, the prospects of a quick victory began to dim. While holding Russia's allies strategically handicapped in the west, the Germans were able, for a time, by mounting an attack in southwest Poland and reinforcing the

Austrian opposition in Galicia, to give the eastern front a different aspect. Recognizing the possibility of Polish defection to the enemy, Nicholas had promised, in return for loyalty, certain postwar changes which "under the scepter of the tsar" would insure the Poles "freedom of religion, language, and self-government." But that precaution notwithstanding, the struggle in Poland during the fall was a hard and costly one. The Germans did not succeed in taking Warsaw, the coveted prize, but they secured their capture of Lodz and kept the Russians uneasy in the possession of what they retained. Meanwhile, the Austrians, stiffened by German leadership and manpower, were able to relieve Przemysl and force the Russians back temporarily. Yet Russia's strength was not broken. Her troops, their morale unshaken, performed admirably against the Turks, who entered the war in October; by November, they were on the advance again, beginning a second investment of Przemysl.

When winter set in, however, it was becoming clear that the plans for a short war were unrealistic: Russia and her allies were farther from their meeting in Berlin than they had been before the war. As the eastern front settled down to the relative inactivity imposed by snow, ice, and mud, the Russians were unquestionably in need of respite.

By this time, the war had exposed a number of important problems relating to both the battle front and the home front. The capital, its name now changed from the "German-tainted" St. Petersburg to the "Russian" Petrograd, had become the forum for some practical discussions that had been needed much earlier.

There were many who still believed that the ultimate military advantage would lie in superior manpower, which Russia had, rather than in superior firepower, which Germany had. Others insisted on examining the evidence accumulated in the first months of the war, when manpower had been put to the test against firepower.

Though the changes made since 1905 had improved the army somewhat, they had not modernized it; the new program of military rehabilitation, planned for completion in 1917, had been abandoned under the urgency of the unanticipated war. Moreover, in all the efforts at reconditioning, reliance on personnel had too far overbalanced the consideration of supply. Already thousands of Russian men had paid with their lives for the shortage that had developed in the most vital of supplies, arms and ammunition. As the fighting continued, men had been sent to the front without rifles, to be equipped there with weapons gathered from those fallen on the battlefield. The artillery had been so short of ammunition at times that enemy guns had been able to rake the Russian lines as they would mere field targets.

The end-of-the-year reckoning pointed up the tragic conse-quences: one-fourth of the four million men under arms at the be-ginning of the fighting were dead, wounded, or in the hands of the enemy. The hope that conditions would improve was nowise upheld by recent reports. The ammunition famine was not being overcome, the medical services were running short of surgical instruments and hospital beds, the commissariat was running short of boots, replace-ments were moving up too slowly to keep the front-line units at full strength, and those who reached the front were more poorly trained and equipped than the men whose places they took. To speak of increasing supplies and moving men and materiel more rapidly only brought up another problem, the coal shortage. Cut off by the German navy from England, their normal source of coal, many northern Russian factories were on short supply, limited to the coal that could be brought from the south. Locomotives on some lines were being fired with wood. Somewhere, somehow, things had to change.

The recognition of such shortcomings did not, at this time, mean any appreciable lessening of public support for the war effort. Patri-otic fervor was still sufficient to take precedence over attention to social and political problems, but it had in no measure obliterated it. When Milyukov had declared for the liberals, "We demand nothing," he might honestly have added, "but we expect a great deal." To him, as to many others, the war was an interlude. Liberals expected Russia to develop into a truly constitutional monarchy after it was over; Poles hoped for the restoration of the kingdom of Poland; Jews hoped for equal rights, peasants for more land, work-ers for the eight-hour day. Those expectations and hopes, under the strain of a long war, could develop into a desperation that would put a practical construction on the words of the SR Duma deputy Alexander Kerensky, who had spoken just before Milyukov at the July session and advised that those who sought the "happiness and welfare of Russia" should "while defending the country, set it free."

Yet Nicholas' belief in the boundless devotion of his subjects led him to the complacent view that victory was the only reward they would seek for serving throne and fatherland. His ministers, with the exception of Sazonov (a liberal by ministerial standards), agreed with him, maintaining that the emergency of the war should not be allowed to bring about any change in the structure of the state or of society. Besides Goremykin, the guardian dragon of the tsarist tradition, the outstanding defenders of the status quo were Minister of Interior Maklakov, Over-Procurator Sabler, and Minister of Justice Shcheglovitov, who viewed with the gravest mistrust any group or activity that could be construed as threatening to it, even though that group or activity was aiding the war effort.

Theirs were the ready voices among those who decried as subversive the voluntary groups organized for the relief of sick and wounded soldiers, the All-Russian Union of Zemstvos and the All-Russian Union of Cities. Though the unions had been founded, at the beginning of the war, with the tsar's approval and provided with government funds, the doubters were soon charging them with seeking to exploit the war for the political ends of the liberals. The fact was that these organizations, made up of thousands of local committees, were exactly what they claimed to be, and their members worked diligently at the tasks to which they were set. Moreover, their chief figure, Prince George Lvov, chairman of the All-Russian Union of Zemstvos, was a dedicated man hostile to the very thought of using the organizations for political ends. It could not be denied, of course, that the unions were *potential* sources of subversion: the leading elements in each were liberals opposed to the prewar policy of the government, they had under their jurisdiction tens of thousands of civilians and soldiers, and they gave little account to higher authorities for what they did. Yet they were providing services which no established government department was able adequately to provide; to disband them would be to permit an inexcusable increase in suffering, distress, and death among the men returned from the battle front. In short, they were essential to the war effort. In these unions was the intimation of a very critical question that the government had to face at this time: how to win the war without accepting popular assistance that might prove to be the forerunner of political and social change.

Regardless of problems below the surface, during the winter both civilian and military morale appeared to be holding up, sustained by the expectation of victory in the spring, when large-scale operations were to be resumed after the winter lull. Likewise, the *Union Sacrée* among the legislators seemed to be enduring, though when the Duma met briefly in January 1915, many deputies fulminated privately about the reactionary policies of Goremykin, Sabler, Shcheglovitov, and Maklakov. They criticized the high-minded manner in which Yanushkevich was employing his authority as chief of staff, particularly in the arbitrary treatment of civilians in the zones of military activity. They also expressed doubt about the ability and honesty of Minister of War Sukhomlinov, now promising that the army would have more than enough rifles and ammunition by early spring. Publicly, however, the Duma still spoke in altruistic and patriotic phrases. "One says *Rodzyanko's* speech was splendid," the empress was pleased to report.*

When, on the first day of spring, the news arrived that the Austrian fortress of Przemysl had finally surrendered with 120,000 men and more than 2,000 officers, it was hailed briefly as a good omen of what would follow. The tsar called it a "ray of sunshine." For the Russian forces already fighting for the control of the Carpathian passes, the capitulation of the fortress meant that the way was open for a broad attack. And beyond the Carpathians lay Budapest and Vienna. This was the greatest military achievement of Nicholas II's reign, and he prepared to celebrate it to the full. His elation was unaffected by the somber advice of Rasputin (transmitted by the empress) that he should restrain himself until the end of the war, and he left as soon as possible for Przemysl to savor his first triumphal entry into conquered territory.

The capture of Przemysl was, unfortunately, to be the last "ray of sunshine" for many months. As the thrill of victory wore off, it was necessary to face the fact that the accumulation of home-front burdens was beginning to depress civilian morale. The peasants, who from the beginning had displayed less enthusiasm for the war than had the city dwellers, grew less enthusiastic as the war progressed and the number of casualties among the fighting men—largely of the peasantry—mounted. At the same time, they were becoming more vocal, more ready to complain about such things as the discrimination authorities practiced against them in requisitioning their horses for use by the army and in assigning prisoner-of-war farm labor more generously to the landlords than to them. Moreover, when the government was forced by shortage of personnel to

* Alexandra always used English in both her conversation and her written communications with Nicholas. Her grasp of the language was imperfect, and her phrasing was often awkward. But, since she considered English her mother tongue and since it was the foreign language that Nicholas found easiest to use, it proved an agreeable compromise.

reduce the number of officials and police in the countryside, the peasants were all the freer to voice their complaints.

Workers in the cities also were feeling the pinch of the war and, in many ways, finding their life grimmer than that of the rural population. With some exceptions, the standard of living among laborers, miserably low to begin with, was being depressed as prices rose more rapidly than wages and as housing, fuel for heating, and even that staple of their diet, kasha, were becoming scarce. Those who endured the privations were the more resentful because they knew that wealthy citizens could still frequent restaurants and cabarets where they might pass their leisure hours in spendthrift gaiety instead of wartime austerity, even buy liquor in defiance of prohibition if they chose.

Peasants and workers were not the only ones whose tolerance of war conditions was wearing thin. For many people, the Galician success could not erase memory of the previous year's Prussian disaster, nor could their cooperation in the war effort eliminate their prewar prejudices and tensions. Evidence of that fact was to be seen in early April, when newspapers published a brief dispatch from *Stavka* reporting that Colonel Sergei Myasoedov, of the Tenth Army, a man whom many remembered as Sukhomlinov's protégé, had been tried and hanged as an enemy spy. The public at once supplied interpretations of what lay behind it. A skeptical minority took the hanging as the first move in a campaign by the Grand Duke Nicholas Nicholaievich to oust his enemy Sukhomlinov, and they encouraged speculation as to whether or not the colonel had received a fair trial. The majority accepted the guilt of Myasoedov as proven, assumed that Sukhomlinov was thereby compromised, and went on to suspect that the army was infiltrated by spies carrying on their nefarious work with the aid of the "German party."

By the "German party" was meant those of German birth or origin in the armed forces, the bureaucracy, the court, and the imperial family (whose German blood-ties dated from Peter III) as well as certain other Russians reputed to be pro-German. All these were assumed to be, at least occasionally, guilty of divided loyalty or—even worse—treason. Suspicion and resentment of Germans had been building up among the Russian people since the eighteenth century, when the imperial policy of Westernization drew many of them into positions of importance in the administration and the army, and when the government began inviting and assisting German colonization along the Volga and in the south, where the settlers prospered and became unwanted competitors. Since that time, the feeling of antipathy for Germans had become traditional, and its revival during a war with Germany was especially easy. Though there was no "German party," the suggestion was sufficient to rouse the war-addled emotions of a host of Russians and lead them to believe that they were fighting an enemy within as well as an enemy without. It was the kind of "evidence" that a people at war could keep in safe reserve against the possible need to establish blame for reverses. In this instance, the turn of events was soon to call it forth.

While Nicholas had been sharing the triumph of Russian arms at Przemysl and Russian military intelligence had been dozing, the Germans had been concentrating men and guns near Gorlice, some seventy-five miles west of Przemysl, in preparation for a massive offensive to relieve the Austrians, now threatened by an Italian assault in the rear, and to protect Hungary, the granary of the Central Powers. And on April 18, nine days after the tsar had left for the north, the enemy artillery roared out against the Russians along a twenty-five-mile stretch near Gorlice.

The Austro-German forces now had all the advantages: the brilliant General August von Mackensen in command, rested and tested troops, twice as many infantrymen, forty times as many heavy guns with more than enough ammunition, and an infinite superiority in reconnaissance planes—since the Russians had none. The Russian artillerymen, despite the assurance of Sukhomlinov as well as the inspector general of artillery, the Grand Duke Sergei Michaelovich, were still on short allowance, sometimes as low as three shells a day per gun. The enemy, their big guns far outranging those of the Russians, tore bloody holes in the helpless advance lines, killing and maiming men and horses by the thousands and spreading panic throughout the ranks. Then their infantry and cavalry poured through, able at first to take prisoners almost at will.

Once the first shock was over, the Russians began to fight back, and reinforcements were rushed up; but they could not halt the drive. The necessity for the enemy high command to deal simultaneously with renewed Franco-British operations in the west, Italy's entry into the war in early May, and the continued allied threat in the region of the Dardanelles made no apparent difference in the concentration on this offensive. The Russians were forced out of Przemysl on May 21, and all along the Galician front, the Austro-German armies moved ahead on an average of six miles a day until, in early June, most of Galicia was in their uncontested possession.

As the southern front collapsed, the men had been forced to abandon supplies, guns, and sometimes even the wounded. When the final tally was made, the results were seen to be the most disastrous of the war: Russian casualties were about 800,000, among them virtually all that had been left of the standing army. The enemy had dealt Russia a truly devastating blow. At the same time Austria, rescued from certain defeat, had been able to free sufficient forces to turn and overrun Serbia.

Russian military censorship muted the tragic news but could not suppress it. What civilians in the rear did not learn from military dispatches, they learned from soldiers' letters, word of mouth, or the evidence of their own eyes as they saw hospital trains and freight trains bringing back the sick and wounded by tens of thousands. Moscow received the brunt of the shock, for it was the central clearing station for the dispersal of sick and wounded. There on May 27, the overmeasure of suffering and distress all around them seemed suddenly to madden the observers, and many of them turned vengefully on the "German party." Mobs invaded stores and factories owned by persons with German names, beating whomever they believed to be German and frequently destroying property, then took to the streets, seeking out and assaulting any who appeared to be German. At first, their "pogrom" was tolerated by the police as misdirected patriotism. But, on the third day, when the indiscriminate condemnations had grown to include the empress as German and the French and English as the kind of allies who would "fight to the last drop of Russian blood," the authorities ordered out troops to help the police restore order.

The Moscow "pogrom" was a sign of overtaxed endurance and dissatisfaction with the progress of the war, a sign that some civilians were feeling the urge personally to do something about the situation. Within a matter of days, there were other meaningful expressions of public opinion. Industrialists formed a military-industrial association, the War Industries Committee, for the mobilization of industry throughout the country in aid of national defense—a gesture of cooperation, to be sure, but at the same time an unspoken criticism of a government that had permitted the supply shortage to develop, a criticism made explicit by the election of Alexander Guchkov, known to be in the bad graces of the government, as chairman of the central committee. Cadet deputies in the Duma demanded the formation of a ministry of confidence, such as Witte had tried to organize. Zemstvo leaders began to enter politics, actively supporting the Cadets. The public did not speak with a single voice; yet one voice, that of the Cadets, was heard above all others. That was the result of their having adopted the formula, "ministry of confidence," to which both the right and the left could adhere, rather than the more liberal one, "responsible ministry," which individually they would have preferred but which the right would have rejected. The *Union Sacrée* still held, but it was becoming unsteady.

The tsar, as usual, was little concerned with this latest manifestation of what some understood as public opinion; he prided himself on ignoring the Petrograd press and avoided discussion of politics with members of his entourage. More than ever he saw in the simple countrymen—the peasants, the soldiers in general and the Cossacks in particular—the "real Russia," on which the future would be built. So dissociated from reality, he would be unlikely to recognize the developing political crisis unless someone he trusted intimately could bring him to an understanding of what was going on around him. For that task, the Grand Duke Nicholas Nicholaievich seemed the man most likely to get a hearing with him.

Though the grand duke had the name of a reactionary, and the instincts of one as well, he had slowly come to make peace with the view that Russia must move with the times. He was known to be susceptible to arguments for change and, at this time, he was in an especially good position to be reached. At *Stavka*, he was in what amounted virtually to a state within a state: he not only directed military operations but also controlled civil administration in the areas (including Petrograd) occupied by the field armies and conducted diplomatic negotiation with the allied powers on matters affecting military operations. He was therefore frequently a host to diplomats, bureaucrats, and Duma deputies.

Among the grand duke's visitors were a number of men deeply concerned with the realities that the tsar persisted in overlooking. One of the most direct and insistent was Michael Rodzyanko. As chairman of the Duma committee to aid soldiers' families, he had the right to visit the front as well as to call at *Stavka*; as chairman of the Duma, he had the privilege of audiences with the tsar. He had earned the sobriquet "Jupiter of the Duma" by a self-confidence that led him to undertake anything he believed to be needful or useful. Early in the war, he had cast himself as one of the organizers of victory, and he had no intention of relinquishing the role despite the fact that some judged him unfit for it. Goremykin thought him half-mad, the tsar found him fat and foolish, and a number of generals regarded him as a bombastic busybody. Others —and they were to be found in the imperial family, at court, at *Stavka,* in the Duma, and in the diplomatic corps—took him at face value, accepting him as a symbol of Russia's will to win, the interpreter of public opinion, a man decidedly knowledgeable on matters both military and civilian. Just now he was annoying the one group and raising the hopes of the other by his efforts to reduce what he considered the barriers to the winning of the war.

At first, among the members of the cabinet, he had the favor only of the foreign minister, Sazonov; but, as the military situation worsened, a number of other ministers came to approve his conclusion that to win the war, Russia must make better use of her human and material resources. They agreed also that, to do so, it was necessary for the government to win public cooperation by liberal acts.

Among the liberal acts that Rodzyanko had in mind was the replacement of certain unpopular high-ranking officials by men who would draw popular support. Like the Grand Duke Nicholas Nicholaievich, he believed Sukhomlinov to be the chief weakness of the army. After some run-ins with other reactionary ministers, he was convinced that the tsar should rid himself not only of Sukhomlinov but also of Goremykin, Sabler, Shcheglovitov, and Maklakov—all of whom he saw standing in the way of essential government rapport with the public.

When he laid his case before the tsar, Rodzyanko made no headway, but in the Grand Duke Nicholas Nicholaievich he found a more receptive auditor. Once convinced of the need, the grand duke agree to join in the effort to win over the tsar. Accordingly, in June, when Nicholas was visiting *Stavka,* the shock of the military disaster on the southern front and the Moscow "pogrom" fresh in his mind, the grand duke led the arguments for change.

The tsar needed no convincing that the war was going badly, that men were dying needlessly for lack of ammunition; he was quite agreeable to any measures that seemed to offer direct help in winning the war. He offered no objection to the organization of conferences, including representatives from government, management, and labor, to deal with shortages of materiel. On steps beyond that, however, he was not so readily agreeable.

It was always difficult for Nicholas to interpret what others chose to call "the voice of the people" as anything more than the chirpings of the intelligentsia; he was not easily convinced that the public

was losing confidence in the government. Yet he could not conscientiously disregard the impassioned arguments of men like the
grand duke, whom he respected as a good soldier and an honorable
man, devoted to tsar and fatherland, and whom, he had noted with
approval, the war and increased responsibility had changed for the
better.[8] So now, under the pressure of what he could not but accept
as sincere pleading and of the necessity to meet the military emergency, he reacted as he had under the pressure that had led to the
appointment of Svyatopolk-Mirsky, in 1904: he agreed to offer a sop
to this so-called public opinion. Though most emphatically he
would not remove his trusted premier, Goremykin, he would replace
Maklakov, Sabler, Shcheglovitov, and Sukhomlinov with more popular men. And he would summon the Duma to meet at a date earlier
than the one he had planned.

The tsar was not reluctant to name a new over-procurator of the
Holy Synod, for he had come to the conclusion that Sabler was not
the "clean, pious, and well-meaning" man he had thought him to be.
The man he chose, Alexander Samarin, had a good reputation and
could be expected to be reasonably conservative even though, in his
very active work with the Red Cross during the past year, he had
shown some favor for a unified effort of society as an aid to the war
effort. When he turned over Sukhomlinov's portfolio to General
Alexis Polivanov, he knew that the ministry of war would now have
the support of the Duma majority; but he did not subscribe to the
idea that Sukhomlinov's acts had been either dishonorable or criminal—irresponsible or mistaken perhaps, but nothing more. It was
clear that his confidence in both Maklakov and Shcheglovitov was
still unshaken. The men he chose as their successors—Prince Nicholas Shcherbatov as minister of interior and Alexander Khvostov as
minister of justice—had the warm recommendation of officials whose
judgment he trusted; that at least was a comfort. Shcherbatov, who
had recently been doing outstanding work as head of the state stud
farms, was endorsed by Krivoshein; and Khvostov, little known outside legal circles, was well liked by Goremykin.

In sum, these men would be generally more acceptable than those
they replaced; but, as long as Goremykin remained premier, their
presence in the ministry could not make it a ministry of confidence.
Moreover, Nicholas' attitude of grudging acquiescence to most of
the changes to which he agreed, an attitude that almost always
marked his concessions, lessened the effectiveness of his agreement as

a gesture of goodwill. But the very fact that he had relented at all inspired some hope for improvement.

For the time being, however, the hopes for the future had to be subordinated to the realities of the present. Even as the Austro-German forces were driving the Russians out of Galicia, their high command was preparing a second offensive—this one, in the kingdom of Poland—expecting that, between an Austrian force in the south and a German force in the north, it would be possible to trap and annihilate what remained of Russia's military strength. When the new offensive began, early in July, the Russians were not as surprised as they had been at the opening of the Galician offensive, but their foreknowledge helped very little: they were manifestly outclassed in everything except the courage of their fighting men. The Russian soldier was respected even by the enemy as a brave man who could subsist on little, endure much, and fight stubbornly; but, dispirited by defeat and lacking adequate arms, ammunition, and the support of good medical and transport facilities, the best he could now do was to retreat courageously. That he was being forced to do, step by step, following almost every stand as the Polish offensive began to move.

On the home front, any conciliatory effects that Nicholas' recent measures might have produced were lost in responses to more tangible particulars. When the Duma was again convened, on July 19, the first anniversary of the war, the "voice of the people," to which the tsar had generously made reference in his manifesto announcing the session, was a voice of panic. The reports from *Stavka* were daily more distressing. Enemy forces were again approaching Warsaw, and there was little hope that it could be held. If the advance continued at its present rate, perhaps Petrograd, Moscow, and Kiev would have to be evacuated. The number of casualties brought from the front—4,000 a day through the Moscow center alone—was proof of the price being paid in lieu of surrender. Civilian refugees also were pouring eastward by tens of thousands. Many of them were Jews, brutally and indiscriminately expelled from their homes by order of Chief of Staff Yanushkevich. Others were families fleeing the war zone because they feared for their lives or because their homes had been burned by the military authorities to discommode the enemy. The number of refugees, by official count, reached a total of three million—an influx that could mean only misery for the displaced persons as well as for the already distressed cities in which they stopped.

Under these chaotic conditions, the spirit of *Union Sacrée* sank, and the Duma became bitter and more openly contemptuous of the government and the high command. Every day, the meetings were loud with demands—for the still unrealized ministry of confidence, for the arrest and trial of Sukhomlinov, for the investigation of shortages, for a prolonged session of the Duma.

At the same time, Duma and State Council leaders, ranging from the Cadets to the moderate right, were meeting privately to settle on a common program which, they hoped, would be acceptable to the government. They worked at the task for a month, during which they agreed on certain measures based on "the conviction that only a strong, firm, and active government can lead the fatherland to victory."

This group and those who supported its principles—the great majority of the Duma and a large part of the State Council—became known as the Progressive Bloc. Its aim was to urge the tsar to accept, not a program of the political right or of the political left, but simply one involving political changes that would give Russia a government displaying its trust of "public initiative" and itself having the trust of the public—a truly "united government." It called for the creation of a cabinet enjoying "the confidence of the country" as well as the support of the majority of the legislature. Beyond that, it called for specific demonstrations of the government's goodwill toward the people: among them, reestablishment of Polish autonomy, reaffirmation of the rights of Finland, elimination of most of the laws discriminating against Jews, restoration of the right to form labor unions, removal of legal disabilities of peasants, and establishment of more zemstvos.

Those favoring such a program could, of course, expect unreserved opposition from extreme rightists in the legislature, leading members of the Council of the United Nobility, and many generals. These were men who would prefer to see the tsar recess the Duma for the duration of the war, silence the opposition press, and arrest the troublemakers. They would, however, admit the wisdom of making certain changes: for instance, replacing Goremykin by a strong, though not necessarily popular, premier whom the tsar could trust with the necessary authority to reestablish order; and replacing Chief of Staff Yanushkevich, now under attack from both right and left, by someone of the caliber of General Michael Alexeev, who had already proved himself one of the ablest commanders of the war.

While those associated with the Progressive Bloc were hoping to draw the tsar in one direction and the extremists of the right were hoping to draw him in another, he was unobtrusively becoming involved in circumstances that would draw him in a third. These circumstances, like many that had become basic factors in the decisions of his reign, originated within his private life.

At the beginning of the war, Nicholas had appointed Alexandra to the chairmanship of the Supreme Council for the Care of Soldiers' Families, established to coordinate the work of the many organizations engaged in humanitarian work associated with the war effort. It was an honorific post, befitting her station. Another woman might have taken it less seriously, but despite the deterioration of her health, Alexandra took it very seriously. No one in the position could have shown herself more loyal, more competent, or more sincerely concerned with the physical and spiritual welfare of the soldiers and their families. She was not one to neglect any phase of a duty she assumed; since this post gave her the right to deal directly with various organizations, ministries, and the Holy Synod in matters affecting her work, she soon felt a freedom of association with them that she had not experienced before the war. The fact that the tsar was now often away from Tsarskoe Selo (their residence for the duration) led her to make more and more use of that association, impelled not only by her pent-up energy but also by her burning desire to help "poor Nicky," who now needed her more than ever, she believed.

As this arrangement enlarged the range of Alexandra's connections, so also it extended the reach of Rasputin's influence. Though he continued his Petrograd residence in quarters on Gorkhovaya Street, near the station from which trains left for Tsarskoe Selo, his rent secretly paid by the tsar and his person protected by special plainclothes policemen,[9] he managed to insinuate himself noticeably into Alexandra's public activities and offer appropriate encouragement. As her influence continued to expand, seekers after his alleged influence became more numerous and ever more flatteringly respectful of his "position."

The fact was that Rasputin's influence over the empress was far overrated. He served her as a reflector rather than a beacon. While he had ideas of his own, his effectiveness lay in radiating the feelings to which he knew she would be receptive. He learned from his talks with her and from the prattlings of Anna Vyrubov ("Alexandra's gramophone") about her ideas and beliefs concerning such subjects as family, autocracy, and religion, and he made a point of reinforcing them whenever possible.

One instance of his reinforcing was especially acceptable to Alexandra. Having learned of her dislike of the Grand Duke Nicholas Nicholaievich and her fear that he was overshadowing the tsar, Rasputin was able to invest her attitude with signal importance and give it a religious aura. After commending her perceptive interpretation of character, he went on to explain that the grand duke was, in fact, the object of even God's wrath because of his hatred for a man of God—himself. Thus encouraged, the empress undertook a quiet campaign to undermine Nicholas Nicholaievich, accusing him at first of exercising authority that was rightfully the tsar's, later of plotting to usurp the throne.

Nicholas, for all his love of Alexandra, had a shrewd appreciation of some of her weaknesses. Though she had inveighed, in June, against his making concessions at the grand duke's urging and argued that dismissal of the commander in chief was more in order, he had resisted her arguments. A month later, it is true, he did decide to remove Nicholas Nicholaievich and take over the command himself, but there is no reason to believe that he was influenced by Alexandra's plea alone.[10]

There were a number of circumstances contributing to this decision: the disastrous retreat of the Russian forces before the Austrian and German armies in Poland, the mounting panic within the country, and the cabinet's recent denunciation of *Stavka* policies. There was also the attitude of members of the imperial family who were highly critical of the grand duke for permitting the Montenegrin princesses to carry on what amounted to a private publicity campaign for him and for conducting himself in such a manner that some were moved to speak of him as "Nicholas III." But the deciding factor was in the mind of the tsar himself. At this time, he was a man of frustrated pride, who still resented having been dissuaded from going to the front as commander in chief when the war began, who still felt that his place was with his men, and who sincerely believed that he would be fulfilling his duty to his country by uniting in his person direction over the front and the rear.[11]

His mind made up, Nicholas proceeded at once to specific plans.

With Alexandra pressing him to be strong, it would be easier than it had been a year earlier for him to hold fast to his resolve. He charged General Polivanov, his new war minister, with carrying the notification of change to *Stavka,* which, as the enemy drove the battle front eastward, had been pulled back to Mogilev, on the Dnieper, a day's journey from the capital. The message was contained in a confidential letter to the Grand Duke Nicholas Nicholaievich, explaining that he was to be relieved by the tsar and reassigned to the viceroyship of Transcaucasia and the command of the Transcaucasian front. Nicholas planned that, after his message had reached the grand duke, he would apprise the cabinet of the *fait accompli,* and that he would leave for *Stavka* on August 15. Thereafter, he would divide his time between *Stavka* and Tsarskoe Selo, between military and civilian administration.[12]

Such were his intentions. But when Nicholas Nicholaievich, who took his removal with surprising docility, suggested that the change of command be postponed for a week, during which time the front line was expected to become more stable, the tsar agreed. Thus, he provided would-be dissuaders a period in which to press their case.

Although the official announcement of the change had yet to be published, word of what was afoot spread rapidly through *Stavka* and the two capitals. A number of people immediately expressed their approval to the tsar. Most of the grand dukes and grand duchesses were extremely pleased that Nicholas Nicholaievich was being removed from the supreme command. However, the overwhelming majority of responsible people in government and society felt that the tsar's decision was a dreadful mistake, that if he personally assumed the military command, he would be inducing further trouble by neglecting grave problems at home while permitting the empress to spread her wings. Many of them tried, some at the risk of their careers, to get him to reverse himself.

There was plenty of evidence that, if ever the internal affairs of Russia demanded the full attention of the head of state, it was just when Nicholas was preparing to assume the duties of both a military and civilian administrator and, presumably, to apportion his attention accordingly.

Rasputin's behavior alone was developing into a demanding problem. It was common knowledge that he had begun to boast of his influence with the empress and that his acquaintances and associates had come to include princes, churchmen of rank, cabinet members, and a variety of other officials. It was common belief—unjustified, but accepted by important and otherwise responsible men and women—that he was working hand in glove with the "German party." It was common joviality to relate stories, real or fanciful, of his carousing and lechery. And it was common practice, to make satiric allusion to his imperial connections; for instance, a specially printed playing card (the king of spades) showed in one corner the tsar holding his scepter, and in the other Rasputin holding a bottle of wine and a bishop's crosier.

One sensational story grew out of Rasputin's making an indecent spectacle of himself when befuddled by drink and music at the Yar, a Moscow gypsy restaurant. General Vladimir Dzhunkovsky, chief of the corps of gendarmes, had made a confidential report of the episode to the tsar, and the tsar had ordered Rasputin to return to his home in Pokrovskoe. But the public, knowing that Rasputin had often returned from his village, was still confident—justifiably, it proved—that he would do so again. Only a few days before Nicholas was to leave for *Stavka*, interest in the incident was renewed by the outcome of the publication in the influential *Stock Exchange Gazette* of a scathing attack on Rasputin. The writer quoted phrases from Dzhunkovsky's confidential report, asked how highly placed persons could associate with "such canaille," and concluded that their association constituted the "most horrible accusation that one can make against the regime." [13] On the day it was published, Nicholas peremptorily dismissed Dzhunkovsky without explanation, probably because of the breach of confidence. But again the public supplied its own conclusion: that anyone who undertook to expose Rasputin would be punished.

Another matter that Nicholas might have recognized as one of immediacy for the regime was the formulation, then in progress, of the program and tactics of the Progressive Bloc. Here was a manifestation that the tsar could ill afford to ignore, for many of those instrumental in the organization of the bloc were not from the usual sources of trouble for the government but from the natural supporters of the government. They included such men as Duma deputy Vasily Shulgin, publisher of the conservative, nationalist *Kievan,* a newspaper that boasted of being the only publication to appear at the height of the general strike in October 1905. He, as well as others of his political disposition, had deliberately sought to offer the hand of friendship to the Cadets—the moderate right joining the liberal left. It was obvious to many that this development was a sign, a dangerous one, indicating the accelerating defection of friends of the regime.

An even more ominous sign was the sudden and sharp increase in the number of labor strikes in the summer of 1915. Most of these were wildcat strikes set off by the rising prices that were eroding the workers' already mean standard of living. But many strikers were expressing, in addition to their personal complaints, a recently exaggerated disrespect for both government and management, having come to accept the accusations that many officials and industrialists were guilty of pro-German leanings and sabotage of the war effort; thus while acting from motives personally understood as patriotic, they were themselves unwittingly disrupting the war effort. Some strikers—in particular those in the work force of the huge Putilov ironworks in Petrograd, who were already under the influence of Bolshevik propaganda—were beginning to respond to the antiwar propaganda now being systematically disseminated by the Bolsheviks and other socialists.

Antigovernment sentiment was further aroused by an incident in Ivanovo-Voznesensk, where, on August 10, police and soldiers fired on textile strikers demonstrating before the city hall, killing or wounding more than one hundred of them. All around the country, anger flared and workers went on brief strikes to express their sympathy with the victims and their outrage against the government. Even employers, who had been carping at the authorities for alleged leniency toward strikers, censured the government for playing into the hands of the radicals by such brutality.[14]

This current prevalence of problems—apropos of Rasputin, the Progressive Bloc, labor unrest, refugees, economic chaos—lent urgency to a series of last-minute efforts to induce Nicholas to remain at the seat of government. Pleas came from all sides: Rodzyanko implored "on bended knee" that the tsar not thus endanger throne and dynasty; the dowager empress sent Nicholas' favorite young cousin, the Grand Duke Dmitri Pavlovich, to beg him not to go; the aged Count Vorontsov-Dashkov timidly suggested in a letter to him that, if the army should continue to retreat after he took command, the prestige of the throne might suffer; members of the Moscow municipal council were demanding that the tsar form a ministry of confidence, even as they were sending a message of confidence to the Grand Duke Nicholas Nicholaievich; students of Petrograd University were threatening a public protest if the grand duke were removed from command.

By far the most concerted effort at dissuasion was made by the cabinet, whose members—excepting the imperturbable Goremykin—were astounded by the news of Nicholas' intention. Convinced that the fate of Russia was at stake, that a revolutionary mood was spreading through the land, they addressed the tsar with unparalleled boldness when he presided over a cabinet meeting on August 20. Their reasoning with him followed a view stated by minister of agriculture Krivoshein at their meeting on the previous day: "The result of the [tsar's] decision to asume the command has been to increase uneasiness at all levels of the populace. I agree wholeheartedly that this decision is . . . a fatal one. . . . We must implore him to rescind the removal of the grand duke, also to make fundamental changes in the nature of the internal policy. . . . To continue playing with fire is dangerous." [15]

But Nicholas, refusing to accept that view, proved again how obstinately resistant he could be when pushed too hard. He clung firmly to his decision.

The next day, a majority of the ministers resolved on an even bolder step: to repeat their request that the tsar renounce his decision and to ask that, if he still held fast to it, they be permitted to resign. Such unprecedented audacity led Goremykin to accuse them of trying to serve the tsar with an ultimatum. The arguments that followed ranged beyond the immediate issue to the larger issue of the nature of the monarchy, Goremykin insisting that the will of the tsar was God's will, to be executed by the ministers. The foreign minister, Sazonov, replied that, while God might be infallible, tsars were not, and that the responsibility of the ministers was to the nation. Goremykin's was the voice of the past. Whether or not Sazonov's was the voice of the future remained to be seen. Eight of the ministers (the majority), true to their resolution, composed and signed a letter containing their alternative requests, and it was put into the tsar's hands on August 22. As an expression of civic courage, it was admirable; as a plea, it was singularly ineffective. It served only to arouse Nicholas' anger. He ordered Goremykin to inform the rebels of his "displeasure" and to tell them that they were not permitted to resign.[16]

Later that day, he left for *Stavka,* to assume the supreme command. There, where he had the able assistance of General Michael

Alexeev as chief of staff (an improvement over General Yanush-kevich, who was to accompany the Grand Duke Nicholas Nicholaievich to Transcaucasia), his problems perforce took on a different order of precedence.

The finality of the tsar's departure was felt keenly among those in court and government circles, some moved to uneasiness, others to greater energy for their home-front responsibilities. Dowager Empress Marie Fedorovna lamented that the times reminded her of the last days of Tsar Paul. She did not presume to judge the outcome, however, only the cause: "Where are we going? Where are we going? This is not Nicky—he is so gentle, honorable, good—it is all her [Alexandra's] work." [17]

On August 25, the Progressive Bloc, speaking for the great majority of the Duma, formally adopted the program on which its promoters had been working for a month. They hoped that the liberal ministers in the cabinet would be willing and able to persuade the tsar to put it into effect and to take the first step, the establishment of a cabinet "enjoying the confidence of the country," without delay. Optimists among them envisioned the first change: the replacement of reactionary Goremykin by a premier acceptable to them, perhaps Krivoshein.

They were trustingly following a chimera. When Nicholas left for *Stavka,* he had not the least intention of forming a ministry of confidence. That would be the first step, as he properly interpreted it, toward the adoption of the principle of ministerial responsibility, a measure as unthinkable as abdication. He remained agreeable to acts of conciliation, but he would not consent to the limitation of his prerogatives.

By way of clearing the political atmosphere and dismissing annoying issues, he sought first to rid himself of the noisy Duma; on his orders, Goremykin prorogued it on September 2. Then, when the ministers continued their bitter contention with the premier, the tsar summoned the whole group to *Stavka* to set them straight. "From all the corners of Russia come the warmest congratulations from my truly loyal subjects," he told them, and added: "It would be useful for you worthy ministers to spend some time here at the front and to refresh your minds: I hope that henceforth you will unhesitatingly follow my orders as well as the instructions of Ivan Logginovich Goremykin, whom I intend to retain at the head of the Council of Ministers for a long time." [18]

XV

Disintegration

NICHOLAS II, 1915–1917

BY rejecting a ministry of confidence, Nicholas II was unwittingly assuring the future growth of opposition. By not appointing a strong premier, he was unwittingly depriving himself of the power of effective control. He was again displaying his kinship with Alexander I, "too weak to rule, too strong to let others rule," and condemning himself to walk a lonely road.

He extended a further invitation to adversity by asking Alexandra to act in his absence as his assistant. "What a pity," he wrote to her from *Stavka,* "that you have not been fulfilling this duty for a long time, or at least since the beginning of the war." [1] She, quite naturally, accepted the suggestion with alacrity: "I am so touched you want my help, I am always ready to do anything for you, only never like mixing up without being asked." [2] Nicholas needed her moral support—he had so little from others—to sustain him in the belief that he was doing the right thing by assuming the supreme command. Also, he wanted her to keep in touch with Goremykin and give the old man moral support in his struggle with the recalcitrant ministers.

Establishing himself at headquarters was, in itself, a satisfying experience. In Mogilev, a quiet provincial capital over four hundred miles away from what he considered the depressing environment of

Petrograd, he had at last reached the place where, he believed, "there is only one thought—the determination to conquer." [3] It was an easy matter for him to feel remote and removed from the capital and its pressures, for he refused to read any Petrograd newspapers but the ministry of war publication *Russian Invalid* and continued his stern prohibition of political talk in his presence by members of his suite. In addition, he had by his side the seventy-six-year-old minister of court, Count Vladimir Fredericks, whose presence gave his *Stavka* quarters a comforting atmosphere of home despite the old man's advancing, and sometimes trying, senility.

The shortsightedness of the step Nicholas had taken was not immediately discernible. On the contrary, just after his arrival at Mogilev, the Russian forces began to hold against both the Austrian and the German armies and, in some places, to counterattack. It could not be said that the tide had turned; but Russian resistance was such that the enemy gradually disengaged, the front was stabilized, and the threat to Petrograd, Moscow, and Kiev was lifted. Moreover, the military collapse that many had feared in view of the Russian losses since May—two million casualties and the territories of Poland, Lithuania, Courland, and parts of Little and White Russia—had been averted. To some, this shift of fortune was an indication that the tsar's presence had inspired the troops and that heaven had favored his undertaking, though skeptics credited rather the autumn rains, the mud, and the shortened fighting lines. In any case, it helped to reassure Nicholas and provide another needed respite.

As General Alexeev, the new chief of staff, used the winter interval, he proved himself a most fortunate choice as replacement for Yanushkevich. "My cross-eyed friend," as the tsar called him, was no military genius but an unaffected man of peasant stock who served ably, honestly, and indefatigably. In effect, he carried the combined load of commander in chief and chief of staff, for Nicholas could do little more than act as intelligent observer, give support when needed, and resolve conflicts. The arrangement appeared promising, however; as *Stavka* prepared for the resumption of major fighting in the coming spring, indications were that it would exercise more effective control over military operations and avoid some of the excesses of the former command.

At the same time, new levies of conscripts were beginning to fill the gaps left by the crippling spring and summer engagements. The demand for munitions was finally being satisfied through the cooperation of the central government, zemstvos, municipalities, industry, and labor with the conferences and committees authorized by the tsar. A railroad line was being pushed through from Murmansk, on the Barents Sea, to Petrograd for the delivery of materiel from Russia's allies.

Understandably, the tsar saw no reason to regret having taken the supreme command.

The eighteen months during which Nicholas II commanded the army were so overlaid with the bizarre melodrama featuring Alexandra and Rasputin that the period, in retrospect, appears unique. Yet, in their political essence, these months were but a continuation of the period begun just after Stolypin's death and dedicated to the tsar's renewed policy of conserving the prerogatives of the crown. The application of that policy now entailed rejection of the Progressive Bloc's demand for a ministry of confidence, restriction of the Duma to its negligible role, and the practice of replacing ministers who continued to oppose the tsar's position by men more amenable—and, conditions being what they were, less able—than the ones they replaced. Under any circumstances, Nicholas's policy would have driven society and government further and further apart. But the circumstances of these eighteen months accelerated the process.

Alexandra provided one of the circumstances. She lost no time in beginning her work as "assistant" to Nicholas with all the energy she possessed, supplemented by the jealousies, suspicions, and dislikes that she had developed over the years. In her daily letters to the tsar, she advised ("One must be severe"), declared judgments about public figures ("Oh, could not one hang Guchkov!"), and made suggestions about ministerial changes: "But about *Sazonov* what do you think, I wonder? I believe, as he is a very good & honest (but obstinate) man, that when he sees a new collection of Ministers who are energetic, he may pick himself up and become once more a man—the atmosphere around him cought [sic] hold of him and cretinised him. . . . I cant [sic] believe he is as harmful as *Shcherbatov* & *Samarin* or even my friend *Krivoshein*—what has happened to him? I am bitterly disappointed in him." [4]

Keeping in touch with the developments in the government, she received Goremykin often, listened to his confidences, and encouraged him to hold fast. Inevitably, his visits gave rise to the fiction that the empress had been secretly appointed regent. When that idea was added to the conclusions invited by Rasputin's swaggering about and boasting of his influence, both friends and foes began to lower their confidence in the government.

Among those beginning to revise their positions were such men as Prince George Lvov, popular leader of the Union of Zemstvos, who had refused to be drawn into politics at the beginning of the war but who was now asserting that the war could not be won by this government and that the country could be rescued only by revolution—not that he proposed to start one. As long as there was a lack of evidence to counteract such a conclusion, the number of persons who endorsed it would continue to grow at an increasing rate.

The next significant change in the government most assuredly did not provide such evidence. Having finally to admit that Goremykin, now seventy-six, was too old and too tired to maintain a tight hold over the cabinet, Nicholas superseded him with Boris Stürmer. Although Stürmer's sixty-seven years did not place him in the ranks of vigorous young men, he had qualities that appealed to the tsar. He was a seasoned bureaucrat, having spent more than thirty years at various government posts, including two years in the ministry of interior under Plehve and twelve years in the State Council. He had proved himself politically a dependable rightist, yet one who could serve the government without unduly offending the opposition (that some chose to see this talent as "carrying water on both shoulders" apparently did not concern the tsar). He could be expected to handle forcefully any position of authority, for he enjoyed administration and loved the attributes of power. Nicholas saw him as a man who could be friendly, yet resolute, with the Duma, firm with the cabinet, and capable of directing the "super-ministry" now being proposed by Alexeev for coordinating supply agencies. For a premier with such qualities, he could accept the liability suggested by his Germanic name.

When he made the appointment of Stürmer, Nicholas announced it without any advance intimation of his intention, hoping thus to avoid efforts to dissuade him from the appointment: he wanted it to "come like a clap of thunder" to the people. He achieved his aim, but the shock proved extremely unpleasant. The public knew Stürmer as an unqualified reactionary, whose career justified a current evaluation of him as a vapid nonentity with a mind like "a peculiar kind of sponge than can absorb from morning to night without producing a single drop when it is squeezed." [5] They readily accepted the suggestion, borne out by his surname, that he was of the

"German party" and, in view of his reputation, that he was simply a tool chosen at the inspiration of what the French ambassador Maurice Paléologue called "the Empress's camarilla" and recommended to the tsar by Rasputin.

Although the appointment seemed a deliberate affront to public opinion, both Stürmer and the tsar at once began a campaign of conciliation. The premier sought out leaders of the Progressive Bloc to ask their cooperation and urge them not to attack Rasputin, and he went personally to Rasputin with the request that he not mention the name of the empress in public.[6] Then Nicholas, accepting a suggestion by Count Fredericks, appeared at the Tauride Palace early in February to open a new Duma session. That act, in particular, inspired hope in some: perhaps a new era was about to begin; perhaps the appointment of a ministry of confidence would follow. The hope was further enlivened by the tsar's subsequent acceptance of an invitation from Russia's allies to send a parliamentary delegation on a goodwill tour of the West, and his appointment of two members of the Progressive Bloc among the delegates—Alexander Protopopov, as chairman, and Paul Milyukov.

The hopes raised by these acts were as groundless as many of the fears then current. The tsar had never intended to go beyond conciliatory gestures, and whatever promise there was in Stürmer's initial attitude soon vanished. Having nothing substantial to offer the Duma, he was shortly at odds with it, and he had no more success than anyone else in trying to curb Rasputin's brazen tongue. Relations between government and society, therefore, returned to the familiar state of mutual hostility and suspicion.

The shafts aimed at the government were sharper now and more frequently tipped with acerbity because the targets appeared somehow more provocative, and boldness was becoming a general passion. As a scathing designation for Stürmer, Duma deputy Purishkevich struck upon "Chichikov," the name of Gogol's fictional swindler and conniver, and the government was readily seen to be a prime source of such men. There was Ivan Manuilov, a well-paid factotum attached to the premier's staff, not unfairly described as *"agent provocateur,* spy, sharper, swindler, forger, and rake in one." There was Pitirim, Metropolitan of Petrograd, a sly and oily ecclesiastical version of Stürmer, maintaining a friendship with the empress (openly) and Rasputin (secretly) while indulging his penchant for pretentious dabbling in politics. As an especially noteworthy pair, there were Alexis Khvostov, whose appointment as minister of interior had followed Shcherbatov's brief stint, and his assistant, Stepan Beletsky. Both were intriguers to their fingertips and walking invitations to caricature—the one with a face so broad and cheerful as to suggest unbelievable goodness, the other with the turned-up mustaches, elegant beard, and general mien of a middle-aged roué. Their devious acts, as finally exposed by themselves, made them leading contenders for the Chichikov role. The minister, once Rasputin's secret friend and now his secret enemy, engaged Beletsky to arrange an "accidental" death for the man. Beletsky, being more anxious to be rid of his chief than of Rasputin, revealed the plan to the empress; with that, both men became involved in a preposterous game of betrayal and counterbetrayal.

When the tsar finally cleared the ministry of interior by dismissing the indiscreet officials, he was not inclined to seek replacements among the untried. He asked that Stürmer add the ministry to his already heavy obligations. This move, of course, indicated to the public that, if the premier remained in favor with Alexandra, the meager chances for change would be still further reduced. In fact, the likelihood seemed foregone in view of his sustained effort to remain a favorite with the empress, ready with agreeable advice on ministerial changes and careful of her sensibilities (she never learned of his prediction that she would go mad) as well as those of Rasputin.

Rasputin also emerged from the abortive assassination episode with advantage. He was more than ever the object of Alexandra's solicitude, the one on whom she relied to continue the spiritual aid without which, she was positive, Russia would long since have perished. Public deriders, however, exercising a freedom of speech that once would have earned them Siberian exile, embellished with fanciful detail whatever they observed concerning either Rasputin or the empress. In their versions, he was in the pay of the German general staff, he was the master of the Church, he dictated to the tsar as well as to Alexandra and Stürmer, he had been given the post of icon-lamplighter in order that he might be free to prowl Alexander Palace, she was the "German woman" and the real ruler of the country. Some even urged openly that Rasputin be assassinated and that Alexandra be subjected to the old Muscovite punishment of confinement in a convent.

This kind of disrespect and criticism reached the height of excess among members of the imperial family, many of whom now felt completely estranged from the tsar's household. As they saw conditions going from bad to worse for the regime, some of them had grown desperate; moved by hostility for Alexandra and a vestige of sympathy for "poor Nicky" as well as by patriotism and self-interest, they no longer troubled to disguise their feelings. The dowager empress, who had chosen to take up residence in Kiev (with Alexandra's fervent approval), was outspoken among both old friends and new acquaintances. The Grand Duke Nicholas Michaelovich shared his feelings with fellow members of the Imperial Yacht Club. The Grand Duchess Marie Pavlovna, socially influential widow of the Grand Duke Vladimir, invited herself to the French embassy, there to denounce Alexandra as "mad" and Nicholas as "blind"—probably not unmindful that, in the imperial succession, her sons followed heir apparent Alexis and the tsar's brother, Michael. The Grand Duke Michael's morganatic wife, Countess Brassov, exercised little restraint in her public comments, which could easily be interpreted as promoting the interests of her husband, who would serve as regent during the minority of young Alexis if Nicholas were to be removed from the throne.

Most of the charges bandied about were groundless: Rasputin rarely appeared at the Alexander Palace, he was not in the employ of the German general staff, he did not dictate to the tsar, ministers who ignored him remained in office. Rasputin did not rule Russia; Alexandra did not rule Russia; in fact, no one ruled Russia—that was the real tragedy.

But what was true or untrue mattered little beside the unmistakable fact that the good name of the monarchy was disappearing in the quagmire of abuse, the confidence of the public was vanishing, and the self-confidence of the bureaucracy was ebbing. The very government seemed to be lapsing into a farce: in the ministry of interior, which had seen four ministers in the space of one year, cynical officials were proposing to put up a sign, "Picadilly Theater—new bill every week." Those who wished the tsar and the monarchy well fixed their hopes on reaching him with enlightenment and an appeal to reason, but he maintained his remoteness. When unpleasant gossip from the home front came to his attention, a typical response was, "Thank God, here at *Stavka,* we hear little of such nonsense." [7]

In the spring of 1916, when the Russian forces were to begin large-scale operations again, interest in the concentrated attack on the government was temporarily diverted. In view of the improvements that had been made to facilitate the war effort, the replacement of Sukhomlinov by Polivanov as minister of war and the co-

operation of government and private interests to provide needed
materiel, the prospect had brightened somewhat; however military
experts knew that the Russians would still be at a disadvantage when
facing Germany's heavy armament.

As in the previous spring, the first reports were heartening. In
Transcaucasia, the forces under the Grand Duke Nicholas Nicholaievich moved on from victory to victory, and is was understood
that the great eastern front was being readied for assured reprisals.
In March, the Russians were urged into an unpromising engagement of the Germans in the north (again, as in 1914, to draw enemy
strength away from the west—this time, from the French at Verdun).
The undertaking cost heavily and ended inconclusively, but revived
optimism persisted. Then, in the latter part of May, General Brusilov, now commanding operations in the south, began an offensive
against the Austrians that promised to be a genuine morale-builder.
Like the northern effort, its purpose was to relieve pressure on an
ally, Italy, then battling the Austrians in Trentino. Though it had
begun before the date Brusilov had set for action (he had intended
it to coincide with England's offensive at the Somme), it had a spectacular beginning and progressed with encouraging success for three
months along a front that expanded to three hundred miles. The
Russians took some 400,000 prisoners and so weakened Austria that
she would have made peace if Germany had permitted. In August,
Rumania abandoned neutrality and added her army to the Russian
offensive; but her effort unfortunately proved a greater disadvantage
to Brusilov than to the enemy forces, for he had to extend his front
in a futile attempt to protect the territory that her forces could not
hold. Then, as the end of the fighting season approached, reverses
came: the Germans again supplied the Austrians with sufficient reinforcement to stop the Russian drive, and losses began to mount at
a fearful rate.

By the time of the winter slowdown, it had to be admitted that
the military balance sheet for 1916 was another disillusionment.
Though the spring and summer fighting had erased much of the
shame of the previous year's routs in Galicia and Poland, it had
brought Russia very little material or strategic advantage, and the
latest encounters with the enemy now overlay that. The loss had been
staggering: one and a half million men killed, wounded, or taken
prisoner. And, with Rumania's entrance, the eastern front was
stretched from the Baltic to the Black Sea.

The time had come when leaders, military and civilian, were beginning to experience what had already reached the public, the onset of desperation. One disturbing factor was the realization that the sources of Russian manpower were not unlimited, as plans had appeared to take for granted. Sufficient replacements for both combatant and noncombatant needs of the army were no longer availble from regular sources. Yet, so far, efforts to supply them from other sources had not succeeded. The tsar had ordered the conscription for noncombatant duty of the Moslems within the empire, hitherto exempt from military service. But when the resistance of the Central Asian Moslems had resulted in attacks on enforcement personnel, the smashing of administrative offices, and the personal humiliation of officials (one governor was compelled publicly to kiss the Koran), the enforcement of the order was seen to be more difficult than anticipated, and a plan to summon the Transcaucasian Moslems for duty was abandoned.

That situation was one of a number that caused some of the men well acquainted with military operations to begin seriously questioning the capability of Russian arms to hold out if the pressure continued. As early as the first part of the 1916 campaign, General Alexeev had come to the conclusion that the Russian peasant soldiers would not endure much more combat. As he viewed the prospect, the tasks he would face when Russia was forced out of the war— which, he conceded, her allies might still win—were to keep the demoralized soldiers from running amok at the time of demobilization and to insure that Russia accept defeat with as much honor and dignity as possible.[8]

Duma chairman Rodzyanko also had grown pessimistic, but for a different reason. After visiting the front in the summer of 1916, he charged the high command with inadequate strategic preparation and with reckless expenditure of lives, accused generals of lack of concern for their men, and reported that officers as well as enlisted men were losing faith in their commanders and giving credence to the most monstrous rumors.[9] Even the tsar had been affected by the darkening outlook. On learning that the Austrian efforts to escape from the war had been frustrated by Germany, he had speculated dispiritedly about how long the war would drag on and what would be in store for "poor Russia."[10]

Still, many responsible persons in the country, obsessed by the slogan "war to the end," would not admit that Russia had assumed a military burden too heavy for her. Rather, they continued to blame the tsar and to insist that, if he would only accept the terms of the Progressive Bloc, the country would experience such a change and public confidence would be so stimulated that there would be no difficulty in bringing the fighting potential to capacity and insuring improvements on both battle front and home front. This view gained wide popularity in 1916, drawing support even from such rightists as those in the nationwide Congress of the United Nobility and failing to impress only a few right-wing extremists intolerant of any changes involving political concessions by the tsar.

So far, such considerations had been quite pointless. The tsar had not displayed any convincing desire to court public confidence, and it had continued to decline. During the summer, when there were rumors that Alexandra and Rasputin were conspiring to arrange a separate peace for Russia, perhaps with the tsar's knowledge, the possibility had seemed entirely reasonable to many. When, in July, Nicholas had installed Stürmer in Sazonov's place as foreign minister, the shift had been readily taken as proof that the "German party" was now in full control. Stürmer was actually a Great Russian chauvinist, but that fact was easily overlooked by the public. So also was the fact that there was some rationale—though patently not wisdom—behind the tsar's action: Sazonov was ill and at odds with the premier, and Stürmer had asked to exchange the burden of the ministry of interior with the "lighter" one of the ministry of foreign affairs in anticipation of taking charge of the proposed "super-ministry" for coordinating supply agencies. The change had appeared logical enough to the tsar.[11]

To replace Stürmer in the ministry of interior, Nicholas chose Alexander Protopopov, a Duma deputy and member of the Progressive Bloc—unfortunately another unwise choice. Again, the tsar had his reasons. In this case, as in the case of Stürmer, he perceived one man, the public another. He saw Protopopov as a man of strength, a no-nonsense man, brimming over with energy and vitality which he would apply ably and willingly to the problems of the ministry, a man who would execute the imperial will and at the same time please the Progressive Bloc; he even had the recommendation of Rodzyanko—though for another position. But Protopopov, once settled in office, presented a quite different character to the public: a slightly demented version of Plehve, a tool of Alexandra and Rasputin and, despite his Russian name, another of the "German party." That he was sympathetic to the Germans was a canard fabricated from an innocent meeting with a German emissary when he was in Sweden with the parliamentary delegation. Otherwise, each adverse evaluation of him had some basis: there was indeed a psychopathic quality about him that grew more pronounced with time; he fought public opinion as Plehve had, though he was no Plehve; he was the friend and protector of Rasputin, though not his tool; while no more Alexandra's tool than Rasputin's, he played up to her egregiously.

Stürmer alone had been indefensible enough in a government that needed support. Combining Stürmer as premier and foreign minister with Protopopov as minister of interior was enough to raise the apprehensions of reasonable men and women, and reason was in short supply in Russia just now. Ideas that had once seemed fatuous were being taken with a degree of seriousness by persons of responsibility. They came from generals, grand dukes, grand duchesses, Duma leaders, zemstvo leaders, and industrialists—all seeking some way to correct the government's misdirection. They opened the old discussions, now frequent and open, of assassinating Rasputin, of somehow getting Alexandra out of reach of the government, and of ousting the tsar and establishing a regency under the Grand Duke Michael. Though most of these went no further than talk, a few daring men tried to match deeds to words. Guchkov, for example, worked feverishly to organize a *coup d'état,* attempting to enlist the aid of such men as the Grand Duke Nicholas Nicholaievich and General Alexeev, but he was given no encouragement.

Reliable military men like Alexeev would not support a *coup d'état* because they feared that such a move would detonate a revolution and that, in the resulting breakdown of authority, army discipline would be destroyed. Such men were perceptive enough to read the signs about them. Though some police officials continued to report regularly that the mood of Petrograd was "comparatively quiet," little effort was required to see that unmistakably revolutionary sentiment was welling up among the workers in the capital. The number of strikes was increasing at an unprecedented rate; while most of them were for higher wages, many were in defiance of regular labor leaders and socialist Duma deputies whom workers had previously respected—for example, Nicholas Chkheidze and Alexander Kerensky, who denounced strikes at this time as unpatriotic. Moreover, many striking groups were displaying outright hostility to the government by hurling charges of treason and demanding a ministry of confidence, while others—the minority, but a growing number—were taking inspiration from Bolshevik propaganda and declaring unequivocal opposition to the war. The dangerous contagion of this mood was clearly demonstrated in mid-October, when soldiers of a reserve rifle regiment fraternized with strikers in Petrograd and had to be subdued by Cossacks. Just a little later, 60,000 Petrograd workers and students came out on strike to express sympathy for a number of sailors on trial for mutiny.

In view of this temper in the capital, the next session of the Duma, scheduled to open on November 1, threatened to be a stormy one. Yet, though some of Nicholas's well-wishers, among them his mother, begged him to take some kind of conciliatory measures before the opening date, he chose to follow Stürmer's advice, that he remain firm.

When the Duma assembled, Paul Milyukov set the tone that was to characterize its meetings until it was prorogued, six weeks later. He did so in a speech dramatically particularizing the inadequacies and incompetencies in the government, asking after each whether it was an instance of "stupidity" or "treason." His hearers provided the answer repeatedly: "Treason!" The clear implication was that the government was in treasonable hands and that the empress was the archtraitor. Reproduction of the speech was forbidden by the censors, but tens of thousands of typewritten and mimeographed copies were distributed and read at all levels of society.

The sensation produced by Milyukov's speech prompted a renewal of efforts by the friends of the tsar. Father George Shavelsky, chief chaplain of the armed forces, advised him that there was no longer any right or left in the Duma, but only one party—of opposition. Others tried to direct him to the way out of his predicament. The Grand Duke Nicholas Michaelovich cautioned him that his wife was being used by "unworthy" persons and that, unless he freed himself from "the chains" binding him and agreed to a ministry of confidence, he would be inviting danger to throne and fatherland. The Grand Duke Nicholas Nicholaievich, on a visit from his Transcaucasian headquarters, pleaded with him to become master in his own house.[12]

As so often happened, the tsar was being drawn in two directions, reason on one side and personal disposition on the other. Alexandra, well aware of the pressures to which he was being subjected and well advised of the current disparagement of her participation in policymaking, bombarded him with frantic pleas for support. The heart of her appeal, in varying versions, was: "You must back me up, for your and Baby's [young Alexis'] sake." Nicholas had no thought of following the public suggestions which she apparently feared most, that he send her to a convent or dispatch her and their children to Livadia for the remainder of the war. Yet, isolated though he was, he could no longer avoid recognition of some of the home-front problems. He was anxiously aware that strikes were becoming more serious and food shortages more acute. He was coming to the conviction that there was indeed something slightly mad about his latest minister of interior, Protopopov; also, that he needed a premier who could do better than Stürmer at appeasing the oppositional factions in the country. He decided, therefore, that he could afford to make a gesture of compromise: he would dismiss both Stürmer and Protopopov, choose an acceptable man as premier, and allow him to recommend new ministers. He had in mind, for the post of premier, Alexander Trepov, brother of the late General Dmitri Trepov, who had stood loyally beside him during the ordeal of 1905. Trepov, the incumbent minister of ways and communications, was conservative and was not, of course, the kind of man preferred by the Progressive Bloc; but he was beholden to neither the empress nor Rasputin, and his appointment might placate opposition.

Again, as in June of the preceding year, Nicholas was willing to yield only to the extent of taking half-measures, and he was frustrated in executing even those. He replaced Stürmer with Trepov without Alexandra's prior knowledge, but he was unwise enough to let her know that he planned to dismiss Protopopov and weak enough to grant her wish that he reserve further action until she could discuss it with him at *Stavka,* where she was due for a visit. The outcome was predictable: he succumbed to her impassioned insistence that Protopopov was the sheet anchor of the throne, that "real Russians" wanted no political changes, and that the ministry of interior should not be disturbed.

By leaving Protopopov at his post, the tsar condemned the new premier to certain failure. Trepov, having counted on being rid of the unpopular minister, had no heart for the difficulties promised by his continued presence in the government. After little more than a month, therefore, the premiership was passed on again—to Prince Nicholas Golitsyn, an almost anonymous figure in politics, who had last held responsible governmental office some twenty years earlier.

While Nicholas busied himself with changes that he hoped would prove innocuous, his responsible subjects were left in their uneasiness about the future of Russia as they observed the threatening growth of popular disquiet at a time when the country was already imperiled by war reversals and a suspect government. But for the most part, like characters in a Chekhov play, having said all they had to say, they could only continue an interchange of speech, expecting disaster yet helpless to act.

An exception was one of the tsar's nephews-by-marriage, Prince Felix Yusupov, at twenty-nine a somewhat overaged cadet in the Corps of Pages, who had become deeply affected by the general hatred directed at Alexandra and was morally certain that Rasputin was about to sell Russia out to the enemy. He was profoundly stirred by a speech of Duma deputy Purishkevich, who, in a tirade against the "dark forces" menacing Russia, submitted the verdict that "a scoundrelly peasant may no longer be permitted to rule Russia." Those words, which aroused an approving response in many, moved Yusupov to dedicate himself immediately to the task of saving Russia by removing Rasputin.

Not the most intrepid of men, he first proposed to hire an assassin; then, advised by Purishkevich of the danger of blackmail, he joined forces with the deputy, the tsar's cousin the Grand Duke Dmitri Pavlovich, and two other trustworthy conspirators to carry out the deed directly. In the early hours of December 17, the five murdered Rasputin; then, shaken by their own daring and wholly inept at their grisly undertaking, they quickly disposed of the body in the icy Neva, where it was readily located by the police. Their detection followed, and news of what they had done spread quickly.[13]

"Horrified and shaken," the tsar rushed back from *Stavka*. He tried to console his wife for the loss of her friend and did what he could to temper the sensation created by the death of Rasputin. He allowed a private burial in Tsarskoe Selo, limited the investigation, withheld prosecution, and arranged that the assassins leave the capital at once. He was grieved that the incident had smirched the imperial family, particularly through the Grand Duke Dmitri Pavlovich and Prince Yusupov; yet he could not bring himself to impose severe punishment on them. He ordered the grand duke off to Persia with a Russian detachment then on its way to that area, and he exiled the prince to the Yusupov estate in Kursk.

Nicholas remained at Tsarskoe Selo for two months, now more hardened than ever in his resistance to pleas for political concessions and more protective of Alexandra. Learning that his cousin the Grand Duke Nicholas Michaelovich was regaling his Yacht Club friends with commentaries insulting to the empress, he commanded him to leave Petrograd for his Grushevka estate and to remain there. Such acts, of course, only encouraged further embitterment. Those who were affected usually reacted as did the grand duke, who wrote in his notebook as he left the capital on the last day of 1916: "Alexandra Fedorovna is gloating, but how long will the vulture hold onto power? How well will I meet the new year! What will it bring us? Nothing good." [14]

"Nothing good," as far as the regime was concerned, was an appropriate label for 1917. As the year began, the atmosphere that enveloped Petrograd was unchanged by anything that the tsar was willing to do or that the security forces could do. Rumors of impending *coups d'état* continued and became more specific in detail. A widely circulated one alleged that the Grand Duke Nicholas Nicholaievich, in collaboration with ninety guards officers, was planning to kill Protopopov, Alexandra, and Nicholas, then to assume the crown. This rumor received serious attention even in some foreign offices of Europe; when William II learned of it, he at once sensed a plot by the English—always suspect to him—and expressed the hope that his cousin Nicholas would hang the grand duke forthwith. [15]

More portentous than rumors was a strike that began on January 9, the twelfth anniversary of Bloody Sunday, with the walkout of 140,000 Petrograd workers. In their demonstrated and proclaimed sentiments, the tsar was no longer their "leader," but the "butcher" of Bloody Sunday, and the husband of a traitor—if not, indeed, one himself.

The mounting militancy of the workers alarmed Protopopov as nothing else had. Unruliness on their part, he knew, could so overtax the police and the Cossack cavalry at his disposal that troops would be required—and therein lay the weakness of the capital's security at that time. Though there were more than 150,000 soldiers in the Petrograd garrison who might supplement the regular security forces, they were only temporarily on call in the capital, for they were soon to be sent to the front. Moreover, Protopopov was far from certain of their reliability. Most of them were new conscripts, either nineteen-year-olds called up two years before their time or men in their thirties and early forties who represented the tail-end of available manpower. They were a fair sampling of what remained after fifteen million men had been fed into the military maw. They were peasants for the most part, but among them was a considerable sprinkling of industrial workers, hitherto exempt because of their employment in war industries. With few exceptions, they were ill-trained, poorly motivated, and lacking in the *esprit de corps* necessary to insulate them from civilians. In their mood were combined the dissidence of Petrograd and the restlessness of the villages, where little sympathy for the war remained.

Distrusting the worth of such troops in a crisis, Protopopov urged that a number of them be removed from Petrograd and replaced by reliable cavalry units. His lack of confidence was not shared by the lethargic commander of the Petrograd Military District, General Sergei Khabalov, who had recently been given direct administrative authority over the city. But he had support from a higher authority: the tsar ordered *Stavka* to withdraw four guards cavalry regiments from the front for rest, and to send them to Petrograd. When *Stavka* for some reason provided a contingent of sailors instead of cavalry-men, it could not be said that the security of the city was much im-proved.

Protopopov had good cause to be concerned, but his judgment as to how to translate his concern into effective action played him false. Predicting violent socialist-led demonstrations for the opening day of the coming Duma session, scheduled for February 14, he put ex-cessive energy into plans for forestalling them. He arrested labor members of the War Industries Committee as potential trouble-makers and arranged an intimidating show of police, gendarmes, and Cossack strength. Then, when there were no demonstrations on the opening of the Duma, he found himself in unforeseen difficulties: the public at large, and labor in particular, concluded that he had intended to provoke a clash in order to impress them with his power of reprisal. Consequently, hostility against him continued to grow; even soft-spoken Premier Golitsyn vainly suggested to the tsar the advisability of ridding himself of this liability.

There had been cries of "Wolf!" before, and Nicholas refused to be unnerved by this one. Anyway, he did not want to become in-volved in any unsettling political affairs, for soon, he felt, duty would require his return to *Stavka*. General Alexeev, who had been away in the Crimea recovering from an illness, had just returned to headquarters, and preparations for a great allied spring offensive, recently planned at a conference in Petrograd, were under way. Nicholas was satisfied to leave the keeping of order in the capital to Protopopov and Khabalov. He knew that Golitsyn, by simply en-tering a date on the signed imperial order of prorogation which he had in his possession, could take care of any difficulty with the Duma. Even when Protopopov counseled him not to leave until after the Duma was prorogued (for again the minister expected trouble), he would not delay his departure. His only concession was a promise to return as soon as possible. But first, he intended to concern himself with the next phase of the military operations and, meanwhile, to determine the reason for *Stavka's* sending sailors to Petrograd when he had asked for cavalry.

On February 22, as the two blue imperial trains carrying the tsar and his staff left Tsarskoe Selo and moved on through the countryside toward Mogilev, there was no intimation of the unusual. Nicholas appeared depressed and bored, but not worried. He whiled away the hours in passage with a French translation of Caesar's *Gallic Wars*. On arriving at Mogilev the following day, he found a telegram from Alexandra stating that two of their children, Olga and Alexis, had contracted measles, and only then did worry assail him: he knew that Alexis might suffer complications from the disease.

He was not aware that, in Petrograd, the current of revolutionary turbulence was, at last, breaking into the open—this time, with such force that it would soon be lapping at the base of the imperial throne.

On February 23, there came together in the capital the first ingredients for the concerted defiance of tsarist authority about which many had speculated during the past century—more often in apprehension than in anticipation. The passion underlying the events of that day and the week that followed was an accumulation from a number of circumstances related, in many cases, only in the participants' common understanding of the source of the injustices they protested. The initial manifestation of defiance was so commonplace, its development so unpredictable, that it caught everyone by surprise, even those who were soon to be directing it.

On that day, Petrograd stores ran short of black bread, the basic food whose lack meant hunger for the majority of the inhabitants. On that day, 90,000 Petrograd workers were out on strike. On that day 28,000 at the Putilov ironworks were idle, having been locked out on the previous day because of a wage dispute. On that day, socialists were celebrating International Women's Day. The commingling of these thousands as well as the intensification and endurance of their rebellious temper was due, to a great extent, to chance.

Early on the twenty-third, striking workers and locked-out workers began tramping the grimy, slushy streets of the industrial districts—Narva, Vyborg, parts of Vasilevsky Island—shouting "Bread!"

and occasionally stopping streetcars and pocketing the keys to the motors. Later in the day, workers who had attended the meeting connected with the Women's Day celebration joined them, and the fraternizing groups kept up the improvised demonstration, now varied with bursts of "The Marseillaise" and cries of "Down with autocracy!"

As the authorities observed this disorderly activity in the industrial areas, they judged it to be no different from any they had handled previously. They believed that once a few of the most boisterous crowds had been dispersed and night had sent all of them to their quarters, their zest for public demonstration would begin to subside. Yet there was a difference, though it was not observable at the time: the shortage of bread was giving an unusual intensity to the anger of these workers, and the men detailed to control them were developing an unusual disinclination for such work.

Still, no one had reason to anticipate, on February 23, that only eight leaves remained on the calendar of Russian tsarism.

Friday, February twenty-fourth. The zest of the demonstrators did not subside overnight; they were now out in force again. Their number was soon increased by 100,000 more strikers, and, on Vasilevsky Island, they were joined by enthusiastic students from the university and other higher schools. Though the moiling crowds still appeared leaderless and uncoordinated, a common mood was spreading through them; they were becoming more assertive and more inclined to display their anger. Many hurled cobblestones and chunks of ice at policemen, and others continued the malicious sport of stopping and immobilizing streetcars.

On this day of such revolutionary promise, there were no major leaders available to plan strategy for the massed strength, most of them being either in exile or in prison. Lenin, Trotsky, Martov, Plekhanov, Chernov—all were frustratingly impotent to take advantage of the long-coveted possibilities of such a situation. But hundreds of minor leaders, many of them socialists, were available. They strove to make the most of the opportunity by trying to give direction to the unwieldy throngs and egging them on toward the center of the city. There was nothing unusually ambitious about their intentions: they were not urging the workers to overthrow authority but simply to make an impressive showing, to declare their position.

In times past, protesting workers attempting to reach the center of the city had usually been easily halted short of their goal and turned back, since streets from the industrial districts led into the city proper by way of bridges and gates that could be effectively manned by small numbers of men. Today, however, circumstances were favorable. The pressing multitude was both numerous and daring; when they found the police and soldiers at the barriers less vigilant and less resistant than they ordinarily were, many reached the main city streets by crossing on the heavy ice of the Neva while others sneaked by the guards or simply pushed through. Then most of them made their way to the great central thoroughfare, Nevsky Prospect, where they formed groups in front of City Hall and the Kazan Cathedral and around the forbidding equestrian statue of Alexander III, in Znamensky Square. A few hoisted banners denouncing autocracy or the war, and some displayed red ribbons on their coats. Self-selected speakers, usually socialists, harangued any willing listeners about the bread shortage or made abusive attacks on the government.

Surprisingly, none of this created any conspicuous response at any level of authority. Security patrols watched the goings-on passively for the most part, apparently finding more cause for approval than for action. At the Marie Palace, the cabinet held its regular Friday meeting without disturbance and, when it adjourned, the ministers were astonished to find the streets so jammed that they had difficulty in making their way home. General Khabalov, after consulting Protopopov, let the public know that there was now enough bread for all and warned against disorderly conduct. Beyond that, scarcely any precautionary measures were taken. Those that were taken were scattered and without focus: some sections of the city were cordoned off, others not; occasionally the Cossacks broke up crowds, at other times just observed. At *Stavka,* a sense of urgency was so lacking that Nicholas was able to write to his wife, "My brain is resting here—no Ministers, no troublesome questions demanding thought." [16] Alexandra, having been informed that there were some "bread riots" in the capital, sent word that bread should be distributed fairly to the workers and that they "should be told that they must not picket." If, at the end of this day's demonstration, the inexperienced leaders evaluated the effect of it, they could only have concluded that, though the participants had disregarded restraint and reached the center of the city, their achievement had been neither intimidating nor particularly impressive.

The fact was that both Khabalov and Protopopov lacked the

capacity required for their positions at this point. Khabalov had no appreciation of what he was facing and no clear plan for controlling mass lawlessness or preventing small crowds from coalescing into larger ones. Protopopov began to lose his nerve at the first evidence of concerted disobedience. The men who, because of their ineptness at the time of the 1905 troubles, had been called "frightened hens" by the tsar were brave eagles by comparison with these two.

Saturday, February twenty-fifth. Overnight, the strike fever had spread and, with it, the mood of defiance. There was evidence that demonstration was beginning to give way to purposeful action. Routine affairs of the city were slowing down as a result: printing establishments and higher schools had to be closed; more factories were shut down, some of them taken over by the workers; many places of public accommodation failed to open; even some police stations near the center of the city were barricaded, the police staying safely inside. Meanwhile, students, workers, and many middle-class adults were surging freely through the central streets or gathering in Znamensky Square, about which Cossack patrols still rode placidly, watching the waving of red banners and listening to speakers shouting from their perches on the base of the Alexander statue such views as would have driven that short-tempered tsar into a fury of reprisal. Aims were broadening and being expressed in terms which, though at first varying from person to person—"bread, peace with the Germans, and equality for the Yids," as one passerby heard them—were becoming realistic battle cries. A few incidents occurred, the most notable one about three o'clock in the afternoon. A police inspector was summarily killed when, accompanied by a detail of mounted police, he rode up to the square and ordered dispersal. And with that gesture of defiance, the issue between authority and insubordination became seriously joined, authority readily winning the first engagement: the police responded with a volley, and the assembled throng panicked and fled.

By the end of the day, the prevailing atmosphere was one of uncertainty. Neither the authorities nor the defiant crowds controlled the capital. Protopopov had ordered the arrests of revolutionary leaders, but the ones arrested were quickly replaced by others, and everything went on as before. Leaders and would-be leaders on both sides, caught up unexpectedly in what now seemed to be fast approaching unqualified rebelliousness, were bewildered.

The socialist leaders found it difficult to grasp the idea that this was a truly insurrectionary manifestation or to conceive of its being the first phase of a revolution. Their immediate concern was to keep the fires fanned and to provide the strikers with direction. To accomplish that, they proposed to follow the precedent set in 1905, to organize a council of workers, a soviet, to act as the nucleus of authority and determine procedure.

The Duma leaders also were hesitant about the nature of their duty. They were fearful that the turn of events would imperil the war effort, for the Petrograd industrial production, now at a standstill, was an important part of it. Yet they were not averse to riding on the shoulders of the crowd to gain their prime goal, a ministry of confidence. Accordingly, chairman Rodzyanko called on Golitsyn and made an urgent request that he resign. The premier thereupon with some heat revealed his superior advantage: he was calling the tune at this point, for he had at his disposal the tsar's order to prorogue the Duma. Impervious to Rodzyanko's arguments, he refused to consider the request; he simply would not admit that authority was faltering.

General Khabalov was just as stubborn in his refusal to admit the existence of an emergency. Advising General Alexeev, by wire, of the day's events, he noted the spread of the strike and the street disorders, but indicated no cause for alarm. When he received a direct order from the tsar to "end all disturbances" without delay, he finally called his officers together and instructed them to use the troops against the strikers; but he did so reluctantly.

Sunday, February twenty-sixth. The quiet of the morning in Petrograd was broken only by the sound of church bells. But in the afternoon, the cacophony in the streets was resumed as the strikers and their growing throng of supporters, still free of effective restriction, poured out of the industrial districts for the third day. More revolutionary symbols were in evidence—red ribbons, banners, arm bands —and there were more shouted denunciations of the government as well as invectives against the tsar and individual officials.

The ministers were no longer making any pretense of ignoring the obtrusive challenge. But, for the time being, they could decide on no better measure than what they finally planned for the following day—to prorogue the Duma.

The tsar, too, began to feel the grip of anxiety, but he still saw the situation only as another instance of deluded workers responding to pernicious leadership; he felt that he was adequately discharging his obligations in the matter from *Stavka*. He had already sent the general order to Khabalov; now he held onto the delusion that Protopopov would provide the necessary "clear and definite instructions" for clearing the Petrograd streets and that Golitsyn would "not lose his head." When Fredericks handed him a telegram from Rodzyanko reporting the capital in "a state of anarchy" and warning that to delay granting a ministry of confidence would be "tantamount to death" for the monarchy, he dismissed it as "rubbish" not worth his attention; Rodzyanko's repeated sounding of the tocsin had become a nuisance.

Nicholas' disregard of this warning probably made no difference whatsoever: the Petrograd crowds had now become too inflamed to be mollified by anything as tepid as a ministry of confidence. And the one measure he had taken—ordering Khabalov to "end all disturbances" forthwith—was already beginning to make matters worse. At first, the troops from the Petrograd garrison responded well enough when ordered to break up gatherings and subdue resistance. They had even fired on a few stubborn crowds, killing or wounding a number of those who resisted orders to disperse. But, as the day wore on, hostile thousands still surged through the streets, gathering almost at will and moving only with sullen reluctance, while the troops quite evidently were becoming more and more disinclined to continue the use of force. Some of the soldiers in a company of the Pavlovsky Guards reserve battalion (the regulars were at the battlefront) denounced the bloodshed and resisted the orders of their officers. Their minor mutiny was readily quelled, but it was an indication that the time against which Ermolov had warned the tsar in 1905 was at hand, the time when soldiers would refuse to act against civilians. At the end of the day, however, the police report showed "order restored."

That night, enlisted men in the barracks of the Volhynsky Guards training detachment, taking stock of the day's events, argued about the moral justification of what they had been doing—using force against fellow Russians, attacking them with intent to kill. Though a few insisted that a soldier's duty was to respond without question to all commands, the majority came to a different and highly significant conclusion: no man should be made to bear arms against his own people.

Monday, February twenty-seventh. At morning assembly, the officer commanding the training detachment was informed that the men were refusing to serve against civilians. Then, as he hurried away—perhaps to summon help—he was shot in the back. With this mark of mutiny against them, the Volhynsky men knew that there could be no reconsideration; they had not planned to lead a mutiny, but they were now criminally involved and to stand on formality was out of the question. Their immediate need being support, they hurried to the nearby barracks of the Preobrazhensky Guards and the Moscow Guards and, from there, to other units within the garrison, gathering what followers they could. Their procedure, reminiscent of the beginning of the Decembrist Revolt, nearly a century earlier, was different in one very noteworthy respect: on that occasion, officers had been seeking support for mutinous action; on this, the enlisted men were the seekers. Though some units refused to join them and some were divided in their response, the majority remained neutral at first but benevolently inclined toward the rebels.

The men who maintained their loyalty were at a disadvantage since they were not only scattered but also lacking in sufficient leadership. Some of the officers had gone with the mutineers, some were now distrustful of all enlisted men, and some had become so frightened that they had simply left their units. Khabalov was hard put to find enough officers and reliable forces even for the protection of the central offices of the government.

The tide was with the mutineers. Meeting little resistance, they pushed on through the streets of the capital, fraternizing with the strikers, attacking the police (in the traditional hatred of garrison soldiers for local civil authority), setting police stations afire, breaking into arsenals to arm civilians, and opening the gates of prisons. Gradually their number coalesced with the excited throngs who welcomed them in Znamensky Square and elsewhere along Nevsky Prospect.

Defiance was now backed by arms. The revolution was progressing as men like Lenin had dreamed that it would—and had often been disappointed when mass assertiveness had dwindled into submission. The first phase, the Petrograd general strike, was now giving way to the second phase, the armed rising.

In the afternoon, at the Tauride Palace, two miles from Znamensky Square, the Duma received from the premier the tsar's order of prorogation. It was a blow that the more daring deputies wanted to ignore, but the majority insisted on following the letter of the law and obeying the tsar's will. So the Duma stood prorogued. But the spirit of its deputies was unchanged. It was agreed that, regardless of legal considerations, the Duma should assume the responsibility which the crumbling administration in the city could not discharge, and that it should take steps to prevent the Petrograd disorders from exploding into a country-wide revolution. As a side benefit, there was the good chance of exploiting the disorders to force a ministry of confidence from the tsar. While Rodzyanko continued to bombard Nicholas and his generals with telegrams of urgency, at the same time enlisting the help of the Grand Duke Michael and conferring now and then with the ministers, the Duma deputies, following the instructions of their leaders, remained in the Tauride Palace—but in a different chamber, to avoid the appearance of disobeying the order of prorogation—and held themselves ready for further action.

The rebels, now virtual masters of the capital, looked to the Duma for leadership. But when their representatives came to the Tauride Palace for instructions, the majority of the deputies again overruled the militant minority (who had become fired with the idea of the Duma's responding as the French Estates General had in 1789) and refused to subscribe to revolution. They were willing, however, to empower the leaders of the various factions in the Duma to create a provisional committee to administer Petrograd until order was restored. They still believed that Nicholas had only to agree to a ministry of confidence in order to appease his rebellious subjects.

By evening, there was a general realization that the contest for authority was fast approaching a showdown. The Duma leaders, the Council of Ministers, the revolutionary leaders, the imperial family— all felt the urgency. In meeting after meeting, some begun earlier and lasting through the night, there were soul-searchings, decisions, and actions that would have been unthinkable a week earlier.

The Duma leaders met as directed and proceeded to elect the Provisional Committee of the Duma, with Rodzyanko as chairman. Thus to accept provisional authority was as far as that body was willing to go at the time.

About thirty socialist leaders, a self-appointed "action committee," met—appropriately enough, in the left wing of the Tauride Palace— to complete plans for organizing a soviet of deputies to speak and act for the Petrograd insurgents. The initiators of this move, most of whom were Mensheviks, Bolsheviks, Jewish Bundists, and SR's, were acting out their doctrinaire vision of reality. They accepted what was happening in the capital as the revolution that would complete the work of the "bourgeois" revolution of 1905 by destroying tsarism and establishing a "bourgeois-democratic" regime. The soviet's function, as they saw it, would not be to seize power but to guide the revolution and protect its achievements. They chose a temporary executive committee and sent out word that deputies chosen by workers and soldiers were to meet them to complete the organization of the Petrograd Soviet. Within a few hours, scores of enthusiastic deputies from workers' organizations and military units began pouring into the palace, ready for action. First, they approved a central leadership, the Executive Committee of the Petrograd Soviet, socialist in composition and dominated by Duma deputies Nicholas Chkheidze and Alexander Kerensky. Then, having discussed immediate problems of revolutionary procedure and designated their meeting place as the "headquarters of the rising," they adjourned.

In a meeting some distance away, the ministers had come to the conclusion that the removal of the unpopular Protopopov from the government would be the act most likely to appease the insurgents, and he, now completely unnerved and desperate, had offered to commit suicide. He was, of course, dissuaded. In any case, no one could recommend an available replacement, and, even if one were found, his appointment would be up to the tsar, not the Council of Ministers. Yet all of them, including Golitsyn, now believed that the only alternative to change was catastrophe. The Grand Duke Michael finally agreed that, if the tsar approved, he would take temporary responsibility for the government—an arrangement that the tsar, apprised of it, promptly vetoed.

While his government officials sat thus helpless and his capital was being taken over, block after block, by the rebels, Nicholas remained at *Stavka,* still the autocrat and still unwilling to compromise.

Tuesday, February twenty-eighth. During the early hours of the morning, the tsar was contemplating his latest affirmative decisions concerning the distant troubles. Some hours earlier, he had received a message from Khabalov, describing the mutiny and making a plea for help. Here was something to which he could respond with satisfaction: he would send help. After some deliberation, he had decided to send General Nicholas Ivanov, one of his generals adjutant, to smash the mutiny and replace the palpably inadequate Khabalov. He was taking a position quite different from the one he had taken in 1905, when he had withheld force and tried conciliation. To a message from his brother, Michael, inspired by Rodzyanko, suggesting that he appoint as premier either Rodzyanko or Prince George Lvov, he had answered with a flat "no." To a similar appeal from Golitsyn, who was now thoroughly chastened, he had replied emphatically that he would consider no ministerial changes now, that he was investing the premier and General Ivanov with broad powers, and that all he wanted was decisive action.

He did not know that, by the time his reply to Golitsyn reached the capital, there was no cabinet; its despairing members had already gone their separate ways. Some had taken refuge at a distance from the besieged government buildings; others had joined Khabalov and the Grand Duke Michael, who were holding out against the rebels with some 1,500 troops, first at the Winter Palace, then at the Admiralty, waiting for relief.

The tsar instructed Ivanov to take with him from *Stavka* the St. George battalion, every man of whom had been decorated with the St. George cross for valor. He was to pick up four reliable brigades along the way and, with only one stop—at Tsarskoe Selo, to make sure that Alexandra and the children were in no danger from the mutineers—to proceed to his assignment. Ivanov was no novice at punitive action, having to his credit the successful suppression of a mutiny of Kronstadt sailors; the tsar confidently expected that he would have no difficulty with this one.

After the battalion from *Stavka* had entrained, Nicholas himself prepared to leave for Tsarskoe Selo. In order not to impede Ivanov's troops, he planned to have the imperial trains take a longer and less direct route than that assigned to them. He left at five o'clock in the morning, in disregard of Alexeev's insistence that he was needed at *Stavka* to cope with rapidly changing circumstances. He was now more worried about the safety of his family than about being out of touch with events during the day's journey ahead of him.

So far, his family was unmolested, but as the hours passed without word from him, Alexandra's anxiety grew. Though her informants did not give her full and true accounts of developments in Petrograd, she realized that there was real danger when she heard that "some of the troops" had mutinied.

The tsar's confidence that Ivanov would have the situation under control before his own arrival might have faltered if he had known the latest developments. In Petrograd, Khabalov and the remaining small contingent of loyal troops had ended their resistance. The Grand Duke Michael had quietly made his way from the Admiralty to the nearby apartment of a friend, Princess Putyatin. Protopopov had managed to reach the Tauride Palace, where he placed himself under the protection of the Provisional Committee, now acting as the governing body of the city. Other ministers were being sought out by soldiers, arrested, and brought to the palace. The newly formed Petrograd Soviet was sitting in continuous and turbulent session in the Catherine Hall of the palace, where Repin's famous painting of Nicholas II, which had hung behind the speaker's chair, now lay mutilated by soldiers' bayonets.

Worse yet, the revolution was beginning to reach out from Petrograd. The Kronstadt naval base and the cities surrounding the capital were being taken over by rebel troops. A general strike was beginning in Moscow.

In the meantime, the tsar was traveling across the snowy countryside, again reading the *Gallic Wars*.

Wednesday, March first. At two o'clock in the morning, when Nicholas reached Malaya Vishera, a hundred miles from Tsarskoe Selo, he was shocked to learn that part of the remaining route was in rebel hands. He ordered the imperial trains to change course, aiming to approach Tsarskoe Selo by way of Dno, and wired Rodzyanko to meet him in that town. He was realizing at last that pacification would not be as simple a matter as he had thought and that it was expedient for him to deal with Rodzyanko, odious though the step might be.

When Rodzyanko received the order to meet the tsar at Dno, he anticipated a painful meeting, but he considered it entirely appropriate that he be the one chosen for it. As chairman of the Provisional Committee, he seemed just now to be the center of whatever responsible authority still existed in Petrograd. When the committee had taken upon itself the administration of the city, almost all the troops within it and its environs had accepted the committee's authority. Even the Grand Duke Cyril Vladimirovich (now wearing a red arm band), who commanded the naval guards, had placed his men at the disposal of the committee and the Duma. All this had added to Rodzyanko's generous view of his own importance; yet it had not sustained his self-confidence intact. On the day before, he had believed that, at an announcement of his or Lvov's appointment to form a cabinet, the strikers and soldiers would toss their caps into the air and parade in celebration. But, having observed the mounting fury of the crowds and heard their angry shouts against the dynasty, especially against the tsar, he had changed his view. He now believed that, to save the dynasty and keep the mutiny from spreading and breaking down the whole army, it was necessary for Nicholas to abdicate in favor of Alexis, with the Grand Duke Michael as regent. That belief was what he intended to communicate to the tsar at Dno.

Rodzyanko was not, in fact, the powerful figure that either he or the tsar and the generals thought him to be. As head of the Duma's Provisional Committee, he represented the temporary legal authority in the capital; but the physical authority of the armed masses, represented by the Executive Committee of the Petrograd Soviet, was not to be overlooked. That fact was impressed on him when he sought to leave for Dno and realized belatedly that the Executive Committee now controlled the Petrograd railroadmen and that the decision about his leaving was, therefore, up to them. At first, the committee would not allow him the use of a train, suspecting that he would sabotage the revolution. When, at Kerensky's insistence, they agreed to his departure, it was too late to make connection with the tsar's trains at Dno.

Not finding Rodzyanko at the appointed place, Nicholas directed his trains to push on to Pskov and wired orders that the meeting be at that point. But now, uneasy because of the speed with which the revolution was spreading, Rodzyanko decided to remain in the capital, near the center of activity.

When the tsar arrived at Pskov, soon after nightfall, the railroad station was under guard by the troops of General Nicholas Ruzsky, commander of the northern front, with headquarters in Pskov. Since there could be no clearance for his trains before the next day, he had no choice but to have them pulled onto a siding and spend the night there. It was an unappealing prospect: the station was gloomy; the waiting telegrams bore grim news; and Ruzsky, with his stooped shoulders, his sunken eyes behind gold-rimmed spectacles, and his air of gravity added to the general depression.

The delay gave Ruzsky an opportunity to introduce to the tsar the development of a new stage of the accelerating revolution, a stage in which the senior generals were to help decide Russia's future. He tried to show Nicholas that Russia was now facing a critical threat and that drastic and immediate action was required to prevent the imminent breakdown of her ultimate security, the army. If the mutiny in Petrograd was not checked forthwith, he argued, the chance to save the army would be lost. Reports were that Ivanov had already lost some of his troops to the rebels and was now waiting in Tsarskoe Selo for further instructions from the tsar; he was not likely to crush the mutiny. Ruzsky gave it as his belief, which was supported, he pointed out, by other senior generals, that there now remained no alternative; it was necessary to pay the price set by the "victors," which, as he understood from Rodzyanko's earlier telegrams, would have to be a ministry responsible to the legislature. He was not implying that he and the other generals intended to push the tsar off the throne; they had merely come to agree with Rodzyanko and Guchkov—especially Guchkov, who had relentlessly propagandized the generals—that the tsar was pursuing a suicidal course. That was not to say that all of them admired either Rodzyanko or Guchkov by any means; they had just accepted the view that political concessions were unavoidable.

With the tsar almost literally in his hands, Ruzsky hoped to get a decision from him before the dawn of another day.

Thursday, March second. The contention between the stubborn tsar and his determined general went on intermittently well past midnight, Ruzsky driving home his points and flourishing telegrams from Alexeev, Brusilov, and other generals, insisting that to prevent "further disintegration of the army," the tsar must instruct Ivanov not to move against Petrograd and must permit Rodzyanko to form a responsible ministry. The general kept urging on Nicholas the draft of a manifesto, prepared by Alexeev, announcing the imperial decision to form such a ministry.

For Nicholas, the ordeal was much like that through which he had suffered in October 1905, and it offered no more escape than the former one. It ended only when he had exhausted all his arguments and reluctantly accepted the need to do what was advised. In final capitulation, he authorized Ruzsky to transmit the text of the manifesto to Rodzyanko and to send instructions that Ivanov remain in Tsarskoe Selo until further advised.

By the time Ruzsky had accomplished what he had set out to do, events in Petrograd had proceeded far beyond the point at which he expected to stop them. While he was dictating to the tsar on the basis of what Rodzyanko had believed earlier to be political reality, a revolutionary government had been in the making at the Tauride Palace. A strikingly varied group of "victors"—Prince George Lvov, just arrived from Moscow, members of the Provisional Committee, and representatives of the Petrograd Soviet—had assembled in one of the large halls of the palace and had been struggling as dili-

gently as had Ruzsky. On one side, there had been the middle-
and upper-class liberals, many of them representative of the Great
Russians and the intelligentsia, who sought to contain and confine
the revolution; on the other side, the socialists of the intelligentsia—
three of them (two Jews and a Georgian) representing minority
groups—who were anxious to push the revolution along. Though
differing in aspirations, both sides had been anxious to avoid delay
in organizing a new government. The Provisional Committee, whose
members would have preferred to act legally, by authority of the
tsar, had felt that to wait any longer for that authority was to risk
a runaway revolution; the Soviet representatives, while not wishing
to forestall revolution, had felt that safety lay in acting before the
undisciplined mutineers had to face the opposition of loyal troops.

The struggle for a decision in the tsar's train at Pskov had reached
its post-midnight climax well before that in the Tauride Palace. The
architects of the new government kept doggedly at their task, hour
after hour, while the tables became littered with papers, voices grew
hoarse, and eyes smarted from the smoke of countless cigarettes;
postponement was no part of their intention. An unforeseen break
came when Rodzyanko was summoned to the telegraph office to con-
verse with Ruzsky. But the pause lasted only long enough for brief
speculation. Then proposals and arguments were resumed.

The once ostentatiously brave Rodzyanko demanded, and was
granted, an armed escort to the telegraph office. There, his conversation with Ruzsky, carried on by means of the cumbersome Hughes
apparatus, consumed four precious hours. He had to make the almost incredulous general understand that the time had passed when
the tsar could appease the people by allowing the formation of a
ministry of confidence and that the only way he could stay the revolution was by abdicating in favor of the young heir, Alexis, and
appointing the Grand Duke Michael as regent. That arrangement,
he asserted categorically, would be acceptable to both the troops and
the civilians of Petrograd. Once the tsar had abdicated, the country
would quickly return to normalcy without any unnecessary sacrifice,
he assured Ruzsky, adding in the familiar Rodzyanko manner that
he, whom the soldiers still obeyed, would not permit such sacrifice.

Ruzsky promised to relay Rodzyanko's affirmations to the tsar at
once, and the conversation ended. (Actually, he reported them to
Alexeev instead and then retired for a short rest before making the
momentous revelation to Nicholas.)

While Rodzyanko was away from the Tauride Palace, negotiations there had finally ended. Though the conferees had been unable to agree on the immediate fate of the monarchy, they had decided to form a provisional government, a cabinet, to exercise executive authority until a constituent assembly could be democratically elected to decide the political future of the country. Accordingly, they had chosen cabinet members for the "Provisional Government" and directed that it begin to function at once. Its program was to provide complete civil freedom, end "all restrictions based on class, religion, and nationality," and grant full political and religious amnesty. With one exception, the chief figures in the new cabinet were men whose political sentiments were known to be those of the Progressive Bloc. Prince George Lvov was chosen as premier and minister of interior; Paul Milyukov, as minister of foreign affairs; Alexander Guchkov, as minister of war; and Alexander Kerensky (the exception), as minister of justice.

While the conference worked behind closed doors, many anxious people gathered in the palace and waited to hear the results. When the worn and hoarse Milyukov finally appeared to make the "official" announcement, he had a most intent audience. As he named the members of the new cabinet, someone shouted a query about who "elected" them; his quick reply, "The revolution!" was agreeably accepted. When asked about the dynasty, he responded with a statement that he was not, in fact, empowered to make, since it did not have the assent of the Soviet: "The old despot who has brought Russia to the brink of ruin will either voluntarily abdicate or be deposed. The power will pass to a regent, the Grand Duke Michael Alexandrovich. Alexis will be the heir." [17]

Even then, the question of the abdication was the subject of messages being passed back and forth among the men of the military and naval high command, while Nicholas II sat alone in his private compartment in one of the immobile trains at Pskov, unaware that the future of the Romanov dynasty was being weighed by others. General Alexeev, informed of the last report from the capital and assuming that Rodzyanko could support his guarantee of a quick return to normalcy after abdication, had notified the other front commanders and the fleet commanders of the turn of events and urged Ruzsky to lose no time in explaining the situation to the tsar.

It was about ten in the morning when Nicholas received Ruzsky and listened to his distressing message. He heard it through with his usual lack of emotional display. Then, still without giving any indication of what was going on behind his mask of composure, he said

simply that he would withhold his decision on the matter until he
had the opinion of all the other front and fleet commanders. Intermediary Ruzsky hastened to pass that information on; and from
Stavka, Alexeev began to poll the commanders, emphasizing his own
belief that the tsar's abdication would insure that the army remain
a cohesive fighting force and that his refusal to abdicate would unquestionably bring civil war.

There was nothing to lessen the burden that had finally fallen
on Nicholas. Merely postponing the decision could not relieve the
gravity of his responsibility. As he stared through the window of his
compartment, the dirty snow outside could not have appeared more
depressing than his future. He had no way of knowing that members
of the imperial family, whose personal concern with his affairs he
had neither encouraged nor appreciated, were then endeavoring to
rescue him from his predicament. His uncle the Grand Duke Paul
was leading a family effort to forestall the necessity of his abdication.
Believing that Rodzyanko and the Grand Duke Michael's wife were
conspiring to press for abdication in order to promote their own
interests—his being to become premier, hers being to clear the way
for her husband to become regent—they had hurriedly drawn up a
constitution in the belief that, if Nicholas would issue it, the turmoil
would cease and the throne be saved. Knowledge of their undertaking did not reach the tsar until it was too late for him to consider
it. In any case, their plan had no chance of success.

Early in the afternoon, Ruzsky delivered four messages to the
tsar: one, from the Grand Duke Nicholas Nicholaievich, implored
him to give up the throne for the sake of Russia and Alexis; the
three others, from Generals Brusilov, Evert, and Alexeev, also counseled abdication. Later, responses from the other commanders were
brought in—all of them in the same vein. Ruzsky, who had come
with two members of his staff to wait for the tsar's response, had
brusquely added his own vote for abdication.

Nicholas, face drawn, reviewed the messages from these men who
had sworn to lay down their lives for him and now seemed united
in betrayal. How could he understand that behind their advice lay
a disenchantment with their tsar which weighed almost as much in
their decision as their lack of confidence in the present morale of
their men and their ill-advised confidence in Rodzyanko as the man
who could save the day for the Russian army and navy. Only twelve
hours before, Nicholas had yielded to their advice and made one
concession; now they were asking him to relinquish his right even

to make concessions. When he had yielded in October 1905, the results, he well knew, had not borne out the arguments he had accepted. Perhaps on this occasion, there was some other way. He asked Ruzsky if the troops in the south, Cossacks, might not be used to suppress the Petrograd mutineers. The general's silence was answer enough. Nicholas turned to the two officers who had accompanied Ruzsky and asked their opinion. They saw no way out but through abdication.

Without the support of his generals, the tsar could not hope to hold out. He did not believe that his abdication was what Russia needed; but if it would satisfy his generals and Petrograd, he could hope that it would be of some benefit to the country. Whatever his faults, Nicholas had ever been, and would remain, a loyal Russian. After a brief pause, he solemnly faced the waiting men and made two statements: he would abdicate; he trusted that they would serve faithfully the one who would succeed him—his son, Alexis. Then he crossed himself and, calling Fredericks to the compartment, told him of the decision. The old man hurried away to the members of his suite waiting outside and reported, *"Tout fini!"* Only a cold formality remained, the arrangement for a public announcement. Nicholas picked up copies of two telegrams he had already prepared —one to Rodzyanko, the other to Alexeev—containing his statement of abdication and handed them to Ruzsky.

The final act of the drama had not been concluded, however. Before the prepared statements could be sent, word came to Pskov that two men, Alexander Guchkov and Vasily Shulgin, were on their way from Petrograd to ask personally for abdication; Nicholas agreed to delay the telegrams.

In the interval that followed, the tsar questioned his physician more closely than ever before about the life expectancy of his twelve-year-old son. The doctor told him frankly that, if there were miracles, there were no limits to the age Alexis might attain despite his hemophilia; but, as far as could be predicted scientifically, he was not likely to reach his forties. Then, knowing the tsar's deep attachment for his son, he remarked that the new government would be unlikely to allow the boy to remain with him. This intimation of separation from Alexis was all that Nicholas needed to set his course; he would abdicate in favor of Michael and keep his son at his side. It remained for him only to see that his manifesto of abdication included this important specification.

Guchkov and Shulgin arrived about ten o'clock that night, aboard one of the first civilian trains to reach Pskov since the revolution began. They were carrying out an undertaking which, strictly speaking, was a personal one, unauthorized by what was now the actual established authority in the capital. They had Rodzyanko's approval, but not that of the Petrograd Soviet. In fact, they were acting without the knowledge of the Soviet and at cross-purposes to it.[18] They had left Petrograd with the hope—supported by Rodzyanko—that, if Nicholas would abdicate immediately and make it possible for Michael, as regent, and the Provisional Government to gather up the reins of authority, order could be restored and the monarchy saved.

They were admitted directly to the tsar's compartment, where they found Fredericks with Nicholas, and where the four of them were later joined by Ruzsky. It was a strange scene. Guchkov, the tsar's inveterate enemy, spoke haltingly and at length of the urgent need that Nicholas abdicate to save the country from disintegration. The tsar endured this redundance with patience, then startled him and Shulgin by stating that he had already reached the decision to abdicate. He startled them even more by stating that Michael, not Alexis, would succeed him. Next, he showed them his abdication manifesto, a forthright declaration of his last imperial decision and his acceptance of a principle never before endorsed by a Russian tsar:

At a time of great struggle with a foreign enemy . . . God has chosen to visit Russia with a new and heavy burden. . . . We have deemed it Our moral obligation to strengthen the close unity and solidarity of all forces of the nation in order that victory may be won as quickly as possible; and, in agreement with the State Duma, We have acknowledged it as right to abdicate the Throne of the Russian State. . . . We hand over Our Succession to Our Brother the Grand Duke Michael Alexandrovich and bless Him on His accession to the Throne of the Russian State. We direct Our Brother to conduct the affairs of the State in full and inviolable union with the representatives of the people in their legislative institutions, taking an inviolable oath to this effect. . . . May the Lord help Russia.[19]

After reading the manifesto, the visitors requested that Nicholas sign two ukases: one, naming Prince Lvov as premier; the other, naming the Grand Duke Nicholas Nicholaievich as commander in chief. When he had done that, he complied with their further request that he date the ukases "March 2, 1:00 P.M." and the manifesto

"March 2, 3:00 P.M." (the time at which he had actually decided to abdicate).

So far as Nicholas was concerned, political matters were now the responsibility of others. He rose and shook hands with his guests. Shulgin fatuously suggested that this scene might have been avoided if concessions had been made two weeks earlier. "Do you really think so?" asked Nicholas, politeness still concealing his contempt.

Back in his private quarters, alone again, Nicholas wrote in his diary: "All around are treason, cowardice, and deceit." Later, he sent a telegram to Michael, expressing regrets that he had been unable to keep in touch with him and vowing to remain a "faithful and devoted brother."

Friday, March third. When Guchkov and Shulgin arrived back in Petrograd after their all-night trip from Pskov, they learned that their efforts had already been bypassed by the fast-moving events of the revolution, just as Ruzsky's had been bypassed the day before. They had thought to save the Romanov dynasty by their alertness in obtaining evidence that its unpopular representative had abdicated; now they were informed that the vocal elements of the populace, shouting as one voice for the end of the dynasty, had made Rodzyanko and his associates doubtful that it could be saved. The news that Nicholas had designated Michael to succeed him had reached the capital before their arrival, and it had already been decided not to publicize the abdication until after consultation with the grand duke. Their next step therefore was to join a group called together in the apartment of princess Putyatin, where Michael was staying, guarded by a detachment of officers and officer-candidates (who had been able, so far, to prevent enlisted men from searching the apartment as they had searched others in the building).

With Michael were members of the Provisional Committee and the Provisional Government. Most of them had come to the conclusion that his acceptance of the throne would set off more furious riots, and they counseled him to refuse. But Milyukov argued that, for the government to survive, it must have the support of the historical symbol of authority, the monarchy. While he conceded that it might be advisable for Michael to begin his reign in Moscow, where the soldiery was still reliable, he insisted that the dynasty should not be brought to an end. Only Guchkov supported him.

Finally Michael rose—a man much like his brother, slight of build, quiet, unassuming—and, asking Lvov and Rodzyanko to join him, excused himself from the group. In the adjoining room, after receiving answers to a few questions and learning the misgivings of Lvov and Rodzyanko about their ability to provide for his personal safety if he became tsar, he made up his mind: he would not accept the throne. Those who knew him would not have charged this decision to a lack of courage; he had courage, but he lacked the temperament to lead a battle.

Returning to face the meeting, he began, "Under the circumstances, I cannot take the throne, because . . . " and broke off in tears.[20]

Later in the day, Nicholas II's abdication was published, along with a statement by Michael that contained these significant words:

I have firmly resolved to assume the Supreme Power only in the event that such is the will of our great people, upon whom the duty now rests to determine the form of government and the new fundamental laws of the Russian State, acting through their representatives, chosen by universal suffrage, in a constituent assembly.

Therefore, invoking God's Blessing, I ask all citizens of the Russian State to pay allegiance to the Provisional Government. . . .[21]

Epilogue

ON the occasion of the Romanov tercentenary, in 1913, the eminent French historian Marquis Pierre de Ségur, in affirming a fellow Frenchman's statement that "Russia is the Emperor," declared his own conviction that between the Russian people and their ruler there existed an "intimate, close, indissoluble" link of "tender familiarity analogous to the relations between the patriarchs and Jehovah in Biblical times." It was a widely held conviction, which resisted the force of contrary evidence revealed by the turn of events in 1917.

The Russian monarchy had weathered countless storms, and it was not readily believable that the link between the people and throne could actually be broken by the prevailing upsurge of opposition. Nor was it readily believable that the Romanov dynasty was doomed at the time of Nicholas II's abdication and Michael's conditional renunciation of the succession. In fact, it was difficult to comprehend the nature of the revolution, to understand that it was inspired by hatred for existing institutions as well as by distaste for the reigning tsar, that it was telescoping years of sought-after change into days.

The sweep of the revolution could not be long misinterpreted, however. It was fast, and it was drastic. Although the Provisional Government did not proclaim a republic until six months after the abdication, both the Romanov dynasty and the Russian monarchy came to an end on March 3, 1917. Thereafter, the men connected with the government of Russia dared not support the notion of monarchy or associate themselves with the Romanovs.

The deterioration of the armed strength that had sustained the autocracy through past crises followed the abdication without delay. Military discipline, undercut by the spirit of mutiny radiating from Petrograd, began to break down everywhere, and enlisted men proved quick to reveal long repressed hatreds and to demonstrate openly their distaste for further fighting. This development added to the insecurity of the Provisional Government, whose chief justification for existence was to lead the country to victory; but its leaders, striving to overlook the obvious, refused to admit the weakening of the army either to themselves or to Russia's allies. Even after the short-lived offensive in June, when only picked troops were found willing to advance under fire, the government kept up a courageous front. Yet the woeful reality was that Russia no longer had an army, only a few million tired civilians in uniform.

Nicholas himself, despite his acquiescence to the first demands of the revolution, was soon entrapped by its development. Since he had no wish to leave Russia, his first thought was to retire with Alexandra and their children to Livadia. But, after Michael's renunciation of the throne, well-wishers persuaded the tsar that it would be more politic to leave the country and remain abroad until after the war.

Deciding on a possible sanctuary involved, quite logically, a consideration of the ties between Russia's imperial family and members of other ruling houses of Europe. The most numerous ties—those with Germany—were valueless in a time of war with Germany, of course; in any case, both Nicholas and Alexandra would have preferred death to rescue by William II. There were others, however. Denmark's King Christian X was Nicholas' cousin. Another cousin was King Constantine I of Greece, whose Romanov mother, Dowager Queen Olga, was now residing in Russia. Queen Eugenia, wife of Spain's King Alfonso XIII, was Alexandra's cousin—like her, a granddaughter of Queen Victoria. King Nicholas I of Montenegro was close to the Romanovs, being father-in-law of the grand dukes Peter and Nicholas Nicholaievich. Yet, with respect to each of the countries represented by these relatives, there was some drawback which made it an unlikely sanctuary. Denmark, a neutral country, was probably reluctant to harbor a former head of a belligerent state, and it could be reached only by passage through German-controlled waters; though the Greek government was pro-Entente, the king himself was pro-German; Spain, where the ties with Russia were tenuous at best, was neutral; and Montenegro was under Austrian occupation. One bright prospect remained: England. After all, Nicholas was an honorary field marshal in the English army, a nephew of the dowager queen, and a cousin (as was Alexandra also) of King George V. Moreover, England, maintaining a northern sea route to Russia, was in a position to provide safe passage for the family.

In view of what seemed most advisable, the Provisional Government requested, and received, from the English government an offer of asylum for the former tsar and his family, and promised them safe conduct to a port of exit where they might board an English warship.

Final arrangements for that trip were never made. The Petrograd Soviet, insisting that Nicholas be tried as a criminal, barred the departure and compelled the Provisional Government to arrest him, then to guard him and his family as prisoners in the Alexander Palace at Tsarskoe Selo. There they experienced, and bravely bore, the humiliation of being held almost incommunicado, submitting to the direction of insolent soldiers, and enduring the curiosity of unfriendly sightseers. Though the Provisional Government kept assuring them that they would soon be on their way to England, there was no longer any likelihood of that escape. The Petrograd Soviet was adamant in its refusal to permit them to leave Russia; the English government, under pressure from its own leftists, ultimately preferred not to grant them sanctuary. Instead of freedom, their lot was removal to stricter imprisonment and further restrictions on both comfort and outside contacts. In July, they were taken 1,500 miles from Petrograd to Tobolsk, in Siberia, where they could be guarded more effectively.

Nicholas and his family were still confined at Tobolsk when the Bolsheviks overthrew the Provisional Government, in October 1917, and established the Russian Socialist Federated Soviet Republic, which became their official jailor. This shift in power made their future grim indeed, for the new government was determined to try Nicholas for "crimes against the people," fully expecting to find him guilty and execute him. It was not until late in the spring of 1918, however, that the busy Bolshevik leaders could take time to prepare the trial, which they intended to be a public spectacle, with Leon

Trotsky as chief prosecutor. By that time, the prisoners had been transferred to another Siberian town, Ekaterinburg.

Since this place was close to the scene of fighting between former Czechoslovak prisoners of war and Soviet troops, Trotsky urged a speedy trial to forestall the possibility of having to change plans because of the military operations. But even that was not to be. While Trotsky was away from the capital, leaders of the local soviet with headquarters at Ekaterinburg, seeing that their town was in imminent danger of being taken by the Czechoslovaks, decided that the prisoners were too much of a liability. Accordingly, with the concurrence of Premier Lenin, they took the responsibility for executing them forthwith without a trial, to prevent their being taken from their guards and used as "living banners" by anti-Bolshevik forces.

There were no elaborate arrangements. Shortly after midnight of July 16/17, 1918 (N.S.), in the dingy cellar of the house being used as a prison, twelve armed executioners faced the twelve condemned victims—eleven human beings and the family's spaniel, Jimmy. Nicholas, Alexandra, and their five children were cold-bloodedly shot, along with four who had been allowed to remain with them: the physician Dr. Botkin, the maid Demidov, the cook Kharitonov, the valet Trup. So that no living trace would be left in the room, the little dog was clubbed to death.

It was not to be expected, of course, that Nicholas be given burial with his Romanov predecessors in the Cathedral of SS. Peter and Paul. His body and the bodies of the other dead were immediately taken from Ekaterinburg to an isolated area of abandoned iron ore diggings a few miles away; there, after crude efforts at destruction by fire and chemicals, the remains were finally thrown into one of the partially water-filled excavations.

The name of Russia's last tsar was added to the roster of retribution simply as Nicholas Romanov. It was just another name on a list that was extended to thousands by the succession of other official executions and deaths incurred through "attempts to escape," the stark evidence of the Bolsheviks' intention literally to expunge tsarism by disposing of any adherents who failed to escape from Russia —as more than a million did.

For the outside world, the truth about what had happened at Ekaterinburg was obscured as long as possible. The first official report was a deliberate falsification. To publish the facts would have been highly inexpedient for the government, for they were undeniably in disagreement with what it had been affirming in order to allay foreign concern about the safety of Nicholas and his family. When the German government, for instance, had warned that the whole world would condemn Russia if they were executed, the new government had given its assurance that officials in Ekaterinburg fully understood the importance of insuring the safety of the prisoners. After the executions, embarrassing explanations were avoided by the official announcement that the Ekaterinburg authorities had executed Nicholas "in accordance with the will of the people," to prevent his escaping judgment, and had removed the other members of the family to "a place of greater safety." For months, the fiction that Alexandra and her children were alive and would soon be permitted free exit from Russia was maintained in official communications. When the whole truth was finally made known, bit by bit, it caused so little stir in the rest of the world—by that time, like Russia, almost inured to protracted hardships and reports of mass deaths—that there seemed little need to justify the earlier misinformation.

When the Russian people were informed that Nicholas had been executed, a few wept privately and some cheered publicly, but most of them responded dispassionately. Their "boundless loyalty" to the Little Father seemed to have disappeared like morning fog in the heat of the sun. So far as the Romanov dynasty was concerned, it was as if life were imitating art, making reality of the epilogue of the opera *The Golden Cockerel*, in which the astrologer explains that, though "the tale might seem gory, woven with a saddening touch," the characters were merely "pallid specters at the most."

The relationship of the Romanov tsars to circumstances affecting the Russian monarchy during its final hundred years and their responsibility for the turn of events in February 1917 has been examined from many points of view and interpreted in a number of ways.

Some interpretations place all the blame for ultimate failure on Nicholas II. They are founded on the argument that he permitted obvious provocations to revolution without sufficient regard for the consequences and, therefore, actually instituted the reaction that brought about the collapse of the dynasty. There is a compelling ring to this argument; it makes everything fall neatly into place— the Alexandra-Rasputin scandal, the repeated warnings of disaster, and Nicholas' persistent obduracy. On close examination, however, it will be seen to have two grave defects. It mistakenly assumes that those who made the revolution, the striking workers and the workers and peasants in uniform, were striving for roughly the same ends as those sought by the men who had been warning the tsar of the need for a ministry of confidence, and it mistakenly assumes that by the beginning of World War I Russia had reached a state of internal equilibrium which could have been maintained if it had not been disturbed through the influence of Alexandra and Rasputin.

Of other interpretations, the most uncompromising are to be found in the writings of some latter-day Russian monarchists and the Marxists. The monarchists see the February events not as an actual revolution but a large-scale *coup* executed by generals, grand dukes, and liberal politicians acting cooperatively with German-financed Bolsheviks (though not necessarily aware of their coopera-tion). Theirs is a view in which identification with a cause obscures facts. The Marxists recognize the revolutionary nature of the events, give ample attention to the long-range factors behind them, but virtually ignore the influence of the tsars upon the fall of the mon-archy. While admitting that men affect history, they insist that in-dividuals act under conditions so constricting that, even in positions as powerful as those of the tsars, they can do no more than slightly impede or slightly assist the operation of historical law. The Marxist view, which forces facts into preconceived patterns, is more agree-able than any other to "prophets who look backward."

If the facts are allowed to speak for themselves, unqualified by attempts to read between the lines, by political orientation, or by preconceived theories, they will be found to indicate conclusions much less emphatic than those so qualified—conclusions that are also less sensational, less accusatory, less dependent on defense by complicated manipulation of evidence.

It is not to be denied that each of the men who ruled during the last century of the Romanov dynasty put his ultimate trust in the *jus divinum* of tsarism and was, in that respect, a Dadon relying on the vigilance of his golden cockerel to the neglect of the realities about him. But that fact alone does not justify sweeping condemna-tion. The last five tsars were not free to solve all of Russia's prob-lems, and they should not be blamed for what they could not do. Their freedom was limited by the training they received, the nature of the bureaucracy through which they ruled, the administrative unwieldiness of their empire, and the nature of the international community in which they lived. That is not to say that they were helpless, however. Restricted though they were, they had sufficient freedom to adopt policies that could have altered the course of Russian history, and they failed to use their freedom as they might have.

Yet, with all their human frailties, individual shortcomings, culpable misdeeds, and power-oriented policies, these five tsars did, or allowed others to do, much for their great Eurasian empire. Under their rule, it developed, broke with many shackling traditions, grew more integrated, and generally confuted Diderot's often-repeated barb that Russia "decayed before it could mature."

There were achievements at all levels. The empire gained and retained eminence among the powers, a position which, though tenuous and often inordinately expensive to maintain, assured a Russian voice in international affairs. There were widely recognized accomplishments in the arts and sciences attributable in significant degree to the regime's continuation of the policy of Westernization and to the support given to special schools, conservatories, and theaters by imperial subsidy even during the most reactionary years of the century. In addition, there were other advances that could be compared favorably with those of countries that had previously been considered far superior to Russia. With the construction of a great railroad network, the people were drawn more closely and profitably together and Russia moved into the modern industrial age. Twenty-two million serfs and twenty-four million state peasants were given their freedom, provided with land, and treated more generously than were their emancipated contemporaries, the former Negro slaves of the United States. The antiquated and iniquitous legal and judicial system was replaced by a far more modern and equitable one staffed by capable and honorable men. Provision for higher education was expanded more than a hundredfold. A system of universal primary education was introduced and developed with promise in the years before the outbreak of the First World War.

The prevailing irony of all this was that, despite specific contributions to what was accompished, a personal love for Russia, and a sincere regard for the progressive possibilities of the system he administered, each of the last Romanov tsars contributed in an individual way to the decline and fall of the dynasty. Each, influenced by the traditions in which he was reared and humanly indulging some aspect of his personality, responding to the advice of some mentor, or failing to distinguish between practical and impractical counsel, led the dynasty a step closer to its disintegration.

Alexander I lacked the consistency of character needed to carry out the commission imposed upon him by the times and by his own education—to rule as an enlightened despot. He alienated liberals by encouraging expectations that he could not, or would not, fulfill. He alarmed and confused conservatives by arousing fears that proved unjustified. By carrying his faith in the goodness and rationality of mankind to extreme lengths, he pursued idiosyncratic fancies while neglecting the affairs of state. When he died, he left a legacy of impoverished serfs, precariously situated nobles, embittered Poles, and a generation of youths whose education had led them to active discontent with the system under which they lived. The margin of safety within which tsarism could take risks had become narrower than it was when he came to power.

Nicholas I, though a ruler of greater strength than his brother, proved even less successful in his efforts to remodel the regime for the effective handling of Russia's problems. Placing his faith in his own goodness and rationality rather than in the goodness and rationality of mankind, he set out to exemplify the Confucian ideal of a ruler—one embodying beneficence, omnipotence, and omniscience. Commendable as the ideal was, conditions opposing his achievement of it, particularly the physical immensity of Russia and the backwardness of her people, were far from favorable. Even if conditions had been favorable, Nicholas would have been impeded by his own efforts to pursue mutually antagonistic goals: to maintain Russia as a great power while preserving her essentially agrarian society in a world becoming industrialized and to advance education among his people while doing his utmost to prevent the development of political thinking and dissent among them. Because of the course he followed, certain malignant characteristics of tsarism-on-the-defensive —heavy reliance on political police and censorship, Russification of troublesome national minorities, and excessive preoccupation with the Jews—became manifest during his reign. By the time of his death, the serfs were more impoverished, the nobles more precariously situated, the Poles more embittered, and the educated youth more restive than when he began his reign. Moreover, he had helped to embroil Russia in the unnecessary and ruinous Crimean War, the only beneficial consequence of which was to be that his successor had to face some unpleasant truths.

Alexander II, despite the fact that he acted boldly and expeditiously to exorcise some of the dangers threatening the regime, unwittingly stored up trouble for his successors by accelerating the process of change just when he was attempting to create a stable agrarian society and by exciting his subjects' political expectations without providing legal means for realizing them. Then, with his renunciation of the spirit of reform, in 1866, he made inevitable further conflict between the ruler and the ruled. In short, he also left the realm in a perilous state, changed in some respects but still without the means necessary to satisfactory development. In 1881, Russia was a drifting ship, broken loose from its moorings and desperately in need of firm control.

Alexander III proved himself a firm but not a wise helmsman. He stifled the spirit of reform, used police power to silence dissent, intensified the policy of Russification, and fixed on the Jews as scapegoats. He was credited with a successful reign because he was able to subdue the opposition, because he followed a circumspect policy abroad and, above all, because he had the good fortune to die before he had to face the consequences of his actions.

Alexander III did not bequeath a revolution to Nicholas II, as Trotsky liked to say that he did, but he left him a realm in a state of disarray far more serious than was then obvious. He had not been able to arrest the economic deterioration within either the nobility or the peasantry, he had not been able to tame the educated youth, he had not won the support of the bulk of the educated class, he had not destroyed Polish nationalism. Moreover, during his reign, significant new difficulties had been added to the old ones: the rise of an industrial proletariat susceptible to revolutionary ideas, the increasing receptivity of the peasantry to urban influences, the burgeoning of minority nationalism, and the beginnings of a politically aggressive middle class.

Although the tsarist regime, as Alexander III left it, was out of joint with the times, the monarchy was not therefore doomed. But the son to whom he left it was not a promising savior. Apparently immune to "crown prince fever," which had driven some of his predecessors to dream of reversing parental policies, Nicholas II attempted to follow in the steps of his strong, imperious father without the strength to do so. Had he been endowed with administrative competence, with diplomatic prudence in the handling of affairs in the Far East, and with luck, he might have avoided that first fateful loss of footing—in the Revolution of 1905.

That revolution was, as Lenin later observed, truly a "dress rehearsal" for 1917. The cast on stage in 1905 was the same cast that appeared in 1917: rebellious workers, mutinous soldiers, turbulent peasants, disaffected intelligents, and dissident national minorities—

all engaged in the practice of procedures through which, they were beginning to realize, autocratic power could be effectively challenged.

While 1905 taught revolutionaries how they might gain power, it did not advance Nicholas II's understanding of how he might preserve power. Even after he had blundered into this first revolution, if he could have seen it for what it was, a popular uprising, rather than what he quickly judged it to be—the effort of native demagogues and international Jewry—and had he been favored by an extended period of peace, he might have avoided a repetition of it. When both advantages eluded him, he was unable to stay the consequences.

The disruption of peace that came with Russia's entry into the First World War created conditions propitious for revolution. The war effort made more nearly insufferable than ever before the impositions and oppressive measures that the Russian people had been enduring for a century while the tsars clung jealously to the principles of autocracy, failed to interpret properly the changes taking place about them, and refused to grant their subjects a reasonable share in the government. When military reverses began to accumulate, this war, like the Crimean and Russo-Japanese Wars, lowered the prestige of the regime and thereby its ability to inspire respect or to command obedience. The stage was set for the final production. When the developments of a century crowded in upon Nicholas II in February 1917, his course was virtually predetermined. The restrictions that had been tightening with each succeeding reign had critically reduced the autocrat's freedom of choice, and Nicholas was not the man to take advantage of what was left.

His abdication of authority resulted in the closing of an era in Russian history. The three-hundred-year-old Romanov dynasty, which had brought the country both renown and progress in the past century, had hastened its own undoing by adherence to unrealistic principles and a too meager, too belated sharing of power. Its dissolution ended a thousand years of monarchical rule and nine hundred years of the established Church. Russia faced an uncharted future.

THE ROMANOV DYNASTY, PETER III–NICHOLAS II*

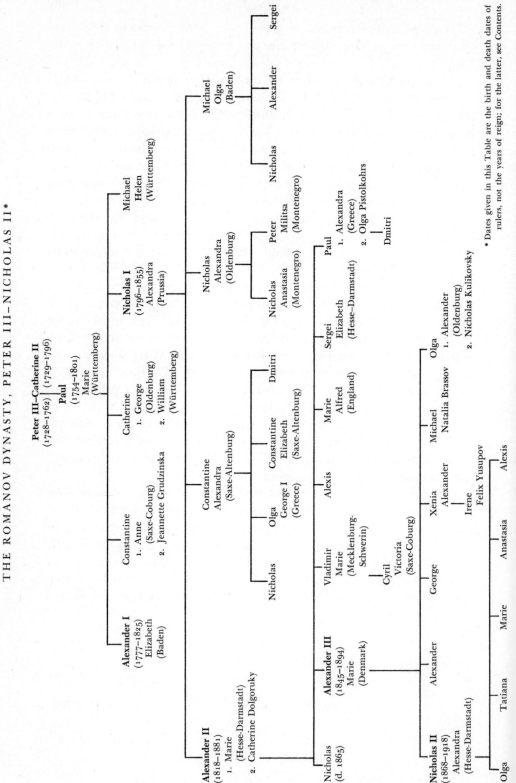

* Dates given in this Table are the birth and death dates of
rulers, not the years of reign; for the latter, see Contents.

Bibliography and Notes

Listed below are sources used in preparation of this book. Beginning on page 497 is a brief, general list of works in English for those who wish to read further on this period.

PREFACE

1. The Russian text of Pushkin's "Tale of the Golden Cockerel" will be found in his *Sochineniya,* I (Moscow, 1962), 454–59. A free English translation by Babette Deutsch is to be found in *The Poems, Plays and Prose of Pushkin,* edited by Avrahm Yarmolinsky (New York, 1936), 322–29.
2. The Russian text of the libretto will be found in *Le Coq d'Or* (Moscow, 1908). *The Golden Cockerel* (New York, 1945) is an English translation of the libretto by Tatiana B. Drowne.

ALEXANDER I

Caulaincourt, A. de. *With Napoleon in Russia.* New York, 1933.

Chaadaev, P. *Sochineniya i Pisma.* 2 vols. Moscow, 1913–1914.

Choiseul-Gouffier, A. de. *Historical Memoirs of Alexander I.* Chicago, 1900.

Czartoryski, A. *Memoirs of Prince Adam Czartoryski.* 2 vols. London, 1888.

Dubrovin, N. *Pisma Glavneishikh Deyatelei v Tsarstvovanie Imperatora Aleksandra I.* St. Petersburg, 1883.

Gershenzon, M. *Griboedovskaya Moskva.* Moscow, 1922.

Karamzin, N. *A Memoir on Ancient and Modern Russia.* Cambridge, 1959.

Kohl, J. G. *Russia.* London, 1844.

Lyubimov, L. "Taina Startsa Fedora Kuzmicha," *Voprosy Istorii,* XLI (1966), 209–15.

Metternich, C. von. *Aus Metternich's nachgelassenen Papieren*. III. Vienna, 1881.
——. *Memoirs*. 8 vols. New York, 1880–1884.
Nechkina, M. V. *Dvizhenie Dekabristov*. 2 vols. Moscow, 1955.
Nicholas Michaelovich, Grand Duke. *Le Tsar Alexandre Ier*. Paris, 1931.
——. *Legenda o Konchine Imperatora Aleksandra I*. St. Petersburg, 1907.
Pypin, A. N. *Obshchestvennoe Dvizhenie v Rossii pri Aleksandre I*. St. Petersburg, 1900.
Raeff, M. *Michael Speransky*. The Hague, 1957.
Schilder, N. K. *Imperator Aleksandr Pervyi*. 4 vols. St. Petersburg, 1904–1905.
Skabichevskii, A. M. *Ocherki Istorii Russkoi Tsenzury (1700-1863)*. St. Petersburg, 1892.
Speransky, M. M. *Proekti i Zapiski*. Moscow, 1961.
Vernadsky, G. *La Charte Constitutionelle de l'Empire Russe de l'An 1820*. Paris, 1933.
Vigel, F. F. *Zapiski*. 2 vols. Moscow, 1928.
Vosstanie Dekabristov: Materialy. 11 vols. Leningrad, 1925–1958.
Wilson, R. T. *Narrative of Events during the Invasion of Russia by Napoleon Bonaparte*. London, 1860.

Notes, chapter I, pages 3–26

1. Caulaincourt, 52.
2. Schilder, IV, 553.
3. *Ibid.*, 114.
4. Wilson, 117.
5. Czartoryski, I, 325.
6. *The Writings of Thomas Jefferson*, XI (Washington, 1903) 291–92.
7. Isaiah 41:25 (R.S.V.).
8. Metternich, *Memoirs*, I, 318.
9. *Ibid.*, 338.

Notes, chapter II, pages 27–44

1. Schilder, IV, 214.
2. Vigel, II, 175.
3. The Free Economic Society, established in the reign of Catherine II for the purpose of "promoting useful knowledge in agriculture," was officially permitted, even encouraged, to study the problem of serfdom and propose possible solutions.
4. Czartoryski, I, 64.

Notes, chapter III, pages 45–73

1. Kohl, 407.
2. Russia, *Polnoe Sobranie Zakonov*, XXIV, No. 27106.
3. Schilder, IV, 87.
4. "Volnost: Oda," *Sochineniya*, I, 88–91.
5. Nicholas Michaelovich, *Le Tsar Alexandre Ier*, 255.
6. Metternich, *Aus Metternich's*, III, 352.
7. "The Age of Bronze," stanza X.
8. Dubrovin, 481.
9. *Ibid.*, 357–59.
10. Nicholas Michaelovich, *op. cit.*, 309.
11. The pamphlet in question was Gesner's *Geist des Leben und der Lehre Jesu Christi*.

12. Dubrovin, 388.
13. Nechkina, I, 306
14. Chaadaev, I, 2–3.
15. Schilder, IV, 214.
16. "The Trouble with Reason," *An Anthology of Russian Plays,* ed. and transl. F. D. Reeve, I (New York, 1961), 110, 116.
17. *Ibid.,* 142–43.
18. Cf. Nicholas Michaelovich, *Legenda o Konchine,* and Lyubimov.

NICHOLAS I

Aksakov, I. *Ivan Aksakov i Ego Pismakh.* 4 vols. Moscow, 1888–1896.
Annenkov, P. B. *Literaturnye V₁ospominaniya.* Moscow, 1960.
Barsukov, N. *Zhizn i Trudy M. P. Pogodina.* 22 vols. St. Petersburg, 1888–1910.
Belinsky, V. G. *Selected Philosophical Works.* Moscow, 1948.
Benckendorff, A. "Graf A. X. Benkendorf o Rossii v 1827–1830 Gg.," *Krasnyi Arkhiv,* XXXVII (1929), 138–74; XXXVIII (1930), 109–47.
Berlin, I. "Russia and 1848," *Slavonic and East European Review,* XXVI (1948), 341–60.
Bolsover, G. H. "Nicholas I and the Partition of Turkey," *Slavonic and East European Review,* XXVII (1948), 115–45.
Curtiss, J. S. *The Army of Nicholas I.* Durham, 1965.
Custine, A. de. *Journey for our Time.* New York, 1951.
Dubbelt, L. V. "Zametki," *Golos Minuvshago,* March, 1913, 127–71.
Foster, J. W. *Diplomatic Memoirs.* I. Boston, 1909.
Granovsky, T. N. *T. N. Granovsky i Ego Perepiska.* 2 vols. Moscow, 1897.
Grunwald, C. de. *Tsar Nicholas I.* New York, 1955.
Herzen, A. I. *Byloe i Dumy,* 2 vols. Moscow, 1962.
Koshelev, A. I. *Zapiski A. I. Kosheleva.* Berlin, 1884.
Lampert, E. *Studies in Rebellion.* New York, 1957.
Lemke, M. K. *Nikolaevskie Zhandarmy i Literatura.* St. Petersburg, 1908.
Linkov, Y. I. *Ocherki Istorii Krestyanskogo Dvizheniya v Rossii v 1825–1861 Gg.* Moscow, 1952.
Mazour, A. G. *The First Russian Revolution, 1825.* Berkeley, 1937.
Monas, S. *The Third Section.* Cambridge, 1961.
Nesselrode, K. *Lettres et Papiers.* 11 vols. Paris, 1908–1912.
Nicholas I. "Iz Zapisok Nikolaya I o 14 Dekabrya 1825 G.," *Krasnyi Arkhiv,* VI (1924), 222–34.
Nikitenko, A. V. *Dnevnik.* 3 vols. Leningrad, 1955–1956.
Pogodin, M. *Rechi.* Moscow, 1872.
Polievktov, M. A. *Nikolai I.* Moscow, 1918.
Predtechenskii, A. V., ed. *Krestyanskoe Dvizhenie v Rossii v 1826–1849 Gg.* Moscow, 1961.
Riasanovsky, N. V. *Nicholas I and Official Nationality in Russia, 1825–1855.* Berkeley, 1959.
Schiemann, T. *Geschichte Russlands unter Kaiser Nikolaus I.* 4 vols. Berlin, 1904–1919.
——, ed. *Zur Geschichte der Regierung Paul I und Nikolaus I.* Berlin, 1906.
Shevyrev, S. *Istoriya Imperatorskago Moskovskago Universiteta.* Moscow, 1855.
Smolitsch, I. *Geschichte der russischen Kirche, 1700–1917.* Leiden, 1964.
Solovev, S. M. *Zapiski S. M. Soloveva.* Petrograd, n.d.

Stackelberg, N. "Zagadka Smerti Nikolaya I," *Russkoe Proshloe*, No. 1, 1923, 58–73.

Stählin, K. "Aus den Berichten der III Abteilung S. M. höchsteigener Kanzlei an Kaiser Nikolaus I," *Zeitschrift für Osteuropäische Geschichte*, VI (1932), 477–512; VII (1933) 20–51, 229–69, 357–86.

Tarle, E. *Krymskaya Voina*. 2 vols. Moscow, 1950.

"Trete Otdelenie Sobstvennoi E. I. V. Kantselyarii o Sebe Samom," *Vestnik Evropy*, LII (1917), 85–125.

Uvarov, S. S. *Desyatiletie Ministerva Narodnago Prosveshcheniya, 1833–1843*. St. Petersburg, 1864.

Zhikharev, M. I., "Petr Yakovlevich Chaadaev," *Vestnik Evropy*, VI (1871), 9–54.

Notes, chapter IV, pages 74–88

1. Schiemann, *Zur Geschichte*, 124.
2. *Ibid.*, 110.
3. Nesselrode, VI, 229–30.
4. Schiemann, *op. cit.*, 94.
5. Schiemann, *Geschichte Russlands*, II, 32–33.
6. Nechkina, II, 275.
7. *Ibid.*, 276.
8. The official report of Nicholas' participation in the suppression of the mutiny (cf. Nesselrode, VI, 263–66), an idealized version issued by the foreign ministry on the following day, overreached the facts somewhat to present the tsar in a heroic light, riding bravely up to the rebels at the head of a loyal battalion, "with firm intention of employing force only after *all* other means of persuasion had been exhausted." For more satisfactory accounts, based on well-documented and circumstantial evidence, see Nechkina, II, 255–324, and Mazour, 169–80.

Notes, chapter V, pages 89–120

1. Of the known influential society members, only Nicholas Turgenev eluded the roundup; he fled abroad, not to return to Russia until 1857.
2. The material collected by the committee was not published until a century later, by the Soviet Government, in an eleven-volume work entitled *Vosstanie Dekabristov*.
3. Under civilian law, capital punishment could not be imposed. However, the military code permitted capital punishment, and civilians, under certain circumstances, could be tried under that code.
4. Nesselrode, VI, 280.
5. Custine, 124–25.
6. Benckendorff, 153.
7. *Russkaya Starina*, LX (1888), 495.
8. Benckendorff, 132.
9. Dubbelt, 133.
10. Nesselrode, VI, 275.
11. *Ibid.*
12. Solovev, 58–59.
13. Nikitenko, I, 174.
14. Pogodin, 271–72.
15. Gogol, *Dead Souls* (New York, 1944), 123.
16. Barsukov, IV, 83.
17. Smolitsch, 286.

18. White, A. D., *The Autobiography of Andrew D. White* (New York, 1907), I, 470.
19. Schneider, L., *Aus meinem Leben*, I (Berlin, 1879), 366.
20. Uvarov, 107–108.

Notes, chapter VI, pages 121–162

1. Benckendorff, 150, 153.
2. Herzen, I, 226, 258–64.
3. Grunwald, 238 n.
4. Chaadaev, I, 77 ff.
5. Skabichevskii, 246.
6. Zhikharev, 37–38n.
7. Tyutchev, F. I., *Polnoe Sobranie Sochinenenii* (St. Petersburg, 1913), 190.
8. Lampert, 264.
9. Aksakov, III, 290.
10. Lemke, 176.
11. Belinsky, 503–12.
12. Stählin, VII, 367–68.
13. Predtechenskii, 343–44.
14. Skabichevskii, 347.
15. Predtechenskii, 817.
16. Polievktov, 197.
17. *The Letters of Queen Victoria*, II (New York, 1907), 196.
18. Polievktov, 363.
19. Skabichevskii, 343.
20. "Trete Otdelenie," 10.
21. Schiemann, *Geschichte Russlands*, IV, 236.
22. Foster, I, 196.
23. Herzen, I, 443–44.
24. Bolsover, 139.
25. Quoted in Tarle, I, 452.
26. *Ibid.*, II, 107.
27. Linkov, 97–99.
28. Barsukov, XIII, 65–66.
29. Sukhomlinov, M. I., *Izsledovaniya i Stati po Russkoi Literature i Prosveshcheniya*, II (St. Petersburg, 1889), 515.
30. Schiemann, *Geschichte Russlands*, IV, 430.
31. White, I, 470.
32. Shevyrev, 469–70.
33. Stackelberg gives the argument for suicide: he succeeds in raising doubts about the reliability of official reports, but he does not prove his case.
34. Dubbelt, 169.

ALEXANDER II

Akademiya Nauk SSSR, Institut Istorii. *Die Bauernbewegung des Jahres 1861 in Russland.* Berlin, 1958.
Dostoevsky, F. *Diary of a Writer.* New York, 1954.
Dzhanshiev, G. *Epokha Velikikh Reform.* Moscow, 1900.
Fedorov, A. V. *Russkaya Armiya v 50-70 Gg. XIX V.* Leningrad, 1959.
Feoktistov, E. M. *Za Kulisami Politiki i Literatury.* Leningrad, 1929.

Garmiza, V. V. *Podgotovka Zemskoi Reformy 1864 G.* Moscow, 1957.
"Konstitutsiya Grafa Loris-Melikova," *Byloe,* April-May, 1918, 125–86.
Kornilov, A. A. *Obshchestvennoe Dvizhenie pri Aleksandre II.* Moscow, 1909.
Lemke, M. *Epokha Tsenzurnikh Reform.* St. Petersburg, 1904.
Leroy-Beaulieu, A. *Un Homme d'État (Nicolas Miliutine).* Paris, 1884.
Lukashevich, S. *Ivan Aksakov.* Cambridge, 1965.
Lyubimov, N. A. *Mikhail Nikiforovich Katkov.* St. Petersburg, 1889.
Milyutin, D. *Dnevnik, D. A. Milyutina. 4 vols. Moscow, 1947–1950.*
"Nezabvennyya Mysli Nezabvennykh Lyudei," *Byloe,* January, 1907, 236–42.
Portal, R. et al. *Le Statut des Paysans Libérés du Servage, 1861–1961.* Paris, 1963.
"Revolyutsionnoe i Studencheskoe Dvizhenie 1869 G. v Otsenke Tretego Otdeleniya," *Katorga i Ssylka,* No. 10, 1925, 106–21.
Schweinitz, H. L. von. *Denkwürdigkeiten.* 2 vols. Berlin, 1927.
Sumner, B. H. *Russia and the Balkans, 1870–1880.* New York, 1937.
Tatishchev, S. S. *Imperator Aleksandr II.* 2 vols. St. Petersburg, 1903.
Tyutcheva, A. F. *Pri Dvore Dvukh Imperatorov.* 2 vols. Moscow, 1928–1929.
Valuev, P. A. *Dnevnik P. A. Valueva.* 2 vols. Moscow, 1961.
Venturi, F. *Roots of Revolution,* New York, 1964.
Vogué, E. M. de. *Spectacles Contemporains.* Paris, 1891.
Zaionchkovsky, P. A. *Krizis Samoderzhaviya na Rubezhe 1870–1880 Godov.* Moscow, 1964.

Notes, chapter VII, pages 163–194

1. Tyutcheva, II, 229.
2. Tatishchev, I, 144–45.
3. *Russkaya Starina,* XXXIX (1883), 220.
4. Linkov, *Ocherki,* 106–142.
5. Barsukov, *Pogodin,* XIV, 207.
6. Russia, *Polnoe Sobranie Zakonov,* 2nd Series, XXXI, Pt. 1, No. 30273.
7. *Krasnyi Arkhiv,* XXXII (1929), 233-34.
8. *Russkaya Starina,* XXXI (1881), 228.
9. Koshelev, *Zapiski,* 93–94.
10. Smolitsch, *Geschichte der russischen Kirche,* 301.
11. *Ibid.,* 207.
12. Dzhanshiev, 325–26, n.1.
13. Valuev, I, 19–20.
14. Russia, *Polnoe Sobranie Zakonov,* 2nd Series, XXXVI, Pt. 1, No. 36650.
15. Akademiya Nauk, *Die Bauernbewegung,* 69–74.
16. Valuev, I, 89.
17. Feoktistov, 348.
18. Valuev, I, 218.
19. Garmiza, 159.
20. Valuev, I, 218.
21. *Kolokol,* February 15, 1864.
22. Garmiza, 246.

Notes, chapter VIII, pages 195–242

1. Garmiza, 161.
2. Tatishchev, I, 534.
3. *Russkaya Starina,* CX (1902), 500.
4. Cf. Valuev, II, 83–84, 86.
5. "Nezabvennyya Mysli," 238.

6. Tatishchev, II, 8–10.
7. Lyubimov, 343.
8. "Revolyutsionnoe i Studencheskoe Dvizhenie," 119.
9. Valuev, II, 44.
10. *Ibid.*, 381.
11. Zaionchkovsky, 148.
12. "Konstitutsiya Grafa Loris-Melikova," 154–61; Tatishchev, II, 635–42.
13. Milyutin, IV, 78–79.
14. Cf. *Byloe*, No. 1, 1925, 92.
15. Kornilov, 257.
16. Dostoevsky, 1032, 1034.
17. Cf. *Otechestvennyie Zapiski*, XLII (1880), 164–68.
18. "Konstitutsiya Grafa Loris-Melikova," 165.

ALEXANDER III

Bing, E. J., ed. *The Secret Letters of the Last Tsar.* New York, 1938.

Bogdanovich, A. V. *Tri Poslednikh Samoderzhtsa.* Moscow, 1924.

Egiazarova, N. A. *Agrarnyi Krizis Kontsa XIX Veka v Rossii.* Moscow, 1959.

Firsov, N. V. "Aleksandr III," *Byloe*, No. 1, 1925, 85–108.

Frank, V. S., ed. "Iz Neizdannoi Perepiski Imp. Aleksandra III i Nikolaya II s Kn. V. P. Meshcherskim," *Sovremennyya Zapiski*, LXX (1940), 165–88.

Katkov, M. *Sobranie Peredovykh Statei Moskovskikh Vedemostei, 1881 God.* Moscow, 1898.

Korolkov, K. *Zhizn i Tsarstvovanie Imp. Aleksandra III.* Kiev, 1901.

Krivenko, V. S. *Puteshestvie Ego Imperatorskago Vysochestva Naslednika Tsesarevicha.* St. Petersburg, 1891.

Kshessinska, M. *Dancing in Petersburg,* London, 1960.

Lopukhin, V. B. "Lyudi i Politika," *Voprosy Istorii*, XLI, No. 9 (1966), 120–36.

Meshchersky, V. A. *Moi Vospominaniya.* 3 vols. St. Petersburg, 1897–1912.

Nicholas II. *Dnevnik Imperatora Nikolaya II.* Berlin, 1923.

Perets, E. A. *Dnevnik E. A. Peretsa.* Moscow, 1927.

Pobedonostsev, K. P. *Pisma Pobedonostseva k Aleksandru III.* 2 vols. Moscow, 1925–1926.

Polovtsov, A. A. *Dnevnik Gosudarstvennogo Sekretarya A. A. Polovtsova.* 2 vols. Moscow, 1966.

Savelev, A. A. "Dva Vosshestviya na Prestol Russkikh Tsarei," *Golos Minuvshego*, V, No. 4 (1917), 91–104.

Von Laue, T. H. *Sergei Witte and the Industrialization of Russia.* New York, 1963.

Witte, S. Yu. *Vospominaniya.* I. Moscow, 1960.

Zaionchkovsky, P. A. "Aleksandr III i Ego Blizhaishee Okruzhenie," *Voprosy Istorii*, XLI, No. 8 (1966), 130–46.

Notes, chapter IX, pages 243–284

1. Zaionchkovsky, *Krizis Samoderzhaviya*, 302.
2. Pobedonostsev, I, 318–19.
3. Schweinitz, *Denkwürdigkeiten*, II, 153.
4. Witte, I, 269, Zaionchkovsky, *op. cit.*, 304 n.
5. Gernet, M. N. *Istoriya Tsarskoi Tyurmy* (Moscow, 1941–1954), III, 104.
6. *Byloe*, Sept. 1917, 39.

7. Tyutcheva, *Pri Dvore Dvukh Imperatorov,* II, 225.
8. Pobedonostsev, I, 315–16.
9. Perets, 40.
10. Pobedonostsev, I, 317.
11. Quoted in Zaionchkovsky, *op. cit.,* 338.
12. *Ibid.,* 382 n.
13. Cf. Tyutcheva, II, 225.
14. Russia, *Polnoe Sobranie Zakonov,* 3rd Series, I, No. 118.
15. Katkov, 209.
16. "Konstitutsiya Grafa Loris-Melikova," 162.
17. Zaionchkovsky, *op. cit.,* 381.
18. *Ibid.,* 419.
19. Perets, 133.
20. Pobedonostsev, I, 381.
21. Korolkov, 56–57.
22. *Ibid.,* 57.
23. Nicholas II, *Dnevnik,* 23.
24. *Ibid.,* 40.
25. Cf. Russia, Ministerstvo Vnutrennikh Del, *Ot Vladivostoka do Uralska.* St. Petersburg, 1891.
26. Nicholas II, *Das Tagebuch des letzten Zaren* (Berlin, 1923), 73–74. The German edition of Nicholas' diaries has some entries not in the Russian.
27. Schweinitz, II, 305–06; Bing, 61.
28. Lopukhin, 120.
29. Bing, 64.
30. Nicholas II, *Dnevnik,* 83.

NICHOLAS II

Because the list of sources used for the period of Nicholas II is so long, it has been subdivided. Sources listed under Alexander III and used as well for the reign of his son are not repeated.

General

Buxhoevden, S. *The Life and Tragedy of Alexandra Feodorovna.* London, 1929.
France, Ministère des Affaires Étrangères, Archives. *Russie, Correspondence Politique,* 1894–1896.
——. *Russie, Politique Intérieure, Dossier Général,* 1896–1914.
——. *Russie, Questions Dynastiques et Cour,* 1896–1914.
Germany, Auswärtiges Amt, Archiv. Russland 82. No. 1. *Akten betreffend der russischen Kaiser Haus,* 1894–1918.
——. Geheim. *Geheime Akten betreffend die russische kaiserliche Familie,* 1894–1918.
Gilliard, P. *Thirteen Years at the Russian Court.* London, 1921.
Gurko, V. I. *Features and Figures of the Past.* Stanford, 1939.
Mamontov, V. I. *Na Gosudarevoi Sluzhbe.* Tallin, 1926.
Milyukov, P. N. *Vospominaniya.* 2 vols. New York, 1955.
Mossolov, A. A. *At the Court of the Last Tsar.* London, 1935.
Nicholas II. *Polnoe Sobranie Rechei Imperatora Nikolaya II, 1894–1906.* St. Petersburg, 1906.

Oldenburg, S. S. *Tsarstvovanie Imperatora Nikolaya II.* 2 vols. Belgrade and Munich, 1939–1949.

Romanov, G. K. *V Mramornom Dvortse.* New York, 1955.

Russia. *Svod Vysochaishikh Otmetok po Vsepoddanneishim Otchetam General-Gubernatorov, Gubernatorov, Voennikh Gubernatorov i Gradonachalnikov za 1881–1904.* St. Petersburg, 1893–1907.

Vyrubova, A. *Memories of the Russian Court.* New York, 1923.

William II. *Letters from the Kaiser to the Czar.* New York, 1920.

Witte, S. Yu. *Vospominaniya.* II–III. Moscow, 1960.

Chapters X-XI

"Dokumenty o Khodynskoi Katastrofe 1896 G.," *Krasnyi Arkhiv,* LXXVI (1936), 31–48.

"K Istorii Pervoi Gaagskoi Konferentsii 1899 G.," *Krasnyi Arkhiv,* L–LI (1932), 64–96.

Lamsdorf, V. N. "Dnevnik V. N. Lamzdorfa," *Krasnyi Arkhiv,* XLVI (1931), 3–37.

Maniguet, L. *Contributions a l'Étude de l'Influence des Empiriques sur les Malades . . . Philippe.* Lons-le-Saunier, 1920.

"Novye Materialy o Gaagskoi Mirnoi Konferentsii 1899 G.," *Krasnyi Arkhiv,* LIV–LV (1932), 49–79.

Otchet Osoboi Kommissii, Obrazovannoi dlya Vyyasneniya Lichnosti Pogibshikh na Khodynskom Pole. Moscow, 1897.

Polovtsov, A. A. "Dnevnik A. A. Polovtsova," *Krasnyi Arkhiv,* III (1923), 75–172; IV (1923), 63–128; XLVI (1931), 110–32; LXVII (1934), 163–86.

Russia, Ministerstvo Imperatorskago Dvora. *Koronatsionnyi Sbornik.* St. Petersburg, 1899.

Shipov, D. N. *Vospominaniya i Dumy o Perezhitom.* Moscow, 1918.

Suvorin, A. S. *Dnevnik A. S. Suvorina.* Moscow, 1923.

Vannovsky, P. *Doklad Vannovskago po Povodu Studencheskikh Bezporyadkov 1899 G.* St. Petersburg, 1900.

Vinogradoff, I. "Some Russian Imperial Letters to Prince V. P. Meshchersky," *Oxford Slavonic Papers,* X (1962), 105–58.

Chapters XII-XIII

Ascher, A., ed. "The Coming Storm," *Survey,* October, 1964, 148–64.

Bok, M. P. *Vospominaniya o Moem Otse P. A. Stolypine.* New York, 1953.

Ermolov, A. S. "Zapiski A. A. Ermolova," *Krasnyi Arkhiv,* VIII (1925), 49–69.

Ezhegodnik Gazety Rech na 1914 God. St. Petersburg, n.d.

Girs, A. *Dokladnaya Zapiska o Meryakh, Mogushchikh Ukrepit Natsionalnoe Samosozanie Belorussov i Protivodeistvovat ikh Polonizatsii.* Minsk, 1914.

Harcave, S. *First Blood.* New York, 1964.

Izvolsky, A. *The Memoirs of Alexander Izvolsky.* London, 1920.

Kokovtsov, V. N. *Iz Moego Proshlago.* 2 vols. Paris, 1933.

——. *Out of My Past.* Stanford, 1935. An abridged English translation of *Iz Moego Proshlago.*

"Konets Russko-Yaponskoi Voiny," *Krasnyi Arkhiv,* XXVIII (1928), 182–204.

Kryzhanovsky, S. E. *Vospominaniya.* Berlin, 1938.

Kuropatkin, A. N. "Dnevnik A. N. Kuropatkina," *Krasnyi Arkhiv,* II (1922), 5–112; V (1924), 82–101; VII (1924), 55–69; VIII (1925), 70–100; LXVIII (1935), 65–96; LXIX-LXX (1935), 101–26.

Louis, G. *Les Carnets de George Louis.* 2 vols. Paris, 1926.

Maiskii, B. Yu. "Stolypinshchina i Konets Stolypina," *Voprosy Istorii*, XLI (1966), No. 1, 134–44; No. 2, 123–40.

Maklakov, V. A. *Vlast i Obshchestvennost*. 3 vols. Paris, 1936.

Nicholas Michaelovich, Grand Duke. "Zapiski N. M. Romanova," *Krasnyi Arkhiv*, XLVII-XLVIII (1931), 140–83; XLIX (1931), 92–111.

Ozerov, I. Kh. *Politika po Rabochemu Voprosu*. Moscow, 1906.

"Perepiska N. A. Romanova i P. A. Stolypina," *Krasnyi Arkhiv*, V (1924), 102–28; XXX (1928), 80–88.

Planson, E. A. "V Shtabe Adm. E. I. Alekseeva," *Krasnyi Arkhiv*, XLI-XLII (1930), 148–204.

Polivanov, A. A. *Iz Dnevnikov i Vospominanii*. Moscow, 1924.

Shavelsky, G. *Vospominaniya Poslednego Protopresvitera Russkoi Armii i Flota*. 2 vols. New York, 1954.

Spiridovich, A. *Les Dernières Années de la Cour de Tzarskoie Selo*. 2 vols. Paris, 1928–1929.

Stolypina, A. *L'Homme de dernier Tsar*. Paris, 1931,

Svyatopolk-Mirskaya, E. A. "Dnevnik Kn. Ekateriny Alekseevny Svyatopolk-Mirskoi za 1904–1905 Gg.," *Istoricheskie Zapiski*, LXXVII (1965), 240–93.

Taube, M. *La Politique Russe d'Avant-Guerre*. Paris, 1928.

"The Tsar," *Quarterly Review*, CC (1904), 180–209.

"Tsarskoselskiya Soveshchaniya," *Byloe*, Sept. 1917, 217–65; Oct. 1917, 183–245; Nov.–Dec. 1917, 289–318.

Chapter XIV

Andrei Vladimirovich, Grand Duke. *Dnevnik*. Leningrad, 1925.

Danilov, Yu. *Velikii Knyaz Nikolai Nikolaievich*. Paris, 1930.

Golovin, N. N. *Voennyya Usiliya Rossii v Mirovoi Voiny*. 2 vols. Paris, 1939.

Kautsky, K., coll. *Outbreak of the World War*. New York, 1924.

Kohn, S., and Meyendorff, A. F. *The Cost of the War to Russia*. New Haven, 1932.

Naumov, A. N. *Iz Utselevshikh Vospominanii*. 2 vols. New York, 1954–1955.

"Nikolai Romanov v Pervye Dny Mirovoi Voiny," *Krasnyi Arkhiv*, LXIV (1934), 130–38.

Paléologue, M. *An Ambassador's Memoirs*. 3 vols. New York, 1924–1925.

Perepiska Nikolaya i Aleksandry Romanovykh. III-V. Moscow, 1923–1927. For the English texts see *The Letters of the Tsar to the Tsaritsa, 1914–1917* (London, 1929) and *Letters of the Tsaritsa to the Tsar, 1914–1916* (London, 1923).

Pourtalés, F. *Meine letzte Verhandlungen in St. Petersburg Ende Juli 1914*. Berlin, 1927.

Rabochee Dvizhenie v Petrograde v 1912–1917 Gg. Leningrad, 1958.

Rudnev, V. *La Verité sur Famille Impériale et les Influences Occultes*. Paris, 1920.

Russia, Gosudarstvennaya Duma, Chetvertyi Sozyv. *Stenograficheskii Otchet, July 26, 1914*. St. Petersburg, 1914.

Russia, Ministerstvo Inostrannykh Del. *How the War Began in 1914*. London, 1925.

Sazonov, S. *Fateful Years, 1909–1916*. London, 1928.

Semennikov, V. P., ed. *Monarkhiya pered Krusheniem*. Moscow, 1927.

——. *Politika Romanovykh nakanune Revolyutsii*. Moscow, 1926.

Spiridovich, A. *Raspoutine*. Paris, 1935.

——. *Velikaya Voina i Fevralskaya Revolyutsiya, 1914–1917* Gg. 3 vols. New York, 1962.

Sukhomlinov, V. "Dnevnik," *Dela i Dni,* I (1920), 219–38; III (1922), 121–36.

——. *Vospominaniya.* Berlin, 1924.

Tikhobrazov, D. "Raspoutine: exerça-t-il une influence sur la conduite de la guerre," *Miroir de l'Historie,* March, 1958, 280–87.

Voeikov, V. N. *S Tsarem i bez Tsarya.* Helsingfors, 1936.

Yakhontov, A. N., ed. "Tyazhelye Dni," *Arkhiv Russkoi Revolyutsii,* XVIII (1926), 5–136. An English translation has been published under the title *Prologue to Revolution* (New York, 1967), edited by M. Cherniavsky.

Chapter XV

Andrei Vladimirovich, Grand Duke. "Iz Dnevnika A. V. Romanova za 1916–1917 Gg.," *Krasnyi Arkhiv,* XXVI (1928), 185–210.

Browder, R. P., and Kerensky, A. F., eds. *The Russian Provisional Government.* 3 vols. Stanford, 1961.

Buchanan, G. *My Mission to Russia.* 2 vols. London, 1923.

Danilov, Yu. "L'Abdication du Tsar Nicolas II," *Revue des Deux Mondes,* Jan. 1929, 45–71.

Dubenskii, D. "Kak Proizoshel Perevorot v Rossii," *Russkaya Letopis,* III (1922), 11–111.

"Fevralskaya Revolyutsiya 1917 Goda," *Krasnyi Arkhiv,* XXI (1927), 3–78; XXII (1927), 3–70.

Ignatev, P. N. *Ma Mission en France.* Paris, 1933.

"K Istorii Poslednikh Dnei Tsarskogo Rezhima," *Krasnyi Arkhiv,* XIV (1926), 227–49.

Lemke, M. *250 Dnei v Tsarskoi Stavke.* Petrograd, 1920.

Lettres des Grands-Ducs à Nicolas II. Paris, 1926.

Lukomsky, A. S. "Iz Vospominanii Gen. Lukomskago," *Arkhiv Russkoi Revolyutsii,* II (1922), 14–44.

——. "Dokumenty k 'Vospominaniyam' Gen. A. Lukomskago," *Ibid.,* III (1922), 247–70.

Melgunov, S. *Na Putyakh k Dvortsovomu Perevorotu.* Paris, 1931.

Mordvinov, A. "Otryvki iz Vospominanii," *Russkaya Letopis,* V (1923), 67–177.

Nicholas II, "Dnevnik," *Krasnyi Arkhiv,* XX (1927), 123–52.

"Nikolai Romanov, 28 Fevralya–4 Marta 1917 Goda," *Krasnyi Arkhiv,* VIII (1925), 244–46.

"Progressivnyi Blok v 1915–1917 Gg.," *Krasnyi Arkhiv,* L-LI (1932), 117–60; LII (1932), 143–96.

Rodzyanko, M. V. "Gosudarstvennaya Duma i Fevralskaya 1917 Goda Revolyutsiya," *Arkhiv Russkoi Revolyutsii,* VI (1922), 5–80.

——. *Report about the General Situation on the Front in 1916.* No. 14, Documents of M. V. Rodzyanko, Hoover Institution, Stanford University.

Russia, Chrezvychainaya Sledstvennaya Komissiya. *Padenie Tsarskogo Rezhima.* 7 vols. Leningrad, 1924–1927.

Seraphim, E. "Der Sturz des Zaren Nikolaus II und die russische Generalität," *Jahrbücher für Geschichte Osteuropas,* II (1937), 433–62.

Shulgin, V. V. *"Tage."* Berlin, 1928.

Solovev, M. E. "Kak i Kem Byl Ubit Rasputin," *Voprosy Istorii,* XL, No. 3 (1965), 211–17.

Sukhanov, N. N. *Zapiski o Revolyutsii.* 7 vols. Berlin and Petrograd, 1919–1922.

An abridged English translation was published under the title *The Russian Revolution, 1917* (New York, 1955).

"Ubiistvo Rasputina: Ofitsialnoe Doznanie," *Byloe,* July 1917, 64–83.

Vilchkovsky, S. N. "Prebyvanie Gosudarya Imperatora v Pskove, li Marta 1917 Goda," *Russkaya Letopis,* III (1922), 161–87.

Yusupov, F. F. *Lost Splendor.* London, 1953.

Epilogue

Benckendorff, P. *Last Days at Tsarskoe Selo.* London, 1927.

Bulygin, P. *The Murder of the Romanovs.* New York, 1935.

Germany, Auswärtiges Amt, Archiv, Russland 30. Weltkrieg: Grosses Hauptquartier. *Die russische Kaiserfamilie: Ermordung des Zaren.*

Melgunov, S. *Sudba Imperatora Nikolaya II posle Otrecheniya.* Paris, 1951.

Nicholas II. "Dnevnik," *Krasnyi Arkhiv,* XXI (1927), 79–96; XXII (1927), 71–91; XXVII (1928), 110–38.

Sokolov, N. *Ubiistvo Tsarskoi Semi.* Berlin, 1925.

Notes, chapter X, pages 285–299

1. Lamsdorf, 10.
2. Nicholas II, *Dnevnik,* 87.
3. *Ibid.,* 92. Because the diary is referred to so frequently hereafter, references to it will not usually be given in the notes. The date given in the text should be reference enough.
4. Polovtsev, LXVII, 170.
5. Boisdeffre to Ministère des Affaires Étrangères, Nov. 17, 1894 (N.S.) and Nov. 22, 1894 (N.S.), France, Ministère des Affaires Étrangères, Archive, *Correspondence Politique,* Vol. 303.
6. *Russkaya Letopis,* V (1923), 156; Stead, W. T., "Alexander III," *Review of Reviews,* X (1894), 634.
7. Bing, *Secret Letters of the Last Tsar,* 33.
8. *Koronatsionnyi Sbornik,* 119.
9. *Otchet . . . Pole,* 1–89; "Dokumenty o Khodynskoi," 76.
10. Suvorin, 132–33.
11. *Krasnyi Arkhiv,* XVII (1926), 219–20.
12. Suvorin, 330.

Notes, chapter XI, pages 300–323

1. "Novye Materialy," 58–62.
2. See also "K Istorii Pervoi Gaagskoi Konferentsii."
3. Polovtsov, XLVI, 128–29.
4. Cf. Vannovsky.
5. Vinogradoff, 124.
6. *Ibid.,* 130.
7. Nicholas II, *Polnoe Sobranie Rechei,* 32.
8. Maniguet provides a solid account of Philippe's background.

Notes, chapter XII, pages 324–363

1. Ozerov, 131.
2. Milyukov, I, 204.
3. Kuropatkin, II, 43.

4. Valuev, *Dnevnik,* II, 140–41.
5. Bogdanovich, *Tri Polednikh Samoderzhtsa,* 290.
6. Witte, II, 291; Kuropatkin, II, 93.
7. Planson, 155–59.
8. Nicholas II to William II, January 11/24, 1904, Germany, Auswärtiges Amt, Archiv, Russland, 82, No. 1, Geheim, Vol. 5–6.
9. Nicholas II to William II, February 5/18, 1904, *ibid.*
10. "The Tsar," 209.
11. Suvorin, 224.
12. Ascher, 155.
13. Suvorin, 314.
14. *Ibid.,* 313.
15. Svyatopolk-Mirskaya, 241.
16. Buxhoevden, *Alexandra,* 109–10.
17. Varnashëv, N. "Ot Nachala do Kontsa s Gaponovskoi Organizatsiei," *Istoriko-Revolyutsionnyi Sbornik,* No. 1, 1924, 205.
18. *The Times* (London), Jan. 25, 1905.
19. *Osvobozhdenie,* Jan. 12/25, 1905.
20. Maklakov, II, 352.
21. Ermolov, 51–52.
22. Bing, *Secret Letters of the Last Tsar,* 185–86.
23. Harcave, 289–92, *passim.*
24. Russia, *Polnoe Sobranie Zakonov,* 3rd Series, XXV, Pt. 1, No. 26805.

Notes, chapter XIII, pages 364–406

1. Bing, 184.
2. Witte, III, 53.
3. Milyukov (I, 329) is not certain that he was quoted correctly but agrees that the words attributed to him represent his thought at the time.
4. Nicholas II to William II, May 12/25, 1906, Germany, Auswärtiges Amt, Archiv, Russland, 82, No. 1, Geheim, Vol. 6–7.
5. Hintze to William II, Jan. 28, 1909 (N.S.), *ibid.*
6. Nicholas II, *Polnoe Sobranie Rechei,* 73.
7. Bompard to Bourgeois, July 14/27, 1906, France, Ministère des Affaires Étrangères, Archives, Russie, *Politique Intérieure,* III.
8. Polivanov, 32.
9. Spiridovich, I, 333.
10. Controversy over responsibility for Stolypin's death still rages. For the most recent, and probably the most adequate, account see Maiskii.
11. Kokovtsov, *Out of my Past,* 283.
12. Kokovtsov, *Iz Moego Proshlego,* I, 493.
13. Bok, 331–32; Stolypina, 118.
14. Cf. Shavelsky, I, 282.
15. Polivanov, 117, 129.
16. *Ezhegodnik Gazety Rech na 1914 God,* 23.
17. *Ibid.,* 35.
18. Cf. Girs.
19. Nicholas Michaelovich, XLVII-XLVIII, 143.

Notes, chapter XIV, pages 407–435

1. Hintze to William II, Jan. 6, 1910 (N.S.), Germany, Auswärtiges Amt, Archiv, Russland, 82, No. 1, Vol. 59–60.

2. Kautsky, 295.
3. Sazonov, 204.
4. Russia, Gos. Duma, *Stenograficheskii Otchet, July 26, 1914,* cols. 2–3.
5. *Ibid.,* cols. 24–25.
6. "Nikolai Romanov v Pervye Dny Mirovoi Voiny," entries for July 19, 24, 31, 1914; Danilov, 57–58.
7. Milyukov, *Vospominaniya,* II, 193.
8. Nicholas to Alexandra, Jan. 26, 1915.
9. Rudnev, 12.
10. Nicholas to Alexandra, August 8, 1916; Polivanov, 203–206; Shavelsky, I, 302–310; Semennikov, *Politika,* 84–85; Andrei, 69–75, *passim.*
11. Andrei, 96.
12. Polivanov, 208–12.
13. Spiridovich, *Raspoutine,* 164.
14. *Rabochee Dvizhenie v Petrograde,* 331.
15. Yakhontov, 84–85.
16. Sazonov, 295.
17. Andrei, 76–78.
18. Naumov, II, 306.

Notes, chapter XV, pages 436–471

1. Nicholas to Alexandra, August 25, 1915.
2. Alexandra to Nicholas, August 28, 1915.
3. Gilliard, *Thirteen Years at the Russian Court,* 137.
4. Alexandra to Nicholas, Sept. 20, 1915.
5. Naumov, *Iz Utselevshikh Vospominanii,* II, 429.
6. Russia, *Padenie Tsarskogo Rezhima,* I, 235.
7. *Krasnyi Arkhiv,* XXXI (1928), 32.
8. Lemke, 648–50.
9. Rodzyanko, *Report about the General Situation on the Front in 1916.*
10. Ignatev, 166.
11. *Padenie Tsarskogo Rezhima,* I, 240–41.
12. *Lettres des Grands-Ducs,* 256–60.
13. Cf. Solovev and "Ubiistvo Rasputina."
14. Nicholas Michaelovich, *Krasnyi Arkhiv,* XLIX, 102.
15. Marginal comment by William II on despatch from von Eisendecher to Bethmann-Hollweg, Jan. 22, 1917 (N.S.), Germany, Auswärtiges Amt, Archiv, Russland, 82, No. 1, Geheim, Vol. 7.
16. Nicholas to Alexandra, Feb. 24, 1917.
17. Milyukov, *Vospominaniya,* II, 311–12.
18. Shulgin, 187; Sukhanov, *The Russian Revolution,* 109–112; *Padenie Tsarskogo Rezhima,* III, 69.
19. Russia, Vremennoe Pravitelstvo, *Sobranie Uzakonenii i Rasporyazhenii Pravitelstva,* I, Pt. 1, No. 344.
20. Shulgin, 255–65; Milyukov, II, 316–19.
21. Russia, Vremennoe Pravitelstvo, *op. cit.,* No. 345.

OTHER SOURCES CONSULTED

Akademiya Nauk SSSR, Institut Istorii. *Ocherki Istorii Leningrada.* II-III. Leningrad, 1956–1957.

Bozheryanov, I. *Detstvo, Vospitanie i Leta Yunosti Russkikh Imperatorov.* St. Petersburg, 1915.

Gernet, M. N. *Istoriya Tsarskoi Tyurmy.* 4 vols. Moscow, 1941–1954. *Obyazannosti Gosudarya.* St. Petersburg, 1854.

Ovsyaniko-Kulikovskii, D. N., ed. *Istoriya Russkoi Literatury XIX V.* 5 vols. Moscow, 1908–1911.

Russia. *Polnoe Sobranie Zakonov Rossiiskoi Imperii.* 240 vols. St. Petersburg, 1830–1916.

Russia, Komitet Ministrov. *Statesman's Handbook for Russia.* 2 vols. St. Petersburg, 1896.

Sliozberg, G. B. *Dorevolyutsionnyi Stroi Rossii.* Paris, 1935.

Volkov, N. E. *Dvor Russkikh Imperatorov.* St. Petersburg, 1900.

GENERAL LIST OF BOOKS IN ENGLISH

Alexander Michaelovich, Grand Duke. *Once a Grand Duke.* New York, 1932.

Baddeley, J. F. *Russia in the 'Eighties.* London, 1921.

Baryatinskaya, Princess M. *My Russian Life.* London, 1923.

Botkin, G. *The Real Romanovs.* New York, 1931.

Buxhoevden, S. *Before the Storm.* London, 1938.

Chamberlin, W. H. *The Russian Revolution.* 2 vols. New York, 1935.

Charques, R. *The Twilight of Imperial Russia.* London, 1958.

Charykov, N. V. *Glimpses of High Politics.* New York, 1931.

Cyril Vladimirovich, Grand Duke. *My Life in Russia's Service.* London, 1939.

Eckardt, J. W. A. von. *Distinguished Persons in Russian Society.* London, 1873.

Florinsky, M. T. *The End of the Russian Empire.* New Haven, 1931.

Graham, S. *Tsar of Freedom.* New Haven, 1935.

Ignatev, A. *A Subaltern in Old Russia.* London, 1944.

Katkov, G. *Russia, 1917.* New York, 1967.

Kleinmichel, M. *Memories of a Shipwrecked World.* London, 1923.

Leroy-Beaulieu, A. *The Empire of the Tsars and the Russians.* 3 vols. New York, 1893–1896.

Lowe, C. *Alexander III of Russia.* New York, 1895.

Marie Pavlovna, Grand Duchess. *Education of a Princess.* New York, 1931.

Massie, R. K. *Nicholas and Alexandra.* New York, 1967.

Paléologue, G. M. *The Enigmatic Czar: The Life of Alexander I of Russia.* London, 1938.

Paley, Princess O. *Memories of Russia, 1916–1919.* London, 1924.

Pares, B. *The Fall of the Russian Monarchy.* New York, 1939.

Poliakoff, V. *The Empress Marie of Russia and Her Times.* London, 1926.

Polovtsov, P. A. *Glory and Downfall: Reminiscences of a Russian General Staff Officer.* London, 1935.

Seton-Watson, H. *The Russian Empire, 1801–1917.* Oxford, 1967.

Troyat, H. *Daily Life under the Last Tsar.* New York, 1962.

Vorres, I. *The Last Grand Duchess*. New York, 1965.
Wallace, D. M. *Russia*. New York, 1912.
Williams, R. H. *Russia of the Russians*. New York, 1915.
Witte, S. Yu. *The Memoirs of Count Witte*. Garden City, N.Y., 1921.
Zetlin, M. *The Decembrists*. New York, 1958.

Index

Index

The Russia of the last Romanov Tsars

BARENTS SEA

SWEDEN

FINLAND

Baltic Sea

Helsingfors

GERMANY

Riga

Baltic Provinces

Neva

ST. PETERSBURG

POLAND

Warsaw

Baranovichi

Vilna

Minsk

AUSTRIA

Carpathians

Mogilev

Kiev

Moscow

U r a l s

S

Tobolsk

RUMANIA

Dnieper

Don

Volga

Ekaterinburg

Trans~

Tomsk

Danube

Crimea

Sevastopol

Livadia

Black Sea

Omsk

CONSTANTINOPLE

OTTOMAN EMPIRE

Kars

Transcaucasia

Caspian Sea

TURKESTAN

PERSIA

AFGHANISTAN

INDIA

JP